Dasbodh

Spiritual Instruction for the Servant

Spiritual Discourses Between a Master and Listeners

by

Saint Shri Samartha Ramdas

Saint Shri Samartha Ramdas

Dasbodh

Spiritual Instruction for the Servant

Spiritual Discourses Between a Master and Listeners

by

Saint Shri Samartha Ramdas

Translation by

Mrs. Shilpa Joshi *and* Dr. Shrikrishna Karve

Edited by David Moe

© 2023 Sadguru Publishing

2023, First International Edition

ISBN: 978-1-7376607-6-7

No part of this book may be reproduced or utilized in any form or by any means, electronic or mechanical for commercial or social media usage without written permission from Sadguru Publishing.

Contact Information:
sadguru.publishing@gmail.com

Cover Art and inset:
Original portrait of
Shri Samartha Ramdas:
David Joaquin

Cover Design:
Andrew Vernon
David Moe

A Sadguru Publishing Publication

SADGURU

Introduction to Dasbodh

India is a land rich in spiritual and cultural heritage that has brought forth many saints and sages into this world. Many of them have left behind a legacy of spiritual literature that has been a great gift to mankind. In particular, the region that is now known as Maharashtra state has been the homeland to many of these great saints. The *Jnaneshwari* of Saint Jnaneshwar, the *Tukaramachi Gatha* of Saint Tukaram, the *Ekanathi Bhagwat* of Saint Eknath, and *Dasbodh* of Saint Samartha Ramdas are considered by many to be the Marathi equivalent of four Vedas that expound upon spiritual knowledge and the path of devotion. Samartha Ramdas is one of the most highly revered saints of Maharashtra who has a vast amount of literature to his credit. *Dasbodh* is regarded as the crown jewel of the writings attributed to Shri Samartha Ramdas.

This greatly treasured classic text has now become available in English to non-Marathi speaking spiritual seekers and aspirants so that they may be benefited by the comprehensive exposition of instruction given by Shri Samartha Ramdas on how to succeed and excel in both worldly life and spiritual life. According to historical accounts, the content of this book was originally dictated by Samartha Ramdas to his disciple Shri Kalyan Swami. Afterwards, copies of the text were distributed to various monasteries founded by Samartha Ramdas where they were further prepared and then recorded for the masses by some of his main disciples.

Dasbodh is a large volume that is comprised of two hundred chapters which are divided into twenty main chapters called Dashaka, each consisting of ten sub-chapters called Samasa. Each of the sub-chapters has a varying number of stanzas that were composed in a meter form called Ovi. The original Marathi text was written in a poetic style that was not only spoken, but was usually sung. Even in this modern age, in many towns and villages in Maharashtra state in India, *Dasbodh* is still widely being sung on a daily basis. It is now even possible to find recordings on the internet of *Dasbodh* being sung in Marathi. *Dasbodh* is an original text in the sense that it is not a commentary on any Sanskrit books that were written prior to it. Although it is supported by the authority of many scriptures, it is mainly the voice of direct experience.

The book is written in the style of questions and answers between a Master and listeners, among whom were several knowledgeable disciples that were familiar with the finer subtle aspects of Advaita Vedanta teachings. This English translation is presented in a free prose style. It is simply not possible to capture the poetic style, or meter and rhyme of the original Marathi text in a modern-day English translation. However, great efforts have been made to ensure that the correct meaning that Samartha Ramdas intended to convey is accurately being presented to you the reader. It is also not possible to give an exact translation from the original text, as it was written in what is now called "Old Marathi," which is not spoken anymore, however there are many modern Marathi language editions available, so every attempt has been made to keep as close as possible to the original wording that appears in those Marathi texts.

Three English translations of *Dasbodh* have been used as reference when editing this book. Two word-for-word translations containing the Marathi transliterations where specifically commissioned for this book, and a third translation, which was published shortly after those two translations were completed in 2004, was also used. The two word-for-word translations were done between the years 2002 and 2004 by Dr. Shrikrishna Karve and Mrs. Shilpa Joshi. The third translation that was used, which does not include the word-for-word Marathi transliteration, was done by the venerable Shri Diwakar Ghaisas who has also done many other English to Marathi, and Marathi to English translation projects on Advaita Vedanta and other spiritual topics. Because of his expertise and knowledge of the subject matter, the translation of Shri Ghaisas has been particularly helpful in making determinations of the meaning that Samartha Ramdas was intending when the two word-for-word translations were not in agreement. Not being a native speaker of the Marathi language myself, I am very grateful that his translation was available to provide a degree of certain clarity that may have been lacking otherwise.

If the readers or any scholars find some error in the text (and surely there will be some in this first edition), know that mistake to be mine only. Additionally, the readers are asked not to harbor any negative thought towards *Dasbodh* or Samartha Ramdas because of any perceived shortcomings. I welcome any knowledgeable people to present any perceived errors in this text for consideration for correction in a future edition of this book. As for commentary, it is often seen that spiritual texts such as this are filled with commentary about each and every line or stanza, but you will not find any such heavy commentary in this book. I feel that the words of Samartha Ramdas stand clear on their own, and for the most part do not need much additional commentary.

Dasbodh presents teachings about many subjects in a methodical and orderly manner. The reader is strongly encouraged to read the text completely from beginning to end at least once, as this is how it is intended to be read or heard. Many of the more subtle points and principles presented in the text build upon points that have been explained previously. By skipping around the text, some benefit will surely be gained, but without having an understanding of points that have been made previously, some confusion will naturally occur in the reader's mind. To this day, *Dasbodh* is read from beginning to end in many households and monasteries across India and then it is reopened to be reread and studied from the beginning again. In this way, its pages always remain open to provide lessons in daily life.

The editing style of this book has been tailored for the minds of western readers who may not be familiar with Sanskrit or Marathi terms. The intention behind the style of editing that has been used is to help ensure that any serious aspirant, regardless of their background, may be able to understand without having any familiarity with Indian terms and phrases. This has been a challenging task because many of the words used in the text simply have no English equivalent. For the benefit of aspirants who wish to study a bit more in-depth, some Sanskrit and Marathi words have been included, mostly in-line, in parentheses, following the English word. This style has been adopted in order to minimize the use of footnotes, so as not to distract the reader's attention away from the points being made. As this book is an English translation, for the most part, the English words appear in the sentences and the Indian words are in parenthesis, rather than the other way around. The intent behind this is to try as much as possible not to confuse the minds of English speaking readers with foreign words. However, it should be said that if the reader can become comfortable with the foreign words, it will surely be an aid to a more subtle understanding. If there are many requests, a word-for-word transliterated version of the text may be made available for the student who is familiar with Marathi or Sanskrit and wishes to try to gain a deeper understanding through the Indian words. Because of the size of *Dasbodh*, it is not really practical to offer a word-for-word transliteration here in this book. Any such work would certainly need to be broken up into three or four large volumes, possibly in a workbook format.

Dasbodh is a compilation of various discourses and dialogues that took place on different occasions over a number of years from 1659 to 1681 A.D. during the latter part of the lifetime of Samartha Ramdas. Samartha Ramdas was an active political and spiritual leader who was a key figure in the religious revival movement that was occurring during a time in Maharashtran history when Mogul rulers were ruling in the region. Samartha was the guru and an advisor to the great king Shivaji who was fighting the Moguls on many fronts and who was working to establish a Hindu kingdom, a campaign which finally became successful in 1674. Those were very tumultuous and chaotic times. The Hindu religion was in a terrible state of decline as a result of political pressures and ongoing wars with the ruling Moguls. The Moguls were Muslim rulers in India from the sixteenth to eighteenth centuries. In the times of Mogul rule, Hindu villages were attacked and burned, many native people were forced to flee from their homes or become enslaved, and there was a general decline in social and moral values. This was at a time when Europeans were just beginning to explore the coastal regions of India, so in the west, we are still largely unaware of the history of extreme chaos and calamity that was going on in India during that time. However, there are many detailed historical accounts of the dozens of fierce and bloody battles and attacks of epic proportions that were going on throughout the land during Samartha's lifetime.

Samartha Ramdas has many literary works attributed to him, of which, *Dasbodh* and *Manache Shlok* are the two most well-known. Millions of devotees in India continue to study and benefit from these texts even in modern times. *Manache Shlok*, which is a conversation with the mind that is meant for spiritual aspirants, is still very popular in India today, where its 205 verses are often studied in schools and learned by heart by teenagers. It has also been heavily commented upon by various scholars over the past several centuries. *Dasbodh* is also very highly revered and commonly studied, even in many business and management courses. The sound principles contained within its pages help people from all walks of life to be successful not only in spiritual practice, but in business, politics, society, and family life as well.

Samartha Ramdas is considered to be somewhat unique when compared to other previous or contemporary Maharashtran saints such as Jnanadev, Eknath, and Tukaram, in that their teachings for the most part focused exclusively on the topics Vedanta, devotion, mysticism, and spiritual practice. The teachings of Samartha Ramdas not only includes these topics, but in them, we also find messages of the importance of the wise use of positive effort, discrimination, determination, and practical shrewdness in daily life and politics. Samartha is recognized as having been a great leader and an advocate for sociopolitical and religious reforms, regeneration, and reorganization. He is well-known for promoting the ideal of establishing and maintaining a harmonious, happy, and morally healthy society supported by a solid foundation of deep spirituality.

At this point, a few words expressing gratitude are warranted. First and foremost, it must be said that inexpressible gratitude is felt for my spiritual master, Shri Ranjit Maharaj, who was the main inspiration behind the undertaking of translating this book into English. By drawing upon his teaching and power the project has finally been brought to completion. The understanding that He, along with Shri Siddharameshwar Maharaj and Samartha Ramdas have given has ensured that a clear presentation of Samartha's teachings has become available in the English language. *Dasbodh* is one of the main spiritual texts that is held in the highest regard by the masters of this lineage (sampradaya) including the well-known master Shri Nisargadatta Maharaj. By the grace of a long succession of realized masters, especially Shri Bhauseheb Maharaj, who founded the Inchgiri Sampradaya, this text is now becoming available outside of Maharashtra state in India.

On a relative level, there are a few key people without whose support this project certainly would not have been completed. I'm sure that they would probably rather remain nameless, but my gratitude is such that their support will not be forgotten. I bow deeply in gratitude to you all for the encouragement and support that you provided in times of need which resulted in the successful completion of this book. There were several occasions when this project seemed in danger of not getting finished, and because of your encouragement and support, this English translation of Dasbodh has now been made available to the world. Thank You!

A few additional words should be said about this book. Some readers may feel the inclination to dismiss this text as merely being a book of do's and don'ts, or of should's and should not's. In addition to being a sublime treatise of spiritual instruction, this text also provides practical instruction for those who wish to live a life of service and excellence. Thus, out of necessity, some of the phrasing in the text is presented in terms of do's and don'ts so that the reader may be able to recognize the best qualities and attributes of a human being as well as undesirable qualities and attributes. Please do not simply dismiss the contents of this text based upon this. Additionally, the reader is advised to keep in mind that the instruction contained in the text is broad in scope, and that many different types of people from many different walks of life are being addressed. Some sections of the text are specifically intended for spiritual leaders or wandering monks, while other sections are meant for householders and business people. Without keeping in mind the diverse audience and specific listeners that are being addressed, there is bound to be confusion in the mind of the reader. The instruction to a monk is not meant for the householder. Lastly, the reader is asked to keep in mind that the original Marathi text is usually sung, so there is often quite a bit of repetition at the end of many stanzas. Great efforts have been made to make the presentation of this text as pleasing to the mind of western readers as can be hoped for without sounding too repetitive, while at the same time not deviating too much from the original Marathi wording. Within the pages of *Dasbodh* Samartha Ramdas himself cautions the reader not to dismiss this text without having read it in its entirety. I ask the same. I also ask the reader to please forgive any spelling, grammatical, punctuation, or any other errors appearing in this first edition of the text.

David Moe / July, 2023
Editor and Publisher

A Short Biographical Sketch of Shri Samartha Ramdas (1608-1681)

For the benefit of the readers, a short biography of Samartha Ramdas is being provided so that you may have some knowledge of the life of this extraordinary saint of the seventeenth century. This is by no means a complete biography of his life and many great accomplishments. There is not a great deal of information about him available that has been written in English at this time, and there a many conflicting accounts of the details of his life and exact dates of when various events occurred. Thus, what is presented here is a general overview of his life and events that are generally agreed upon by most sources and various biographers. In doing the research for this biography many stories and events relating to the life of Samartha were found, but the accuracy of those statements could not be verified, so they have not been included. Much of what is presented here has been adopted from the life-sketch of Samartha Ramdas that is found in the book *Dasboadh* translated by Shri Diwakar Ghaisas. Many thanks are offered to him for his work on *Dasboadh* and his lifetime of selfless service.

Early Life

Samartha Ramdas was born in a small village called Jaamb, in the Aurangabad district of Maharashtra in the year 1608 A.D., on the auspicious day of Ram Navami, a day that is celebrated as the birthday of Lord Rama (an incarnation of Vishnu, much like Christ). His family belonged to a brahmin community in Jaamb that had a long history of worshipping Lord Rama and the Sun for over ten generations. It was the long held tradition of his family to celebrate the birth anniversary of Lord Rama, and it so happened that this was also the day that Samartha was born. He was given the name Narayana which is a name of Vishnu.

The childhood of Narayana is said to be filled with many extraordinary and wondrous happenings. Narayana had an older brother named Gangadhar, who by all accounts was a peaceful and obedient son, while Narayana was a strong mischievous boy who was very inquisitive and adventurous. There are many stories of him playing rough games, swimming, and roaming around deep in jungles. At the age of five, he was taught various Sanskrit prayers from the Vedas, as well as given other spiritual teachings. Narayana's father was an authority on spiritual teachings and it is said that when his older brother Gangadhar was given initiation on the spiritual path, Narayana also asked for initiation at that time, but was refused. Being disappointed, he began to become more introspective and often retreated to the jungle to meditate for hours at a time.

There are many stories telling about how that from a young age, Narayana was concerned about the general wellbeing and spiritual welfare of the people of the world. Probably the most well-known story about his early life is about how when Narayana was twelve years old, his mother insisted that he should get married. Narayana refused, but his mother was determined in her insistence, and eventually he consented to be married. However, when standing upon the wedding platform, towards the end of the marriage ceremony, he heard the word from the priest "Savadhan" which means "Be alert!" and he immediately ran away from the wedding and left his home village.

At the young age of twelve, when he left Jaamb, he went to the town of Nasik which is located on the banks of the Godawari river. He stayed alone there at a quiet place called Takli where he began doing intense spiritual penance with the intent of gaining the blessings of Lord Rama. Historical accounts tell us that he was repeating the Gayatri Mantra and the mantra "Shri Ram, Jai Ram, Jai Jai Ram," for many hours every day from early morning to mid-day while standing waist deep in the flowing waters of the river. It is also said the he believed that having a healthy body was essential for successful spiritual practice, so he was doing many repetitions of the yogic practice of the Sun Salutation every day in order to maintain a strong healthy body.

He lived there in Nasik for twelve years doing penance, during which time it is said that Lord Rama, the embodiment of the Godhead, blessed Narayana with his darshan. It is told how on one occasion he was fasting for 21 days at the doorsteps of Lord Rama's temple in order to get His blessings. Seeing his intense yearning for God, Lord Rama himself is said to have thrown open the door and initiated him with spiritual knowledge. He is considered to be one of the rare saints who did not have a guru in human form, and received initiation directly from Lord Rama. It is said that it was during this period in his life that people began calling him Ramdas because of his intense spiritual practice and great devotion to Lord Rama. By the time he was twenty-four years old, he was well known as an accomplished Siddha of the highest caliber who had mastery not only over spiritual powers, but who also possessed a perfect athletic body. It was during this period of penance that one of the great miracles attributed to him occurred. It is told that he had come across a dead brahmin man by the name of Girdhar Kulkani, and how he brought him back to life by sprinkling some sacred water on his body. Later, Uddhava the first born son of Girdhar Kulkani went on to become a disciple of Ramdas.

Mid-life Years

At the age of twenty-four Ramdas began to feel the desire to travel around the countryside and see the condition of his country and countrymen for himself. Ramdas had two main objectives in mind when he set out on his travels. First, he wanted to see for himself the terrible conditions that the people were forced to live in under the reign of the cruel Mogul rulers. Secondly, he wanted to instill in the Hindu population not only a sense of deep spiritual devotion, but also to inspire them not be lazy when the country was in a time of need, and to inspire some to embrace the values of the warrior caste that were desperately needed during that time of oppression and great despair.

From the age of twenty-four to thirty-six, Ramdas traveled extensively throughout the north and south of the country establishing Hanuman temples and a large network of monasteries, several of which are still in existence today. At the age of thirty-six, after having traveled the country for twelve years, Ramdas decided to stay in one location for some time and settled down at a place on the banks of the river Krishna. It was shortly after his arrival there that he received word that his ailing mother was requesting for him to come home to be at her side. There is a well-known story from this time period that when he arrived at his mother's home, she was having trouble with her eyes and was in an advanced stage of blindness, and that Ramdas cured his mother's blindness by touching her eyes with his hands. It is also told that on one occasion, by a single utterance of the name of Lord Rama, he brought back to life a bird that he had killed.

He stayed with his mother for a short period of time to please her, and then continued on with his mission of restoring and revitalizing the Hindu religion in Maharashtra. He constructed many more temples of Hanuman, who is the embodiment of strength, devotion and intellect. It is during this time that he obtained some statues of Rama, Sita, and Laxman from Angapur and moved them to Chapal where he built a temple to Lord Rama. He also started the tradition of celebrating the festival of the birth anniversary of Lord Rama there. The festival continues to be celebrated at that temple to this day.

It was around that same time that Ramdas first met King Shivaji, who accepted him as guru. Shivaji had just captured the fort at Torna and as a result of his meeting with Ramdas was inspired to establish his kingdom as a Hindu kingdom. As a sign of respect for Ramdas, Shivaji adopted the orange Hindu flag, a symbol of desirelessness and valor. During this time in his life, Ramdas began meeting with many young men, as well as men of power, to inspire them to work for freedom, religion, and to support the strong leadership of King Shivaji. Many monasteries and temples were built and began to be used as meeting places and centers for communications and training during that time of war.

It was also around that time that Ramdas first met Saint Tukaram. There are many stories of miraculous events that occurred during that time when he was visiting Pandharpur. The numbers of his followers began to steadily grow as his life progressed. One of the most well-known among his disciples was a devotee named Ambaji. There is a story about how one day Ambaji fell into a deep well. Concerned about his welfare, Samartha called down to him asking if he was alright. It is said that Ambaji shouted up from the well, "All is well by the grace of Maharaj!" From that incident, when he called up using the word "kalyan," which means welfare, he was given the name Kalyan by Ramdas. The historical record states that it was Kalyan who scribed *Dasbodh* as it was narrated by Ramdas in a cave located on a cliff-side at the place called Shivtarghal, which is near the hill-town of Mahad in the Raigad district of Maharashtra. The cave at Shivtarghal is considered a sacred place where life-size statues have been installed of Samartha Ramdas and Kalyan being depicted writing *Dasbodh*. Celebrations that attract throngs of devotees and pilgrims are held there to this day. The cave at Shivtarghal is truly a beautiful and holy place worth visiting.

Ramdas was unique among saints because his teaching was not focused exclusively on giving spiritual advice. He was heavily involved in political activities aimed at removing the cruel Moguls from power, and reviving Hinduism. Ramdas was instrumental in inspiring the people of Maharashtra to give up laziness and worldly ways and to take up the path of devotion. His message moved the people to make positive efforts in joining the wars of Shivaji against the Moguls and to fight for establishing a kingdom of righteousness and justice.

Later Years

Learning of the death of his mother, Ramdas returned to his home village of Jaamb in 1655. Afterwards, in his travels around the country, he met the brother of Shivaji, named Vyankoji, who also became his disciple. During this time, his disciples began to number in the thousands, and he established many more monasteries and temples. In 1672, Ramdas again met with Shivaji and spent time giving him extensive advice and knowledge about political and administrative affairs, as well as spiritual teachings and instructions for doing spiritual practice. In 1674, Shivaji's goal was achieved, and with Ramdas in attendance, he was coronated king of the newly established Hindu kingdom. Shivaji donated a fort named Parali to Samartha Ramdas to establish a permanent monastery that was renamed as "Sajjangad," meaning the place where good men gather. The monastery still stands there today and attracts many devotees and pilgrims.

There are many stories of that time, but probably the most well-known story is about how Shivaji made an offering of surrendering his entire kingdom to Samartha Ramdas. It is said that Ramdas asked Shivaji what he proposed to do with himself now that he had disposed of his kingdom. Shivaji is said to have prostrated himself before Ramdas and said that he would be very happy, and would consider himself blessed, if he could spend the remainder of his life in service to Ramdas. Ramdas then told him to take up a begging bowl and go begging for alms with him. It is said that Ramdas and Shivaji then went around the town of Satara begging for food. After returning to the place they were staying, Shivaji then asked Samartha what he was going to do with him now after reducing him to a beggar. Ramdas then told Shivaji to rule the kingdom under the orange colored Hindu flag, and to remember that the kingdom did not belong to him, and that it was only being entrusted to him, to be ruled justly before God.

Shivaji's reign lasted only 6 years after being officially established, as he passed away in 1680. His son Sambhaji assumed power upon his father's death. There is a famous letter that Ramdas wrote to Sambhaji which is considered a great and important historical document. Ramdas admonished Sambhaji to remember his father and to live and rule with the same values that Shivaji had upheld his entire life. Ramdas continued to keep abreast of all events that happened in the kingdom, and he encouraged Sambhaji to resist the attempts of the Mogul warlords to regain the territories that they had lost to Shivaji.

Samartha Ramdas passed away in the year 1681 at the monastery at Sajjangad. His ashes were kept for some time at Chapphal. After 36 years, Keshav (a disciple of Kalyan) removed some of the ashes from Chapphal to immerse them in the sacred river Ganga, and it was on that same day that his dear disciple Kalyan passed away. Later on, more of the ashes of Samarth Ramdas and some of the ashes of his disciple Kalyan were immersed in the Ganga during a special ceremony honoring them both.

This "Grantharaj," a king among spiritual books, named **Dasbodh – Spiritual Instruction for the Servant** is being presented as an offering to you the reader. It is a garland of word-gems that will surely illumine your consciousness and inspire devotion to God.

Jai Raghuveer Samartha!

Table of Contents

Chapter 1. Salutations and Praises
Chapter: 1, Sub-Chapter: 1
  The Beginning of the Book 1
Chapter: 1, Sub-Chapter: 2
  In Praise of Lord Ganesha...................3
Chapter: 1, Sub-Chapter: 3
  In Praise of Goddess Sharada...................5
Chapter: 1, Sub-Chapter: 4
  In Praise of the True Master...................7
Chapter: 1, Sub-Chapter: 5
  In Praise of the Saints...................9
Chapter: 1, Sub-Chapter: 6
  In Praise of the Listeners...................10
Chapter: 1, Sub-Chapter: 7
  In Praise of the Great Poets...................12
Chapter: 1, Sub-Chapter: 8
  In Praise of the Audience...................14
Chapter: 1, Sub-Chapter: 9
  In Praise of Supreme Meaning...................16
Chapter: 1, Sub-Chapter: 10
  In Praise of the Human Body...................17
Chapter 2. Signs of Fools
Chapter: 2, Sub-Chapter: 1
  The Signs of a Fool...................21
Chapter: 2, Sub-Chapter: 2
  The Signs of the Best Qualities...................24
Chapter: 2, Sub-Chapter: 3
  The Signs of Wrong Knowledge...................27
Chapter: 2, Sub-Chapter: 4
  Discourse on Devotion...................29
Chapter: 2, Sub-Chapter: 5
  The Quality of Worldly Activity (Rajas).31
Chapter: 2, Sub-Chapter: 6
  The Quality of Ignorance (Tamas)...................33
Chapter: 2, Sub-Chapter: 7
  The Quality of Purity (Sattva)...................35
Chapter: 2, Sub-Chapter: 8
  The Explanation of Pure Knowledge...................40
Chapter: 2, Sub-Chapter: 9
  The Attributes of the Dispassionate One
 42
Chapter: 2, Sub-Chapter: 10
  The Signs of a Learned Fool...................44
Chapter 3. Commentary on Life
Chapter: 3, Sub-Chapter: 1
  The Suffering at Birth...................47
Chapter: 3, Sub-Chapter: 2
  The Miseries of Life...................49
Chapter: 3, Sub-Chapter: 3
  Miseries of Life - Assessment of the Self (1)..53
Chapter: 3, Sub-Chapter: 4
  Miseries of Life - Assessment of Self (2)...................55
Chapter: 3, Sub-Chapter: 5
  Miseries of Life - Assessment of Self (3)...................58
Chapter: 3, Sub-Chapter: 6
  The Bodily Tortures...................61
Chapter: 3, Sub-Chapter: 7
  Tortures of the Elemental World...................64
Chapter: 3, Sub-Chapter: 8
  The Cosmic Tortures...................68
Chapter: 3, Sub-Chapter: 9
  Explanation of Death...................70
Chapter: 3, Sub-Chapter: 10
  Explanation of Desirelessness...................73
Chapter 4. Nine-Faceted Devotion
Chapter: 4, Sub-Chapter: 1
  Devotion Through Listening...................77
Chapter: 4, Sub-Chapter: 2
  Narration About God (Kirtan)...................79
Chapter: 4, Sub-Chapter: 3
  Remembrance of God's Name...................81
Chapter: 4, Sub-Chapter: 4
  Serving the Feet of the Guru...................83
Chapter: 4, Sub-Chapter: 5
  Devotion Through Worship...................84
Chapter: 4, Sub-Chapter: 6
  Devotion Through Bowing...................86
Chapter: 4, Sub-Chapter: 7
  Devotion Through Service...................88
Chapter: 4, Sub-Chapter: 8
  Devotion of Communion with God...................89
Chapter: 4, Sub-Chapter: 9
  Self-Surrender...................91
Chapter: 4, Sub-Chapter: 10
  The Four Types of Liberation...................93
Chapter 5. Mantras
Chapter: 5, Sub-Chapter: 1
  The Importance of the Guru...................95
Chapter: 5, Sub-Chapter: 2
  The Signs of a Guru...................97
Chapter: 5, Sub-Chapter: 3
  The Signs of a Disciple...................101
Chapter: 5, Sub-Chapter: 4
  The Signs of Teachings...................107
Chapter: 5, Sub-Chapter: 5
  Explanation of Knowledge...................109
Chapter: 5, Sub-Chapter: 6
  Explanation of Pure Knowledge...................111
Chapter: 5, Sub-Chapter: 7
  Signs of a Bound Person...................115
Chapter: 5, Sub-Chapter: 8
  The Signs of a Seeker...................118
Chapter: 5, Sub-Chapter: 9
  The Signs of an Aspirant...................121

Chapter: 5, Sub-Chapter: 10
  The Signs of an Accomplished One.....124
Chapter 6. The Search for God
Chapter: 6, Sub-Chapter: 1
  The Search for God..................127
Chapter: 6, Sub-Chapter: 2
  Attainment of Brahman..................129
Chapter: 6, Sub-Chapter: 3
  The Appearance of Illusion..................131
Chapter: 6, Sub-Chapter: 4
  Narration About Brahman..................134
Chapter: 6, Sub-Chapter: 5
  Narration About Reality and Illusion...135
Chapter: 6, Sub-Chapter: 6
  Discourse on Creation..................137
Chapter: 6, Sub-Chapter: 7
  Worship of God With Attributes..........140
Chapter: 6, Sub-Chapter: 8
  Dissolution of the Visible World 142
Chapter: 6, Sub-Chapter: 9
  In Search of Essence..................145
Chapter: 6, Sub-Chapter: 10
  The Indescribable 147
Chapter 7. Fourteen Brahmans
Chapter: 7, Sub-Chapter: 1
  An Auspicious Introduction..................151
Chapter: 7, Sub-Chapter: 2
  Explanation of Brahman..................155
Chapter: 7, Sub-Chapter: 3
  The Fourteen Brahmans..................158
Chapter: 7, Sub-Chapter: 4
  Explanation of Pure Brahman 161
Chapter: 7, Sub-Chapter: 5
  Discarding the Imagination of Duality 164
Chapter: 7, Sub-Chapter: 6
  Explanation of Bound and Liberated ..166
Chapter: 7, Sub-Chapter: 7
  Establishment of Spiritual Practice......170
Chapter: 7, Sub-Chapter: 8
  The Importance of Listening..............174
Chapter: 7, Sub-Chapter: 9
  The Importance of Listening (2)..........177
Chapter: 7, Sub-Chapter: 10
  The End of the Body..................180
Chapter 8. The Origin of Maya
Chapter: 8, Sub-Chapter: 1
  Perceiving God..................184
Chapter: 8, Sub-Chapter: 2
  A Subtle Doubt..................187
Chapter: 8, Sub-Chapter: 3
  A Subtle Doubt (2)..................190
Chapter: 8, Sub-Chapter: 4
  The Five Subtle Elements..................193

Chapter: 8, Sub-Chapter: 5
  The Five Manifest Elements 196
Chapter: 8, Sub-Chapter: 6
  Explanation of Restlessness..................200
Chapter: 8, Sub-Chapter: 7
  The Signs of Liberation..................202
Chapter: 8, Sub-Chapter: 8
  The Perception of Self..................206
Chapter: 8, Sub-Chapter: 9
  Signs of the Accomplished One..........210
Chapter: 8, Sub-Chapter: 10
  Clarification About the Void..................213
Chapter 9. Attributes and Form
Chapter: 9, Sub-Chapter: 1
  Questions..................218
Chapter: 9, Sub-Chapter: 2
  Narration on Brahman..................219
Chapter: 9, Sub-Chapter: 3
  Narration on Doubtlessness..................222
Chapter: 9, Sub-Chapter: 4
  Narration on Knowledge..................224
Chapter: 9, Sub-Chapter: 5
  Removing Guesswork..................227
Chapter: 9, Sub-Chapter: 6
  Explanation of Attributes and Forms. ..229
Chapter: 9, Sub- Chapter: 7
  Removal of Doubts..................233
Chapter: 9, Sub- Chapter: 8
  The End of the Body..................236
Chapter: 9, Sub- Chapter: 9
  Removal of Doubt..................238
Chapter: 9, Sub-Chapter: 10
  The State of the Self..................241
Chapter 10. The Universal Flame
Chapter: 10, Sub-Chapter: 1
  The Oneness of the Inner-Mind..........244
Chapter: 10, Sub-Chapter: 2
  Doubt About the Body..................246
Chapter: 10, Sub-Chapter: 3
  Clearing Doubts About the Body.........248
Chapter: 10, Sub-Chapter: 4
  Description of the Seed..................249
Chapter: 10, Sub-Chapter: 5
  The Five Dissolutions..................252
Chapter: 10, Sub-Chapter: 6
  Explanation of Delusion..................253
Chapter: 10, Sub-Chapter: 7
  Worship of God with Attributes...........256
Chapter: 10, Sub-Chapter: 8
  Explanation of Actual Experience........257
Chapter: 10, Sub-Chapter: 9
  Primordial Existence and Manifestation....260
Chapter: 10, Sub-Chapter: 10
  The Moving and the Unmoving..........262

Chapter 11. Bhima Dashaka

Chapter: 11, Sub-Chapter: 1
Explanation of the Final Conclusion...266

Chapter: 11, Sub-Chapter: 2
The Four Types of Gods......................268

Chapter: 11, Sub-Chapter: 3
The Teaching..271

Chapter: 11, Sub-Chapter: 4
Discrimination of Essence...................272

Chapter: 11, Sub-Chapter: 5
Discourse on Politics...........................274

Chapter: 11, Sub-Chapter: 6
Signs of a Spiritual Leader..................276

Chapter: 11, Sub-Chapter: 7
The Ever-Changing River....................277

Chapter: 11, Sub-Chapter: 8
The Inner-Self......................................278

Chapter: 11, Sub-Chapter: 9
The Teaching..279

Chapter: 11, Sub-Chapter: 10
Desireless Behavior..............................281

Chapter 12. Discrimination and Desirelessness

Chapter: 12, Sub-Chapter: 1
Description of Purity...........................283

Chapter: 12, Sub-Chapter: 2
Explanation of Direct Experience........284

Chapter: 12, Sub-Chapter: 3
Signs of a Devotee................................286

Chapter: 12, Sub-Chapter: 4
Discrimination and Detachment..........288

Chapter: 12, Sub-Chapter: 5
Self-Surrender......................................289

Chapter: 12, Sub-Chapter: 6
The Sequence of Creation....................291

Chapter: 12, Sub-Chapter: 7
Renunciation of Sense Objects............293

Chapter: 12, Sub-Chapter: 8
The Form of Time................................295

Chapter: 12, Sub-Chapter: 9
The Teaching About Effort..................297

Chapter: 12, Sub-Chapter: 10
Narration About the Best Person.........298

Chapter 13. Name and Form

Chapter: 13, Sub-Chapter: 1
Discrimination of Self and Non-Self....301

Chapter: 13, Sub-Chapter: 2
Explanation of Essence and Non-Essence. 303

Chapter: 13, Sub-Chapter: 3
Explanation of Creation......................305

Chapter: 13, Sub-Chapter: 4
The Dissolution...................................306

Chapter: 13, Sub-Chapter: 5
A Story...307

Chapter: 13, Sub-Chapter: 6
Summary of the Teaching...................309

Chapter: 13, Sub-Chapter: 7
Explanation of Experience...................311

Chapter: 13, Sub-Chapter: 8
Explanation of the Doer......................312

Chapter: 13, Sub-Chapter: 9
Explanation of the Self........................314

Chapter: 13, Sub-Chapter: 10
The Teaching..317

Chapter 14. Constant Meditation

Chapter: 14, Sub-Chapter: 1
Description of Desirelessness..............319

Chapter: 14, Sub-Chapter: 2
Explanation of Taking Alms................324

Chapter: 14, Sub-Chapter: 3
The Art of Poetry.................................325

Chapter: 14, Sub-Chapter: 4
Narration About Praising God............328

Chapter: 14, Sub-Chapter: 5
Narration About God (Lord Vishnu)...330

Chapter: 14, Sub-Chapter: 6
Description of Discernment.................333

Chapter: 14, Sub-Chapter: 7
The State of Present Times..................335

Chapter: 14, Sub-Chapter: 8
Uninterrupted Meditation...................337

Chapter: 14, Sub-Chapter: 9
Explanation of the Eternal Reality.......340

Chapter: 14, Sub-Chapter: 10
Explanation of Illusion........................342

Chapter 15. Chapter on the Self

Chapter: 15, Sub-Chapter: 1
The Signs of Wisdom...........................344

Chapter: 15, Sub-Chapter: 2
Detachment from Worldly Life............346

Chapter: 15, Sub-Chapter: 3
The Greatness of the Inner-Self...........348

Chapter: 15, Sub-Chapter: 4
Eternal Brahman.................................349

Chapter: 15, Sub-Chapter: 5
Explanation of the Moving..................351

Chapter: 15, Sub-Chapter: 6
Description of Wisdom........................353

Chapter: 15, Sub-Chapter: 7
Explanation of Above and Below.........355

Chapter: 15, Sub-Chapter: 8
Explanation About Microscopic Creatures. 358

Chapter: 15, Sub-Chapter: 9
The Creation of the Body....................360

Chapter: 15, Sub-Chapter: 10
Explanation of the Final Conclusion...362

Chapter 16. The Qualities of the Elements

Chapter: 16, Sub-Chapter: 1
In Praise of Valmiki..................365

Chapter: 16, Sub-Chapter: 2
In Praise of the Sun....................366

Chapter: 16, Sub-Chapter: 3
In Praise of the Earth..................367

Chapter: 16, Sub-Chapter: 4
Explanation of Water..................369

Chapter: 16, Sub-Chapter: 5
Explanation of Fire....................371

Chapter: 16, Sub-Chapter: 6
In Praise of the Wind..................373

Chapter: 16, Sub-Chapter: 7
The Great Element....................375

Chapter: 16, Sub-Chapter: 8
The Self That is Lord Rama..........377

Chapter: 16, Sub-Chapter: 9
The Many Forms of Worship........379

Chapter: 16, Sub-Chapter: 10
The Gunas and the Elements........381

Chapter 17. Prakriti and Purusha

Chapter: 17, Sub-Chapter: 1
The Power of God....................383

Chapter: 17, Sub-Chapter: 2
Explanation of Shiva and Shakti........385

Chapter: 17, Sub-Chapter: 3
The Importance of Listening..........387

Chapter: 17, Sub-Chapter: 4
Dissolution of Imagination..........389

Chapter: 17, Sub-Chapter: 5
The Continuous Sound of Soham........391

Chapter: 17, Sub-Chapter: 6
The Body and the Self..................392

Chapter: 17, Sub-Chapter: 7
Life in the World......................394

Chapter: 17, Sub-Chapter: 8
Explanation of the Principle Elements 396

Chapter: 17, Sub-Chapter: 9
The Four Bodies........................400

Chapter: 17, Sub-Chapter: 10
Signs of a Dull-Minded Person..........401

Chapter 18. Description of Various Objects

Chapter: 18, Sub-Chapter: 1
The Description of Various Deities......404

Chapter: 18, Sub-Chapter: 2
The Company of the Knowledgeable......405

Chapter: 18, Sub-Chapter: 3
The Teaching About Detachment........407

Chapter: 18, Sub-Chapter: 4
The Importance of the Body............408

Chapter: 18, Sub-Chapter: 5
The Signs of an Unfortunate Person....411

Chapter: 18, Sub-Chapter: 6
The Signs of the Best Person..............413

Chapter: 18, Sub-Chapter: 7
The Nature of Ordinary People..........414

Chapter: 18, Sub-Chapter: 8
Explanation of the Inner God..........416

Chapter: 18, Sub-Chapter: 9
Explanation of Sleep..................417

Chapter: 18, Sub-Chapter: 10
Negative Signs of Listeners..................419

Chapter 19. The Teaching

Chapter: 19, Sub-Chapter: 1
The Art of Writing....................422

Chapter: 19, Sub-Chapter: 2
Discourse on Giving Explanations......423

Chapter: 19, Sub-Chapter: 3
Signs of an Unfortunate Person..........424

Chapter: 19, Sub-Chapter: 4
The Signs of a Fortunate Person..........426

Chapter: 19, Sub-Chapter: 5
The Importance of the Body..............428

Chapter: 19, Sub-Chapter: 6
Explanation of Intelligence............430

Chapter: 19, Sub-Chapter: 7
Discourse on Making Effort..................432

Chapter: 19, Sub-Chapter: 8
The Description of Endeavors..........434

Chapter: 19, Sub-Chapter: 9
Discourse on Politics..................436

Chapter: 19, Sub-Chapter: 10
The Signs of Discrimination..............438

Chapter 20. The Chapter of Completion

Chapter: 20, Sub-Chapter: 1
The Complete and the Incomplete......441

Chapter: 20, Sub-Chapter: 2
The Three-Fold Creation..................443

Chapter: 20, Sub-Chapter: 3
Subtle Terms..........................445

Chapter: 20, Sub-Chapter: 4
Explanation of the Self..................447

Chapter: 20, Sub-Chapter: 5
The Four Substances..................449

Chapter: 20, Sub-Chapter: 6
The Attributes of the Self..................451

Chapter: 20, Sub-Chapter: 7
Explanation of Self..................453

Chapter: 20, Sub-Chapter: 8
The Field of the Body..................455

Chapter: 20, Sub-Chapter: 9
Explanation of the Subtle..............457

Chapter: 20, Sub-Chapter: 10
Explanation of Pure Brahman............458

Chapter 1. Salutations and Praises

Chapter: 1, Sub-Chapter: 1

The Beginning of the Book

|| ShriRam ||

1. The listener asks, "What is this book, and what is contained in it? What does one gain from listening to it?
2. The name of this book is **Dasbodh**. It is a dialogue between the Master (Guru) and listeners. This is a book of knowledge, and in this book, the path of Devotion (Bhakti) is explained in detail.
3. The explanation of the "Nine-Faceted Path of Devotion" (Navavidha Bhakti), the "Path of Knowledge" (Jnana), as well as a narration of the characteristics of Desirelessness (Vairagya) are contained here in this book. But mostly, this text is an explanation of the "Spiritual Science of Self-Knowledge" (Adhyatma).
4. The significance of this book is that it clearly states that human beings can surely realize God through devotion.
5. Mainly, this book makes clear statements regarding devotion, declarations as to the nature of Pure Knowledge, and indications as to the nature of one's "Being," the Self (Atman).
6. Presented here is pure spiritual instruction (upadesha) regarding the significance of attaining Liberation (Moksha), and the meaning of obtaining "Liberation through Union" (Sayujya Mukti).
7. This book makes clear statements about Reality, the pure "True Form" (Swaroopa; also translated as True Nature and Self Form). Also given here is confirmation of the formlessness beyond body-consciousness, and the meaning of detachment is clearly explained as well.
8. Provided here are clear statements regarding the nature of God and the nature of the devotee, as well as explanations regarding the nature of the distinction between the "individual consciousness" (Jiva) and "Pure Consciousness" (Shiva).
9. Explained herein are clear statements about Reality (Brahman), as well as confirmed declarations and information that is provided from many sources as to the true nature of the Self.
10. The basic nature of the various ways to worship, many different poetic styles, and many signs of wisdom are explained here.
11. The appearance of Illusion (Maya), the nature of the Five Elements, and the explanation as to the nature of the true "doer" is told here.
12. Many wrong notions are cleared away, many doubts and fears are removed, and many questions are answered.
13. Comprehensive knowledge from many ancient scriptures, which forms the main substance of this book, has been translated and is explained herein. It is impossible to tell all that is contained in this book in only a short introduction.
14. The complete *Dasbodh* is comprised of twenty chapters. Each chapter clearly discloses and reveals knowledge about various subjects.
15. The knowledge presented here is in accordance with many ancient texts, especially the *Upanishads* and Vedanta. Mainly this knowledge has been passed down from

word of mouth after listening, and has resulted in "Self-experience" that is supported by spiritual scriptures.
16. Many texts and scriptures agree with what is presented in this book so it should not be considered to be invalid. However, explanations are given so that what is presented can be verified and confirmed in your experience.
17. Some say that what is said in this book is not true. In doing so, they also deny the knowledge that is contained in ancient scriptures and the teachings of God.
18. Many great texts (gitas) are referred to here such as *Shivagita*, *Ramagita*, *Gurugita*, *Gharbhagita*, *Uttaragita*, and *Avadhutagita*, as well as knowledge from the *Vedas* and Vedanta.
19. Other supporting texts referred to here are the *Bhagavadgita*, the *Hansagita*, the *Pandavagita*, the *Ganeshagita*, the *Yamagita*, the *Upanishads*, and the *Bhagwat*.
20. All of these texts with their various teachings are relied upon, and the divine teaching of God, full of meaning, is presented here.
21. One who doubts and disbelieves the teachings of God contained here can be said to be downfallen, as everything said in this text is nothing other than God's own statement.
22. Without first studying the complete text, one who finds fault with it and criticizes it, does so out of pride and arrogance and will surely suffer a downfall in life.
23. With pride comes envy, and with envy comes hatred. This hatred then breeds anger, which continues to grow stronger.
24. In this way, one becomes spoiled and full of desire and anger, and the false ego affects one's attitude. This can be clearly seen in one's behavior.
25. How can it be said that one who is overwhelmed by desire and anger can be considered a good person? In ancient legend, even Rahu the demon[1] died after drinking the immortal nectar because of being evil-mindedness.
26. For now, let this talk end. Everyone takes according to one's own capacity. However, the reader should know that the best thing is to give up all pride.
27. The listeners have originally asked what is contained in this book, so this short explanation has now been given.
28. The fruit of listening to this text is that there is an immediate transformation in the activities of the listener, and that the root of doubt is quickly cut.
29. Here, one comes to easily know the correct path, and the real meaning of "Liberation through Union" (Sayujya Mukti). Difficult and torturous practices are not required.
30. Here, ignorance, sorrow, and delusion are destroyed, and there is an immediate acquisition of Knowledge (Jnana). This is the gain that one receives from this book.
31. Desirelessness, which is considered the ultimate fortune for yogis, can be acquired in one's life, and the development of skill in correct understanding through discrimination (viveka) can be gained.
32. Even those who are deluded and who have many negative qualities, understanding the importance of the wise utilization of time, become logical, discerning, and virtuous.
33. The lazy become alert, the sinful repent, and even critics come to worship on the Path of Devotion (Bhakti Marga).

---

[1] In Hindu mythology the demon Rahu attempted to partake of the nectar of immortality when it was being served to the gods, but he was detected and beheaded by Lord Vishnu. In this story, the nectar could not make him immortal because he was evil-minded.

34. The ignorant become aspirants, the foolish become attentive, and even non-believers can attain liberation through the path of devotion.
35. Many defects are destroyed, the downtrodden become pure, and human beings can attain the highest realization by listening to what is contained in this text.
36. Many dangers of bodily identification, and many doubts and miseries of the worldly life are destroyed by listening to what is contained in this text.
37. These are the benefits derived from this book. By listening to its contents, one can avoid downfall in life, and the mind will remain pacified and content.
38. One will receive the benefits according to their own understanding. Likewise, those who hold envy and malice in their mind will receive the same.

Thus in Shri Dasbodh, a dialogue between the Guru and disciple, Sub-Chapter 1 of Chapter 1, named "The Beginning of the Book" is concluded.

Chapter: 1, Sub-Chapter: 2

In Praise of Lord Ganesha

|| ShriRam ||

1. OM. Salutations to Lord Ganesha. You are the lord of the organs of perception and action, of the mind, and of the intellect. You are the one who is the giver of the fruits of all accomplishments. You are the destroyer of ignorance and delusion. You are the very form of instruction and understanding itself.
2. Reside within me at all times, and fill me with your intellect. Make me, who is deficient in speech, able to speak by means of your benevolent compassion and blessings.
3. By the power of your blessings the clouds of delusion disappear, and Time, who devours the entire universe, is made a servant.
4. When you bestow your blessings, obstacles and problems become powerless and run away at the mere mention of your name.
5. Therefore, you are called the "Destroyer of Obstacles." You are the shelter for the destitute, and even the gods Shiva and Vishnu worship you.
6. By bowing to you, who are the reservoir of all that is auspicious, all endeavors are accomplished, and calamities, obstacles, and troubles cannot create any obstruction.
7. Upon remembering your form, one experiences supreme contentment. When the concentration of the mind is fixed on you, the body becomes powerless as if paralyzed with great peace.
8. Your form with attributes is a treasure to behold. It is overwhelmingly beautiful and attractive. When you are performing your dance, all of the gods become motionless and spellbound.
9. You are continuously in ecstasy, always dancing blissfully. Your face shines with joy and delight.
10. Your form is immense and you stand as a massive figure with great strength. Your large forehead is adorned with red powder.
11. Many different fragrances ooze from your temples. The spreading of the aroma has brought swarms of honeybees that make a joyful humming sound.

12. Your trunk, both bends and is straight, and the humps of your forehead shine radiantly. Your lower lip droops elegantly with a most pleasing benevolent smile.
13. You are the master of the fourteen different streams of knowledge. Your tiny eyes move around while your huge ears flutter, making a flapping sound again and again.
14. Your crown, adorned with gems, shines with beautiful colors spreading their brilliance. Your earrings are adorned on the top with blue gems that sparkle and radiate their light.
15. Your tusks are white and strong surrounded with a golden ring inlaid with gems. At the rim of the ring are beautifully hung ornamental metallic leafs that sparkle and shine.
16. Your large belly is girdled tightly with a serpent. Tiny bells make a sweet soft jingling sound as your belly sways and moves to and fro.
17. You, with four arms and drooping belly, have a yellow silk cloth tied around your waist, and the hooded cobra around your belly makes a constant hissing sound.
18. Swaying his head, with his tongue sliding in and out, he is coiled around your waist with his head rising up to the region of your naval, as he glances around.
19. You wear garlands of many varieties of flowers that hang down from your neck to your naval region where the serpent is wrapped. A beautiful pendant studded with gemstones glimmers as it embellishes the garland that adorns your lotus heart.
20. You brandish an axe in one hand, hold a lotus in your second, a shiny piece of sharp broken tusk in your third hand, and your favorite little round sweet in the forth.
21. You act and dance in a skilled performance. You dance to the rhythms of cymbals and drums while making sweet sounding verbal expressions all the while.
22. Not remaining still for even a moment, you excel in swiftness. Your figure is extremely attractive and beautiful and adorned with auspicious markings. You are a mine of elegance and beauty.
23. The anklets with small bells at your feet make a jingling sound that is pleasing to the mind, and both of your feet look exquisitely graceful as you dance.
24. The assembly of gods is graced by your presence as the dazzling light of your glorious divine raiment spreads its radiance. All of the various types of literature stand ready at your service.
25. You, who are handsome like this, are the storehouse of all of the streams of knowledge. I prostrate with highest regard to you with all of my limbs outstretched and all parts of the body touching the floor.
26. Upon hearing the description of your form and qualities, the intellect that was confused becomes illumined. While listening to the description of your good qualities even the "Goddess of Wisdom," Shri Saraswati, is delighted.
27. Even Lord Brahma and the other gods worship Lord Ganesha. In comparison to those gods, human beings are so petty, yet this does not matter, even human beings who are of dull intelligence should meditate upon lord Ganesha.
28. Not only the foolish and unfortunate, but also these who are lower than the lowest, can be transformed and become alert and expert in all subjects.[2]
29. Like this, is Lord Ganesha, who is such a powerful and accomplished deity that realization can be gained by the one who sings his praises. In this, the Kaliyuga, it is Lord Ganesha and Shri Saraswati who are the main deities who bestow blessings.

---

[2] Lord Ganesha is considered to be the seat of intellect in human beings. So it is considered that all learning and accomplishment comes from him.

30. With all my intellect I have praised Lord Ganesha as per my capacity, keeping in mind the desire for "Supreme Truth" (Paramartha), which is the ultimate objective in life.

Thus in Dasbodh, a dialogue between the Guru and disciple, Sub-Chapter 2 of Chapter 1, named "In Praise of Lord Ganesha," is concluded.

Chapter: 1, Sub-Chapter: 3

In Praise of Goddess Sharada

|| ShriRam ||

1. Now I bow down to Goddess Sharada (Saraswati) who is the mother of Vedas. She is the daughter of the Creator (Brahma). She is the origin of words, the deity of speech, and the original "Great Illusion" (Mahamaya).
2. She is the origin of the sprouting of words, the one who speaks the limitless number of words so that they may be heard, and it is she who is the one that reveals the inner meaning of words.
3. She is the one who is not different from the state of absorption (samadhi) of the yogis, the one who is the prudence of the courageous, and the one who destroys the limitations of both knowledge (vidya) and ignorance (avidya).
4. She is the one who is the wife of "Original Being" (Purusha). She is the "Fourth State" of consciousness (Turya; SatChitAnanda) that is the great objective for which sages undertake heroic efforts to attain.
5. She is the peace of the "Great Ones" (Mahantas), she is the Power (Shakti) of the Almighty Lord (Ishwara). She is the detachment of the "Self-Realized" (Jnanis) that keeps them free of worldly entanglements.
6. It is her play (lila) that creates and destroys a limitless number of universes easily while she always remains hidden in the oneness of Primordial Being.
7. She is all that is visible, yet when inquired into, she cannot be found with thought. Her limitless nature is not understood even by Brahma and the other gods.
8. She is the essential root of all activity, pure awareness, and the inspiration that is the dawning of realization. She is of the nature of the "Bliss of the Self," and the "Power of Knowledge."
9. She is of the nature of radiant beauty, the brilliance of "Absolute Reality" (Parabrahman). She is the one by whose words creation arises and is sustained, and it is by her words that Vedic Knowledge destroys the illusion of mundane worldly existence.
10. She is the one who bestows liberation and good fortune. She is the fullness of the vitality of Life, the purity in righteousness, and the source of beauty.
11. She is the manifest form of unmanifest Being (Purusha). She is the expression of the expanse of His unlimited willpower. She is the one who is the controller of Time which devours all, and she is the benevolence of the "True Guru" (Sadguru).
12. She is the one who reveals the pathway to spiritual life and self-inquiry. By her power of words, she reveals the difference between Essence and non-essence that enables one to cross over the ocean of worldly life.

13. Like this, the Great Goddess, the incomparable accomplished Sharada has adorned herself with many different forms and is full with the four different types of speech[3].
14. The three inner types of speech become manifest in the fourth type that is named Vaikhari, which is the actual words that are verbally spoken. In this way, all that appears takes place because of the Goddess Sharada.
15. She is the mother of Brahma, Vishnu, Shiva and all of the other gods. All of the three worlds are the expanse of her manifestation alone.
16. She is the origin of spiritual life, and it is she alone who is "True Knowledge." She is the pure and changeless "True Form" (Swaroopa).
17. She is the meditation of the yogis, the contemplation of the aspirants, and the inner-mind of the accomplished ones (Siddhas) in the form of absorption in Reality.
18. Her identity is without attributes, yet it is she only who is recognized in all experiences. She completely pervades all forms.
19. All of the ancient scriptures (*Shastras, Puranas, Vedas, Upanishads*) praise her incessantly, and all living beings give praise to her in all of her various forms.
20. She is the greatness of the *Vedas* and *Shastras*. She is that which cannot be labeled, yet is referred to as the "Supreme Self" (Paramatman).
21. She is the many various streams of knowledge, the many varieties of accomplishments, and the resolve of the intellect. She is the subtlest of principles and the purity of Pure Knowledge.
22. She is the Self-worship of the devotees of God, the inner state of those true to the Inner-Self, and the liberation of the "liberated" (Jivanmukta), which is the union with Reality.
23. She is the limitless "Illusion of God" (Lord Vishnu) that cannot be comprehended, and her play of enchanting tricks makes even the wisest among wise, with high intellect, confused.
24. She is all that is seen with the eyes, all that is identified by words, and all that is felt by the mind. All of manifestation is her form.
25. Prayers, singing praise, and all expressions of devotion cannot exist without the presence of Illusion (Maya). The meaning of this statement will be known to the experienced ones.
26. Therefore, to Her, who is greatest of the great, the "God of Gods," I offer salutations, being a part of her expression.

Thus in Dasbodh, a dialogue between the Guru and disciple, Sub-Chapter 3 of Chapter 1, named "In Praise of Goddess Sharada" is concluded.

---

[3] The four types speech are "Para" or original arising of thought or primal arising of speech at the region of the navel, the "Pashyanti" which is the subtle formation of the word at the level of the heart, the "Madhyama" which is the subtle manifestation of the sound of words in the form of a whisper at the region of the throat, and the "Vaikhari" which is the gross manifestation of speech or thought at the level of the mouth. Later on in the text Samartha Ramdas gives a detailed explanation of the four types of speech (Chapter 18, sub-chapter 8).

Chapter: 1, Sub-Chapter: 4

In Praise of the True Master

|| ShriRam ||
1. Now, salutations are offered to the "True Master," the Sadguru, who cannot be described. He is that "True Form" (Swaroopa) where Illusion cannot touch. How can an ignorant person like me understand his greatness?
2. Where the knowledge of the *Vedas* falls short saying "Not this, not this" (Neti, neti[4]), how can the foolish intellect try to describe him?
3. It is not possible to comprehend him in thought. I salute you from a distance, Oh Lord Guru (Gurudeva)! Reach out to bring me across the ocean of worldly life.
4. There was a feeble hope of praising you, but the confidence of being able to describe you with the help of Illusion is shattered. You are as you are, Oh Sadguru!
5. The mind was hoping to praise you with the help of the strength of Illusion (Maya), but Illusion itself became unwilling to try. What can I do?
6. Because the greatness of the Supreme Self (Paramatman) cannot be known, imagery is used as a pointer. Like that, with the help of Illusion I shall try to describe the greatness of the True Master.
7. With a feeling of devotion in the mind one should remember God in meditation. In the same way, I shall praise the Sadguru now.
8. Jai! Jai! Praises to the "King of Gurus"! You are the one who is the seed of the universe, *and* the one who permeates the universe. You are "Supreme Original Being" (ParamaPurusha), the triumph of Liberation, and the brother of the downtrodden.
9. Because of your assurances, the overwhelming uncontrollable Illusion disappears, in the same way that darkness disappears in the presence of sunlight.
10. The sun dispels darkness, but afterwards at night the universe is once again filled with darkness.
11. The Sadguru is not like that. He destroys the cycle of birth and death by completely uprooting ignorance.
12. Gold can never be transformed into iron. In same way, one who is a servant of the guru will never again fall back into doubt.
13. If a river merges with the Ganges (the sacred river Ganga) it becomes the Ganges. Even if one were to try to separate it, it cannot be done.
14. In this example, before joining with the Ganges, the river is known by the world only as a small separate stream. However, it is not like that in the case of the disciple of the Sadguru. He is not separate. He immediately becomes the Master.
15. The philosopher's "touchstone" is said to transform iron into gold, but it cannot change a stone into a stone like itself, and the gold it produces cannot turn iron into gold. However, with the teachings of the Sadguru, the disciple is able to give teachings to many people.
16. The disciple becomes the same as the guru, while the transformed gold cannot turn iron into gold, therefore, the simile of the philosopher's stone is not really applicable to the Sadguru.

---

[4] Neti, Neti - The Vedas could not describe in words the nature of the Sadguru (the words fall short; he is beyond words), therefore they said that he is "Not this, Not this," because it is not possible to say what he is.

17. The simile of the ocean is sometimes used, but the ocean is very salty. Even if he is compared to an "ocean of sweetness," that ocean would still be destroyed at the time of the final destruction of the universe. The Sadguru will not be destroyed.
18. Sometimes the comparison with the huge mythological Meru Mountain is used, but that mountain is heavy and made of hard stone. The Sadguru is not like that at all. He is soft and compassionate towards meek and miserable people.
19. The simile with the sky is often used, yet the sky has attributes, and the Sadguru is without attributes (nirguna), so this comparison also falls short.
20. Sometimes a bold comparison to the solidity of the Earth is used, but the Earth will also be destroyed at the time of the final destruction. Thus, the comparison with the Earth is also not suitable.
21. Sometimes the Sadguru is compared to the Sun, yet science tells us that the Sun has limits to its light, while the Sadguru is limitless.
22. Therefore, the comparison of the Sadguru to the Sun also falls short. His "Light of Knowledge" is exceedingly vast. The Sadguru cannot even be compared with Shesha[5], the great serpent of legend, because Shesha carries the burden of the world, and the Sadguru removes the burden of the world.
23. Sometimes the comparison with water is used, however water will dry up at the time of the final dissolution, while the Sadguru is everlasting. He will never be destroyed.
24. The Sadguru is sometimes compared with the "Nectar of Immortality." However, even the gods who consume that nectar will eventually disappear. It is only the blessings of the Sadguru that truly make one immortal.
25. The Sadguru is compared to Kalpataru[6], the wish-fulfilling tree, but the Sadguru takes one beyond all desires and wishes, so how can such a comparison be considered acceptable?
26. The Sadguru does not leave any worries in the mind. When there is no worry in the mind, who will bother with Chintamani, the mythological stone that removes worries? Similarly, why would one without desires have any need for the milk of Kamadhenu[7], the wish-fulfilling cow?
27. The Sadguru is often compared to great wealth, but wealth is destructible. The great wealth of liberation awaits at the door of the Sadguru.
28. The "Kingdom of Heaven" and even the wealth of Indra, the "King of the Gods," all gets destroyed after a period of time. However, the blessings of the Sadguru do not get destroyed by time.
29. All of the gods including Shiva, Vishnu and Brahma will be destroyed after a period of time. The only thing that is indestructible is the existence of the Sadguru.
30. What label can one give to him? The entirety of creation is destructible so not even the vast play of the five elements[8] works as a comparison.

---

[5] In Hindu mythology, Shesha is a giant snake who is said to be the support of the world. The literal translation of the word Shesha means "remainder." At the time of the great dissolution of the world, what is left over, or what "remains," is Shesha. Thus, it is said that Shesha is the support of the world.

[6] In rural India, the village people leave pieces of old clothing on Kalpataru, the wish-fulfilling tree, in the hope of having their desires fulfilled.

[7] In Hindu mythology, the magical stone Chintamani removes the worries of whomever possesses it, and Kamadhenu, the wish-fulfilling cow, fulfills one's desires with it's milk.

[8] The Five Elements, or Panchabhooti, are Sky (Space), Air (Wind), Fire (Light), Water, and Earth.

31. The Sadguru truly cannot be described. What has been said here is only my description. The indications of his inner state are understood only by those who are devoted to the Inner-Self.

Thus in Dasbodh, a dialogue between the Guru and disciple, Sub-Chapter 4 of Chapter 1, named "In Praise of the True Master" is concluded.

Chapter: 1, Sub-Chapter: 5

In Praise of the Saints

|| ShriRam ||

1. Now, I offer salutations to the virtuous ones. They are the abode of spiritual life. It is through them that the hidden Self-Knowledge gets revealed to the people.
2. Keeping the company of saints (santasanga) provides incomparable benefits. "That" which is rarely realized, and which is difficult to grasp, becomes easily realized in their company.
3. Reality is evident everywhere. However, it cannot be attained or located through spiritual practice (sadhana) or by undergoing various austerities.
4. In looking for it, many expert examiners get deceived, and even for those who have visions and mystical experiences, it is if they are blind. By the very act of looking they are missing "That" which is already the closest thing.
5. It cannot be seen with the help of a lamp, nor with any other forms of light. Even if one applies ointments to the eyes, it cannot be seen.
6. Neither the light of the moon in any of its sixteen phases, nor the extreme bright light of the sun can reveal it.
7. The sunlight can reveal the fine threads of a spider's web, as well as microscopic particles and atoms, but it cannot reveal Reality.
8. The sunlight can reveal the split end of a hair, but not Reality. Reality can only be realized by the aspirant who keeps the company of saints.
9. It is only where arguments disappear, efforts are exhausted, and logical thinking cannot work, that That which is already one's own can be found.
10. In trying to see Reality, discrimination fails, words falter, and the faculties of the mind are of no use.
11. Even Shesha, the serpent which is the support of the world who is said to have one-thousand mouths, becomes completely exhausted while trying to describe "That."
12. The knowledge contained in the *Vedas* has shed light on everything. There is no greater knowledge that compares to Vedic Knowledge, yet even the *Vedas* cannot reveal Reality.
13. Reality becomes realized in one's own experience in the company of saints. The importance of their company cannot be expressed in words.
14. Illusion (Maya) has many strange forms and modes of expression, but it cannot say anything about Reality. Only the saints can explain the way of reaching That which is beyond Illusion.

15. Reality cannot be described with words and the saints are of the same "True Form" (Swaroopa) as Reality. Thus, it is not possible for words to describe them.
16. The saints are the abode of bliss and satisfaction itself. They are the very root of contentment. Such are the saints.
17. The saints are the tranquility of liberation, and the contentment of one's own Self. Another way of saying this is that they are the fruit of devotion. Such are the saints.
18. Saints are the true religion, which is one's own Self-religion, they are the true form of contentment, and they are the true sacred place of purity.
19. The saints are the temple of absorption (samadhi), the reservoir of the power of discrimination, and the home of "Ultimate Liberation."
20. The saints are the firm resolution of Truth, and the fulfillment of Victory. The saints are the success of the proper utilization of time. The saint's realization is the form of accomplishment itself.
21. The saints are adorned with the wealth of liberation. Because of this, they have made many poor beings rich like themselves.
22. The saints are powerful, benevolent, and charitable without limits. They are capable of giving the knowledge of inquiry and thoughtfulness that others cannot give.
23. There have been great kings and emperors in the past and now in the present, and there will be more in the future, yet none of them can ever offer liberation.
24. That Reality which cannot be found in all the three worlds (Trailokya; heaven, earth, and netherworld, or waking, dream, and deep sleep states) is what the saints and virtuous men offer that no one else can give. Their greatness cannot be described with words.
25. That which cannot be obtained in the three worlds, and cannot be understood through studying the *Vedas* and *Upanishads* is the Absolute Reality (Parabrahman) which can only be realized within when revealed by the saints.
26. Such is the greatness of the saints. The more that is spoken, the more the words fall short in any attempt at some comparison. It is because of them that the revelation of the Supreme Self (Paramatman) occurs.

Thus in Dasbodh, a dialogue between the Guru and disciple, Sub-Chapter 5 of Chapter 1, named "In Praise of the Saints" is concluded.

Chapter: 1, Sub-Chapter: 6

In Praise of the Listeners

|| ShriRam ||
1. Now, I bow in reverence to the listeners who are comprised of devotees, knowledgeable people, saints, renunciates, the virtuous, yogis, those who are full of good attributes, and those who speak the Truth.
2. Some are the ocean of purity, some are reservoirs of intellect, and some are like mines of the gems of words.
3. Some enjoy the nectar of knowledge from many texts, and some are eloquent speakers who can clear the many doubts of men at the appropriate times.

4. Their capacity is limitless, and they are like incarnations of God (Ishwara), or actual gods themselves, sitting in the audience.
5. They are a group of sages (rishis) who are themselves the very form of peace and purity. Because of them, the audience is supremely magnificent.
6. In their heart dwells the essence of the *Vedas*, in their speech resides Shri Saraswati the goddess of speech and learning, and when they speak, it is as if the guru of the gods is speaking.
7. They are pure like fire. They are like rays of inspiration from the sun. Nothing in the entire universe can be compared to their knowledge.
8. They are continuously alert, and they have the knowledge of all of the three aspects of time (past, present and future). They are Self-realized and always without pride.
9. There remains nothing that has gone unnoticed by them. They have given careful consideration to everything that has appeared in their mind.
10. Whatever comes to mind to tell them, they already know. What remains to be explained to them from a position of authoritative knowledge?
11. They are appreciative of virtuous qualities, therefore I speak to them without any hesitation or doubt. These fortunate ones receive and retain what is presented.
12. Those who always eat the best food sometimes want simple meals for a change. My words and expressions are like that, simple and common.
13. Each one worships the Supreme God with one's heart according to their capacity, but nowhere is it said that one should not worship God.
14. I am an unskilled speaker, and the audience is none other than God. I try my best to worship them with my inadequate speech.
15. I do not have scholastic knowledge or artistic flair. I am not clever with words, nor do I have great poetic skill with sweet sounding words when speaking about Devotion (Bhakti), Knowledge (Jnana), and Desirelessness (Vairagya).
16. Such is my clumsy play with words, yet still I speak, because the Lord of the Universe (Jagadisha) enjoys the feeling of devotion that is conveyed in my words.
17. You, the audience, are the form of this Almighty Lord. I am not skilled in giving explanations of ancient scriptures, but with the small intellect and simple thoughts, I can give informal explanations to you.
18. The son of the powerful man, even if dull-minded, is still powerful. Similar to this is the relationship I have with you and the saints.
19. While the lion and tiger are fierce and we are struck with fear when seeing them, their cubs play in front of them fearlessly.
20. Similarly, I am the child of saints, and I am speaking to you saintly people, so I am confident that my concern will surely be viewed with compassion in your thoughts.
21. Just as when one's own speech is incorrect, some action is required to correct it, likewise, if there are shortcomings in my talks, please make them complete.
22. The sign of affection is that it comes automatically for the mind. Similarly, you saintly and virtuous people are the parents of the world.
23. Understand the inner meaning of my words, and do that which is appropriate. "Give your full attention to the narration that comes after this," says the humble servant of the servant of God.

Thus in Dasbodh, a dialogue between the Guru and disciple, Sub-Chapter 6 of Chapter 1, named "In Praise of the Listeners" is concluded.

Chapter: 1, Sub-Chapter: 7

In Praise of the Great Poets

|| ShriRam ||

1. Now I bow to the great poets who are like the gods of the mastery of words. It can be said that they are the Supreme God of the *Vedas* incarnate.
2. They are the dwelling place of Shri Saraswati, the goddess of speech and learning, they are the life in many arts, and it can rightly be said that they are the home of words.
3. They are adorned with the power and richness of the words that are used to describe the importance of the "Lord of the Universe." Because of their skill at describing the glory of God, they are called poets.
4. They are the ocean of the jewels of words, the lake of liberation of the liberated, and the reservoir of intellectual skill that has been specially created.
5. They are the mines of the books of spiritual knowledge, they are like the stone that removes worries (Chintamani), or the milk from the wish-fulfilling cow (Kamadhenu) that is flowing down to the audience.
6. They are like the wish-fulfilling tree of the imagination, the majesty of the expression of Freedom, and the vast expanse of Ultimate Liberation.
7. They are of the embodiment of That which is one's Self beyond this world appearance. They reveal the secret path of the yogis, and they bring to form the words of the "Ultimate Truth" of the Jnanis.
8. They are the sign of That which is beyond Illusion, the indication of That which is attributeless, and they fittingly describe the wondrous Illusion.
9. They are the inner meaning of the *Upanishads*, and they easily reveal the rare knowledge of the Supreme God. They are Self-Realization in the form of the poet.
10. Poets are the ointment that opens the eyes of those desirous of liberation, the spiritual practice of aspirants, and the satisfaction of the accomplished ones. This is definite.
11. The poets are the shelter of one's own "True Religion" (Swadharma) which gives victory over the mind. They are humble in their ways, and they spread their humility to others.
12. The poets are the proper guardians of desirelessness, the adornment of devotees, and the preservers of True Religion.
13. Poets are the affection of the affectionate, they are the object of meditation of the meditators, and they spread the fame of great devotees.
14. They are the origin of spiritual practices, and the fruit of all efforts. Many tasks are accomplished by only listening to the words of the poet. Their words are like an offering from God to the devotee (prasad).
15. Upon first hearing the poet's skill with words, happiness swells within. It is because of the words of the poets that the intellect is enlightened.
16. Poets are the qualification of the scholars, the power of the powerful, and the skill of clever people in many various ways.

17. The poets are their poetic compositions. They write in various styles, expression, and meter, and they bring out the differences between prose and poetry, as well as initiate many new linguistic methods.
18. Poets are the jewels of language in the universe. They are the adornment of the "Goddess of Prosperity" (Lakshmi), and the resolve leading to all accomplishments.
19. The poets bring prestige to a gathering. They are adornments of good fortune, and protectors of happiness.
20. Poets describe the forms of many gods, they tell the importance of sages, and they praise and reveal the power of scriptural spiritual science (*Shastras*).
21. Without the activities of the poets, the upliftment of the world would not be possible. Therefore, they are the support of the universe.
22. Access to the many streams of knowledge is not possible without these great poet gods. All knowledge of everything flows from the poets.
23. In earlier times, many poets like Valmiki, Vyasa, and others have come and gone. From them, the power of discrimination has been offered to all people.
24. In earlier days, many poems and narrations were composed and compared, and scholarly knowledge was gained by scholars that enhanced their capabilities.
25. Many such great poets lived in the past, are alive today, and many will come to live in the future. I offer salutations to them all.
26. The poets are the form of wisdom, just like the "Guru to the Gods" (Brihaspati). The *Vedas* and other scriptures speak through their mouths and words.
27. Because of their generous nature, many doctrines are translated, and ultimately the poets speak the entire Truth without any doubts whatsoever.
28. The poets are like the clouds showering the nectar of immortality on us. It can be said that they are the flowing rivers of the nine types of emotions[9] expressed in literature, or lakes overflowing with happiness.
29. They are the treasure-trove of discrimination appearing in human form. They are overflowing with thoughts about Reality.
30. They are the storehouse of the "original primal power of manifestation" (Adishakti). Compared to them, all other things seem to be lacking. It can be said that it is only by great fortune that they have become manifest for all people.
31. They are like ships that are forever overflowing with happiness, and they are very useful to mankind, offering many different ways of exploration.
32. They are the wealth of Reality. They are the realization of the oneness of God for the yogis, and the fruition of devotion.
33. They are the greatness of God (Ishwara) that is greater than space, and their poetic compositions are more extensive than the created universe.
34. Now, let this be enough of these thoughts. The poets are the support to the world. I offer salutations to them lying prostrate in reverence with all eight parts of the body outstretched.[10]

Thus in Dasbodh, a dialogue between the Guru and disciple, Sub-Chapter 7 of Chapter 1, named "In Praise of the Poets" is concluded.

---

[9] The nine types of emotions according to vedic literature are love, joy, wonder, courage, peace, sadness, anger, fear, and disgust.
[10] The eight parts of the body are - two feet, two knees, two arms, torso, and forehead, laying flat on the ground.

Chapter: 1, Sub-Chapter: 8

In Praise of the Audience

|| ShriRam ||

1. Now, I bow to all who are present in the audience. Liberation is easily attained here for the audience where the "Lord of the World" (Jagadisha) is himself waiting with affection.
2. The Lord said to Narada (a great devotee of Narayana, Lord Vishnu) "My place is not in heaven (Vaikuntha, the abode of Vishnu), nor in the hearts of the yogis. I dwell where my devotees are singing my praises."
3. Because of this, the gathering of devotees is superior. The Lord says, "My abode is where devotees sing and chant the name of God aloud, with joyful voices."
4. The abode of God is where devotees sing of God's glory with great love, where the narration of the stories of God are told, where music is used to praise him, and where the discourses and listening to the knowledge contained in the *Vedas* goes on continuously.
5. Where the qualities of God are expounded upon and many commentaries are given, and where discussions about the various aspects of the science of Self-Knowledge are taking place, this is the abode of God.
6. God resides where many doubts are cleared and many suspicions are removed to satisfaction, and where the mind becomes fixed in the object of meditation through the eloquent play of words that are being spoken.
7. In such gatherings, devotees are full of love and devotion, they are good natured, deeply thoughtful, virtuous in nature (sattvic; inclined towards spirituality), and there are many singers singing delightful songs full of devotional feeling.
8. The devotees are dutiful, well behaved, generous, and on the right path. They are pious, virtuous, pure in their thoughts, and kind in their deeds.
9. There are yogis who are free of anger, ascetics who are disciplined in austerities, and some who are indifferent and desireless, who reside in the forest.
10. Some are renunciates (sanyasins) with matted hair belonging to the Nath sect, some are wearing the marks of the worshippers of Vishnu (vaishnavas), some are young celibates, and some are great "Masters of Yoga" (Yogeshwaras).
11. There are some who are reciting mantras and performing austerities while residing in holy places, and some are great yogis who have controlled their minds to such an extent that they behave like common people while remaining aloof in a crowd.
12. Some are accomplished (siddhas), some holy men (sadhus), and some are aspirants (sadhakas). Some are proficient in the use of many mantras, and some are loyal worshippers who are full of good qualities.
13. There are saints, virtuous men, and scholars. There are some who are knowledgeable of vedic literature and spiritual science. There are many great men who are highly intelligent knowers of everything who are fully content, and whose actions are flawlessly pure.

14. There are many yogis, many who are experts in scholastic knowledge, and there are great sages (rishis). There are shrewd and logical great poets, and there are those who have conquered the mind and are abiding in silence and nakedness.
15. There are knowers of Brahman and the Self who understand the nature of Reality and the nature of the body. There are students of yogic science, and those who are accomplished in yogic austerities who are not involved in worldly life at all.
16. There are scholars and narrators of the ancient mythological stories (*Puranas*), learned priests who have studied and recite the *Vedas*, and there are those who are knowledgeable in the ancient rituals in the *Yajur Veda* (a part of the *Vedas* that contains instructions on various rituals).
17. There are many good natured and versatile listeners, there are some who perform sacred fire rituals, there are healers and medicine men, and some who are very charitable to others.
18. There are some who have the knowledge of all the three times (past, present and future), and there are some who have heard a great deal of knowledge yet have no pride or expectations.
19. There are those who are full of peace, forgiveness, compassion, and virtue. There are those full of the sattva quality whose mind is clear, being full with Knowledge (Jnana).
20. Such are the leaders of the gathering where there is discrimination between the permanent and impermanent. Their greatness is divine. How can it be described?
21. Where people are gathering to listen to discourse about "Supreme Meaning" (Paramartha; Supreme Truth), the way is made easy and effortless.
22. In this gathering is found people with the best qualities. They are by nature peaceful, calm, pleasing, and always happy and fresh.
23. There are many people who are endowed with knowledge of various arts, and who have special good qualities of God. They are adored wherever they gather together.
24. There are some who are engaged in worldly life, and there are those who have turned their back to the world. There are some who are leading a family life, and those who are solely on the path of spirituality and have retired from family life to live as hermits and ascetics.
25. They are old and young, and men and women, and all are continuously meditating upon the Lord (Vishnu; the Christ Consciousness) within.
26. Like this are the people of God. To them I give my regards. Because of them, we get great satisfaction.
27. I bow to those who comprise such a gathering where the praises of the beloved Lord are always going on.
28. Where images of the Lord are present, satisfaction is obtained. This is confirmed in many texts given to us by great saints.
29. In the present Kali Yuga (according to Hindu cosmology, the current age) it is through the singing of the praises of God (kirtan), and in hearing the narration of the stories of God in gatherings, that many doubts are dispelled and completely eliminated.

Thus in Dasbodh, a dialogue between the Guru and disciple, Sub-Chapter 8 of Chapter 1, named "In Praise of the Audience" is concluded.

Chapter: 1, Sub-Chapter: 9

In Praise of Supreme Meaning

|| ShriRam ||
1. Now I shall praise the "Supreme Truth" (Paramartha) that is of the nature of the ultimate welfare of aspirants. Of all the powerful yogas this is the most powerful means for liberation.
2. Actually, it is very easy, but it has become difficult for people because they have missed the importance of the association with wise and virtuous people (satsang).
3. There are many practices which offer results in the future, but the realization of Brahman and the essence of vedic science can be experienced immediately.
4. It is present everywhere, but it is not perceived. It is indifferent to everything. It sees everything, yet always remains ever unseen itself.
5. It is open like the sky, but it is only the competent yogis who know this hidden path. Others generally do not easily come to know the hidden meaning.
6. It is the essence of Self-essence. It is permanent and never suffers any damage or loss. Thieves can never take it away, no matter how hard they may try.
7. It has no fear of king or government, nor of fire or fierce animals. It would not be correct to say anything such as this.
8. The "Absolute Reality," Parabrahman, cannot be moved. It will never leave its place even after the end of time. It remains always where it is.
9. It is one's own true belonging that never changes. It never increases or decreases over time.
10. It cannot deteriorate or ever become invisible, yet it cannot be seen without a Sadguru's teaching.
11. Powerful yogis in the past realized Paramartha and called it the "Supreme Secret."
12. For those who tried to find it, the meaning was revealed, while for others, even though it was very close, it became unattainable even after many lives.
13. The wonder of this Paramartha is that once known, the signs of birth and death disappear, and one attains "Ultimate Liberation" (Sayujya Mukti) which is the identification with That which is nearest.
14. With discrimination (viveka), Illusion disappears, and one comes to realize Parabrahman through contemplative thoughtfulness and inquiry.
15. When Brahman is experienced fully, the entire appearance of the creation of the five elements becomes submerged in Brahman and is felt to be insignificant.
16. The worldly life appears untrue, and Illusion is seen as a false story when the "Pure Self" is perceived inwardly through discrimination.
17. When established in Brahman, doubts and suspicions are gone, and the entirety of creation becomes like an old tattered and torn rag that is fit to be discarded.
18. Like this, is Paramartha. One who puts in effort to realize it is one who is acting in their own best interest. To what extent can I describe the capacity of this most powerful and effective path?

19. Because of this Paramartha, Brahma and other gods find contentment, and yogis become absorbed in Absolute Reality.
20. Paramartha is the contentment of all who are accomplished with the "Supreme Experience." Even the ignorant become pure in the company of saints.
21. Paramartha makes life worthwhile. This Supreme Meaning is the real savior of the world, and is the true spiritual life that gives realization which is beyond this world.
22. Paramartha is the support of the ascetics and aspirants. It shows the way to cross over the ocean of the worldly life.
23. One who has this Paramartha is like a true ruler, while one without this Paramartha is the equivalent of a beggar. This Supreme Truth cannot be compared to anything.
24. Only through the merit of innumerable lives does one arrive at this Supreme Truth through which the Supreme Self (Paramatma) is directly experienced.
25. One who has realized the Supreme Self has made his life worthwhile, while all others can only be said to have been born and neglected their rightful inheritance.
26. Now let all of this be. Without any attention to realizing God, those people who only strive for success in worldly life are fools who do not even see his face.
27. Those who are wise follow the path of Paramartha and make life worthwhile. With devotion to Lord Vishnu the fame of those great ones who have come before is enhanced.

Thus in Dasbodh, a dialogue between the Guru and disciple, Sub-Chapter 9 of Chapter 1, named "In Praise of the Supreme Meaning" is concluded.

Chapter: 1, Sub-Chapter: 10

In Praise of the Human Body

|| ShriRam ||

1. Blessed is this human body. See how unique it is. The one who uses it to follow this path of Supreme Truth becomes successful.
2. With this human body, some take to the path of devotion while others become extremely detached and go to live in the hills and mountains.
3. Some wander to different places of pilgrimage while some practice various vows and rituals, and some put complete faith in the continuous chanting of the name of God.
4. Some begin undertaking various austerities, some become good people by practicing yoga, and some become scholars by learning the *Vedas* and *Shastras*.
5. Some follow the path of hatha yoga with great determination and torture their bodies, and some realize God through the strength of Devotion (Bhakti).
6. Some get the greatest experience of Reality and become well known devotees, and some gain extraordinary powers and roam in the sky.
7. Some become the brilliance of Light itself. Some become merged with Water, and some suddenly disappear in the form of the Wind.
8. Some gain the ability of taking on many different forms, some suddenly disappear, and some roam around to many places and even go under the ocean while remaining seated in one location.

9. Some ride on ferocious beasts, some are able to make the immovable move, and some can bring dead bodies to life with supernatural powers.
10. Some can make light become dim, some can dry up water, and some can obstruct the breathing of all of the people in the world.
11. There are many who have gained various supernatural powers with their strong determination and keen intellect. Millions of such accomplished ones have lived in the past.
12. Some have accomplished control of the mind, some have accomplished control over speech, some have accomplished only a few things, and some have accomplished all things. Thus, there have been many kinds of accomplished ones who have become famous.
13. Some followed the royal path of "Nine-Faceted Devotion" (Navavidha Bhakti). some have gone beyond this world appearance in their own self-interest and were saved, and some yogis have followed the hidden path and attained the state of Brahman.
14. Some have reached the abode of Vishnu, others remained in the abode of Brahma, and some reside in the abode of Shiva, remaining as his true form.
15. Some have reached the abode of the gods and lived as Indra, the "King of the Gods." Some became great like their ancestors. Some became established in the constellations, while others became established in the divine "Ocean of Milk."
16. The four types of liberation (mukti) that are attained according to one's own wish are (1) to abide in God's residence, (2) to be near to God, (3) to identify with God's form, and (4) to be one with God.
17. Like this, with the aid of the human body, the accomplished ones, sages, and saints have gained infinite benefit in their own self-interest. In this regard, how much can the body be praised?
18. With the help of the human body and various spiritual practices, mainly the utilization of the power of discerning inquiry, many have become free.
19. With the help of the human body many have attained the highest state. Giving up the ego they have become blissful and happy.
20. It is with the human body alone that all have become emancipated. It is only with the aid of the body that the root of doubt gets snapped.
21. One cannot gain spiritual knowledge with an animal body. This statement is found everywhere. It is only with the human body that one can realize Reality beyond this world appearance.
22. Because of the human body there are saints, great beings, sages, hermits, the accomplished ones, ascetics, the contented, devotees, the liberated, the detached and the Self-realized.
23. Because of the human body, there are philosophers, students of yoga, celibates, ascetics who live without clothes, renunciates, hermits, and those with the knowledge of the six traditional streams of philosophy[11].
24. Thus, it can be said that the human body is important and superior to all other bodily forms. With proper use of the human body one can avoid the suffering associated with death.
25. The human body is mostly under one's own control, and it rarely comes under the control of outside influences. The best use of the body is that it be used for the purpose of helping others. In this way, one can gain lasting fame.

---

[11] The six traditional streams of philosophy are Sankhya, Yoga, Nyaya, Vaisheshika, Mimansa, Vedanta

26. If horses, bulls, cows, buffaloes, or other domestic animals, as well as women and household servants are allowed to roam freely, someone will surely try to catch them.
27. This is not the case with those who have gained Knowledge (Jnana) while in the physical body. Whether they desire to remain where they are or leave, no one can keep them in bondage.
28. If the human body is disabled, or is without hands and arms, it is of little use for helping others.
29. If the human body is blind, it is nearly useless for performing common duties, and if it is deaf it cannot hear explanations.
30. If the human body is dumb it cannot ask about doubts. If it is weak and diseased it is basically useless.
31. If one uses the body foolishly, or if it is constantly having fits and seizures, it is truly sorrowful to have such a useless body.
32. If there are no disabilities and the human body is fit, without disease, one should follow the path of Supreme Truth without wasting any time.
33. If a healthy human body is acquired, and one does not use the intellect to follow the path of Paramartha, such a person is a fool who is merely caught in the web of Illusion.
34. By digging up the earth, one builds a house and strongly imagines that it belongs only to him. He does not know that it really belongs to many (insects and pests).
35. The mice, lizards, and flies all say that it is definitely their house.
36. Spiders, big ants and small ants, all say that the house is theirs.
37. The scorpions, serpents, and cockroaches say that it is their house.
38. The black bees, and wasps say that the house is theirs, and the worms that live in the wood say that the house is theirs.
39. The cats, dogs and mongoose all say that the house is theirs.
40. Moths, flies, and fleas say that the house is theirs.
41. Bugs, mosquitoes and sand-flies all say that the house is theirs.
42. The large fleas, stinging insects, germs and large flies all say that the house belongs to them.
43. There are so many such irritating creatures that are spread out all over. How many shall I describe? All of them say that the house is theirs.
44. The pets, servants, and the owners of the house all say that the house is theirs.
45. The guests say it is their house, friends say it is theirs, and all of the villagers say that the house is theirs.
46. The thieves and government officers alike say that the house belongs to them. The fire says that the house belongs to it, and that it will turn the house into ashes.
47. All of them say that the house is "mine." Even the foolish builder of the house says "It is mine, mine," yet in the end, it becomes a heavy burden and he leaves the place.
48. All houses eventually collapse over a period of time, and even the site of the village turns to ruins. Afterwards, wild animals come and live in the broken down houses.
49. The house really belongs to the insects, ants, worms, and mice. The foolish people will all vacate it in the end.
50. Such is the state of houses. One should have the experience for oneself that life is also like this. The duration of one's life is only temporary.

51. Even if the body is said to be one's own, it is really created for many. On the head there are lice that eat away at it.
52. Germs destroy the roots of the hair, boils appear and germs live in them, and worms can be seen that live in the abdomen.
53. Worms can be found in the teeth and eyes, and flies even get inside the ears.
54. Leeches drink the blood, lice pierce the flesh, and mosquitoes bite and fly away quickly.
55. The bees and wasps bite and sting, ticks and leeches drink the blood, and scorpions, serpents, centipedes and millipedes also bite and sting.
56. Having been born with a physical body, we take care of it, but at any time it may be taken away and forcefully be eaten by a tiger or a wolf.
57. The mice and cats bite, horses and dogs can tear the body to pieces, and bears and monkeys will beat and suffocate it.
58. The camels bite and cast it away, elephants can crush it with their feet, and bulls can pierce it with their horns.
59. Thieves beat up and break down the body, and ghosts hunt it and kill it. Now, let this be enough of this talk. Such is the state of the human body.
60. The state of the physical body is like this. The foolish say "It is mine," but it is really food for many creatures. This will be discussed further in the chapter on the "Three Tortures."
61. Unless the physical body is used for realizing the Supreme Truth, it only goes to waste, suffering many blows and dangers on the way to death.
62. Let this talk be. Those who are merely foolish householders will never know the happiness of the Supreme Truth. Their signs of foolishness will be told in the next chapter.

Thus in Dasbodh, a dialogue between the Guru and disciple, Sub-Chapter 10 of Chapter 1, named "In Praise of the Human Body" is concluded.

Chapter 2. Signs of Fools

Chapter: 2, Sub-Chapter: 1

The Signs of a Fool

|| ShriRam ||

1. Om. Salutations to Lord Ganesha who has one tusk and three eyes. Cast your blessings upon the devotees.
2. We bow to you next auspicious Goddess Sharada, the Mother of the *Vedas* and the daughter of Brahma. Oh bestower of Grace, dwell in the heart in the form of inspiration.
3. Touching the Sadguru's feet, and remembering the name of Lord Rama, I will now tell the signs of a fool that are to be abandoned.
4. One type of fool is simply a fool, and another is a "learned fool." Listeners should give thought to both with attentiveness and discernment.
5. The signs of "learned fools" are explained in a later sub-chapter. Remain alert and discerning, and listen to what follows now.
6. Now, I will present some thoughts about the many signs of fools. Please pay attention to them as you listen.
7. I shall describe now the attributes of people who are attached to the householder's life, those who have no Self-realization, and people who are simply ignorant.
8. One who opposes his mother in whose womb he was born, and considers only his wife close to his heart, is a fool.
9. One who breaks off all relations and lives under the control of his wife, and tells all the secrets of his mind to her, that one is a fool.
10. One who loves somebody else's wife, who stays in his father-in-law's house, or who marries a girl who does not come from a good family, is a fool.
11. One, who out of pride, considers oneself equal to those who are more competent, or who without proper qualifications tries to dominate, that one is foolish.
12. One who praises himself, one who faces thousands of problems in his own country, and one who brags about his ancestors' fame, is a fool.
13. One who laughs without reason, one who does not use discrimination even after having been told to do so, and one who has many enemies, is a fool.
14. One who keeps away from his own people and makes friends with strangers, or who blames others after the day is finished, he is a fool.
15. One who sleeps where many people are awake, or who eats excessively in a stranger's house, he is a fool.
16. One who speaks arrogantly regardless of whether somebody respects or insults him, or who is addicted to various bad habits such going to prostitutes, gambling, stealing, etc., he is a fool.
17. One who expects help from others and gives up his own efforts, or who takes satisfaction in being lazy, is a fool.
18. One who understands everything at home, but in public meetings is afraid to even speak a word, he is a fool.
19. One who tries to be intimate with his superior, or who dislikes good advice, he is a fool.

20. One who teaches those who do not listen to him, or one who shows off in front of wise elders, or one who deceives good people, is a fool.
21. One who impulsively and passionately overindulges in sensual activity, and who crosses his limits and behaves in a shameless manner, is a fool.
22. One who does not take medicine when sick, or who does not take care with regard to his food, or one who is not satisfied with the things that come to him, he is a fool.
23. One who goes to a foreign land without any companionship, or who makes friends with a person without knowing them, or who jumps into a flooded river, is a fool.
24. One who goes again and again to a place where he is praised by others, but does not protect his own self respect, he is a fool.
25. When a servant becomes wealthy and the master starts serving him, the master is foolish, or when one is constantly doubting with a restless mind, that one is foolish.
26. When one does things without considering the outcome, or punishes someone who has not committed any offense, or when one is a miser for even small things, that one is a fool.
27. One who always blames God and one's ancestors, who acts without the proper authority, or who speaks using foul language, he is a fool.
28. One who gets angry at home, but is meek and shy when outside, or one who acts mad and stupid, is a fool.
29. One who keeps the company of lowly people, or who likes the intimate company of another's woman, or who continues eating even after getting up from a meal, is a fool.
30. One who does not help anybody, or does not know how to act properly if someone helps him, or who talks a lot but does very little, he is a fool.
31. One who is hot tempered, greedy, lazy, or crafty, or who has no courage, he is a fool.
32. One who has no knowledge, no prosperity, no wealth, no goal in life, or no strength or respect, or has nothing, yet who still carries on pridefully in vain, he is truly a fool.
33. One who is deceitful, fraudulent, cunning, ill-behaved, and crafty, or who is excessively fond of sleep, he is a fool.
34. One who changes his clothes in an open exposed place, or who sits to go to the toilet on the street, or who is seen naked all the time, he is a fool.
35. One whose teeth, eyes, ears, hands, clothes and feet are dirty all the time, he is a fool.
36. One who sets out on a journey at inauspicious or ill-advised times ignoring bad omens only to go on ahead and meet with ruin, he is a fool.
37. One whose intellect strays with anger and insults, one who commits suicide, and one whose intellect is unstable, is a fool.
38. One who brings a lot of pain and sorrow to close relatives, one who does not even utter a word of kindness, or one who bows before lowly people, he is a fool.
39. One who constantly cares for and protects the body by any and all means, one who disrespects someone who has surrendered, and one who believes he will always have wealth, he is a fool.
40. One who considers his sons, wife and family as his only support while forgetting God, he is a fool.

41. One who does not understand that he obtains results according to what his actions are, is a fool.
42. Women have been given a gift from God of being eight times more passionate than men. One who marries many such women is a fool.
43. One who behaves badly going beyond his limits based on the advice of bad people, or who does all sorts of wrong things even in the day time, is a fool.
44. One who is hostile towards God, guru, mother, father, or a brahmin (priest), is a fool.
45. One who is happy to see others' sorrow, or feels sorrow when seeing others happy, or who laments over lost belongings, he is a fool.
46. One who speaks disrespectfully, one who becomes a witness without being asked, or who adopts bad habits, he is a fool.
47. One who puts down others by his speech, who strays from a good path in life, or who makes friends with poorly behaved people, is a fool.
48. One who cannot keep his respectability, one who is always joking around, or one who feels irritated and wants to start a fight if somebody laughs at him, he is a fool.
49. One who makes foolish bets, who indulges in worthless talk, or who does not speak when required, he is a fool.
50. One who is not well groomed, one who has no knowledge but occupies a high place, or one who places too much trust in his close relatives, is a fool.
51. One who gives the thief all of his personal information, one who demands everything he sees, and one who brings harm to himself because of anger, he is a fool.
52. One who behaves in the same manner as lowly people, one who keeps arguing and reacts aloud, or one who eats with the left hand, he is a fool.
53. One who is jealous of great men, who envies what he cannot have, or who steals in one's own home, he is a fool.
54. One who does not have faith in the Lord of the Universe and relies only on human beings, and who spends his years without doing anything fulfilling or worthwhile, he is fool.
55. One who upon facing the sorrows of worldly life curses God, or who talks about the shortcomings of a friend, is a fool.
56. One who cannot forgive small offenses of others, one who is always strict to everyone, and one who betrays others, is a fool.
57. One who is not liked in the minds of great people, one whose presence spoils meetings, and one whose moods change from one moment to the next, he is a fool.
58. One who removes servants who have been with him for a long time, and replaces them with someone new, and one who holds meetings without keeping order, he is a fool.
59. One who accumulates wealth wrongfully, one who gives up proper conduct, good principles and justice, or one who breaks association with close friends, he is a fool.
60. One who frequents the house of other women even though he has a wife, and one who accepts food that has already been tasted by many others, is a fool.
61. One who gives one's wealth away, yet still desires the wealth of others, or one who gets involved in transactions with lowly people, is a fool.
62. One who wears out the patience of a guest, one who lives in a village with a bad reputation, and one who worries all the time, he is a fool.

63. When two people are talking, and another person sits idly by as a third person and scratches his head with both hands, he is a fool.
64. One who gargles and spits it into good water, and one who serves people but has no morals, he is a fool.
65. One who becomes too intimate with women and children, one who sits close to someone possessed by a ghost, or who raises a dog but does not control it, he is a fool.
66. One who quarrels with another's woman, one who beats dumb animals cruelly, and one who keeps company with fools, he is a fool.
67. One who stands by when seeing a quarrel and does nothing to try to resolve it, or one who accepts something as true even though he knows it is false, is a fool.
68. One who upon acquiring wealth forgets his past acquaintances, and one who thinks that he is superior to gods and priests, is a fool.
69. One who remains humble only as long as his own selfish interest is not fulfilled, but afterwards does not do any work, he is a fool.
70. One who reads and omits words or inserts things in his own way, or who does not take proper care of books, he is a fool.
71. One who does not read at anytime, nor gives any books to others for reading, but instead keeps them locked away, he is a fool.
72. Such are the signs of a fool. Upon listening to them one acquires wisdom. The wise will give thoughtful consideration to what has been said.
73. The signs of the fool are many, and I have told but a few according to my capacity so that they may be discarded by the listeners. Please excuse any shortcomings.
74. Adopt the best qualities, and drop the attributes of the fool. In the next sub-chapter the best qualities are explained.

Thus in Shri Dasbodh, a dialogue between the Guru and disciple, Sub-Chapter 1 of Chapter 2, named "The Signs of a Fool" is concluded.

Chapter: 2, Sub-Chapter: 2

The Signs of the Best Qualities

|| ShriRam ||

1. The listeners are asked to please remain alert. Now, I shall tell you about the best qualities, with which, upon acquiring, one becomes all-knowing.
2. One should not proceed to go somewhere without first enquiring about the way, nor eat a piece of fruit without first identifying it, nor suddenly pick up dropped objects that are lying around without thinking first.
3. One should avoid over-indulging in argument, avoid holding any malice in the mind, or marrying someone without knowing their family ancestry.
4. One should not speak without proper thinking, or go out without proper preparation, or act in any way without proper consideration to the rules of conduct.
5. One should not show anger towards another unless one has a close relationship with that person. One should not ask to be introduced to a thief, and one should not hastily begin a journey alone at night.

6. One should behave with modesty when among other people. One shouldn't accumulate wealth through improper means, nor abandon a virtuous lifestyle.
7. One should not blame or hate anyone, keep bad company, or forcibly take another's money or wife.
8. One should not interrupt a speaker, behave in a way that breaks up unity, or leave the study of knowledge, no matter what happens.
9. One should not quarrel with a foul mouthed person or argue with a talkative person, and one should not lose the love for keeping the company of saints from one's heart.
10. One should not indulge in excessive anger. One should not hurt near and dear ones, and one should not become disinterested in spiritual teachings.
11. Do not get puffed-up about small things from moment to moment, or speak about false virtue, or of achievements without actual accomplishment.
12. One should not forget whatever one has said. In difficult situations one shouldn't hesitate to show one's strength, and one should not criticize others about something if one has not done that thing oneself.
13. One should not take pleasure in laziness, one should not be bitter about others in the mind, and one should not undertake any task without proper discernment.
14. One should not be too attached to bodily comfort, one should be courageous and not give up making efforts, and one should not get annoyed at any time while doing hard work.
15. One should not feel shy to speak in a meeting, one should not indulge in loose talk, and one should not bet or wager on what will happen.
16. One should not worry a lot, one should not stay idle, and one should not look at another's spouse with lust in the mind.
17. One should not be under anyone else's obligation, and if some obligation is accepted, it should be quickly cleared away. One should not cause trouble to others or betray anyone.
18. One should maintain a clean appearance and not wear dirty clothes. One should not ask where someone is going when he is going out.
19. One should not give up a broad outlook, and one should not become dependent upon another, or become a burden to anyone else.
20. One should not enter into transactions unless the agreement is put into writing. One should not take a loan from a person of low character, and one should not go to represent oneself at a place of government without proper evidence.
21. One should not take the side of false claims. One should not go against the verdict passed in the meeting, and obviously one should not speak in a place where one is not respected.
22. One should not be envious when seeing others belongings. One should not do any injustice or harass anybody, and one should not behave like a bully because of one's physical strength.
23. One should not eat or sleep excessively, and one should not stay very long in the place of a person with a bad reputation.
24. One should not falsely vouch for someone close. One should not speak about one's own fame, and one should not become involved with the telling of gossip and stories.
25. One should not consume intoxicating drink or smoke, and one should not be too friendly with those who are overly talkative.

26. One should not remain without work, one should not be tolerant of insulting remarks, and one should not take food even from elders without doing some work.
27. One should not be abusive when speaking, nor laugh at others, and one should not focus on the small faults of good people.
28. One should not steal things that are seen laying around, one should not be a cruel miser, and one should not quarrel with near and dear ones at anytime.
29. One should not deceive or destroy anybody's reputation, or give any false evidence against anyone. One should not exhibit irrational behavior.
30. One should not be abusive or a thief. One should not become involved with another's woman, or speak about another's deficiencies behind his back.
31. One should be courageous when the times call for it. One should not abandon spiritual inclinations or virtuous qualities (sattva), and one should not punish an enemy who has surrendered.
32. One should not become intoxicated by a little wealth. One should not be ashamed of becoming devotional to God (Vishnu), and one should not behave arrogantly among virtuous people.
33. One should not keep relations with the foolish. One should not put one's hand into a dark place. One should not forget where and what one's own things are due to absentmindedness.
34. One should perform one's customary rituals and devotional singing. One should not fall into loose behavior out of laziness.
35. One should not give up the appreciation of hearing about God, and one should not interrupt during narrations. One should not give up on spirituality because of being too involved in family life.
36. One should not fail to follow thru with commitments that one has made to God. One should not disregard one's own duty. One should not get carried away and do things without first giving thought as to what is appropriate.
37. One should not be cruel to, or kill living beings. One should not go out when heavy monsoon rain is expected, or at ill-advised times.
38. One should not lose courage when being in a gathering or in a public place. One should not avoid answering at critical times. One should not lose courage if condemned or criticized
39. One should not remain without a guru, nor should one have a guru of a low caliber. One should not assume that life and wealth are eternal.
40. One should not give up the path of righteousness and adopt a path of falsehood. One should never take pride in what is false.
41. One should give up infamy and notoriety and instead should try to increase one's good reputation. One should use the power of discrimination (viveka) and hold firmly to the path of Truth.
42. If one does not adopt the best qualities it is a sign of being unfortunate. Listen to the signs of misfortune in the next sub-chapter.

Thus in Shri Dasbodh, a dialogue between the Guru and disciple, Sub-Chapter 2 of Chapter 2, named "The Signs of the Best Qualities" is concluded.

Chapter: 2, Sub-Chapter: 3

The Signs of Wrong Knowledge

|| ShriRam ||

1. Now listen to the signs of "wrong knowledge," which are indicative of low character. They are told here so that they may be given up upon the hearing of them.
2. Listen to how one wastes one's life as a human being due to wrong knowledge. I will describe these negative attributes so that they may be easily identified.
3. A person with wrong knowledge does not like to listen to spiritual discourses. He finds them boring and difficult to understand because he has many negative qualities.
4. Such a person is full of passion, anger, arrogance, lust, pride, spitefulness, hatred, rigidity, ego, malice, depression, and doubt.
5. He is full of hopes, affections, wants, imagination, worries, vanity, desires, feelings, envy, ignorance, rivalry, tendencies, discontent, and impatience.
6. He is full of deception and demands. He is overly critical, vicious, a troublemaker, rude, full of pride about his knowledge, disrespectful, quarrelsome, he has evil-minded intentions, and is full of trickery.
7. He is one who is always competing, bothersome, overactive, careless, overly hasty and pushy, and always complaining about all sorts of physical ailments. These are all attributes of wrong knowledge.
8. Because of these negative attributes he appears ugly, weak, indecent, poor, and excessively miserly.
9. He is lazy, gluttonous, weak, harsh, uncaring, and conniving.
10. Such a person is foolish, hot-tempered, stupid, and over talkative. He speaks falsely and is very foul mouthed and abusive.
11. He is not able to understand, and does not listen to others. He does not know and does not learn. He does not do anything, does not see clearly, and does not have any intention of studying.
12. He is ignorant and does not have any confidence in anyone. He harasses others while he is himself full of faults. He has no devotion or appreciation for devotees.
13. Such a person who is full of wrong knowledge is unrepentant while being critical of others. He is always in anguish. He is dangerous, sorrowful, and prone to violence.
14. Being of lowly character, he is a pretender who is sick and engaged in wrongful deeds. He is unscrupulous and revels in tendencies that are contrary to his own best interest.
15. Having a feeble body, he boasts about being athletic. Even though he is hypocritical and lacking moral standards, he advises others about discrimination.
16. He is rowdy and arrogant, or useless and idle, but walks around puffed up with pride. He is a coward that talks of courage.
17. He is junior in status yet proud, overly indulgent in sensual pleasures and destructive, hateful and excessively corrupt.
18. He is proud and shameless, always in financial trouble and wicked-minded. He is prone to falsehood and is lacking in self discipline.

19. He is dirty with diseased mind, deceitful and unobliging. Having many negative attributes he is quick to turn against others.
20. He is of dull intelligence and argumentative. He has many faults himself but is harshly critical of others, and he minutely observes insignificant faults and points them out with irritating abusive words.
21. He makes harsh statements, and speaking loudly he uses crafty words and creates doubts in people's minds. He says things that cause grief for others, and he is cruel, heartless, and evil-minded.
22. He constantly criticizes others and slanderously speaks of other's shortcomings. His speech is mean, immoral and envious. He engages in false and meaningless talk, and he shows disdain towards others.
23. He is crafty, scheming, secretive, devious, evasive in work, hypocritical, hot tempered, and earns wealth from and makes jokes at the expense of others.
24. He is short tempered, ignorant, thoughtless, vicious, problematic, and he goes into fits as if haunted by ghosts.
25. He may be suicidal or violent towards others, and may even be a killer of women, priests, or cows. Such a person might even kill his own parents. Like this, is his downfallen state.
26. His character is lacking good qualities, he is undeserving, illogical, treacherous, a betrayer of friends, ungrateful, and he frequents brothels. People like this are rebellious and boastful.
27. He is always quarreling and suspicious of others. He is argumentative and always makes a big commotion. He is irreligious and given to vices. He is prone to addiction, and he is domineering.
28. Such a person is mischievous, unsuccessful, shabby, an instigator, a miser who is annoying and selfish. He is possessive, problematic, and never charitable. Such people are shameless and malicious.
29. Such a one is a rascal and a fool who is a coward that interferes. He is deceitful, rebellious, heretical, a thief, and a fraud.
30. One with wrong knowledge is reckless, uncontrollable, and undisciplined. He is an incessant babbler who always makes frivolous comments and falsely accuses others. He is an arrogant liar with a corrupt and wayward intellect.
31. He may even be a killer, a looter, or a gang member. He is a cheat who indulges in hurting people. He is an imposter, an adulterer, and someone who is fascinated by performances of black magic.
32. He is unhesitating, shameless and quarrelsome. He is thick headed, rough and tough, outspoken but illiterate, overly dramatic, overly passionate, and does not get along with anybody.
33. He is impatient, a liar, and misbehaved. Even if he is blind, lame, always coughing, deaf, or asthmatic, he still does not give up his rigidity.
34. He is not knowledgeable, he is without prosperity or good family background, and without any real power or ability. He is unfortunate like a beggar.
35. He is without strength or ability, without any understanding of religious symbols or spiritual initiation, he is lacking in good attributes, and troubled by physical ailments.
36. He is without dexterity, intelligence, or good conduct. He is lacking in thoughtfulness (vichara), right actions, spiritual inclination (sattva), proper discrimination (viveka), and he is always doubting.

37. Those people with wrong knowledge have no devotion or deep feelings. They have no Self-Knowledge or desirelessness. They have no peace or forgiveness, and are petty about everything.
38. One with wrong knowledge does not understand the importance of time, or what is appropriate to the occasion. He does not understand the significance of study or effort. He does not know friendship, and is truly an unfortunate ignorant person.
39. Let this be enough of such talk. Like this are the many faults of the one who holds to many false concepts. Such a person is a storehouse of wrong knowledge. The listeners should now be able recognize these signs.
40. These are the signs of wrong knowledge. Upon hearing their description, one should give them up. Holding on to them due to pride is not in one's own best interest.

Thus in Shri Dasbodh, a dialogue between the Guru and disciple, Sub-Chapter 3 of Chapter 2, named "The Signs of Wrong Knowledge" is concluded.

Chapter: 2, Sub-Chapter: 4

Discourse on Devotion

|| ShriRam ||

1. To get a human body is a result of many virtuous deeds of the past. Among those with a human body, there are some that are fortunate who are rewarded with finding the path of righteousness.
2. Among all human beings, those born into the brahmin caste are special. If in addition to that, they are moved to perform rituals and behave according to beneficial desires and be devotees of God, it is because of past merit.
3. Devotion to God is the best, and in addition to that, keeping the company of saints makes life worthwhile and should be understood to be supremely beneficial.
4. There is divine love and goodwill found in gatherings of devotees, and with the narration of God's stories, the love for God is multiplied.
5. Upon acquiring the human body one should do something that makes life worthwhile and results in going beyond the worldly life. This is extremely rare.
6. Devotees make use of rituals, exercise compassion, and are charitable. They sing the praises of God which are easy to follow.
7. The devotee should see one's own errors and renounce them, hold to the path of devotion, and keep the company of saints.
8. The devotee should study spiritual scriptures and make some pilgrimages to holy places. Repetition of the name of God is a good way to lift one's sight from objectivity.
9. One should be charitable to others, inquire into Self-Knowledge, and discern the Essence from non-essence by utilizing the power of discrimination.
10. The devotee should observe the teachings in the *Vedas*, and have an understanding of actions and worship. In this way one becomes authoritative in Knowledge (Jnana).

11. With body, speech and mind, by offering leaves, flowers, fruits or water, and singing God's praises, one should partake in some form of devotion to make one's life worthwhile.
12. Having received the fruit of human birth, one should do something that makes that life fruitful. Otherwise, one's life is fruitless, and a burden to the earth.
13. The purpose of the human body is to do good for the Self. Offer your mind and wealth as per your capacity to the Almighty, for His use.
14. One who does not reflect upon this in the mind is like a dead body that is just moving around. Such a person is wasting their difficult to come by human birth, and has caused his mother to suffer the pain of giving birth unnecessarily.
15. Such a person does not do any worship, does not sing any bhajans, and makes no offerings to the Lord. He doesn't do any chanting or repetition of God's name, he does no meditation, and he does not even perform any mental worship.
16. He has no devotion, no affection, no faith, and no discipline. He has no God, no religion, and does not even welcome guests and visitors.
17. He does not have an intellect for doing beneficial things, nor does he have any good qualities. He does not enjoy listening to narrations of scriptures, nor does he listen to any spiritual discourses at all.
18. He does not keep the company of good people, his thinking is not correct, and he does not attain liberation because of false pride.
19. He has no moral values, no sense of justice, and no virtue to allow him to go beyond the worldly life. He does not give any thought as to what is proper and what is improper.
20. He has no knowledge, no prosperity, no signs of wisdom, no skill, no attractive qualities, and no beneficial learning.
21. He has no peace, no forgiveness, no initiation, no good friendship, no way to distinguish between good fortune and misfortune, and no spiritual practice.
22. He has no sense of sanctity, no sense of his own duty, and no sense of appropriate behavior. He is not thoughtful, and he is not successful in the material world nor in the spiritual world. He behaves according to the uncontrolled activity of the mind.
23. He does no good actions, and has no spiritual practice. He has no Knowledge, no detachment, no unity, and no courage. If you observe him, there is nothing worthwhile to be seen.
24. He does not do anything to change his ways, he does not renounce anything, he has no signs of equanimity, no signs of virtue, and he has no respect or love for God.
25. Such a person is not pleased to see good qualities in others, and does not get any pleasure from helping others. He does not even have the slightest thought of devotion to God.
26. When seeing such people, it is like seeing living dead bodies. Virtuous people should not even waste their time talking with such people.
27. If there is some accumulation of virtue, one finds the devotional path. Everyone receives according to their actions.

Thus in Shri Dasbodh, a dialogue between the Guru and disciple, Sub-Chapter 4 of Chapter 2, named "Discourse on Devotion" is concluded.

Chapter: 2, Sub-Chapter: 5

The Quality of Worldly Activity (Rajas)

|| ShriRam ||

1. Basically, the body consists of three qualities or attributes (the three gunas). These qualities are named Sattva, Rajas, and Tamas. Among them Sattva is the best quality.
2. It is because of Sattva (purity; virtue) that one turns to devotion for God. It is due to Rajas (worldly activity) that one returns again and again to worldly affairs. It is due to Tamas (ignorance) that a downfall is experienced in human beings.
3. These three qualities (gunas) are each classified into two types. The first is pure which means that it is unpolluted or untainted. The other is tainted and undesirable. This should be understood.
4. Listen carefully to the signs of purity and of the mixed qualities and understand. Purity (Sattva) is of the nature of spiritual life (Paramartha), and the mixed qualities are of the nature of worldly life.
5. Those who are obsessed with worldly life take their position to be in the body which is subject to the three attributes (Sattva, Rajas, Tamas). When one of the three becomes more dominant, it is as if the other two were not there.
6. The lives of living beings move according to these three qualities of Sattva, Rajas, and Tamas. Now, I will describe the activity of "worldliness" (Rajas).
7. Listen now to the behavior of one in whom the Rajas, or "worldly" quality, is dominant in the body. Listen carefully, and become alert to what is being said.
8. One who says, "This is my house, my family. Where does God come in?," and has such a firm resolution, has the worldly quality dominating.
9. When one constantly worries for mother, father, wife, sons, daughters-in-law, daughters, etc., this is all due to the worldly, or Rajas quality.
10. When one constantly feels they should eat good meals, wear good clothes, and harbors desires for others' things, that is due to the worldly quality.
11. When one has no care for religion, or charity, or chanting the name of God or meditation, and does not bother to enquire as to what is correct and what is not, this is due to the worldly quality.
12. When one does not understand the significance of holy places or traditions, or taking care of guests, and instead is involved in misdeeds, this is due to the worldly quality.
13. When one indulges in storing wealth and grain, when the mind always has lust for money, this miserly type of life is due to the worldly quality.
14. When one says "I am young, beautiful, strong, clever, and the greatest among all," that is due to the Rajas quality.
15. When one takes pride in country, village, house and property, such attachment in the mind is because of the worldly quality.
16. When one thinks that others' belongings should get destroyed, and only his should remain intact, this is due to the worldly quality.
17. Treachery, jealousy, hatred, and desire in the thoughts are all because of the Rajas quality.
18. When one feels affection for children, or attachment to wife, or a liking for always having others close, this is all due to the worldly quality.

19. When one sees the worries about their friends and family coming into one's own thoughts over time, it should be recognized as this happens that this is the activity of the Rajas quality.
20. There are many hardships encountered in worldly life. How will this end? It ends when one remembers the calamities that arise from this worldly quality.
21. Whatever suffering that one has gone through which is remembered in the mind, and the grief that is often felt, is the worldly quality.
22. When one sees the glory of others, and desire arises in the mind and it becomes filled with hopes and sorrows, that is the Rajas quality.
23. When whatever is seen by the eyes is longed for by the mind, and when whatever is demanded is not acquired and there is resulting sorrow, all of that happens due to the worldly quality.
24. When the mind is filled with amusement, or music and songs of romantic love, or being consumed with emotions, this is the Rajas quality.
25. When one is fooling around and joking and criticizing all the time, and engaging in talk that results in dispute, it is because of the worldly quality.
26. When there is a strong feeling of laziness, or interest in many different games and types of entertainment and enjoyments, that is confusion that is the Rajas quality.
27. When one acts out many roles and enjoys watching plays, and spends a lot of money on games, this is the worldly quality.
28. When one is prone to indulging in intoxicants, or is always interested in mischief, or keeps the company of mischievous people, this is due to the effect of the Rajas quality in the mind.
29. When thoughts of stealing arise, and when one likes to talk about the shortcomings of others, or when the mind is fed up with one's daily duties, this is the worldly quality.
30. When one is shy to do service for God and only works to fill one's stomach instead, or when one is painstakingly attached to family life, this is the worldly quality.
31. When one is greedy about eating sweets, or if one is always very careful to nourish the body with good food and will not even consider fasting for even a day, this is due to the Rajas quality.
32. When one's enjoyments are romantic, when one is engrossed in arts and exhibition, and when one has no liking for devotion or detachment, this is due to the worldly quality.
33. When one does not know the Supreme Self (Paramatman) and only adores objects, this force that brings about the cycle of birth and death is called the Rajas guna.
34. Like this is the "worldly quality," the Rajas guna. It offers death and birth for one who is attached to family life. Understand the power of this Rajas quality and see that it causes one to suffer extreme sorrow.
35. Now, this is the description of the Rajas guna which does not easily leave for the one who is entangled in worldly life and latent desires and tendencies (vasanas). What is the remedy?
36. There is one remedy if dispassion towards worldly life does not occur, and that is to sing the praises of God or Guru according to one's capacity.
37. Devotion should be with body, speech and mind, making offerings of leaves, flowers, fruits, and water. One should offer one's mind to God and make one's life fulfilled.

38. Be charitable as per your capacity, and be attached to God. In joy, or in sorrow, think of God always.
39. In the beginning and in the end, there is the one God, alone. What is present in between is Illusion, or "Maya" (Maya literally means "that which is not"). Therefore, let there be a fullness of deep feelings for God.
40. Like this is the power of the worldly quality, the Rajas guna. It has been described briefly here. Now, listen to the description of the pure, unmixed Rajas quality as it pertains to the aspirant.
41. The identifying sign of Rajas in its pure form is that it is like Sattva which is the origin and completeness of all devotional activity.
42. Like this, the "worldly quality," or Rajas guna has been explained. The listeners can experience this in the mind. Now, listen further to the explanation on the "Quality of Ignorance," the Tamas guna.

Thus in Shri Dasbodh, a dialogue between the Guru and disciple, Sub-Chapter 5 of Chapter 2, named "The Attribute of Worldly Activity (Rajas)" is concluded.

Chapter: 2, Sub-Chapter: 6

The Quality of Ignorance (Tamas)

|| ShriRam ||

1. Like this, the attributes of the "worldly quality" (Rajas) and its activities, have been explained. Now, listen to the explanation of the quality of "ignorance," or the Tamas guna.
2. Worldly life creates sorrow which makes one feel bound. When one feels that sorrow, and when anger can suddenly rise up and set in, this is all an indication of the Tamas quality.
3. When the mind is full of anger and one cannot recognize or respect one's own mother, father, brother, sister or wife, and even beats them, this is Tamas quality.
4. When one feels the inclination to kill someone else or oneself, and even loses affection for one's own life, that is Tamas.
5. When one is filled with the madness of anger and behaves like a person possessed by a ghost who cannot be controlled by any remedy, that is a sign of Tamas.
6. If such an occasion occurs when one injures one's own body or someone else with a weapon, that is the quality of Tamas.
7. When one has the feeling that one must see a battle with one's own eyes, or go to visit the battlefield where dead bodies are lying around, these thoughts arising in the mind are the sign of the Tamas quality.
8. When one is continuously in a state of confusion and cannot make decisions, or likes excessive sleep, this is due the Tamas guna.
9. When one has an excessive appetite, does not understand bitter or sweet, or when one is very dull, this is all due to the quality of Tamas.
10. When a loved one dies and one feels inclined to kill oneself, this is due to the Tamas quality.

11. When one likes killing insects, ants, and animals, and is very unsympathetic and inhumane, that is all due to the Tamas quality.
12. If there is the killing of women and children, or the killing of brahmins (priests) and pious people or sacred cows for money, this is due to the Tamas quality.
13. When one is agitated with anger and feels like taking poison, or if the thought of killing others comes in the mind, this is the Tamas quality.
14. When one holds malice in the mind for others and wishes for their misfortune, or when one is unrestrained in one's arrogance, this is due to the Tamas quality.
15. When one feels inclined to engage in disputes and quarrels, and even takes to physically fighting because of jealousy in the mind, this is the appearance of the Tamas guna.
16. When one wants to see or hear about war, or wants to become involved in warfare and indulge in killing, and even dying, this is due to the quality of Tamas.
17. When out of jealousy one gives up on devotion, and even destroys temples and cuts down fruit trees, this is because of the Tamas quality.
18. When one does not like to do good deeds and is involved in misdeeds, and has no sense of propriety, that is due to the quality of Tamas.
19. When one does not respect the tradition of the brahmins, or causes sorrow to living beings, or enjoys committing crimes, this is due to the Tamas quality.
20. When one likes to set things on fire, or fight using weapons, or prey on or poison others, or because of jealousy causes damage to another's body, that is all because of the Tamas quality.
21. When one feels happy when giving trouble to others, or when one enjoys being ruthless and cruel to others, and never gets tired of worldly life, this is the Tamas quality.
22. When one initiates quarrels and enjoys watching them, or when one's intelligence is full of evil intentions, that is called Tamoguna, the quality of ignorance.
23. When one acquires wealth yet gives trouble to others and has no compassionate thoughts arising, this is due to the Tamas quality.
24. When one does not like devotion (bhakti) or devotional feelings, or pilgrimage places or God, and when one feels that the knowledge of the *Vedas* is not required, know that this is a sign of Tamas quality.
25. When one does not have any discipline regarding the performing of daily worship, and has no sense of one's own "Self religion" (Swadharma), and only indulges in corrupt activities, this is because of the Tamas quality.
26. When one does not like to hear the advice of an elder brother, or father and mother, and immediately gets angry and leaves the home, this is due to the Tamas quality.
27. When one eats unnecessarily, or always remains idle, or stays where his presence is not required, or when one is very forgetful, this is all due to the quality of ignorance.
28. When one takes up studying black magic and weaponry, or is very interested in wrestling, this is because of the Tamas attribute.
29. When one takes up various bodily tortures such as burning and piercing the body, this is due to the Tamas quality.
30. When one burns the head, or puts a lighted torch on the body, or pierces oneself with a sharp weapon, this is due to the Tamas quality.

31. When one offers to sever his head for God, or slay the body as an offering, or jump off a cliff for God, know that these are all attributes of Tamas.
32. When one sits on the doorstep of a temple with a determination to hang oneself and give up his life if his desires are not fulfilled, this is due to the quality of ignorance.
33. When one undergoes intense fasting without food, or inhales smoke, or lights fires all around the body, or buries oneself in the hopes of some spiritual experiences, this is due the Tamas quality.
34. When one performs religious rituals or holds one's breath desiring some fruits from it, or from even just always laying around, know that this is the Tamas quality.
35. When one takes up such penances as growing the nails and hair long, or holding one's arms up above the head, or takes a vow of silence, this is all due to the Tamas quality
36. When one tortures the body, or complains in anger when experiencing some pain, or when one breaks idols of the Gods out of anger, this is due to the Tamas guna.
37. Know that when one criticizes God, is bound by hopes and desires, has inclinations towards cruelty, and does not keep the company of saints, all of this is due to the quality of ignorance.
38. Like this, is the "Tamoguna." It is impossible to describe its expanse completely. This explanation has been given so one may recognize and give up a few of these qualities upon hearing about them.
39. One whose behavior displays the Tamas quality shows the signs of the cause of downfall. These are not the indications of one who is liberated.
40. Know that whatever actions (karma) have been done, the fruits flowing from them will surely be acquired, and birth, which is the root of sorrow, is not easily broken off.
41. To break the birth cycle, the attribute of "Purity," the "Sattva Guna" is required. This is explained in the next sub-chapter.

Thus in Shri Dasbodh, a dialogue between the Guru and disciple, Sub-Chapter 6 of Chapter 2, named "The Attribute of Ignorance (Tamas)" is concluded.

Chapter: 2, Sub-Chapter: 7

The Quality of Purity (Sattva)

|| ShriRam ||

1. In the previous sub-chapter I have just told about the "Attribute of Ignorance," the Tamas Guna, which brings great sorrow in life. Now listen to the description of the "Attribute of Purity," or Sattva Guna, which is very rare.
2. The Sattva guna is that which forms the basis for singing the praises of God and the Guru (bhajans), that which is an anchor for the yogis, and that which destroys the worldly life that is the root of all sorrow.
3. It is that which is the progress on the path of spirituality, it is the pathway that leads towards God by which one can attain liberation, and that which is the Oneness of the Self.

4. It is that which protects the devotees and gives assurance to help one to swim across the worldly life. The wealth of liberation is the adornment of the Sattva guna.
5. Sattva is the adornment of Supreme Truth (Paramartha), the ornament of the great spiritual leaders (Mahantas), and that by which one wards off the attributes of worldliness (Rajas) and ignorance (Tamas).
6. It is that which is the supreme giver of happiness, that which brings waves of bliss, and that which removes the cycle of birth and death.
7. It is that which ends ignorance, is the root source of all things and actions that are considered sacred, and it is that by which one finds the way beyond worldly life.
8. Like this is this attribute of purity (Sattva). The signs of the activity when it arises in the body by itself is what is being described.
9. When one has great love for God, and continues to perform one's worldly affairs in an appropriate manner, and when one always utilizes correct discrimination (viveka), this is the attribute of purity.
10. That which makes one forget the sorrows of the worldly life, that which shows the pure path of devotion, and that which inspires the activity of singing the praises of the Guru and his teachings (bhajans), is the Sattva guna.
11. When the liking for Supreme Truth and inner meaning arises, and when one feels an earnest need to help others, this is due to the quality of purity.
12. When one is inclined to observe ritual prayers and bath, or when one is righteous and pure in heart and clear in mind, or is presentable in one's dress, this is all due to the Sattva guna.
13. When one performs sacred fire rituals, and inspires others to perform sacred rituals, or when one is both a learner and a teacher, and when one understands the importance of being charitable in auspicious work, know all of this to be due to the attribute of Sattva.
14. When there is a liking for spiritual explanations, and when one has an interest in the meanings of the stories of God (Lord Vishnu), and when upon the hearing of these stories there is an immediate affect and change in one's behavior, this is the activity of the Sattva guna.
15. When one generously donates things such as livestock, or land, or gems and jewels, this is due to the quality of Sattva.
16. When one donates money, clothes, and food and water, and brings together knowers of Brahman and satisfies them with meals, this is due to the attribute of purity.
17. When one is inclined towards performing various rites and rituals, charities, pilgrimages, or fasts without any selfish expectations, this is due to the Sattva guna.
18. When one offers meals to thousands, or is involved in a variety of different charities, not desiring any fruits from their donations, this is due to the attribute of purity. Desire for some fruits of one's charity is a sign of the attribute of worldliness, the Rajas quality.
19. When one donates land to be used for holy purposes, builds wells and lakes, and temples and domes, this is due to the quality of purity.
20. When one builds places of sanctuary, steps, lamps, special structures, and plants trees, this is due to the quality of Sattva.
21. When one makes forests, gardens, flower beds, water reservoirs, and brings comfort to the minds of hermits, this is the Sattva guna.

22. When one constructs places for prayer and meditation, or steps to the river bank, or storage places for food, and kitchens for food at temples, this is due to the attribute of Sattva.
23. When one arranges for the continuous burning day and night of the lamps at many temples, and even offers one's own jewelry and ornaments, this is the quality of purity.
24. When there is a gathering of various beautiful musical instruments like drums, string instruments, metal cymbals, and many other wonderful instruments being played as the intermingling of their sounds creates a great melody, this is Sattva.
25. When there are many kinds of beautiful decorations used in preparing the temple, and when people are keen to sing songs in praise of God, that is due to the attribute of purity.
26. When one makes offerings and decorations of umbrellas, comfortable cushions, and ornamental flags and posts, this is due to the quality of Sattva.
27. If one is inclined towards making structures for plants and gardens, arranging for the cleaning of roads and rooms in temples and shrines of holy men, and loves all of this, then know this is as the Sattva guna.
28. When there are many beautiful vessels that are used for worship, and decorative roofs and seats are offered to the temple, this is a display of the Sattva attribute.
29. When one offers various foods and exotic fruits for worship, this is the attribute of purity.
30. When devotees who like to serve at the temple do lowly services like sweeping and cleaning of their own volition, this is the attribute of Sattva.
31. When one is involved with religious festivals at auspicious times, and when one offers body, speech and mind, this is the Sattva guna.
32. When one is keenly attentive when listening to the narrations of the Lord, and when one carries special perfumes, garlands and fragrant powders while standing at the doorstep of God, this is due to the attribute of purity.
33. When men and women carry articles of worship according to their capacity and are standing at the doorstep of God, this is the quality of purity.
34. Leaving behind one's great personal works, when one rushes towards God with devotion in the mind, this is the Sattva attribute.
35. When one gives up one's sense of superiority, and accepts work of a low status, and stands waiting at God's doorstep, this is the attribute of purity.
36. When one partakes in fasting, or avoids always indulging in one's habits or taking food in favor of regularly engaging in chanting and meditation, this is the quality of Sattva.
37. When one does not speak harsh words, is disciplined in one's behavior, and has the satisfaction of the yogis, this is the Sattva guna.
38. When one drops all pride and sings chants about the glory of God (kirtan) without any expectation of return, and when upon hearing this kirtan one becomes absorbed and one's hair stands upright, this is the quality of Sattva.
39. When the inner-mind is in meditation on God that overwhelms the eyes, and the body-consciousness drops off, this is the quality of purity.
40. When one has a great love for listening to the stories of God (Vishnu), and there is no change in that love for the story from the beginning until the end of the narration, this is the quality of Sattva.

41. When one chants the name of the Lord, and claps one's hands while singing the praises of the Lord, and takes the dust from the Lord's feet and applies it to one's forehead, this is all Sattva guna.
42. When one drops the pride for the body, and develops detachment for sensual objects, and understands the falseness of Illusion, this is the Sattva attribute.
43. When the feeling dawns in the heart that there should be some remedy when one gets entangled in the worldly life, this is the quality of Sattva.
44. When one gets fed up with worldly life and sings bhajans praising the guru, the guru's teaching arises there in the mind providing knowledge. This the quality of Sattva.
45. When one attends to one's own discipline, and has a great respect and commitment to always feeling a deep love for the Self, Lord Rama, this is the Sattva attribute.
46. When one becomes disinterested in everything and feels drawn to Supreme Truth, and when one is courageous during times of calamity, this the quality of Sattva.
47. When one remains always disinterested and fed up with the many worldly enjoyments, and instead the mind remembers the praises of the Lord, this is due to the Sattva attribute.
48. When one's thoughts do not get attached to any objects, and instead the mind always remembers God with a firm deep inner feeling, this is Sattva guna.
49. When people say that a devotee is eccentric, but still his love for God grows within and remains firm, this is the attribute of Sattva.
50. When inspiration about one's True Nature (Swaroopa) arises within and logic prevails, and evil thoughts and doubts disappear, this is the Sattva guna.
51. When the human body is used for good works, and when such thoughts arise in the inner-mind (antahkarana), this is the creative activity of Sattva guna.
52. When peace, forgiveness, and compassion arise in one, know that the inner meaning of the Sattva Guna has become understood by such a person.
53. When guests and visitors arrive and one does not allow them to go without food, and when one naturally gives gifts according to one's abilities, this shows the activity of the Sattva guna.
54. When one gives aid and shelter to those who are poor if they arrive on the doorstep, this the quality of Sattva.
55. If there is a scarcity of food in the house, but one is not sad, and if one is always ready to give as per one's capacity, this is the attribute of Sattva.
56. When one has control over one's tongue, and when one's habits are satisfied while one harbors no desires, this is the quality of Sattva.
57. When things happen as they do, and some calamity befalls the family, yet one is not disturbed in one's thoughts, this is the quality of Sattva.
58. When God is everything for the devotee, and the seeking for pleasures in things and the body-consciousness is dropped, this is the Sattva guna.
59. When one does not become distracted by the tendency of the mind to follow after sense objects, and when one's strength does not waver, this is the attribute of Sattva.
60. When the body is affected by some calamity, or suffers hunger and thirst, and one still does not give up one's conviction, this is the Sattva quality.
61. When one utilizes "listening" (Shravana), along with "contemplation" (Manana), and "verification by experience" (Nididhyasana), and becomes satisfied in Self-Knowledge, this is the Sattva guna.

62. When one does not have any ego sense, when detachment is apparent in one's behavior, and kindness and generosity are present, this is the Sattva attribute.
63. When one speaks with humility to everyone, is disciplined in one's behavior and is able to satisfy all of the people, this is due to the attribute of Sattva.
64. When one is polite with all the people and there is no place for opposition, and when one spends one's life helping others this is due to the Sattva attribute.
65. When one forsakes one's own works for the sake of the achievements of others, and when the fame of that work survives even after one's passing, this is the activity of the Sattva guna.
66. When one sees with one's own eyes the merits and demerits of others, and keeps quiet about them in one's mind without even speaking about them, like the sea retains water, this is the quality of Sattva.
67. To listen to humiliating remarks and to not answer back, and to not hold on to any anger that may arise, this is the attribute of Sattva.
68. When one is unjustly harassed in different ways and bears all of it silently without any thoughts of complaint, this is the quality of Sattva.
69. When one bears the presence of physical suffering, and can bear bad people and even feels obliged to one's critics as well, this is the Sattva guna.
70. When the mind runs in the wrong direction towards objectivity and one controls it with discrimination (viveka), and when one brings the sense organs under control (dama), this is the activity of the Sattva guna.
71. When one engages in activities that are aligned with Knowledge (sat) and abandons those activities which are not so aligned (asat), and adheres to the path of devotion, this is a sign of the Sattva guna.
72. When one likes early morning bathing, listening to the mythological stories, and enjoys many mantras and worshipping God, this is the Sattva guna.
73. When one worships respectfully during the auspicious religious periods and celebrates holidays associated with great men, this is due to the quality of Sattva.
74. When one takes care attending to the performing of the last rites of someone who died in a foreign land, this is the activity of the Sattva attribute.
75. When one sees that someone is being beaten and he goes to protect him and frees him from his bondage, this is the activity of the Sattva quality.
76. When one engages in the worship of the Shiva Lingam, and has faith in chanting the name of God, and takes the time to go and have a glimpse (darshan) of God or the Guru, this is the quality of Sattva.
77. When one sees a saint and runs to him rejoicing in overwhelming happiness, and when one bows down to the saint with complete sincerity, this is the Sattva guna.
78. One who receives the blessing of the saint's teaching uplifts one's family, and exhibits the qualities of godliness. This is the Sattva guna.
79. When one shows the right path to the people, gets them to sing God's praises, and teaches Knowledge to the ignorant, this is the quality of Sattva.
80. When one likes virtuous deeds, making circumambulation in reverence at the temple (pradakshina), bowing down to God, and memorizing scriptures and prayers, this is the attribute of Sattva.
81. When one has a great yearning for devotion, and collects spiritual texts and even idols which assist in his worship, this is the functioning of the Sattva guna.
82. When one has shiny accessories and flower garlands for worship set at a special place, and wears clean clothes especially for worship, this is the attribute of Sattva.

83. When one shares with others in their sorrow, feels happy with others in their joy, and rejoices when seeing detachment, this is the Sattva guna.
84. When one feels honored when others are honored, accepts the blemishes of others as one's own blemishes, and feels unbearable sorrow at other's sorrow, this is the attribute of Sattva.
85. Now, let this talk be enough. When one's mind is attentive to God and one's duties, and when one worships without any desire or expectation, know that to be the quality of Sattva.
86. Like this is the untainted pure quality of Sattva which is the savior from the ocean of worldly life and suffering. By this Sattvaguna, the power of discrimination (viveka) arises which puts one on the Path of Knowledge (Jnana Marga).
87. The Sattva guna is devotion to God, the acquisition of Self-Knowledge, and liberation through identification with Brahman.
88. This is the state of the "Sattva Guna." I have told about it in short detail according to my capacity. Now, let the listeners become alert and pay attention to what is given next.

Thus in Shri Dasbodh, a dialogue between the Guru and disciple, Sub-Chapter 7 of Chapter 2, named "The Attribute of Purity (Sattva Guna)" is concluded.

Chapter: 2, Sub-Chapter: 8

The Explanation of True Knowledge

|| ShriRam ||

1. Listen now to the signs of "True Knowledge" (Sadvidya) whose attributes are extremely pure manifestations. When thought over repeatedly, they are acquired in one's own self.
2. One with this Sadvidya has the best of special qualities. Upon hearing of these qualities one feels supremely satisfied.
3. He is one who is sattvic in his demeanor, loving, peaceful, forgiving, compassionate, humble, always eager to help in good work, and his speech is like nectar.
4. One with such True Knowledge is supremely beautiful and adept, supremely strong and patient, supremely wealthy and benevolent.
5. He is very knowledgeable and a devotee, a great scholar who is detached, and a great ascetic who is very peaceful.
6. He is a good speaker, but is not involved in it for any gain. He has knowledge of all, and is respectful to everyone. He is great, yet modest with everyone.
7. He is like a king who is both religious and courageous. He uses discrimination, and is disciplined.
8. He is one who shows appropriate respect due to elders and family traditions. He is frugal in his diet and detached. He has basic knowledge of health sciences, has a helping nature, and he is lucky and successful with whatever he lends his hands to.
9. He does his work with no pride, and he is a devotee of God (Vishnu) among people. His wealth is his devotion and he praises God with great respect.

10. He is a philosopher and is detached. He is familiar with scriptures, and a gentleman. He is familiar with mantras and has many good qualities and values.
11. He is a sage who is holy and is given to good deeds, inner purity, and Self religion. He is untainted in his own duties and free of greed, yet he is also remorseful.
12. He has an interest and love for spiritual life, he lives a righteous life filled with good activities done with determination and courage. He has studied the *Vedas* and scriptures with ease, and is praised for his intelligence and introspective observation.
13. He is alert, shrewd, appropriate, logical, truthful, well-read, precise, diplomatic, agile, and unusual in many ways.
14. He knows how to give respect and honor, how be discerning, and he knows what action is appropriate in each situation as well as being aware of the signs of cause and effect. He is an expert speaker.
15. He is an alert, industrious aspirant and student of the *Vedas* and other scriptures. He is knowledgeable about spiritual science with firm resolution.
16. He engages in chanting and repetition of mantra. He visits holy places with firm discipline even if experiencing bodily discomfort. He is a worshipper with firm resolution and understanding.
17. He speaks the truth with auspicious words. He is soft spoken and true to his word, and he always speaks with confidence in a pleasing manner.
18. His desires are fulfilled. He is a yogi of great depth. He is grand, pleasing, non-attached, mild, pure, on a righteous path, straightforward, and has no addictions.
19. He is knowledgeable and appreciative of the qualities of music, he is diplomatic in gatherings of people without any selfish motives, and he is friendly with everyone and all living beings.
20. He obtains money by proper means, he is faithful to his wife and behaves in a just way. He is clean within, clean in the activities of his life, and clean in his renunciation of them. He is clean in everything without any attachment.
21. Out of friendship, he does good for others. The sweetness of his words makes sorrow disappear. He is a powerful servant of all. He is a friend of all because of his great strength.
22. He is a great speaker who can clear all doubts. He understands all of the thoughts of the listener, and in his explanations he does not say anything that is not full of meaning.
23. He can have a dialogue without any argument. He speaks without any attachment, obstructions, or anger. He is faultless without any jealousy.
24. One with this True Knowledge is firm in the Self and a content worshipper. Being both the accomplisher and the accomplished, he exemplifies spiritual practice.
25. He is of the nature of ease and contentment, and joy and cheerfulness. His nature is of unity. He is one with the Self and with everything.
26. He is fortunate, victorious, successful, has a nice appearance, good qualities, and is well behaved when engaged in activity. He is steadfast in his thoughtfulness (vichara).
27. He is successful, famous, strong and powerful. He is heroic and benevolent, truthful and virtuous.
28. He is knowledgeable and an artist with abundant good qualities. He is from a good lineage, has a history of holy deeds, and is strong and kind.

29. He is tactful and virtuous and senior in standing, as well as intelligent and courageous. He is initiated, and is always content. He is desireless and unattached.
30. Let this talk be. These are some of the best qualities of True Knowledge. In order that these qualities may be studied, a few have been spoken about.
31. The beauty of one's appearance cannot be obtained with studies, and there is no remedy for the attributes that one has naturally acquired at birth. However, some study should be done to acquire attributes of Sadvidya.
32. These are some of the attributes of this Sadvidya. Everyone should have them, but especially the dispassionate one should certainly develop them.

Thus in Shri Dasbodh, a dialogue between the Guru and disciple, Sub-Chapter 8 of Chapter 2, named "The Explanation of True Knowledge" is concluded.

Chapter: 2, Sub-Chapter: 9

The Attributes of the Dispassionate One

|| ShriRam ||

1. Listen now to the best qualities of the dispassionate one so that you may become detached from everything and live with the power of the yogi (one who lives in conscious union with the Supreme Self) within.
2. With detachment good fame increases, and the dispassionate gain fulfillment and importance.
3. By detachment, the Supreme Meaning (Paramartha) is gained, and bliss (ananda) grows. Dispassion increases greatly with discrimination (viveka).
4. With dispassion, happiness overflows, true knowledge (sadvidya) prevails, and good fortune is strengthened with liberation.
5. With dispassion, one's purpose is complete, one is finished with desire, and the "Goddess of Speech" (Saraswati) resides in one's mouth, speaking sweet words.
6. Listen to these attributes of dispassion. Hold strongly to them in life and you will become well-known in the world.
7. With dispassion and discrimination be detached and spread spiritual science. With dispassion and courage exercise control over sensual indulgences.
8. The dispassionate one maintains spiritual practice (sadhana), sings God's praises (in bhajans and kirtan), and reveals the special knowledge of Brahman.
9. The dispassionate one increases devotion, exhibits peace, and puts forth effort in detachment.
10. The dispassionate one gives prestige to good activities, spreads the spirit of non-involvement in objectivity, and remains strong in the absence of hopes and expectations in life.
11. The dispassionate one establishes virtue, follows good moral behavior, and upholds forgiveness with respect.
12. The dispassionate one glorifies the Supreme Truth, understands through inquiry, and keeps to the good path of the quality of purity (sattva guna).
13. The dispassionate one takes care of the faithful, shows them the satisfaction of divine love, and does not shun simple people who seek refuge.

14. The dispassionate one is supremely alert, utilizes inner observation, and stands up for Supreme Truth.
15. The dispassionate one continues studying, is hard working and industrious, and with his excellent speaking skills is able to uphold Paramartha where it is lacking.
16. The dispassionate one speaks of true knowledge, and praises detachment. With firm conviction he gives satisfaction with his speech.
17. The dispassionate one holds religious celebrations on a large scale, organizes groups of devotees, and in different ways glorifies the path of worship.
18. The dispassionate one sings songs of God, gives many discourses, and with the path of devotion he humbles critics and hateful people.
19. The dispassionate one helps many people, revives goodness, and expands the path of virtue with strength.
20. The dispassionate one performs rituals, does repetition of mantra, meditates, goes on pilgrimages, and sings the praises of God with reverence and a clear mind.
21. The dispassionate one is firm in his resolve, leads a happy life, and uplifts the people of the world by his association with them.
22. The dispassionate one is courageous, generous, and always ready to provide explanations.
23. The dispassionate one is alert, follows the correct path, is of service to others, and is glorified in leaving a lasting legacy.
24. The dispassionate one seeks out others who are dispassionate, identifies other sages, and makes friends with saints and yogis.
25. The dispassionate one understands the use of mantras, and visits different pilgrimage places, as well as other beautiful places.
26. The dispassionate one performs many different kinds of tasks while inwardly maintaining a disinterested attitude, and he does not hold to any hopes or desires for anything.
27. The dispassionate one is true to himself, is not corrupt in is his activities, and does not assume an inferior status by being overly dependent upon someone else.
28. The dispassionate one properly understands the significance of time and various situations, and is intelligent in all ways.
29. The dispassionate one is not overly biased in one way of thinking and studies many things. He understands things as they are.
30. The dispassionate one knows the stories of God and their meanings, and understands the significance of singing the praises of the Knowledge of Brahman. He has a good understanding of the body, and good knowledge of philosophy. He truly has a good knowledge of everything.
31. The dispassionate one understands the path of action, the path of worship, the path of knowledge, the path of the investigation of truth, as well as the paths of being engaged in worldly activity and the renunciation of worldly activity.
32. The dispassionate one understands the characteristics of the states of love, depression, balance, meditation, bodilessness, and the natural state of one's own being.
33. The dispassionate one understands the nature of the attributes of sound, hand gestures (mudras), body postures (asanas), words and diagrams used in meditation practices (mantras and yantras), and various religious procedures and assertions. He knows about all of them and gives them up.

34. The dispassionate one is friendly with everyone, truly marvelous, and has many diverse qualities.
35. The dispassionate one is detached, a devotee of God, free from the sense of individuality, and untainted by involvement in activity.
36. The dispassionate one studies many types knowledge in depth, challenges various opinions, and guides aspirants to the correct path.
37. The dispassionate one speaks about the correct path, removes doubts, and treats all of mankind as his own.
38. The dispassionate one respects his critics, gives explanations to aspirants, and motivates the ignorant with explanations about the desire for liberation.
39. The dispassionate one adopts the best qualities, abandons undesirable qualities, and overcomes obstacles by utilizing the power of discrimination.
40. Like this are the best signs of the dispassionate one. Listen to them with concentration of mind. The dispassionate one does not look on them with indifference.
41. All of this has been said naturally. Accept whatever is agreeable in it. The listeners should not become disinterested because so many things have been said.
42. If instead of accepting these good attributes after hearing them, one adopts negative attributes and does what is inappropriate, he becomes a learned fool.
43. The signs of the learned fool are explained in next sub-chapter. The listener is asked to listen attentively to what is said next.

Thus in Shri Dasbodh, a dialogue between the Guru and disciple, Sub-Chapter 9 of Chapter 2, named "The Attributes of the Dispassionate One" is concluded.

Chapter: 2, Sub-Chapter: 10

The Signs of a Learned Fool

|| ShriRam ||

1. Previously, the attributes which can change a fool into someone who is wise were described. Now, listen to the description of those who are intelligent, yet are fools.
2. One such as this is called a learned fool. The listeners should not feel uneasy when hearing about these attributes. Know that by giving them up, one can become truly content.
3. Having heard a lot of explanations one becomes knowledgeable and may even speak clearly about the "Knowledge of Brahman." However, if he holds on to pride and groundless hopes he is called a learned fool.
4. One who advocates unrestrained actions, does not believe in the worship of God with attributes, and criticizes one's own inherent duty (swadharma) and spiritual practice (sadhana), is a learned fool.
5. Considering himself to be knowledgeable, he criticizes others and sees defects in all living beings. He is a learned fool.
6. One who asks his disciples to do something which causes them to be disobedient or causes them misfortune, or with his words hurts someone's mind, is a learned fool.

7. One who is full of worldliness (rajoguna) and ignorance (tamoguna), is scheming and cruel within, and who upon seeing wealth and prosperity praises it, is a learned fool.
8. One who criticizes an entire text without reading all of it, who unnecessarily finds fault in it, and who only looks for its negative attributes, is a learned fool.
9. One who gets bored when hearing about the good attributes, who out of jealousy bothers others, and who is arrogant and does not act with morality and justice, is a learned fool.
10. One who is knowingly stubborn, cannot control his anger, and whose actions are not in accord with his speech, is a learned fool.
11. One who speaks without being knowledgeable, who goes to great trouble to do so, and whose words are harsh, is a learned fool.
12. The listener who has heard a lot of things and argues with the speaker, and insults him by his over talkativeness, is a learned fool.
13. One who finds fault with his elders, even though he has the same faults that he does not see, is a learned fool.
14. One who studies and acquires all types of knowledge but does not use it to console others, is a learned fool.
15. When one is entangled in family matters he is like the elephant caught in a spider's web, or a honey bee who goes to his death because of greed[12], he is a learned fool.
16. One who enjoys keeping the company of women and engages in various conversations with them, and in general engages in undesirable habits, is a learned fool.
17. When one firmly holds onto things which lead to a low status, or when one is identified with the body and intelligence, he is a learned fool.
18. One who instead of praising God only praises men and whatever his eyes see, is a learned fool.
19. One who goes on describing the body parts of women and their various expressions and gestures, meanwhile forgetting God, is a learned fool.
20. One who is full of pride in excessive wealth and prosperity, who considers others lowly and inferior, and is outspoken about his atheistic opinions, is a learned fool.
21. One who is well educated and detached, or who is a great yogi with the Knowledge of Brahman yet indulges in fortune telling, is a learned fool.
22. One, who while listening, constantly analyzes the virtues and defects of the speaker, and becomes jealous about the virtues of others, is a learned fool.
23. One who has no devotional practice, no detachment, nor does any singing of the praises of God or Guru, and does not practice what he preaches, is a learned fool.
24. One who does not recognize various pilgrimage and holy places, or the *Vedas* and other ancient scriptures, and one who is born into a holy family yet does not recognize what is holy himself, is a learned fool.
25. One who is respected and feels puffed-up about it in the mind, or who praises someone who has no reputation and then turns around and criticizes him, is a learned fool.
26. One who says one thing before and a different thing afterwards, and whose reputation is that he is not consistent in his actions, is a learned fool.
27. One who eagerly takes to family life, has disrespect for Supreme Truth, and instead knowingly holds to ignorance, is a learned fool.

---

[12] These metaphors are attributed to ancient Indian myths about lust and greed in worldly life.

28. One who gives up the real meaning of true statements, who only speaks what is liked by the mind, or whose welfare is dependent on others, is a learned fool.
29. One who puts up a facade on the surface, does what he knows he should not do, and stubbornly follows the wrong path, is a learned fool.
30. One who listens to explanations day and night yet does not give up undesirable attributes, and who does not know what is in his own best interest, is a learned fool.
31. When there are noble people sitting in the audience, and yet the speaker speaks to them discourteously and treats them disrespectfully, know that he is a learned fool.
32. One who continues to hold onto hope for the disciple who is not serious and only insults him again and again, is a learned fool.
33. One who develops uneasiness in the body and gets irritated when listening to discourses, as well as generally gets irritated with bodily problems, is a learned fool.
34. One who gets carried away with pride in wealth, and one who ignores the tradition of the Sadguru, yet claims the guru's tradition for himself, is a learned fool.
35. One who speaks of Self-Knowledge yet behaves selfishly, accumulates money like a miser, and takes advantage of spiritual lifestyle to become wealthy, is a learned fool.
36. One who does not practice what he preaches, uses speaking about the Knowledge of Brahman for earning money, and becomes dependent on others for his livelihood, is a learned fool.
37. One who interrupts the continuity of the path of devotion, and who creates divisions among people is a learned fool.
38. One whose family life slips through his hands, who does not know anything of Paramartha, and who hates God and the knowers of Brahman, is a learned fool.
39. The qualities of the learned fool are described so that you may drop them. The one who is thoughtful should understand the significance of these attributes, and forgive any shortcomings of what has been said.
40. The learned fool is a fool among fools who considers mundane worldly life to be a happy one, and who does not see that there is nothing more sorrowful than worldly life.
41. The description of the sorrow of birth and the grief of the experience of the time in the womb is narrated in the next sub-chapter.

Thus in Shri Dasbodh, a dialogue between the Guru and disciple, Sub-Chapter 10 of Chapter 2, named "The Signs of the Learned Fool" is concluded.

Chapter 3. Commentary on Life

Chapter: 3, Sub-Chapter: 1

The Suffering at Birth

|| ShriRam ||

1. Birth is the origin of suffering, an ocean of grief, and a mountain of fear which seems immovable.
2. Birth is the collection of actions (karma), a mine of wrongdoing, and an ever new and cruel harassment by time.
3. Birth is the fruit of wrong knowledge, a lotus of greed, and a veil of Illusion without Knowledge (Jnana).
4. Birth is bondage for the individual being, the cause of death, and the cause of confusion and entanglement without reason.
5. Birth is the forgetting of happiness, a reservoir of worry, and an extensive expanse of passion.
6. Birth is the misfortune of living beings, the stamp of imagination, and the spell of the witch called attachment.
7. Birth is the deception of Illusion, the bravery of anger, and an obstacle in the way of liberation.
8. Birth is the assertion of individuality by living beings, the quality of ego, and is itself the forgetting of God.
9. Birth is the fondness for sense objects and the bonds of greed. Birth is like a cucumber that is being devoured by time.
10. Birth is itself difficult times, a false time, and a downfall into a heap of filth.
11. If one looks at the origin of the physical body, where birth takes place it is very dirty, being formed in the discharge of menstruation.
12. The body is a statue that is made from the discharge of menstruation. How can the body be considered pure when it is made from what is considered to be very dirty?
13. The discharge of menstruation becomes thickened and stabilizes, and it is that dirt which takes the form of the body.
14. Outwardly, the body looks magnificent, but inside it is like a sack of odorous filth and fluids that should not be opened.
15. While a garbage container becomes clean by washing the inside of it, the dirt and odor of the body, even if washed everyday, never becomes clean.
16. The body is made up of an erect bone skeleton that is wrapped in blood vessels and nerves, and the space inside the skin, which is filled to the brim with fat and flesh.
17. That which is unclean (ashuddha) cannot become clean (shuddha). The body is filled with that which is unclean (the word for blood is also ashuddha) as well as many afflictions and diseases residing inside it that cause sorrow.
18. The body is like a storehouse of filth, inside and outside it is covered with dirt. It is a bag containing foul smelling urine.
19. The intestines are full of worms, that looks like many small bags containing foul smelling things, and the skin covering over them looks very disgusting.

20. The head is considered the best part of the body, yet mucus runs from the nose and the ears and emits a foul smelling odor.
21. The eyes give out secretions, the nose is filled with accumulated dirt, and in the morning the mouth throws out dirty saliva.
22. From the face, saliva along with other dirty mucus and phlegm are spit out, and yet it is compared to a lotus, or said to be beautiful like the moon.
23. That the face is dirty, and the bowels are full of fecal matter can easily be seen. This is clearly evident in the world and does not require any proof.
24. Even if one fills the stomach with the best food, it is eliminated as feces or sometimes is vomited out. Even if one drinks pure Ganges water, it becomes urine.
25. Understand thus, that dirt, urine, and vomit (gastric fluids) make up the life of the body. The body grows because of these only. There is no doubt about this.
26. If there is no feces, urine, and vomit, then there is death. This is the same for everyone. Whether a king or a beggar, one cannot escape having feces in the abdomen.
27. If one tries to take these things out the body to try to keep it clean, it will die. Such is the arrangement of the body.
28. Such is the state of the body as seen in a healthy condition. My mind doubts that it should even be described when it is in a diseased condition.
29. Like being in a prison, the body suffers for nine months in the womb. All of the nine openings are closed, and there is no air.
30. The vomit and hellish juices percolate in the stomach and become heated up with the gastric fire. It's as if the bones and flesh are being boiled inside.
31. Without skin, the fetus moves around in the womb, and because of that the mother feels the ill effects of pregnancy. The bitter and hot food consumed by the mother makes the whole body of the child burn.
32. When the skin is developed, the fetus is like a bundled packet surrounded by feces in the abdomen of the mother, and it receives food in foul liquid form through the placental cord.
33. Drenched in the dirt of feces, urine, vomit, bile, with worms in the nose and mouth, the thoughts of the fetus are exceedingly agitated.
34. Like this, a living being is in a condition like being imprisoned, having fallen into a very cramped place. Moaning, he asks God to release him from there right away.
35. Oh! God, please release me from here. I shall do good for myself, and once I escape from this womb, I shall not come back here again.
36. Because of this suffering in the womb, such a vow is made. By then, the time of birth comes near and the mother begins screaming at the time of delivery.
37. There is flesh in the mouth and nose so the fetus is not able to breathe, and the head is completely blocked from coming out at the time of birth.
38. With the opening for the head closed off, the thoughts of the living being become frightened and be begins moving in agony, feeling suffocated.
39. The feeling of suffocation from not being able to breathe in or out makes the fetus very anxious. Not seeing the way out, he feels lost and restless.
40. The thoughts are very frightened and the fetus gets stuck in a horizontal position. With that, people say that an obstruction has occurred and that the fetus must be cut into pieces to get him out.

41. So, by cutting the fetus into pieces, they take it out. First the hands and legs are cut and removed. Then, whatever comes into their hands such as the face, the nose, and the abdomen, is all is cut up and removed.
42. In this way, the life force of the child is given up and the mother also gives up her body.
43. His own death has occurred, and his mother's life is taken away as well. Such is the sorrow that is suffered in the womb.
44. However, but even if due to past good deeds the fetus finds its way to the vaginal opening, it may still get caught at the neck and shoulders.
45. Restricted in this way, the fetus is forcefully removed and taken out, and in this manner the life force goes out of the child.
46. When in the end the child loses his life force, this results in forgetfulness. With that, past memories and even the memory of oneself is forgotten.
47. In the womb the fetus says "I Am That, I Am That" (Soham, Soham). After coming out, he says "Who am I?" (Koham). Like this, he undergoes much suffering during the stay in the womb.
48. After having been afflicted by a lot of suffering and coming out of the womb with great effort, after a short time he forgets the suffering of that time in the womb.
49. Becoming devoid of knowledge and not remembering anything in his thoughts, delusion occurs through ignorance, and is considered to be happiness.
50. The body becomes affected by happiness and sorrow, and like this it gets caught in the web of Illusion. Let it be.
51. It is like this that the suffering in the womb happens to living beings. Therefore one should surrender to God.
52. One who is the devotee of God becomes liberated from birth. With the strength of Knowledge (Jnana) one becomes detached for all time.
53. Like this, the calamities of staying in the womb have been explained according to my ability. Listeners, remain alert, and pay attention to what is said next.

Thus in Shri Dasbodh, a dialogue between the Guru and disciple, Sub-Chapter 1 of Chapter 3, named "Description of the Sorrow of Birth" is concluded.

Chapter: 3, Sub-Chapter: 2

The Miseries of Life

|| ShriRam ||
1. Worldly life is itself the root of sorrow. It inflicts misery like the sting of a scorpion. Previously I told you about the suffering in the womb.
2. The suffering that occurred in the womb is soon forgotten by the child, and the child begins growing day by day.
3. During childhood the skin is delicate and upon feeling pain the child suffers, but at that time it cannot speak to tell anyone about either its happiness or sorrow.
4. If there is any suffering felt in the body, or when feeling hunger, the child cries, but no one can know what goes on inside its mind.

5. The mother caresses him all over his body, but his suffering is on the inside. The mother cannot know from the inside what suffering is occurring for the child.
6. Again and again the child sobs and cries. The mother takes it in her arms to try to pacify it, but she does not know the agony the poor little one is suffering in its life.
7. Many ailments come upon the child and it gets agitated with its suffering. It cries when it falls or gets burned.
8. The child cannot protect its body, and many injuries happen to it. Sometimes, being mischievous, the child may lose a limb.
9. If accidents and mishaps are avoided and the child escapes death, day by day it begins to recognize its mother.
10. If it so happens that if for even a moment the child does not see its mother, it cries and screams with grief. At that time it is as if nothing else exists for it except its mother.
11. With hope the child keeps waiting and looking for her. The child cannot bear to be separate from its mother even for a moment, after having remembered her.
12. Even if Brahma and other gods were to come, or the child would have the blessing of seeing the Goddess Lakshmi, still, no words can console it without its mother.
13. Even if she is ugly, or less fortunate, or more useless than everyone else, still, nobody on earth can be a substitute for her.
14. Like this, the child is pitiable. Without its mother it seems to be lacking something. Even if she pushes it away in anger, it still screams and clings to her.
15. The child gets happiness being with its mother. When she does get away, the child suffers. Because of excessive love at that time, the child gets attached to its mother.
16. Then, if death comes to the mother and the child becomes an orphan, it begins to suffer crying "Mother! Mother!"
17. The child looks for its mother, but can't find her. In a sorry pitiable state it begins to look towards other people while the mind clings to hope, thinking that the mother will come.
18. Thinking another woman's face to be its mother's, the child then sees that she is not its mother, and becomes very disappointed and disheartened.
19. Being separated from its mother the child becomes miserable. It suffers in the mind and becomes weak in the body as well.
20. Or, it may happen that the mother survives, and the mother and child are reunited again, and the young child's childhood continues day by day.
21. Soon childhood passes, and day by day the child grows wiser, and the craving for its mother's affection is left behind.
22. Later on, the child develops an interest in playing games. He gathers together with a group of boys, and wining or losing the games makes him feel happy or sad.
23. The parents teach the child with great affection, and they feel great sorrow when he forms the habit of keeping the company of his friends and does not want to leave them.
24. While playing among the other children he does not remember his mother and father. However, he unexpectedly meets with sorrow there as well.
25. The teeth get knocked out, an eye is damaged, or he breaks a leg and becomes lame. His enthusiasm is now gone, and bad times begin to set in.
26. He gets infected with small-pox and measles. He gets headaches, fevers, and always has stomachaches and problems with intestinal gases.

27. He gets attacked by ghosts, takes a beating from water spirits, spirits of the dead, and a host of other malevolent spirits and demigods.
28. A fierce phantom holds him, or a ghost of a brahmin enters within him and he doesn't know whether or not he has been cursed by a sorcerer. He cannot understand anything about his troubles.
29. Some say that all of his misfortune is the work of one god, and others say it is the work of another god, and some say that it is all the work of a ghost of a priest.
30. Some say that some entity has entered the body and that is the cause, and others say that something must have gone wrong when performing the rituals at the time of birth.
31. Some say that all of this suffering is because of past actions. Many diseases appear in the body and eventually good doctors and even exorcists are asked to come.
32. Some say he will not live, others say he is not dying. Still others say that all of this trouble is the pain and suffering resulting from past deeds.
33. He has forgotten the pain of being in the womb, but he gets burned by the three types of tortures[13], and experiences much grief coming from his family.
34. If he escapes all of this trouble and survives, his parents still beat him to make him learn and study. He eventually becomes respected in society and upholds his family name.
35. Afterwards, out of greed, his parents hastily plan to arrange his marriage. They put on an outward show of prosperity so they can select a girl from a wealthy family.
36. Upon seeing the great wealth that is evident at the wedding party, the young man feels great happiness, and his mind becomes enamored with his in-law's home.
37. Staying in his parent's house he was unconcerned about his prosperity, but when he goes to the in-law's house he must always be wearing nice clothes, and if he has no money he even takes out a loan with interest.
38. He becomes involved at his in-law's house while his own parents remain in a pitiable condition. He feels that they have completed their duty towards him.
39. Having come home with his bride, he feels very enthusiastic in his love for her. He says, "Surely there is no one else as lucky as me!"
40. If his wife is not with him he does not even feel happy to see his parents or brothers and sisters. He becomes very heavily influenced by many wrong types of behavior and he is easily deceived by ignorance.
41. Before having a sexual life with her, he was very much in love with her, and then when she comes of age to engage in sex[14], he exceeds all limits of indulgence. He develops such a love for sex that he becomes entangled in lust.
42. If he does not see his wife even for a moment, he becomes anxious. His beloved one has taken away his inner peace of mind.
43. He is enticed by hearing her tender sweet words and by seeing the modesty on her blushing face. Her speech and eyes are a great source of distraction.
44. He cannot control his yearning for her. His body is helpless and out of control. He cannot concentrate on anything else because of the longing that he feels.
45. Even while doing his work elsewhere his mind clings to thoughts of her at home. Every moment he is remembering his wife in his mind.
46. By saying with extreme sweetness, "You are the life of my life", she becomes the focus all of his thoughts.

---

[13] The three tortures; bodily tortures, worldly tortures, and cosmic tortures, are explained later in this chapter.
[14] In ancient times in India, a young girl was often hastily married off before puberty.

47. When he comes near to the end of life, it is as if his whole life has been spent associating with thugs who are ready for his life to end, so they can take all of his possessions.
48. Being very much in love with his wife, if anyone scolds her, he feels extremely insulted in his mind.
49. Defending his wife, he makes insulting remarks to his mother and father. He speaks to them with hatred and separates himself from them.
50. For this woman he loses his dignity, he gives up his friendships, and his relationships with his family members get spoiled.
51. For a woman, he sells his body into a life of servitude, and gives up his power of proper discrimination.
52. Because of the woman he becomes addicted to pleasures, and he becomes submissive and dependent.
53. Because of the woman he becomes greedy, he gives up his virtue, he is deprived of going on pilgrimages to holy places, and he gives up his own Self nature.
54. Because of the woman he never gives thought as to what is good or bad. In his sincere commitment to her, he gave her his body, mind, and all of his wealth.
55. Because of the woman, he gave up the spiritual life, he neglected his own best self-interest, became disinterested in God, and developed a lustful intellect.
56. Because of the woman, he gave up devotion, he gave up detachment, and he considered liberation unimportant.
57. Because of one woman he considered himself to be greater than the whole universe, and he came to feel like those who were dear to him were enemies.
58. He had such a heartfelt love for his wife that he gave up everything because of her. Then, suddenly, his wife passed away.
59. Because of her death, his mental grief gets greatly increased. He says "Such a great tragedy has happened. Now my family life is destroyed."
60. He had left the company of his friends, and now there is a sudden collapse of his household. In his grief he says, "Now I will be finished with Illusion."
61. Laying the woman's body down, he beats his chest and abdomen in agony. Giving up all shame, he carries on praising her in front of other people.
62. He proclaims, "Now that my household is destroyed, I don't want to have a family life." He cries profusely in a loud voice filled with grief.
63. Due to his loss he becomes confused, and gets fed up with everything. Due to his grief, he decides to become an ascetic or some great spiritual being (Mahatma).
64. However, he does not actually go in that direction. Instead he goes on to get married again, and his mind becomes very engrossed in his second marriage.
65. As a result of his second marriage, he once again considers himself joyful. The listeners should continue to remain alert to what is said in the next sub-chapter.

Thus in Shri Dasbodh, a dialogue between the Guru and disciple, Sub-Chapter 2 of Chapter 3, named "The Miseries of Life" is concluded.

Chapter: 3, Sub-Chapter: 3

Miseries of Life - Assessment of the Self (1)

|| ShriRam ||

1. The second marriage took place and the man forgot about the sorrow of the past. He remained in the family life, thinking to himself that he was happy.
2. He became very miserly and did not even take enough food to fill his own stomach. He was even ready to give up his life for the sake of money.
3. Even in the most difficult times he would not spend any money. Whatever he accumulated, he just kept adding to it. How can it be possible for him to have good desire within?
4. He did not give out anything in charity, and he would prohibit anyone else from giving. He was always criticizing saintly people.
5. He does not know anything about visiting holy places or engaging in spiritual activity, and he does not welcome any special guests or visitors. He even picks up and accumulates small pieces of grain from the mouths of ants.
6. He does not do any good deeds himself, and cannot stand to see anybody else doing them. He ridicules such people in his mind because he does not find that kind of activity appealing.
7. He harasses devotees of God. With bodily force he hurts others, and with harsh words he causes pain in the minds of living beings.
8. Having already given up moral conduct he behaves immorally, all the while puffed up with pride.
9. He slanders his ancestors, does not observe any customary rituals after their death, and somehow even disregards his family's accepted deity.
10. Disregarding tradition, he gives an invitation to his sister and brother-in-law in order to avoid having to give anything to outsiders.[15]
11. He never likes to listen to narrations about God, and says that God is not required at all. He also speaks out against daily prayers, saying they are unnecessary.
12. He greedily accumulates money and betrays others. He becomes intoxicated with uncontrolled arrogance in his youth.
13. With his body still filled with youth, he can not take control and hold back his enthusiasm, so he commits a grave misdeed that one should not do.
14. He was married to a woman who had not yet come of age, and due to his lack of patience, he gives in to lust and makes the acquaintance of another woman.
15. In this way, he does not show respect to his sister or mother and he commits adultery with the other woman. Even when punished at the king's court, he still does not change his ways.
16. On seeing the other woman, lust for her arose within him. Because he was unable to control himself, he once again became miserable.
17. In this way, he committed plenty of misdeeds, and had no sense of what was right and wrong. As a result of his reckless behavior, he suddenly began to experience disease in his body.

---

[15] For some religious occasions, it is customary to invite a married woman and a priest for food. In his miserliness he only invites family to come to his house.

18. His body became filled with all sorts of diseases. He contracted tuberculosis and immediately began suffering because of his misdeeds.
19. Filled with diseases, his whole body came to have ruptures, and his nose became flat. His pleasing attributes disappeared and he became filled with unpleasant qualities.
20. His body became weak, and many ailments arose. His youthful energy was gone, and he became emaciated.
21. His body came to be in a miserable state. He experienced pain all over, and lacking energy, his body began to tremble and shake.
22. His limbs began to deteriorate, and his entire body became infected with worms. Young and old alike began spitting at him upon seeing him.
23. He had dysentery and the foul smell of his own feces was all around. He became very emaciated, and his sorrowful life would not leave him.
24. He cried, "Oh God! Give me death now! I have experienced so much suffering. Is the stock of my misdeeds not yet finished?"
25. He cries incessantly in his sorrow. Every time he looked at his body, he felt more and more miserable. His body had become pitiable, and he was suffering greatly.
26. Like this, great suffering was experienced. His life was in ruins, and then thieves came into his house and robbed him of all of his money.
27. He had neither worldly life nor spiritual life. His destiny was so terrible that he even consumed his own urine and feces in utter misery.
28. Eventually, the accumulations of his misdeeds was exhausted. Day by day, his suffering became less as the treatments and medicines that the doctor gave him began to take effect.
29. He almost died, but he was saved. It was as if he had been born again. People commented about how he had come back into society.
30. He was reunited with his wife once again, and he put his household back in order. And once again, he became very selfish like before.
31. He worked to obtain and accumulate some wealth once more, but the household was on the verge of collapse because there was no child.
32. Not having a son, he was very unhappy and people labeled him as childless. So he wished that he might at least have a daughter.
33. Many efforts were made to have a child. He made vows to many different gods, went on pilgrimages, undertook many types of worship, and went on fasts. He participated in many ceremonies, and prepared various religious meals.
34. He was not happy sexually because being childless filled him with sorrow. Then, it so happened that the family deity blessed him with a child.
35. The couple had extreme love for the child. Neither one of them would leave the child for even a single moment. If anything ever happened to the child, they would cry loudly.
36. In this way they were saddened, so they were worshipping many deities. Then, suddenly the child died, as a result of past deeds.
37. Because of the child's death, they were greatly saddened. Becoming without child in the household, they asked, "Why has God kept us childless?"
38. "What is the use of money? Let it all go. We must have a child even if we have to give up everything."

39. The label of being childless was gone, but now the label of being a family whose children die was put on them. They could not get rid of this label by any means, and because of this they cried aloud with grief.
40. "Why has our family tree been cut off? The means to continue our family has been destroyed. Our family deity has put out the light of the heir of our family."
41. Now, if we can have a child, then I will even walk over burning coals with joy, or pierce my body with hooks in front of the family deity.
42. Oh, Goddess Mother, I shall do a form of offering to you, or give the child some terrible name, or even put a bridle in my nose. Please fulfill our wish."
43. They made vows to many gods, sought out many ascetics, and even swallowed scorpions.
44. The tried using mediums and spirits and offered coconuts, bananas, mangoes, and clothes to priests.
45. They performed many types of strange things in order to fulfill their desire for a son, but it was not to be their destiny. They did not get a son.
46. They tried things like bathing under trees, thereby scorching even the roots of fruit bearing trees. They committed many misdeeds out of their greed for a son.
47. Giving up all of their wealth, there was great anxiety in their life. Then, God and their family deity blessed them with a child.
48. Now their longing had been fulfilled and the couple rejoiced. The listeners should continue to remain alert, and give your attention to what follows.

Thus in Shri Dasbodh, a dialogue between the Guru and disciple, Sub-Chapter 3 of Chapter 3, named "Miseries of Life - Assessment of Self (1)" is concluded.

Chapter: 3, Sub-Chapter: 4

Miseries of Life - Assessment of Self (2)

|| ShriRam ||

1. After some time, many children were born, and the family's wealth had gone away. They became poor and began begging because they could not get anything to eat.
2. Some small children were crawling and playing, and one was still in the mother's womb. Thus, the house became crowded with daughters and sons.
3. Day by day their expenses increased, and the income that they had previously stopped coming in. The daughters became of marrying age but there was no money (for dowry and wedding expenses) to get them married.
4. The man's parents (the grandparents of the family) were wealthy and had plenty of money. Thus they had prestige and were respected among the people.
5. Because of his parent's wealth people had the wrong idea about him and thought that he was also wealthy. However, he did not have the same stature as his parents, and day by day, the poverty in the household increased.
6. Because of the expansion of the family's needs and the number of mouths to feed had increased, the man began to worry and was filled with sadness.
7. The children were of marrying age. The sons got their wives, and then he needed to get his daughters married.

8. If the children were to remain unmarried, it is a shameful thing in society. People would ask what the purpose was of even giving them birth into such poverty.
9. In this way, the man was facing public shame and his father's good name would be ruined. Who would loan him enough money to get the daughters married?
10. A previous loan that he had already taken out was not paid back. It was like a sky of despair had fallen upon him.
11. He was thinking, "We eat the food, but the food is also eating us." Day and night he was worried like this in his mind.
12. All of his credit was totally gone, and all of his belongings were in mortgage. He exclaimed, "Oh God, now the time has come for me to become bankrupt."
13. He took out another loan and was able to buy some household things, as well as some cows and buffaloes.
14. He became more in debt in order to make an outward show in society. The people all commented about how he had maintained the reputation of his father.
15. In this way it happened that he became deeply in debt and was surrounded by creditors, so he departed for a foreign country.
16. For two years he went into hiding, and accepted lowly service. His body suffered with many calamities.
17. Eventually, he earned some money abroad, and he began remembering his family back home. After asking permission from his employer, he returned home.
18. Meanwhile, his family had become very agitated, because they had been waiting anxiously to see him. They asked, "Oh God, what is the reason he has been gone for so long?"
19. They were wondering, "What shall we eat? Will we be forced to starve to death? Oh God, why have you put us in the family of such a man?"
20. In this way, they saw their own discomfort but they did not care to know anything of his suffering, and in the end when his strength was gone, none of them would have even come to his aid.
21. While they were waiting for him like this, suddenly, the children saw their father, and ran to him saying, "You have returned!"
22. Upon seeing him, his wife was very happy. She said, "Now our miseries are over." Then he gave out bundles that he had brought with him into the hands of his family.
23. Everyone in the family was happy. They said, "Our father has come, and he has brought us clothing and caps."
24. Their joy lasted for four days and then they began complaining saying, "If he leaves, we will be miserable again."
25. The family decided that whatever he had brought should remain there, and that he should return to the foreign country. He should return home again with some money when everything that they had to eat was gone.
26. It was agreed that this was the desire of all the family members. Everyone in the family was concerned only for their own comfort. Even his wife, who he loved very much, was only interested in her own comfort.
27. The man had worked very hard in the foreign country and had come home to take some rest. But he had barely taken a breath of rest when the time came for him to leave again.

28. The man consulted an astrologer, and discussed with him the auspicious time for his departure. However, the man's mind was entangled with his family, and he did not want to go.
29. He packed some medicine and some other things he would need, as well as some money. He looked at his children and said his good-byes before he went on his way.
30. He looked at his wife and felt the great sorrow of separation. Destiny had cut the connection of their being together.
31. He became choked up and could not speak, and he could not control his sobs. The children and the father were once again to be separated.
32. He said, "If it is our destiny, then we will meet again. If not, then this gathering is our last meeting."
33. Saying this, he rode away on horseback, looking back again and again. He could not bear the sorrow of separation, but nothing could be done.
34. He left his village behind, but his thinking was confused and he had become miserable because of the attachment and pride for his family life.
35. At that time, he remembered his mother, and said, "Oh! How blessed I was to have such a mother. She suffered so much for me but I was a fool and did not understand.
36. If she were still here today, she would not have allowed me to go abroad. She would have cried about separation from me, but her affection was of a special type.
37. Even if her son becomes a pauper, a mother accepts him like that. Seeing his sadness causes her to feel sadness within.
38. If thought is given about the family, it can be seen that a family can be re-acquired but one cannot get another mother, the one from whom this body has come into existence.
39. Even if the mother is a witch, the love she has for her child cannot be equaled, even by a thousand wives. But I forgot that, and wasted my time pursuing my sexual desires.
40. Because of sexual desire, I fought with those close to me, and made enemies out of my friends."
41. He said, "Blessed are those family people who cherish their parents, and are not cruel towards their relatives.
42. The association with wife and children will remain for one's life, but one cannot get their parents back after they are gone.
43. I had heard this before, but did not understand at that time. My mind was drowned in the pond of sexual pleasure.
44. These relatives who are my family are like enemies because they come to me only for my wealth. I would feel very ashamed to return to them empty-handed.
45. Now, I will have to do whatever I have to in order to earn money to take back to them. If I go back to them empty-handed, naturally it will cause everyone much grief."
46. In this way, he continued brooding, feeling overwhelmed with grief within. He was drowned in a flood of worries.
47. In this way, this body of ours becomes enslaved. One even turns their back on God and becomes a slave for the sake of family.
48. For fulfilling sexual desire one will spend the whole life working, and then at the end, when one has lived out all of their years, one only ends up going away alone.

49. In this way, he repented in his mind for a moment, and then once again, he got caught up in the net of Illusion.
50. He remembered his daughters and sons and felt sorrow in his mind beyond limit. He said, "Now, my children are separated from me."
51. He remembered his past sorrows and all of the sufferings that he had undergone. Then he started to cry out loud.
52. Crying there alone, there was no one to console him. Then, he started to question his own mind.
53. "Why should I weep now? I must accept whatever comes." Saying this to himself, he gathered courage.
54. Like this, troubled by his sorrows he continued on to a foreign land. The listener should listen attentively to the description of the situation that follows.

Thus in Shri Dasbodh, a dialogue between the Guru and disciple, Sub-Chapter 4 of Chapter 3, named "Miseries of Life - Assessment of Self (2)" ends.

Chapter: 3, Sub-Chapter: 5

Miseries of Life - Assessment of Self (3)

|| ShriRam ||

1. Afterwards, when the man was abroad, he started working there and he suffered from many difficulties.
2. Like this, the mundane life is full of difficulties. He worked very hard and after a few years he was able to save some money.
3. Then came time for him to go back to his own people. When he arrived he saw that there was a famine in his country, and that the people were undergoing great hardship.
4. Some had hollow cheeks, some had lost the power of their eyes, and some were shaking with tremors. Everyone was miserable.
5. Some people were just sitting around pitiably, some had swollen limbs, and some were dead. Suddenly, he saw with his own eyes that his daughters and sons were also suffering like this.
6. Upon seeing this, he became full of grief, and began crying aloud miserably.
7. When his family became aware of him, they said, "Father! Father! Give us food," and they mobbed him for food, and clung to him.
8. Opening the packets he carried, they searched for food. Whatever came into their hands they ate immediately. Some died with food in their mouths, and some with food their hands.
9. He began to feed them in a great hurry, but some died while eating, and some were so hungry that they died of overeating.
10. Like this, most of his family died. Only one or two children survived, but they were miserable because of the loss of their mother.
11. It was like this that his household was destroyed by the famine. Afterwards, there were conditions of plenty in the country for everyone.

12. The man was not able to raise his children well. He had to make them their meals with his own hands. Having to do the cooking created a lot of trouble in his mind.
13. People encouraged him, so he got married another time, and all the money that he had was spent for the wedding.
14. Once again, he went to a foreign land to earn some money. When he came back home a quarrel started between the stepchildren.
15. The new wife that he took was a very young woman. The sons would not accept her as their mother, and the man had also lost his youth and vitality.
16. His sons were always fighting amongst themselves, and nobody listened to anybody else. He came to love his wife very much and she became his only precious loved one.
17. There was distrust in the minds of all the siblings and they could not agree on anything, so he called five respectable people to gather together.
18. He divided everything into five parts for all to share. However, his sons did not agree on this decision, and in the end, a quarrel ensued.
19. The father and his sons began to quarrel, and the sons beat their father. At that time the mother began shouting loudly.
20. Upon hearing the shouts, people gathered and watched what was going on. They all said that these sons were of no use for the father.
21. They were the reason that all of the vows had been taken and for whom all the troubles had been endured, and now his sons were being seen beating the father.
22. Such was the terrible quarrel that took everybody by surprise. The people of the town that were standing around them tried to settle the dispute.
23. The five people standing in front settled the dispute between the father and sons by dividing everything into five parts equally.
24. The father was kept separated in a small hut that was built for him, and his mind became thoroughly attached to his wife with selfish motives.
25. The wife was young and the man was old, but they came together and gave up their sorrow and began to consider that their life was a joy.
26. He had found a beautiful woman who was talented and clever. He said, "My luck is great in old age."
27. In this way, he regarded his life joyful, and he forgot all of his previous sorrows. Then, disaster occurred when an enemy invaded the country.
28. The attack came suddenly. They kidnapped his wife, and all of the people's belongings were taken away.
29. Once again, he suffered much grief. He cried loudly and in his mind he remembered his beautiful wife and all of her good qualities.
30. Then some news of his wife arrived. Upon hearing the news that his wife had been raped, he threw his body down on the ground.
31. He rolled around right and left with tears running down from his eyes. Upon remembering her, his thoughts burned with the fire of sadness.
32. He thought, "The money earned was spent for marriage, and now my wife has been taken away by villains.
33. Old age has come to me, and my children have kept me separated. Alas, Oh God, why has such misfortune come upon me?
34. I have no money, no wife, no home, and no strength. Oh God, for me, there is nobody except you."

35. Previously he did not worship God. He had become intoxicated upon seeing wealth, but in the end he repented in his old age.
36. His body had become very weak, and his skin dried up. The gases and bile had increased abnormally, and his throat was choked up with phlegm.
37. His tongue hung drooping in his mouth and he lost the power of speech. Phlegm filled his throat and made a peculiar sound. A foul odor was coming from his mouth, and his nose was running with mucus.
38. His neck moved and trembled, and tears flowed from his eyes. The horrible condition of old age had become his lot in life.
39. His dentures had become broken and his mouth became hollow. Saliva was dripping down from his mouth with a bad smell.
40. His eyes could not see, his ears could not hear a word, and he could not speak with a loud voice because breathlessness had set in.
41. The strength of his feet was gone, he could not sit properly without his body falling over, and the wind passing out through his anus was making loud sounds.
42. He could not control his feelings of hunger, and could not get food quickly enough. And even if he did get it, he could not chew properly with his teeth gone.
43. Due to excess bile he could not digest his food, and he was vomiting out what he ate or quickly passing it out through the anus as diarrhea.
44. The area around him was getting so spoiled with feces, urine, and vomit that the people passing by could not breathe.
45. Suffering from many sorrows and ailments, and the unsteady intellect of old age, his life was still not over.
46. The hair from his eye lashes and eyebrows greyed and then fell off completely, and his flesh was hanging like rags all over his body.
47. His bodily functions all became dependent on the few friends that remained. All of the people asked why he was not dying.
48. Those to whom he had given birth and raised turned their back on him. Difficult times had come upon him in the end.
49. His youth and energy was gone, his desire for family life was gone, and everything was in ruins including his body and wealth.
50. His whole life he had been selfish, and everything had gone to waste. How very difficult his condition had become at the end of his life.
51. He had labored for happiness, yet had ultimately ended up sad and unhappy. Now, still ahead was coming the danger of the pains of death.
52. Birth is the root of sorrow and gives misery like the stings of the scorpion. Therefore, without losing a moment, look after after your own self-interest.
53. Now, let this talk be. Old age is terrible for everyone. Therefore, surrender to God.
54. That same repentance which happens in the womb should also happen in old age at the end of life.
55. Afterwards, he again takes the birth after a stay in the mother's womb, and the miserable mundane life, which is difficult to cross, once again becomes his destiny.
56. Without worshipping and praising God one cannot escape birth in this world. Next, I shall tell of the suffering coming from the three types of tortures.

Thus in Shri Dasbodh, a dialogue between the Guru and disciple, Sub-Chapter 5 of Chapter 3, named "Miseries of Life - Assessment of Self (3)" is concluded.

Chapter: 3, Sub-Chapter: 6

The Bodily Tortures

|| ShriRam ||

1. Now, I will give narration on the signs of the three categories of tortures. The listeners should listen with appropriate concentration.
2. The one who has been scorched by these three types of tortures gets cooled in the company of saints, just as one who is thirsty gets satisfied when he gets what he longs for.
3. He is like the one who is hungry and gets food, the one who is thirsty and gets water, or one who is imprisoned and gets happiness when his bondage is broken.
4. He is like the one who reaches the shore when caught up in a huge flood, or the one who is awakened from a sorrowful dream.
5. He is like someone who is dying and is given life, or wards off calamity and becomes happy.
6. He is like one who is sick and gets the appropriate medicine and becomes joyful upon being cured.
7. Similarly, the one who has suffered with the family life, and has been burned by the three types of tortures, is the right one to receive instruction about the spiritual path.
8. Now I shall tell the listeners about the three types of tortures. There is support for this description from ancient Sanskrit statements.
    * The torture that arises from the pleasures and pains of the body, senses and prana is called Bodily Torture (Adhyaatmika).
    * The torture that arises from the pleasures and pains from the contact with the elemental world is called Worldly Torture (Adhibhautika).
    * The torture that arises from virtuous and non-virtuous actions done by one in life that cause one to enjoy heaven or to suffer after death is called Cosmic Torture (Adhidaivika).
9. The first torture is the torture pertaining to one's body, the second torture is from contact with the elemental world, and third torture comes from one's own behavior. The listeners should understand these.
10. The listeners asked, "What is the torture from one's body, and how does one recognize it? What are the characteristics of torture from the elemental world, and how can one understand what they are?
11. What is the torture of human behavior, and what is its nature? Please explain in detail in such a way that we can understand."
12. The speaker agreed, and began narrating in detail the torture pertaining to the physical body. Be alert and listen attentively
13. Understand that one becomes troubled by the pleasures and pains arising from the body, senses, and life force (prana), and this is what is called "Bodily Torture."
14. That which comes from the body, senses, and prana, and which causes unhappiness, is called bodily torture.
15. That suffering which comes from the body, and gives sorrow to living beings will now be explained.

16. Scabies, diseased scalp on the head, pimples, guinea worms, sores in the nails, tumors in arm pits, small pox and measles are afflictions in the body and are called bodily tortures.
17. When one gets boils in the armpits, boils at the hair roots, putrefied sores, black carbuncles, unbearable pain from diseases like piles, this is called bodily tortures.
18. Inflammation on the finger tips, swollen cheeks, unusual itching all over the body, swollen gums, and small particles filling the tooth cavities are bodily tortures.
19. Unusual boils coming up, swelling all over the body, and flatulence giving continuous pain and spasms are bodily tortures.
20. Ringworm, bone injuries, ear scabies, the stomach enlarged with dropsy, closure of the palate, and ear infections are bodily tortures.
21. Leprosy and wet leprosy, sickle shaped anemia, and great suffering from tuberculosis are bodily tortures.
22. Pain in the knee, diseases in the breasts of women, pains in the abdomen, pain in the hands and legs, and aching that leads to dizziness from time to time are bodily tortures.
23. Infections and rashes on the skin, unbearable stomach pains, and migraine headaches are bodily tortures.
24. Pain in the waist, in the neck, swollen throat and face, aching bones, and joint pain are all bodily tortures.
25. Indigestion based vomiting and diarrhea, jaundice, glandular tuberculosis, acne boils, and infections from dirty water are bodily tortures.
26. Dehydration, malaria, vertigo, loss of sight in the eyes, and relapsing fever with shivers are bodily tortures.
27. Feeling extremely cold, hot or thirsty, chronic hunger, too much sleep, chronic diarrhea, and excessive sexual hunger are bodily tortures.
28. Laziness, foolishness, lack of success, always being fearful in the mind, forgetfulness, and mental agitation day and night are bodily tortures.
29. Trouble with urination, gonorrhea, leprosy, incurable blood disease, and the terrible pain of kidney stones are bodily tortures.
30. Amoebic dysentery, burning sensation with urination, uneasiness associated with constipation, and illness that cannot be diagnosed are bodily tortures.
31. Hernia, bloody stool, intestinal worms, and passing undigested food in the stool are bodily tortures.
32. Bloated abdomen with stiffness in the belly, sprained muscles, sores causing obstruction of food in the throat, and boils that are extremely painful to a light touch are bodily tortures.
33. Hiccups, choking on food, vomiting with excessive gastric fluids, boils on the tongue, and a cold with cough are bodily tortures.
34. Asthmatic attack with breathlessness, infection of uvula, cough with phlegm, and fever with fits of anger are bodily tortures.
35. Eating food with toxins in it which causes internal disturbances, and the irritation of a boil in the throat are bodily tortures.
36. Diphtheria, mutilation of the tongue, foul smell from the mouth, teeth falling out, and infection of gums are bodily tortures.
37. Spleen disorder, nasal hemorrhage, scrofula, loss of an eye from a sudden accident, and cuts on one's finger are bodily tortures.

38. Body pains and stiffness, teeth getting knocked out, and the lips and tongue getting bitten are bodily tortures.
39. Ear troubles, eye troubles, suffering from many various pains, being born blind, and impotency are bodily tortures.
40. White spots in the eyes, cataracts, glaucoma, worms in the eyes, night blindness, mental confusion, depression, and mental retardation are bodily tortures.
41. Deafness, dumbness, cleft-lip, being without hands, eccentricity, madness, being lame, or being hunchbacked, are bodily tortures.
42. Having wild eyes, twisted neck, crossed eyes, crooked eyes, being cat eyed, being a dwarf, having a defective walk, having six fingers, and having an ugly appearance are all bodily tortures.
43. Protruding teeth, front teeth missing, an excessively long nose, having no ears, being flat nosed, babbling meaninglessly, being very thin, and being very fat are bodily tortures.
44. Stammering speech, inarticulate speech, being weak, being diseased and ugly, having a scheming mind, jealousy, being gluttonous, and having a hot temper are bodily tortures.
45. Being habitually angry and then showing immediate repentance, being hateful, being lustful, being envious, being insulting, having a propensity towards doing mean deeds, being vicious, and having mental ailments are bodily tortures.
46. Difficulty in getting up, general stiffness, stiff neck, sprains, and swelling and pain in the leg joints are bodily tortures.
47. An undeveloped fetus, abortion, tumors in the breast, delirium with high fever, difficulties in the family, and the premature death of a family member are bodily tortures.
48. Infections in the nails, a boil in the nose, bad food, indigestion because of stale food, and getting tetanus lock-jaw are bodily tortures.
49. Loss of hair from the eyelashes, swelling of the eyebrows, infection in the eyes, and requiring glasses at an early age are bodily tortures.
50. Brown spots on the skin, moles, black fungus pustules on the skin, warts, mumps, outgrowths of flesh, and delusion in the mind are bodily tortures.
51. Having swelling all over, ganglions, foul smells and body odor, balding patches of hair loss, and saliva drooling from the mouth are bodily tortures.
52. Having many worries creating darkness under the eyes, miseries agonizing and burning in the mind as if seared in, and uneasiness without any disease are bodily tortures.
53. Calamities, disease, and weakness associated with old age are bodily tortures.
54. Many various diseases, pains, and injuries that cause living beings uneasiness and sorrow are called the "Bodily Tortures" (Adhyatmika).
55. Such is the suffering of bodily tortures which is the result of past deeds. There is no end to the description of it because it is like a limitless ocean of sorrow.
56. How much more should I say? The listeners should be able to understand by these examples. Naturally, I will speak next about about the tortures pertaining to the elemental world.

Thus in Shri Dasbodh, a dialogue between the Guru and disciple, Sub-Chapter 6 of Chapter 3, named "The Bodily Tortures" is concluded.

Chapter: 3, Sub-Chapter: 7

Tortures of the Elemental World

|| ShriRam ||

1. Previously, the narration on the attributes of bodily tortures was given. Now, I shall tell about the tortures pertaining to the elemental world.
2. The happiness and sorrow that arises from the contact of living beings with the elemental world and disturbs the mind is called "Worldly Torture."
3. Now a clear explanation of the characteristics of worldly torture will be given. This will help to enable one to fully recognize and understand the three categories of tortures.
4. When the foot gets injured upon stumbling, or a thorn breaks inside the flesh, or the blow from a weapon causes some injuries, or when some object like a pointed stick penetrates the skin, these are known as worldly tortures.
5. When the unexpected contact with plants or herbs gives burning and scratching sensations, or when a bee stings, these are called worldly tortures.
6. When insects such as a fly, a cattle fly, bees, ants, oil ants, or mosquitoes bite, or when a leech sucks the blood, these are worldly tortures.
7. When fleas, or red birds, red ants, bristles of grain, black ants, bugs, worms creating eczema, black bees, or cattle lice bite or irritate the skin these are worldly tortures.
8. When a scorpion stings, or a centipede, or tiger, or wolf, or wild pig, or birds, or an elk bite, these are worldly tortures.
9. When one is bothered by wild cows, buffaloes, bison, bears, elephants, or when someone is maddened by ghosts, these are worldly tortures.
10. When a crocodile carries one away, when one suddenly gets drowned or falls into flowing water, these are worldly tortures.
11. There are many poisonous snakes, many water animals, and many wild animals. They are countless. This is named as worldly torture.
12. Disobedient animals such as horses, oxen, donkeys, dogs, pigs, foxes, and cats are known as worldly tortures.
13. Many different types of animals that make terrible noises and cause severe grief are called worldly tortures.
14. Walls and terraces that fall, cliffs and tunnels that collapse, and trees that break and fall on the body are worldly tortures.
15. When the effects of someone's curse or black magic are seen, or when someone suddenly becomes mad, these are worldly tortures.
16. When someone provokes, hypnotizes, abuses, or kidnaps another, these are worldly tortures.
17. If someone gives poison, blames another, or puts a noose around your neck, these are worldly tortures.
18. When poisonous plant secretions infect the body, or some nut oil causes an allergic reaction, or one becomes suffocated with smoke, these are worldly tortures.
19. When one's foot steps on a burning coal, or one's hand is crushed under a large stone, or one stumbles and falls while running, these are worldly tortures.
20. When one falls suddenly in a well, tank, a ditch, or from a cliff or river bank, these are worldly tortures.

21. When one falls down from a fort or a tree and screams loudly in pain, these are worldly tortures.
22. When the lips crack from the cold, when the hands, feet and heels get cracked from dryness, or when one gets fungal infections between the fingers or on the nails, these are worldly tortures.
23. When the tongue gets burnt with hot foods while eating, or when the teeth crack and get cavities, these are worldly tortures.
24. In childhood, when one is at the mercy of others, or is harassed and abused, or is deprived of proper food and clothing, these are worldly tortures.
25. When a girl is staying at her in-law's place and is pinched, beaten, or burned with a hot iron, and starts crying out of control, these are worldly tortures.
26. If by mistake an ear gets twisted, or asafetida (a spice) goes into an eye, or if one is constantly harshly berated, these are worldly tortures.
27. If one is beaten by wicked people in many ways, or if one's mother's home is far away, these are worldly tortures.
28. If someone forcibly pierces one's ears or nose, holds one down and makes tattoos on the body, or if one mistakenly gets burned on a hot iron bar, these are worldly tortures.
29. When one gets kidnapped by enemies, or one gets sold to people of a lower caste, or if one gets into a miserable state and dies, these are worldly tortures.
30. When many diseases arise that are described as bodily torture, but practitioners of exorcisms are brought in to try to cure them, this is a worldly torture.
31. When one is forcibly given terrible medicines to try to cure various ailments, this is a worldly torture.
32. When the juices of bitter plants or herbs, boiled extracts, or powders and pastes are given making one feel uncomfortable, these are worldly tortures.
33. If laxatives are given, or medicine to make one vomit, or a difficult diet regime is observed which causes difficulties, these are worldly tortures.
34. If an incision is made on a wound with a sharp blade to remove infection, or the skin is branded with a with hot iron rod causing great pain, these are worldly tortures.
35. If plant sap or extract from some nut is applied to the skin causing pain, or blood vessels are cut, or leaches are applied to extract blood from the body, these are worldly tortures.
36. There are so many diseases, and even more medicines that are prescribed for them. It is impossible to mention them all. When one is caused pain and sorrow because of medicines, these are worldly tortures.
37. When someone who wards off ghosts is called and uses excessive smoke and gives beatings, these are worldly tortures.
38. When thieves break into someone's house and assault and beat those who live there bringing great pain and suffering, this is worldly torture.
39. When one gets burned with fire causing great pain, or when one suffers the loss of something that causes crying and groaning, these are worldly tortures.
40. When many beautiful temples, stores of jewels, and attractive clothing gets burned, these are worldly tortures.
41. When many things such as grains, various objects, many animals, precious belongings, and even people, are burnt to ashes, these are worldly tortures.

42. When someone deliberately sets one's field on fire and the grains, piles of grass, heaps of husks, and sugarcanes are burned suddenly.
43. And when such a fire brings about great loss, and causes severe sorrow, this is worldly torture.
44. When there are many such fires taking place causing misery and sorrow in the mind, this is called worldly torture.
45. When one forgets, loses, drops, spoils, breaks, or topples over one's belongings, or misplaces them so they cannot be found anywhere, these are worldly tortures.
46. When a person loses one's position because of corruption, or loses one's pets, or one's sons and daughters cannot be found, these are worldly tortures.
47. When thieves or enemies make a sudden attack and go around looting houses, and taking away the animals, these are worldly tortures.
48. When vandals cut down crops and banana plantations, or put salt in the fields to ruin the crops, or carry out other such crimes, these are worldly tortures.
49. When cheaters, pickpockets, robbers, gold snatchers, hypnotists, looters, thugs or killers attack and raid people's houses.
50. When bags, or parcels are stolen and opened and one's money and jewelry is taken away, or if rats take away many various belongings, these are worldly tortures.
51. When lightning strikes, or there is a hailstorm, or when one gets caught in heavy rain, or is drowned in a big flood, these are worldly tortures.
52. When there are rushing torrents of water with whirlpools and dangerous bends, and waves and ebbs that carry around scorpions and vicious insects and snakes.
53. And if a person gets caught in that, or is trapped under rocks or on an islet, and almost drowns but survives, this is all worldly torture.
54. When the family life is not to one's satisfaction, or the wife is ugly, harsh, and cruel, or when one's daughters are widows or one's sons are foolish, these are worldly tortures.
55. When one is haunted by ghosts, or the body gets paralyzed, or by the incorrect incantation of some mantra a person goes mad, these are worldly tortures.
56. When some spirit comes in to one's body and causes many troubles, or when Saturn is in an inauspicious place in one's horoscope and creates calamities, these are worldly tortures.
57. When there are hard times according to the position of the planets, stars, and lunar phases, or position of the moon that cause one uneasiness, these are worldly tortures.
58. When one sneezes at the wrong time, or the song of a fortune bird, or a sound of a lizard, or a hoot of an owl, or the song of some other ill-omened bird or crow makes an inauspicious sound and one starts worrying about these things, these are worldly tortures.
59. When a wandering fortune teller predicts some misfortune to come and one worries and gets nightmares, this is worldly torture.
60. When a fox barks, or a dog cries, or when a lizard falls on the body, or other such omens increase one's worrying, these are worldly tortures.
61. If at the time of leaving on a journey bad omens appear in various ways and the mind becomes depressed, these are worldly tortures.
62. If a person is put in a prison and is made to suffer much pain and injury, these are worldly tortures.

63. If a person is given punishment from the court, or is caned, or hit with a stick on the souls of the feet, or thrown from a cliff, these are worldly tortures.
64. If one is tied to a tree and thrashed with sticks, or is beaten by many people in many ways, these are worldly tortures.
65. If one is punished in various ways such as blocking the anus with a plug, or being enclosed in a barrel, or stretched and beaten with bamboo or fists, or being strangled by the neck, or beaten on the knees, these are worldly tortures.
66. If one is abused by being kicked, slapped, having dung thrown on his body, or stones thrown at him, or the ears twisted, or hit in many different ways, these are worldly tortures.
67. If one is hung, pinched, has one's hands tied behind them, or is bent over the trunk of the tree and beaten, or put in a wooden trap and kept guarded, these are worldly tortures.
68. If one has harsh or acidic things inserted into their nose such as lime, or salt, or mustard, these are worldly tortures.
69. If one is immersed again and again in water, or is bound and thrown in front of an elephant, or dragged and beaten like a bull, these are worldly tortures.
70. If one's ears, nose, hands, legs, tongue or lips are forcibly pierced, these are worldly tortures.
71. If one has arrows shot at them, or is put to the gallows, or has one's eyes or testicles removed, or is pierced with nails or needles, these are worldly tortures.
72. If one is harassed and constantly put on the scales, or pushed from a cliff, or tied to the mouth of the cannon and had it fired, these are worldly tortures.
73. If one has wooden blocks hammered in the ears or anus, or has parts of their skin peeled away, these are worldly tortures.
74. If one is skinned from head to toe, or has their skin pierced with fingers, or has a hook put around their neck, or forks put into their testicles, these are worldly tortures.
75. If one is made to drink lead or some other poison, or is cut on the head, or put under the foot of an elephant, these are worldly tortures.
76. If lizards or cats are put in one's clothing, or one is hanged until death, or tortured in many cruel ways, these are worldly tortures.
77. If one is endangered by dogs, tigers, ghosts, crocodiles, or weapons, or lightning, these are worldly tortures.
78. If one has their veins or blood vessels pulled and stretched out, or if one is burned by lit torches, or is affected by any of so many calamities, these are all called worldly tortures.
79. If one suffers the loss of human beings, money, importance, animals, or any objects, these are worldly tortures.
80. If one's mother dies in childhood, or one's wife dies in youth, or one's son dies when one is in old age, these are worldly tortures.
81. If one suffers the sorrow of poverty and debt, or other calamities while in a foreign country, or has difficulties due to bad food, or is otherwise somehow deprived of necessities while abroad, these are worldly tortures.
82. If many die due to a cholera epidemic, or because of defeat in battle, or if death happens to one's friends, these are worldly tortures.

83. If in difficult times, there is famine, or if the mind is doubtful during hard times, or one becomes depressed because of sadness and the poison of worries, these are worldly tortures.
84. If one gets crushed under a crushing machine, or gets caught in the wheels of some vehicle, or falls into fire, these are worldly tortures.
85. If one gets wounded by many weapons, or eaten by wild animals, or put into imprisonment, these are worldly tortures.
86. If one gets suffocated and made uncomfortable with bad smells, or is made to feel ashamed by many insults, or is weakened by many sorrows, these are worldly tortures.
87. Like this, the descriptions could go on endlessly. There are unlimited mountains of sorrow. The listeners should think about and understand the "Worldly Tortures" coming from the elemental world (Adibhootika).

Thus in Shri Dasbodh, a dialogue between the Guru and disciple, Sub-Chapter 7 of Chapter 3, named "Tortures of the Elemental World" is concluded.

Chapter: 3, Sub-Chapter: 8

The Cosmic Tortures

|| ShriRam ||

1. Previously, I told you about the Bodily Tortures, and the Worldly Tortures. Now, I shall tell you about the tortures arising from one's own behavior, or the "Cosmic Tortures." Please listen with alertness.
2. People experience heaven or hell at the time of the destruction of the body according to the good and bad actions done in their life. This is called the cosmic torture.
3. Due to arrogance and indiscrimination, many wrong deeds and faults are done that give grief and cause one to suffer great misery.
4. With physical strength, the power of money, with manpower, and with support from rulers, many wrongful deeds are committed with these various powers that give strength.
5. Giving up the principles of morality, one does what one should not do, and suffers great misery at the time of death.
6. Closing his eyes in selfishness, he uses his injurious intellect to engage in trying to satisfy many greedy desires by acquiring the land, money, women or possessions of others.
7. Intoxicated with arrogance he kills living beings and their families, and commits all kinds of offensive activities, and accordingly suffers great misery at the time of death.
8. When people behave without exercising any restraint, and abandon propriety and justice, the village is punished by the head of the village and a region is punished by the ruler of the region.
9. The ruler of the region is in turn punished by the king. If the king is not upholding propriety and justice, he is punished by God, and suffers miserably accordingly.

10. If the king behaves immorally and acts only out of selfishness, and engages in many offenses against the people, yet remains king, at the time of the end of his kingdom he suffers a hellish existence.
11. If the king commits politically wrong actions and gives up the control over the senses, affections and passions, the fear of death hounds him, and he is punished by the Death God (Yama). If Death abandons his duty, God punishes him.
12. In this way, the gods have put into place some principles by which beings should behave. Giving up morality, one suffers misery at the time of death.
13. The gods send Death, therefore this type of torture is named as "Cosmic Torture." This third type of tortures that are the cosmic tortures, are unbearable.
14. The punishment of Death is the great suffering and misery that happens at the time of death. The ancient sciences (*Shastras*) have told of the many types of suffering of destiny that cannot be escaped. This is called the cosmic torture.
15. The suffering of the tortures of destiny are told in detail in the *Shastras*. One's misdeeds remain in the subtle body in many ways.
16. The good and bad deeds are there in the subtle body. According to the many kinds of good or bad deeds, one experiences their subtle body as being heaven, or as suffering in hell.
17. If the impressions of many good deeds are there, then one experiences the joys of heaven, and if there are many wrongful deeds, one experiences harsh suffering. The *Shastras* have spoken of this, and they should not be disbelieved.
18. If one does not behave according to the edicts of the *Vedas*, and has no devotion to God, they will suffer great misery at the time of death. This is a cosmic torture.
19. There are lots of subtle bodies of beings causing commotion in the various types of hell. In one type of hell, the irritation is like that of having one's hands and feet bound, with worms biting at them. This is a cosmic torture.
20. Another type of hell is like being in a big pot with a small opening, and the beings there are boiling alive in a foul smelling liquid inside. This is a cosmic torture.
21. In another type of hell the beings feel that they are placed on the hot floor which burns them while a burning log is rolled over them and many forks pierce their bodies. This is a cosmic torture.
22. The beatings of the misery of death are many, and there are limitless types of torture and suffering that those who commit many wrongful deeds must endure. This is cosmic torture.
23. In the world the tortures are many, but there are many more miseries that are suffered after death. There, the relief that comes from dying does not exist and the beatings do not stop. This is cosmic torture.
24. From all four sides, the servants of death pull the being, they swing and throw him and drag him away, beating him all the while. This is cosmic torture.
25. He feels that he can't get up, he can't sit, he can't cry, he can't lie down. Tortures one after the other are unending. This is cosmic torture.
26. The being cries and sobs in a loud voice, and with the exertion after struggling, he becomes weaker and weaker, until he is emaciated, remaining like a living skeleton. This is cosmic torture.
27. Harsh statements, harsh beatings, and a great variety of tortures and troubles must be endured by those who have lived a life of wrongful deeds. This is cosmic torture.

28. Previously, I spoke about the punishment given by kings, but the miseries experienced after death are far more severe. There, the tortures are very immense and miserable.
29. Now I have spoken about Bodily Tortures, Worldly Tortures, and even worse than those, the extraordinary Cosmic Tortures. Only a few examples were given to you for your understanding.

Thus in Shri Dasbodh, a dialogue between the Guru and disciple, Sub-Chapter 8 of Chapter 3, named "The Cosmic Tortures" is concluded.

Chapter: 3, Sub-Chapter: 9

Explanation of Death

|| ShriRam ||

1. The mundane worldly life is like a race, where the ending, which is death, cannot be postponed. From the very beginning of the physical body, death keeps track of its time, moment by moment.
2. Always living in the company of Time[16], people cannot understand what is going to happen next. According to one's actions, one may die in one's own country or in a foreign land.
3. Upon the exhaustion of the remainder of one's accumulated actions, one has to meet with death without a moments delay.
4. Suddenly in life, the messengers of Time begin beating you continuously, and put you on the path of death.
5. When death arrives, no one can be protected. Sooner or later, death claims all.
6. When the powerful stick of death hits, even one who is strong, or a great powerful king, cannot remain.
7. Death does not say that someone is cruel, or that he is a fighter, or that he is a warrior on the battlefield.
8. Death does not say that he is hot tempered, or that he is adventurous, or that he is fierce, or that he is a big crook.
9. Death does not say that he is strong, he is wealthy, he is arrogant, or that he is endowed with all virtues.
10. Death does not acknowledge that anyone is famous, rich, or exceptionally brave.
11. Death does not say that someone is the ruler of the world, or that he is someone who knows tricks and magic.
12. Death does not say that he is the owner of horses, he is the owner of elephants, or that he is the leader of the people and a famous king.
13. Death does not say that he is superior among people, or he is a politician or one with a huge salary, or one who is paying salaries to others.
14. Death does not say that someone is a revenue authority, a businessman, or an evil king known in many places.

---

[16] Here Ramdas is using the word "Kala" which has a dual meaning. One meaning is time, and the other is a word for death.

15. Death does not acknowledge that one is wearing religious marks, or that he is a trader, or that she is somebody's wife, or she is a princess.
16. Death does not care about cause and effect, or that someone is of a high or low caste, or a priest doing good works.
17. Death does not say that anyone is a scholar, or prosperous, or highly learned among the people.
18. Death does not say that someone is clever, well respected, a vedic scholar, or of great character.
19. Death does not say that he is a narrator of mythology, or that he is a follower of the *Vedas*, or he is one who performs fire sacrifices, or he is an astrologer.
20. Death does not care that anyone takes care of the sacred flame, or is a listener to scriptures, or a chanter of incantations, or one who has "Complete Knowledge."
21. Death does not say that he is a scientist, or he is a knower of the *Vedas*, or that he is a knowledgeable person who knows everything.
22. Death does not say that anyone is a killer of a priest, or a killer of a cow, or that he has killed many women and children.
23. Death does not say that someone is an expert in classical music, or a knower of rhythms, or a knower of philosophy and a teacher.
24. Death does not say that he is a practitioner of yoga, or he is a renunciate, or that he knows how to deceive death.
25. Death does not care that someone is alert, or is accomplished, or a famous doctor, or an exorcist.
26. Death does not say that he is a hermit, he is an ascetic, or that he is one who is detached from his mind.
27. Death does not say that someone is a great sage, or a great poet, or one who is naked and in a state of total absorption (samadhi).
28. Death does not say that someone is an expert in a hatha yoga, or in raja yoga, or in a detached state forever.
29. Death does not say that he is a bachelor, or he is one with matted hair, or he is a yogi living without food.
30. Death does not say that anyone is a saint, or a spiritual leader who can disappear.
31. Death does not say that he is independent or dependent on others. It is death alone who consumes all living beings.
32. Some are almost on the pathway to death, some have reached half-way to death, and some have reached to the end of life in their old age.
33. Death does not say that he is a child or young, or one with good qualities, or one who is discerning, or very talkative.
34. Death does not say that he is a support to many, he is generous, or he is a beautiful and clever man.
35. Death does not say that he is a man with many merits, or he is a servant of God, or he is a man who has done special good deeds.
36. Now, let this talk be. Who can escape from death? Know with confidence that sooner or later, all must go down the path of death.

37. All beings coming from the four streams of life[17] with the four types of speech[18], comprising the 8.4 million species[19] that have come to life, must eventually arrive at death.
38. If you try to run away from death in fear, death still does not go away. Death cannot be avoided, no matter what you try to do.
39. Death does not say that this one is in his own country, or he is a foreigner, or he is one who is always fasting.
40. Death does not say that he is a great person, or he is Lord Vishnu or Lord Shiva, or that he is an incarnation of God.
41. The listeners should not be angry. Death is known to all. The living being who is born is bound to go down the path of death.
42. Do not have any doubt about this. Death is well known and clearly understood by all, large and small.
43. Even if one has doubt about it, death is still there. Everything that is born will die.
44. Realizing this, one should have fulfillment in life, and even continue to live after dying, in the form of fame.
45. All living beings large or small, will die. This is for sure. One should not suppose that there is any other answer about death than this.
46. Many who were wealthy are gone, many who were long lived are gone, and even those who were highly influential have all gone down the path of death.
47. Many who were brave are gone, many who have done clever deeds are gone, and many great warriors on the battlefield are gone.
48. Many who had great strength are gone, many who lived in great times are gone, and many kings and their great dynasties are gone.
49. Many who were supporters of others are gone, many great intellectual speakers are gone, and many great logical debaters are gone.
50. Many who were great oceans of knowledge are gone, many who were mountains of strength are gone, and even great gods of wealth have gone down the path of death.
51. Many men of great achievements are gone, many men of great adventure are gone, and many organizers and workers of great capacity are also all gone.
52. Many who have wielded weapons are gone, many who were benevolent are gone, and many protectors of religion of all kinds are gone.
53. Many men of great valor are gone, many with great fame are gone, and many ethical kings of great character are gone.
54. Many opinionated people are gone, many dedicated workers are gone, and many who were clever debaters of all topics are all gone.
55. Many groups of scholars are gone, many grammatical analysts are gone, and many extraordinary arguers with many different opinions are all gone.
56. Many great ascetics are gone, many detached renunciates are gone, and many thinkers who used keen discrimination have all gone down the path of death.
57. Many householders are gone, many men who played many different roles are gone, and many who have enjoyed many different hobbies are gone.

---

[17] The four streams of life are (1) life from seed, (2) life from eggs, (3) life born through live birth, and (4) life born from the combination of heat and moisture.

[18] Four types of speech are also explained in more detail later in the text (Chapter 17, sub-chapter 8).

[19] In Hindu mythology it is said that there are 8.4 millions species of beings in the cycle of death and rebirth.

58. Many groups of priests, as well as many teachers are gone. So many beings have gone in so many ways. How much more can I say?
59. Now, let this talk be. Like this, one and all have gone. Only those remain who have gained Self-Knowledge and realized their "True Nature." (Swaroopa; having the form of, or being identical with Brahman).

Thus in Shri Dasbodh, a dialogue between the Guru and disciple, Sub-Chapter 9 of Chapter 3, named "Explanation of Death" is concluded.

Chapter: 3, Sub-Chapter: 10

Explanation of Desirelessness

|| ShriRam ||

1. Worldly life is like a great flood with unlimited water animals and poisonous serpents running around biting.
2. Hopes, and the sense of "mine," are like shackles for the human body. They are like alligators tearing one into pieces. They drag one towards sorrow and put one into difficulties.
3. The ego is like a crocodile which throws one into the lower world and drowns one there. It is difficult for living beings to escape or be freed from there.
4. Desires hold tightly like an alligator that does not loosen its grip. When one develops hatred and it does not go away, and when pride and jealousy are never reduced, this is being caught in Illusion.
5. The habits and latent desires (vasanas) are like serpents that strangle one around the neck with tongues that vomit dangerous poison.
6. Taking the burden of family life on the head, one says "It's mine." Even when drowning one does not leave it and only takes pride in one's family name.
7. One gets caught in the darkness of delusion. The thief by the name of pride robs one of everything, and the ego haunts one like a ghost.
8. The majority of beings are caught in a whirlpool and are swept away, but some call to God for help, with a deep feeling of devotion.
9. God himself jumps into the flood and takes them to the other shore, while those who are without devotion get swept away.
10. God is hungry for devotion. He is enticed by seeing devotion, and helps the devotee in danger and protects him.
11. The sorrows of worldly life disappear for the one who loves God and calls upon him.
12. Those who give their allegiance to God enjoy the celebration of their own happiness. Such devotional people are blessed with good fortune.
13. Whatever type of faith one has in God, God is like that for them. He is the innermost knower of the thoughts of all beings.
14. If one is deceitful, God becomes a great deceiver. It's a wonder to see his reciprocation.
15. Whatever way in which one praises God, in the same way, God gives contentment. If one's faith becomes a bit less, God moves away.
16. The image in the mirror appears just as one is. The control of that reflection lies with oneself.

17. Whatever one does, the image in the mirror will appear the same way. If one looks with eyes widened, it will also appear to have big eyes.
18. If one looks angry by raising the eyebrows, the image will also raise the eyebrows. If one laughs, the image looks happy.
19. Just like one's feelings are reflected, God is also like this. According to how one worships God, he receives back in the same way.
20. With faith in the "Supreme Truth" (Paramartha), the ways of devotion lead to the highest state of liberation when keeping the company of saintly people.
21. Those who give praise with deep feeling are purified and become one with God. By the power of their devotion they liberate their ancestors as well.
22. They have saved themselves and have become helpful to other people. Hearing of their salvation, those who were not devotional become full of faith.
23. Blessed are the mothers of those who sing the praises of God (Vishnu), as they alone among people have fulfilled their life.
24. How can their greatness be described, whom God himself protects? By his power, He tears down their sorrow.
25. At the end of many lives one escapes the cycle of birth and death. It is only with this human body that one can meet God.
26. Therefore, blessed are those devotees who have acquired the great treasure of God. It is the merit of countless lives that has born fruit.
27. Life itself is a box of jewels. The beautiful gems inside are in the form of singing the praises of God (in bhajans). In offering such praises to God one gets great joy.
28. The devotee of God may be inferior with regard to riches, but he is superior to Brahma and the other gods as he is always content and without any desires.
29. Those devotees who have given up attachment to worldly life and who hold to the support of God are protected by the "Lord of the Universe" (Jagadisha) from all sides.
30. For those who use discrimination feel happy even in the sorrows of worldly life, while those who are learned fools get caught due to greed for worldly pleasures.
31. Those who have love for God rejoice in the bliss of the Self. Their wealth is different from that of other people. It is never-ending.
32. They become happy, and remain forever happy. Having forgotten the sorrows of worldly life and having become disinterested in the enjoyment of sensual gratification, they take pleasure in being one with the Lord, who is pleasure itself.
33. They have profited from the treasure box which is the human body and used it for the purpose of devotion to God. Others who are non-devotees are truly unfortunate and have lost the opportunity provided by having a human body.
34. In the same way that when one gets a treasure suddenly and then exchanges it for a small sum, the life of a non-devotee goes to waste.
35. One who has practiced severe austerities for a long time receives the prized touch-stone[20] as a result, yet he is unfortunate. Because of his ignorance, he does not know how to use it.
36. In the same way, one who comes into the worldly life gets entrapped in the net of Illusion, and in the end goes away alone and empty handed.
37. It is with the proper association of the human body that many have attained the best spiritual state. Other poor people remain caught in the cycle of birth and death.

---

[20] The touch-stone, or Parisa, is a mythological stone that had the power to turn iron into gold by its touch.

38. With the human body one should rush to fulfill one's life by keeping the company of saints. A great deal of suffering has been experienced in previous births in lower species.
39. No one can know or give any kind of assurance about what situation will come next, just like the birds that are carried away in all ten directions.
40. In the same way, one's own glory or prosperity is like that. Who knows how the future will be? One's wife or children may leave or become separated from you at any time.
41. This very moment is not ours to hold on to, and one's entire lifetime also passes away. When the life is wasted, one is placed in a lower birth as soon as the body dies.
42. In the lower births such as a dog or a pig, one is made to suffer many calamities. There is no chance there to attain the best spiritual state.
43. In the past you have suffered the miseries of residence in the womb, and you have had the good fortune to escape from there with great difficulty.
44. You suffered sorrow there all alone. There were no others for you there. In much the same way dear one, in the end, you will have to go alone.
45. What mother or father, or sister or brother, what well wishers, wife, son, or daughters will go with you?
46. You must realize that they are illusory. All of your relatives are there for their own happiness. They are not with you in your pleasure and pain.
47. What will become of your family life, and your family name? Why do you become tormented? All of your money, grains and wealth will be gone.
48. What about your house, and worldly life? Why are you worrying and carrying the burden of these things all of your life when in the end you drop them and go away.
49. What about youth and glory, or rejoicing and celebration? Understand all of this to be hollow and nothing but the deception of Illusion.
50. If in this moment one was to die saying "Everything is mine, mine!," it is as if they are separated from God.
51. You have undergone repeated births and deaths. How many parents, wives, daughters and sons have you had? Millions!
52. All have come together by the association of previous deeds (karmic connections), yet only those who come to be born in the same household are considered as one's own. This is the belief of a fool!
53. Even the body is not your own, what thought can be given to others as "yours"? Only God is one's own. You should hold to him with strong devotion.
54. Just to fill the stomach one has to serve many lowly people, as well go out of one's way to praise and flatter them.
55. One puts the body into slavery for someone who provides food for the stomach, but how can you forget God who gave you life?
56. It is God who is concerned day and night for all beings, and by whose authority the clouds rain, and the ocean is kept within its limits.
57. Due to God's authority alone, the earth is supported, and the sun shines.
58. The benevolent "God of Gods" is such that we can't understand his skills. It is He who takes care of all beings with affection.
59. This God, Lord Rama, is the Self in everyone. Those who put him aside and instead take to sensual desires are lowly-minded and degraded people who suffer from their own actions.

60. You should understand that everything that is desired, except for Lord Rama, only disappoints. Saying "mine, mine," only results in fatigue in the end.
61. Those who are only constantly thinking about sensual pleasures end up becoming fatigued, and when they do not get the object of enjoyment, they become agitated.
62. God is complete joy (ananda) itself. How can one who forgets him, and who is constantly running around thinking of sensual pleasures and indulging in passions ever be content?
63. One who feels that they need to be happy should adore God (Rama), and give up the attachment to other people, which is the root of grief.
64. When one has a burning passion for something it is like a wound that causes grief. Accordingly, when one gives up the desire to pursue sensual pleasure, one becomes happy.
65. All the happiness that one gets from sensual pleasures only gives rise to sorrow in the end. It is unavoidable that what pleases in the beginning brings sorrow in the end.
66. Like the fish that feels happy when swallowing the hook, but gets its throat torn when it is pulled out, or a deer that is taken down by a hunter after being enticed by some sweet grass.
67. In the same way, when chasing after sensual pleasures, one feels they are enjoying happiness, but in the end what was pleasurable causes misery. Therefore, one should only have desire for God.
68. After listening to this, one who is faithful asks, "How can one make life worthwhile? Swami,[21] please tell how one can escape suffering in death.
69. Where does God reside? How can I meet him? How can the root of misery that is worldly life be broken?
70. You who are the living image of compassion, please tell me the sure way to realize God and avoid downfall. Please tell a poor person like me, what is the remedy?"
71. The speaker says, "You should adore God with single-minded devotion. With that, contentment will come naturally."
72. The listener asked, "How should God be adored, and where should this mind be concentrated? What are the attributes of devotion to God? Please, explain them to me."
73. Asking like this, he held tightly to the feet of the speaker. Full of emotion, he was choked-up and could not speak, as tears were falling down his face.
74. Seeing the unusual loyalty and deep feelings of the disciple, the generous Sadguru was moved. Now, in the next sub-chapter, overflowing "Self Joy" (Swa-ananda) will proliferate.

Thus in Shri Dasbodh, a dialogue between the Guru and disciple, Sub-Chapter 3 of Chapter 3, named "Explanation about Detachment" is concluded.

---

[21] The word Swami is a title or appellation signifying status that is used to refer to someone who is held in high esteem. The western equivalent would be something like "Honorable One."

Chapter 4. Nine-Faceted Devotion[22]

Chapter: 4, Sub-Chapter: 1

Devotion Through Listening

|| ShriRam ||

1. Jai! Jai! Salutations to you, Lord Ganesha! You are the powerful magnificence of Knowledge, Self-Knowledge, and Ultimate Truth. So that others may know, help me to speak.
2. Salutations to Goddess Sharada who is the mother of the *Vedas*. Spiritual accomplishment is possible because of her. She is the inspiration that moves the mind to meditate.
3. And now let us remember the Sadguru, the True Master, who is the greatest of the greatest. It is because of him that one begins to understand the investigation of Knowledge (Jnana).
4. The listeners have asked a good question. "How should one adore God?" Therefore, naturally I will speak about it in this text.
5. The listeners should be alert and listen to the nine types of devotion.[23] In sacred scriptures it is said that upon hearing about these one becomes purified.
6. The nine types of devotion will be clearly explained now. The listeners should pay close attention.
7. Understand that the first type of devotion is listening (shravana). People should listen to explanations and ancient stories about God, and continue listening to many explanations about spiritual science and Self-Knowledge.
8. Listen to explanations about the path of action (karma), the path of knowledge (jnana), the path of conclusive truth (siddhanta), the path of union (yoga), and the path of desirelessness (vairagya).
9. Listen to the importance of religious observances and vows, pilgrimage places, and various types of charity.
10. Listen to what is said about many great people and many places, various mantras and spiritual practices, as well as different types of austerities and initiations.
11. Listen about how some people live on only milk, or without food, or only on fruit, or on leaves or grass, and how some live on many different types of food.
12. Listen to how some people live in extreme heat, or in water, or in extreme cold, or in the jungles, or buried underground, or how some roam about in the air.
13. Listen to how some are engrossed in the repetition of the name of God, how some engage in difficult practices, how some are hot tempered yogis, how some practice

---

[22] The word "bhakti," and the word "bhajan," are used somewhat interchangeably throughout the text meaning to: adore, worship, cherish, respect, honor, revere, pay homage to, praise, devotion to, love for, or to be exceedingly delighted with or fond of. To a lesser degree, the words "bhava/bhavana" are also used extensively in the text, to indicate commitment to, faith in, and adoration of, with the connotation of a sense of deep feeling and a sense of naturalness to one's being associated with these attitudes.

[23] The nine types of devotion are; (1) listening to narrations about God, (2) singing God's praises (3) remembrance of God's name, (4) service at the guru's feet, (5) worship, 6) bowing down, (7) service, (8) friendship with God and (9) self-surrender.

hatha yoga, some are worshippers of spiritual energy (shakti), and some are yogis practicing sorcery.
14. Listen to the explanations of various signs and gestures (mudras), the postures (asanas) practiced in yoga, various wondrous happenings, concentration points, and the knowledge of the body and various philosophies.
15. Listen to explanations about the composition of various living forms, geographical facts, and the many creations of nature.
16. Listen to the descriptions of the sun, the moon, galaxies of stars, planets, clouds, twenty one heavens, and seven hells.
17. Listen to the description of the abodes of Brahma, Vishnu, Shiva, Indra, and the gods of wind, rain, and wealth.
18. Listen to the description of the nine continents, fourteen worlds, protectors of the eight directions, as well as many jungles, gardens and secret places.
19. Listen to the descriptions of the various groups of celestial warriors, scholars, singers, offspring of gods, celestial singers and experts with musical instruments, and various opinions in the field of music.
20. One should listen to the descriptions of musical moods, rhythms, classical dance, various percussion instruments, appropriate timing, and how to handle situations wisely.
21. One should listen to the explanations of the fourteen sciences or streams of knowledge, the sixty-four arts, palmistry, the attributes of all arts, and the thirty-two signs of auspicious times.
22. One should listen to the knowledge of medicinal mantras and gems, mystical remedies, many types of accomplishments, many herbs, medicinal substances, metals, chemicals and diagnoses that are made using the pulse.
23. Listen to the knowledge about which fault or excess causes which disease, which treatments are for which diseases, and what are the correct times and the combinations of treatments.
24. Listen to the descriptions of the creatures in hell, the pains in the realm of death, and how one experiences the pleasures of heaven and the sufferings of hell.
25. Listen to the description of the nine types of devotion, four types of liberation, and how to attain the best path of spiritual upliftment.
26. Listen to the description of the creation of the human body and the universe, and their organization, the explanation of the consideration of various principles, and the investigation of the True and the false.
27. Listen to how one becomes liberated through absorption in Brahman, and how to attain liberation. For this purpose, many opinions should be sought.
28. Listen to the knowledge of the spiritual sciences (*Shastras*), of the *Vedas*, of the mythological texts (*Puranas*), of the four great statements (Mahavakyas[24]), and the explanations of the four bodies[25], their origin, and their negation.
29. Like this, everything should be listened to. However, one should search for and obtain the True, and discard the false through understanding. This is called devotion through listening.

---

[24] The Mahavakyas are the gist of the Upanishads put into four statements:
    Pradnyanam Brahma - **Consciousness is Brahman**.
    Ayam Atma Brahma - **The Self is Brahman**.
    Tat Tvam Asi - **You are That**.
    Aham Brahmasmi - **I am Brahman**.

[25] The four bodies are: (1)Gross (2)Subtle (3)Casual (4) and Great Casual - These are explained later in the text.

30. One should listen to the narration about God with attributes (saguna), and one should listen to the discourses on That which is without attributes (nirguna). Like this, one should understand the attributes of devotion through listening.
31. One should continue to listen to the narration of God with attributes and how to use certain symbols for understanding "That" which is without attributes. Both of these are very holy.
32. Listen to the descriptions of the significance of various celebrations, fasting, spiritual practices, mantras, usage of meditation techniques and concepts, repetition of God's name, the speaking about God's praises and fame, and all different kinds of songs of God's glory.
33. In this way, one should listen to the description of God with attributes, which is the Self, as well as to the explanations about the attributeless. Give up the belief in separation from God by seeking out the root of devotion.
34. Now the narration about devotion through listening has been explained so that you may gain understanding. Next, the attributes of devotion through the narration of stories about God, and singing the praises of God will be explained.

Thus in Shri Dasbodh, a dialogue between the Guru and disciple, Sub-Chapter 1 of Chapter 4, named "Devotion through Listening" is concluded.

Chapter: 4, Sub-Chapter: 2

Narration About God (Kirtan)

|| ShriRam ||

1. The listeners have asked about devotion to God. It is described as being of nine types. The first type which is "Listening" (shravana) has been explained. Listen now to the explanation of the second type which is the "Narration about God" (kirtan).
2. One should give narrations about God (Vishnu) with qualities, and enhance the fame of God in the most appropriate way, through the use of speech.
3. One should learn by heart a lot about God, and be able to explain about the differences in the various texts, and continuously give narrations about God.
4. For one's own self-interest one should talk about God again and again. One should not forget to talk about God.
5. One should have a thirst for being able to talk about God in new ways while keeping a methodical approach. Fill the entire universe with the narrations and songs about God.
6. One should always be enthusiastic for hearing the narrations about God with a deep liking in the mind, and with great interest in the heart.
7. Narrations are loved by God, and by hearing about God one gets contentment. The narration about God is a remedy for the people in the Kali Yuga.[26]

---

[26] Kali Yuga: According to the ancient scriptures the whole time span from the creation until the destruction of the universe is divided into four ages, or yugas. The current yuga, which is the last of the four, is the Kali Yuga. During this time it is said that human beings will have great intellectual capacity, but it will predominantly be a time of indulgence in sensual pleasures and passions.

8. One should be able to describe the various ways to meditate on God, as well as elaborate upon the adornments of God. The object of meditation should be focused on with the inner-mind (antahkarana) while one is giving explanations.
9. One should be able to explain about success, fame, bravery, and greatness with great sincerity. One should also be able to talk about the Self (Atman), and the Supreme Self (Paramatman) in such a way that devotees will become content.
10. Give explanations of logical connections and various interpretations. Chant God's name aloud with music and clapping. Give appropriate illustrations and anecdotes according to the occasion.
11. Accompany the singing of God's praises with cymbals and drums, and with music and dancing in such a way that the continuity of praise is unbroken.
12. Compassion flows in the narration about God. The explanations should be told vigorously in such a way that the ears of the listeners are filled with joy.
13. The singing of God's praises should be done with such inspiration that tears of love flow, and the hairs on one's skin stands up. One should salute God by bowing at the doorsteps of the temple.
14. According to the occasion one should use poetic songs, verses, gestures, and compositions of various styles. On occasion, one should use such speech that arouses courage, as well as make use of humor as appropriate.
15. Narrations about God should be of various sentiments with an appreciation of prose and poetry. Many quotations should be used and what is said should be supported by scriptures.
16. One should be able to explain the attributes of devotion, knowledge, detachment, appropriate morality, and of one's duty and self nature. The path of spiritual practice (sadhana) and the means to Self-Knowledge should be clearly explained.
17. According to the occasion, one should give narration about God with attributes (saguna) while praising His qualities, while on other occasions, one should keep to the explanation about That which is without attributes (nirguna), thereby spreading Self-Knowledge.
18. Leaving behind the explanations about God with attributes, one should give correct explanations on the final doctrine (siddhanta) using normal and organized speech and logic.
19. For some, reading from the *Vedas* is appropriate, while to others, one should tell mythological stories. One should be able to speak about and give detailed explanations regarding Reality (Brahman) and Illusion (Maya).
20. One should protect and respect the ways of the brahmins and the ways of worship and adoration, and should serve and preserve the tradition of the Guru with firm determination.
21. One should protect the qualities of detachment, and the attributes of Knowledge, and one should be extremely alert and discerning in taking care of all.
22. If while giving narrations, one says things that creates doubt upon hearing, truth and satisfaction go away, and people's morals and sense of justice get broken. One should not say anything that causes this to happen.
23. Speaking about God with attributes is known as narration, or kirtan. When giving explanations of non-duality (advaita) one can give emphasis to That which is without attributes (nirguna) while still giving appropriate importance to God with attributes (saguna).

24. One who is giving narrations must have authority behind his speech. One with only a little knowledge cannot give correct replies. A good speaker should be well experienced.
25. One should speak in such a way as to protect Knowledge, that does not contradict the authority of the *Vedas*, and that puts human beings on the best path.
26. Continuing on and leaving aside these details, let it be said that one should give narration on the attributes of God. This narration about God (kirtan), and singing the praises of God (bhajan) is the second type of devotion.
27. With the narration of God many faults disappear and one gets the best upliftment. Through narration, one can attain Godhood. There is no doubt with respect to this.
28. Through narration one's speech becomes pure, one becomes truthful, and living beings become virtuous.
29. Narrations brings about concentration, foster determination, and remove doubts of both the listeners and the speakers.
30. Narada, the son of Brahma, the creator, is always engaged in praising God, and is therefore said to have become God, Narayana, the one who dwells in the hearts of all.
31. The greatness of the narration about God is unparalleled. The Supreme Self, Paramatman, is contented by such narration. All places of pilgrimage, and indeed the Universal Self reside in the praising of God.

Thus in Shri Dasbodh, a dialogue between the Guru and disciple, Sub-Chapter 2 of Chapter 4, named "Narrations About God" is concluded.

Chapter: 4, Sub-Chapter: 3

Remembrance of God's Name

|| ShriRam ||

1. Previously, I have explained the "Devotion of Narration" through which everyone becomes free. Now, listen to the "Devotion of Remembrance of God" (Vishnosmarana) which is the third type of devotion.
2. One should have constant remembrance of God. The name of God should be repeated continuously. This will bring about freedom and contentment.
3. One should have the discipline to continuously remember the name of God in the morning, in the afternoon, and in the evening.
4. One should not be without the name of God at anytime, whether in a state of happiness, sorrow, distress, worry, or joy.
5. Remember God in times of enjoyment, in unfavorable times, auspicious times, festive times, at the time of rest, and at the time of sleep.
6. Remember God's name in times of trouble, in awkward times, in danger, in the worldly life, and when beginning any endeavor.
7. Remember God while walking, talking, during your work, while eating simple meals or fancy meals, or while enjoying many various pleasures.

8. In wealthy times or poor times or in whatever times that come, don't give up the remembrance of God.
9. Whether in the midst of power, authority, the goings on of many activities, or enjoying the greatest of fortunes, don't give up the remembrance of God.
10. Whether in pitiable conditions in the beginning and good conditions later, or the other way around, no matter what the circumstances may be, don't give up the remembrance of God.
11. With the remembrance of God, dangers are overcome and obstacles removed. One can attain the best state with the remembrance of God.
12. All types of troubles from ghosts, malevolent spirits from astral worlds, problems arising from the incorrect chanting of mantras, to being haunted by a spirit of a brahmin can all be destroyed with faith in God.
13. With the remembrance of God the effects of poison become ineffective and all sorts of black magic get destroyed. With remembrance of God, one is on the best path at the time of death.
14. In childhood, in youth, in difficult times, in old age, and at the time of death, there should be remembrance of God.
15. The greatness of chanting the name of God was told by Lord Shiva. By chanting the name of Lord Rama, Shiva made the holy city of Varanasi the place of liberation.
16. Even by chanting the name of Rama in reverse order (ma-ra), the sage Valmiki was easily saved[27] and went on to write the great biography of Lord Rama before it even happened.
17. Pralhad, who was a devotee of God, escaped from many dangers and was saved by the name of God, and a demon named Ajamela became purified by the name of God (Narayana).
18. By the name of God, stones have floated on water, an unaccountable number of devotees have been uplifted, and even the worst scoundrels have become completely free.
19. The names of God are endless. By remembering God, one is protected. Even death cannot affect you.
20. Out of a thousand names of God, if even one name is remembered, one's life becomes fulfilled. One who remembers God becomes sacred and godliness itself.
21. Even if one does nothing else except repeat the name of Rama, God becomes satisfied and takes care of that devotee.
22. The body of one who always remembers the name of God should be considered an auspicious body. Mountains of wrongful deeds and faults are destroyed by the name of Rama.
23. The greatness of God's name is such that it cannot be told with words. Many people have been uplifted with God's name. Lord Shiva himself escaped from the effect of poison[28] with God's name.
24. Everyone, in all classes of society, has the right to chant the name of God. There is no such thing as inferior or superior when remembering God. Even foolish and

---

[27] Valmiki, who was a member of a gang of robbers, chanted the name of Rama in reverse, as "mara" which means to die. When mara-mara is chanted, it becomes Rama Rama. Thereby, with reverse chanting of Rama, he was saved, and became a great sage who went on to write the spiritual epic "Ramayana."

[28] In Hindu mythology, when the sea was churned by the gods and the demons, fourteen precious objects were dispelled along with a lot of poison that was consumed by Lord Shiva. It was by chanting the name of Lord Rama that the poison was rendered ineffective.

materialistic people have reached the other shore by remembering the name of God.
25. Now it has been explained that one must remember the name of God continuously, and his form should be meditated on in the mind. This is the third type of devotion which has been explained in a very natural way.

Thus in Shri Dasbodh, a dialogue between the Guru and disciple, Sub-Chapter 3 of Chapter 4, named "Remembrance of God's Name" is concluded.

Chapter: 4, Sub-Chapter: 4

Serving the Feet of the Guru

|| ShriRam ||

1. Previously, I have given the explanation of the "Devotion of Remembering God's Name." Now, listen to the fourth type of devotion, "Serving the Feet of the Guru."
2. Understand that serving the feet of the Guru is to serve the True Master (Sadguru) with body, speech, and mind with the aim of Self-Realization.
3. What is meant by serving the feet of the Sadguru is to be one with him, and to step out of the troubles associated with the birth and death cycle.
4. Without the Sadguru's blessings (teaching), there is no other remedy for escaping the miseries of the world. For this reason, one should serve the feet of the Sadguru as soon as possible in life.
5. The Sadguru points to what is true and provokes the thought of discrimination between the True and the false. He inspires the inner determination with which one realizes Parabrahman, the Absolute Reality.
6. "That" which cannot be seen with the eyes, and which does not appear to the mind, cannot be experienced without renouncing all attachments.
7. When one says "I have the experience," detachment is not possible, and when one is detached, there is no "I" that has the experience. This statement is understood only by one who is experienced, for others it is but a source of confusion.
8. Detachment, self-surrender, being beyond body-consciousness, aloneness, the natural state, no-mind, and Supreme Knowledge, are given seven different names, but they are the same.
9. Terms such as these, as well as other statements and indications become clear by serving the feet of and being one with the Guru.
10 The *Vedas*, the essence of the *Vedas*, Vedanta, the "accomplished one" (the Siddha), the inner meaning of the final doctrine of accomplishment (siddhanta), the indescribable, actual experience, and the Truth, are one thing.
11. Most of the various aspects of experience are understood by keeping the company of the saints. However, with this fourth type of devotion, "That" which is hidden becomes evident.
12. What is not seen is revealed, what is hidden becomes apparent, and That which is beyond appearance and non-appearance comes to be known only by taking the path shown by the Sadguru.

13. The initial steps on the inner path are indicated by saying that everything that is seen is not the Self, and as one makes progress in this, it is understood that the Self cannot actually be seen or pointed out.
14. One must become the Reality that one gives their attention to and looks for, and is That which is meditated upon in meditation. This is verified in three ways. (Verification from scriptures, the teaching of the Guru, and in one's own experience).
15. The doors of experience are opened by understanding how to utilize the investigation into what is True and what is false. Only in the company of saints can the true answer come to be known directly.
16. When one sees the Truth, the false disappears. When seeing the false, the Truth is not seen. Whether one sees the True or the false depends upon the one observing.
17. When the seer and the seeing are realized to be one with the seen, one's pervasiveness is realized and One is content.
18. There are many means of contentment which are gained through the Sadguru. Without the Sadguru it is not possible to take the correct path by any means.
19. Even by utilizing many experiments, spiritual practices and efforts, or hard work and studying holy texts, one cannot come to know the secret knowledge that can only be acquired from the Sadguru.
20. How can That which cannot be learned by studying, and which is unattainable through practice, be realized without the Sadguru?
21. For this reason, to truly understand the path of Knowledge (Jnana), one must keep the company of saints. One cannot speak of the possibility of understanding without them.
22. Serving the feet of the Guru is known as the fourth type of devotion which has now been briefly explained here.
23. God, the knowers of Brahman, and those with true Self-experience, are the truly free and worthy of praise. One should hold them in high regard.
24. All of this practical talk is being given for one's protection in worldly affairs, but what is really important is the service to the feet of the Sadguru.
25. "Serving the Feet of the Sadguru" is the fourth type of devotion. It gives freedom in all the three worlds, and gives the disciple liberation of merger with the Self.
26. Because of this fourth type of devotion, one becomes greater than the greatest, and with it many people have been able to cross beyond the world to the other shore.

Thus in Shri Dasbodh, a dialogue between the Guru and disciple, Sub-Chapter 4 of Chapter 4, named "Serving the feet of the Guru" is concluded.

Chapter: 4, Sub-Chapter: 5

Devotion Through Worship

|| ShriRam ||

1. Previously, I gave the explanation on the attributes of the fourth type of devotion. Now, be attentive and listen to the explanation of the fifth type of devotion.

2. The fifth type of devotion is "Devotion Through Worship." Worship means the worshipping of God with respect to what has been laid out in ancient scriptures.
3. Worship means that many types of seats should be prepared, instruments of worship used, decorative clothing and ornaments offered, and that mental worship and meditation on the forms of God should be done. This is known as the fifth type of devotion.
4. Worship can be of God, Brahman, fire, saints, sages, guests, those with great experience, and the Gayatri mantra. This is known as the fifth type of devotion.
5. Worship can be of idols made of metal, stones, clay, pictures, respected pious elders, and the gods of one's own household. This is known as the fifth type devotion.
6. Worship can be of various stones representing various gods, or stones that have come from some sacred place or river.

Note: Verses 7 to 13 of this sub-chapter give names of various incarnations and deities from Hindu mythology that are worshipped in different regions of India.

7. Bhairava, Bhagavati, Mallaaree, Munjyaa, Nrusiha, Banashankari, the cobra, coins of different varieties, and a group of five gods called Panchaayetna are worshipped.
8. The various idols of Ganesha, Sharada, Vithal, Ranganatha, Jagannaatha, dancing Shiva, Krishna, Hanuman and eagle vehicle of Lord Vishnu are worshipped.
9. The fish, tortoise and bear incarnations, Nrusiha, Vaamana, Bhargava, Lord Rama, Lord Krishna, and Hayagreeva, are all forms of gods that are worshipped.
10. The idols of Keshava, Narayana, Madhava, Govinda, Vishnu, Madasudana, Trivikrama, Vaamana, Shridhara, Rhishikesha and Padmanabha are all worshipped.
11. There are idols of Daamodara, Sankarshana, Vaasudeva, Pradyumna, Aniruddhava, Purushottama, Adhokshaja, Naarasiha, Achyuta, Janaardana, and Upendra that are worshipped.
12. There are many idols of Vishnu, Shiva, Jagadatma, Jagadeesha, Shiva/Shakti and others that are worshipped.
13. Ashvathanarayana, the Sun, Laxmi/Narayana, Trimallanarayana, Shreeharinarayana, Aadinaarayana, Vishnu reclining on the serpent, and Paramatma are all worshipped.
14. There are innumerable images and incarnations of God. If you look, you will see that there are plenty. Worship can be done to any of these. This is the fifth type of devotion.
15. Aside from these, there are many family duties and routines that are followed, and one should give their best performance to them.
16. One can worship various household gods and goddesses as per family traditions.
17. One should visit pilgrimage places and worship the god there. One should make offerings to God of many various things while worshipping.
18. Offer liquids like honey, milk, ghee, curds with sugar, as well as sandalwood paste, rice grains, flowers, perfumes, incense, lit oil lamps, and lamps burning with camphor.
19. Many types of good food, many fruits, varieties of betelnut leaves, money, ornaments, decorative clothes, and garlands of flowers should be offered.
20. Offerings of umbrellas, comfortable seats, canopies, huge flags with various symbols, small flags and banners, and music with cymbals, big drums and tabor.
21. Many celebrations should be made with musical instruments and there should be many groups of devotees gathering to sing with feelings of devotion towards God.

22. Water tanks, wells, lakes, temples with special ornaments on the tops, temple yards, beautiful structures, plants, and meeting halls should be offered.
23. Monasteries, marketplaces, dormitories, doorsteps of the temple, and resting houses should be decorated with many adornments and garlands in worship of God.
24. Many decorative curtains, decorative roofs, and clusters of jewels hanging nicely should be made. One should donate to temples for the care of the horses, elephants, and chariots.
25. Ornaments and ornamental boxes, money and money boxes, food vessels and many varieties of utensils for preparing and serving food should be given.
26. One should make offerings for the upkeep of forests, gardens, flower gardens, and the huts of the hermits. These are all ways of worshipping God.
27. Birds like parrots, chakrawaks, chakors, singing birds, peacocks, ducks, nightingales, cuckoos, and animals like deer and antelope should be offered to the temples.
28. Musk deer, cats, cows, buffaloes, bullocks, monkeys, as well as many other objects should be offered to the temples.
29. Body, speech, mind, heart, money, life, and indeed the entirety of your being, should be offered with devotional feelings as worship to God. This is what is known as devotion through worship.
30. Praising the Sadguru like this, one becomes one with God. This is known as "Devotion Through Worship," the fifth form of devotion.
31. If worship is not done in the ways described, then worship should be done with the mind. Doing mental worship is essential for realizing the Supreme God (Parameshwara).
32. God should be worshipped in the mind. Conceive that everything is in God, and is offered to God. Understand this to be the sign of worship in the mind.
33. Whatever one wants, should be imagined as God's, and offered to God. This is the way to worship in the mind.

Thus in Shri Dasbodh, a dialogue between the Guru and disciple, Sub-Chapter 5 of Chapter 4, named "Devotion Through Worship" is concluded.

Chapter: 4, Sub-Chapter: 6

Devotion Through Bowing

|| ShriRam ||
1. Previously, I explained the attributes of the fifth type of devotion. Now listen with alertness to the sixth type of devotion.
2. The sixth type of devotion is the "Devotion of Bowing." One should bow down to God as well as the saints, sages, and virtuous people.
3. One should bow to the Sun, God, and to the Sadguru with deep devotion.
4. Bow in full prostration to honor God and the Guru. For everyone else the degree of bowing should be decided according to the designation of the person.
5. The earth is very large, and in it there are innumerable images of God. Bow to them with love when you are before them.

6. By seeing images of Shiva, Vishnu, and the Sun, blemishes in one's character are diminished. Similarly, one should bow down to Hanuman.
7. When seeing devotees, the Self-realized (Jnanis), the dispassionate, ascetics and yogis with Self-experience, one should be quick to bow to them.
8. When seeing those with knowledge of the *Vedas*, scientists who are knowers of all, scholars, experts in telling mythology, great learned people, and pure men performing sacred rituals from the *Vedas*, one should bow to them.
9. When seeing extraordinary qualities in someone, know that the Sadguru is residing in those qualities, and bow to that person with great respect.
10. There are the great powers of Lord Ganesha, of Sharada, and the incarnations of Vishnu and Shiva. There are so many gods with their powers, how many can be mentioned for the purpose of giving examples?
11. When one bows before any god, that salutation reaches the one God. There is one statement in Sanskrit which says the same thing.

"Like the rainwater eventually becomes one with the sea, salutations to any number of gods all reach the one God (Keshava)."

12. For this reason, one should bow to all gods with respect. Cognizant that all gods are abiding only in the one God, one feels happy in honoring them.
13. The one God and the many gods have their abode in men of Truth and the Sadguru. Therefore, one should bow to all of them.
14. By bowing, one becomes humble, doubts are removed, and friendship develops with many good people.
15. Due to bowing, faults are cleared away, injustices are pardoned, and strained relationships are repaired, bringing about a sense of contentment.
16. It is said that there is nothing so humbling as making one bow one's head in surrender. For this reason, one should bow down before God and his devotees.
17. By bowing, blessings are bestowed and happiness is enhanced. By bowing in surrender, the Guru is pleased with his disciples.
18. By bowing without any motives mountains of faults are destroyed, and the one Supreme God (Parameshwara) bestows blessings.
19. By bowing, the downtrodden are uplifted. If one bows in surrender to the saints, the cycle of birth and death is left far behind.
20. If someone commits some great wrong, and then later bows down and prostrates himself, a great person should pardon him for that offense.
21. There is nothing else like bowing, and therefore it should be done. By bowing, a person develops a good intellect.
22. For bowing there is no money, nor any hard work, nor any instruments, nor any additional materials required.
23. There is nothing so easy as bowing. When bowing is done, it should be done with complete surrender, and as such, one should not trouble oneself making great efforts or with many rituals and instruments of worship.
24. When the aspirant bows down in devotion, the saint takes care of him and takes away his worries and puts him on the right path so that he arrives at his goal.
25. For this reason, bowing is superior. By bowing, one's elders are pleased. Now, I have clearly explained the sixth type of devotion.

Thus in Shri Dasbodh, a dialogue between the Guru and disciple, Sub-Chapter 6 of Chapter 4, named "Devotion Through Bowing" is concluded.

Chapter: 4, Sub-Chapter: 7

Devotion Through Service

|| ShriRam ||

1. Previously, I have given the explanation of the attributes of the sixth type of devotion. Now, listen carefully to the seventh type of devotion.
2. Know that the seventh type of devotion is "Devotion Through Service." Remain always at the doorstep of God and do whatever service that you are called upon to do.
3. Cherish the magnificence of the one God who is all. One should not allow for any deficiencies in their devotion, but should increase and spread the adoration of God.
4. One should work to repair broken-down temples, and broken reservoirs and dormitories in the temple yards, or even build them anew if necessary.
5. One should renovate structures that are old and in a bad state. Do the work that comes to you without delay, and do it with care.
6. One should renovate the places for elephants, chariots, horses, thrones and sitting areas, beds, stages, hammocks, and vehicles. All these should be taken care of.
7. One should renew the canopies, umbrellas, ceremonial fans, totems with the sun's image, and flags, and care for them them with great respect.
8. One should make efforts to care for the varieties of vehicles, the sitting arrangements, and varieties of seats.
9. Houses, store rooms, boxes, iron trunks, earthenware pots, large vessels, and pots and pans of different types should all be taken care of.
10. Tunnels, basements, underground cells, places with secret doors, and storage areas for keeping precious objects should all be looked after.
11. Ornaments, jewelry, decorative clothes, beautiful gems, golden items, and other metal objects should all be looked after properly.
12. Flower beds, forests, and gardens with big trees should be looked after. Care should be given to keep them alive.
13. One should take care of animal zoos, bird sanctuaries, painting galleries, many musical instruments, drama theaters, and talented singers.
14. One should construct large kitchens, dining halls, storage spaces to keep cooking utensils and grains, dormitories for guests, and comfortable places for resting and sleeping.
15. One should make storage places for various fragrant preparations, various types of food and fruits, and many different kinds of juices.
16. One should take care of many places and many objects, and if they are broken or run-down, one should make them as if new. The magnificence of serving God is such that it cannot be described, so how many words should be used to try?
17. One should be respectful to all in all places. One should be eager and ready to serve, and not forget to do the work allotted.
18. Special celebrations of birth anniversaries, auspicious periods, and festivals should be done on such a grand scale that upon seeing them even the Gods will be spellbound.

19. In these ways, one should propagate the magnificence of God, and one should not hesitate to do any types of menial service. Whatever circumstances come, be alert and act appropriately at all times.
20. Whatever is required should be done or given immediately. Do all service willingly with enjoyment.
21. On various occasions one should go to get water for washing of feet, or bathing, or for some other purposes, or go to get colored rice grains, clothes, ornaments, seats, or various flowers, incense, lamps, and food.
22. One should offer the best places for sleeping and keep water in a cool place, and arrange to have traditional enjoyments readily available, or organize some musical entertainment.
23. One should offer fragrances and essences, and many beautiful smelling oils, and wonderful foods and fruits should always be kept near.
24. One should sprinkle water around to clean various places, fill water vessels with water, and bring the clothes around after washing.
25. One should be welcoming to everyone, and guests should be looked after well. Understand that what is being described is the true seventh type of devotion.
26. Speak words of compassion and find many ways to give praise and pacify the minds of everyone. One's speech should be pleasant in this way.
27. Like this is the seventh type of devotion, explained to the best of my ability. If one cannot do all of this actually, then in one's thinking one should do mental worship.
28. Like this, one should be in service to God which is the same as serving the Sadguru. If it is not possible to always serve like this actually, then do the worship in the mind.

Thus in Shri Dasbodh, a dialogue between the Guru and disciple, Sub-Chapter 7 of Chapter 4, named "Devotion Through Service" is concluded.

Chapter: 4, Sub-Chapter: 8

Devotion of Communion with God

|| ShriRam ||

1. Previously, I gave the explanation of the seventh type of devotion. Now, listen attentively to the eighth type of devotion.
2. One should come into supreme communion with God. When one takes delight in, and loves only God, this is the sign of "Devotion Through Communion," the eighth type of devotion.
3. When one takes extreme gratification in God, he behaves accordingly. In this way, one is always in communion with God.
4. God likes the deep feelings of devotion and adoration, the explanations of stories, and the narrations and singing about God by his devotees.
5. If one behaves in such a way that what one likes is the same as what God likes, it is naturally pleasing to the mind, and one is definitely always in communion with God.

6. For the sake of communion with God, one should give up one's sense of personal happiness. Becoming one with him, one gives up the sense of a separate life, self, and body.
7. Giving up the concern for the miseries of worldly life, one should be concerned only about God. Speak only about explanations and narrations, and stories of God.
8. For the sake of communion with God, one should be willing to even break away from those who are dear. Everything, even one's own life, should be given to God.
9. Even if everything one owns should go away, one should stay in communion with God. One's life should have such a deep feeling of gratification in God such as this.
10. God means one's own Self. One should not give away one's own Self. This is the attribute of having supreme gratification only in God.
11. When one holds to supreme communion with God, God himself begins to look after the devotee.
12. In communion with God, one stays with one's Self. This is the secret of staying with oneself. Just as how one speaks, the same echo comes accordingly.
13. When we remain with the Self, God is immediately attained. If one becomes troubled with oneself, God is troubled accordingly.
14. The way in which one adores God, in that same way, God himself is. Therefore, one should understand that everything is only one's Self.
15. When things don't happen according to the liking of the mind, one's faith gets diminished. Even this quality is naturally due only to oneself.
16. If the rain clouds do not rain, the Chataka bird remains unchanged in its devotion. If the moon does not rise on time, the Chakora still remains true to the moon.[29]
17. Like this should be one's communion with God. Hold on to what is pure (sattva) using discrimination (viveka). Do not give up the sense of connectedness with God.
18. One should consider God as one's closest friend. Mother, father, relatives, knowledge, money, wealth, property, all is only the Supreme Self, Paramatman.
19. There is nothing except God. Everyone says this, however somehow their faith does not always hold firm.
20. Do not be like this. Be true to communion and hold firmly within to the one Supreme God (Parameshwara).
21. If one gets angry with God for unfulfilled desires, this is not a sign of devotion through communion.
22. Whatever is the will of God is what is right for oneself. One should not forsake God in order to pursue one's desires.
23. One's actions are according to God's will. Accept whatever God does as the way things should be, and naturally God is kind.
24. When seeing God's kindness, even a mother's kindness is of no comparison, because in adverse times, it is possible that a mother might even kill her child.
25. It has never been heard of nor seen that a devotee has ever been killed by God. God becomes a protective armor to one who has surrendered to him.
26. God is the protector of devotees, the downtrodden, and the destitute.
27. God is the protector of the needy, and keeps them from many dangers. Being the one who is innermost, God himself came to the rescue of the elephant Gajendra.[30]

---

[29] The Chataka and Chakora are birds. The Chataka bird is believed to live only on rain water, and the Chakora lives on the moon light. Even if it doesn't rain, or the moon does not rise on time, their love never diminishes.

28. God is the ocean of kindness and the blanketing cloud of compassion. It will never happen that God will forget his devotees.
29. God knows how to maintain communion. Make God your most beloved. Those who are around you are all selfish and will not come to your help.
30. Communion with God is never broken, and the gratification and delight in God never disappears for one who has surrendered.
31. Therefore stay in communion with God, and talk to him with intimacy from the heart. Understand the attributes of the eighth type of devotion are like this.
32. The Sadguru is the same as God. This is told in the ancient scriptures. Therefore, one should have this kind of communion with the Sadguru.

Thus in Shri Dasbodh, a dialogue between the Guru and disciple, Sub-Chapter 8 of Chapter 4, named "Devotion of Communion with God" ends.

Chapter: 4, Sub-Chapter: 9

Self-Surrender

|| ShriRam ||

1. Previously, I gave the explanation of the eighth type of devotion. Now, listen attentively to the description of the ninth type of devotion.
2. Understand that the ninth type of devotion is "Self-Surrender." This will be explained naturally making it clear.
3. Listen to the attributes of surrender. One should offer oneself to God completely. One should analyze the meaning of this principle and then you will understand.
4. It is absurd for one to call oneself a devotee and yet still adore God with a sense of separation.
5. The sense of separation from God is essentially the One that is without attributes taking himself to be with attributes. While being Knowledge himself, he is ignorant, and while taking himself to be a devotee, he is without true devotion.
6. To be a devotee means not to be separate, and to be separate means to not be a devotee. Without properly thinking this over, one does not get satisfaction.
7. Therefore, one must think deeply and investigate who God is, and understand him. One should search within oneself.
8. One should find out "Who am I?" Upon looking into and analyzing what one takes oneself to be, the investigation clearly reveals that there is nothing that can be called "I."
9. When misidentifications are cast off one by one, how can this "I" remain? This is the way that self-surrender happens very easily.
10. When, through using discrimination (viveka), everything that is taken to be oneself is discarded, the "I" is clearly seen to be non-existent. When even creation (Prakriti) itself is cast off and only the Self remains, how can any "I" be found there?

---

[30] There is a story in Hindu mythological stories (the Puranas) of how Lord Vishnu protected the elephant Ganjedra from a crocodile.

11. The one true identity is the one "Supreme God" (Parameshwara). The second identity that appears is creation (Prakriti) which is in the form of the universe. Where has any third identity such as an "I" come in between?
12. When it is proven that there is no "I" the misidentification with the body is dispelled, and with further investigation, it is seen that nothing really exists.
13. Upon investigation into one's identity and the nature of one's body along with all of creation, it is seen that the many forms in the universe appear to spread out because of what one takes one's own identity to be.
14. By being the witness, misidentifications disappear, and with the experience of the Self (Atman), even the witness itself does not remain. Only the Self exists in the beginning and at the end, so how can there be any independently existing "I"?
15. The Self is One, the fullness of "Self-bliss." With the understanding that "I am the Self," where is there any separate "I" remaining?
16. When one investigates into "What is this I?," "I Am That" (Soham) is the answer, and one sees only the Self. How can any separate "I" exist there?
17. The Self is without attributes (nirguna), and contains no darkness. Be one with it. To be one with it means that there is no other. How can any separate "I" exist?
18. The Self (Atman) means that which is non-dual. Where both dual and non-dual do not exist, how can the question of any separate individual remain?
19. The Self is complete and full in itself with neither qualities nor absence of qualities. In that which is untainted by any attributes, who else can be there?
20. When the labels of "You," and "Are," and "That" (together making Tat Tvam Asi; You Are That), are dissolved, removing all distinctions of differences, the Self is alone without distinctions. How can any "I" exist there?
21. Removing the labels of individual self (Jiva) and God (Shiva), how can there be any first occurrence of two things. When the intellect becomes firm in the oneness of one's "True Form" (Swaroopa), how can there be any separate "I"?
22. The "I" is false, God is true. God and the devotee are inseparable in oneness. The meaning of this statement is known to the one with Self-experience.
23. This is known as self-surrender which is the satisfaction of the knowledgeable (Jnanis). Now, the explanation of the attributes of the ninth type of devotion have been given.
24. In the same way that among the five elements, the sky (akasha; space) is the greatest, and among all the gods, the "Lord of the Universe" (Jagadisha) is the greatest, among the nine types of devotion, the ninth, self-surrender is the greatest.
25. The ninth type of devotion is self-surrender. If one does not arrive at self-surrender, the cycle of birth and death cannot be escaped. This is a proven truth without any doubt.
26. If the nine types of devotion are practiced, one can gain the greatest "Liberation of Identification with the Self" (Sayujya Mukti). This liberation does not change even after the final destruction of all creation.
27. With the other three forms of liberation, there is change, or reversion. Understand that the "Liberation of Identification with the Self" is unchangeable. Even when all of the three worlds get destroyed, "Self-Identity" does not change.
28. The *Vedas* and ancient scriptures (*Shastras*) talk of four types of liberation. Among them, three get destroyed, and the fourth is indestructible.

29. The first liberation is being in the abode of God (Swalokata), the second is to be near to God (Samipata), the third is to have similar appearance to the form of God (Swarupata), and the fourth is the liberation of Self-Identity with God (Sayujya).
30. These are the four kinds of liberation which the human beings can attain through devotion to God. This itself will be clearly explained in the next sub-chapter. The listeners are asked to remain alert and listen attentively to what follows.

Thus in Shri Dasbodh, a dialogue between the Guru and disciple, Sub-Chapter 9 of Chapter 4, named "Self-Surrender" is concluded.

Chapter: 4, Sub-Chapter: 10

The Four Types of Liberation

|| ShriRam ||

1. Brahman is basically without form. In it, the sense of ego (ahankara) or "I Am" arises in the form of an inspiration. From that arises the five elements. The investigation into this is explained later in the chapter on Knowledge.
2. The ego is in the form of wind, and from that movement of wind the energy of light takes its form. On the support of that light, water takes its form and proliferates, covering everywhere.
3. On the support of that expansive covering of water, the expanse of the earth is spread out.
4. On the earth, there are seven seas. In the middle, there is the great mountain Meru, that is surrounded by the eight directions.
5. The great mountain Meru has a vast expanse, and is the support of the earth.
6. It is tall and beyond measurable limit, and surrounded by the range of mountains called Loka-aloka.
7. Prior to that are the Himalayas where all of the Pandavas fell except for Dharma who went beyond.
8. There is no way to get there as there are huge serpents spread along the way, lying happily in the pleasant coolness, looking like the mountains.
9. Before that place, are located the holy places of Badrika and Badrinarayana where great ascetics go to abandon their bodies.
10. And, before that, is the Badrikedar, which is visited by many pilgrims. Such is the great the expanse of the great mountain Meru.
11. Located on Meru mountain there are three peaks in a line. These are where the Gods Brahma, Vishnu, and Lord Shiva stay with their families.
12. The peak of Brahma is made of stones and rocks, the peak of Vishnu is made of emerald, and the peak of Shiva is named Kailash and is made of crystal.
13. Vaikuntha is the name of the peak of Vishnu, the mountain of Brahma is called Satyaloka. Below that is the place called Amaravati which is the abode of Lord Indra.
14. There around that golden mountain dwell many categories of Gods and celestial singers, and the various aspects of nature.

15. There one finds stables of wish-fulfilling cows, forests of wish-fulfilling trees, and lakes full of nectar that are ebbing and flowing from place to place.
16. There are innumerable wish-fulfilling stones, mines of diamonds, philosopher's stones, and the land is made of gold and shines brightly.
17. There are precious stones of great value, and nine gems whose radiance is extremely enchanting. There ecstasy and happiness abound continually.
18. There, the meals are delicious nectar, everywhere there are divine fragrances and flowers, and divine music and celestial songs always fill the air.
19. There, youth never ends, diseases don't exist, and old age and death do not ever come around.
20. There, each being is more beautiful, more clever, more composed, more generous, and more courageous than the other, beyond limit.
21. There, divine bodies are in the form of light which dazzle like lightening. There, success, fame, and bravery extend beyond all limits.
22. Like this is the realm of heaven, the residing place of the gods. It's greatness is beyond description. It is impossible to try.
23. Whichever God one worships here in this world, he goes there to that God's abode. Understand that the sign of the liberation of being in the same abode as God (Swalokata Mukti) is like this.
24. Swalokata Mukti means to live in the same abode as God. Samipata Mukti is being near God. The third form of liberation, having the same appearance as God, is called Swaroopata Mukti.
25. One can take on the appearance (Swaroopata) like that of God while having bodily existence, yet he cannot get the possessions or wife of God. This is the difference between that state of Swaroopata Mukti and God that one should recognize.
26. As long as some merit remains for one, he may enjoy many pleasures like God, yet when the merits are exhausted, then that one is pushed out, while the Gods remain as they themselves are.
27. One should understand that all of the first three types of liberations are perishable, and only the "Liberation of Identification with the Self" (Sayujya Mukti) is permanent. This I will explain now. Please listen with full attention.
28. In the final destruction the entire universe will be destroyed. The earth along with the mountains will be burned away. At that time, even the gods will have their end. How then can any of these first three types of liberation be there?
29. At that time, only the "Attributeless Supreme Reality" (Nirguna Paramatman) remains, unchanged. Attributeless Devotion (Nirguna Bhakti) alone is permanent. Understand that it is only the "Liberation of Identification with the Self" (Sayujya Mukti) that is like this.
30. Being that one attributelessness itself is being "Self-identified." Being Self-identified means to be the same Self-nature that is "Attributeless Devotion."
31. Devotion with form and attributes comes to an end while "Attributeless Devotion" is indestructible. This can only be clearly understood with the help of the "True Master," the Sadguru.

Thus in Shri Dasbodh, a dialogue between the Guru and disciple, Sub-Chapter 10 of Chapter 4, named "The Four Types of Liberation," is concluded.

Chapter 5. Mantras

Chapter: 5, Sub-Chapter: 1

The Importance of the Guru

|| ShriRam ||

1. Jai Sadguru! Salutations to you, the one who is completely content. You are Supreme Being, the Self within that is Rama. Being beyond all expression of words, your greatness cannot be described.
2. Through you, the true disciple is directly able to attain That which is difficult to attain, That which is difficult for the *Vedas* to tell, That which is not understood with words.
3. You are That which is the personal secret of the yogis, That which is the abode of Lord Shiva, That which is the resting place of peace, That which is the unfathomable ultimate secret.
4. Because of you, the disciple realizes that he is one with Brahman, and he does not become bound by worldly life at any time.
5. Now, because of the kindness of the Guru, I will describe the attributes of the Guru and disciple in such a way that the one seeking liberation will surrender himself.
6. The brahmin priests (Brahmana[31]) are the gurus of the masses. Even if one is not performing rituals, one should surrender to a brahmin with a sense of dedication.
7. It is because of the brahmins that God (Vishnu) has taken incarnation. The opinions of others need not to be considered.
8. With the approval of a brahmin even someone from the lowest caste can become a brahmin. Even metal and stone idols are instilled with godliness by the mantras chanted by the brahmins.
9. Before the sacred thread ceremony[32] one is considered to be of a low caste. The thread ceremony is the second birth when one is born into the spiritual life.
10. The brahmin priest should be respected by all. This is clearly stated in the *Vedas*. That which is not in accord with the *Vedas* lacks authority.
11. The disciplines of yoga, sacred fire rituals, various types of spiritual worship, charities, and pilgrimages, are all performed by the brahmins.
12. Brahmins are the manifestation of the knowledge of the *Vedas*. The brahmin is himself God. Desires are fulfilled with the blessings of a brahmin.
13. By worshipping a brahmin one's attitude becomes pure and one's life gets turned towards God. Beings are uplifted and arrive on the best path by taking the sacred water from brahmins.
14. In the traditional feast where one-hundred-thousand brahmins are served, only a brahmin is respected there and people of other castes are not served at such a

---

[31] The word Brahmana in it's common usage is a priest of the Brahmin caste, which is the highest of the four classes of Hindu society. It is also used to indicate a "knower of Brahman."

[32] In Hindu culture, at the age of eight, a boy of the Brahmin caste is initiated by the Guru who performs the sacred thread ceremony where a string is draped over one shoulder around the body in a loop. It is said that one's first birth is at the parent's home, and the second birth (the spiritual life) takes place when one arrives at the Guru's feet.

gathering. However with God, only devotional feelings are appreciated. Things such as caste and status are not relevant to God.

15. Let all of this be as it is. The gods respect the brahmins so human beings should do so even more. Even if a brahmin is dull-minded, he should still be respected by all.
16. Someone born of a low caste may well be a Jnani, but it is not proper that he should be put next to a brahmin and worshipped alongside a priest. This will not happen ever.
17. Whatever is done by the people, but is rejected by the *Vedas* is not considered acceptable, and is therefore referred to as being heretical.
18. Let all of this be like this. Many who are devotees of God have put their faith in brahmins, and by worshipping the brahmins have become purified.
19. One may ask why should one go to a Sadguru if it is possible to attain the state of the greatest of gods by worshipping a brahmin? One may say this, but understand that one cannot get the most precious treasure without the Sadguru.
20. For religious rituals and activities the brahmin is worshipped, however, Self-Knowledge cannot be gained without the Sadguru, and without the Knowledge of Brahman that he gives, one cannot avoid the cycle of birth and death.
21. Without the Sadguru, one can never get Self-Knowledge, and ignorant beings get carried away by the current of worldly life.
22. Whatever is done without Self-Knowledge becomes the root of birth. Therefore, one should hold firmly to the feet of the Sadguru.
23. One who wants to see God must hold on to the company of saints. Without the company of saints, the God of gods cannot be realized.
24. Without a Sadguru many practices become wasted and may even make one go mad. Without the teachings of the Sadguru, one's efforts are futile.
25. I will give some examples: Some perform bathing rituals or do other rituals and make celebrations upon the completion of vows, some give in charity, some sit next to a fire, or consume smoke, or perform other practices like sitting in the midst of fire on all sides.
26. Some listen to narrations of God's stories, or listen to the *Puranas* (ancient myths), and some respectfully give explanations and travel to difficult pilgrimage places.
27. Some use shining vessels (usually silver and copper) for worship, perform rituals after bathing, make seats of grass, put a red powder mark on their forehead, and make offerings of garlands, sandalwood, and plates marked with various auspicious symbols.
28. Some offer pots and special vessels for water, or pots to keep idols of God in, or copper plates marked with symbolic diagrams of gods and goddesses, or other varieties of beautiful articles used in worship.
29. Some bang and ring bells loudly, some recite spiritual verses, prayers, and praises. Some do various postures, meditation, and offer salutations to various deities.
30. Some worship a set of five gods, some make a hundred thousand symbols of Shiva, and some offer betel leaves and coconuts. Some do many types of worship that are complete in all respects.
31. Some people do regular fasting faithfully, and some take vows or do other practices with great effort. They acquire the fruits of their actions, but still the inner meaning is missed.
32. Various rituals and actions are done while inwardly imagining the expectation of fruits. In this way, one's own desires are the ground for next birth.

33. One may make many efforts to study the various fourteen streams of knowledge, and may even become accomplished in these types of knowledge.
34. However, without the teachings of the Sadguru, it never happens that one is able to uplift oneself, and escape the tortures and pain of death.
35. Without acquiring Self-Knowledge through the teachings of the Sadguru, one is unable to escape the cycle of birth and death, and avoid the return to the womb.
36. Meditation, concentration, symbols, body postures, devotional feelings and devotional songs are all useless as long as one does not obtain the Knowledge of Brahman.
37. One who does not receive the teachings of the Sadguru roams around in the wrong directions like a blind person who eventually stumbles and falls into a ditch or a pit.
38. Like when upon the application of ointment to the eyes one is able to see what was not seen before, in the same way, the words of the Sadguru give the light of Self-Knowledge.
39. Without the Sadguru, life is useless, everything causes sorrow, and anxiety never goes away.
40. While in the protective hands of the Sadguru, God is revealed and the unlimited miseries of worldly life are destroyed.
41. In the past there were many great saints, sages and spiritual authorities of the highest order. They also received the instructions about investigation into Self-Knowledge (Jnana) and Supreme-Knowledge (Vijnana) from the Sadguru.
41. Lord Rama, Lord Krishna, and other incarnations of God like them eagerly worshipped the Sadguru. The accomplished (siddhas), sages (sadhus), and saints all served the Guru.
43. Those who are running the functioning of nature, and even the gods Vishnu, Shiva, and Brahma are humble at the feet of the Sadguru. They did not rise to their eminent positions without the Sadguru.
44. Let this talk be. Know for certain that the one who wants liberation should go the Sadguru. Without the Sadguru it is not possible to attain liberation. Even until the end of the universe, it will not happen.
45. Now, how to know who is a Sadguru, a True Master? He is not like other gurus who give various kinds of knowledge. He is the one by whose teachings the light of Pure Knowledge shines forth.
46. The way to recognize the Sadguru is told and explained in the next sub-chapter. The listeners should listen to the explanations given here in sequence.

Thus in Shri Dasbodh, a dialogue between the Guru and disciple, Sub-Chapter 1 of Chapter 5, named "The Importance of the Guru" is concluded.

Chapter: 5, Sub-Chapter: 2

The Signs of a Guru

|| ShriRam ||

1. There are those who perform miracles and call themselves "Gurus," but they are not the "True Master" (Sadguru) who can help one attain liberation.

2. There are some who perform mass hypnotism, mesmerizing a whole audience, or some who perform magic tricks, or who use the evil powers of mantras, or do extraordinary feats and amazing things that are not possible for a common man.
3. Some teach about medicines, or alchemy, or how to get things one desires through eye contact (something like hypnosis).
4. Some teach literature, musical knowledge or knowledge of singing, some teach dance and performances, and some teach various musical instruments to the people. They are all gurus.
5. Some teach occultism, or the use of amulets and talismans, and others teach skills so one can earn a living and fill the stomach.
6. Those who teach the professions that are traditional to a particular caste so that one may earn a livelihood are also gurus, but not a true Sadguru.
7. In principle, one's own mother and father are also a type of gurus in life, but the one who makes it possible to cross over beyond the worldly life is the Sadguru.
8. One who teaches the pronunciation of Gayatri Mantra is a guru of the family, but without Self-Knowledge, it is not possible to cross beyond the worldly life.
9. The "True Guru" teaches about the Knowledge of Brahman, removes the darkness of ignorance, and reveals that the identity of the individual self (jivatma) is one with the Supreme Self (Paramatma).
10. When the imagination that there is separation between God and devotee is there, the Sadguru reveals that there is no duality of the individual (jiva) and God (Shiva), thus unifying God and devotee.
11. Understand that when the tiger of the world illusion has separated the cow and the calf (God and devotee), it is the Sadguru who quickly jumps in and reunites them.
12. When living beings are caught in the net of Illusion, and suffering because of the miseries of worldly life, it is the Sadguru who liberates them.
13. Know that when living beings are being drowned in the great flood of the river of desires, the one who jumps in and saves them is the Sadguru.
14. The time of residence in the womb is very difficult, and afterwards in the world there are the shackles and bondage of desires. The one who gives relief by imparting Self-Knowledge is the Sadguru.
15. One who opens up the inner meaning of words and reveals the essence of one's true identity is the True Guru who is himself the resting place of the seeker.
16. The individual is a pitiable limited being. By a single statement, the Guru reveals that the individual is Brahman and breaks the bonds of worldly life.
17. He extracts the essence of the *Vedas* and speaks statements to the ears of the disciple like one who is feeding morsels of food to one's own child.
18. That which is the essence of the *Vedas*, spiritual scriptures and the highest experience, are all one, and that is the form of the Guru.
19. He burns all remnants of doubts. He respects and protects one's true "Self Religion" (Swadharma), and does not indulge in loose talk that is not in accord with the *Vedas*.
20. One who freely indulges in whatever the mind wishes is not liberated, but is like a beggar who is hungry for any objects that come along.
21. Such gurus do not advise their disciples to do spiritual practice, or to get their senses under control. Even if you could get three gurus like this for a fraction of a rupee, they should be abandoned as worthless.

22. The one who gives instruction on Self-Knowledge and prescribes control over the senses cuts ignorance at the root. He is a "True Guru."
23. Some gurus sell themselves for money, some are subservient to their disciples, and some become very pitiable due to excessive desires.
24. Some gurus agree with whatever whims appear in the mind of the disciple and accept the same whims in their own mind and embrace a lustful and passionate lifestyle.
25. The guru who makes himself a subordinate of his disciples is lower than the lowest. He is a robber and a deceptive rascal who is after money.
26. He is like an ill behaved doctor who takes away everything from the patient, and because of the hesitancy of the patient, the doctor ends up completely betraying him in the end.
27. The Sadguru is nothing like that doctor. He does not allow for there to be any notion of distance from God, nor does he allow for any bondage.
28. Where there is pure Knowledge of Brahman and where correct spiritual practice is taking place, that itself is the treasure of the Sadguru who shows the disciple how to see clearly.
29. Some gurus make a show of religion or whisper mantras into the ears of seekers, and this is all that they know. These poor fellows do not have closeness with God.
30. The one who is in accord with the threefold verification (that of the scriptures, the guru, and through actual experience) is the True Guru with good qualities. The one who desires liberation should surrender to only him, with respect.
31. There are some who give great explanations of non-duality but are captivated by sensual pleasures. One will not get true fulfillment from such a guru.
32. Some gurus let their mind wander while giving explanations, and their speech meanders like their mind. It will never happen that anyone will establish the correct intelligence from such a guru.
33. Some give explanations about powers and accomplishments, and the listeners develop desires for such things. While thinking about miracles and powers, the intellect becomes unsteady.
34. In the past, there were knowledgeable and detached devotees who were equal with God, and they had amazing power because of their yogic accomplishment.
35. Their powers were such that they believed that Self-Knowledge alone was useless. Like this, selfish desire for powers dwells in the mind.
36. Only when such extreme desires are snapped can one meet with God. Those who hold on to vain expectations are full of desire and only have knowledge of words.
37. There are many who only have word knowledgeable and have wasted their lives because they were crazed with lust. Those poor fools died thinking only of sensual gratification.
38. It is rare to find a saint who is totally without any remnant of desire and whose opinion is always very different from others.
39. The indestructible treasure of the Self is in all, but because the attachment to body-consciousness has not been cast off, many miss the correct path of God.
40. When one gets powers and becomes more powerful, they give more importance to the body. With that attachment, body-consciousness only gets stronger.
41. Giving up eternal happiness, those who desire powers are foolish. There is no other grief greater than that caused by desire.

42. Whatever is desired other than God is sure to bring many sorrows and creates many entanglements and downfall.
43. When the body comes to an end, one's power also goes away. The end result is that one has wasted life and turned away from God because of desires.
44. It is the Sadguru alone who instills the thought of desirelessness firmly in the intellect, and it is he alone who is able to take one beyond worldly life.
45. The main sign of the Sadguru is that first and foremost he should have pure Self-Knowledge and firmness of contentment in the realization of his "True Form."
46. Over and above this, he has strong dispassion, an attitude of non-attachment to the world, and especially, his conduct is stainless with regard to his True Nature.
47. In addition to this, going on around him there is listening to discourses on Self-Knowledge, narrations about God, and explanations of Supreme Truth at all times.
48. Where there is the investigation into the True and the false there is upliftment of the people. Additionally, many people get support from the nine types of devotion.
49. The listeners should recognize that a sign of the Sadguru is that he emphasizes the nine types of devotion, as well as that one have an established spiritual practice.
50. Where one is found who has the pure Knowledge of Brahman inside, and loyal devotion on the outside, many devotees get contentment there.
51. Without the support of devotion, spiritual attainment is baseless. Without some spiritual discipline one merely becomes misbehaved.
52. Recognize the signs of Self-Knowledge, dispassion, devotion, acting in accord with the realization of one's True Nature, spiritual practice, narration of stories about God, explanations about God, listening, reflection, appropriate morality, justice, and appropriate behavior.
53. If even one among these qualities is lacking, then the whole spiritual life looks like it has missed the mark. Therefore, all of these qualities will shine in the Sadguru.
54. He is a protector of many, he has concern for many, and he has many powerful ways to protect them.
55. Those who seek spiritual attainment only stray from the path without spiritual practice (sadhana), therefore it is important to be prudent and gain Self-experience.
56. Those who give up appropriate behavior and worship have the appearance of being corrupt and non-devotional. Let their greatness go to hell. Who wants it!
57. Where discipline in one's actions and worship are lacking, corruption becomes established. Such a person is ridiculed among the people, and even householders laugh at his conduct.
58. If the guru is of a lower caste, it becomes awkward and he is thought of as an intruder in a gathering where Brahman is being discussed.
59. In a gathering of brahmins, they cannot take sacred water or prasad from a guru of a lower caste. If someone were to take it, it is as if they have become unclean.
60. If one does not accept the sacred water and prasad from the guru, that shows the lower caste of the guru, and the devotion of the people to the guru is suddenly spoiled.
61. If one shows respect to the guru of a lower caste then those of the brahmin caste get angry, and if the proper respect is shown to the brahmins, then an awkward situation is created with the guru.
62. Such difficulties occur on both sides and negative situations arise. For this reason, one with a low caste should not have the status of guru.

63. In spite of all this, if one takes a liking to such a guru, then let him keep that relationship to himself. To disrupt an assembly of many people would only create a bad reputation.
64. Now, let these thoughts be. One should have a guru of one's own caste. If not, then awkward situations will definitely be created.
65. All of the best qualities that have been described are attributes of the Sadguru. Still, I will tell some some other things which will help you recognize the Sadguru.
66. There are some gurus who give mantras, some who teach technical knowledge, some who teach methods of spiritual rituals, some who teach gymnastics, and some who are called the "Guru of the Royal Family."
67. There are some traditional family gurus, some who are considered as gurus, some who are teachers of knowledge, some who are teachers of harmful knowledge, some who are false gurus, and some who are gurus who give the punishment to the various castes of people.
68. One guru is the mother, one is the father, one is the guru of the king, one is the guru of the Gods, and one is the guru of the world, who is accomplished with all sorts of knowledge.
69. Like this they are many types of gurus. Other than those already described, there are many more types of gurus. Listen and give some thought to their descriptions which I shall tell now.
70. One is a guru who teaches in dreams, one gives initiations, one says that idols are the guru, and one says that oneself is one's own guru.
71. Whatever business or occupation is pursued there are just as many gurus. If one gives thought to this, it can be seen that there are many of them.
72. Let it be like this. There are many types of gurus who teach many different opinions. Know that the one who gives liberation, the Sadguru, is totally different from all of these.
73. The listeners should understand that where there is Pure Knowledge accompanied with the many good qualities and the kindness that has been described, these are the attributes of the Sadguru

Thus in Shri Dasbodh, a dialogue between the Guru and disciple, Sub-Chapter 2 of Chapter 5, named "The Signs of a Guru" is concluded.

Chapter: 5, Sub-Chapter: 3

The Signs of a Disciple

|| ShriRam ||

1. Previously, I described the signs of the Sadguru in detail. Now, listen attentively to the identification of a good disciple.
2. Without the Sadguru, a good disciple definitely goes wasted, and without a good disciple, the Sadguru only becomes fatigued.
3. For example, the best quality land may be found, but the seeds sown there are rotten, or the seeds of the best quality may be found but they only come in contact with rocky soil.

4. Similarly, there may be a good eligible disciple, but if the guru only teaches some mantra or trivial techniques as a practice, he gets no benefit either in worldly life or in spiritual life.
5. Or, there may be a guru who gives the best complete instruction, but the disciple is not qualified. He is like one who is a beggar even though he is the son of a man with a great fortune.
6. Like this, having one without the other is useless, and it does not allow for the fulfillment of spiritual life.
7. However, when the Sadguru and a good disciple come together, no strenuous efforts are required. The intentions of both are achieved at the same time.
8. Just as the best seeds will not grow in fertile land without rain, similarly, there will not be spiritual growth without having a base of good explanations on one's "Self Nature."
9. The field is sown and the crops grow, but without proper care all goes to waste. The same thing happens with the disciple without correct spiritual practice (sadhana).
10. Until the crop is ready to be harvested, proper care needs to be given to it, and then, when the crop is ready, that is not a time to be inactive.
11. Similarly, upon gaining Self-Knowledge some practice must still be done. It is like the example of how even though we have eaten an ample meal, there is still a need to make sure that groceries are acquired.
12. Therefore, spiritual practice, study, the Sadguru, a good disciple, deep thinking about spiritual teachings, appropriate action, and virtuous desires, all together make it possible for one to cross beyond worldly life.
13. These should be accompanied by correct worship, virtuous actions and conduct, commitment to one's True Nature, keeping in association with saintly people, and keeping some regular routines.
14. When all of these come together, only then does pure Self-Knowledge become clear. Otherwise, heretical opinions spread vigorously among the people.
15. What was just said are not just words for the disciple. All of this rests on the Sadguru, for it is he who transforms the undesirable qualities of the disciple with many efforts.
16. Because of the Sadguru, a bad disciple may be transformed, but a good disciple does not transform a bad guru because the reputation of that guru would become diminished.
17. Therefore, the Sadguru is required. Only he points out the correct path. Without him, the disciple comes under the influence of many incorrect teachings and heretical opinions.
18. These things are the responsibility of the Sadguru and not the responsibility of anyone else (the disciples). In spite of this, I shall tell the signs of how to recognize a good disciple
19. The main sign of a good disciple is that he has complete faith in the teachings of the Sadguru. If he surrenders himself totally in the feeling of oneness, he is a good disciple.
20. The disciple should be pure, acting with appropriate behavior, and he should be detached, lifting his attention from objectivity.
21. The disciple should be loyal, clean in appearance, and well disciplined.

22. The disciple should be hard working and extremely alert, and he should be able to perceive "That" which is cannot be conceived.
23. The disciple should be very patient, very generous, and very committed and sincere regarding spiritual life.
24. The disciple should be obliging, should not be envious, and should be deeply involved in understanding the inner meaning of spiritual teachings.
25. The disciple should be very pure and extremely alert. The disciple must be overflowing with virtues.
26. The disciple should have good intuitive capacity, he should be a loving devotee, and should be disciplined in moral behavior.
27. The disciple should be resourceful, intelligent and should have the capacity to discern what is right from wrong
28. The disciple should be courageous, firm in his convictions, and should have a good upbringing.
29. The disciple should be spiritually inclined (sattvic), he should be one who worships, and he should be an aspirant doing spiritual practice.
30. The disciple should be trustworthy, should be one who has experienced physical suffering, and he should be one who knows how to enhance the spiritual life.
31. The disciple should be independent, he should be a friend to the world, and should be endowed with all good qualities.
32. The disciple should have True Knowledge, he should be endowed with good feelings, and should be supremely pure in the mind.
33. The disciple should not be without discrimination, the disciple should not be born into excessive physical comforts, and should have experienced the sorrows of the worldly life and the physical bodily.
34. Only the one who is experienced the grief of the worldly life and who has been burned by all of three tortures (bodily, worldly, cosmic tortures) is really ready to enter into the spiritual life.
35. One who has suffered much sorrow understands the significance of spiritual life. It is only when one has experienced the suffering of worldly life that dispassion arises within.
36. One who has suffered from worldly life gets faith in the spiritual life, and with the strength of that faith holds to the teachings of the Sadguru.
37. Those who give up their faith and let go of the Sadguru's teaching get drowned in the ocean of worldly torture and are swallowed up by the creatures of pleasure and pain that are in that water.
38. Understand that the one who has firm faith is a good disciple and a leader among those who are deserving of liberation
39. One who derives inner peace from the teachings of the Sadguru is entitled to liberation, and is never affected by the entanglements of worldly life.
40. One who thinks that God is greater than the Sadguru is misguided and loses his glory and prosperity by thinking that the power of God is superior.
41. The "True Form" (Swaroopa) of the Sadguru is such that it has no end, while the gods will have their end at the time of the dissolution of the universe. How can even gods such as Vishnu and Shiva remain then?
42. Like this, the power of the Sadguru is more than that of Brahma and all of the other gods who will eventually cease to exist. However, humans beings of small intellect are like beggars to these gods, and cannot understand what is being said.

43. One who considers that the gods are equal to the Guru is a disciple with wrong understanding. Such a disciple harbors delusion in his mind and does not understand the established truth.
44. God is imagined by man, and with the use of mantra, one can attain godhood. However, it cannot happen that the Sadguru can be imagined, even by God.
45. The Sadguru in his fullness is millions of times greater than the gods. Even the *Vedas* and ancient scriptures failed when trying to describe him.
46. It should be understood that nothing is superior to the status of the Sadguru. The power of the gods is great, but even their power has its origin in Illusion.
47. The one who has understood the teachings of the Sadguru has power that cannot be equaled by anyone. With the power of that Self-Knowledge, such a one considers worldly wealth to be as significant as a blade of grass.
48. With the strength of the understanding given by the Sadguru arises the experience of Self-Knowledge in which the entire universe and Illusion is not seen.
49. Like this is the wealth of a good disciple. The one who is absolutely devoted to the teachings of the Sadguru becomes God himself.
50. When one turns within, away from the objective world, that fire within purifies the mind which becomes pacified by the teachings of the Sadguru. One such as this is a good disciple.
51. When one is on the path of the Sadguru's teachings, even if the whole universe were to come down around him, his pure devotion does not get diminished.
52. These who have surrendered to the Sadguru are good disciples and have been selected. Their activities are purified and they are transformed into God.
53. Those who have pure devotional feelings inside are deserving of liberation. Others only put on an outward show of appearances and are considered bad disciples.
54. They feel happy with sensual pleasures and want to acquire fame through spirituality. They are learned fools who make a show of surrendering.
55. Their obsession with sensual pleasures becomes uncontrollable, and they hold firmly to worldly life. Giving thought to discussions about spiritual endeavor is of no concern to them.
56. Once one turns away from the spiritual life, one holds on to the lust for the worldly life, and becomes like a servant carrying the burden of family.
57. One such as this considers only the family life to be happiness, and makes jokes about spiritual life. He is a confused unintelligent fool who is immersed in sensuous desires.
58. One who is engrossed in sensual pleasures and is given the teaching about discrimination (viveka) and the Knowledge of Brahman is like a pig that is worshipped with perfume, or a buffalo that is smeared with sandalwood paste.
59. A donkey rolls around in a garbage heap, so what enjoyment can he have from a nice smelling fragrance, and the owl flies in the dark, so how can he enjoy flying with swans in the daylight?
60. Similarly, how can one who is but a beggar at the door of sensual pleasures, which is to jump on a downward path, develop a liking for God and the company of pious people?
61. Just like a dog that is obsessed will continue chewing on its bone, similarly, the passionate person is always restless for sensual pleasures.

62. How can the dog who is so obsessed take good food into its mouth, or how can a throne be given to a monkey? Similarly, how can one attached to sensual pleasures digest Knowledge?
63. Just as one whose life has been spent tending to donkeys is not asked to sit among scholars, similarly, one who is has a weakness for sensual pleasures does not attain the Supreme.
64. He is like a raven who arrives in the gathering of royal swans looking for a lump of feces, wanting to call himself a swan.
65. Similarly, are those who are in the company of saintly people and who call themselves saintly while their thoughts are focused on feces.
66. Like the man who is going around with his wife in his arms asking to be called a renunciate (sanyasi), are those who are addicted to sensual pleasures while going around babbling on about Knowledge (Jnana).
67. But let this be as it is. How can such learned fools ever understand the true happiness of non-duality? They are in the hell of their own desires and they suffer in that hell.
68. How can one who seeks the services of a prostitute be called a minister, and likewise, how can one who is a slave to sensual pleasures be considered a true devotee of God?
69. For those who are pitifully attached to sense objects, from where will the True Knowledge come to them? They are always talkative and wordy in order to put on a show.
70. Such disciples are very lost and destructive. They don't use proper discrimination and are harmful scheming pretenders who are not really good people.
71. Like this are those troubling people in whom many faults have become strong over a long period of time. However, liberation is possible for them with the recognition of their error, and a turning away from the addiction to sensual pleasures.
72. They should once again surrender to the Sadguru, which pleases him. By following his teachings they become stainless once again
73. One who loses faith in the Sadguru falls into hell as long as the sun and moon are in existence, for there is no way out other than by following the teachings of the Guru.
74. If some detachment arises in one after seeing someone die and he feels humbled and bows down to a guru, this will not result in the establishment of Self-Knowledge.
75. Because of feelings like this, one may go to a guru and take initiation and receive mantra, but their commitment is only for a few days and only goes as deep as temporarily taking up the mantra.
76. In this way, one may go to many gurus and learn some spiritual words only to go on to become one who arrogantly and rudely prattles on.
77. In one moment he may fall down crying, in another moment he feels risen to detachment, and in the next moment he takes pride in Knowledge.
78. In one moment he holds on to faith, and in the next moment roars on arrogantly about himself. Like this, he carries on like a mad person.
79. Lust, anger, arrogance, jealousy, greed, and temptations of many kinds along with pride, treachery, and hatred dwell in his heart.

80. He is filled with ego and attachment to bodily comforts. He is misbehaved and addicted to sensual gratification and worldly pleasures, and is agitated within by his family life.
81. He is a procrastinator and an ungrateful person who indulges in harmful acts and ways of thinking. He is of a doubting nature and has no devotional feelings. He is short tempered, hard hearted, and betrays others.
82. He is heartless and lazy, thoughtless and unreliable, impatient with wrong ways of thinking, and firmly holds doubts in his mind.
83. He is full of hopes and attachment, thirst, imagination, harmful intellect and attitude, shallow thinking, and desire for sensual pleasures always dwells in his mind.
84. He is overly ambitious, envious, scornful, and always eager to criticize others. He is proud of his body and shows off with his knowledge.
85. He cannot control his hunger and thirst, and cannot control his sleep. His worries about his family never subside and he is easily confused.
86. He speaks too much and does not have a bit of detachment or courage to turn away from his addiction to sensual pleasures. He does not follow the path of spiritual practice.
87. He has no devotion, no renunciation, and no peace. He is not good natured or humble, and does not show any generosity, kindness, or compassion. He is not content nor does he have any good intelligence.
88. He avoids the suffering of the body and physical labor. He is very miserly when it comes to charity, and he does not change his hard hearted behavior.
89. He is not friendly with the people, and is not liked by gentlemen. All of his life he thinks day and night about the shortcomings of others.
90. He always tells lies and false stories. When looking into his thoughts and actions, he is not true to his words.
91. Eager to harass others, and like a scorpion with its poison, his tongue is sharp with hurting words that pierce the hearts of others.
92. He is quick to cover up his own bad qualities, speaks harshly to elders, and without examining whether something is true or not, he points out faults.
93. He is full of wrongful thinking within and does not have compassion for others. Like a violent person who is ill behaved, he does not having any feelings when others are hurting or are in pain.
94. He cannot understand the sorrows of others, and like someone who is torturing someone who is already being tortured, he takes pleasure in seeing them suffer.
95. He suffers from his own sorrows, but laughs at other's sorrow. He is surely in hell and is tortured by the thought of death.
96. Let all of this be as it is. How can those poor people who are blind with arrogance meet God? They don't like virtuous thinking due to their prior wrongful deeds.
97. At the demise of the body, their physical sense organs will become weak and non-functional, and they will realize that those who are close to them will leave them at that time.
98. Let it be enough with this description. Those who do not have these qualities are different and are considered good disciples. They are firm in their conviction and enjoy the glory of "Self-Bliss."
99. Those in whose minds doubts arise, and in whom the pride of the family tradition overshadows them, become depressed in family life.

100. Because of the things that have made them feel unhappy, they hold on to those feelings firmly in the mind, and as a result repeatedly feel miserable.
101. To get happiness in family life has neither been seen nor heard of. Even while knowing this, one goes against their own good, and becomes unhappy of their own accord.
102. These who believe that happiness is found in family life are dull-minded. Such learned fools knowingly close their eyes to the facts.
103. One should lead a comfortable family life, but should also enhance the spiritual life. It is not proper that one should ever neglect the spiritual life.
104. Previously, I gave the explanation on how to recognize a good Guru and a good disciple. Now I will describe the attributes of a good teaching.

Thus in Shri Dasbodh, a dialogue between the Guru and disciple, Sub-Chapter 3 of Chapter 5, named "The Signs of a Disciple" is concluded.

Chapter: 5, Sub-Chapter: 4

The Signs of Teachings

|| ShriRam ||

1. Listen to the attributes of teachings. There are numerous types of teachings and it would be impossible to tell them all, but I shall describe a few.
2. Many types of teachings of sacred words, or mantras[33], are given. Some give a mantra which is a name of God and some prescribe only the repetition of "OM" (Pronounced "AUM" in three syllables with a lingering emphasis on the M syllable).

Verses 3 through 7 list various names of deities used as mantras.

3. Teachers tell aspirants to repeat mantras of Shiva, Bhavaani, Vishnu, Mahalakshmi, Dattatraya, Ganesha, and Maartanda.
4. They say to chant the mantras of various incarnations of Vishnu in the form of a fish, a tortoise, a bear, and the deity that is half man and half lion. There are mantras of Vamana, Bhaargava, Lord Rama, and Lord Krishna.
5. They give mantras of various deities like Bhairava, Mallaari, Hanuman, Yekshini, Narayana, Panduranga, and of various spirits.
6. There are mantras of Shesha, Garuda, Vayu, Vitthala, Aghora, etc. How many can be told?
7. There are mantras of various Goddesses like Balaa, Bagula, Kali, Kankali, and Batuka. There are many mantras offering many powers.
8. There are as many independent different mantras as there are deities. Some are easy, some difficult, some strange, some with severe effect and some even having effects on the sky.
9. If one looks around the world, many deities can be seen. Who can count them all? There are as many mantras as there are gods. How many can be mentioned?

---

[33] Mantras are sacred words or sacred syllables which are used for the purpose of meditation or achieving some effect. They are usually given by a Guru at the time of initiation. The mantras for meditation are usually repeated over and over again. This repetition is called "japa." The Mantra is usually repeated silently in the mind, but can be spoken or chanted out loud.

10. Innumerable are the strings of names used as mantras. Each one different from the other. Strange is the play of Illusion. Who can understand it?
11. There are mantras by which ghosts can be driven away, illnesses can be cured and poison stings from scorpions can be healed.
12. Like this, there are many varieties of mantras that are spoken into the ears of disciples. There are many teachings on the repetition of mantras (japa), meditation, ritual worship (puja), and various symbols of concentration (yantras).
13. Some say to repeat the name of Lord Shiva, some say to repeat "Hari" (Vishnu), and some give the name "Vitthala," for chanting.
14. Some say chant "Krishna, Krishna," and some say chant "Vishnu, Vishnu." Some say to repeat the name "Narayana."
15. Some say to repeat "Achyuta," and some say repeat "Ananta," while some say to repeat "Datta."
16. Some say to chant "Rama, Rama," some tell to repeat only "Om, Om," and some say to chant the many names of "Meghashama" (Krishna)
17. Some say to repeat "Guru, Guru," some say to repeat "Parameshwara," and some say to go on only deeply remembering Lord Ganesha.
18. Some say to chant "Shamaraj" (a name of Krishna), and some say to chant "Garudadhvaja," some say to repeat "Adhokshaja[34]."
19. Some say repeat "Deva, Deva" (God, God), some say repeat "Keshava, Keshava," and some say to go on repeating "Bhargava."
20. Some say to repeat "Vishvanath," and some say repeat "Malhari," and some say to repeat "Tukai."
21. How many more should I give of these many names? Lord Shiva and his power (Shakti) have an endless number of names. Different names are given as per one's wish or according to one's temperament.
22. Some teachers talk about the four types of gestures (mudras) like turning towards the sky (khechari), turning towards the earth (bhuchari), or that which is not fixed (chachari), or that which is said to reveal the Self (agochari), and some advise yogic postures (asanas) according to one's capacity.
23. Some show things that are normally unseen, some teach how to experience clairaudience, and some gurus teach thorough knowledge of the physical body.
24. Some speak about the way of action (karma), some the path of worship, and some speak about the eight limbed yoga (ashtanga yoga), while others talk about the energy centers of the body (chakras).
25. Some tell about various austerities, some tell about the internal chanting that is going on by itself, and some teachers who are knowledgeable expound upon the principles of creation.
26. Some tell about God with form (saguna), some explain the attributeless (nirguna), and some advise aspirants to go to pilgrimage places.
27. Some tell about the four great statements from the *Vedas* (Mahavakyas[35]), saying that they should be chanted, and some give the explanation of them, saying "All is Brahman."

---

[34] There are one thousand names of Vishnu, each describing different qualities. There are many names of Lord Krishna also describing him. The point being made is that one can repeat any one of these multitude of names according to the instruction given or one's liking.

[35] The Mahavakyas, the four "Great Statements" are - Prajnanam Brahmma (from Righveda), Aham Brahmasmi (from Yajurveda), Tat Tvam Asi (from Samveda), Ayamatma Brahmma (from Atharvaveda).

28. Some tell the path of worship of the Goddess (Shakti), some talk about unrestricted liberty, and some speak of worship of the sex organs.
29. Some tell about hypnotism, some tell ways to make a person unable to do his activities or how to entice someone into some action or cause them some destruction, and some tell about black magic.
30. There are so many types of teachings. How many should I describe? Let it be as it is that there are innumerable teachings.
31. There are many teachings, but without Self-Knowledge all of them are meaningless. On this subject there is one statement made by Lord Krishna:
"Many people read many scriptures, and worship many deities, but without Self-Knowledge, everything is meaningless. The opinion of the shaivas, shaktas (devotees of Shiva and Shakti), or others, are many. There are many faulty doctrines of individuals in illusion who are confused. There is nothing which purifies like Self-Knowledge."
32. There is nothing that can be found that is as pure as Self-Knowledge. Therefore, one must first acquire Self-Knowledge.
33. Of all teachings, the teachings about Self-Knowledge are special. This has been said by God in many places.
34. The greatness of Self-Knowledge is not known to even the four-faced Brahma[36], what can mere individuals understand?
35. The value and status of Self-Knowledge is billions of times greater than the benefit of all pilgrimages, the results of all sacred baths, or the merit of giving in charity.
36. Therefore, know that Self-Knowledge is what is the most profound type of knowledge. Listen to attributes of Knowledge which I will now tell.

Thus in Shri Dasbodh, a dialogue between the Guru and disciple, Sub-Chapter 4 of Chapter 5, named "The Signs of Teachings" is concluded.

Chapter: 5, Sub-Chapter: 5

Explanation of Knowledge

|| ShriRam ||

1. As long as Self-Knowledge is not clear everything else is useless. Without Self-Knowledge, agitation does not go away.
2. When talking about Knowledge, one feels confused and thinks, "What is the real meaning of Knowledge?" Therefore, I shall explain it now, step by step.
3. Knowing the past, future and present, is called knowledge, but that is not the real "Knowledge" (Jnana).
4. One may do a lot of study and become educated in the science of music, or the moods of notes and melodies, or the various spiritual sciences (*Shastras*) and the *Vedas*, but this also is not Knowledge.
5. There is knowledge of many occupations, knowledge of many initiations, and knowledge tested by many examinations, but this is not Jnana.

---

[36] Brahma, the creator, is depicted with four faces, as if he is telling the knowledge of all four Vedas. This point being made here is that even the four Vedas cannot tell the greatness of the Self-Knowledge.

6. There is knowledge of many women, knowledge of many men, and the judgements about many people, but this is not Knowledge.
7. There is knowledge of the value of horses, the value of elephants, and knowledge about wild animals, but these are not the true Knowledge.
8. There is knowledge of various beasts, of birds, and ghosts, but this is not Jnana.
9. There is knowledge of many vehicles, of clothes, and of many weapons, but this is not Knowledge.
10. There is knowledge of many metals, of many coins, and of many gems, but this is not the true Knowledge.
11. There is knowledge about the value of many stones, of many woods, and of many varieties of musical instruments, but this is not Knowledge.
12. There is knowledge of many kinds of land, of many types of water, and of many types of lights, but this is not Jnana.
13. There is knowledge of many kinds of extracts, many seeds, and of many sprouts, but this is not Knowledge.
14. There is knowledge of flowers, of fruits, and of creepers, but this is not true Knowledge.
15. There is knowledge about many kinds of miseries and many diseases and their many signs and symptoms, but this is not Knowledge.
16. There is knowledge about many sacred words (mantras), many diagrams of contemplation (yantras), and many idols, but this is not true Jnana.
17. There is knowledge of many pilgrimage places, many houses, and many types of vessels, but this is not true Knowledge.
18. There is knowledge about future events, auspicious times, and many types of logic, but this is not Knowledge.
19. There is knowledge of many types of inferences, rules and regulations, and knowledge about many varieties of objects, but this is not true Knowledge.
20. There is knowledge about many streams of learning, many arts, and many types of wisdom, but this is not Jnana.
21. There is knowledge of many words and their many meanings, and of many languages, but this is not Knowledge.
22. There is knowledge of many alphabets, various consonants, and many writings, but this is not the true Knowledge.
23. There is knowledge of many opinions, the identification of many types of information, and knowledge of attitudes of people, but this is not true Knowledge.
24. There is knowledge of many shapes, many flavors, and about many fragrances, but this is not Knowledge.
25. There is knowledge of creativity, of the universe and its expansion, and of many types of objects, but this is not true Knowledge.
26. To speak exact words, give ready answers, and compose a poem in moment's time, are types of knowledge, but this is not Jnana.
27. There is knowledge of the movement of the eyes, the art of music, hand movements, different types of arts, melodious singing and various forms of expressions, but this is not true Knowledge.
28. There is knowledge about skill in poetry, the art of singing, song composition, the art of dancing, and mastery of words in addressing gatherings, but all of this is not Knowledge.

29. There is knowledge of the art of charming others with words, the art of engrossing others with melodies, and knowledge of jokes and humor, but this is not true Knowledge.
30. There is knowledge of the art of making attractive paintings, the art of playing many musical instruments, and many exceptional arts of various kinds, but this is not Knowledge.
31. There are all of these types of knowledge and more. There is the knowledge of the sixty-four arts, as well as many other types. There are the fourteen streams of learning, and knowledge about extraordinary powers, but this is not Jnana.
32. One may be an expert in all arts, and have complete mastery in all types knowledge, but still all of that is only expertise and cannot be called true Knowledge.
33. All of these appear to be knowledge that one has gained, but the principle Knowledge where the creation of Illusion is absent, is completely different.
34. To understand the minds of others appears to be Jnana, but this is not an indication of Self-Knowledge.
35. A very experienced sage was committing some mistake while doing mental worship, and someone came to know of it and told him that he was making an error.
36. The one who told him this came to know the other's inner state of mind as a result of his worship, and he was called very knowledgeable. However, this was not the Knowledge with which one can attain liberation.
37. There are many types of knowledge. It is impossible for me to tell them all. The Knowledge by which one can attain "Liberation through identification with the Self" (Sayujya Mukti) is a Knowledge that is quite different.
38. The listener asked, "What is this Knowledge you speak of, and what are the attributes of its peace and contentment? Please explain it so it may become clear."
39. Like this, the question was asked about Pure Knowledge. The explanation will be given in the next sub-chapter. The listener should remain alert and pay close attention to what follows.

Thus in Shri Dasbodh, a dialogue between the Guru and disciple, Sub-Chapter 5 of Chapter 5, named "Explanation of Knowledge" is concluded.

Chapter: 5, Sub-Chapter: 6

Explanation of Pure Knowledge

|| ShriRam ||

1. Listen now to the signs of Knowledge. Knowledge means Self-Knowledge where the Self sees only itself. This is called "Knowledge" (Jnana).
2. Primarily this means to know God. To reflect deeply upon the Eternal and the ephemeral, and to know one's "Self Nature" (Swaroopa) is called Knowledge
3. Where the visible creation ends, the five elements dissolve, and where the root of duality does not arise, is called Knowledge.

4. That which is not perceptible to the mind and intellect, what logical thinking cannot comprehend, and which is said to be beyond the source of speech, is called Jnana.
5. Where there is no awareness of the visible world, and where consciousness (knowledge) is ignorance, this is called the stainless and pure "Knowledge of Reality."
6. That which is called the fourth state (Turya; SatChitAnanda) is the witness of all, and is said to be Knowledge, but understand that this also falls short because this indicates a knowledge of objects. (Knowledge of "all" involves a subject/object duality.)
7. Understand that knowledge of visible objects is called objective knowledge. Understand the pure untainted "Self Nature" is itself the "Knowledge of Reality."
8. Where there is originally no "all," how can there be any witness of all? Therefore, the knowledge that is the Turya state should not be considered as "Pure Knowledge."
9. Knowledge (Jnana) means non-duality. The Turya state is in fact duality. "Pure Knowledge" is always quite different than this.
10. Listen to the indications of "Pure Knowledge." The listeners should understand that the pure "Self Nature" is one's own Self, and is called the "Pure Knowledge of one's own Self Nature" (Shudda Swaroopa Jnana).
11. The teaching of the four "Great Statements" of the *Vedas* (Mahavakyas) is good, but simply repeating these statements over and over is not advised. The purpose of them is that the aspirant should deeply think over their meaning.
12. The teaching of the four great statements is the essence of the *Vedas*, but deep thought must be given to their meaning. By merely repeating these statements the darkness of Illusion is not dispelled.
13. When contemplating the meaning of the four great statements, one understands that one is "That" oneself. Simply repeating the statements is useless effort.
14. Upon inquiry into the meaning of the great statements, the main attribute of this Knowledge is seen to be that the pure Reality which is being indicated is one's own Self.
15. To gain one's own Self by one's Self is Knowledge, and is extremely rare. It is That which is, in the beginning and at the end, alone, in its own "Self Form."
16. It is that from where everything appears, and to where everything disappears. When that Knowledge is gained, it removes the misconception of bondage.
17. By using minute observation and keen subtle thinking one sees Oneness, and many differing opinions become meaningless.
18. That which is the origin of this animate and inanimate universe is the pure, untainted Self Form (Shudda Swaroopa). It is this alone that is called Knowledge according to *Vedanta*.
19. Upon discovering our origin, ignorance disappears automatically. This is called the Knowledge of Brahman that bestows liberation.
20. When one knows oneself, one gains complete Knowledge within. With that, the concept of one's existence being limited disappears completely.
21. When one has the intention to find out "Who am I?" one sees beyond the body. When one contemplates this regularly, one's "Self Nature" is confirmed.
22. In the past there were many great ones, who with Self-Knowledge truly crossed beyond worldly life. Listen, and I will tell some of their names now.

23. Vyasa and Vasishtha and many great ascetics, along with Shuka and Narada were all content with Knowledge. King Janaka and others were great Jnanis with this Self-Knowledge.
24. Vamadeva, Vaalmiki, Atri, Shaunaka, and others were accomplished with Self-Knowledge that is in accord with Vedanta.
25. Sanaka and others, mainly Adinath, Meena, and ascetics like Goraksha along with many more. There are too many to say all of their names.
26. There are many accomplished ones and ascetics with the "Great Experience" (MahaAnubhava) who have attained the inner happiness which pleases Lord Shiva who is always nodding with satisfaction.
27. That which is the essence of the *Vedas* and *Shastras* and is the established conclusion of direct experience resulting from introspection and deep thought, is acquired according to one's good fortune by sincere devotees.
28. That which is the Knowledge of sages, saints and virtuous people, the secret Knowledge of the past, future and present, I shall tell now.
29. That Knowledge is not gained by going on pilgrimages, taking religious vows, by giving in charity, or by undergoing many various austerities.
30. That which is the fruit of all spiritual practices is the pinnacle of Knowledge that alone cuts the root of doubt completely.
31. There are so many languages and so many spiritual texts, of which the foremost are the *Upanishads* (the vedic teachings on non-duality also called Vedanta). Of all these, there is only one real meaning at the center.
32. That which is not given in the mythological books (*Puranas*), and where the teachings of the *Vedas* became exhausted, I shall explain with the blessings of the Guru, now this very moment.
33. Not having seen the Sanskrit texts, nor having been introduced to the knowledge of Marathi texts, it is the understanding given by my Master, the Sadguru that dwells in my heart.
34. Now, neither the Sanskrit texts, nor the Marathi texts are required. The understanding of my Master dwells in the heart.
35. Without studying the *Vedas* or putting in hard work, but by listening to the Sadguru, excellent understanding comes without effort.
36. Sanskrit texts are considered superior to Marathi texts, and of the Sanskrit texts, the *Upanishads* (the end part of the *Vedas*) are clearly the greatest.
37. There are not any texts that are superior to the *Upanishads*. There, the essence of the *Vedas* is revealed.
38. So, let Vedanta (Ved and anta is the end of the *Vedas*) be understood like this. Of that Vedanta, the inner meaning is very deep. Listen now to that Supreme Truth.
39. Dear one, know that there is one statement of the Sadguru that is the deepest of deep statements. With that statement of the Sadguru there is definite contentment.
40. That statement of the Sadguru is itself Vedanta. That statement of the Sadguru is itself the final doctrine. That statement of the Sadguru is itself the Truth, and my true experience now.
41. The statement of my Master is very deep, and has given great contentment.
42. This is the secret of my life which I am going to tell to you now. If you give your complete attention to me at this very moment.
43. The disciple with an eager look on his face held firmly to the Sadguru's feet (held to his every word) and asked to be taught. Then, the Sadguru started to speak.

44. "I am Brahman" is the "Great Statement," or Mahavakya, the meaning of which is beyond logical understanding. I shall tell about this, where the identity of the Guru and the disciple is one.
45. Dear disciple, listen, and understand that the secret here is that you are Brahman. Do not harbor any doubt or illusion about this matter.
46. Of the nine types of devotion, the most important is self-surrender. I will explain that fully to you now.
47. At the dissolution of the universe the five elements that have been created in order get dissolved, one back into the other in order, just as they originated, and even the primordial female principle (Prakriti - manifest creation) and the primordial male principle (Purusha - unmanifest formless existence) which are not two, also become Brahman only.
48. When visible objects disappear, in truth, one's Self also does not remain. Only the one Absolute Reality exists alone from the beginning.
49. There is no existence of creation. There is always only oneness. If we look with the eye of this Oneness, where will we see a physical body and a universe?
50. When the fire of Self-Knowledge reveals itself, the dirt of the visible world is burned up and disappears. In Oneness, the illusion of separateness is destroyed before it begins.
51. By understanding what is unreal, one's experience changes. The visible world that appears to be existing disappears, and self-surrender happens effortlessly.
52. Understand like this. If there is oneness with the Guru, then what is there to worry about? Do not remain as a separate non-devotee.
53. Now, in order to make this oneness very strong, one should worship the Sadguru. With the adoration of the Sadguru there is definitely contentment.
54. Dear disciple, Self-Knowledge is itself the attainment of contentment. With Self-Knowledge the bondage of the fear of worldly life is seen to be false at its root.
55. When one feels that "I am the body," it is if that person is committing suicide. With the pride of the body (bodily identification), one suffers from the sorrows of the cycle of birth and death.
56. Your understanding should be that you are different from the four bodies (gross, subtle, casual, and great-casual or turya), and that you are different from the birth of the body, its appearance, and its actions. You are entirely different from all that has a visible appearance.
57. No one is in bondage, but due to the wrong assumption of body-identification, people believe in Illusion.
58. The aspirant should take some time to go and sit alone and rest in one's "Self Nature." With that practice, one becomes firmly rooted in "Supreme Truth."
59. When there is continuous listening and reflection one can gain full contentment. Having complete Knowledge of Brahman, desirelessness (vairagya) naturally fills one within.
60. Dear disciple, know that uncontrolled liberty and the indulgence in sensual pleasures will not make your longings and desires go away.
61. Only the one who is detached and dispassionate throws away the objects of the world that are taken by all to be gems. Only he alone, can gain complete Knowledge.
62. It is illustrated best by the story of the king who gave away his kingdom for a gemstone, and only got his kingdom back when he threw away the gem.

63. Dear disciple, be alert and listen to what I tell you now. That which one meditates upon is what he obtains.
64. Therefore, give up ignorance and wrong knowledge and adopt wise knowledge. With that, one realizes God and is respected in the world.
65. If one is suffering from high fever, he may experience hallucinations of things appearing in front of the eyes. However by taking the right medicine, he feels happy and joyful.
66. In the same way, with the fever of ignorance, when the false appearances are seen by the eyes, the medicine of Knowledge (Jnana) is to be taken. By taking that medicine, it is understood that at the root Illusion does not exist.
67. One who is terrified in a dream may cry out in fear, but when he is awakened, he returns back to his normal state which is free of that fear.
68. If what is false is conceived to be true, one feels sorrow because of that, but there is no such thing as the dissolution of the false, as it was never really existing.
69. The dream events are untrue for the one who is awake, but the one who is asleep feels totally affected by them. It is only when becoming awake that the fear is dispelled.
70. The sleep of ignorance fills one with darkness. For complete awakening, one should listen, and reflect upon what is heard.
71. Understand the sign of identifying one who has fully awakened. He is the one who is completely detached from sensual pleasures.
72. It should be understood that the one who does not have this detachment is still an aspirant. He should give up his pride in realization and continue with spiritual practice (sadhana).
73. One who is not inclined to do any spiritual practice is bound by his pride of being in an accomplished state. Compared to him, one who is a serious seeker desirous of liberation is better off and more entitled to Self-Knowledge.
74. Then the disciple asked, "What are the signs of one who is bound, one who is a seeker, one who is an aspirant, and one who is accomplished? How to can one understand and identify these?"
75. The answer to this will be given for the listeners in the next sub-chapter. The listeners should give their full attention to the narration that follows.

Thus in Shri Dasbodh, a dialogue between the Guru and disciple, Sub-Chapter 6 of Chapter 5, named "Explanation of Pure Knowledge" is concluded.

Chapter: 5, Sub-Chapter: 7

Signs of a Bound Person

|| ShriRam ||

1. This universe is full with the animate and inanimate. There are innumerable living beings which are said to be classified into four types.
2. Listen to the signs of these four types of beings, and know that they are (1) the person who is bound (baddha), (2) the seeker (mumuksha), (3) the aspirant, or practitioner (sadhaka), and (4) the accomplished one (Siddha) or Master.

3. Other than these four types, there is no fifth type. Now, understand this as I explain all of these four types of beings.
4. I will describe what it means when it is said that one is bound, and I will tell how to know and identify the signs of seekers, aspirants, and the accomplished.
5. The listeners are asked to remain alert as you listen to what is being presented about the person who is bound, the seeker, the aspirant, and the accomplished.
6. Now, understand what it means to say one is bound. It is like a blind man's eyes. For him, all the ten directions are dark and empty.
7. One who is bound would not even be able to recognize devotees, the "Knowledgeable" (Jnanis), ascetics, yogis, renunciates, or hermits, even if they were right in front of his eyes.
8. He cannot see or know which actions are to be done and which are to be abandoned. He cannot see or know what is one's proper duty and what is improper, and he cannot see the path towards the realization of Supreme Truth.
9. The one who is bound does not recognize what are good scriptures, the value of keeping the company of those with Self-Knowledge, or even good people, and he does not recognize the pure correct path.
10. He does not understand the importance of deeply thinking about what is True and what is false, and he does not understand his own True Nature. He does not know how to behave appropriately, and he does not know how to help others or give in charity.
11. He has no compassion for other living beings, he does not have a clean or healthy body, and does not offer any soft speech to comfort people.
12. When one does not understand anything about Knowledge (Jnana), devotion (bhakti), desirelessness (vairagya), meditation (dhyana), liberation (moksha), or spiritual practice (sadhana), this is what is called being in bondage.
13. When one does not have any firm understanding of God, does not understand anything of the discrimination (viveka) that is prescribed by the saints, and does not understand the play of Illusion, this is called being bound.
14. When one does not understand the signs of Supreme Truth, does not understand the explanations about the Self-Knowledge, and does not understand oneself, this is called being bound
15. When one does not understand the root cause of the birth of living beings, does not understand the fruit of spiritual practice, and does not understand the Oneness that is alone, this is called being bound.
16. When one does not understand what bondage is, does not understand the signs of liberation, and does not understand about Reality, this is called being bound.
17. When one does not understand the meaning of what is said in scriptures, does not understand what is for one's own benefit, and does not understand that he is entangled in imagination, this is called being bound.
18. Where there is no sign of Self-Knowledge, this is the main sign of being bound. One such as this knows nothing of pilgrimages, nor of religious or charitable merit whatsoever.
19. When one has no kindness, no compassion, no simplicity, no friendship, no peace and no forgiveness, this is called being bound.
20. If one is lacking Self-Knowledge, how can there be any signs of Self-Knowledge? To the contrary, mostly bad attributes are seen in such a one. This is called being bound.

21. When one takes great pleasure in doing many types of wrongful deeds and has an intense longing for behaving wildly, this is called being bound.
22. When one has too much passion, too much anger, too much pride, too much arrogance, too much divisiveness, or too much sorrow, this is called being bound.
23. When one does too much boasting, has too much hypocrisy, too much greed for objects, speaks too many harsh words, and believes in many bad omens, this is called being bound.
24. When one is too much of a bully, has too much malice, too much envy, too much hatred, does too many harmful deeds, and is not right in the mind, this is called being bound.
25. When one has too much love of praise, is too demanding, has too much ego, too much intrusiveness, or too much accumulation of hurtful deeds, this is called being bound.
26. When one is too crafty, too argumentative, too illogical in their thinking, or is too cruel and ruthless, this is called being bound.
27. When one criticizes too much, is too jealous, commits excessive misdeeds, has too many expectations, or has many kinds of bad qualities, this is called being bound.
28. When one is excessively corrupt, indulges in vile destructive misconduct, has no morality and is thoughtless, this is called being bound.
29. When one is excessively cruel, treacherous, having the attitude of a murderer, exceedingly hurtful, hot tempered, and entertains many kinds of knowledge about black magic, this is called being bound.
30. When one harbors too much hope, is excessively selfish, engages in too much conflict, has too much misfortune, and thinks too much about jealousy and revenge with harmful intentions, this is called being bound.
31. When one is engaged in too much imagination, too much lust, too much thirst, too many desires, too much affection, and is too emotional, this is called being bound.
32. When one has too much suspicion, too much depression, too much foolishness, excessive attachment to relatives and family life, or is involved in too many activities, this is called being bound.
33. When one is too talkative, too heretical, excessively hurtful to others, pretends too much, is too clever, or too mischievous, this is called being bound.
34. When one is excessively negative, excessively confused and prone to delusion, is exceedingly ignorant, too whimsical, or too lazy, this is called being bound.
35. When one is too miserly, too rough in their speech, is harboring too much hatred and too much contempt, is performing many bad deeds, and is excessively manipulative, this is called being bound.
36. When one is completely ignorant of Supreme Truth and has excessive knowledge regarding a worldly lifestyle, and is not content in one's Self, this is called being bound.
37. When one is disrespectful of spirituality but shows excessive attraction for family life, and constantly feels the heavy burden of the yoke of worldly life, this is called being bound.
38. When one does not like the company of the virtuous and wise, criticizes saints, and is shackled to the identification with the body and the intellect, this is called being bound.

39. When one's mind is constantly repeating thoughts about money, is focused on women all the time, and has no association with virtuous people, this is called being bound.
40. When one sees only money and women with his eyes, only hears about money and women with his ears, and only thinks of money and women in his thoughts, this is called being bound.
41. When one is worshipping money and women with his body, speech, and mind with every breath his whole life, this is called being bound.
42. When one focuses the sense organs towards money and women without thinking of anything else, this is called being bound.
43. When money and women alone are considered to be the only reason for pilgrimage, they are one's religion and one's motivation. The one who thinks like this is bound.
44. When one spends his entire time thinking about the worries of worldly life and is always only talking about them, this is called being bound.
45. When one is always feeling affected by many worries, many sorrows, is always feeling miserable, and has given up spirituality, this is called being bound.
46. When the one who is bound is not feeling depressed even for a few moments, he spends that time only thinking about money, women and family.
47. He never gives any thought about pilgrimages, giving in charity, devotion to God, explanations and narrations about God, mantras, chanting, or meditating. Such a one is consumed by thoughts of money and women.
48. When one is very attached to passion day and night without a moments rest whether being awake or while in the dream state, this is being bound.
49. Like these are the signs of a bound person. Understand that one's attributes change when they come into the stage of being a seeker. Listen to the signs of the seeker in the next sub-chapter.

Thus in Shri Dasbodh, a dialogue between the Guru and disciple, Sub-Chapter 7 of Chapter 5, named "Signs of a Bound Person" is concluded.

Chapter: 5, Sub-Chapter: 8

The Signs of a Seeker

|| ShriRam ||

1. Because of intoxication with worldly life one acquires many lowly and undesirable qualities. Even by looking at such a person one feels affected by his worldliness.
2. One who is bound and who behaves in an uncontrolled manner in worldly life becomes miserable over time.
3. When one has suffered from the miseries of worldly life and knows what it is to feel scorched by the three tortures (bodily tortures, worldly tortures, and cosmic tortures), he begins to turn inward and away from worldly life when he hears the explanations about God.

4. When one becomes disinterested in the family life, his mind begins to lose interest in worldly objects, and he says to himself, "Enough with this greed for mundane worldly life!"
5. He sees that the family life will eventually only go away, and that all efforts undertaken there will not really bear any fruit. He begins to think "Now I should make something of my life that will bear fruit."
6. Like this, there is a change in the intellect. There arises a feeling within that his time is almost gone and that he has been wasting his life.
7. He remembers all of the misdeeds that he has previously committed, and the memories of them stand strongly in his mind.
8. He is reminded of his fears about death. That fear of death is felt strongly in his mind because he has done so many wrongful deeds in his life.
9. His whole life he gave no thought to doing any good deeds while a mountain of wrongful deeds were committed. Now he worries about how he can cross beyond this ocean of worldly life.
10. Hiding his own faults, he was always commenting on the faults of good people. He thinks, "Oh God, I have unnecessarily criticized saints, sages, and virtuous men.
11. There is no other fault worse than that of criticism. I have done so many wrong things that it is as if the sky could be drowned in them.
12. I have not recognized saints, nor done any worship of God, and I have not even respected and honored guests and visitors.
13. The past misdeeds are now coming to fruition. Nothing good was ever done by me and my mind was always engaged in wrongful ways of thinking.
14. I never worked hard, nor did anything to help others, and I didn't observe any good conduct due too much lust and pride.
15. It is as if I have drowned devotion, which is like a mother, and foolishly I have disturbed the peace and spoiled good intellect and virtuous desire.
16. Now, how can I make life worthwhile? By unnecessarily committing so many wrongful acts, I have no capability to see with proper discernment.
17. What is to be done to remedy my situation? How can one go beyond the worldly life? What qualities will enable me to realize God?
18. I have never had any devotional feelings. I achieved a good name in the world, but all of my efforts and actions were hypocritical and even deceitful.
19. I gave narrations about God and sang his praises only to make a living. I made a show for earning money in the name of God and spoiled my own intellect in ways only I know.
20. I was harboring pride within while outwardly saying that I am without pride, I was sitting in a meditation posture while inwardly, in the mind, I was desiring money.
21. I fooled people by showing the scholarly knowledge of scriptures, and criticized saints in order to make a living. I am filled with so many kinds of vices.
22. I put down the Truth and encouraged and praised the false. All these things I did only for the sake of filling the belly."
23. If in this way, one recognizes and turns away from worldliness, and goes on to expose oneself to spiritual discourses, one can change and become a seeker (mumuksha) such as described in sacred texts.
24. When one holds to a virtuous inward path, has a desire for the companionship of good and virtuous people, and begins to become detached from worldly life, this is called being a seeker.

25. When one sees that even great kings and emperors have passed away, and how much less one's own prosperity is compared to theirs, and feels inclined to have the companionship of good and virtuous people rather than pursue material gain, this is called being a seeker.
26. When one recognizes one's own vices and begins to develop detachment in the mind, and criticizes oneself with remorse, this is called being a seeker.
27. When one says to oneself, "What an unhelpful person I am. What a pretender I am. What a misbehaved person I am." This is called being a seeker.
28. When one says, "I have fallen, I am a hurtful person who is always engaging in harmful conduct. I am nothing but a wrongdoer." This is called being a seeker.
29. When one says "I have no devotion. I am lower than the lowest. My life has been useless like a stone." This is called being a seeker.
30. When one says, "I am stubborn. I am hot tempered with people, and I have many addictions." This is called being a seeker.
31. When one says "I am lazy and reluctant to work. I am crafty and a coward. I am foolish and thoughtless." This is called being a seeker.
32. When one says "I am an idle braggart. I am a heretic prone to constant quarrels. I am filled with bad intellect and always scheming." This is called being a seeker.
33. When one says, "I know nothing, I have more fault than anyone," and describes his negative qualities. This is called being a seeker.
34. When one says, "I am without any authority, I am from a poor family background, and I am a dangerous person who is mean in all respects." This is called being a seeker.
35. When one says, "What a selfish person I am. What a harmful criminal I am. I am not spiritual at all." This is called being a seeker.
36. When one says "I am a heap of bad qualities. I have wasted my life in vain. I am a burden to the earth." This is called being a seeker.
37. When one criticizes oneself at length, is inwardly tired of the troubles of worldly life, and is eager for the company of virtuous people. This is called being a seeker.
38. The seeker then begins going to many pilgrimage places, does many practices for controlling the mind and the sense organs, and reads many books trying to find their inner meaning.
39. Still, with all that, he does not find contentment. He feels that everything so far has only been guesswork. Finally he says, "I must go and surrender myself to the saints." This is called being a seeker.
40. The one who is proud of the body, has pride in one's family name and pride in wealth, and who then goes and drops all of that pride at the feet of the saints is called a seeker.
41. When one begins leaving behind one's egotism, starts criticizing oneself in many ways, and holds to the expectation of liberation, this is called being a seeker.
42. One who begins to feel ashamed of personal greatness, who begins making efforts for a spiritual life, and who begins to develop faith in the saints, is called a seeker.
43. One who begins dropping the selfish interest in family life and begins having a strong liking for spiritual life and who begins serving virtuous people is a seeker of liberation.
44. Understand one such as this to be a seeker of liberation and recognize the signs of this stage. The listener should now pay attention as I explain the signs of an aspirant in the next sub-chapter.

Thus in Shri Dasbodh, a dialogue between the Guru and disciple, Sub-Chapter 8 of Chapter 5, named "The Signs of a Seeker" is concluded.

Chapter: 5, Sub-Chapter: 9

The Signs of an Aspirant

|| ShriRam ||

1. Previously, I have given the explanation of the signs of a seeker. Now listen with alertness to the signs of an aspirant.
2. One who is renouncing his vices, and begins keeping the company of saints is then called an aspirant. Listen attentively.
3. In other spiritual texts as well, it is said that one who surrenders to the saints, is assured by them, and has developed faith in what they say, has come to be called an aspirant.
4. Once having received instruction in Self-Knowledge, the bondage of the worldly life breaks off. One who does spiritual practice in order to remain firm in that Knowledge is called an aspirant.
5. When one has a great liking for listening to the explanation of non-duality, and with reflection finds out the inner meaning, he is called an aspirant.
6. One is an aspirant when he begins thinking deeply and inquiring into what is True and what is false, and when he is becoming eager for firmness in Self-Knowledge while destroying doubts.
7. In developing the attitude of clearing many doubts, the aspirant keeps to the company of the virtuous and utilizes the threefold verification. This verification is the realization that the experience of the Self, and the statements of the scriptures and the Guru are one.
8. One who disregards the bodily focused intellect with discrimination and holds the focus of the intellect strongly on the Self, and who is always listening (shravana) and reflecting on what has been heard (manana), is called an aspirant.
9. One who is doing away with the perception of the visible world and firmly holding to Self-Knowledge with correct thinking, and who is remaining content, is called an aspirant.
10. One who is breaking conceptual duality, whose practice is itself the non-dual Reality, and who attains the state of absorption in undivided Oneness (samadhi) is called an aspirant.
11. When Self-Knowledge becomes old and decays in one generation, one who rejuvenates and restores it and crosses over the worldly existence is called an aspirant.
12. One who adopts the best attributes of the sages as well as their explanations, and with some effort realizes one's "Self Nature," is a called an aspirant.
13. One who gives up wrongful and harmful activities and increases virtuous activity, and who becomes strong in one's Self Nature is called an aspirant.
14. One who gives up negative qualities day by day and adopts the best qualities, and who is constantly verifying one's Self Nature inwardly is called an aspirant.

15. One who by the force of strong conviction nullifies the existence of the visible world, and who is constantly dissolving himself into his Self Nature, is called an aspirant.
16. One who ignores the appearance of Illusion, and who instead turns his attention inwardly to the unseen and holds his concentration in the Self, is called an aspirant.
17. The one who holds firmly to that which is hidden from common people, and which cannot be conceived of or imagined by the mind, is called an aspirant.
18. One who makes efforts to realize That which upon speaking about it leaves one speechless, and upon trying to see it makes one as if blind, is called an aspirant.
19. One who acquires That which cannot be acquired and which cannot be seen when one tries to see it, is called an aspirant.
20. One who through correct effort brings about the experience of rendering logic useless, and the dissolution of the mind, is called an aspirant.
21. The one who through the strength of "Self-Experience" attains immediate identification with Reality is called an aspirant.
22. One who knows the various aspects of experience and acquires the attributes of a yogi (one abiding as Oneness) while not becoming anything, but is just "being" is called an aspirant.
23. One who gives up attachments and with correct spiritual practice realizes That which is the unattainable Absolute Reality, and whose intellect remains fixed in one's Self Nature, is called an aspirant.
24. The one who searches everything and finds the root of God and the devotee, and who succeeds in the immediate attainment of it, is called an aspirant.
25. The aspirant is one who through the power of discrimination effortlessly dissolves himself and becomes invisible. Even though he seems to be visible, he really cannot be seen by anybody.
26. The one who has left the sense of "I" behind, who has discovered one's Self by oneself, and who has crossed over the fourth body (Turya), is called an aspirant.
27. The one who afterwards, in the state of no mind (unmana), meets permanently with one's own Self, and who is the One who sees continuous Self-experience is called an aspirant.
28. The one who breaks through duality, who destroys the appearance of appearances, and who while still having a bodily form is bodiless (videha), is called an aspirant.
29. One who is permanently in the state of being one's Self Nature, who has no ego of bodily activity, and is free from all doubt, is called an aspirant.
30. One who feels the expanse of the five elements to be like a dream, and who is firm in That which is which is without attributes, is called an aspirant.
31. The one who has seen that what was previously felt as fearful in the dream is no longer seen once awakened, and has thereby concluded that everything is false, is called an aspirant.
32. The Illusion that has the feeling of Reality and is felt to be true by the common people, is realized to be unreal in the experience of the aspirant.
33. Like the one who is relieved of the fear felt in a dream upon becoming awake, the aspirant gives up Illusion and rests in Self Nature.
34. The one who has attained the inner state like this and outwardly lives in a state of desirelessness, and who gives up attachment to worldly life, is called an aspirant.
35. The aspirant is one who has become free of lust and anger, and who has dropped arrogance and jealousy.

36. One who has given up the pride of family name, has put to shame the "public shame" of the public's eye (doesn't care for social status), and who nourishes spirituality by the strength of his detachment, is called an aspirant.
37. The aspirant is one who breaks the connection with ignorance, escapes from the bondage of family entanglements, and quickly slips out of the hands of greed.
38. The aspirant is one who is not concerned about greatness or wealth, and is uninterested in personal importance because of the strength of his detachment.
39. The aspirant is one who has broken duality, given up and thrown away the ego, and smashed the enemy named doubt.
40. The aspirant is one who kills the imagination of alternative arguments, who with a mighty blow destroys the ocean of mundane worldly life, and who cuts off and throws away any opposition from all of the five elements.
41. The aspirant scorches the fear of worldly bonds, breaks the legs of time, and beats and breaks the head off of the cycle of birth and death.
42. The aspirant is one who attacks being haunted by bodily identification, annihilates desires, and quickly kills the deception of imagination.
43. The aspirant beats up all inner fear, wins over the subtle body (mind, intellect, thoughts, etc.), and overpowers heretical talk with the power of discrimination.
44. The aspirant has beaten down pride, destroyed selfishness, and has put to destruction the immoral life and shown it to be meaningless by living a virtuous life and upholding justice and morality.
45. The aspirant tears apart temptations, cuts away pain, and throws away sorrows.
46. The aspirant banishes envy, casts away non-devotional feelings, and makes illogical thoughts and behavior flee.
47. For the one who is an aspirant, Self-Knowledge is strengthened by discrimination, conviction becomes firm, and vices are destroyed with the power of detachment.
48. For the one who is an aspirant, the lack of any true religion is wiped out by one's own "Self Religion," (Swadharma) and one's Self Nature. Wrongful deeds are replaced by good deeds, and thoughtlessness is replaced by right thinking.
49. The aspirant enthusiastically crushes hatred, carves out and discards envy, and always remains happy by smashing down sorrows.
50. The aspirant has thrashed down anger, pounded out the scheming from within, and is considered a friend to all of the people of the world.
51. The aspirant has renounced outwardly oriented activities, given up the association of worldly friends, and achieved "Union through Knowledge" (Jnana Yoga) on the path of turning away from worldly concerns.
52. The aspirant deceives the thieves of sense objects, engulfs and puts an end to the wrong knowledge, and frees oneself from relatives who are like robbers.
53. The aspirant gets angry with dependence, wrathful with attachment to affection, and quickly gives up on and abandons excessive hopes.
54. The aspirant merges the mind in Self Nature, makes pain for life's pains, and has established diligence and right effort.
55. The aspirant holds the companionship of studying, sets out to accomplish that which is not easy, and makes the best efforts on the path of spiritual practice.
56. One who is alert and vigilant is an aspirant. He sees with discrimination the permanent and impermanent, and giving up relationships with everyone holds only to the companionship of the saints.

57. With deliberate effort the aspirant gives up worldly life, with discriminating thought gives up all worry, and with purity of behavior removes bad conduct.
58. The aspirant forgets to forget his Self Nature, becomes lazy about laziness, and is inattentive towards doubts.
59. Now, enough of this talk. The one who gives up vices with the help of this explanation is an aspirant. Recognize the signs of an aspirant to be like this.
60. The one who is strong in his renunciation of everything is called an aspirant. Now, in the next sub-chapter, understand the signs of an "Accomplished One" (Siddha).
61. Here a doubt was raised by the listener, who asked, "If only one who is desireless can become an aspirant, is someone who is unable to renounce the family life not able to become an aspirant?"
62. Like this, a question was asked by the listener. What is the answer to this question? Listen to the reply with full attention in the next sub-chapter.

Thus in Shri Dasbodh, a dialogue between the Guru and disciple, Sub-Chapter 9 of Chapter 5, named "The Signs of an Aspirant" is concluded.

Chapter: 5, Sub-Chapter: 10

The Signs of an Accomplished One

|| ShriRam ||

1. Previously, the question was asked if a family man can become an aspirant without renunciation. Dear listeners, hear the answer to this question utilizing the power of discrimination.
2. The way of renunciation for a family man is to keep to a path of good morals and virtuous behavior, and to give up inappropriate behavior.
3. Unless one sacrifices the wrong intellect, proper intellect cannot operate. One should see that renunciation for a householder is like this.
4. Only when one becomes disinterested in the mind, which has the passion for sense objects, can one follow and make progress on the path of Supreme Truth (Paramartha).
5. There must be a renunciation of the lack of faith, renunciation of the doubting mind, and renunciation of ignorance, and this happens step by step.
6. This subtle inner renunciation must be there for both the householder and the one who is without desires. However, for the desireless one, external renunciation has special significance.
7. For the householder, there must be some external renunciation on occasion as well. Some letting go of daily worldly affairs, such as taking some time to listen to spiritual discourses, or having some regular daily spiritual practice or ritual, must occur.
8. Now, the question has been answered, and the doubt cleared. Without some renunciation one cannot be an aspirant. Listen with alertness to the explanation of the subject before us in the sequence of the narration.

9. Previously, I gave the explanation of the signs of an aspirant. Now, I shall tell the signs of an accomplished one.[37]
10. The accomplished one has merged his identity with the Absolute, has banished all doubt from the bliss of Brahman, and is unmovable in his conviction.
11. Understand that the vices of one who is bound are not found in the seeker, and the signs of a seeker are not found in the aspirant.
12. Initially there is doubt in the mind of the aspirant which is later dispelled, and he becomes doubt free. When the aspirant is free from all doubt, he can be recognized to be an accomplished one.
13. Knowledge that is free of all doubt is the sign of a sage. How can there be any doubt, which is a sign of a lower stage, in the one who is accomplished?
14. The path of action is full with doubts, and while doing spiritual practice one is confused by doubts. Doubt is found everywhere. The sage alone is doubtless.
15. Knowledge with doubt is false, detachment with doubt is without power, and worship with doubt is untrue and fruitless.
16. The concepts of God with doubt and devotion with doubt, and the notion of one's True Nature with doubt, are all useless
17. Vows with doubt, pilgrimages with doubt, and spiritual life with doubt are all useless.
18. Devotion with doubt, affection with doubt, and friendship with doubt, are also useless, and only serve to increases doubt.
19. Living with doubt, making decisions with doubt, and all actions done with doubt are useless and done in vain.
20. Reading a spiritual text with doubt, gaining scholastic knowledge with doubt, and listening to ancient scriptures with doubt are all useless. Doubt cannot help one on the spiritual path gain unshakable conviction.
21. Alertness with doubt and doctrine with doubt are as useless as liberation with doubt. It cannot happen.
22. A saint with doubt, a knowledgeable person with doubt, and a well-read listener with doubt are all useless, and lack firm conviction.
23. Greatness in worldly life with doubt, higher education with doubt, and a scholar with doubt are all useless, and without conviction.
24. Without firm conviction everything is unreliable. Everything that falls into the river of doubt is useless.
25. Speech that has no conviction is tiresome and irrelevant. One who speaks without firm conviction babbles on meaninglessly.
26. Let that be enough about doubt. Without any firm conviction, big talk and boasting is all ridiculous. When one has doubt, there can never be satisfaction within.
27. Therefore, know that Self-Knowledge is free of all doubt and is conviction and contentment itself. This is definitely the sign of an accomplished one.
28. At this point, the listener put forth a question. "What is the firm conviction that one should have, and what is the main sign of that conviction? Please explain this to me."
29. Samartha Ramdas answered, "Listen to what this conviction is. Find out the one Supreme God. One should not be confused about God with regard to many gods."

---

[37] The word Siddha means "accomplished." The words Jnani, siddha, sadhu, saint and sage, and are often used interchangeably for one who is Self-Realized.

30. One should think deeply about who has created this entire animate and inanimate universe. With the power of pure discrimination one should recognize the one Supreme God (Parameshwara).
31. Recognize the one Supreme God and the signs of a devotee, and by giving up the identification with what is false, hold to That which is true.
32. Recognize God, and then find out "Who am I?" Give up attachment to the false and remain as the form of the Supreme Self.
33. One should cast off the doubts that one has about being in bondage and gain conviction about liberation. One should examine the elements in creation and see them as temporary and ephemeral.
34. The premise of the final doctrine (siddhanta) should be understood. One should see the end of creation and remain at peace in the conviction of the one Supreme God.
35. Association with the form of the body creates doubt and destroys contentment. One should not swerve from the firm conviction of one's true "Self Form."
36. Accomplishment is Self-Knowledge. Identification with the gross body increases doubt. For this reason, on should hold firm to the contentment of Self-conviction.
37. When remembering body-consciousness, the power of pure discrimination is gone. For this reason, one needs to make the intellect firm in the conviction that one's true identity is the Self.
38. The firm conviction of the intellect fixed in the Self is itself the state of liberation. The fact that "I am the Self," should not be forgotten at anytime.
39. I have explained the signs of conviction, however what has been said cannot be fully understood without the company of saints. Having surrendered to the saints, doubts are completely destroyed.
40. Now, let this talk be enough. Listen to the signs of the accomplished one. Primarily the one who is completely free of doubt is called "accomplished" (a Siddha).
41. The "True Form" of the accomplished one is not the body so how can there be any doubt? Therefore, you should see the Master as being completely without doubt.
42. The quality of being identified with the body has many signs, but for the one who is bodilessness itself, and who has no bodily identification, what signs can be described?
43. How can the attributes of That which cannot be seen with the eyes, be described? The Master is pure Reality, how can he be described by any signs?
44. To have signs means to have attributes. Reality is without attributes (nirguna). That itself is the sign of the accomplished one, the Master, who is the form of Reality.
45. The explanation of signs is given in the chapter on Knowledge, so this talk will end here. I ask the listeners to please excuse anything that is lacking, or anything that has been told in excess.

Thus in Shri Dasbodh, a dialogue between the Guru and disciple, Sub-Chapter 10 of Chapter 5, named "The Signs of an Accomplished One" is concluded.

Chapter 6. The Search for God

Chapter: 6, Sub-Chapter: 1

The Search for God

|| ShriRam ||

1. Now, make your thoughts still, sit quietly for a moment, and become alert so that you may retain what is said.
2. If one wants to stay in some village or country, one has to go and meet the ruler of that area. Otherwise, how can there be satisfaction in that place?
3. Therefore, wherever one wants to stay, one must get to meet the head person there so that everything will be smooth and acceptable.
4. Without meeting with the head person, how can there be any recognition? One's importance will be lost in no time.
5. He may be anyone from a beggar to a king, but someone is the head person there. The wise understand that the proper action is to meet him.
6. If you stay in a city without meeting the ruler, you might be taken away and put into some servitude, or even blamed for some theft one has not committed.
7. So, one who is wise should understand that he must go to meet the ruler, otherwise, to not do so may result in making life miserable.
8. In the city the head of the city is the greatest of the people. Above him, the ruler of the region is greater, and even greater than the ruler of the region is the king of the country. This should be understood.
9. The ruler of the country is the king. Above him, the ruler of many countries is a greater king, and above the greater king is an emperor.
10. There may be one man who is the lord of men, and one man who is a lord of the elephants, and one man who is the lord of horses, and one man who is a lord of land. Above all of these is the emperor who is the greatest king.
11. Okay, so let all of this be as it is. For all of these rulers there is one who has created everything who is called Brahma. But above this, who is the creator of that creator?
12. The one who has created the entirety of creation in the form of Brahma, Vishnu, and Shiva, is the greatest. One should recognize that Supreme God (Parameshwara), by putting in whatever effort is necessary.
13. If one does not come to know that one God, the sufferings of death cannot be avoided. If one does not recognize the "Lord of the Universe," it is not proper.
14. If one does not recognize the God who has put us into this world, and who has created the entire universe, that one is considered to be downfallen.
15. Therefore, recognize God and fulfill your life. If you do not understand this, hold on to the company of saints, and then you will understand.
16. One who knows God is called a saint. He understands what is permanent and what is ephemeral.
17. God is changeless and never has any modification. One whose inner experience is like this, is the one with "Great Experience" (MahaAnubhava) who is called a saint or sage.

18. One who moves around among the people yet speaks differently from the ordinary person, and who is awake in Self-Knowledge, is a sage.
19. Understand that the Supreme Self (Paramatman) that is without attributes is alone what should be called Knowledge. Aside from that, all other knowledge is ignorance.
20. For filling the belly (to make one's living) it is necessary to study various streams of knowledge. This is called knowledge, but with these types of knowledge there is no real fulfillment.
21. One should recognize God. That alone is the only knowledge that is worthwhile. Everything else is totally meaningless "belly knowledge," which is only useful for making a living.
22. The whole life is spent working to fill the stomach and protect the body. Eventually, all of that effort is gone to waste at the time of death.
23. Therefore, the knowledge that is useful only for the purpose of filling the stomach should not be called true knowledge. Only that knowledge with which the omnipresent Reality is immediately realized is "True Knowledge."
24. Understand that only the one who has this Self-Knowledge is considered to be a virtuous gentleman (sajjana). One should ask him how to obtain contentment.
25. When an ignorant person meets with another ignorant person, how can knowledge be found there? When an unfortunate person meets with another unfortunate person, how can any good fortune be found there?
26. When a diseased person goes to another diseased person, how can good health come to him? How can one who is without strength give support to another who is weak?
27. If a ghost meets with another ghost, what worthwhile thing can come out of that meeting? If one arrogant person meets with another who is arrogant, who can make them be able to understand each other?
28. Of what good is going to beg for alms from a beggar, or going for initiation from one who is uninitiated, and how can one observe moonlight during the time of the new moon phase?
29. If an ill-behaved person goes to another ill-behaved person, how will that person ever become well-behaved? If a bound person meets with another bound person, he cannot become an accomplished one.
30. When one who is identified with the body goes to another who is identified with the body, how can he realize bodiless Consciousness? The path of Knowledge cannot be followed without the aid of one who has Self-Knowledge.
31. For this reason, look for one with Self-Knowledge and gain the blessing of his teaching. By investigation into the changeless and the ephemeral, living beings can attain liberation.

Thus in Shri Dasbodh, a dialogue between the Guru and disciple, Sub-Chapter 1 of Chapter 6, named "The Search for God" is concluded.

Chapter: 6, Sub-Chapter: 2

Attainment of Brahman

|| ShriRam ||

1. Listen to the signs of the teachings with which one attains the liberation of "Identification with the Self" (Sayujya Mukti). Looking for many opinions about this is of no use at all.
2. Teachings without the "Knowledge of Brahman" are not important. It is the like husk without the grain that should not be eaten.
3. Such teachings are useless like beating grass that has no grain in it, or churning milk which has no butter in it, or drinking the water used for washing the rice instead of taking the rice itself.
4. It is like eating the hard skin of some fruits, or chewing the fiber of the sugarcane after the juice has been extracted, or eating the coconut shell after having thrown out the kernel.
5. Like in these examples, teachings without the Knowledge of Brahman only cause unnecessary troubles. What wise person will take the unsubstantial thing, giving up the substantial, which is the Essence?
6. Now, the listeners are asked to listen with a pure inner-mind (antahkarana), while I give the explanation about attributeless Brahman.
7. Understand that the structure of the universe is composed of the five elements and that these do not last forever.
8. Understand that at the beginning and at the end, there is only the attributeless Brahman that has as its indication indestructible permanence. Everything else is composed of the five elements and is destructible.
9. When one looks into these five elements, it is seen that they are ephemeral like a ghost[38]. How then can they be called God? If one were to call a human being ephemeral or a ghost, that would be considered a lowly insult.
10. Likewise, to say that the creator of the universe, Paramatman, whose greatness is not understood even by gods such as Brahma and others, is similar to an element is ridiculous.
11. To say that God is like an element is to make an incorrect statement. Only the truly great beings understand correctly.
12. The Lord of the Universe (Jagadisha) is within the five elements of earth, water, fire, air, and space, but also exists outside of them. The five elements are destructible, but the Self is indestructible.
13. Understand that all that has a name is totally an illusion. That which is beyond name or form is understood as Essence through actual experience.
14. The name the "Eightfold Creation" is given to the visible universe because it is made up of eight aspects. The eight aspects are the five elements and the three attributes (space, wind, light, water, earth, rajas, tamas, and sattva).
15. The *Vedas* and *Upanishads* say that the entire visible manifestation is destructible and that the Knowledgeable One (Jnani) realizes the eternal attributeless Brahman.

---

[38] Bhoota is the word for ghost, but it also is the word for element. This play on words is being used to indicate that the elements are insubstantial or ghostlike. The word for the five elements is PanchaBhooti (Panch is five, and bhooti is the plural form of element).

16. It is That which cannot be broken with a weapon, cannot be burned with fire, and cannot be dissolved with water.
17. It is That which cannot be blown away by the wind, which never falls or deteriorates. That which cannot happen or be hidden, is the Absolute Reality, Parabrahman.
18. It has no color and is quite different from everything, yet is continuously existing alone eternally.
19. It does not matter that it cannot be seen. It pervades everywhere. It is present here and there in the most subtle way.
20. Our eyes have the ability to see only what has an appearance. However, one should understand That which is secretly hidden from the eyes.
21. Understand that whatever has an appearance is false, and That which is hidden from the eyes is true. With the help of the words of the Guru, the meaning of this begins to be understood.
22. That which cannot be understood should be understood, which cannot be seen should be seen, and which cannot be known should be known. This is only possible through the power of discrimination.
23. That which is concealed should be uncovered, which is unattainable should be attained, and which is difficult to understand should be studied with perseverance.
24. That extraordinary Absolute Reality which the *Vedas*, Brahma, and Shesha the divine serpent, became completely exhausted trying to describe, should be attained.
25. Now, the question arises, "How *can* That be attained?" The answer to this question is given quite naturally. The Absolute Reality is attained by listening to discourses on Self-Knowledge.
26. It is not earth, it is not water, it is not fire, it is not air, it does have any color, and it is indescribable.
27. It is what should be called "God." To people of a superficial nature there are as many gods as there are villages full of people.
28. One should have definite conviction about God. One must have experiential realization of God without attributes. One has to think deeply and investigate to find this out for oneself.
29. When one says, "This is my body," it should be understood that the one who says this is different from the body. When one says, "This is my mind," it should be understood that the one who says this is different from the mind.
30. When investigating into the nature of the body, it is seen to be made up of only the five elements. By eliminating each element one after another until all are gone, only the Self remains.
31. There is no residence for any "I" as such. It cannot be seen anywhere. The elements are separate and are all in their proper place.
32. The body appears to be a bundle of the five elements tied together. However if one investigates into this with proper thinking and minute observation and unties the body (dissolving the elements), the bundle called the body disappears.
33. This body is made up of elements. Looking into this and thinking it over, it is seen that only the eternal Self can be found. There is no "I" existing there.
34. When the "I" does not exist, how can there be anything called birth or death? When seeing that oneself is the Absolute Reality, there is no place for such things as virtues or vices.

35. Virtues and vices, and the sufferings of death do not exist in That which is attributeless. When one's Self is That which is without attributes, how can birth and death exist?
36. One feels bound by body-consciousness because of the identification with the body. By the power of discrimination one is freed from this body-identification. This is what is called the attainment of the state of Liberation.
37. To know oneself to be the Self without attributes is the fulfillment of life. In order to realize this, one has to look again and again using the power of discrimination.
38. When one is awakened, the dream ends. When seeing with proper discrimination, the visible disappears. Continuous abidance as one's "Self Form" is the salvation of living beings.
39. One must become identified as the Self. With discrimination it is seen that an independent "I" does not exist. Understand that this is what is called self-surrender, or realizing one's true Self-identity.
40. First there is listening to spiritual discourses, then comes serving at the feet of the Sadguru (following his instructions), and finally there is "Identification with the Self" through the blessings of Sadguru.
41. Beyond this "Identification with the Self" there is only the eternal Absolute Reality. This is the inner understanding that the Self always has of itself.
42. With that Self-Realization of Brahman, the sorrow of the worldly life goes away and the fate of the body is effortlessly given up to follow out it's due course.
43. This is called Self-Knowledge. With this Self-Knowledge one obtains complete satisfaction. The devotee is inseparable from the Absolute Reality, Parabrahman.
44. Now whatever happens, let it happen. Whatever is to go, let it go. The doubt about birth and death has now been cleared from the mind.
45. God and devotee are recognized to be one, and the suffering associated with the troubles of worldly life is avoided. Mainly, God is recognized due to keeping the company of the Self-Realized (in satsang).

Thus in Shri Dasbodh, a dialogue between the Guru and disciple, Sub-Chapter 2 of Chapter 6, named "Attainment of Brahman" is concluded.

Chapter: 6, Sub-Chapter: 3

The Appearance of Illusion

|| ShriRam ||

1. The Self is without attributes and pure like space. It is homogeneous, never tainted, and never moving.
2. Brahman is continuous, so it is said that it is not broken. It is larger than the largest, and more vast and subtle than the sky.
3. The Absolute Reality, Parabrahman, cannot be seen or felt. It is That which does not appear nor disappear, and has no coming nor going.
4. The Supreme Reality does not move, nor fall down. It does not get cut, nor does it break. It does not get constructed, nor does it collapse.

5. It is That which is always in front of us untainted and pure. It is spread out everywhere, permeating the space, the sky, the earth and the nether region below the earth.
6. Brahman is That which is indestructible and has no attributes, and Illusion (Maya) is what has attributes and gets destroyed. That which has no attributes (nirguna) and that which has attributes (saguna) are intermixed together.
7. Like the great Royal Swans[39] who select only the milk from a milk and water mixture, the accomplished ones know how to think of this mixture correctly.
8. The five elements are intermingled in the material world, and the Self permeates that entirely. Looking with discrimination into what is permanent and what is temporary, this can be understood.
9. Like with the sugarcane when the juice is extracted, the fiber remnants are thrown away, similarly with discrimination, the "Lord of the World" should be recognized as separate from the world.
10. However, understand that this is just an example. The juice is destructible and fluid, while the Self is permanent and steady. The juice has imperfections and is not complete, whereas the Self alone is pure and complete.
11. There is nothing like the Self that can be used as a good simile. However, in order to help you understand I must give some simile.
12. So, understand that the Self is such that there is nothing similar to it. How then, does Illusion occur in the Self? It is like a puff of air moving in the sky.
13. From the air, came the light. From the light, water came to existence. From the water, the earth was formed.
14. From the earth many beings have been generated. It is not known how many have come into existence, but Brahman pervades all from the beginning through the end.
15. Everything that comes to into existence gets destroyed, but Brahman, which is the origin, remains as it is.
16. For example, there is space existing before the appearance of a pot, and in that space there is the appearance of a pot. When the pot breaks, the space is the same. It is not destroyed by the coming and going of the pot.
17. Similarly, the Supreme Reality is alone, unmoving and immovable. In it, everything animate and inanimate appears and disappears.
18. Brahman is spread out everywhere. It is prior to anything being created, it permeates all that comes into existence, and it remains after everything is destroyed. It is indestructible.
19. This indestructible Brahman is itself the experience of the Knowledgeable Ones (Jnanis). With the dissolution of the elements, one gains oneself by oneself.
20. When the elements are mixed together in a particular way, a form comes into being that is given the name as "the body." The Jnanis examine and analyze each element.
21. Utilizing the power of discrimination, when the elements are examined and cast off leaving nothing remaining, the misidentification with the body vanishes, and one attains the identity of the attributeless Brahman.
22. When the body is examined with discrimination, and one by one the elements are dissolved, it is experienced that there is no "I" that can be found.

---

[39] In Hindu mythology, the Rajhansa, or Royal Swan drinks only the pure milk from a mixture of milk and water.

23. When one searches oneself it is seen that the sense of "I" is illusory. At the end of the elements, what remains alone, is the attributeless Brahman.
24. Attributeless Brahman without the false sense of "I" is the essence of one's true Self-identity. With the separation and dissolution of the elements, the illusion of "me" and "you" also disappears.
25. When one searches for the "I" it cannot be found. Attributeless Brahman is unmoving and is one's own Self. However, this cannot be understood without the Sadguru.
26. When the investigation into Essence and non-essence is thorough, the non-essence disappears. What remains is only the Essence, attributeless Brahman.
27. First is it is explained that Brahman alone is spread out everywhere, permeating everything. Then, it should be understood that when everything that has an appearance is completely destroyed, Brahman alone remains.
28. When with the power of discrimination, Essence and the non-essential have been examined and the non-essential has been discarded, one comes to know oneself by oneself.
29. The sense of oneself as "I" is only imagination. Upon searching into this sense of "me" and "mine," it is understood to not really exist. When this false sense of "I" disappears, one realizes one's true identity as the attributeless Self by oneself.
30. After having gone through the dissolution of the elements the attributeless Self knows itself. How can any "I" be seen after the elimination of the elements?
31. The sense of "me" and "mine" disappears along with the elements. Then the attributeless Self effortlessly remains. The realization of Self-identity is the sense of "I Am That" (Soham).
32. With the realization of one's identity as the Self, having given up the sense of separateness, God and the devotee are one.
33. There is no birth or death, and no virtue or vice in the attributeless. When one realizes oneness with the attributeless, this itself is liberation.
34. Engulfed in the appearance of the elements, the living being gets wrapped up in doubt and forgets himself. In his confusion, he asks "Who am I?"
35. When entangled in the elements he asks "Who am I?" and when he begins looking with discrimination he says "I am That." Realizing Oneness, the concept of "I," as well as the concept "I am That," both disappear.
36. What remains beyond this, is the "True Form" (Swaroopa) of the saints. Understand that it is both in the body and beyond the body.
37. Because the arising of doubts does not disappear, I have had to tell again that which has already been said according to the situation. I ask that the listeners please excuse me.

Thus in Shri Dasbodh, a dialogue between the Guru and disciple, Sub-Chapter 3 of Chapter 6, named "The Appearance of Illusion" is concluded.

Chapter: 6, Sub-Chapter: 4

Narration About Brahman

|| ShriRam ||

Note: The first five stanzas of this sub-chapter outline the entire time-span of creation according to traditional vedic cosmology. In vedic cosmology the time-span of creation is divided into four epochs, or separate divisions of time, called "yugas."

1. The first yuga (Kruta Yuga), is comprised of 1,728,000 years. The second yuga (Treta yuga) is 1,296,000 years long. The third yuga (Dvapara Yuga) is 864,000 years long. Now, we are in the time of the fourth yuga, the Kali Yuga.
2. The fourth yuga is 432,000 years. The passing of 1,000 rounds of these four yugas constitutes 1 day of Brahma.
3. The passing of 1000 days of Brahma constitute 24 minutes of Vishnu. The passing of 1000 of these "24 minutes of Vishnu" make up a fraction of a minute (one pala, or 24 seconds) of the "Almighty God" (Ishwara).
4. When 1000 of these fractions of a minute of God passes, that makes up 12 seconds (half of a pala) of the primordial energy (Shakti). This is the calculation that is given in the ancient scriptures.
5. Like this, the primordial energy, Shakti, comes into existence and passes away an endless number of times. Even with the coming and going of all of this creation, the condition of the Absolute Reality, Parabrahman, remains continuously uninterrupted.
6. To speak about the condition of Parabrahman is just a manner of speech. The *Vedas* and *Upanishads* have already said, "Not this, Not this," with regard to saying anything about Parabrahman.
7. Four thousand and seven hundred years have elapsed in the Kali yuga. The information about the remaining years of the Kali yuga is as follows:
8. 427,240 years are remaining in the Kali Yuga. During this time, there will be many inter-caste marriages. (This calculation was done in the days of Ramdas, probably sometime in the mid to late 1600's, so there would be somewhere around 300 to 350 years less remaining of the current Kali Yuga at the time of the first printing of this English translation of *Dasbodh in 2010AD*.)
9. The animate and the inanimate creation is such that there is always one thing greater than another. When giving thought to it's extent, one cannot find an end to it.
10. Some say that Vishnu is the greatest, some say that Shiva is the greatest, and some say that the primordial energy, Shakti, is the greatest of all.
11. Everyone speaks according to one's own understanding, but know that all will be destroyed with the ending of creation. It is said in the *Vedas* that whatever has an appearance will be destroyed.
12. Many people take pride their own teachings and understanding, but firm conviction cannot be gained without the help of sages.
13. Only the sages have the conviction that the Self permeates everywhere. Everything else that is animate and inanimate is of the nature of Illusion.
14. If a picture is drawn of an army, ask yourself who is great and who is small in that picture.

15. So many things are seen in a dream, and many things are imagined to be small and large in that dream. However, upon becoming awake, look and see what happens.
16. If one gives some thought to what is small and what is big after awakening, the entirety of what was seen is known to have only happened in the dream.
17. The entire thing is only illusory thought, how can there be any small or big? This understanding about small and big is understood by the Knowledgeable.
18. One who is born, dies, saying, "I am great." However, one should investigate into this and see the illusory nature of this appearance.
19. Those who have Self-Knowledge are the truly great beings. Throughout history and in the ancient scriptures they are called sages and saints.
20. The greatest of the great is the one Supreme God (Parameshwara) who is alone. It is in him that the other gods such as Vishnu and Shiva, come and go.
21. He is attributeless and formless, without creation or expansion. The thoughts of space and time are only recent concepts.
22. Name and form, and space and time are all only imagination. All of this will be resolved at the time of the final destruction of the universe.
23. Brahman is beyond all name and form and is indestructible. Brahman remains the same, as it is, regardless of time.
24. Understand that those who who know Brahman completely and give the explanation about Brahman, are the true Brahmins (Brahmanas), the "Knowers of Brahman."

Thus in Shri Dasbodh, a dialogue between the Guru and disciple, Sub-Chapter 4 of Chapter 6, named "Narration About Brahman" is concluded.

Chapter: 6, Sub-Chapter: 5

Narration About Reality and Illusion

|| ShriRam ||

1. The listener asks, "What is this Illusion (Maya) and what is Reality, or Brahman?" Now, please listen to the explanation that is given in this dialogue between the listener and the speaker.
2. Brahman is without attributes and is formless. Illusion has attributes and form. Brahman has no boundaries or limits, Illusion does.
3. Brahman is pure, and changeless. Illusion is active and restless. Brahman alone is untainted by any color or form while Illusion is color and form.
4. Illusion is seen, Brahman cannot be seen. Illusion is perceptible, Brahman cannot be perceived. Illusion gets destroyed, Brahman is indestructible, even at the final dissolution of all creation.
5. Illusion is created, Brahman cannot be created. Illusion can deteriorate, Brahman cannot. Illusion is liked by the ignorant, Brahman is not.
6. Illusion is born, Brahman cannot be born. Illusion dies, Brahman cannot die. Illusion can be conceived of, Brahman cannot comprehended by the intellect.

7. Illusion breaks, Brahman cannot break. Illusion can be cut off, Brahman cannot be cut off. Illusion gets old and tattered, Brahman does get old and tattered as it is indestructible.
8. Illusion is subject to modification, Brahman is changeless. Illusion does everything, Brahman does nothing. Illusion assumes many forms, Brahman is formless.
9. Illusion is of the nature of the temporary five elements and is many, Brahman is eternal and One. The difference between Illusion and Brahman is understood by those who utilize the power of discrimination.
10. Illusion is inferior, Brahman is superior. Illusion is the non-essential, Brahman is the Essence. Illusion is on the side of the world, Brahman does not have sides.
11. All of Illusion is spread out covering Brahman, but the sages have sifted out Brahman.
12. Clearing out the moss, one should take the water. Throwing away the water from the milk and water mixture, one should take the milk. Similarly, giving up Illusion, one's experience should be of Brahman.
13. Brahman is clean and untainted like the sky, Illusion is messy like the earth, Brahman alone is subtle, while Illusion is gross form.
14. Brahman is not observable, Illusion is observable and seen. Brahman is undifferentiated everywhere, Illusion is differentiated forms.
15. Illusion is a visible object, Brahman is not. Illusion is witnessed, Brahman cannot be witnessed. In Illusion there is always two sides (duality), Brahman has no sides.
16. Illusion is the assertion of an argument, Brahman is the final statement. Illusion is ephemeral, Brahman is Eternal. Brahman does not have a cause for its existence, for Illusion there is a cause.
17. Brahman is homogeneous and solid, Illusion is made up of the five elements and hollow. Brahman is always flawless, Illusion is old and tattered.
18. Illusion becomes, Brahman does not become. Illusion falls, Brahman cannot fall. Illusion gets spoiled, Brahman cannot get spoiled. It is just as it is.
19. Brahman always exists, Illusion disappears upon dissolution. Illusion ends, there is no end to Brahman even after the final dissolution.
20. Illusion is hard, Brahman is subtle. Illusion is very small, Brahman is vast. Illusion can be destroyed, Brahman always remains.
21. Brahman cannot really be spoken of, or said to be like anything. Illusion appears to be however it is spoken of. Brahman cannot be extinguished by time while illusion is consumed by it.
22. A multitude of forms and colors are the occurrence of Illusion. Illusion breaks, but Brahman is unbreakable, always just as it is.
23. Now, enough of this narration. The entire animate and inanimate creation is all Illusion. The one Supreme God (Parameshwara) pervades everything.
24. The Supreme Self, Paramatman, is different from qualities, like with the reflection of the sky that is in the water, the sky itself is not found in the water.
25. Through listening to explanations and with the inquiry into Illusion and Brahman one can escape birth and death. When one seeks refuge in the saints, one can attain liberation.
26. There is no limit to talking about the greatness of the saints. Because of them, one gains the inner realization of one's identity with the "Universal Self."

Thus in Shri Dasbodh, a dialogue between the Guru and disciple, Sub-Chapter 5 of Chapter 6, named "Narration About Reality and Illusion" is concluded.

Chapter: 6, Sub-Chapter: 6

Discourse on Creation

|| ShriRam ||

1. "Before creation Brahman was existing. At that time creation did not exist. Now we can see creation. Is it true, or is it false?
2. You are a great sage who knows everything. Please clear my doubt." In this way, the listener pleaded with the speaker.
3. The benevolent speaker who is the knower of everything began to talk, and said, "Now, listen to the answer to your question. Remain alert as I explain."
4. In the *Bhagavad Gita* it is stated that "The Eternal exists in every living being." According to this statement, creation is true.
5. However, according to the statement, "Whatever is seen, gets destroyed," creation is false. Who can decide what is true and what is false?
6. If we say it is true, it gets destroyed. If we say it is false, it is still seen. Now, I shall tell you how it is.
7. In the world there are many varieties of people. Some are ignorant and some are knowledgeable, so it is difficult for one to get satisfactory answers.
8. The opinion of the ignorant is that creation is permanent, and the gods, religion, pilgrimages, and religious vows are all true.
9. The Jnani says that idol worship is for fools. The foolish are ready to bet on the reality of their idols, but where will those idols be after the entirety of creation is dissolved?
10. An ignorant person asks, "Why then should one perform rituals and do chanting, and why sing the praises of the Sadguru and go to various pilgrimage places?"
11. It is advised by Lord Shiva himself to worship the Sadguru. His explanation of the worship of the Sadguru is given in the *Guru Gita*.
12. How is one to worship the Guru? First, one must recognize him. Then, one should gain contentment for oneself by using discrimination as advised by the Guru.
13. The *Guru Gita* states, "When one meditates on the Sadguru, how can the illusory creation remain?"
14. The Jnani speaks like this. When the Sadguru is recognized, one gets the firm conviction that all of creation is unreal.
15. The listener in the audience does not agree with this at all. He begins to argue saying, "How can you say that what Lord Krishna has said is ignorance?"
16. The statement of the *Bhagavad Gita* says, "I am the Eternal in living beings." How can you say that this is ignorance?
17. The listener felt sadness in his mind as he expressed his doubt in this way. The answer to this question should be listened to carefully by the alert listeners.
18. You do not understand what Lord Krishna has said in the *Gita*, therefore you unnecessarily feel worried.
19. Lord Krishna said, "My grandeur is like the great ficus tree." Yet, a tree breaks when it is cut down.
20. My True Form cannot be broken with tools, it cannot be burned with fire, and it cannot be dissolved in water.

21. Meanwhile, the ficus tree can be broken with tools, can be burned with fire, and can be dissolved in water, as it is destructible.
22. The ficus tree breaks, burns, and dissolves. If the Lord is like this, how can there be oneness? The meaning of this can only be understood through the teachings of the Sadguru.
23. Lord Krishna says, "I am the mind among the sense organs." If he says that God is the mind, then why should one control the waves of the restless mind?
24. Lord Krishna said this in order to show steps on the path of spiritual practice, just as one would teach the alphabet. Similar to placing one stone after another.
25. The seeming contradictions in the meanings of his statements are like this. God is the knower of all. Any arguments based on body-identification (thinking oneself to be the body) are of no use.
26. In the *Vedas*, *Upanishads*, and other ancient scriptures there are differences in many of the statements. Only with the teachings of the Sadguru can these differences be resolved.
27. Can anyone resolve the differences in the *Vedas* and other scriptures? No one except the sages can give the correct understanding.
28. The primary proposition or assertion, and the final doctrine are indicated with the use of pointers in the ancient scriptures. However, the definite conviction of the meaning can only be understood through the words of the sages.
29. Diverse and contrary opinions are given as answers to arguments. Each one proclaims to be better than another. The various arguments in the scriptures and *Vedas* are too numerous to tell.
30. Therefore, one should give up arguments, and instead be engaged in spiritual dialogues which aid in gaining the "Bliss of Brahman" as one's own Self-experience.
31. From one concept an endless number of creations appear and pass away. How can the descriptions of these creations be true?
32. God is created out of imagination, and from that one develops a strong feeling towards that God. If anything happens to that imagined God, the devotee is miserable with sorrow.
33. If an image of God is made of stone and one day it gets broken, the devotee is filled with sadness and sorrow and falls down crying and lamenting.
34. Anything can happen to an image of God. It may get lost somewhere in the house, or stolen and taken away, or be broken by ill-behaved people.
35. An image of God may get corrupted, or thrown in water, or taken away and crushed under someone's feet.
36. Or, for example, how would one able to recognize the greatness of a pilgrimage place which has been completely destroyed by mischievous people? One cannot understand what has happened to the great purity that was once there.
37. Some images of God may be made out of gold by a goldsmith or out of metal from a mold, and some may be sculpted out of stone.
38. On the banks of the rivers Narmada and Gandaki there are stones numbering in the millions that are considered to be images of God.
39. In sacred places like Chakratirti, there are countless stones with natural circular corrugations in them that are considered to be images of God. With so many images of God the mind does not get a definite conviction that there is only one God.

40. There are many temples where various things like arrows, rice grains, copper coins and flint stones are worshipped, and the people don't know if these Gods are true or false.
41. One day a person worships a God made of silk thread, and then, when that gets broken, the next day he begins to worship a God formed out of clay.
42. All say, "Our God is the true God, He favors us when we are having difficulties, and fulfills our yearnings and wishes all the time."
43. Then after something happens to their image of God, they say, "Now the state of his purity has gone. Whatever happens is our destiny to happen. Now, it is not possible for our God to change our destiny."
44. What fools! One should see that these are only metal, stones, mud, and wood. How can this be God? All of this type of thinking is only delusion.
45. Like this, fruits are acquired according to one's imagination. The sign of the one true God is altogether different.
46. Everything in creation is Illusion. Creation is false. The *Vedas* and ancient scriptures declare this hundreds of thousands of times.
47. The sages and saints with the highest experience also say that their experience is the same as these declarations. God is beyond the five elements and all of creation is false.
48. Before the appearance of creation, during its existence, and after its destruction, the one eternal God alone exists, at the beginning and the end.
49. This is the definitive conclusion of all. There is no doubt about it. Connection with cause and effect, and negation through nullification all appear in imagination.
50. Out of imagination it is said that there are eight types of creations, or worlds. Listen carefully to the narration of these eight worlds.
51. One is the world of imagination, the second is the world of words, and third is the visible world known to all.
52. The fourth is a world that is painted, the fifth is the dream world, the sixth is the world of celestial beings, and the seventh is the world that is hallucinated due to high fever.
53. The eighth world is the world created from hypnosis. Understand these to be the eight worlds. Which among them can be considered to be superior? Which can be considered to be true?
54. The entire creation is destructible. This is understood by the saints and sages who say that worship of "God with Attributes" (saguna) should definitely be done with firm resolve.
55. One arrives at the certainty of the attributeless (nirguna) only with the help of the one with attributes (saguna). This happens by the power of thinking about Essence and the non-essential in the company of saints.
56. Now, let this talk be enough. One can definitely understand what has been said in the company of the saints. Otherwise, one's thoughts only become restless and full of doubts.
57. At this point, the disciple raised an objection. He said, "I have understood that creation is false, but if all of this does not exist, why is it still seen?
58. What is visible is clearly seen with the eyes and therefore it is felt to be real. Oh Master, tell me, what can one do about this?"
59. A proper reply is given to this in the next sub-chapter. The listeners are asked to listen attentively to the explanation that comes next.

60. Knowing that the entire creation is unreal, one should still respect the one with attributes. Only those who have experienced this sweetness will understand.

Thus in Shri Dasbodh, a dialogue between the Guru and disciple, Sub-Chapter 6 of Chapter 6, named "Discourse on Creation" is concluded.

Chapter: 6, Sub-Chapter: 7

Worship of God With Attributes

|| ShriRam ||

1. The listener asked, "With Knowledge (Jnana), the visible becomes false, so why should one be required to worship God with attributes? What is to be gained by that? Please explain this to me.
2. If there is nothing more superior than Knowledge, then why is worship necessary? What do people attain with worship?
3. The Essence is attributeless (nirguna), and there the one with the attributes cannot be seen. What is the point of worshipping the one with attributes? Please explain this to me.
4. Everything is destructible, so what reason is there to worship what can be destroyed? Who wants to give up the real by worshipping the unreal?
5. Having the experience of Truth, why should one follow any discipline of worship? Why should one go to the trouble of giving up the Real?
6. The verified experience is that one attains liberation only in the attributeless (nirguna). What does the one with attributes (saguna) give? Please, explain this dear Master.
7. You are telling us that the one with attributes is destructible, and at the same time you are saying to do worship. Please tell me, for what reason should one engage in worship and singing praises (singing bhajans)?
8. Out of respect for you Master, I hesitate to ask this question, but this does not make sense and does not seem acceptable. Having attained that which is to be attained, why should one do any further spiritual practices?"
9. The speaker replied, "The listener, being confused, has asked these questions. Now, listen to the reply."
10. To follow the teachings of the Guru is the main sign of spiritual life. To go against the teachings, one will surely meet with adversity.
11. Therefore, one should respect the instructions of the Guru, and accept the worship of God with attributes. Again the listener asks, "What is the need for this?
12. What is to be considered as a reason for any obligation to worship? Has anyone become realized by it, or has God wiped out anyone's fate because of it?
13. Whatever is going to happen is not going to change. Of what use is it that people should worship? When thinking about this, one does not come to any reasonable conclusion.
14. The instructions of the Guru are clear and should be followed. Who can say that he is without authority? However, what is the benefit of this? Please, explain it to me."

15. Upon hearing this, the speaker asks, "Consider carefully, and tell me, what are the signs of Knowledge? After acquiring Knowledge, do you still need to do things in life, or not?
16. You still have to eat meals and drink water, and the activities of passing the feces and urine out of the body also cannot be avoided.
17. You continue to feel that those close to you should remain content, and you continue to recognize those who are close to you and those who are strangers. You do all of this, and yet you feel that you want to break away from worship. What type of Knowledge is this?
18. With the Knowledge born of discrimination, everything is known to be false, yet all of your activities are not given up, so why do you want to only give up the worship of God? Please tell me.
19. You act like a lowly person and bow down to your boss, and yet you do not want to believe in God. What kind of Knowledge is this?
20. Vishnu, Shiva, Brahma and others, are all obedient to God. If you, a mere human being do not worship Him, what does it matter?
21. Lord Rama is our lineage. Lord Rama is the Supreme Truth. He is the most powerful of the powerful, and he has liberated gods.
22. We are his servants. We have acquired Knowledge by serving him. If one does not have any devotional feelings for him, certainly there will be downfall.
23. The Guru tells about the Essence and the non-essential. How can what he says be called non-essential? How can the significance of this thought be conveyed to you? Only the wise understand.
24. Understand that those who contradict the minds of the great realized ones have lost a great fortune, like the luckless person who has been thrown down from holding a kingdom and the throne.
25. One who feels in his mind, "I am great" does not have the "Knowledge of Brahman." If one observes closely, it can be seen clearly seen that he is harboring pride for the body.
26. Understand that the one who claims to be realized, but who does not worship the Reality, and says that he will not worship, has the belief in body-identification remaining hidden inside.
27. If there is no worship, there is no Knowledge (Jnana). The pride for the body (body-identification) is unnecessarily being held. This is not conjecture, but what one actually experiences.
28. Do not be like this. You should begin worshipping Lord Rama. Only then should you speak of the Knowledge of Brahman which is eternal.
29. God with attributes is the one who causes the destruction of proud and malicious people, and who protects devotees. It is like this that the miracle is actually experienced.
30. With Lord Rama's blessings the experience comes that whatever wish you have in the mind gets fulfilled, and all obstacles get totally destroyed.
31. Knowledge is obtained by the worship of Lord Rama, and one's greatness is increased by the worship of Rama. Therefore, you should do the worship.
32. This is already the fact and verified experience, but you don't feel it true. Therefore, you should prove it to yourself and realize it with actual experience.
33. Start every task by remembering Lord Rama, and it is immediately successful. Keep it in the mind that Rama is the real doer.

34. "The doer is Lord Rama, and not myself. There is no me." Like this, one offers everything including oneself to God with attributes, and only then does one become identified with the attributeless and actually become attributeless oneself.
35. If you say that you are the doer, then you will not get success. If you are looking for the true experience, then you can verify it immediately.
36. If you say, "I am the doer," you only become tired. By saying that Rama is the doer, one obtains success, fame and power.
37. If one has the feeling that "I am the doer," there is a feeling of being cut off from God. When one feels that God is the doer, then one feels blessed.
38. We exist only for a few days, but the existence of God is for a long time. We are known to but a few, but God is known in all the three worlds.
39. For this reason, many people respect the one who worships Rama. Even Brahma and the most prominent and respected people are eager to sing the praises of Rama.
40. If we who are devotees do not respect the worship of God with attributes because of our Knowledge, then there will be downfall because of the lack of devotion.
41. If because of pride one ignores the greatness of God, then it is he who suffers a loss. This is incorrect understanding and is not acceptable for the great ones.
42. With the worship of God one's body-identification is diminished, and with discrimination the sense of "I" does not remain. In this way, one becomes virtuous.
43. Everything is known to be false through the worship of Lord Rama. The visible world appearance is like a dream from the perspective of the Knowledgeable Ones (Jnanis).
44. Just as the occurrences of the events in a dream are unreal, the saints and sages know that the visible world is false.
45. Here, the listener raises an objection. "If it is false, then why does it still appear to us?" The answer to this is given in the next sub-chapter.

Thus in Shri Dasbodh, a dialogue between the Guru and disciple, Sub-Chapter 7 of Chapter 6, named "Worship of God with Attributes" is concluded.

Chapter: 6, Sub-Chapter: 8

Dissolution of the Visible World

|| ShriRam ||

1. Previously, the listeners had asked, "If the visible is false, then why is it still seen?" Now, I will tell the answer to this. Please listen attentively.
2. For the Jnani what is seen is not presumed to be real simply because it is seen. It is the dull-minded foolish and ignorant beings who consider what is seen to be real.
3. If what is seen with the eyes is considered to be real, then thousands of spiritual texts, and the teachings of great saints and sages must be considered false.
4. If only what I see with my own eyes is considered to be true, everything said here and other places is considered to be mistaken or foolish, and one gets filled with doubts. One should not be filled with such doubts.

5. The deer sees a mirage and runs after it thinking it to be real. Who can convince the deer that the water seen there is not real?
6. In a dream it is seen that one has found a large sum of money and has made many transactions with many people. How can what happened in the dream be considered as true?
7. If a skillful artist creates a painting with many wonderful colors, there arises a great love inside one for the images upon seeing it. However, what is actually there is only colored mud.
8. In the low light of nighttime, one may see images of many women, elephants and horses and the mind gets fascinated by them. However when seen in the daylight, they are seen to only be hides that have been hung out.
9. There may be statues that are made to look very realistic and felt to be very beautiful, but they are only made from wood and stone.
10. On many temples there are statues of women with beautiful bodies that appear to be looking at you with expressive eyes. Seeing these statues one feels enchanted by their beauty, but the only thing there is cement (made from lime, sand, and jute).
11. In a theatrical play about the ten incarnations of God, the properly dressed male actors play the roles of beautiful women using their eyes artistically. However, they are really always only men.
12. The entire creation is very colorful but it is unreal. The activity of many visible forms is seen and felt to be true, however you should understand that this is ignorance.
13. The false appears to be real, but this must be inquired into. If something appears in front of one's eyes when their vision is affected, how can that be considered real?
14. If one looks up, it appears that the sky is facing downwards all around us. If we look at the reflection of the sky in a pool of water, it looks like the sky is facing upwards and the stars are shining inside the water, but all of this is not true.
15. A king may have sculptors make statues that look exactly like people, and the statues might even be mistaken for those people, but they are all not real.
16. Whatever is seen is reflected in the pupils of the eyes, and it appears that the image is there in the eyes, but there is not really anything there in the eyes. How can that be considered real?
17. There are many reflections of surrounding images that appear in bubbles as they arise. In a fraction of a second they burst, and the images disappear and are seen to be false.
18. If one holds many mirrors in one's hands, just as many images of his face will appear as there are mirrors, but those are all unreal. In the beginning and at the end, there is only one face being reflected.
19. If something is seen floating down a river, it appears that there is second thing that is underneath it which is being seen reflected upside down in the water. Or similarly, when a loud sound is made, the sound of an echo is suddenly produced.
20. On the shore of a lake or some body of water there are many animals, birds, human beings, monkeys, trees and other objects that can be seen, and they appear to be both on the land and in the water.
21. If a weapon is moved around very fast, it appears that two weapons are being seen, or similarly if the strings of an instrument are played, their vibration makes them appear as two strings.

22. If there is a gathering in a hall with large mirrors, it appears to double the size of the room, or if many lamps are lit, they cast many shadows of a single object.
23. Like this, there are many ways in which something appears to be real, but how can one say that because of its appearance it is truly real, and believe it?
24. One should know that Illusion (Maya) is a like a magic trick. It appears to be real but it should not be considered to be true.
25. If the false is felt to be true and someone says, "Why should there be any examination of what is felt to be true?," you should know that this is said out of ignorance.
26. The magic tricks of human magicians are felt to be real by many people, but in the end they are seen with certainty to be false.
27. Similarly, in mythology, the magic spell of a demon was felt to be real by Lord Rama, who was deceived into following after a deer.
28. It's said that some demons can change their bodily forms, or that one demon can become many, such as in the story of where many demons were born from drops of blood.
29. There is the legend of how demons adopted various forms, and then in crafty ways entered the place called Dwarka, and were killed by Lord Krishna.
30. It is told of how the crafty demon Ravana made a fake head of Lord Rama and created a beautiful false monastery by his magic.
31. There are stories of demons with such crafty ways in magic that they could not even be controlled by the gods, and in the end, Shakti, the primal power eventually destroyed them.
32. Like this there are many stories about the tricks of demons that could not even be understood by the gods. Their art of deception is incomprehensible.
33. Human beings perform what is called trickery or misdirection, the demons perform magic, and what God does, which is strange in many ways, is called Illusion.
34. This Illusion appears as if it is real, but upon investigation into it, it disappears. Even though it is known to be false, its appearance continues to be seen.
35. If we say that it is true, it still gets destroyed. If we say that it is false, it is still seen. Whichever way it is told, the mind disbelieves both things.
36. One should understand that Illusion is not real. One should think deeply about the unreality of Illusion and understand that all appearances are like a dream.
37. Please listen. If Illusion is felt by you to be real, know that this is a mistake.
38. The illusion of what is visible is due to ignorance. The body is a part of this illusion, so there is lack of discrimination with regard to it.
39. The visible is seen with the eyes and the mind fixates on that illusion as being true. In this way, the subtle body is made up of ignorance (of the Self).
40. It is ignorance that sees ignorance and then believes that the things that are seen are true. The body is an accumulation of ignorance.
41. To think that "I am the body" is the sign of body-identification, and as a result of this concept the visible world seems to have become real.
42. There is one concept that the body is real, and another concept that you are certain that the visible is true. Together, these two notions create a huge amount of doubt.
43. If you hold strongly to body-identification and try to make an earnest effort to see Brahman, the belief in the visible appearances are an obstruction on the path of Absolute Reality.

44. When having a strong conviction that visible appearances are real, you will quickly see what a big mistake has been made.
45. Now, let this be enough of this talk. Brahman cannot be attained with the notion of an individual "I" intact. The belief in the visible world is the sign of body-identification.
46. The body made up of bones has an eye which is made of flesh, and it wants to see Brahman with that eye. Such a person as that is not knowledgeable, but a mere blind fool.
47. All that is seen with the eyes and appears to the mind gets destroyed over a period of time. The Supreme Reality, Parabrahman, is beyond what is visible.
48. Parabrahman is that which is Eternal. Illusion is temporary. This is a conclusive declaration that is stated in many scriptures.
49. The explanation of the signs of body-identification and how one has come into the wrong conception of who one is will be told next.
50. One should understand "Who am I?" Giving up the false sense of "I" (ego) one should be "Oneness" alone. Then, naturally contentment will be acquired within oneself.

Thus in Shri Dasbodh, a dialogue between the Guru and disciple, Sub-Chapter 8 of Chapter 6, named "Dissolution of the Visible World" is concluded.

Chapter: 6, Sub-Chapter: 9

In Search of Essence

|| ShriRam ||

1. There is a great wealth that is hidden, but what do the servants know of it? They only have the knowledge of what is seen on the outside.
2. A great treasure is kept hidden, but only many outwardly visible things are seen. The wise ones know to search for one's inherent wealth within.
3. Like this, the visible appearances are illusory. All people are looking only at Illusion. However, those who know how to use discrimination know how to see beyond appearances.
4. When a treasure is kept inside a lake that is filled with water, the people seeing it say that the lake is filled with only water. Those with the capacity to know understand what is really inside.
5. Similarly, only the Knowledgeable Ones (Jnanis) are capable of knowing the Supreme Truth, while others are selfish in their pursuit of visible objects.
6. The laborers carry heavy loads, but only the rich people enjoy the profits of precious gems. Like this, everyone gets according to their fate.
7. Some make their living out of collecting wood and some collect cowdung. However, the truly wealthy are not like that, they enjoy the Essence.
8. Those who utilize the power of investigative thought become seated on a platform of happiness, while others feel close to the burden of the world and die while carrying it.

9. Some eat the divine food (of Self-Knowledge), and some eat any kind of dirty food while taking pride in (the identification with) their accomplishments.
10. The Essence is taken by the great ones while others fruitlessly carry the burden of the non-essential. Those who are knowledgeable understand the Essence and the non-essential.
11. Hidden are the wish-fulfilling stones of alchemy while the pebbles and glass beads lie out in the open. Hidden are the mines of gold and precious gems while stones and mud are out in the open.
12. A conch that turns to the right side, the vine that grows in the right direction, and precious herbs are hidden, while common shells and castor and thorn apple plants are readily seen out in the open.
13. A wish-fulfilling tree is not seen anywhere, but the common milk bush trees are spread around everywhere in plenty. Seeing the scented sandalwood tree is rare, but the berries and trees of the gum arabic tree are plentiful.
14. The divine wish-fulfilling cow is known to Lord Indra while the common people see only the world filled with ordinary cattle. Kings enjoy according to their fate and other people according to their fates.
15. People do all sorts of various businesses and call themselves rich, but no one can compare their wealth to that of the "God of Wealth."
16. Like that is the Knowledge of the realized one. He is the God of the hidden treasure while others are slaves to their bellies who constantly seek out different opinions.
17. It is the Essence that is unseen and only the non-essential that is seen by people. This understanding regarding the Eternal and the ephemeral is known to the sages.
18. What is the point of telling this to ordinary people? Who among them knows the True from the false? The saints and sages know the signs of saints and sages.
19. One cannot see the hidden treasure unless one's vision is made clear. The Supreme Self that is hidden should be sought in the company of saints and virtuous people.
20. In the company of rich people, one can easily become rich. Similarly, by keeping the company of saints, Reality is easily realized.
21. Reality meets Reality while confusion meets with confusion. When looking with correct thinking one comes into correct thoughtfulness.
22. With right thought, the entire visible world is seen to be ephemeral. The Supreme Self is changeless and endless, and is different from all visible appearances.
23. Paramatman is different from the visible and within the visible. It is the Self that permeates the entire animate and inanimate creation. One gains conviction within when seeing with right thought.
24. Without abandoning the family life, and without giving up the title of a householder, the life being lived among people can only become fulfilled by utilizing right thought.
25. This advice is based on experience. One should gain experience using the power of discrimination. Those who see experientially this way are wise and others are not.
26. There is a great difference between one's own direct experience versus theory and speculation, or funds in credit versus money in cash, or direct perception of God versus a mental concept of God.
27. The concept that realization will be in the future or in the next life, like some obligation to be paid by God in the future, is totally without substance. The power

of discrimination between the Eternal and the ephemeral, where one's gain is immediate, is not like that.
28. With right thought the benefit is immediate. The living being is freed from worldly life and all the doubts about birth and death are wiped away.
29. In this very life, one can be aloof from worldly life and immediately attain liberation in the moment and remain permanently established in one's True Nature.
30. One who disagrees with this statement as being baseless, even if he is one who is accomplished, will experience a downfall. To the one who says that this is false, I swear to them it is true on the strength of my worship.
31. This talk is full of deep meaning. Become liberated quickly through the power of discrimination. Be among the people, but don't be anything at all (be in the world while being out of it).
32. The state of God is attributeless. Stabilization in the state of God is itself the meaning of complete pervasive contentment.
33. One becomes "without a body" (videha) even though within the body, and even though one is doing, he is not doing anything. The signs of the liberated ones are known by the liberated ones.
34. For others, what has been said does not appear to be true. By only utilizing guesswork and imagination one always feels doubtful. The root of doubts are cleared away by the teachings of the True Master, the Sadguru.

Thus in Shri Dasbodh, a dialogue between the Guru and disciple, Sub-Chapter 9 of Chapter 6, named "In Search of Essence" is concluded.

Chapter: 6, Sub-Chapter: 10

The Indescribable

|| ShriRam ||
1. The listener asks, "What is this satisfaction which is said to be like nothing else, and which cannot be described? Please explain fully what it is.
2. If a mute person eats sugar, he cannot describe its sweetness. Please explain to me what this means.
3. If we ask about the experience of this satisfaction, it is said that it cannot be told in words. Whom can we ask for the answer?
4. Everyone says things which cannot be understood, and the experience does not come to me. Please do something in such a way that the correct thoughtfulness is established with certainty."
5. In this way, the listener asked these questions. Now I shall explain the answer. Listen alertly with your full attention.
6. Is that which is called "the place of satisfaction," merely an experience, or is it one's pure "Self Nature" (Swaroopa)? I shall make it perceptible through speech.
7. It is "That" which cannot be expressed in words but cannot be understood without being spoken about. On trying to imagine or conceive of it, imagination itself gets destroyed.

8. That Supreme Reality, Parabrahman, which is the great secret of the *Vedas* should be understood. It is only by keeping the company of saints that everything is understood.
9. Now I shall tell about that which gives deep satisfaction. Listen to what is being said coming out of the experience of Reality, which is beyond description.
10. To know the sweetness of sugar, one has to be given sugar. Similarly, to understand That which is being described but cannot be described is not possible without the Sadguru.
11. One who searches oneself begins to understand through the teachings of the Sadguru. Such a one goes on to gain the natural understanding and experience of Reality.
12. With firm intellect, one must first find one's own Being. With that, suddenly there is samadhi (absorption in Being).
13. When correctly finding one's own root, the sense of an individual "I" is known to be illusory. What remains is the Reality, which is satisfaction itself.
14. The "primary premise" is that the Self is the witness of all. This has been said in the *Vedas*. However, the "final understanding" is attained by the accomplished ones (the Siddhas) alone.
15. If one tries to attain the "final understanding" with the state of being the witness of all, this is just a state, while the Self is beyond any state. It is stateless.
16. When the knowledge of objects gets wiped out, the seer no longer exists as an individual seer. At that time, the ego, that is the conceit of "I," disappears.
17. Where the sense of "me" disappears, that itself is the sign of the experience of the satisfaction which cannot be described in words.
18. This talk is one of extraordinary thoughtfulness. Even so, the words are all illusory, empty, and superficial. The meaning alone, is what is deep.
19. Because of the words, the meaning is understood. Once the meaning is understood, the words become useless. What the words tell about is That which is full of meaning, but the words themselves are false.
20. Because of the words, the thing becomes apparent. Upon seeing the thing, the words disappear. The words are empty, while the meaning is sustained.
21. Grain is protected because of the husk. The grain is kept and the husk is thrown away. Similarly, words are like the husk and the meaning is the grain.
22. The Essence, which is the grain, is contained within the outer shell. When the grain is removed, the empty shell is discarded. Similarly, in relation to Parabrahman, words are like husks which are abandoned.
23. The simile of the word making the meaning apparent is not totally accurate because while it is true that after the words are spoken, the meaning is apparent, even before any words were spoken, the meaning was existing.
24. Giving up the husk of the words, take the grain of pure meaning which is "Self-experience."
25. When we use the statement "That which is different from the visible," this is what is meant by using words. The meaning of the statement is what should be understood, and that is "Pure Understanding."
26. Similarly, that "Pure Understanding" should be understood to be itself the primary premise, which is the inconceivable Self-experience that cannot be understood.
27. Sometimes it is said that what remains after the sky is strained through a sieve is the experience of Essence, but this concept is only a creation of imagination.

28. The untrue is what is born out of imagination, so how can there be Reality in it? Really, there is no place at all for experience.
29. It is wrong to say that one can get an experience without duality. For this reason, there is no place for experience (in Oneness).
30. In experience, the three factors[40] are present (experiencer, experiencing, and object of experience), but in non-duality, duality is not present. Therefore, the term "beyond words" is appropriate.
31. The root cause of the appearance of day and night is the sun. If the sun was removed, what would there be to say about day and night?
32. The thought of speech and silence exists due to Omkar (the reverberation of Om). If the OM sound itself is not there, what pronunciation can be made?
33. The experience and the experiencer exist because of Illusion. If Illusion does not exist, then what can be said about experience?
34. If we say that "I" am one thing, and an "object" is another, there is differentiation (the experience of separateness). Only if there is experience, is it possible to speak about discrimination.
35. The mother of separateness (Maya) is false like a daughter of a barren woman. Therefore, there is no separateness. Unity is what is original.
36. The unborn was sleeping, and in a dream, he saw a dream where he went to the Sadguru and surrendered the sorrows of the worldly life.
37. With the blessings of the Sadguru, the worldly existence is known to be false. Having gained Self-Knowledge, one asks, "Where is the basis for ignorance?"
38. Whatever was existing never became existent, and that which was non-existent disappeared into nothingness. Thus, when that which is and that which is not are both gone, "That" which remains cannot be said to be nothing or anything.
39. Beyond nothingness is Pure Knowledge that is satisfaction itself. It is the singularity which is not different from the spontaneous state of Beingness.
40. With the explanation of non-duality, duality gets dissolved. When talk about Self-Knowledge is going on, awakening takes place.
41. The listeners are asked to be alert and apply the mind to the meaning of what is being said so that there may be inner understanding, and you may gain true satisfaction.
42. Whatever was said about Self-Knowledge has all disappeared like a dream. What remains is the indescribable happiness, beyond description.
43. There is oneness without words, with neither any experience nor an experiencer. Like this he is awakened.
44. There, he saw the dream within a dream, and he became awake by awakening. Words are a failure there, and the end of that awakeness cannot be found.
45. The root of this explanation will be given again in a simple and direct manner so that you may gain a clear understanding of this inner satisfaction.
46. Then the disciple requested, "Yes Master, please tell us again what you have explained up to now.
47. Please give the explanation again so that the signs of this experience of satisfaction may be known.

---

[40] The three factors, or "Triputi," are always there when there is experience. For example, the trio of observer, observing, and observed, or knower, knowing, known, etc. It is for this reason that the emblem of Shiva is marked with three lines, representing that all of the three aspects are within him, and yet He is beyond them.

48. Who is the one who is not born? How did he see the dream? How is the explanation given in the dream?"
49. Recognizing the respect of the disciple, the Master gives the answer. The listeners should now listen to that answer with focused attentiveness.
50. Dear disciple, listen with attentiveness. Know that the one who is unborn is you, yourself. You have seen the dream in the dream. Now, I shall tell you about this.
51. You should understand that the thought of the dream in a dream is this worldly life. You have come here and utilized thoughtfulness with regard to the Eternal and the ephemeral.
52. Having surrendered to the Sadguru you are taking part in pure discourse with the confirmation of actual experience, and this is happening right now.
53. In the experience of this talk, you understand that whatever has been spoken is false. Resting in the most profound stillness, you will understand awakeness.
54. When all of the noise of the talk about Knowledge has subsided, the meaning is apparent. Giving thought to this, the inner experience is naturally present.
55. You feel that you have acquired this awakeness, and that "this experience has happened to me." This is merely delusion that has not yet disappeared.
56. To say that the experience has dissolved in the experience, and that there is experience without the experiencer, this also is a part of the dream, and indicative that you have not yet awakened, my dear one.
57. If after having awakened from the dream, you say that the "I was the unborn one in the dream," this indicates that the dream's effects, and the memories and feelings of the dream are not yet gone.
58. If in the dream one feels that one is awake, this is a sign of experience in the dream. You feel you that it is true that you are awake, but this is still of the nature of delusion.
59. Awakeness is beyond this. How is it possible to describe That in which even the power of the discrimination does not function?
60. Understand that this satisfaction cannot be described in words. Recognize the sign of it is wordlessness.
61. Total satisfaction is like this. Understand that it cannot be described. With this explanation, there is the coming into this wordlessness.

Thus in Shri Dasbodh, a dialogue between the Guru and disciple, Sub-Chapter 10 of Chapter 6, named "The Indescribable" is concluded.

Chapter 7. Fourteen Brahmans

Chapter: 7, Sub-Chapter: 1

An Auspicious Introduction

|| ShriRam ||

1. Lord Ganesha is the most ancient ancestor of the learned. With the head of an elephant, he is single tusked, has three eyes and four arms, and wields an axe in one hand.
2. From the "Lord of Wealth" comes wealth, from the *Vedas* comes the knowledge of Reality, and from the "Goddess of Fortune" comes good fortune.
3. Similarly, all streams of knowledge come from the origin, Lord Ganesha, who came first. It is due to him that many poets and writers become skillful and write with authority.
4. Just as the children of the rich and powerful look beautiful with many beautiful adornments, the poets write beautifully due to his power. He is the primordial ancestor.
5. Let us bow respectfully to Lord Ganesha, who is like a full moon shining with the light of Knowledge. Because of him, the sea of spiritual Knowledge is full like at high tide.
6. He is the beginning of the power and capability of doing. He is the Original Being, the Primordial Beginning. He is Brahman, which is beyond the visible, and is self-existent, in the beginning and at the end.
7. From his wish is born the young woman who is the "Goddess of Knowledge" (Sharada) who is like a stream in a mirage that flows due to the presence of the sun.
8. She entangles one even though she is false. She is very attractive in her illusory activity, and surrounds even the speaker with her sense of illusory separateness.
9. She is the mother of duality, yet she is also the mine of non-duality. She is the Original Illusion (Moolamaya) that is the covering of an endless number of universes.
10. She is like a very huge vine which grows without any effort and on which a limitless number of universes reside. She is the mother of Primordial Being (Purusha) in the form of a daughter.
11. I bow to this Sharada, who is the mother of the *Vedas*, and who is the power of Original Primordial Being. Now I shall remember the powerful Sadguru.
12. It is the Sadguru who offers his blessings and showers the disciple with bliss. It is because of him that the entire creation becomes filled with happiness and bliss.
13. He is the creator of bliss. He is the authority of "Liberation through Identification with the Self" (Sayujya Mukti), and the one who bestows oneness with Brahman. He is the brother of those who are friendless.
14. The seeker of liberation is like the chataka[41] bird who sings softly to the sky for rain, and the Guru is like the sky which showers the waters of his blessings on the aspirant.

---

[41] The chataka bird is thirsty for the rainwater. He longs and waits and cries, looking towards the sky for the rain shower. Only when it rains does his longing for water become pacified.

15. The Guru is the ship of correct understanding that carries one to the other shore of worldly life. He is the great support for devotees in the whirlpool of worldly existence.
16. He is the ruler of time who provides relief from life's calamities. He is the mother of the devotees who is exceedingly affectionate.
17. He is the support of spiritual seekers that is the Life which is not of this world. He is the place of rest, and the comfort of one's residence that is of the nature of happiness itself.
18. Like this is the Sadguru who is whole and complete. He breaks the delusion of duality and body-consciousness completely. I lay in prostration to him.
19. Finally, I pay respect to the saints, sages and virtuous people. Now, the listeners should remain alert and attentive while listening to the continuation of the narration.
20. As was being explained previously, the world appearance is a long dream. However, people babble on out of greed, how "this is my wife," or "my wealth," or "my daughters and sons," and they become entangled in this dream
21. Like this, when the "Sun of Knowledge" sets, the light fades, and the entire universe is filled with the darkness of ignorance.
22. When there is no light of Truth by which a correct path can be shown, the effect is that nothing but delusion can be seen.
23. Due to the identification with the body and intellect, such people are sleeping (in ignorance) and snoring aloud, crying with grief because of the sorrows associated with their attachment to sensual pleasures.
24. People such as this die asleep in ignorance, and as soon as they are born they are asleep again. Many people have come and gone in this way.
25. In the sleep of ignorance, many have continued along in the cycle of births and deaths, and because they did not know the Supreme God, they suffered many hardships.
26. To do away with the varieties of hardships one must have Self-Knowledge. Therefore, the explanation of Self-Knowledge is given in this text.
27. Among all the streams of knowledge, the essential knowledge is that which contains the thoughts about Self-Knowledge. This has been stated by Lord Krishna in the tenth chapter of the *Bhagavad Gita*.
28. It is for this reason that this text on non-duality, which is a discourse on Self-Knowledge and Supreme Truth, has been written. The one who listens to what is said here with the totality of his being is the one who is capable of realization.
29. However, the one whose mind is restless should not give up this text. Leaving this text aside will make the real meaning contained here unattainable.
30. One who is engaged in spiritual life should become familiar with this text. If one searches here for Supreme Truth, conviction about the Self will be gained.
31. One who is not on the spiritual path will not understand the deeper meaning found here, like one who is blind and without sight cannot comprehend a place of wealth.
32. Some say that because this book was written in the Marathi language virtuous people should not listen to its contents. Such statements are made by the foolish who do not understand the sequence of what is said and the meaning of the words.
33. A box made of iron has many valuable jewels contained inside, but the unfortunate one throws it away saying that it is only an iron box.

34. Similarly, the language of this text is Marathi, but the meaning is that of Vedanta and of "Final Understanding" (Siddhanta). Not knowing this, one who is of dull intelligence is deluded and abandons this text.
35. If wealth is found suddenly and without any effort, it is foolishness to give it up. Take the wealth and don't bother about what the container looks like.
36. It should be considered good fortune if a magic stone is found in the courtyard, or a rare vine with medicinal qualities is seen in a well.
37. Similarly, the knowledge and experience of non-duality comes easily when explained in Marathi. Spiritual knowledge is being made easily available and can be verified immediately, so one should definitely take it without hesitation.
38. The secret of keeping the companionship of saints is that the real meaning of scriptures becomes easy without making strenuous efforts of scholastic learning.
39. That which is not understood through scholastic education can be realized in the company of saints and virtuous people where the meaning of all the scriptures is grasped in one's own experience.
40. The companionship of saints and virtuous people is very beneficial. The real secret to the fulfillment of life cannot be acquired though scholastic endeavors.
41. Even if the explanation is translated in a different language (Sanskrit to Marathi, or Marathi to English), the meaning is not lost. What is being accomplished in this text has to do with the preservation of the meaning.
42. It is because of the commonly spoken Marathi language that the meaning of the Sanskrit words is revealed. Otherwise, who would understand the secret meaning of a language which is not one's own?
43. Now, let this be enough of this talk. Abandoning the language, understand, and keep the meaning, just as one would take the best of the fruit and give up the skin and the shells.
44. The meaning is what is essential, the language is unimportant. Because of pride in the knowledge of Sanskrit, one will only labor unnecessarily to arrive at the meaning by searching through scriptures. Different types of pride such as this are only obstructions on the path of liberation.
45. While on the search for the meaning, how can one place importance on the word over the meaning? One's emphasis should be on the realization of the unimaginable greatness of God.
46. The speech of a mute person is only known to himself. Similarly, to know the signs of "Self-experience," one must be Self-experience.
47. Where can a listener who knows the real meaning of spiritual life be found, so that the explanations about it are satisfying?
48. When a gem is placed in front of one who knows the value of gems, one derives satisfaction from that gem, similarly one feels like speaking about Self-Knowledge to the knowledgeable.
49. The restless mind is entangled in the net of Illusion. Explanations are of no use for those who are engrossed in worldly life. They cannot understand the meaning of what is being said.
50. One who is totally engrossed in worldly affairs cannot understand the explanations given here. Alertness and attentiveness are what is required for understanding.
51. One accepts many types of gems and many coins. However, if one is not attentive he will be fooled, and will take a loss if what is accepted is not examined properly.

52. Similarly, one will not understand the meaning of the explanations if only looking superficially, even if the explanation is being given in simple Marathi language.
53. Where the words of the explanation are spoken from Self-experience, such a spiritual discourse is even deeper than something said with Sanskrit words.
54. One should recognize what Illusion is and what Brahman is. That is what called is spiritual science. First one should understand one's "True Form" (Swaroopa) and with that understanding, one should know the nature of Illusion.
55. Illusion is with attributes and form, and is constantly changing. Understand that Illusion is the expanse of the five elements.
56. Illusion is visible and apparent to the eyes. It is but a false perception that appears to the mind. Illusion is momentary and is destroyed when viewed with proper discrimination.
57. Illusion is the many forms that appear in the world. Illusion is the "Self-Form" of Lord Vishnu. The extent of Illusion is so vast that it is more than what can be said about it.
58. Illusion takes on many forms and colors. Illusion is the companion of God as well. If one goes looking for Illusion, it appears to be uninterrupted, continuous, and pervading everywhere.
59. The composition of the entire creation is illusory. Illusion is one's own imagination. It cannot be broken without Self-Knowledge.
60. Like this, I have given a short explanation about Illusion by way of some small indications. Now, the attitude of the listener must remain alert and attentive.
61. What is to come next is an explanation of Brahman. With the explanation of the "Knowledge of Brahman" the perception of Illusion is dispelled with one stroke.

Thus in Shri Dasbodh, a dialogue between the Guru and disciple, Sub-Chapter 1 of Chapter 7, named "An Auspicious Introduction" is concluded.

Chapter: 7, Sub-Chapter: 2

Explanation of Brahman

|| ShriRam ||

1. Brahman is formless and without attributes. Brahman is without any association or modification. The sages say that there is no limit or end to Brahman.
2. In the scriptures it is told that Brahman is all-pervading, it is the One in the many. With discrimination Brahman is known to be Eternal.
3. Brahman is unmoving and endless. Brahman is always pure without imagination or doubts.
4. Brahman is different from the visible as well as different from the void, or nothingness. Brahman cannot be known through the medium of the senses.
5. Brahman cannot be seen with the eyes. For the foolish, Brahman is not there. Brahman cannot come to be experienced without a sage.
6. Brahman is greater than everything. There is nothing more essential than Brahman. It is subtle and beyond the senses. It is not known even to the Creator (Brahma) and other gods.
7. In words it is said that Brahman is like this and like that, but it is beyond comparison and different from anything that can be said about it. However, by listening to spiritual discourses and by studying, one can attain Brahman.
8. There are endless names for Brahman, but Brahman is beyond all names. To make any comparison of Brahman to any visible object is not suitable.
9. When seeing what is true, there is nothing other than Brahman. It is not possible at anytime to make a statement of comparison about Brahman.
10. In the *Upanishads* (Vedanta) and the "final doctrine" (Siddhanta) it is stated that speech returns from Brahman, and that it is not comprehensible by the mind.
11. Everything that the mind sees is in the form of imagination. In Brahman imagination does not exist. The "Great Statements" (Mahavakyas) of the *Vedas* are not false.
12. Now, the question naturally arises, "How can one acquire that which cannot be acquired by the mind?" If this question arises, the reply must be that "Such rare accomplishment cannot happen without the Sadguru."
13. A storehouse may be packed full, but it is locked. If one does not have the key, nothing inside is available.
14. The listener asks the speaker, "What is the meaning of this, what is that key?"
15. The Sadguru's blessing is the key. Due to his instruction the intellect becomes enlightened, and the doors of duality are thrown wide open in an instant.
16. There, the happiness is overflowing, but there is no entry for the mind. Spiritual effort should be of the type that is not a contrivance of the mind.
17. This satisfaction that is without desire is acquired without the mind. Scholarly knowledge of texts and imagination do not apply.
18. That which is beyond the origin of speech, and beyond the mind and intellect, is immediately attainable after giving up attachment.
19. Give up the attachment to the sense of being an individual and see Him. One who has an experience of what is being said here will rest in happiness.

20. Saying that oneself is "I" or "me," is ego. The sense that one is an individual is what is meant by ego. Ego is ignorance, which means having attachment to the sense of an independent "I."
21. When attachment is given up, there is unity with That which is unattached. This is the authority of the attainment of That which is without imagination.
22. When one does not know one's Self, it is called ignorance. When ignorance is removed by Self-Knowledge, one realizes oneself as Parabrahman.
23. Understand that body-identification is not important in Parabrahman. There the sense of "I" has no place.
24. In Parabrahman the distinctions such as high and low, or of king and beggar do not exist, as all are considered to be One. Whether male or female, all have the status of being only One.
25. It is not the case that the Brahman of a brahmin (priest) is pure, and the Brahman of an untouchable is impure. Such distinctions do not exist in Brahman.
26. It cannot be said that Brahman of the king is superior and Brahman for the servants is inferior. Such differences do not exist in him at all.
27. Brahman is One in all. In Brahman there is no such thing as many. Those who are poor and even the gods such as Brahma the creator and others are all the same there.
28. The knowledgeable know Brahman alone is the place of rest for all the three worlds; Heaven, Earth and the Netherworld[42].
29. The guru and the disciple are One, alone in the same place. There is no difference there, but to understand this the connection with the body must be broken.
30. When the identification with the body and intellect ends, this Oneness alone is the ultimate attainment of all. There is one Brahman and nothing other. This is the teaching of the *Upanishads* (also called Shruti and Vedanta; it is the end part of the *Vedas* and is comprised mostly of teachings on non-duality).
31. Sages appear to be different, but their Self Form is the same. All of them are only the one "True Thing" that is alone and bodiless.
32. Brahman is neither new nor old, and never becomes more or less. One who has these concepts is like a dog that is a slave to the attachment to the body and intellect.
33. The identification with the body and intellect increases doubts and destroys contentment. The opportunity to be content is missed because of the identification with the body and intellect.
34. When one attributes greatness to the body, that itself is the sign of identification with the body and intellect. The wise ones, recognizing it as false, criticize body-identification.
35. One holds strongly to the pride for the body up until the time of the death of the body, and this leads to rebirth where one comes back again with the experience of body-identification.
36. With the feeling of importance or greatness (pride) of the body, contentment becomes less. Eventually, the body with all of its attributes will disappear. Nobody knows when this will happen.
37. The saints have explained that what is truly beneficial and that which is true virtue is to be bodiless. Non-virtue itself begins with body-identification.

---

[42] Patala is called the "netherworld." This is the Causal Body in the form of forgetfulness. In the Patala Loka (netherworld), there is the pitch darkness of ignorance.

38. Even yogis are affected by body-identification due to various powers they have gained though their yogic practices. Powers (siddhis) only increase the misidentification and attachment to the body and intellect.
39. Only when the identification with the body and intellect disappears is the "Supreme Meaning" (Paramartha) realized. The misidentification with the body and mind veils the oneness of Brahman.
40. The power of discrimination turns one towards Reality, while the identification with the body and intellect pulls one away from it. It is because of identification with the body and intellect that one feels separateness from Brahman.
41. For this reason, the wise one should abandon body-identification. By listening attentively about the "True Nature of Brahman," one becomes united with it.
42. At this point, the listener asks the question, "What is the True Nature of Brahman?" Listen now to the answer that the speaker gives to the listeners.
43. It is said that Brahman is one alone yet it appears in many forms and is experienced as many various bodies. There are many different opinions about this.
44. Whatever one has experienced, that is what is acceptable to him, and that is where his faith is placed in his inner-mind (antahkarana).
45. Brahman is devoid of name and form, and yet it has many names. It is described as being untainted, changeless, without disturbance, and Self-Bliss.
46. Brahman is called formless, inconceivable, beyond the senses, immovable, limitless, without boundaries, invisible, beyond logic, and "the One beyond."
47. Brahman is said to be the form of sound, the form of light, the form of Life-Energy, the form of power, the form of the witness, and the true Self Form.
48. It is called the void, the Eternal, Lord of all, Knower of all, the Self in all, and the Life in all.
49. Brahman is said to natural, existing at all times, pure wisdom, beyond everything, permanent, and beyond words.
50. Brahman is said to be gigantic, expansive, filling the entire universe, stainless, the "True Thing," expansive like the form of sky, the Self (Atman), the Supreme Self (Paramatman), and the Supreme Lord (Parameshwara).
51. Brahman is the Supreme Self, Paramatman, that is dense Knowledge. It is continuous and the most ancient. It is the form of universal consciousness and universal energy. Understand that these are some of the names of the "nameless."
52. There are innumerable names for Brahman, yet that one Supreme God is beyond all names. To try to attribute some definite meaning to him many names are given.
53. Brahman is that God who is the Self (AtmaRam), the restfulness in rest, and the Primordial Being (Purusha). All of this is none other than the Absolute Reality (Parabrahman).
54. To understand this Reality, the signs of the Fourteen Brahmans will be told. By listening to them, one develops firm conviction.
55. By removing everything that is false one by one, what remains should be understood to be true. Now, I will tell about the Fourteen Brahmans that are described in the scriptures.

Thus in Shri Dasbodh, a dialogue between the Guru and disciple, Sub-Chapter 2 of Chapter 7, named "Explanation of Brahman" is concluded.

Chapter: 7, Sub-Chapter: 3

The Fourteen Brahmans

|| ShriRam ||

1. The listener is asked to become alert. I shall now speak about the "Knowledge of Brahman" which is the contentment of the spiritual aspirant.
2. To acquire precious gems, soil needs to be collected. Similarly, the description of Fourteen Brahmans are given in order to be understood and then discarded.
3. Objects cannot be described without giving indications, descriptions about non-duality require using dualistic examples, the final understanding cannot be gained without first hearing about the primary premise, and no examples can be given without the power of speech.
4. First, an explanation of the false needs to be given so that it can be identified and given up. Then, the Truth will be naturally be impressed deeply within the mind.
5. Therefore the indications of the Fourteen Brahmans is being told so you can come to know the "Final Conclusion." Here, the listeners should remain attentive during this narration.
6. The first Brahman is called "Brahman as Words." The second is called "Brahman as OM." The third is "Brahman as the Sky." These names are told in the *Upanishads*.
7. Understand that the fourth Brahman is called "Brahman that is All," the fifth is "Brahman as Life-Energy," the sixth is "Brahman that is Power," and the seventh is "Brahman as the Witness."
8. Know that the eighth is called "Brahman with Attributes" (Saguna), the ninth is called "Brahman without Attributes" (Nirguna), and the tenth is called "Brahman of Speech" (the spoken word).
9. The eleventh is called "Brahman as Experience," the twelfth is called "Brahman that is Bliss," the thirteenth is called "Brahman the Form of Reality," and the fourteenth is called "Brahman the Indescribable."
10. These are the names of the fourteen Brahmans. Now the explanations will be given of these names, and then I shall tell the indications of the secret of "True Form" (Swaroopa) itself.
11. Know that the saying of "Brahman as Words" is actually only delusion without experience, as Brahman cannot be experienced with words. Similarly, Brahman as "OM" is only a single word, and Brahman is not a single word.
12. That which is called "Brahman as the Sky" has the quality of expansiveness, and that which is called "Brahman as All" has the quality of being all-pervading which means it is very subtle.
13. The "all" that is seen by the eyes is an intermingling of the five elements, and is essentially only Brahman.
14. That which is named "Brahman that is All" is the essential foundation of the *Upanishads*. Now, I shall tell about Brahman which is called "Brahman that is Life-Energy" (Chaitanya).
15. Brahman that is the Life-Energy is what brings to life the Illusion in the form of the five elements, therefore it is called Brahman as Life-Energy.
16. This Life-Energy requires some power in order that living things may become animated with Life. That which gives this power is the principle that is called

"Brahman as Power" (Satta). That which knows or witnesses this Power and Life-Energy is called "Brahman as the Witness."

17. This "Witness" which is itself the capacity of knowing and observing has attributes present, thus it is called "Brahman with Attributes" (Saguna Brahman).
18. Where there is no presence of attributes, that is called "Attributeless Brahman" (Nirguna Brahman). Now, I will tell about Brahman that can be described by words.
19. That which can be described with speech is called "Brahman as Speech," yet the experience of Brahman is such that it cannot be described with words.
20. That which is called "Brahman as Experience" has as its nature the experience of Bliss, the secret of which, I shall also tell.
21. This "Brahman as Bliss," is continuous and without distinction. It is that which is indescribable, where no dialogue is possible.
22. These are the Fourteen Brahmans described in sequence. When seeing and understanding these the aspirant is not affected by Illusion.
23. Understand that Brahman is Eternal, and Illusion is all that is ephemeral. Now, the final conclusion regarding the Fourteen Brahmans will be presented.
24. The Brahman that is "words" is merely verbal and illusory as it is not based on any experience. With discrimination it is easily seen that it is not permanent.
25. Likewise, Brahman that is OM is but a single word. When thoughtfulness is applied to understanding OM, it can be seen that it is also not permanent.
26. It is said that Brahman is like the sky, but the sky is like emptiness which can be destroyed with Self-Knowledge. Thus, it can be seen that the sky is also not permanent.
27. Everything that appears must come to an end, so the Brahman that is "all" is also destructible. The final dissolution of the universe is described with certainty in the scriptures of Vedanta.[43]
28. Where there is a final dissolution of the universe, how can there remain any existence of the elements? Thus it is shown that there is an end to "Brahman that is All."
29. The wise will not agree that the inert is moveable, or that which is attributeless has attributes or form.
30. The "all" that is created is made up of the five elements and its destruction is inevitable. Thus, how can the conclusion be made that Brahman is "all"?
31. Now that's enough talk about "Brahman as All." Brahman as "all" is destructible, not Eternal. Even the seer that sees and is different from "all" also ends, so who is there to see what?
32. Now, as for that which gives everything Life. Know that all those things are also illusive in nature. That Life-Energy which gives life and moves everything is also destructible.
33. Now for "Brahman as "Power." Power, or satta, means to have power over something. If all things are not real, then what is there to have power over? Similarly, with Brahman as "Witness," if there is nothing objective, the witness is also false.

---

[43] For a detailed explanation on the final dissolution of the universe, refer to the sub-chapter titled "The Final Dissolution."

34. As for "Brahman with Attributes," (Saguna Brahman) it is clearly evident to the eye that all attributes are destructible. Thus, no additional proof is required to know that Saguna Brahman is definitely not Eternal.
35. Now, as for that which is named as "Attributeless Brahman" (Nirguna Brahman), what can be understood to be the relevance of such a name? How can one come to know of something, or speak about something without first bringing to mind some attributes?
36. It is said that Illusion is like a mirage or an imaginary cloud that never existed.
37. If there is no town, how can there be any question of boundaries? Without birth, how can there be any individual being? Likewise, how can similes that are dualistic really ever tell about non-duality?
38. How can there be any such thing as Illusion without "Power," or objects without the "Knower," or a state of inertia without the "Life-Energy"?
39. Power, Life-Energy, and Witness all have attributes. How can that which is without attributes be like that which is with attributes?
40. It is said that Brahman is attributeless, but you should understand that this indication is also only a name which is impermanent. There is no doubt about this.
41. The word attributeless is an indication of Brahman. Many such names are given to it, but one should understand that "Attributeless Brahman" is only a description in speech, and speech is destructible.
42. The experience of bliss is a feeling that is a personal state or attitude of mind. In the completeness of Brahman, there is no place for a personal state.
43. Brahman is indescribable, so indicating that it is a particular attitude or state has its shortcomings, as no mental attitude can be applicable to it.
44. To say that it is indescribable is indicative that it is without any attitude, which is the same as to say that it is the state of no-mind (unmani). It is the resting place of the yogis who are untainted by any identification.
45. Reality is that which is not represented by any identification. It is itself the effortless and "natural samadhi" (Sahaja Samadhi) where the suffering of worldly life is non-existent.
46. That which is the end of identification is itself the "Final Understanding." It is the confirmed Truth of Vedanta, the Self-experience of the Self.
47. Like this, Brahman is Eternal, without any trace of the delusion of Illusion. The experienced understand the secret of Self-experience.
48. By discarding concepts from one's experience, one gains the satisfaction of this Self-experience.
49. If one must imagine something, one should try to imagine that which is unimaginable (inconceivable) and in this way, the imagination is destroyed naturally. Then, "be" without being any thing, as epochs pass away.
50. The one good thing about imagination is that you can turn it in any direction. If one turns it towards one's "Self Form" it becomes pervaded by that which is without modification.
51. When one imagines that which is unimaginable, imagination cannot exist there. When one is without modification, the presence of imagination cannot remain there. When one meets with that which is unattached, one becomes unattached oneself.

52. Brahman is not a visible object, it cannot be given by the hands, or held in the hands. One should understand that it can only be experienced through the words spoken by the Sadguru.
53. After this sub-chapter, the narration will be continued in order to make the conviction in the aspirant strong. In this way, one will gain the experience of "Pure Brahman."

Thus in Shri Dasbodh, a dialogue between the Guru and disciple, Sub-Chapter 3 of Chapter 7, named "Explanation of the Fourteen Brahmans" is concluded.

Chapter: 7, Sub-Chapter: 4

Explanation of Pure Brahman

|| ShriRam ||

1. Brahman is more clear than the cloudless sky that appears empty when looking at it. Like the sky, Brahman is formless, huge, and limitless.
2. Twenty-one heavens and seven lower-worlds (patalas) are all contained within the sphere of creation. The limitless pure Brahman permeates all of this.
3. Brahman is endless above and below the universe. There is no place, or even the smallest particle that it does not permeate.
4. Brahman permeates all of the water, land, wood, and stone. Not a single being is without it.
5. Just as water is in and around water animals, in the same way, this pure Brahman is in and around all living beings.
6. However, this simile with water is not entirely appropriate, because there are dry places which exist apart from water, while it is not possible that anyone can ever go outside of Brahman.
7. If one tries to run outside of the sky, it is not possible because the sky is always found in front of us. Similarly, there is no end to the endless Brahman.
8. But even though it is only Brahman that we meet continuously, it is inseparable from the body, and though it is what is closest to everyone, it is also hidden.
9. One exists within it but does not know it. One imagines to have understood it, but really the Absolute Reality cannot be understood
10. When clouds are seen in the sky it seems as if the sky has somehow become muddied, or that something has been mixed into it, but that is false, the sky remains clear and pure.
11. If one fixes one's gaze at the sky, tiny specks, like little bubbles or droplets are seen to the eyes. Similarly, visible appearances are unreal to the Knowledgeable (Jnanis).
12. Although it is false, it is still seen, like a dream for one who is asleep. Only upon becoming awake does one understand that it is not true.
13. Similarly, one becomes awakened with Self-Knowledge in one's own experience, and thereby begins to understand the nature of Illusion.
14. Now enough of this enigmatic talk. That which is beyond the universe will now be shown by way of explanation and selective analysis so that it may be deeply understood.

15. Brahman is mixed in with the entire creation, permeating all objects and diffused into every particle in existence.
16. All of creation appears in Brahman, and Brahman is in all of creation. However, the experience of this world appearance is but a small fraction of Brahman.
17. Only a small fraction of Brahman is within the entirety of creation. Who can know it's boundaries outside of creation? How can all of Brahman be contained within creation?
18. It is like trying to put the whole sky in a small pot, it is not possible. Therefore, we say that the pot contains a small fraction of the sky.
19. Brahman is mixed in with everything, but it is not disturbed. It exists in everything, yet is still beyond everything.
20. Brahman is mixed in with the five elements but is also beyond them and not limited by them, like the space that permeates the mud, yet is not dirtied by it.
21. No simile can be given for Brahman, yet in order to understand, the simile of the sky (space) is given and some means of explanation are required.
22. The *Upanishads* and other ancient texts say that Brahman is like the sky, so in keeping in accordance with those texts, the simile of the sky is given for Brahman.
23. In the absence of tarnish, brass is only pure gold in color. Similarly, in the absence of the attribute of emptiness, the sky would be untainted pure Brahman.
24. Brahman is like the sky, and Illusion is like the wind that can be felt but cannot be seen.
25. The creation that is formed out of words appears and dissolves from moment to moment. Like the wind it cannot remain still.
26. Illusion is false like this, let it be as it is. Eternal Brahman is One, yet it is seen to be permeating all things.
27. Brahman is permeating the earth but it is not hard like the earth, and no simile can be given for its softness and subtlety.
28. Understand that water is softer than the earth, fire is softer than water, and the wind is softer than fire.
29. Understand, that the sky, or space, is much softer and more subtle than the wind, and that the fullness of Brahman is more subtle than the sky.
30. Brahman has penetrated the hardest of weapons, but still its subtlety is not lost. It is neither hard nor soft. There is no accurate simile for it.
31. Brahman pervades the earth, but the earth is destructible and Brahman is not. Brahman is in water, but water gets dried up, and Brahman does not dry up.
32. Brahman is in fire but cannot be burned. Brahman is in the wind, but it does not move. It is in the sky, but the sky is known, and Absolute Reality cannot be known.
33. It is occupying the whole body, but it cannot be found. It is both very near to us, yet it is far from us at the same time. How amazing this is!
34. It is in front of us an on all sides and all seeing takes place in it. It is Self-evident and Self-established.
35. One's self is in it alone, and only it is in and all around oneself. If we have to give it some comparison, it can be said that it is like the sky without anything other appearing in it.
36. It is not felt to be anything, yet it is filling everything. It is like a great wealth that is one's own yet cannot be seen.
37. Whatever object is seen, it is prior to that. One must solve this mystery in one's own experience.

38. Space is all around and contains all objects, yet it remains the same even without the presence of objects. With or without the presence the earth, the space remains the same.
39. Whatever has name and form is Illusion and non-existent. The secret beyond name and form is known to the experienced.
40. Like a huge cloud of smoke rising into the sky takes on the appearance of mountains, similarly, the Goddess of Illusion (Maya) shows her trick that looks like the creation of the universe.
41. Understand that Illusion is impermanent, and that Brahman is Eternal and spread out everywhere at all times.
42. While reading this spiritual text, Brahman is the letters and words. It is the seeing of them as well as the subtle presence that is in the eyes that are seeing.
43. That which hears the words when listening, that which is the mind that sees thoughts, and that which permeates the mind through and through, is only the Supreme Reality itself.
44. The feet that are walking, the pathway that is being walked on, all that is encountered by the body, and all that is picked up with the hands along the way is only Brahman.
45. Let it be like this. Everything exists in Brahman only. The understanding of this fact is what destroys the desire for the objects of the sense organs.
46. Brahman is that which is closest to us. If one tries to see it, it cannot be seen, but it exists even though it is not seen.
47. Brahman can only be understood by experience. Only the absence of the appearance of the visible leads to the Self-experience that is the realization of Brahman.
48. Correct seeing must be with the eyes of Knowledge and not with the physical eyes. The recognition of this correct inner-seeing is the witness of the inner-seeing itself.
49. Understand that the one who knows both Brahman and Illusion is the one who has the experience of being the "Witness of All," that is called the "Fourth State," or Turya. (The first three states are the waking, dreaming, and deep sleep states)
50. Witnessing is the instrumental cause of the attitudes of mind, or the focus of attention. Understand that the absence of the attitudes of mind is "no-mind" where even the awareness of oneself as an entity is dissolved. That is called "Spiritual Knowledge," or Vidynana.
51. Where Ignorance (Avidya) has disappeared, and Knowledge (Vidya) does not remain, and even the higher Spiritual Knowledge (Vidynana) dissolves, this is Parabrahman, the Absolute Reality.
52. Like this, Brahman is Eternal, whereas all imagination ends. Understand that this is the blissful solitude of the yogis.

Thus in Shri Dasbodh, a dialogue between the Guru and disciple, Sub-Chapter 4 of Chapter 7, named "Explanation of Pure Brahman" is concluded.

Chapter: 7, Sub-Chapter: 5

Discarding the Imagination of Duality

|| ShriRam ||

1. The listener said, "The description of Brahman has been given and the experience of it has come, yet there is still clinging to the thought of Illusion.
2. Brahman illumines and is within all of the visible Illusion. How can this duality be explained so the understanding is clear?"
3. The speaker responds, "Please be still and alert now. Concentrate your mind, and listen carefully to the explanation of Brahman and Illusion."
4. It is only the chattering of the mind that makes the dualistic statements such as "Brahman is real" and "Illusion is unreal."
5. That which knows both Brahman and the Illusion is the Fourth State (Turya). It understands all, and is the witness of all.
6. Listen to the signs of the Turya state which knows all. However, when the "all" is not there, what is there to understand?
7. The creation of imagination and decisions has taken place within the mind, but if that mind itself is proved to be unreal, who is the witness to all of these happenings?
8. The "Witness," the "Life-Energy," and the "Power," are attributes that are ascribed to Brahman. Understand that these are all wrongly applied to Brahman because of Illusion.
9. The three types of space are spoken of by giving the examples of the vast space that is spread out everywhere, the space in a room, and the space in a pot. Similarly, when attributes are ascribed to Brahman, the Illusion seems to be real.
10. As long as Illusion is thought to be true, there is assumed to be a witness to Brahman. With the disappearance of Illusion and ignorance, how can such duality exist?
11. Accordingly, when the mind which is the witness of all becomes no-mind, the Turya state, which is Knowledge itself, also vanishes.
12. When the mind to which duality appears becomes no-mind, the thoughts of duality and non-duality also disappear.
13. Duality and non-duality are indicative of a state of mind, or the focus of attention. When the dualistic state of mind is absent, where is there any duality?
14. That Knowledge which is without any states, is itself the fullness of deep satisfaction where the thoughts of Brahman and of Illusion are banished and absent.
15. The mind has imagined the ideas of Brahman and Illusion as a form of indication. However, Brahman is without imagination. The Jnanis understand this.
16. When that which is beyond the mind and intellect, and beyond imagination is experienced directly, how can there be any duality?
17. If you see duality, Brahman disappears, and if you see Brahman, duality disappears. Both duality and non-duality appear only in imagination.
18. It is the work of imagination that removes Illusion, and it is imagination as well that puts Brahman in its place. It is imagination that raises doubt, as well as removes it.

19. It is imagination that imagines bondage, and it is imagination that imagines satisfaction. It is also imagination that helps one to remember the thought of Brahman.
20. Imagination is the mother of duality, and in principle, Knowledge itself is also imagination. Both bondage and liberation are imagined only in imagination.
21. When the imagination is running strong, it imagines the creation of the universe which is otherwise non-existent, and in an instant it can imagine the pure nature of the Self which is unimaginable.
22. One moment it gets carried away imagining danger, and the next moment it remains steady, and then in another moment it imagines a perplexed state of mind.
23. For a moment it understands, and then for another moment it is in ignorance. One should be able to recognize the many modifications that this imagination creates.
24. Imagination is the root cause of birth, imagination is the fruit of devotion, and it is imagination alone that gives liberation.
25. Let it be like this, there are many aspects of imagination. If engaged with spiritual practice, the imagination gives satisfaction, otherwise it basically becomes the root cause of the experience of one's downfall.
26. Therefore, it should be understood that imagination alone is the root cause of everything, and if it is removed at the root, that is itself the realization of Brahman.
27. Listening, reflecting, and verifying in one's own experience, is what brings about true satisfaction. In this way, the false perception of Illusion is dispelled.
28. The conviction of Pure Brahman conquers imagination. With definite conviction doubt is banished and abandoned.
29. Like darkness that is destroyed in the presence of sunlight, how can the false imagination remain in the light of Truth?
30. In the light of Knowledge, false imagination is destroyed, and the congruity of the thought of duality collapses.
31. Eliminate imagination with imagination. It is like using one animal to catch another animal, or shooting down an arrow in the sky with another arrow.
32. Certain imagination can be considered more correct imagination, and by the power of that imagination, the incorrect imagination can be eliminated. Please listen alertly so this statement can be clarified.
33. The sign of the correct type of imagination is that it imagines oneself as attributeless. This type of imagination helps one not to forget one's Self Nature.
34. Through continuous contemplation on one's identity as one's Self Nature, the thought of duality dissolves, and one gains the conviction of the knowledge of non-duality, which is what is called correct imagination.
35. That which imagines non-duality is considered correct imagination, and that which imagines duality is considered incorrect imagination. The incorrect imagination is what is commonly called tainted or polluted imagination.
36. The meaning of saying that there is something that is considered correct imagination is that it leads to the firm conviction of non-duality, while that which is called incorrect imagination is said to be polluted in the sense that it imagines duality.
37. When the imagination of non-duality is utilized it shines, and at that moment, duality is eliminated. When duality disappears, the incorrect imagination vanishes along with it.

38. The wise understand that imagination is removed with imagination like this. When the incorrect imagination is gone, afterwards only the correct type of imagination remains.
39. That which imagines one's True Form is the correct type of imagination. When imagining one's True Form, one becomes one with it, and the imagination falls off.
40. When imagination is known to be false, one naturally is, as one's True Form, without imagination. With such Self-conviction, imagination is totally annihilated.
41. The very moment that one's conviction becomes shaky, the imagination of duality springs up like the darkness that prevails after sunset.
42. It should also be understood that when Knowledge becomes tainted, ignorance increases. For this reason, one should not stray away from listening to spiritual dialogue.
43. Now, let this be enough of this talk. All doubts can be cleared in one statement. "You are not that imagination in which duality appears."
44. Having cleared the doubt that was asked earlier, this discourse is now finished. The listeners should keep their mind alert for what follows in the next sub-chapter.

Thus in Shri Dasbodh, a dialogue between the Guru and disciple, Sub-Chapter 5 of Chapter 7, named "Discarding the Imagination of Duality" is concluded.

Chapter: 7, Sub-Chapter: 6

Explanation of Bound and Liberated

|| ShriRam ||

1. The listener says, "The explanation of the non-dual Brahman that exists without imagination has been given, and for a moment, oneness with it was experienced directly by means of your explanation.
2. Now, I feel that I should remain like that, that I must become Brahman, and that I should not come back into the mundane worldly life again.
3. The happiness that is without any imagination does not allow for any of the sorrow of worldly life, so accordingly one should try to remain one with Brahman.
4. When listening to spiritual discourses one naturally becomes Brahman, but because of various states of mind, there is a feeling of coming back out from that Oneness. Like this, there is always coming and going that feels like it cannot be avoided.
5. For a moment the mind dives inward and becomes merged in Brahman, and then it falls down from there and gets involved with various states of mind once again.
6. There is a constant coming and going in and out of these states of mind aimlessly again and again. How long must this coming and going continue? It is like an insect that is tied to a string and is constantly being pulled back.
7. When listening to spiritual discourse there is the experience of oneness with Brahman, and that the body has fallen away and there is no such things as 'me' and 'you.'
8. When such talk is going on, it feels that to speak of anything else would be shameful, and that upon becoming one with Brahman it would be contradictory to live the life of a householder.

9. For one who has become Brahman, how is it that one can come back out of that again? My knowledge is like this, it feels that not to stay as Brahman would not be satisfactory.
10. It seems that one should either become Brahman, or should be in the worldly life. How long can one keep swinging to both sides?
11. When spiritual discourse is going on, Self-Knowledge gets stronger, yet when leaving from here, it's strength fades, and once again desire and anger are aroused in Brahman (oneself).
12. How can it be said that one such as this has realized Brahman? Such a one is deprived of success on both sides. His spiritual welfare and his family life are both in shambles.
13. While enjoying the happiness of the bliss of Brahman, the attraction to family pleasures drag him back, and while trying to live a family life the attraction to Brahman once again arises in him.
14. It is as if the Bliss of Brahman has been snatched away by the worldly life, and that the worldly life suffers because of Self-Knowledge. Not just one, but both sides are unsatisfactory.
15. For this reason, my mind has become restless and full of doubts. I do not have any definite conviction as to what should be done."
16. Like this, the listener spoke about his dilemma, and then asked the speaker, "How should I live now, how should I remain? My intellect is not continuously merged in the form of Brahman."
17. Now, the speaker will give an answer to this in a beautiful way. The listeners should remain quiet for a moment.
18. The speaker said, "Do you mean to say that only those who have given up their bodies and become the attributeless Brahman have become liberated? Do you mean to imply that many great sages such as Vyasa and others like him have somehow fallen, or that they have failed?"
19. The listener responded by saying, "In the *Vedas* it is said that only the sages Shukadev and Vamdev were liberated.
20. According to the *Vedas*, all of the rest are said to be in bondage. If the *Vedas* say that only Shukadev and Vamdev are liberated, are we to consider the scriptures lacking?"
21. Making reference to the *Vedas* in this way, the listener asserted that the *Vedas* have emphasized with great dignity that only these two became liberated.
22. The speaker responded to this, saying, "If we say that only two are liberated in the entire creation, what about all of the others? Is there no possibility of liberation for anyone else?
23. Many countless sages, many ascetics, accomplished ones, yogis, and those with Self-Knowledge have become fully content.
24. In addition to those, there have been many great beings like Brahma, Vishnu and Shiva. Foremost among them is Dattatraya who is said to be clothed in space.
25. Those who believe the statement that only Shukadev and Vamdev became liberated, and all others have failed, are simply learned fools."
26. Hearing this, the listener responded, "Then why have the *Vedas* said this, and how can you claim that it is false?" Upon hearing this, the speaker began his reply.

27. The *Vedas* assert many elementary statements, and those who are foolish keep their attention only on what is said in these statements. Sages and those who are wise are alert to this, and do not limit themselves exclusively with these primary premises.
28. If all of these elementary statements of the *Vedas* are accepted as true, then the power of the *Vedas* will be discredited. How many have been liberated by the knowledge in the *Vedas*? The number cannot be told by anyone.
29. If there is no power in the texts of the *Vedas*, who would even care for the *Vedas*? They are very respected because of the power that is there to liberate people.
30. It is said that one who can expound on the knowledge that is contained in the words from the *Vedas* is a mountain of merit. What can be said to be lacking in the power of the *Vedas*?
31. It is said by the sages that one is very fortunate to hear the knowledge that is contained in the *Vedas*, *Shashtras* (books of spiritual science), and *Puranas* (mythological stories filled with spiritual meaning), and with this knowledge, one becomes pure.
32. It is further said, that by listening to a single verse, or half a verse, or even just part of a verse, or just one word, many faults are warded off.
33. There are many powerful statements in the *Vedas* and scriptures, as well as quotes by the great sage Vyasa that are of indescribable importance.
34. The greatness of these texts has been spoken of in many places, and one can be certain that by listening to the knowledge contained therein, one's intellect becomes pure.
35. If there are none other than those two (Shukadev and Vamdev) that have become liberated, then how can the claims of the greatness of these text be true? Simply just let it be like this. The significance of this is understood by the wise, while for others it is only a source of confusion.
36. How can the power of *Vedas*, *Shastras*, and *Puranas* be doubted? And if there is no power in the knowledge contained there, who else will able liberate anyone other than those two sages?
37. If you say that one who has fallen down lifeless like a log has become one with Brahman, how could it be then that Shukadev was able to give so many explanations?
38. Shukadev was liberated, this is a true statement according to the *Vedas*. However, he was not lifeless like a log, even though he was only Brahman.
39. If Shukadev was lifeless because of being Brahman, then it would not have been possible for him to speak about the penetrating discrimination between the Eternal and the ephemeral.
40. If we say that one who has realized Brahman falls lifeless like a log of wood, then Shukadev himself would have not been able to narrate the text of the Bhagavatam in the presence of the King Parikshit.
41. With the explanation about discrimination between the Eternal and the ephemeral, one should think deeply and investigate the entire animate and inanimate universe when looking for examples.
42. In one moment become attributeless Brahman alone, and in another moment investigate the visible world, and in this manner it is possible to come up with many good examples that can be used when giving a talk.
43. In this way, Shukadev himself was able to give the good explanations of the Bhagavatam. We must not say that he was in bondage.

44. It should be understood that one can attain liberation through the teachings of the Sadguru while walking and living a normal life, and not by just simply falling down lifeless.
45. There are many who are liberated, some who are said to be "ever-free," some who are liberated from life but still having a physical body, and some yogis who are liberated without a body, but it should be understood that to be liberated means to be satisfaction itself.
46. Those who are liberated with a body are called Jivan Mukta, and those who are liberated from from a physical body are called Videha Mukta. Aside from these two types of liberation, those who are ever-free are called "Yogeshwara," the Lords of Yoga, or Masters.
47. When one gains some knowledge of one's Self Form there is a stability and stillness of mind. One should understand that stability and stillness of mind are still related to the body.
48. What is being indicated here is the importance of one's own experience. Anything else is really useless. One must gain contentment in one's own Self-experience.
49. One who has eaten to his heart's content cannot correctly be called hungry. Saying that he is hungry would not make him feel disturbed, for he knows the truth.
50. In the realization of one's Self Nature the body is not an issue. About this, there can be no doubt. Bondage and liberation are only feelings that are dependent upon bodily identification.
51. Even Lord Brahma and the others gods cannot be liberated as long as they are holding on to the bodily identification, then what would be the state of liberation for Shukadev?
52. The feeling of liberation is itself bondage. Liberation and bondage are but terms that are not relevant to one's Self Nature, which is complete in itself. Neither bondage nor liberation apply.
53. One who is tied to the concept of liberation is like one who has a stone tied to his belly and is sure to sink down. Unless one is free from body-identification, one cannot realize one's Self Nature.
54. Only the one who is free from the notions of "me" and "mine" becomes liberated. He may speak or he may be a mute, without these notions, he is truly liberated.
55. How can one be bound by that which is essentially false? Likewise, how can there be any feeling of liberation when seeing that both of the notions of bondage and liberation are false, and that they have their basis only in the three attributes (gunas).
56. The one who is the "Knowledge of Reality" is extremely pure. To him there are no such things as liberation and bondage. Liberation and bondage are notions in the mind that are attributes of Illusion.
57. Where name and form do not exist, how can there remain any concept of liberation? When both liberation and bondage are forgotten, even that forgetfulness is forgotten.
58. Who can say that one has become bound or liberated when it cannot even be said that there is an individual that exists? Understand that what is called bondage is only when one holds on to the sense of "I" and feels bound by it.
59. All of this talk about bondage and liberation is delusion that is the trouble which comes from ego. It is a result of not having experienced that rest which is beyond Illusion.

60. Let it be like this. Bondage and liberation are ideas that have arisen out of imagination. In principle, imagination can never be said to be true.
61. Therefore the similes are used that Illusion is like a mirage, or like clouds seen in the sky, and like a dream that is known to be false immediately upon awakening.
62. In the dream, the one who was bound has become liberated, yet he is still dreaming and has not become awakened. How can one who is still in the dream understand what it means to be awake?
63. Really it is only those who have Self-Knowledge who can be considered to be liberated. With this pure Self-Knowledge, the idea of liberation is removed at the root.
64. The concepts of bondage and liberation only create doubts in the imagination. Sages are always without doubt, being the Reality that is beyond all body identification.
65. Now, enough with this explanation. Next, I will give the narration about how to live with the understanding that was gained from the explanation just given. I ask the listeners to please listen to what follows next with alertness.

Thus in Shri Dasbodh, a dialogue between the Guru and disciple, Sub-Chapter 6 of Chapter 7, named "The Explanation of Bound and Liberated" is concluded.

Chapter: 7, Sub-Chapter: 7

Establishment of Spiritual Practice

|| ShriRam ||

1. If we try to imagine a thing that is Reality, it cannot be done, as its nature is without any imagination or concepts. There is no imagination in Parabrahman.
2. Even if one goes on trying to imagine it, it cannot be known in imagination. It cannot be found in thoughts, and one only becomes confused by trying.
3. It is not something that is visible to the eyes or can become apparent to the mind. How can That which cannot be seen, and which does not appear to the mind, be recognized?
4. If one tries to see it, it is formless and appears to be nothing to the mind. When trying to imagine this nothingness, one feels filled with darkness.
5. In the imagination one feels that it is black. However, Brahman is neither black, nor yellow, nor red, nor white, nor blue. It is colorless.
6. How does one recognize that which is without any color, has no appearance, and is without form?
7. Not seeing it, how can it be recognized? How long should one try to see it? One only becomes exhausted by such efforts.
8. Supreme Beingness is without attributes and beyond all attributes. It is invisible and indescribable. It cannot be comprehended as it is beyond the capacity of thoughts.
9. How can one think about That which is beyond thoughts? How can one remember That which is beyond description? How can one recognize That which has no attributes?

10. How can one see That which cannot be seen with the eyes? How can one find That which cannot be known to the mind? How is it possible to see That which has no attributes?
11. How to be attached to That which is not attached to anything? How to reside in a state which is supportless? How to speak of That which is wordless?
12. When trying to think about That which is not of thought, or imagine That which cannot be imagined, or trying to meditate on non-duality, it is only duality that arises from such efforts.
13. Yet, if one gives up the mediation, and breaks from the habit of giving continuous thought to Reality, one falls into a state of great doubt.
14. However, if because one has the fear of falling into duality, one gives up all efforts and does not pursue the realization of Reality, there will never be any satisfaction.
15. If one develops a habit, the habit becomes stronger. By developing the habit of contemplation on Reality, and with perseverance in giving thought as to what is Eternal and what is ephemeral, one gains satisfaction.
16. When thinking about Reality, duality arises, and by simply giving up thinking, nothing is revealed. One only becomes ensnared in doubts about nothingness without the proper use of the power of discrimination (viveka).
17. Therefore, one should properly utilize discrimination. With Self-Knowledge, one should remain aloof from the worldly life (be in the water without getting wet), and get rid of the sense of a separate "I," which is not so easily cast off.
18. Parabrahman, the Absolute Reality, is non-dual. When trying to imagine it, duality arises. While trying to speak of it with examples of cause and effect, or by means of using various similes or examples taken from the visible world, nothing applies.
19. Parabrahman is such that to remember it one forgets it, and by forgetting it, one remembers. The understanding of it is such that it cannot be understood.
20. In not trying to meet it, you meet with it. If you try to meet it, the feeling of separation arises. Like this is the wonderful silent story which cannot be described in words.
21. It cannot be attained by trying to attain it, and in trying to go away from it, it does not leave. Being connected with it, one can never break away from it.
22. It always is as it is. If we try to go see it, it is as if it is not there. Without trying to see it, it shines everywhere, as it is.
23. How can That by which any means to try to achieve it is an impediment, and not to attempt any means is its achievement, be known and understood without actual experience?
24. It is understood by not understanding. Saying that one has understood only shows that it is not understood. Where there are no attitudes of mind, one becomes settled as that which has no attitudes or modifications.
25. It cannot be held on to in meditation, and thought cannot think about it. The Supreme Reality cannot be contained in the mind.
26. If we try to compare it to water, this simile is not fitting as it is pure and motionless, and water is not. Even if the whole universe is drowned, it remains dry.
27. It is not like light, nor like darkness. How can it be described as being like any thing?
28. Like this, Brahman never comes into contact with the world, and is not visible at any time. In what way can one's attention be fixed on it?

29. If one turns one's attention to it trying to see, one does not get the feeling of it and the mind becomes lost in doubt.
30. When trying to see it, the Reality cannot be seen and is thought to be false, and one has no place to go and rest. Thus, the individual is taken to be true, and believed to be one's true nature.
31. If this false belief is said to be true, one would be saying that the *Vedas* and *Shastras* (scriptures considered to be of divine origin) are false. The writing and teachings of the sage Vyasa[44] and others are not wrong.
32. Therefore, one should not say that Reality is non-existent (because it cannot be seen). Many with Self-Knowledge have given explanations that cannot be called false.
33. Teachings of the "Knowledge of Non-Duality" have been given by Lord Shiva to Parvati in the *Guru Gita*.
34. In the *Avadhuta Gita* composed by Dattatraya, the path of Knowledge (Jnana) is given to Gorakshanath.
35. Lord Vishnu, becoming a Royal Swan (Raj Hansa), gave the teaching of Knowledge to Brahma. That text is called the *Hansa Gita* which has been given by the "Lord of the Universe" himself.
36. Brahma gave the sage Narada the teaching of Lord Krishna in four stanzas (the *Bhagavatam*), which later was expanded very much by the sage Vyasa.
37. The sage Vasishtha gave his teaching to Lord Rama in the *Yoga Vasishtha (Maharamayana)*, and Lord Krishna instructed Arjuna in the *Bhagavad Gita*.
38. How many examples like this need to be given? Many sages have stated again and again that this "Knowledge of Non-Duality" is true.
39. Therefore, based upon the strength of the statements of the Jnanis, to say that Self-Knowledge is false, is an indication of delusion. This cannot be understood by those who are without this Knowledge.
40. The ability of Shesha to express Knowledge became exhausted, and the *Upanishads* fell into a state of silence trying to describe that Self Form which knowledge cannot describe.
41. Even though one may not understand it oneself, it should not be called false. To understand, one should hold firmly to the teachings of a True Guru (Sadguru).
42. When the false has been taken to be true and the True is taken to be false, the mind is drowned in an ocean of doubts.
43. Mind has the habit of imagining, but whatever the mind imagines is not true. However, as a result of pride in the imagination of the individual "I," doubt runs down a path out of control.
44. Therefore, the path of doubt must be abandoned. Then one feels connected to the Supreme Self, Paramatman. The root of doubt is cut off by keeping the company of saints and sages.
45. The sense of a separate "I" cannot be cut with weapons, and it cannot be broken. It cannot be given up by doing anything.
46. With the pride in the sense of the individual "I" intact, one cannot understand Reality. With the sense of "I" intact, devotion is diminished, and the power of detachment is weakened.

---

[44]Vyasa is the proper name of a saint and author, the supposed compiler of the Vedas and Puranas. Vyasa is considered to be the founder of Vedanta philosophy

47. Because of pride, the family life is not successful and the spiritual life is lost. Because of the pride in "I," everything including success, fame, and power are lost.
48. Because of this pride, friendship is broken, and affection disappears. Because of this pride for "I," conceit swells within oneself.
49. Because of pride, doubt arises in the mind, disputes take place, and the sweet feeling of unity is lost.
50. One's pride in "I" is not liked by anyone, so how can it be liked by God? Only one who gives up this pride of "me" and "mine" is truly content.
51. The listener asks, "How can one renounce this pride of 'me' and 'mine'? How can one gain the experience of Brahman? How does one arrive at contentment?"
52. Give up the pride in the sense of "I" with understanding. By being Brahman, experience it. By being free of all attachments, one arrives at contentment.
53. Over and above that, there is a contentment in which one knows to do spiritual practices without any sense of an individual "I." Such a one is truly blessed with contentment.
54. If one thinks "Now I have become Brahman, who is there to do any spiritual practice?," and goes on conceptualizing like this in the mind, it only gives rise to more concepts.
55. Concepts do not apply to Brahman, and if one has that concept, one remains with that concept. One who can recognize this, and discard that concept after seeing it, is the true sage.
56. Surely one must conceive of "That" which is without any concepts, however, one should not conceive of any concept of oneself. Give up the sense of a separate "I" in this way.
57. Be in this Knowledge of Brahman, but do not be anything. Only one who is alert and content understands this.
58. Whatever one conceives of, one experiences accordingly. When conceiving of "That" which is without any concepts, conceptualization itself vanishes.
59. To not move from the Knowledge of Brahman, spiritual practice (sadhana) is the only remedy. In this way, one finds the solution to separateness.
60. When the king is seated on his throne, all the workings of his administration function effortlessly. Similarly, when having gained the Knowledge of Brahman, continue with spiritual practices effortlessly.
61. Spiritual practices are a task for the body. Since one's Self is never the body, being a non-doer comes naturally.
62. One can only speak of giving up spiritual practice if one conceives of oneself as being the body. Not being the body, where is the question of the body giving up spiritual practices?
63. There is neither spiritual practices, nor is there a body. When one is only Brahman without doubt, this is being bodiless (videha) while being in the body.
64. When having the Knowledge of Brahman without continued spiritual practice, affection for the body and laziness develop in the name of the realization of Brahman.
65. In the name of spirituality, self-interest is indulged in, in the name of meditation, being asleep to Reality is promoted, in the name of liberation, there is behavior that is full of vices and indulgence that is out of control.

66. In the name of explanation, criticism takes place, in the name of dialogue, arguments occur, and by adding titles to one's name, pride is developed within oneself.
67. Similarly, in the name of the Knowledge of Brahman, laziness enters within, and one says that it is madness that one should do any spiritual practices.
68. Such a one says, "What should I do and where shall I go, and what should I take and what should I leave? Everything is filled with my Self, just as the space is everywhere." Using this statement as a support, one behaves as if he was hitting himself with his own weapon.
69. In this way, the remedy becomes harmful, and by neglecting spiritual practices one's own best interest suffers. Giving up all spiritual practices, one becomes bound in liberation.
70. Such a one is afraid that by doing spiritual practices, he will lose the status of having become accomplished by his own hands. For this reason such a one does not like to do any regular spiritual practices.
71. He is afraid that people will say that one doing spiritual practices is only an aspirant, and he feels shameful about this. He does not know that even Brahma and others do spiritual practices.
72. Now, let this talk about such ignorance come to an end. Knowledge follows the practice of regular study. By studying, one can realize the primordial complete Brahman.
73. The listener asks, "What must be studied? You must explain the spiritual practice which results in the realization of one's Divine Nature."
74. The answer to this question is given for the listeners in the next sub-chapter where the spiritual practice by which one realizes Supreme Truth is explained.

Thus in Shri Dasbodh, a dialogue between the Guru and disciple, Sub-Chapter 7 of Chapter 7, named "Establishment of Spiritual Practice" is concluded.

Chapter: 7, Sub-Chapter: 8

The Importance of Listening

|| ShriRam ||

1. Listen to the means (sadhana) by which one arrives at the realization of "Supreme Meaning" (Paramartha) and gains contentment. Understand that the best means is definitely listening (shravana).
2. By listening, devotion is understood, dispassion arises, and attachment to sensual pleasure gets broken off.
3. By listening, one's thinking becomes clear, one's intellect becomes firm, and the bondage of pride is broken
4. By listening one gains conviction, the sense of "me" and "mine" is broken, and one gains inner contentment.
5. By listening doubts get cleared, misunderstanding is dispelled, and previously existing traits and attributes are changed.

6. Through listening the mind gets controlled and one gains contentment. By listening the bondage of body-consciousness gets broken.
7. By listening the ego sense of individuality disappears, dangers are avoided, and many calamities are burned to ashes.
8. Due to listening one's undertakings are accomplished, one can get the experience of samadhi, and one becomes spiritually accomplished and content.
9. Listening in the company of saints and the virtuous (in satsang) helps one to understand by way of explanation. By listening one becomes one with Brahman.
10. By listening understanding increases, the intellect is sharpened, and the attraction to sensual pleasures is broken off.
11. By listening one understands the meaning of inquiry, or "thoughtfulness" (vichara), Knowledge (Jnana) becomes stronger, and Reality becomes clear to the aspirant.
12. By listening good intelligence is developed, the power of discrimination is awakened, and the mind begins to long for God.
13. By listening, bad company is broken off, passion dies down, and the dangers of life dry up all at once.
14. By listening the fascination with objects gets destroyed, inspiration shines, and Reality is definitively revealed.
15. By listening one gains the best of life, one finds peace, and one gains a firmness in turning away from worldly entanglements.
16. There is nothing that is as essential as listening, by which anything can happen. By listening one can find the way out of the river of worldly miseries.
17. Listening is the beginning of devotion. Listening is the beginning of all things. By listening everything becomes complete by itself.
18. Neither being engaged in worldly activities nor turning away from worldly entanglements can take place without listening. This is the actual experience of everyone.
19. It is well known to all people that without listening one cannot understand. For this reason, the first basic effort in spiritual endeavor is listening.
20. When there is something that one has not heard about in life, one has doubt about it. Therefore nothing can be compared to the importance of listening.
21. If one looks at the various types of spiritual practices, none is equal to listening. Without listening one's work cannot actually be carried out.
22. Without the sun, there would be darkness everywhere. The spiritual aspiration without listening is similar to that.
23. Without listening, the nine types of devotion, the four types of liberation, and the nature of the spontaneous natural state of effortlessness (sahaja) cannot be understood.
24. Without listening, we would not know about the six duties of the priests, or how to do repetition of mantra, or how to perform rituals of worship.
25. Without listening, the significance of many religious vows, charities, austerities, spiritual practices, yogic practices, and pilgrimages cannot be understood.
26. The various streams of knowledge, the knowledge of the body, the significance of the understanding of various principles and the employment of various skills, and the gaining of the Knowledge of Brahman, cannot be understood without listening.
27. The multitude of varieties of herbs and plants exist because of water. Indeed, all creatures are born from one aquatic source.

28. All beings are supported by the one earth, for all beings there is only one sun, and for all beings, their actions come about by the one wind.
29. For all beings there is one space, which is called the sky, and all beings reside in the one Absolute Reality, Parabrahman.
30. Likewise, for all beings, there is one essential spiritual practice which is listening.
31. There are many countries, many languages, and innumerable opinions found on this planet earth. In all of this, there is no other spiritual practice that is greater than listening.
32. By listening there arises a weariness with worldly pursuits. Those who are in bondage become seekers, and those who are spiritual aspirants become committed to regular spiritual practice.
33. By listening, those who are spiritual aspirants become accomplished, acquiring highest understanding. This is well known to everyone.
34. The immediate effect of listening is that even those who are cruel and hurtful-minded people become virtuous.
35. The greatness of listening is such that it cannot be told in words. By listening, even one who has a hurtful intellect and is always committing wrongful deeds becomes virtuous.
36. It is said that one gets the fruits of pilgrimages and spiritual vows in the future. It is not like that with listening. With listening, one gets direct results immediately.
37. An example of the power of listening is that it is similar to how many diseases and ailments are cured immediately by certain medicines. Those who are experienced understand this.
38. When what is heard is thought about and understood, good fortune reigns strongly. Mainly, the Supreme Self, Paramatman, is understood in one's own Self-experience.
39. Understand that it is called "reflection" (manana) when one remains always attentive to the meaning of what has been heard. With reflection comes the verification (nididhyasana[45]) that is constant abidance in the Self and contentment.
40. Only when the meaning of what has been said is understood, does one become content. With this understanding, all doubts are instantly cleared.
41. It can be said that doubt is the root cause of birth, and that by listening doubt becomes rootless and one naturally becomes completely content.
42. Where there is no listening and no reflection, how can there be contentment? Without listening, instead of liberation, one holds on to bondage.
43. Whether one is a seeker, an aspirant (sadhaka), or one who is accomplished (a Siddha), without listening one does not become free from bondage. It is by listening and constant reflection that one's mind becomes subtle and clear.
44. One should know that a place where there is no regular listening is not conducive to spiritual understanding and that the aspirant should not stay there even for a moment.
45. Without listening in one's own self-interest, how can there be any spirituality? Even all that has been accomplished already can become fruitless without continued listening.
46. Therefore, you should listen, and retain in the mind what you have heard and the spiritual practices that you have been given, and you will always be saved from the ocean of worldly entanglements.

---

[45]In Vedanta teachings Shravana, Manana, and Nididhyasana are the three activities of the listening, reflection, and verification used to gain Self-Knowledge.

47. Just as one has to eat food and drink again and again, one must also listen to what has been heard again and again.
48. That person who disregards listening due to laziness, suffers when it comes to their own best interest.
49. One who defends this kind of laziness is effectively losing their spiritual life. For this reason, listening to spiritual discourses must be done.
50. Now, with regard to how one should listen, and which texts should be read, this will be told in the next sub-chapter.

Thus in Shri Dasbodh, a dialogue between the Guru and disciple, Sub-Chapter 8 of Chapter 7, named "The Importance of Listening" is concluded.

Chapter: 7, Sub-Chapter: 9

The Importance of Listening (2)

|| ShriRam ||

1. Now, I shall explain about how to listen. The listener is asked to pay attention and concentrate the mind on what is being said.
2. There is one type of speech where the contentment that one has gets disturbed and one's conviction is suddenly spoiled.
3. Give up that speech which is untrue and illusory in nature, as it is empty and not capable of providing firm resolution leading to conviction.
4. By reading one book conviction is gained only to be erased by reading another book. In this way, doubts are created throughout one's whole life.
5. One should only listen to the spiritual books on non-duality (advaita) where doubts are cleared away and objections are removed.
6. One who is intent on liberation holds to the path of spirituality, and develops within an affection for the texts on non-duality.
7. One who has given up interest in this world and aspires for spiritual realization uses the scriptures on non-duality to help him see using the power of discrimination.
8. For the one who is interested in non-duality, his mind gets agitated when dualistic teachings are put in front of him.
9. If one receives according to what one likes, one feels happy, otherwise the mind gets bored upon hearing.
10. One feels affection for the particular type of spiritual practice that one does, and it does not feel agreeable when something else is being described.
11. The sign of love is that it arises effortlessly and runs downstream on its own like water.
12. Similarly, the person with Self-Knowledge does not care for anything else. This is where the investigation into Essence and non-essence is required.
13. For one whom the family goddess is Bhagavati, there should be discussion on the text of *Saptashati* (a book of 700 verses in praise of Bhagavati). The praising of other gods is not interesting to that person.

14. For one who is involved only in ritualistic worship there is no interest in the teachings of the *Bhagavad Gita*, and for sages there is no expectation of fruits of their actions.
15. Just as a bracelet is not worn like a nose ring, everything should be in its proper place, otherwise it is of no use at all.
16. The greatness of many deities is described in many texts. These descriptions are respected when they are read in their appropriate places, otherwise it seems awkward.
17. If a text describing the greatness of the god Malhari is read at Dwarka, or if the greatness of Dwarka is praised at Kashi, or the greatness of Kashi is praised to Lord Venkatesha[46], these are examples of things not being in their proper place.
18. There are so many examples like this of how things are fitting in their proper place. Similarly, it is only the Knowledgeable (Jnanis) who have a fondness for non-dual texts.
19. If magical tricks are performed in front of yogis, or a common stone is brought before a jeweler, or rustic ballads are performed in front of a scholar, it is not appropriate.
20. It is like a hermit being made to sit in front of one performing rituals, or describing the fruits of action in front of one who is desireless, or reading a text book about sexual positions to one who is Self-realized.
21. It is like an erotic dancer brought before one who has taken a vow of celibacy, or the description of Lord Krishna and the gopis (cowherd girls) making love during an explanation of spirituality, or bringing plain water before the Royal Swan which drinks only milk.
22. In the same way, it is not appropriate if a book about romance is brought before those who are spiritually inclined. How can they feel content with such a book?
23. It is improper that a king would be attracted to the possessions of a pauper, that buttermilk would be praised as nectar, or that the power of a ghost is described to a renunciate (sanyasin).
24. If someone who is involved in performing rituals is given advice about hypnotism or is given some explanations about how to deal with ghosts, he will naturally lose interest.
25. In the same way, those who are on the path of spirituality will not be satisfied reading books which do not deal with the topic of Self-Knowledge.
26. Now, enough talk about this topic, one who is concerned with his own self-interest always thinks about the teaching that is contained in the texts on non-duality.
27. One who is intent upon gaining Self-Knowledge should focus the mind on the principles of non-duality in a secluded quiet place. This will bring contentment.
28. Looking from many different points of view it can be seen that there are no other books comparable to a book on non-duality. Such a book is like a boat taking one beyond worldly life, to Supreme Meaning.
29. Other books which deal with worldly affairs such as humor and things that make one laugh, or that evoke other emotions are not useful on the spiritual path.
30. A book that is considered great is one by which spirituality is increased, changes take place within, and which inspires a fondness for devotional practices.

---

[46]In Hindu culture, there are multitude manifestations of various gods with their particular powers and greatness, and these gods are usually associated with a particular place. So what is being indicated here by Samartha Ramdas is that a text praising a particular deity or place will only have significance in that particular place and only for that particular deity.

31. Upon listening to what is contained in such a book, pride falls away, doubt is dispelled, and the mind suddenly turns toward God.
32. A book which inspires one to give up one's vices, and by listening to its contents it helps one to avoid downfall, is considered a great text.
33. A text which helps one build courage, which inspires benevolence towards others, and which helps to snap the desire for sensual gratification is considered a great text.
34. A book which provides a means to cross over mundane worldly life, by which one gains Knowledge, and which helps one to be free from worldly entanglements, is truly considered a great text.
35. There are many books that make promises of some results, but if such a book does not give rise to detachment and devotion it cannot be considered a great book.
36. A book which does not show the path to liberation, but only speaks about the fruits of actions, is merely a book that offers insatiable hopes which only keep increasing.
37. Upon listening to a book which only instills more desires, one loses sight of the power of discrimination and is haunted by the ghosts of insatiable hopes which bring about a downfall.
38. When listening to the promise of some future results, one says, "At least I will reap the fruits in the next life," and in this way, experiences certain downfall.
39. Many fruits are eaten by many birds and they get satisfied, but the chakor bird longs only for the nectar of moonlight.
40. In the same way, the family man only seeks to fulfill the desires of his family, while the one who is committed to God only longs for God.
41. The Jnani only wants Knowledge, the devotee only wants devotion, and the spiritual aspirant only wants spiritual practices according to his liking.
42. A spiritual aspirant wants spirituality, a selfish person only wants what is in his own self-interest, and a miser only has a desire for money in his heart.
43. The yogis want yoga, pleasure seekers only want pleasures, and sick people want medicine that cures their disease.
44. The poets wants poetry, the logical people want logic, and devotees feel that only discussion about God is enjoyable.
45. Scholars want scholastic knowledge, students want to study, and artists want various forms of art.
46. Servants of God want to sing the praises of God, one who is desirous of purity wants to perform rituals, and those who adhere to particular rituals only want to perform those rituals.
47. A loving person wants compassion, a shrewd person want alertness, and a wise person respects cleverness.
48. A devotee likes to see the form of an idol, the common musician likes the knowledge of rhythms, while the classical musician likes the study of various moods and compositions.
49. Students of hatha yoga want knowledge of the body, the philosopher wants to know various systems of philosophy, and practitioner of Ayurvedic medicine wants the knowledge of the pulse rate and the properties of various herbs.
50. The person with sexual desires wants books about sex, a person who is interested in black magic wants mantras for casting spells, and a mechanical engineer has a keen interest in machines and technical information.

51. The mischievous one likes making fun of others, a person who is undisciplined has many habits, and an ignorant person is prone to making many mistakes.
52. A foolish person gets caught up in musical sounds, a critic always looks for an opportunity to find the shortcomings of others, and one who is prone to wrongful deeds is constantly looking to see if others are committing similar kinds of deeds.
53. Some people want to hear interesting stories, some want lengthy anecdotes, while some want only simple pious devotion.
54. One who knows the *Vedas* wants to see the *Vedas*, one who is courageous wants to see war, and some want to know about many religions according to their liking.
55. One who is liberated wants to see liberation in action, one who is interested in everything wants to see all varieties of things, and an astrologer wants to give prophecies.
56. How many examples of things like this can be given? People only like to read various books and listen to things according to their likes and dislikes.
57. However, when there is no discussion about the spiritual practice used to gain the Knowledge of Brahman, this cannot be called true listening, or shravana. Where there is no Self-Knowledge, such discussions are but mere amusement.
58. Just as something cannot be called sweet that is not sweet, or someone without a nose cannot be called beautiful, explanations about spirituality are useless if one does not have Self-Knowledge.
59. Now, let this be enough of this talk. Listen to what is contained in the spiritual texts. Without spiritual texts, life goes in vain and is frivolous.
60. Therefore, one should only listen to the spiritual texts which speak about the inquiry into that what is permanent and what is temporary, and what is Essence and what is non-essential. Only such a text will help one to cross over the mundane worldly life by telling how to use the power of discrimination.

Thus in Shri Dasbodh, a dialogue between the Guru and disciple, Sub-Chapter 9 of Chapter 7, named "The Importance of Listening (2)" ends.

Chapter: 7, Sub-Chapter: 10

The End of the Body

|| ShriRam ||

1. The false has become true, and the True has become false. This is the delusion created by Illusion.
2. Many explanations are given in order for Truth to be understood, but even then, the influence of the untrue is not lessened.
3. The false becomes firmly fixed in the mind for reasons that have no explanation. Even though the True is present, it is not seen.
4. The *Vedas*, *Shastras* and *Puranas* all give definitive explanations about what is True, but still, realization of one's True Nature does not take place.
5. The True, being covered over, suddenly seemed untrue, and the false, being non-existent, seems to have become true. Such is the strange thing that has taken place.

6. Like this is the play of Illusion. One can come to understand this in a moment by keeping the company of saints and thinking deeply about their explanations.
7. Previously in this text the explanation has been given as to how one sees oneself by oneself. In that way, one realizes Supreme Truth.
8. Becoming contented in this way, one's mind become consciously merged in the Life-Energy (Chaitanya) and one realizes one's Self Nature as being Reality itself.
9. In this realization, the body is given up into the hands of its destiny and all doubt has been cleared away through understanding. Upon knowing that the body is untrue, whether it falls dead or remains alive does not matter.
10. The body of the Jnani is known to be unreal as he is formless and without qualities, so wherever the body falls dead is a sacred place.
11. It is because of the presence of sages that pilgrimage places become sacred, and the aspirations of people gets fulfilled. If sages were not going there in the past, those places would have no value to pilgrims.
12. Common people think that in order to be liberated the body should die on the bank of a sacred river, but the sage is always liberated.
13. Thinking that dying during the time period when the sun is migrating in the southerly direction is unlucky, is a type of delusion and a doubt that is in the mind of the common person. The sage is without any such delusion.
14. Similarly, the common person thinks that dying during the first fourteen days of the lunar phase when the sun is moving in a northerly direction with a lamp lit in the house during daytime is auspicious, or that one only needs to remember God at the very end of their life in order to be liberated.
15. However, the yogi does not think like this. He is liberated even while living, and is the embodiment of virtue. Both sin and merit have been given up by him and do not apply.
16. The ignorant person says that if the end of the body has taken place in a good way, and if the body has passed away without any negative incidents, that that person has been blessed.
17. With the absurd opinion that it is only at the end of life that one meets God, people go about wasting their lives.
18. Their life is not made worthwhile while living, and it simply passes away uselessly. If the grain is not sown, how can anything grow?
19. If one engages in devotional worship to God, then one becomes pure. It is like a practical man who properly manages his money and then becomes wealthy.
20. Without giving, one cannot get anything, and without sowing, the crop cannot be harvested. This statement is well known to all people.
21. A servant who does not perform his work and service and then asks the employer for compensation does not get paid, similarly one who is not a devotee is not looking after his own best interest in the end.
22. If while living there is no devotion to God, how can one become liberated only at the time of death? Let this be as it is. That which one does comes back to him.
23. Without devotion to God during one's life, one does not simply become liberated at the time of death. Even if one has a good or pleasant death, without devotion in life, one suffers a downfall.
24. The sages have properly utilized the body and fulfilled the purpose of life. They are truly blessed.

25. The Jnanis are liberated beings and are not concerned whether the body falls in the forest or in a cemetery.
26. If the dead body of a sage rots unattended, or is eaten by cats and dogs, it is considered to be a bad thing by the people of dull intellect.
27. If the end of the sage's body does not come in a nice way, people become sad. This is due to ignorance, as they do not know the Truth.
28. How can the one who is not born at all, die? By using the power of discrimination, he has swallowed and is finished with the cycle birth and death.
29. By the strength of having realized his Self Nature the entire Illusion disappears. The expanse of his realization is not understood even by Brahma and other gods.
30. He is dead while living, as he is one who has killed death. Through the power of discrimination he does not even hold the concepts of birth and death.
31. He is seen among people but is beyond their sight. He appears to behave like common people, yet he is different. He is stainless, and never touched by visible objects.
32. When the Jnani worships and sings the praises of Reality, other people are uplifted. This is how it is with sages, through devotion and worship of them, people become pious.
33. The aspirant who is under the guidance of the Sadguru should continually use the power of discrimination. With discrimination and sound reasoning, the explanations become easy to understand.
34. This is the formal promise that is given to the aspirant. By receiving the pure explanation of non-duality, you will arrive at the same contentment as that of the sage.
35. One who surrenders to the saints, becomes a saint himself, and becomes an aid to others with his kindness.
36. Such is the greatness of the saints. One gets Knowledge in the company of saints. There is no other practice superior than keeping the company of the saints.
37. With the support of the worship of the Sadguru, by thinking over the explanations with determination, and with clarity in one's actions, one can surely realize Brahman.
38. Adoration of the Sadguru is itself the birthplace of spirituality. In worshipping the Sadguru, one instantly becomes content.
39. Knowing that the body of the individual is unreal, make this life fulfilled by having the feeling of devotional worship and by pleasing the mind of the Sadguru.
40. The Sadguru takes on the worries of the one who has surrendered. He is like a mother who makes every effort to raise and take care of the growth of her child.
41. One who adores the Sadguru is truly blessed. There is no other contentment greater than that which can only be gained with the teachings of the Sadguru.
42. Let this play of words come to an end at this point in the text. I have clearly told the listeners about the worship of the Sadguru.
43. There is nothing comparable to the worship of the Sadguru that can give liberation. If one does not agree with this, one should study the *Guru Gita*.
44. There, it is very nicely explained by Lord Shiva to Parvati how one should serve at the feet of Sadguru with a true feeling of devotion.
45. The spiritual aspirant who gives deep thought to what is contained here in this text and who utilizes the power of discrimination will arrive at the firm conviction of Self-Knowledge.

46. Do not call this text which which tells of non-duality ordinary because it was written in the Marathi language. Understand that what is contained here is true Advaita Vedanta with regard to its meaning.
47. One can understand the teachings of Vedanta through the Marathi (and English) language contained here, and the inner contentment that is the same as described in ancient scriptures can be gained.
48. Do not call this text ordinary, as the means to attain Self-Knowledge is given here. How can a foolish person understand what is contained within this text? It is similar to a monkey with a coconut in his hands.
49. Now, enough of this talk. Each one can take according to their capacity. Do not say that the pearl is of the same value as the shell.
50. Where the *Upanishads* say "Not this, Not this" (Neti, Neti) the cleverness of language does not work. Parabrahman, the Absolute Reality, that is the only thing that exists in the beginning and in the end, cannot be described in words.

Thus in Shri Dasbodh, a dialogue between the Guru and disciple, Sub-Chapter 10 of Chapter 7, named "The End of the Body" is concluded.

Chapter 8. The Origin of Maya

Chapter: 8, Sub-Chapter: 1

Perceiving God

|| ShriRam ||

1. The listeners are now requested to remain attentive to this conversation between the Guru and disciple in which "Pure Knowledge" is made very easy to understand by way of listening.
2. Even if one were to search everywhere in many scriptures for their entire life it still would not be enough to know God, and the affliction of doubt would only continue to increase.
3. There are many famous places of pilgrimage that can be found in this world. Some are easy to find while others are more difficult to find, and they are all said to be auspicious places to visit.
4. Is there anyone in the world who can go to all of these pilgrimage sites? Even an entire lifetime would not be enough time to visit them all.
5. Many types of austerities are undertaken and much is given in charity, and there are various types of yoga and many spiritual practices that are all done for the sake of knowing God.
6. It is a widely accepted opinion that to realize the God of gods, one must endure many types of efforts.
7. There are many paths and opinions with regard to how to realize God, but what is the true nature of God?
8. There are so many various gods in nature, who can count them all? But how does one come to know the one true God?
9. There are many types of worship and spiritual practice. When one gets some desired result, the mind feels satisfied so the person stays with that type of practice.
10. There are many gods with their many devotees who become attached when their desires are fulfilled, and there are many sages who all have differing opinions.
11. When one tries to choose from many different opinions, one does not come to any firm resolution. When there is disagreement even among the scriptures, the aspirant does not know how to gain conviction.
12. There are many differences of opinion stated in the many various scriptures. Because of this, many have spent their lives quarreling.
13. It is only one person among thousands who uses the power of discrimination to try to know God, and even that one does not come to really know the true nature of God.
14. Why do I say that God's nature is still not understood? It is because pride is still present. God remains unknown because of pride (ego).
15. Enough about this for now. The question is, how can this God, for whom all of the various practices of yoga are being done, be realized?
16. Who should be called God? How can he be known? I shall tell this now in simple language.
17. God is the one who has created the world of animate and inanimate things, the one who has put into motion all action, and the one who is the only doer of everything.

18. He has created the fleets of clouds, the coolness in the moonlight, and he gave light and brightness to the sun.
19. He is the One by whose power the ocean stays within its bounds, who has established the support of the universe, and who has created the stars and the sky.
20. The one who created the four streams of life, the four types of speech, the 8.4 million species of living beings, and the three worlds, is called God.
21. Without any doubt, it is certain that it is the one God alone who has incarnated as Brahma, Vishnu, and Shiva (the activities of creation, preservation, and destruction in the universe).
22. The images of God residing in the temples have not gone out and created all living beings, nor have they have created this universe.
23. There are many gods in many places. These small gods have not made the earth, the moon, or the sun, stars and clouds.
24. The one God is the doer of all who has no various parts, and whose mode of operation and divine play of creation is not understood by even Brahma and other gods.
25. Some doubt about this naturally arises which will be cleared in the next sub-chapter, but for now the attitude of the listener's mind must remain attentive.
26. Originally, boundless space was spread everywhere and it was completely empty, containing nothing. In that empty space, the wind was born.
27. From wind came fire (light), and from fire came water. Like this, this wondrous creation took place.
28. From water, all of living creation (plants and living organisms) took place without any obstruction. The One who has done this marvelous thing, is called "God."
29. God created this earth from which stones were formed. Those who do not utilize the power of discrimination call stone idols gods.
30. The One who is the creator of this world existed prior to this creation, and it is by his power that creation appeared afterwards.
31. Just as the potter exists prior to the pot and the pot is not the potter, similarly God exists in the beginning and does not become the stone idol.
32. A toy army is made out of clay while the maker of the army remains distinct from the clay and the army. Even if the clay and the army are considered one, the cause and the effect (the maker and the army) are different.
33. However, in this example, the creator and the creation exist only within the five elements. For that which is without attributes, the distinction between the cause and effect does not exist beyond the five elements.
34. The one who is the creator of the entire creation is different from creation. There should not be any doubt about this.
35. How could it ever happen that the person who makes the puppets dance say that he is himself a puppet?
36. The appearance of creation is like the play of shadow puppets on the screen. The puppeteer pulls the strings but never becomes the many characters.
37. Similarly, God is the creator of the universe, but is not that creation. How can the one who has created many beings be one of those beings himself?
38. When one creates something, how can he become that which has been created? Many poor ignorant people unnecessarily fall into doubt about this.
39. The nature of the universe is like this. One who constructs the beautiful tops of temple towers does not become the tower.

40. Similarly, the one who has created the world is different from it. Some foolishly say that the world is itself the "Lord of the World" (Jagadesha).
41. The Lord of the World is different from his creation which is his work of art. Although he exists in everything, he is still different from everything.
42. Therefore, the Self that is God (AtmaRam) is different from this intermingling of the five elements. It is because of ignorance that this Illusion is felt true.
43. To presume that the creation of Illusion in its amazing immensity is real is contrary to deep investigative thought, and no such statements can be found in any texts on non-duality.
44. This being the case, the world is unreal and the Self (Atman) is real. That Supreme Self (Paramatman) is beyond everything, and is the Inner-Self (Antaratman) which pervades everywhere.
45. Only the Self should be called God, and everything else is false. This is the inner meaning of Vedanta.
46. All objects are destructible. Everyone has the experience of this. In this way it is seen that God is different from objects.
47. God is pure and unmoving. This is stated in all of the scriptures. That which is Eternal can never be called ephemeral.
48. To say that God has come, or that God has gone, or that God is born, or that God is dead, is but an accumulation of wrong thinking which amounts to an estrangement from God.
49. Talk about birth and death never applies to God. How can God, by whose power other gods are made immortal, ever die?
50. To be born and to die, to come and go, and suffering and sorrow are all the creation of God. Thus being the cause, it is clear that he is different from all of this.
51. The inner-mind (antahkarana), the functioning of the five pranas, and the knowledge of the physical body with its many principles, are all impermanent and therefore cannot be God.
52. That which is without any concept is called God. Even the notion of "being God" is not there.
53. Thus the disciple raised a question. "How then is the universe created, and how is the doer, which is the cause, also in the creation, or effect?" (Is the attributeless in that which is with attributes?)
54. Like the seer effortlessly becomes the seen with the act of seeing, similarly, the doer by his doing, gives attributes to the attributeless.
55. The listener asks, "Who is the maker of the universe? How is he recognized? Is God with attributes or without attributes? Please explain all of this to me.
56. Some say that it is by mere will that Brahman has made this creation. Who is the maker of this creation other than Brahman?
57. Now let this be enough of this long talk. From where has all of this Illusion come, must now be explained by the speaker."
58. Upon hearing this statement, the speaker says, "Remain alert, in the next sub-chapter I shall give the explanation.
59. How Illusion was created in Brahman will be explained later on. Now, the listeners must keep their mind alert.
60. The explanation will be given next. By listening to it and analyzing what is said, spiritual aspirants will become content.

Thus in Shri Dasbodh, a dialogue between the Guru and disciple, Sub-Chapter 1 of Chapter 8, named "Perceiving God" is concluded.

Chapter: 8, Sub-Chapter: 2

A Subtle Doubt

|| ShriRam ||

1. Earlier, the listeners raised a doubt that must be explained. How can this universe of animate and inanimate things be created from that which is without any attributes?
2. The answer to this question is as follows, Brahman is eternal, and there in it, the untrue appearance of Illusion appears like ripples on water.
3. The primal One, Parabrahman, the Absolute Reality, is eternally free, and totally beyond any activity. There, in it, the subtle and unmanifest primal original Illusion (Moolamaya) came into existence.
4. The listener asked, "If Brahman is one, formless, free, beyond any activity, and without modification, How can the appearance of Illusion happen in it?
5. As Brahman is continuous and without attributes, how can there be any desire there? In that which is without attributes, there cannot be any desire without that which is with attributes.
6. Originally, the one with attributes was not there, thus Brahman is named attributeless (nirguna). How did attributes come into being?
7. To say that the attributeless has attributes would be foolishness.
8. Some say he is without any attributes, and that while doing everything he is a non-doer. How can the poor ignorant beings understand his divine play?
9. Some say, 'Who can know the greatness of Parabrahman? It cannot be known.' How are poor ignorant individual beings to understand?
10. Some try to explain the greatness of Parabrahman ignoring what is said in the scriptures. They boldly say that the attributeless is the non-doer after having done everything.
11. In the original attributelessness there is no doing of anything. Who is the doer or non-doer? The ideas of a doer and a non-doer are totally false.
12. For That which is fundamentally without any attributes, how can there be any doership, and who is there to have any desire to make creation?
13. Most people say that it is the desire of God, but how can that which is without attributes have any desire? How can this be understood?
14. Still the question remains, who made all of this creation? Has it happened by itself? If so, that would mean that it was constructed without God.
15. If everything was created without God, then where is there any place for God? This would mean that God is absent and cannot be found.
16. If we say that God is the creator of creation, this would mean that he is seen to be with attributes, and there can be no notion of God without attributes.
17. If God is fundamentally attributeless, then who is the maker of this creation? The nature of a doer is to have attributes that are innately destructible.

18. Here one gets into the thought about how were all of these animate and inanimate things created. If we say that Illusion exists independently, this seems to be backwards logic.
19. If we say that Illusion is not made by anyone, that it has happened or expanded by itself, then there can be no talk about the existence of God.
20. If we say that God is self-existent and attributeless, what relationship can he have with Illusion? In saying this, there is contradiction.
21. If we say that the task of creation was entirely the responsibility of Illusion, then how can there be any talk of God who uplifts devotees?
22. If there is no God, and there is only Illusion, then who is responsible for the dissolution of Illusion, and who is there to protect us, the devotees?
23. All of that being said, one cannot say that Illusion has created itself. The one who is the "Lord of All" is alone the creator of Illusion.
24. So, what is God, and what is one to think about Illusion? Please, now all of this must be explained in detail."
25. The speaker said, "Listeners remain alert now, focus your mind, and listen attentively to the explanation that follows."
26. Here a doubt has been expressed about the various experiences of different people. I will tell about them all, in a sequential manner.
27. Some say that God has made and expanded this creation, and that if God had not desired it, then how could Illusion exist?
28. Some say that God is without attributes, so who is there to have any desire, and that Illusion is unreal, as it cannot happen by itself.
29. Some say that because it is seen, one cannot say it does not exist, and that Illusion is only the Power (Shakti) of God from the beginning.
30. Some say that if Illusion is true, then how is it that it can it dissolved with Knowledge (Jnana)? It only appears to be real, but it is really unreal.
31. Some say that it is innately false, so why should anyone do any spiritual practices, and others say that God has said that following the way of devotion is the means for being free of Illusion.
32. Some say that Illusion is unreal and that it appears due to the fever of ignorance, and that spiritual practice is the medicine by which the visible world is seen to be untrue.
33. An endless number of practices have been given, and many opinions have been expressed which create much confusion. And still, Illusion has not been discarded, so how can it be called untrue?
34. The knowledge of yoga, of the *Vedas*, vedic scriptures (*Shastras*), and the mythological books (*Puranas*) all say that Illusion is false. In a great number of explanations Illusion is said to be unreal.
35. Just saying that Illusion is false does not make it disappear. No one has ever heard of this happening. Actually, when one says that it is unreal, it seems more real.
36. For one who does not have Self-Knowledge and who does not know any saints, the unreal Illusion appears to be real.
37. Whatever is one's determination, one gets the results accordingly. In this way, Illusion is like the reflection that one sees of whatever is put in front of the mirror.
38. Some say that when all is only Brahman, where is Illusion? Similarly, with ghee, whether it is solid or liquid, it is only ghee.

39. Some say that the simile of solid and liquid cannot be applied to Brahman, and that even though it is spoken of in these terms, it has not changed, it always remains only one.
40. Some say that all is Brahman, but that this understanding cannot be gained as long as delusion has not gone from the mind.
41. Some say that since there is one God alone, how can there be any thing such as "everything"? Surely such a marvel as "everything is Brahman" has never occurred!
42. Others say that because there is only One alone that is true, it is not possible to bring in any "other," so Brahman has become everything effortlessly.
43. Some say that everything is entirely false and disappears, while Brahman is the only thing that remains, and is real. They say that statements like these have the support of scriptures.
44. Some say that because ornaments are only gold, there is no difference in them, and that it is only unnecessary toil to try to unify them.
45. Some say that any simile about Oneness will fall short, because how can using any concepts about objects apply? It is not possible to make a comparison of manifestation as being similar to the unmanifest.
46. If one has seen gold in its basic melted form and then sees the ornaments, it is understood that the ornaments are only gold.
47. Basically because gold is a manifested form that has the qualities of being heavy and a particular color of yellow, the simile cannot apply to Brahman which is complete in itself.
48. Similes are all limited, but some similes need to be given to help with understanding. For example, the simile of no differentiation between the waves and the ocean is often given.
49. Some similes are the best, some in the middle, and some are inferior. With one simile comes clarity and understanding, and with another clarity is destroyed and doubt is increased.
50. Even the simile of the ocean and the waves does not apply. How can the immovable Brahman be equated with the constantly moving sea and its waves. The magic of illusory objects cannot be considered to be real.
51. The magic of Illusion is only imagination. It shows many appearances, however it is always only Brahman.
52. In these ways, many people argue with one another, and the doubts remain. Now, be alert and listen to the explanation that follows.
53. The unreality of Illusion is understood, but how did it appear in Brahman? Even if we say that it was created by the attributeless, this statement is basically false.
54. The word unreal or untrue means that there is nothing, so who can say that anyone has done anything? It is not possible that anything has happened in that which is attributeless. This is a very wondrous thing.
55. The doer is essentially formless, and what has been made by him is unreal. Even so, the doubt of the listeners shall be cleared.

Thus in Shri Dasbodh, a dialogue between the Guru and disciple, Sub-Chapter 2 of Chapter 8, named "A Subtle Doubt" is concluded.

Chapter: 8, Sub-Chapter: 3

A Subtle Doubt (2)

|| ShriRam ||

1. The speaker said, "Dear one, why are you asking about that which has not happened? Nevertheless, I will give you some explanation so no doubt will remain.
2. It is because of the rope that there appears to be a snake, because of water that ripples appear, and because of the presence of the sun that a mirage appears.
3. It is because of imagination that a dream appears, because of the shell that there is a resemblance of silver, and because of water that ice is formed for a short time.
4. It is because of earth that a wall is constructed, because of the sea that waves appear, and it is because of the eye's lens that an image appears.
5. Because of gold there are ornaments, because of threads cloth is seen, and it is because of the turtle that its claws and limbs are extended and withdrawn.
6. It is because the ghee is present that it becomes liquid or solid, it is because of the water drying in the lagoon that salt is formed, and it is because of an object that its image is reflected.
7. It is because of the earth that trees exist, it is because of trees that there are large shadows, and it is because of metals that the qualities of superior or inferior colors and qualities are considered.
8. So, now let this be enough of these examples which are dualistic. They do not really apply to non-duality, yet one cannot speak of non-duality without making reference to duality.
9. It is because of appearances that the world appears, because of visibility that something becomes visible, and because there is no simile for the invisible, it is said to be beyond comparison.
10. Without conceptualization, there cannot be any intention, without visible objects, there can be no similes given, and without giving examples of duality how can duality be understood?
11. The creation of God is so marvelous that even Shesha, the thousand headed serpent that supports all of creation, cannot describe the endless number of universes with his thousand mouths.
12. The Self, Paramatman, is the Supreme God, who is the doer of everything. Because of him, the vast expanse of this universe has appeared.
13. He bears an endless number of names, and creates innumerable energies. The wise understand that he is Primal Being (Purusha).
14. The recognition of this Primal Beingness is itself the "Primal Illusion" (Moolamaya; Prakriti). The action of doing anything and everything comes only from there.
15. However, this should not be revealed openly because people will put off doing spiritual practice instead of making some effort to see what is true.
16. Everything has come from God, and this is known by everyone. However, this God must be recognized.
17. The explanation of this is given by the accomplished (Siddhas), but it is not understood by aspirants if the mind is not mature.

18. The individual exists because of the attribute of ignorance, Illusion exists because of Consciousness (Shiva), and the "Primal Illusion" (Moolamaya) exists because of God.
19. The Primal Illusion which holds immeasurable energy and active power is the cause (of creation). To understand this, it must be experienced.
20. The Primal Illusion is itself Primal Being. That itself is "Lord of All." It is this "Lord of the Universe" (Jagadisha) that is given an endless number of names.
21. The whole of Illusion is expansive, but it is really non-existent. The depth of this statement is very rarely understood.
22. What is being indicated is beyond words and can only be understood by Self-experience. This type of understanding is not possible without keeping the company of the saints.
23. The statement that Illusion is itself Primal Being is not easily understood by the spiritual aspirant, but still, who is it that is named "Lord of the Universe"?
24. It is a correct statement to say that the nature of illusory objects is to have name and form. The listeners should not have any doubts about this.
25. Now, let this be enough talk about this, the doubt raised earlier still remains. How has the Primal Illusion come from That which is formless?
26. How does this false mesmerism come into play? Now, it will be made entirely clear how this happens.
27. In the still empty space, the wind began to stir. In a similar way, the awareness of the Primal Illusion arose.
28. It can never be said to be true that by the stirring of the wind somehow space became broken.
29. Like this, the Primal Illusion arose while that which is without attributes remains unaffected. By this example, the previously expressed doubt is resolved.
30. The wind was not originally existing. The Primal Illusion should be understood to be like this. Even if you call it true, it only disappears again.
31. What is the form of wind? The Primal Illusion is seen to be similar to this. It is perceived, but its form is not seen.
32. We say that the wind is real but it cannot be shown. If we try to look at it, only dust is seen.
33. The Primal Illusion is similar to this, it is perceived, but it is not seen. Afterwards, it proliferates as "Illusion as Ignorance" (Avidyamaya).
34. Just as appearances disappear in the sky because of the wind, in the same way, the world appearance disappears because of the Primal Illusion.
35. In the sky, the clouds are not there, and then they suddenly appear. Similarly, the world is seen to appear like this, because of Illusion.
36. Nothing is there in the sky, and then suddenly clouds appear. Like this, the visible world appears in the same way.
37. Because of the clouds it seems that the stillness of the sky has disappeared, but as the base, it always remains the same.
38. Like this, because of Illusion it is felt that That "which is without attributes" (nirguna) has become "with attributes" (saguna). However, if we look into it completely, it is as it always is.
39. Even though the clouds appear and disappear, the sky remains as it is. In the same way, attributeless Brahman does not take on attributes.

40. The sky appears to be touching our head, but it just is, as it is. Similarly, one should understand with confidence that attributeless Brahman is as it is.
41. Looking above, the sky appears to be blue everywhere. This should be understood to be a false appearance that is only perceived to be real.
42. If one lays down and looks up at the sky, it looks as if it is curved and that it covers the earth in all directions, but it is really open and free.
43. Mountains, when seen from a distance appear to be blue in color, but they are not really that color. Similarly, understand the attributeless Brahman to be untouched by appearances.
44. While on a moving chariot, it feels as if the land is moving even though it remains motionless. Similarly, understand that the Absolute Reality is attributeless.
45. Because of the passing clouds the moon appears to be moving in the opposite direction, but this is only an illusion. Only the clouds are moving.
46. Because of heat waves, the sky looks like it is vibrating, but it really always remains motionless.
47. Similarly, the Reality, or "Self Form" (Swaroopa) appears to have taken on attributes, but this is only imagination which is untrue.
48. Illusion is like a trick of mesmerism which is ever-changing, while Reality is eternally still, as it is.
49. Reality is without any parts, but Illusion makes it seem to have many parts. The nature of Illusion is like this, it appears, but it is not really there.
50. When looking into Illusion, it is not really there at all, yet it appears to be real. It appears and disappears like the clouds.
51. Illusion arises like this. In the attributeless still expanse of Reality the inspiration of "I Am" (Aham) arose. This inspiration is itself Illusion.
52. All activity appears as the "Illusion with attributes" (Gunamaya). Nothing ever happens in that which is attributeless. Creation and destruction only appear to exist in the one True Form.
53. It is like when one has blurred vision and sees what appears to be an army in the sky, but it is unreal.
54. Now I have explained how the false play of Illusion occurs while keeping aside a lengthy description of the various characteristics of the five elements.
55. The five elements have their origin in the movement of the wind in the form of OM. The meaning of this is understood by the alert Knowledgeable Ones (Jnanis).
56. The restless nature of the Primal Illusion is itself the characteristic of wind. It is in this activity of wind that the subtle elements appear as visible forms.
57. It is in this manner that the previously unmanifest five elements became manifest during the process of creation.
58. Understand that the property of the Primal Illusion is that it is itself the five elements. This can be understood only with the subtlest vision.
59. How can desire as "word" arise without the stirring of the wind in space? Understand that the energy of this desire is itself the form of light.
60. Know that softness is itself water, and hardness is the earth element. Understand the Primal Illusion to be like this in the form of the five elements.
61. In each of the elements, there is the intermingling of all five elements. All of this is understood by seeing subtly with minute observation.

62. Afterwards, the elements appear in more gross form, but even then, they are still intermingled with each other. Like this, Illusion has spread out as the appearance of the five elements.
63. Whether one sees the Primal Illusion at its root, or as ignorance in the world, or heaven, or death, or in the netherworld, it is all only consisting of the five elements.
64. The one True Form exists at the beginning and at the end, and the five elements occupy the space in between. The listeners should understand that the Primal Illusion is itself the five elements.
65. Here a doubt arises. Be alert and listen attentively. The five elements are said to have come into existence from one quality which is ignorance, or Tamas (Tamoguna).
66. As the Primal Illusion is said to exist prior to any attributes, how can the five elements exist there? This is the doubt that listeners have raised.
67. The listeners have raised this doubt, and the answer is given in the next sub-chapter.

Thus in Shri Dasbodh, a dialogue between the Guru and disciple, Sub-Chapter 3 of Chapter 8, named "A Subtle Doubt (2)" is concluded.

Chapter: 8, Sub-Chapter: 4

The Five Subtle Elements

Shri Ram

1. The root of the doubt that was raised earlier will now be made clear. Please keep the attention of your mind clear and focused now.
2. The Primal Illusion (Moolamaya) appeared in Brahman. And that Illusion gave birth to the disturbance of the three attributes (Gunas). Therefore it is also given the name of the producer, or "disturber" of the attributes (Gunakshobini).
3. From that disturbance arose the "Three Gunas," the attributes of Sattva, Rajas, and Tamas, and then the five elements were formed from the Tamas attribute.
4. Once the elements were formed, they continued on to proliferate everywhere. Thus, the five elements came to exist from the quality of ignorance (Tamas).
5. The listeners have previously raised the doubt, that if the Primal Illusion is without attributes, how can the elements be formed there?
6. In addition to that, I will now make clear how all of the five elements are contained within each element.
7. With minute observation, the marvel of how the Primal Illusion contains the five elements can be seen. The listeners must utilize the power of clear thought in order to understand.
8. First come to know and understand the elements. Recognize their forms and then look into their nature with minute observation.
9. As long as one does not have an inner understanding of them, how can one recognize them? Therefore, one should wisely listen to the explanation about the recognition of the elements.

10. All that is gross and hard is indicative of the element of earth. That which is soft and having wetness is indicative of the water element.
11. Wherever there is heat and light, understand that as being the fire element. Now, I will explain the wind element (Vayu) with ease.
12. Know that the Life-Energy (Chaitanya) and its movement is itself the wind element, and understand that the space element (akasha), is by nature still and empty.
13. In this way, the five elements can be recognized by their particular conditions. Now, listen attentively to how all of the five elements are in each element.
14. To understand that which is beyond the three attributes, one should listen very attentively giving subtle consideration to what is heard.
15. How earth is present in the subtle sky must first be explained. Listeners, focus your concentration attentively here.
16. The "sky" means space that is empty, or void. Void means that there is ignorance. Understand that ignorance is inertia or heaviness which is itself earth.
17. Sky has the quality of being soft which is the presence of water in it. Now, the element of light in sky will also be explained.
18. Because of ignorance, visible appearances appear. This is itself the shining of light. Now I shall tell the nature of wind, in a relaxed manner.
19. There is no difference between wind and sky. The sky is still, but the quality of resistance that is experienced in the sky is wind.
20. The sky is infused with the sky element, this much is not required to be explained. Thus, in this way, I have explained the presence of five elements in sky.
21. Listen attentively now and I will explain in sequence how the five elements are present in the wind.
22. Just as a flower is delicate but still it has some weight, similarly, wind is soft, yet it still has density and heaviness that can break down trees with great force.
23. Without weight or heaviness, a tree cannot be broken. That weight which is a part of wind is the element of earth.
24. Here the listener expresses a doubt. "How can you speak of hardness that breaks trees if the forms of trees are not there in the Primal Illusion?" The answer to this is that hardness is inherent in the Primal Illusion in the power of subtle wind.
25. Just as heat is contained in a small spark of fire, similarly there is heaviness contained in the subtle form of wind.
26. The softness in wind is the element of water, the appearance of light is itself the form of light in wind, and the restlessness that is naturally found in the wind is the wind element itself.
27. The space element encompasses everything, so naturally the element of space is present in wind. Thus, I have explained how the five elements are present in wind.
28. Now, as for the element of fire, the appearance of light is itself the hardness which is the element of earth in light.
29. The feeling of softness that is felt in the warmth of light is the presence of water in the fire. Light itself is obviously present in fire, this is not even required to be told.
30. The restlessness or motion of light is the element of wind, and of course the immovable, all-encompassing space is present in light. Now, the presence of all of the five elements in light have been told.
31. Now, the explanation of water. Water has a natural softness to it, yet there is a quality of hardness in water that is the earth element.

32. The water element naturally is present in water, this is easily seen. The appearance, or visibility of water is the element of light. The motion that appears on the stillness of water is the wind element with softness within it.
33. The space element is not required to be told as it by its nature pervades water. Now, I have explained in a subtle way the presence of the five elements in water.
34. Now, I will explain the earth element. The main quality of the earth element is hardness itself, yet in that hardness, sometimes there is a quality of softness which is the water element.
35. The appearance of hardness that it is visible, is the quality of the light element in earth. The quality of resistance in the hardness of earth is the wind element.
36. The space element pervades everything. This can be easily discerned. The very appearance of the earth in space is itself the presence of the space element.
37. Space cannot be broken or split, and no one can go beyond space.
38. Now, let this explanation be enough. The qualities of the five elements and how all of the five elements are present in each element have been shown.
39. However, this cannot be understood by superficially looking, as confusion will only become stronger and many opinions will go on increasing.
40. When looking with subtle observation, all is seen to be principally of the nature of wind, and with minute observation of the wind, the five elements are found.
41. Thus, understand that it is the wind, which contains the five elements and is itself the Primal Illusion. This Primal Illusion is also the subtle Three Gunas (Rajas, Tamas, and Sattva), together with the Five Elements.
42. The elements combined together with the gunas is called the "Eightfold Manifestation" (Prakriti). Understand that the Eightfold Manifestation is itself the five elements.
43. To search without finding out, and to hold on to doubt is foolishness. Look with minute observation and identify what is true.
44. The subtle elements have come out of the gunas, and by becoming visible and gross, they became the manifest elements.
45. The explanation of the manifest elements and their arrangement of the gross body and the subtle body of the universe will be given later so that it will be made clear to the listeners.
46. The intermingling of the elements has been revealed by subtle indications. This happened before the universe was created.
47. Understand with subtle vision that the Primal Illusion existed before the creation of the things in this universe.
48. The enormous seven-sheathed creation[47] as well as the activities of Illusion and ignorance were created afterwards.
49. Brahma, Vishnu, and Shiva, as well as the earth, mountains and seven seas were created afterwards.
50. Many people, many places, the moon, the sun, the galaxies, seven continents, and fourteen universes were created afterwards.
51. The serpent Shesha, the incarnation of Lord Vishnu in the tortoise form, the seven hells, the twenty-one heavens, the eight sentinels of eight directions, and thirty three million kinds of gods, were all created afterwards.

---

[47] The interpretation of the seven sheaths varies, but is generally considered to be the Five Elements, the ego or ignorance, and Chaitanya or the Self which is sometimes referred to as the seven sheathed creation.

52. The twelve suns, the eleven forms of Shiva, the nine serpents, the seven great sages, and many incarnations of gods were all created afterwards.
53. The clouds, the ancestors, the ancient emperors, and the multitude of living beings were all created afterwards. Now, enough of this! How much should be told about the expanse of creation?
54. The origin of the expanse of the universe is the Primal Illusion alone. It has already been explained how everything in creation is made up of the five elements.
55. It has also been explained how the subtle elements, appeared and became manifest afterwards. This will be explained further in the next sub-chapter.
56. The analysis of the five elements will be described in detail. The listeners are respectfully asked to listen attentively and recognize what is being said.
57. This universe is made up of the five elements. One who understands this clearly will attain the Reality by giving up what is visible.
58. Just as one must cross the main door of the temple to get the view of the god within, similarly, one must give up the visible world with understanding.
59. The visible world is full with the five elements intermingling together visibly.
60. The visible world is made up of only the five elements. The listeners are requested to be at ease and listen to the explanation of how the universe was created.

Thus in Shri Dasbodh, a dialogue between the Guru and disciple, Sub-Chapter 4 of Chapter 8, named "The Five Subtle Elements" is concluded.

Chapter: 8, Sub-Chapter: 5

The Five Manifest Elements

|| ShriRam ||

1. Those who are ignorant do no not understand, therefore the explanation of the attributes of the five elements is given.
2. The five elements are intermingled to such an extent that it is impossible to separate them, but some explanation of their differences will now be given.
3. Hills, stones, rocks, mountaintops, rubble, and gravel that is small and large of many colors and varieties are all made of earth.
4. Soil of many colors which is present in many places, and various types of sand are all earth.
5. Beautiful towns and cities, many temples filled with jewels, and many temple tops are all made of earth.
6. How much should be told to describe the land masses and continents that are made of earth?
7. Many gods, kings, languages, cultures, and all of the 8.4 millions species of living beings are all made of earth.
8. Many barren forests, many jungles with huge trees, and many places in the mountains and valleys are all made of earth.
9. The listeners should understand that all the many creations made by gods and all of those created by man are made of earth.

10. Many metals such as gold and others, many various types of jewels, and many types of trees and wood are all made of earth.
11. Now, let this be enough of these many examples. You can have confidence that whatever is firm and hard is of the nature of earth.
12. The nature of earth has been described, now I shall give the description of water. Listeners are asked to remain alert and recognize its nature.
13. The water, which comes from wells, ponds, lakes, many rivers, clouds and the seven seas[48], are all made up of water.
14. The oceans of salt water are visible and easily seen by all. This form of water where salt is formed is called the salt sea.
15. Another form of water is named the sea of milk. In ancient mythology this sea of milk was given by God to Upamanyu, the son of Vyagrapada.
16. Other seas are the sea of wine, one of ghee, and one is the sea of curds (cultured milk; yogurt).
17. There is one that is the sea of sugarcane juice, and lastly, one that is but pure water. Like this, there seven seas found around the earth.
18. Thus, understand that all of the various forms of water found all over the earth, are made of the water element.
19. There is water in many underground sources, on the surface of the earth, and in the covering of moisture all around the earth. The water in all three of these locations is the water element.
20. There are many varieties of vines, the sap of many trees, honey, mercury, ambrosia, and poison that are all made from the water element.
21. There are many other liquids such as juices and oils which look different from water, but they are of the nature of the water element.
22. Liquids that are wet and cool, and fluids in nature such as semen, blood, urine, and saliva, are all made of the water element.
23. Understand the indications of the water element and recognize that its nature is to be soft, cool, and fluid.
24. The signs of liquidity, softness, and smoothness of the water element have now been told. Understand that sweat, phlegm, and tears, are also all made of water.
25. Listen alertly now to the description of the fire element. The moon, sun, galaxies, and shining heavenly bodies, are made of the fire element.
26. That which is seen in the clouds as lightening, that which is the fire that destroys the universe, and is the huge fire the bottom of the sea, is the fire element.
27. The fire that is in the third eye of Shiva, the fire of the hunger of time that devours all, and the luminosity that is around the circumference of the earth is all fire.
28. Whatever is in the form of luminance, and that which has the quality of heating and drying is the of the nature of fire.
29. Understand the wind element to be movement. It is the wind alone that ignites Life-Energy (Chaitanya). The activities of talking and walking are all because of the wind element.
30. All that moves and vibrates is wind. Nothing moves without wind. The primary animating force of nature is the wind.
31. To move, to bend, to expand, to resist, and to contract are the qualities that are the nature of the constantly changing wind.

---

[48] The seven seas are 1) salt water, 2) milk, 3) wine, 4) ghee, 5) curds, 6) sugarcane juice, and 7) pure water

32. Understand that the five vital airs or pranas (Prana, Apana, Vyana, Udana, and Samana), and the secondary airs, the Upapranas, (Naaga, Kurma, Karkasha, Devadatta, and Dhananjaya) to be only wind.
33. Anything and everything that moves is due to the wind. The moon, the sun, and the galaxies are all supported by the wind.
34. Understand that the sky is empty, stainless, and still. Understand that the empty form of space is the sky.
35. The sky permeates all, and everything is contained in the sky. The other four elements have their residence in the sky.
36. There is nothing as essential as the sky. The sky is greater than everything else. Through inquiry, one can see that the sky is similar to the True Form of the Self.
37. Here the disciple raised a doubt. "If both are similar in form, then why do we not say that the sky (space) itself is our True Form?
38. What is the difference between space and our True Form? When looking, there appears to be no difference. Why not call the space as Reality itself?
39. Reality is still, indestructible, pure, and changeless. Similarly, the sky is like Reality."
40. Hearing this, the speaker responds, "Reality is eternal, and without attributes, while the sky has seven attributes that are explained in the scriptures.
41. Desire, anger, sorrow, enticement, fear, ignorance, and emptiness are the seven attributes that are inherent in the sky's nature.
42. The authors of the ancient scriptures have described the sky element with attributes like this, while Reality is formless and cannot be compared to anything.
43. While a glass floor and water look similar, it can be easily understood that one is glass and the other is water.
44. If a clear piece of crystal falls into a pile of cotton, people see only see the cotton. The two look the same, but crystal is hard and could even break one's head while cotton could not.
45. If there are some small white stones mixed in with grains of rice, one does not know the difference in them until biting down on one and breaking a tooth.
46. In the solid concrete, there is stone, lime, and sand which all appear hard, but when looking into their composition, they are seen to be of different hardness.
47. Jaggery (a crude type of brown sugar) may have a small clump of soil in it, yet the soil is hard and dry and different from the sugar. Nagakandi and Vekhanda are two plants that look alike, but they cannot be said to be the same. (One is poisonous and one has medicinal qualities.)
48. Gold and yellow brass appear to be the same, but when coming into contact with a flame, the brass gets coated with black soot.
49. Now, enough of these comparisons which are of low quality. The sky is only an element, how can an element be the same as the boundless Reality?
50. There is no color to Reality while the sky appears to have a blue or black color. How can they be said to be similar.
51. The listener says, "How does the sky have form when it is basically formless? The formless sky is so similar to Reality that there is no difference.
52. The other four elements are subject to destruction, but how can the sky be destroyed? It does not possess color, form, or undergo any modification.
53. The sky is still, how can it be destroyed? If we look into it, it is our opinion that the sky is permanent."

54. Hearing these statements the speaker gives a reply. Listen now to the qualities of the sky.
55. The sky is formed from ignorance (Tamas), and is covered by desire and anger. It is called by the name of the "Void of Ignorance."
56. From ignorance arises desire, anger, enticement, fear and sorrow. These distinctions in the sky are because of ignorance.
57. The atheist rejects the existence of Reality and openly says so. This in itself is a sign of emptiness. People call him empty-hearted and ignorant.
58. The stillness of the sky is empty or void. Being empty means that its nature is ignorance and its form is solid.
59. How can that which is hard, empty, and prone to modification be called permanent? It is only thought to be the same as Brahman by the mind when not seen clearly.
60. Ignorance is infused with the sky, and Knowledge has the capacity to destroy that mixture. Therefore, the sky is destructible.
61. In this way, the sky and Reality seem to one and the same, however there is a difference in the emptiness of them.
62. If one only looks superficially, both appear to be the same, but there is a difference between the sky and Reality
63. The state of deep sleep and "no-mind" (unmani), are basically felt to be the same, but when seen with proper discrimination, there is a difference.
64. When a falsehood is presented to be true, the ordinary person is fooled, but the expert examiner can select what is true. It is similar to the deer that sees a mirage and runs towards it.
65. Now, let this be enough of these similes. These are only examples given to help one understand that the sky element and the immeasurable Brahman are not the same.
66. The sky is seen from the perspective of being apart from it, and Reality is only seen by being one with it. Reality is only seen in this way.
67. Here the doubt has been cleared, and the skeptical attitude has faded away. Reality cannot be experienced by being separate from it.
68. The sky can be experienced, while Reality is beyond all experience. Therefore, the sky cannot be the same as Reality.
69. The Royal Swan (Raj Hansa) can differentiate between milk and water, sipping up the milk and leaving the water. Similarly, the saints understand the difference between the sky and Reality.
70. All of this world appearance is a tumultuous intermixture of Illusion. Only in the company of saints is one able to resolve this. Arrive at the state of liberation in the company of the saints.

Thus in Shri Dasbodh, a dialogue between the Guru and disciple, Sub-Chapter 5 of Chapter 8, named "The Five Manifest Elements" is concluded.

Chapter: 8, Sub-Chapter: 6

Explanation of Restlessness

|| ShriRam ||

1. The listener requested of the speaker, "Please explain the importance of keeping the company of saints. How does one attain liberation and in how many days?
2. By keeping the company of sages, how long does it take for liberation? Please, give the understanding by which a poor person like me may gain conviction."
3. The speaker said, "One becomes liberated at the very moment that one has full faith in the explanation. If the mind is restless and skeptical, one is at a loss."
4. The listener asked; "When there is attentiveness, and then suddenly the mind becomes restless, how does one make it quiet?"
5. The speaker responded, "The mind should be cut off from the many distractions and one should sit attentively listening to explanations with interest and alertness making the time worthwhile from one moment to the next."
6. The meanings of important principles from various texts should be sought out, understood, and retained within oneself. If the restlessness or confusion returns, then listen to the explanations again and again.
7. One who listens but does not see the meaning, is not really a listener, but is a stone, disguised as a human being.
8. Here the listeners may feel disturbed because they are being called stones. So the speaker said, "Be alert, and listen to the attributes of stones."
9. If a stone is broken somehow and then is chiseled out to be made proper, it will remain in its proper condition thereafter.
10. When a slice is cut off of the stone with a chisel it cannot be reattached again afterwards. However, if a person rids oneself of wrongful intellect, that way of thinking can come back again.
11. Negative qualities may be discarded by way of explanation if they are pointed out, but afterwards they return. For this reason a stone is much better than a man.
12. One whose negative attributes cannot be shed is inferior to the stone. Understand that a stone is thousands of times superior to such a person.
13. How can a stone be thousands of times superior to a person? The listeners are asked to remain alert and listen to the qualities of stone.
14. All of the jewels such as rubies, pearls, corals, emeralds, sapphires, turquoise, topaz, and others such as wish fulfilling stones are all essentially only stones.
15. In addition to these, there are sun influenced stones, moon influenced stones, and many others that are well known for their medicinal qualities.
16. Besides these there are many other types of stones. There are stones that are found at many pilgrimage places, some that are utilized for constructing wells and ponds, and some stones that are used for making idols of Vishnu and Shiva.
17. If you consider all of this, you will find that there is nothing more valuable than stones. Human beings are of little value in comparison to stones.
18. Understand that the body of the confused non-devotional person is comparable to a dirty useless type of stone.
19. Now enough of this type of talk. With a restless doubting mind one suffers a loss. With a restless mind one neither enjoys the worldly life nor spiritual life.

20. With restlessness one's work does not get accomplished. With restlessness and doubt, worries get lodged in the mind. With restlessness there is forgetfulness of important things.
21. With the restless and doubtful mind, life is like an enemy, and one is bound in the cycle of birth and death. Restlessness only results in harm to oneself.
22. With restlessness, there is no spiritual practice, worship does not happen, and the aspirant does not gain Self-Knowledge.
23. With restlessness, there is no firm resolution, success is not possible, and there is deterioration of one's own welfare.
24. With restlessness listening and analysis are not possible, and the meaning of the explanations is lost.
25. The person with a restless mind appears to be seated in one place, but really he is not there, as his mind is ensnared in a whirlpool of restlessness.
26. Understand that the life of a human being with a restless mind is like one who is deaf, dumb and blind, or one who is possessed by a ghost.
27. Even though he is awake, he does not comprehend, and although he is listening, he does not hear. He has knowledge, but he is not able to understand the thought regarding the Eternal and the ephemeral.
28. How can one who is restless and lazy, in whose life laziness resides day and night attain that which is beyond this world?
29. Even if the restlessness may disappear, there is still some laziness remaining. Because of laziness, the lazy person never seems to have any time.
30. Laziness obstructs the power of inquiry. With laziness the appropriate behavior gets drowned, and with laziness nothing that is heard is retained.
31. Because of laziness listening is not possible, and there is no understanding of the explanation. With laziness the ability to recognize the signs of spiritual life becomes blurred.
32. With laziness the daily discipline is not followed, one's study gets washed away, and laziness itself increases beyond imagination.
33. With laziness mental focus and patience is lost. With laziness one's mental attitude becomes tainted and the power of discrimination becomes dull.
34. With laziness sleep increases, and one's mental tendencies proliferate. With laziness virtuous intellect becomes void, lacking conviction.
35. Restlessness of mind is associated with laziness and excessive enjoyment of sleep. With excessive enjoyment of sleep, one ruins his own life.
36. Sleep, laziness, and restlessness of mind are signs of a foolish person. Such a person cannot understand the explanations that are given.
37. Where these three signs are present, how can there be any power of discrimination? The ignorant one does not find any other happiness.
38. Feeling hungry, such a person has his meals. After eating he feels lazy. Feeling lazy, he goes off to sleep very comfortably.
39. After waking from sleep, the mind becomes restless again and unable to concentrate. How can there be any self benefit listening to explanations with such a restless mind?
40. Giving explanations to one with a restless mind is like giving a jewel to a monkey, or putting treasure in the hands of a ghost.
41. Let this be enough of this explanation about restlessness. The original question was, "In how many days does one become liberated in the company of saints?"

42. Now, listen to the reply, and with the explanation become cleared of doubts. The effect of keeping the company of saints is like this.
43. Iron that has been touched by the philosopher's stone becomes gold. A drop of water merges into the sea. The river meeting the Ganges becomes the Ganges. All of these things happen in the moment.
44. For the one who is attentive, observant and thoughtful, liberation is immediate. For others it is out of sight, and there cannot even be any talk of liberation.
45. Here, the intelligence of the disciple alone is important. The one who is intelligent does not require any time. Being one with the Self, liberation is immediate.
46. Those with understanding who are one-pointed don't require even a single moment. However, having the thought of being one with the Self in the intellect without having devotion, is of no use.
47. Without intelligence, the meaning is not understood, and without faith Reality is not understood. With faith and intelligence together, one is able to discard the misidentification with the body.
48. With the ending of the misidentification with the body, there is effortless realization of Reality. In the company of saints, there is no delay in realization.
49. For one who is especially alert, observant, intelligent, and who has faith, great effort in spiritual practice is not required.
50. Other devotees who are simple-minded can become liberated as well by means of spiritual practice, and by keeping the company of sages, which enables clear seeing with the power of discrimination.
51. However, spiritual practice and spiritual discourse should not be abandoned. Spiritual discourse is beneficial for everyone.
52. Now, I will explain the nature of liberation, the nature of one's Self Nature, as well as how one gains certainty by keeping the company of saints.
53. Clear explanation of all of this will be given in the next sub-chapter. The listeners are requested to listen with a still and attentive mind.
54. In order to ensure the abandoning of negative qualities it was necessary to use harsh but just words. The listeners are asked not to hold on to any anger about such statements.

Thus in Shri Dasbodh, a dialogue between the Guru and disciple, Sub-Chapter 6 of Chapter 8, named "Explanation of Restlessness" is concluded.

Chapter: 8, Sub-Chapter: 7

The Signs of Liberation

|| ShriRam ||

1. Previously, the listeners asked, "How many days does it take for one to become liberated?" The listeners are now asked to listen to the reply while remaining alert.
2. What is meant by liberation? Who should be called liberated? How does one become liberated in the company of saints?

3. Alright then, bondage means that one is tied down, and liberation means that one is free. Listen now to the explanation about how one becomes liberated in the company of saints.
4. Living beings are only bound by desires and the concept that one is a limited individual being (jiva). One becomes liberated by the sages by means of the power of discrimination.
5. Holding firm to the determination that one is a separate individual over a long time, the living being has become small because of body-consciousness (misidentification with the body).
6. One thinks, "I am a separate individual. For me there is bondage. I have a birth and death. I shall suffer the fruits of actions that I have done.
7. The fruits of wrongful deeds are sorrowful, and the fruits of good deeds are pleasurable. I must certainly experience the fruits of my sins and merits."
8. Like this one's concepts become so fixed that the sufferings of sins and merits cannot be escaped, and that a return to the womb is inevitable.
9. This is what is termed as bondage. The idea of being an individual makes one feel bound. It is like the silkworm that dies in its own cocoon.
10. Like this, the living being is ignorant and does not have the knowledge of God, and does not become liberated from birth and death.
11. One thinks, "Now I shall do some charity that will be beneficial for the next life. With that charity my worldly life will be better.
12. Before I did not do any charity and therefore got poverty. Now, at least I will do something charitable.
13. I will give away the old clothing and one copper coin, and then I shall receive back a thousandfold later."
14. Having heard about the greatness of giving in charity at great pilgrimage places, one goes there thinking of a thousandfold returns.
15. By giving a donation of a coin or two, and by feeding a pilgrim a piece of bread, one thinks that some great amount of food provisions will be received in return many times over.
16. Like this, one imagines about future returns. In this way, the living being becomes entangled in the desire to be born again.
17. Understand that one who imagines that, "Whatever I give now, I will reap in the next life," is bound in ignorance.
18. Only after many lives does one acquire a human body. If one does not gain Self-Knowledge on the true path in this life, the return to the womb cannot be avoided.
19. To return to the womb of the human body is not always possible, and it may happen suddenly that one has to suffer life in a lower species again.
20. Thus, the conviction that has been told in many scriptures and by many people is that to get a human body in this world appearance is very rare.
21. Only if there is a balance of virtuous and non-virtuous deeds does one acquire a human body, otherwise human birth is not possible. This is the statement of Vyasa muni in the *Srimad Bhagavatam* (an ancient Hindu scripture, one of the *Puranas*).
22. The human body is rare, and is obtained by some desire. If the Sadguru is the captain of the ship it becomes possible for one to be content.
23. God does not favor one who is not virtuous. Such a human being cannot go beyond the worldly life. He is considered to be committing suicide.

24. Without Self-Knowledge human beings remain in the cycle of birth and death in the 8.4 million species. He must die many times, therefore he is said to be one who is committing suicide.
25. Without gaining Self-Knowledge in the human body one cannot escape the cycle of birth and death, and one must endure miserable suffering being born into many lower species.
26. Bear, monkey, dog, pig, horse, bull, buffalo, donkey, crow, cock, fox, cat, chameleon, frog and fly are some of the species.
27. Not having Self-Knowledge, one has to suffer through all of these lowly births. Only a foolish person holds on to hopes for the next life.
28. Such a one shamelessly hopes that once this human body falls dead that he will get a human birth again.
29. Who can be sure that he has so much accumulation of virtue that he will once again obtain a human body? Such a one is seen to be holding to false hopes for the next life.
30. Like this, the ignorant foolish people create their own bondage by desire. They become their own enemy in this life.
31. Such is the bondage of desires. Understand that it breaks in the company of saints. Listen, and I shall tell the signs of keeping good company.
32. The body along with the entirety of the animate and inanimate creation is made up of the five elements which act according to their various natures in this world appearance.
33. The bodies, the states of mind, the states of ego, along with the organs, the enjoyments, the degrees of AUM, the attributes (gunas), and the powers, are all categorized into four main categories.

The four bodies: Gross body, subtle body, causal body, and great causal body.
The four states of mind: Waking, dreaming, deep sleep, and Turya.
The four states of Ego: Physical body, subtle body, casual body, and great casual body.
The four places: eyes, throat, heart and head.
Four senses of enjoyment: Physical, selective, desire for joy, and the subtle semblance of joy.
The four degrees: Aum: The generator, the sustainer, the destroyer, the all pervasive.
The four attributes: Sattva, Rajas, Tamas, and Pure Sattva.
The four powers: Action, matter, will, and wisdom.
Together, these make 32 in all. This is described again in detail in Chapter 17, Sub-chapter 9 of this book.

34. The organization of the body and universe is like this. Its expanse is increased by imagination. Asserting knowledge of these principles, many have become confused by various opinions.
35. There are many differences of opinion which only increase arguments. Only the sages truly understand how to discuss all of this as non-duality.
36. The primary indication of this dialogue is that the body is made up of the five elements. Understand that the Self is the cause of the body.
37. In the end, the body is destroyed, so it cannot be called the Self. It is a combination of the principle elements which are found to be present in the form of the body.
38. The scriptures state that the subtle body is composed of intellect, mind, thoughts, ego, and inner-mind (antahkarana), the five life energies or pranas, the five action

organs, and the five sense organs along with the five objects of the senses. This should be understood with subtle discrimination.

39. With subtle investigation and clear seeing, the subtle body becomes purified and one can know that the inner-mind, mind, and intellect are its principle elements, while the Self is altogether different.

40. For the human being, there are four bodies; gross, subtle, casual, and great casual, and at the level of the universe there are four corresponding bodies called the 1) the gross physical universe, or Virat body (2) the universal life energy, or Hiranya body, (3) the unmanifest causal, or Avyakruta body, and (4) and the Primal Illusion, or Moola Prakriti body. Understand these to be the eight bodies.

41. There are four bodies associated the human body, and four bodies of the universe, which are the well known eight bodies. Together with the original unmanifest and manifest male and female principles (Purusha and Prakriti) these make ten bodies in all.

42. The signs of the various principle elements are described like this. The Self is the extraordinary witness, the doer of all activity, and the cause of the visible.

43. The individual (jiva) and God (Shiva), as well as the physical body and the universe, are all the commotion of Illusion and ignorance. There is a great deal that can be said about this, however, it should be known that the Self is different from all this.

44. If we investigate, we can find what are called the four categories of Self. Listen to their signs and retain what has been heard.

45. The first is the Individual Self (Jivatma), the second is the God Self (Shivatma), the third is the Self that is beyond the universe (Paramatma), and fourth is the Self that is unrelated to anything (Nirmalatma). These are the four categories of Self.

46. These appear to be different, and superior or inferior, but really all four are only one Self. I shall explain this with a simile. Listen with alertness.

47. There is the space in a pot, the space in the room, the space outside the room, and space that is Brahman which is beyond the appearance of the universe. However, all of these together comprise only one space.

48. In the same way, the individual Self, the God Self, the Self beyond, and the unalloyed Self all together make up only one Self.

49. There is space that is occupying the pot (Ghatakasha), and similarly there is that aspect of Brahman which is occupying the physical body called the individual Self (Jivatma).

50. There is space that is occupying the room (Mathakasha), and similarly the aspect of Brahman that is occupying the universe is called the Self as God (Shivatma).

51. There is space that is outside of the room (Mahakasha) and similarly, there is that aspect of Brahman which is beyond the universal appearance which is called the Self that is beyond (Paramatma).

52. Lastly, there is the space that is unalloyed with anything (Chidakasha), and similarly, the pure unalloyed Self without any attributes (Nirmalatma), is the Supreme God, and is nameless.

53. Because of the different names, the space appears to be different, however it is really undifferentiated. Similarly, the Self is One, full with bliss.

54. Inside and outside of all visible things is the subtle Self which is always present. Even the great serpent Shesha was not able to describe its greatness with a thousand mouths.

55. When the Self is understood in this way, it is seen that there is no separately existing individual, and one's identity is known to be undifferentiated being, free of all labels and attributes.
56. Believing oneself to be an individual, one feels separate. With this sense of individuality or ego, one suffers birth. How can there be any birth for the one who sees clearly using the power of discrimination?
57. Understand that escaping from the birth and death cycle is what is called liberation. Through investigation and analysis of the principle elements, the Reality is realized.
58. One's Self is Reality itself. This is the meaning of the great statement, "I Am That" from the *Vedas*. The saints give clear explanations from their own experience.
59. The very moment that one receives initiation and instruction, at that same moment, liberation takes place. One cannot speak of any bondage for the Self.
60. Now the doubt has been cleared, and the skeptical attitude has been discarded. In the company of saints, one becomes liberated immediately.
61. The one who was bound in the dream is made free by waking up, and it is with knowledge and discrimination that human beings become liberated.
62. When the night of ignorance comes to an end, the sorrow arising from desires is destroyed, and one immediately becomes liberated.
63. To break the bondage of the dream, no additional spiritual practice is required other than to wake-up.
64. Similarly, for one who has the concept of being an individual, there is no other remedy than clear seeing. By using the power of discrimination, bondage disappears.
65. Without using discrimination, all efforts that are made only become tiresome. Using the power of discrimination, one sees clearly that oneself is the Self alone.
66. In the Self, there is no bondage or liberation, and there is no birth and no death taking place.

Thus in Shri Dasbodh, a dialogue between the Guru and disciple, Sub-Chapter 7 of Chapter 8, named "The Signs of Liberation" is concluded.

Chapter: 8, Sub-Chapter: 8

The Perception of Self

|| ShriRam ||

1. Understand the explanation given previously that you yourself are the Supreme Self, Paramatman. The signs of Paramatman will now be given.
2. These is no birth, no death, no coming, no going, no bondage, and no liberation for the Self.
3. The Self is attributeless, formless, limitless, and endless. It is Eternal and continuous. It is as it is.
4. Paramatman pervades all. It is One in many. The recognition of the Self is beyond logic.
5. Like this, are the signs of the Self, as stated in the *Vedas* and *Upanishads*. The Self can be only be realized with devotion. There is no doubt about this.

6. The signs of devotion are the nine-faceted devotion. With the nine-faceted devotion many devotees have become pure.
7. Within that nine-faceted devotion, the greatest is self-surrender, or identification with the Self. One should inquire into the Self and realize it for oneself.
8. It must be in one's own experience that one identifies with the Self. The devotion of self-surrender is of this quality.
9. In the end, the greatest worship is when one offers one's head to God completely. Such closeness with God is the devotion of self-surrender.
10. There are very few devotees who surrender themselves completely. To them the Self gives liberation immediately.
11. The listener asks, "How should one surrender oneself? Where should one go to bow down? Should one cut one's head off before an image of God?"
12. Hearing such talk, the knowledgeable speaker says "Please remain alert with an attentive mind."
13. The sign of self-surrender is to first find out "Who am I?" and with that comes the recognition of the attributeless Self.
14. By searching out who God is and who the devotee is, self-surrender naturally takes place, and the devotee sees that God is eternal.
15. In the recognition of God there is oneness with God. There is no existence of separation between God and the devotee at all.
16. Because there is no separateness, God is the devotee, and as there is no bondage, there is freedom, or liberation. This talk is not incorrect, it is in accordance with reference to the scriptures.
17. In seeking the root of God and the devotee the sense of separation completely disappears, leaving only the Self, Paramatman, which is different from visible appearances.
18. Being one with it, there is nothing remaining as a second thing. The feeling of there being a difference between God and devotee gets dissolved.
19. With self-surrender there is devotion without any separation. Understand that this is the true total liberation (sayujya).
20. The one who surrenders to the saints, and receives the explanation of non-duality cannot be made separate even if he tries.
21. When the river meets with the sea, how can it be separated? And if iron is turned into gold, it cannot be turned back into iron again.
22. Similarly, once one is merged with God, it never will happen that he can become separate again. The devotee becomes God, never to be made separate.
23. One who has understood with discrimination that God and devotee are one is worthy among sages of offering the promise of liberation.
24. Now enough with this talk. See God through the eyes of a devotee, and immediately enjoy the glory of God.
25. Living only as the body one experiences the sorrows of the human body, and when living beyond the body, one realizes Parabrahman, the Absolute Reality.
26. The listener asks, "How can one go beyond body-identification, how does one realize Parabrahman, and what do you mean by God's glory? Please explain."
27. These were the questions that the listener put forth. Please listen attentively to the explanation regarding the doubts that have been expressed.

28. Reality is beyond the body, and that Absolute Reality is oneself. When you go beyond the identification with the body, you will not be able to tolerate any attachment to the body.
29. The *Vedas* praise one whose intellect is like this. This Knowledge is not readily gained even after searching through many scriptures.
30. In principle, glory is acquired only by giving up body-consciousness. If one thinks, "I am the body," there is downfall.
31. For this reason, do not consider the statements of the sages as unacceptable. If one considers what the sages say to be false, then who is to blame?
32. The listener asks, "What is the statement of the sages, and why should one have faith in them? Please, explain this to me."
33. The statement of the sages is that "I am the Self, full of bliss and unborn. Understand that you yourself are unborn and full of bliss." Hold firmly to it.
34. The meaning of this great statement is that you are always Brahman. Statements such as this must not be forgotten.
35. If one says "When the body comes to an end, then I will become endless," you should not consider this type of talk to be true.
36. Another fool says, "Only when Illusion is destroyed at the time of the final destruction, will there be attainment of Brahman.
37. Illusion must come to an end, either at the time of the final destruction, or when the body comes to an end. I will peacefully attain Parabrahman then."
38. This type of talk is not correct. One does not become satisfied in this way. The true quality of contentment is quite different.
39. This is like ruling a kingdom when the army is all dead. What is the use of such a kingdom? The fool does not understand that one should be ruling as king when the army is still in existence.
40. Understand that Illusion is not real even though it has an appearance. Similarly, even though one has a body, one is already beyond the body. Recognize this and know the contentment that comes with this understanding.
41. When a kingdom suddenly falls into your hands, the administration of the kingdom continues to function just fine as you see everything going on. The kingdom does not become lost because the administrators are seen to be functioning.
42. Similarly, upon gaining Self-Knowledge, the awareness of the body does not disappear. Seeing the body function does not take away one's contentment.
43. If a long root is mistaken for a snake one becomes very frightened, but when giving some thought as to the truth of its nature, there is no need to kill the root.
44. Similarly, Illusion is scary, but when one inquires into its true nature, there is no reason why one should hold on to any fear about it.
45. When seeing a mirage, it looks like a flood and one asks about how to get across the water. However, when the truth is known, there is no worry.
46. When seeing a terrible dream, one feels very scared in the dream. However, upon waking up, there is no reason why one should have any doubt that the events in the dream where not real.
47. Illusion occurs in concepts while the Self is beyond all concepts. How can there be any despair when there are no concepts?
48. It is said that whatever mental state that one has at the time of the end of the body determines what comes after death. It is told like this in all of the scriptures. Therefore, naturally you will also experience according to your own mental state.

49. You are the Self that is different from the four bodies and their birthplace, which is in ignorance and Illusion.
50. One whose state of mind is like this is knowledgeable and is on the path of the Self. For such a one, elevation and downfall do not apply.
51. Where even the intellect of the *Vedas* became incapable of further explanation about the Self, how can there be any question about upliftment or downfall? The verification of oneness comes from oneself, the scriptures, and the teaching of the Sadguru.
52. When the delusion of being an individual is discarded, Reality is realized in one's Self-experience. It is by the teachings of the Sadguru that living beings land on the best path to liberation.
53. When one receives knowledge from the Sadguru he comes to the end of the four bodies, which gives rise to constant contemplation of one's True Form.
54. With that constant contemplation the living being becomes rich in the liberation of identification with Reality.
55. When the visible objects disappear, what remains is only the Self. With careful inquiry, one can see that visible appearances do not really exist.
56. The false is seen to be false and is experienced as unreal. The listeners should listen carefully to this principle which is called liberation.
57. One who holds the teaching of the Sadguru in the heart is entitled to liberation. Such a one listens and reflects upon what has been heard again and again, with great respect.
58. Where both the primary premise and the final statement of the *Vedas* disappear, and where there is neither seeker nor goal, understand that this is the state of the Self which is liberation.
59. Where meditation and concentration end and concepts disappear in That which is without any concepts, there remains only Knowledge which is the most subtle form of Brahman.
60. When the mirage of worldly life dries up, one is released from the false bondage, and That which has no birth is freed from the sorrows of birth.
61. The illness of attachment that has afflicted the one who is innately detached, the body-consciousness which has affected the one who is beyond the body, and the identification as being a limited being in the world, are all destroyed by the power of discrimination.
62. The sense of duality in the non-dual is broken, solitude is given to the one who is alone, and the endless is granted the realization of endlessness.
63. The wakefulness is itself awakened, the awakened is made alert, and that which is knowledgeable is given Self-Knowledge.
64. The immortal nectar is made immortal, liberation is given to the house of liberation, and the individual self and the Supreme Self are forever merged.
65. The attributeless has become attributeless, the meaningful has become meaningful, and one has met oneself after a long time.
66. The partition curtain of duality is snapped, non-distinction has broken distinctions, and the afflictions of the five elements are removed.
67. Spiritual practice has born fruit, the unmoving remains immovable, and by the power of discrimination, That which is stainless and untainted by any appearances remains pure.

68. That which was very near was missed and was then acquired by the one to whom it belonged. Upon seeing oneself, the miseries of birth are removed.
69. A brahmin priest became horrified when he saw himself born into a lower caste in a dream, but upon awakening he realized his real identity.
70. It is similar to this for one with Self-Knowledge. The signs of such a person are explained in the next sub-chapter.

Thus in Shri Dasbodh, a dialogue between the Guru and disciple, Sub-Chapter 8 of Chapter 8, named "Perception of the Self" is concluded.

Chapter: 8, Sub-Chapter: 9

Signs of the Accomplished One

|| ShriRam ||

1. When taking nectar within, the body glows on the outside. What are the signs of a saint who has acquired Self-Knowledge?
2. In order for you to understand how Self-Knowledge is gained I will explain the signs of sages in a natural way.
3. Listen to the signs of the Siddha, the accomplished one. Understand to be "accomplished" means the realization of one's Self Nature (Swaroopa) where separateness does not exist.
4. Consciously being and abiding as one's Self Nature is called being accomplished. Only being accomplished in one's Self Nature is fitting of being called accomplished.
5. It is well known, and it is stated in the *Vedas* and other scriptures, that only one who is accomplished in one's Self Nature is called a Siddha. No other state of consciousness is called accomplished.
6. However, something must be said about the accomplished one so that the aspirant may be able to discern and understand the signs of accomplishment.
7. The question naturally arises, "When one's Self Form is realized, how does the body function afterwards?" It is similar to how the false dream activities occur in the world of the dream.
8. The signs of the accomplished ones will be explained to some extent so that the inner state of the spiritual life can be understood.
9. To be always consciously abiding in one's Self Form is the main sign of a sage. While functioning among people, he is quite different from other people.
10. Once one sees one's Self Form, the worries of worldly life get diminished and one begins to feel a strong affection for spiritual discourse.
11. This is the sign of a spiritual aspirant, but understand that this is also a sign of a Siddha. The accomplished one cannot be described without using the signs of the aspirant.
12. Outwardly he appears to be like a spiritual aspirant while inwardly he is identified with his Self Nature. Only the wise understand the signs of the Siddha to be like this.

13. The accomplished one has no doubt regarding his spiritual practice. His contentment is unshakable within as well as outwardly.
14. When the inner state becomes immovable, how can there be any disturbance? With the entire attitude of mind being fixed in one's Self Nature, one is only one's Self Nature.
15. Then, one is immovable while moving, and changeless while changing. The body is restless and one's Self Nature is unchanging.
16. When one realizes one's Self Nature, then whether he remains lying down or gets up and runs around, he remains unmoving.
17. For this realization, one's inner state must be one of withdrawal or disinterest in the outward going attitudes of mind. Only when one's mind is inwardly fixed on God alone, is he a sage.
18. The outward behavior may be of any type, but inwardly one's attention should be fixed on one's Self Form. These signs are naturally seen in the sage.
19. While sitting on the throne, the royal qualities of a king are naturally present. Similarly when one has realized one's Self Form, the signs of accomplishment are naturally evident.
20. These qualities cannot be acquired by other means such as study. It is only by abiding in one's Self Nature that one realizes one's Self Nature.
21. The crown jewel of spiritual studies is that one remains attributeless. In the company of saints and by listening to their explanations, the attributeless state is easily attained.
22. These are some of the signs of realization of one's Self Form which should be understood. Even renunciates get confused when losing track of their Self Form.
23. Now, enough of this. Listen further to the signs of the sage, so that the aspirant will be content.
24. When all of one's concepts are fully fixed in one's Self Form, how can any desire remain? Therefore, there is no desire for the sages.
25. When some imagined treasured sensual object slips through one's hands, one gets angry. However, the everlasting treasure of the sages will never disappear.
26. Therefore they are without anger. The saints realize their own true nature, giving up all that is perishable.
27. Where there is no second entity, with whom can one get angry? The sages function in this animate and the inanimate universal appearance without anger.
28. Being immersed in one's own Self-bliss, what cause is there for annoyance? Therefore, argument and disputes don't arise.
29. The sage abides in his Self Form which is without modification. How can there be any disgust for him, and who is there to be envious of?
30. Sage is effortlessly Reality. Therefore he does not have any jealousy. The madness of pride and jealousy does not exist in the sage.
31. The sage abides spontaneously in his Self Nature. How can there be any hypocrisy for such a one for whom duality does not exist?
32. For one who has discarded all appearances, how can there be something called a worldly life? For this reason, understand that the sage is without a worldly life.
33. The entire universe is his abode. He quickly realizes that the entire expanse of the five elements is false and abandons it.
34. Because of this, the sage has no greed for anything. He is always without greed and his desires are dissolved in the untainted Self Nature.

35. There being only one's Self everywhere, there is no selfishness in him. Therefore, the sage is without any sorrow or grief.
36. Giving up perishable appearances one abides in one's eternal Self Nature. Understand that because of this, the sage is without sorrow.
37. States of mind are affected by sorrow, but the sage is free of states of mind and is therefore always without sorrow.
38. The mind becomes overwhelmed by fascination with objects, but the sage has become "no-mind" (unmana) and is beyond any fascination for objectivity.
39. The sage is Reality alone. From where can fear be felt? The sage is fearless Parabrahman, the Absolute Reality.
40. Therefore, the sage is fearless and peaceful. Even though everyone will come to an end, the sage is endless.
41. Being Reality itself, the sage is immortal, so what could he possibly fear? It is for this reason that the sages are fearless.
42. Where there is only one's Self without any differentiation, or any distinctions of duality, how can there arise any sorrow related to bodily misidentification?
43. With the proper use of the intellect, the sages have confirmed the truth of the attributeless Brahman which cannot be taken away by anyone. For this reason there is nothing which can cause sorrow for the sages.
44. When one experiences only oneself alone in all places, what is there to be selfish for? When the visible world does not exist, there is no place for selfishness.
45. The sage is only Oneness itself, alone. Being only one, how can there be any sorrow or despair? Where there is no duality or differentiation of "other," the absence of the power of discrimination will also not arise. (There is only clear seeing without differentiation.)
46. By holding only to the desire for the Absolute Reality misplaced desires and selfish expectations are broken. Therefore, lack of desire is the distinguishing sign of the sages.
47. The sign of the sage is like the softness of the sky. Accordingly, there is no hardness to the statements of the sage.
48. Unified, in his own Self Nature, the yogi realizes that he is Reality itself. Therefore he is always free of desire.
49. Once one's Self Nature is realized, worrying about the body is given up, and there is no anxiety about what will happen in the future.
50. When the intellect is merged with Reality all discriminative properties are lost. For this reason the sages are without any differentiation.
51. The sage abides in Reality and does not have any association with anything or anyone "other." Therefore the sage does not pay heed to praise or insult.
52. Having his attention focused on That which is beyond the scope of the mind's grasp, the sage remains extremely alert. He knows how to be established in Absolute Reality.
53. Reality is untainted by any impurity. Therefore, being Reality itself, the sage is untainted and pure.
54. Among all duties (dharmas) one's true "Self duty" (swadharma) is to abide as Reality. Understand that this is the main characteristic sign of a sage.
55. By keeping the company of a sage one realizes one's Self Nature. With the realization of one's Self Nature, one exhibits the signs of a sage oneself.

56. Like this, the signs of the sage come to be acquired through listening to explanations. The main point is to always abide in your Self Nature.
57. By continuously abiding in your Self Nature you principally become Reality itself, and the signs of the sage become yours without delay.
58. When one's intellect resides in Reality, all negative qualities and vices fall away, but for this, the company of saints and listening to explanations is required.
59. In the world everyone has different experiences. This will be told in detail in the next sub-chapter.
60. Ramdas asks the listeners to pay attention to the explanation about the various experiences of different people, and the state in which one should remain.

Thus in Shri Dasbodh, a dialogue between the Guru and disciple, Sub-Chapter 9 of Chapter 8, named "Signs of an Accomplished One" is concluded.

Chapter: 8, Sub-Chapter: 10

Clarification About the Void

|| ShriRam ||

1. When asking various people about their experience, quarrels arise quickly bringing about confusion and a big commotion. The listeners are asked to listen to the narration of this confusion with interest.
2. Some say that just by living a mundane worldly life, one crosses to the other shore naturally because the burden of all the worldly activity is not on the individual being, as it is all only God.
3. Some say that this is not possible because greed comes in and one gets attached to worldly things while earning a living to buy bread and serving one's family.
4. Some say that one should just live a worldly life comfortably and gain some merit by doing charity, and that this is the true path.
5. Some say family life is worthless and one should take up renunciation and roam around the world, and that in this way that the door to heaven will become open.
6. Some say "Where should one go unnecessarily and why should one wander around? It is better that one should remain in one's own house carrying out the proper duties of a householder."
7. Some say "How can anyone speak of one's proper duty when everywhere it is seen that there is a lack of doing one's proper duty? In this worldly life one is forced to do many actions that are not proper."
8. Some say that people should try to have many good habits and a good predisposition, and in this way one can easily cross over the worldly life.
9. Some say that faith is the only means by which one can realize God, and that anything else is unproductive and confusing.
10. Some say that elders and other beings should be honored as God himself, and that one should worship one's mother and father with single-minded devotion.
11. Some say that one should worship idols of God, and in this way Lord Narayana (Vishnu) who is the mother and the father of all will be pleased.

12. Some say that the scriptures should be studied as the explanations there are given by God, and that by following that instruction one can go beyond this world.
13. Some say, "Oh, you people! The scriptures are vast and the study of them is endless. Therefore, one should go and surrender to the sages."
14. Some say to give up all this talk that is worthless, and that one should have compassion for all living beings.
15. Some say that one should behave in whatever way that one thinks is best, and in the last moments of life one should repeat the name of God.
16. Some say that only if one has gained merit in life will one remember to repeat the name of God, and otherwise, during the last moments of life one will forget.
17. Some say that as long as one is living one should make life worthwhile, and some say that life is made worthwhile by wandering around and visiting places of pilgrimage.
18. Some say that this is all going to a lot of trouble just to go to a place with some water and stones, and that while bobbing around in the water there one only become short of breath unnecessarily.
19. Some say to give up such talk, that the greatness of holy places is incomparable on this earth, and by just seeing them the worst of one's wrongful deeds turn to ashes.
20. Some say that the natural pilgrimage means control of the mind, and some say that one should sing songs of praise and narrations about God with a sense of ease and composure.
21. Some say that the path of yoga is the best and should be practiced first, and in this way the body can be made immortal.
22. Some say that this is all just a waste of time and nobody should do it. Some say that one should hold on to the path of Devotion (Bhakti Marga).
23. Some say that the path of Knowledge (Jnana Marga) is best. Some say it is necessary to do spiritual practice (sadhana), and some say that you are always already free.
24. Some say that one should not behave in an uncontrolled manner and should avoid bad behavior, while others say, "Our's is the path of no self-control."
25. Some say that one should not criticize or be envious of others. Some say that one should give up and abandon bad company effortlessly.
26. Some say that one should die serving in front of the one who gives us food, and in that way one will attain the state of liberation.
27. Some say that all of this type of talk should be abandoned from the beginning and that one must have bread first, and only then can one go on conversing comfortably.
28. Some say that there should be rain so that all things will be good and there will not be any drought, and everything will be fine.
29. Some say that by performing various austerities one can acquire all types of powers. Some say that one must first attain the status of "King of the Gods."
30. Some say that one must practice magic in order to please Satan to get his co-operation, and in this way one can attain the status of the gods in heaven.
31. Some say to learn the Aghora Mantra of Shiva and that with this mantra one becomes free and the Goddess Laxmi will be pleased.
32. Some say that all duties happen only because of Laxmi so how can there be any question of performing actions and activities, as even bad deeds are due to her.

33. Some say that one should make effort to chant the healing Mrityunjaya Mantra of Shiva so that all desires will be fulfilled.
34. Some say that it is the worship the child Shiva which gives one prosperity, and some say that it is a ghost that gives all that one desires.
35. Some say that different forms of the Goddess Kali or other female deities should be worshipped if one wants blessings.
36. Some say to worship Lord Ganesha, some say that it is the worship of the form of Shiva as Shankara is best, and some say that only if one worships the Goddess Bhagavati does one receive blessings quickly.
37. Some say that worship of Shiva in the form of Mallari makes one quickly fortunate, and some say that it is best to have great devotion to Lord Vishnu.
38. Some say that what matters are the merits of one's past life, some say that one must make efforts, and some say that all of the burden is on God.
39. Some say, "What is this God who puts all kinds of troubles on good people?" Some say that all troubles are normal things that happen in accordance with the Kali Yuga.
40. Some consider everything as a wonder while some always get surprised. Some get bored and say that we just have to see what is going to happen.
41. These are the signs of the experience of common worldly people. There are many signs, so a few examples have been given.
42. Now, let this be enough of this talk. Please listen with alertness as I explain the experience of the Knowledgeable (Jnanis).
43. Some say that one should have devotion to God, Lord Vishnu, and he will give emancipation. Some say that Brahman can only be attained by actions.
44. Some say that suffering cannot be avoided, nor can the cycle of birth and death be broken. Some say there are many spontaneous uprisings of ignorance.
45. Some say that "Only Brahman exists, so what actions and activities are there in Brahman?" Some say that such talk is not proper and that one should not talk like this.
46. Some say that everything gets destroyed and only Brahman is what remains. Some say that this is not a satisfying statement.
47. Some say that both of the statements "All is Brahman," and "Only what remains is Brahman," are wrong statements based on logic and that the secret of experience is quite different.
48. Some say that Reality cannot be described in words, and that even the *Vedas* and scriptures have become silent when trying to speak about it.
49. At this time, the listener asked, "Who has given the conclusion to all of this? According to the "final conclusion," the doctrine of siddhanta, how can there be any experience?"
50. The listener continued, "The experience of each body is different. You have said this previously. You cannot say something different now.
51. Some speak of being the witness that is different from appearances, and that one's Self, which is the seer, is the state of one's own experience.
52. The seer is different from what is seen, and this is the art of being detached. One's Self is different from appearances and this is one's own experience.
53. When the knower of all appearances is known to be different from the appearances, one easily understands that even though there is the appearance of the body, one is not limited to the body.

54. Some say that because this is one's own experience one should abide as the witness, because the seer of all visible appearances is different from them.
55. Some say that Reality does not have any differentiation, that it is One, alone and undifferentiated. How then can one with dull intelligence bring in any witness?
56. Just as sugar is naturally sweet and no bitterness can be found in it, similarly, how can any separate witness be found in one's experience when all is only Brahman?
57. The expanse of the universe and the Absolute Reality, Parabrahman, are one and not different, but those who take up a dualistic perspective see only division and duality. However, all of manifestation is really only the Self reveling in it's own Self-Bliss while taking form.
58. Just as with ghee where there is a fluid fluid state and a solidified state, similarly, that which is without attributes (Nirguna) has become that which is with attributes (Saguna). What separation is made there by the observer?
59. The witness and all of the visible appearances are only the one Lord of the Universe (Jagadisha), so what is the need to make an effort to be the witness?
60. So, now I have recounted two types of experiences of various knowledgeable people. The first being that Brahman alone exists and has become all forms everywhere.
61. The second type of experience of knowledgeable people is that it is the Self (Atman) that has taken form and that one can never be separate from the Self."
62. After hearing all of this, the speaker replied; "Please listen to a third type of experience. Some say that when all of the visible world is eliminated or forgotten so that nothing remains, that this is God."
63. Some say that when all of the visible appearances are separated out and only the invisible remains that this is the experience of Brahman.
64. However, this should not be called Brahman. It is like a remedy that really causes harm. How can one say that this void, or nothingness, is Brahman!
65. When going beyond all visible appearances, the invisible void remains. Thinking that to be Brahman, one returns back from there.
66. On one side there is what is visible, and on the other side, there is the attributeless God. In between the two, there is nothingness, or the void. It is because of dull intellect that some say that this is Brahman.
67. For example, when one does not recognize the king, the servant is mistaken to be the king. But when the king is seen, the old concept is discarded.
68. Similarly, one thinks of the void as being Brahman, but afterwards when one sees Reality, the delusion of taking the void to be Brahman disappears.
69. This is a subtle obstacle to realization which can be recognized and discarded with the power of discrimination, similar to how the Royal Swan is able to sip and drink only the milk while leaving the water.
70. First, visible appearances are given up. Then, going beyond the void one sees the "Primal Illusion" (Moolamaya). Only from there, can the Absolute Reality, Parabrahman, be realized.
71. When one tries to see from a perspective of being a separate observer, one finds the state of the void, and doubts increase in the mind about this state of nothingness.
72. Experiencing a sense of separateness from it, one labels it as the void. However, if one's goal is the realization of Reality, one must first recognize undivided oneness.

73. Be Reality itself to see Reality. When looking with a sense of separation, one only gets the experience of the void.
74. The experience of the void can never be the realization of the Absolute Reality. By being Reality, one sees Reality with one's own experience.
75. The fact that one is Reality oneself is confirmed. Do not imagine that "I am the mind." The sages teach the true remedy. "You are the Self."
76. The saints have never said that the concept "I am the mind" is true. By whose word should you consider the concept "I am the mind" to be true?
77. Firm faith in the statements of the saints is itself the pure experience of the Self. In this way, it is natural for the mind to say that "I am Reality."
78. One whose experience is that he himself is Oneness spread out everywhere, is in his own experience the very Life of the universe.
79. When a man who is greedy for wealth becomes wealthy, that fortunate man is able to comfortably enjoy that wealth.
80. Similarly, the spiritual aspirant who gives up the identification with the body gains the knowledge and experience of Reality that has been described.
81. Fundamentally one is Reality oneself. This is the Knowledge (Jnana) gained through the power of discrimination. Now, this chapter on Knowledge is complete.
82. Self-Knowledge (Atmajnana) has been explained. I have given the explanation to the best ability of the intellect. The listeners are asked to please excuse any shortcomings.

Thus in Shri Dasbodh, a dialogue between the Guru and disciple, Sub-Chapter 10 of Chapter 8, named "Clarification About the Void" is concluded.

Chapter 9. Attributes and Form

Chapter: 9, Sub-Chapter: 1

Questions

|| ShriRam ||

1. The listener asks, "What is meant by formless, what is meant by supportless, and what is meant by non-conceptual? Please explain this to me."
2. This means that Parabrahman, the Absolute Reality is without form, is not supported by anything, and is without any concepts or imagination.
3. "What is meant by free from affliction, what is meant by to be without appearance, and what is meant by to be without body parts? Explain this to me."
4. This means that Parabrahman is untroubled by any ailment, is beyond perception, and has no limbs or parts.
5. "What is meant by without worldly existence, what is meant by stainless, and what is meant by untainted? Please explain this to me."
6. This means that Parabrahman is beyond the five elements, that it is without any stain or blemish, and that it is free of any covering or coloring
7. What is meant by beyond comparison, what is meant by independent, and what is meant by beyond expectations? Please explain this to me."
8. This means that for Parabrahman there is nothing similar to it, that it is not dependent upon anything else, and that it does have any hope or desire for anything.
9. "What is meant by untouched by the world, what is meant by continuous, and what is meant by attributeless? Please explain this to me."
10. This means that Parabrahman is never touched by the world or ignorance, that there is never any gap or break in its pervasiveness, and that it is completely without attributes.
11. "What is meant by unattached, what is meant by pure, and what is meant by unmoving? Please explain this to me."
12. This means that in Parabrahman there is no other thing to be attached to, that it is unmixed with anything else, and that it is always changeless and unmoving.
13. "What is meant by without words, what is meant by flawless, and what is meant by without any attitudes? Explain this to me."
14. This means that for Parabrahman there are no words to explain it and that it is beyond words, that there are no defects that can be found in it, and that it is without any attitudes or states of mind.
15. "What is meant by desireless, what is meant by detached, and what is meant by actionless? Please explain this to me."
16. This means that in Parabrahman there is nothing else, so there is no desire for anything other, that there is no attachment to any other thing, and that Parabrahman does not do any actions.
17. "What is meant by nameless, what is meant by unborn, and what is meant by imperceptible? Please explain this to me."
18. This means that Parabrahman has no name, that it has never been born, and that it is not perceivable by the senses, or cognizable by the mind or intellect.

19. "What does immeasurable mean, what does dutiless mean, and what does imperishable mean? Explain this to me."
20. This means that Parabrahman cannot be measured, that it does not have any duties, and that it is indestructible and permanent.
21. "What is meant by shapeless, what is meant by objectless, and what is meant by endless? Please explain this to me."
22. This means that Parabrahman has no particular shape, that there are no objects in it, and that there is no end to it.
23. "What is meant by limitless, what is meant by immovable, and what is meant by unimaginable? Explain this to me."
24. This means that Parabrahman has no end or limit to it, that it is unshakable and never deviates from its own nature, and that it cannot be imagined.
25. "What does non-dual mean, what does invisible mean, and what does unswerving mean? Please explain this to me."
26. This means that for Parabrahman there is no duality, that it cannot be seen by the eyes, and that it is always in its place and does not move anywhere.
27. "What is meant by unbreakable, what is meant by nonburnable, and what is meant by indissoluble? Please explain this to me."
28. This means that Parabrahman cannot be affected by the elements, it cannot be broken or split into parts, it cannot be burned or scorched, and it cannot be dissolved in water.
29. Parabrahman, the Absolute Reality is beyond all the visible. Upon seeing it, one becomes That oneself. This is understood through direct experience with the help of the Sadguru.

Thus in Shri Dasbodh, a dialogue between the Guru and disciple, Sub-Chapter 1 of Chapter 9, named "Questions" is concluded.

Chapter: 9, Sub-Chapter: 2

Narration on Brahman

|| ShriRam ||

1. Anything that appears with a form will be destroyed at the time of the dissolution of the universe. Only the True Form (Swaroopa; Self Nature) of the Self exists eternally.
2. That which is the Essence of everything and is eternal is not false. It is That which is permanent and pervasive everywhere.
3. That which is the "True Nature of God" is also called the "True Nature of the Self." He also has innumerable different names aside from these.
4. The name is used as an indication in order to understand the examples given, but the form or nature of the Self is always beyond the name.
5. It fills the inside and the outside of all objects, but it is hidden from the world. It is as if it is not existing even though it is very close to us.
6. Hearing about God like this, there arises a desire to see God. However, when trying to see God, only the visible world is seen all around.

7. When trying to see it, only the objects appearing to the eyes are seen. By seeing in this way one feels some satisfaction, but this is not the true vision of God.
8. Whatever is seen as "the visible" gets destroyed. Regarding this, it is said in the *Upanishads* that whatever is seen with the eyes is not one's True Nature.
9. That Self Nature is without any appearance and is inconceivable, and that which is visible and appears is illusory and unreal. It is told in the science of Vedanta that whatever has an appearance is destructible.
10. When trying to see, only visible appearances are seen. Reality is beyond what is visible. With Self-experience it is seen to be both within and beyond all that is visible.
11. What indication can be said about That which is inconceivable, invisible, and without attributes? Understand that your True Nature is itself the nearest thing.
12. Just as everything appears in space and space is permeating everything, in the same way, understand the Lord of the Universe is within and outside of everything.
13. The True Nature of God is such that it is in the water but does not get wet, it is in the earth but does not get worn out, and it is in the fire but does not get burned,
14. It is in the mire, but does not get drowned, it is in the air but does not fly off, and it is in the gold but it cannot be formed into golden ornaments.
15. Like this, it pervades everywhere, yet it cannot be comprehended. That which creates divisions and distinctions in undivided oneness is called pride, or the ego.
16. Now, some signs of the nature of this pride will be given so that it can be easily recognized. Listen with alertness to this explanation.
17. Pride reaches towards the Reality as if it were a part of the experience, and then tries to speak out words to describe the extraordinary experience.
18. Pride says, "I am the Reality now." That itself is the form of pride. It spontaneously makes distinctions in the formless.
19. The delusion of pride is such that it says, "I am Brahman." This becomes apparent by looking with the most subtle of the subtlest seeing.
20. Imagination brings about desires and intention, while Reality is beyond the imagination. Therefore, the end of the endless cannot be comprehended.
21. Explanations that progress in a logical order and fanciful conjectures are all within the realm of the differences of words. The discrimination of "wordless silence" must be pursued inwardly.
22. First take the apparent meaning of words, and then recognize what is being indicated by the words. Once what is being indicated by the words is seen, the apparent meaning doesn't remain.
23. Statements such as "All is Brahman" and "Pure Brahman" are only words that are used to indicate some deeper meaning. However, when discovering That which is being indicated, the indications themselves don't remain.
24. "All" and "pure" are but two perspectives about Brahman that exist only in words. When one's attention becomes fixed in That which is being indicated, both concepts (that everything is Brahman, and that Brahman is pure and untainted by any "things") drop away.
25. That which is being indicated must be experienced. Here the words that are being spoken to indicate it are of no use. When that "main principle" is experienced, the desire to begin speaking about it does not arise.
26. When the four types of speech (the inner inspiration of sound, the sound at the level of the heart, the sound at the level of the throat, and the sound that is actually

spoken aloud[49]) all disappear, where is there any place for articulate language and skill with words?

27. Once a word is spoken, it immediately disappears by itself. Where is there anything permanent about speech? This is the actual case, no proof is required to observe this fact.

28. Words are truly all perishable, accordingly, all opinions and arguments will fall away. Concepts such as "All is Brahman" and "Pure Brahman" don't exist in the actual experience itself.

29. Listen to the signs of experience. Understand that experience means that there is "nothing other." Listen to the signs of this Oneness without other.

30. "Nothing other" means that there is no other thing. In self-surrender all attachments are broken and the Self remains alone by itself.

31. For the Self there is no sense of separate selfhood. This is itself the sign of detachment. These words are being used only so that you might understand.

32. Otherwise, how can That which is being indicated be told in words? By listening to the explanations of the great statements (mahavakyas) of the saints, one begins to easily understand.

33. By listening to the explanations about Reality one should find the attributeless Brahman. In order to understand, one must see oneself by oneself.

34. Without speaking, the meaning of That which is being indicated should be considered again and again while remaining dissolved in it. Thus it is said that the absence of speaking is the adornment of great men.

35. Words have become silent, and the *Vedas* fall speechless saying "not this, not this," (neti, neti). This must now become actual Self-experience.

36. If after having obtained experience one continues to indulge in conjecture and guesswork, this is a sign of obstinate pride. This is basically saying, "I am ignorant, I cannot understand anything."

37. Instead say, "I am false, my speech is false, my behavior and walking is false. 'I' and 'mine' is false, everything is false. All is only imagination.

38. For 'me' and 'mine' there is no place at all. All of my speech is entirely meaningless. All of this is the nature of manifestation which is Illusion, and all of manifestation is false."

39. Manifestation (Prakriti) and the "Primordial Being" prior to manifestation (Purusha) are both bound to disappear, so how can there be any independently existing individual?

40. Where everything has disappeared without anything remaining, how can there be anything remaining? It is like breaking the silence to say "I am silent."

41. Therefore, now don't break the silence. While doing, don't do anything. While being, don't remain as anything. This is only understood through the power of discrimination.

Thus in Shri Dasbodh, a dialogue between the Guru and disciple, Sub-Chapter 2 of Chapter 9, named "Narration on Brahman" is concluded.

---

[49] These four types of speech are explained in detail in Chapter 17, sub-chapter 8.

Chapter: 9, Sub-Chapter: 3

Narration on Doubtlessness

|| ShriRam ||

1. After hearing what has been said, the listeners asked, "How is it that the "Knowledge of Brahman" is not a thing, yet it still exists? How can this be possible?
2. How can Brahman be doing everything while not being the doer, how can Brahman be enjoying everything while not being the enjoyer, and how can Brahman be detached while being in the midst of all?
3. You say that the yogi who is one with Brahman is not the enjoyer or sufferer even while enjoying or suffering. Does this also mean that such a one does not enjoy heaven or suffer in hell?
4. It is clear that everyone feels the suffering associated with birth and death, but you say that the yogi is not a sufferer. Doesn't he experience the many pains in life?
5. Does a great yogi not get a beating even though he is beaten, is he not crying even though he cries, and does he not moan while making strenuous efforts?
6. Has he no birth even though he has been born, has he not fallen even though he has committed wrongful deeds, and is he above pain and sufferings even though he experiences them in many ways?"
7. Like this is the conjecture put forth by the listeners who have taken up a wrong line of thinking, so now a satisfactory answer must be given to these questions.
8. The speaker asks the listeners to remain attentive. You speak of good things, but what you have said is only based your own experience of what happens to you.
9. Everyone speaks according to one's experience, but if one speaks courageously without the wealth of Knowledge (Jnana), that speech is meaningless.
10. Without the wealth of Knowledge, there is the calamity of poverty in the form of ignorance, and one suffers from the limitations of the knowledge which is limited to words.
11. A great yogi is recognized by another yogi, a great Jnani is recognized by another Jnani, and one who is very clever is recognized by one who is also clever.
12. The one who is experienced knows one who is experienced, one who is detached feels a sense of common contentment when meeting with another who is detached, and one who has given up the body misidentification recognizes one who is without the body-consciousness.
13. It goes without saying that the one who thinks that an "accomplished one," a Siddha, is the same as one who is in bondage, and the one who is in bondage is the same as a Siddha, is a fool.
14. The one who is possessed by some ghost or spirit and the one who is an exorcist both have a body, but how can they both be considered as equal?
15. Similarly, how can it be correct that one who is ignorant and self absorbed should be considered the same as one who is knowledgeable and liberated?
16. Let this be enough of these similes. Now I shall speak with the purpose that the listeners may gain some experience. The listeners are asked to remain attentive for a moment while listening.

17. One who is "Knowledgeable," a Jnani, is one who is dissolved, and who has seen with the power of discrimination that a separate individual does not exist. Being one with the Self, he has not remained as anything at all.
18. How does one find That? Having found it, one becomes That itself. Having become That, it is not necessary to say anything.
19. If one is looking only in the body it cannot be seen there, if one is searching only in the elements, it does not appear there. However, being only One, Brahman cannot be separated out from anything.
20. The Jnani appears to be having a bodily appearance but does not have any feeling of being within a body. How can one understand his inner experience when only looking at him superficially?
21. To know him, one must search within, and he is found to be existing there eternally. Upon finding That, one's disturbed state of mind falls away and one becomes changeless, without any attributes.
22. That alone is the Supreme Self, Paramatman. In it, there is no impurity of Illusion. Undivided, it is never affected by desires or hopes.
23. One such as this is the "King of Yogis" who is effortlessly and spontaneously always the Self, the completeness of Brahman, the origin of the *Vedas*. This cannot be understood by one who takes oneself to be the bodily form.
24. Looking only at his body, he appears to be the body, but his inner experience is totally different. Finding That, one becomes free of the cycle of birth and death.
25. Who is there to have any birth and death? That is not its nature at all. How can that which does not exist be brought in from anywhere?
26. If the attributeless is imagined to have taken birth or to be subject to death, these notions of birth and death are only one's own imagination.
27. This is similar to how if one spits at the sun at high noon, the spit only falls back on oneself, or if one inwardly has ill wishes for another, those negative effects are felt for oneself.
28. When coming to know the greatness of a Self-realized person, one feels contentment. And even if a dog begins to bark at him very loudly, his greatness is not diminished, while the dog continues to remain only a dog.
29. The Jnani is the True Form of the Self, but the ignorant one looks at him only as being the form of a human being. Accordingly, as one's feelings are towards God, God is reflected back in the same way.
30. God is formless and attributeless, yet people worship stone idols. Stones break, but how can That which is attributeless ever break?
31. God is always pervading everywhere. People think of him as being many, but it cannot happen that God can actually become many.
32. Similarly, the Jnani is full with Self-Knowledge, and completely content in that Knowledge. Through the power of discrimination he has surrendered in the Self, and is actually the True Form of the Self.
33. When fire burns wood, the fire appears to take on the shape of the wood, but we can never say that the fire has become the wood.
34. By analogy, camphor can be seen when it is burning, just as the body of the Jnani is seen, however, once the camphor has been burnt, it cannot be put back into the plant from which it originated. (Once the Jnani leaves behind bodily identification he does not return to identifying with the body again.)

35. A seed that has been burned will not sprout, a piece of fabric that has been burned cannot be properly spread out, and a stream that has merged with the Ganges cannot be separated out again.
36. A separate river can be seen prior to its merging into the Ganges, but afterwards it cannot be seen separately. The Jnani is not the body that has an appearance, but is the Self which pervades everything.
37. Just as gold is not iron, the birth of a Jnani has never occurred. However, this is not understood by the ignorant being who is dull and foolish.
38. Just because a blind person cannot see anything does not mean that all other people are blind.
39. One who is dreaming and is terrified by events in the dream screams aloud with the fear caused by the dream. How can one who is awake be affected by the fear caused by the dream?
40. When a root that is shaped like a snake is seen by two people, one person gets scared and the other recognizes it as a root. How can it be said that the states of both people are the same?
41. Even when holding it in his hand, it does not bite him, but because of his imagination it does not appear to be a root and he is still affected by his fear of it.
42. Even when a scorpion or snake bites someone, only that person is affected. How can other people be affected with that pain?
43. Now the conjecture has been cleared away. Those who are knowledgeable understand this Knowledge. For the ignorant, the cycle of birth and death cannot be avoided.
44. People undertake many efforts in order to know the one Self. Because of not knowing it they bear the sufferings of birth and death.
45. The continuation of this explanation will be given in the next sub-chapter, so the speaker says, "Remain alert and attentive!"

Thus in Shri Dasbodh, a dialogue between the Guru and disciple, Sub-Chapter 3 of Chapter 9, named "Narration on Doubtlessness" is concluded.

Chapter: 9, Sub-Chapter: 4

Narration on Knowledge

|| ShriRam ||

1. The listener asks, "On this earth there are all types of people. Some are prosperous, some are poor, some are clean and some are dirty. Why is this so?
2. There are many who enjoy royalty and many who suffer from poverty. There are many who are in the best positions and many that are in poor pitiable positions.
3. For what reason has this happened? Please explain this to me." Now the answer to this will be told to the listeners.
4. All of this happens according to our qualities. Those with good qualities, enjoy good fortune, while those with negative qualities experience poverty. There is no doubt about this.

5. One who masters the profession that he enters into is called a good worker by the people.
6. One who knows a profession does his work well, while the one who does not know any profession does nothing. The one who knows a profession can earn money to satisfy his hunger, and the one who does not know anything begs for his food.
7. This is quite evident and can be clearly seen among the people. One without any education or knowledge lives an unfortunate life, while one with knowledge is fortunate.
8. If one does not acquire any education along some line of knowledge, then one will have to go around begging to get their meals. Elders everywhere speak of this basic wisdom.
9. Many times it is seen that an elderly person becomes unfortunate because of a lack of education, and a younger person becomes powerful because he is more educated and knowledgeable.
10. One who has no knowledge, no intellect, and no discrimination, who does no hard work, has no skill, and no occupation becomes destitute.
11. Where all of these qualities are present, prosperity is not lacking there, and even if the prosperity is dropped, it comes again quite easily.
12. Sometimes it is seen that the father is powerful but the son is a pauper. This happens because the son does not pursue an occupation like the father has done.
13. According to the knowledge one has, their ambition is along the same lines. According to the occupation one is in, the prosperity is likewise. People do the activities that are appropriate to their capacity.
14. Where there is no knowledge and no prosperity how can there be cleanliness? Being unfortunate, a man appears unpleasant and destitute.
15. Even powerful people show kindness and appreciation towards animals and birds that have good qualities. However, if a living being is without any good qualities, their life is basically useless.
16. When a person has no good qualities he is not respected, if he has no power, he is given no importance, and if he has no skillful capacity, he is not able to make good decisions.
17. For these reasons, to have the best qualities is itself the sign of good fortune. Without good qualities, one naturally becomes ill-fated.
18. If there is one among the people who is knowledgeable and educated he is respected. Anyone who has knowledge is important in society.
19. Whether in worldly life or in spiritual life, the one who is knowledgeable is powerful. Understand that one who is ignorant remains useless without any purpose.
20. Being ignorant, a person gets bitten by scorpions and snakes, and is unable to recognize something that is a threat to life. Due to ignorance even one's work gets spoiled.
21. Being ignorant, a person gets cheated, and behaves in strange ways. The ignorant person easily gets deceived, and even forgets about their own belongings.
22. Because of ignorance a person's enemies can conquer him. Because of ignorance people bear great losses, lives get destroyed, and even massacres are carried out.
23. Those people who don't know what is in their own best interest suffer pain and sorrow in life. Without knowledge, the ignorant being experiences a downfall.

24. One should have knowledge and an understanding of Illusion and Brahman, as well as of the individual (jiva) and God (Shiva), the Eternal and the ephemeral, and of meaning and lack of meaning, so that the birth and death cycle becomes non-existent.
25. When one understands who the doer is, and for whom there is bondage and the liberation, one becomes free from the birth and death cycle.
26. Realize that God is without attributes, understand who the "I" is, and understand the sign of becoming one with the Self, and you will be liberated.
27. When whatever is known is given up, and when one goes beyond all that is visible, then one knows the "knower," and the root of the ego sense is snapped.
28. If one does not gain Self-Knowledge, he will not become liberated even if he does millions of types of practices.
29. By recognizing Illusion and Brahman and understanding the Self by oneself, one naturally escapes the birth and death cycle.
30. By knowing the mind of the realized saint and by practicing according to his instruction, one naturally achieves great fortune and unlimited prosperity.
31. Therefore, to have knowledge is not an ordinary thing. With knowledge one becomes popularly respected by everyone, but by not knowing anything, one does not get respect anywhere.
32. An ignorant person may see some object in the dark and even give up his life thinking that it's a ghost, while the knowledgeable person understands that it is just some imaginary thing.
33. The knowledgeable person understands the secret to success while the ignorant person generally commits mistakes leading to misfortune. The knowledgeable person knows what is one's proper duty and what is not.
34. The ignorant person suffers the agonies of death, and the Knowledgeable One is not hurt by anything. Having knowledge, the one who thinks things over properly becomes liberated.
35. If one does not know how to act properly according to the various situations, he may cause insult to others and even take away someone's life. The behavior of an ignorant person creates difficulties for everyone.
36. Therefore, to remain ignorant is not proper. Those who have no knowledge are truly unfortunate. Having knowledge and utilizing clear thinking are what break the cycle of birth and death.
37. Therefore do not be negligent. Knowledge itself is the remedy. By gaining knowledge one finds the way beyond the worldly life.
38. Having knowledge is accepted as being right for everyone. Only the foolish think that it is wrong. It is only with knowledge that true detachment is understood.
39. Who has the power to help other living beings aside from those who have knowledge? No work can be carried out that is not understood with knowledge.
40. To know means to remember, and to not know means to forget. The wise person knows which of the two is correct.
41. Those who are knowledgeable are wise, and the ignorant are pitiable and destitute. Even Self-Knowledge is gained by way understanding knowledge.
42. Where knowledge reaches its limit, and where even words disappear, there is contentment that is desireless.

43. The listener says, "With correct knowledge, one has become supremely content, but now the signs of that "whatever is in the human being is also what is in the universe," must be explained.
44. Many say that whatever is the case for the universe is also true for man. (What is true for the microcosm is true for the macrocosm.) However, there must be some actual perception and realization that this is true. Please explain this."

Thus in Shri Dasbodh, a dialogue between the Guru and disciple, Sub-Chapter 4 of Chapter 9, named "Narration on Knowledge" is concluded.

Chapter: 9, Sub-Chapter: 5

Removing Guesswork

|| ShriRam ||

1. The listener asks, "The structure of the universe is like that of man. This is not just imagination, however when seeing many opinions people don't have this experience and become confused.
2. That which is in man is the same as that which is in the universe. Philosophers make this statement again and again.
3. It is common for people to say that whatever is in man is in the universe, but the actual experience that this is true does not last.
4. The gross body, the subtle body, casual body, and the great casual body (Sthoola, Sukhma, Karana, and Maha-Karana) are the four bodies of the human being. Accordingly, there are the gross form of universe, the subtle life energy, the unexpressed causal, and the Primal Illusion (Virata, Hiranya, Avyakruta, and MoolaPrakriti) that are the four bodies of the universe.
5. It is understood that this is the classical description from ancient scriptures, but how does one go about getting the actual experience of this? When trying to see this, one becomes confused."
6. The speaker responds, "Understand that in the human being there is the inner-mind (antahkarana) which is the same as Lord Vishnu on the universal level. And what is called the mind (manas) in man is equivalent in significance as the moon on the universal level.
7. Understand that what is called the intellect (buddhi) in the human is what is Brahma, or the creator, on the universal level. And what is called activity of thoughts (chitta) in the human is recognized as Narayana at the universal level.
8. What is called ego (ahankara) in man, is Lord Shiva in the universe. The ancient scriptures have declared all of this to definitely be the case."
9. The listener said, "Then please explain how Vishnu is the inner-mind, how the moon is the mind, and how Brahma is the intellect.
10. How is the activity of thought Lord Narayana, and what is the nature of Lord Shiva? These thoughts must be investigated thoroughly using the power of discrimination.
11. True conviction gained from experience cannot be compared to guesswork and mere conjecture. Like putting a dog in front of a lion, how can what is untrue stand up to the truth?

12. To understand this, examination and verification is required. It is only with accurate examination and investigation that one will gain firm conviction. Without proper examination one is left only with guesswork, and remains full of doubts."
13. The listener continued, "Oh Swami, please explain to us the fivefold aspects of the inner-mind of man and how they correlate to Lord Vishnu, the Moon, Lord Brahma, Lord Narayana, and Lord Shiva in the universe."
14. The speaker replied, "Here, experience is the proof. Even the references to the scriptures are not required when one sees directly and gains the actual experience.
15. Any speech that doesn't have the support of actual experience is simply boring. It's like a dog howling loudly with its mouth wide open.
16. Listen to what has been said and then look for yourself and see if what has been said is true. When what has been said is just empty words, one cannot gain any experience.
17. Where is there a place for a man with vision where everyone else is blind? When the eyes of experience are not present, there is only darkness.
18. Where there is no milk nor water present, and only fecal matter is spread around everywhere, only ravens will be found picking through it.
19. Everybody speaks according to their own liking, imagining that the physical body is like the universe. But what is important is how this can be experienced.
20. Therefore all of this kind of talk is but conjecture and guesswork. It is all just a jungle of imagination. The wise people do not enter into that jungle, only the thieves go there.
21. It can be said that mantras were created in imagination and that the various gods are influenced by these mantras. Thus it follows that the gods are also only products of imagination.
22. What is being said here should be understood without discussion but through the power of discrimination. Just as a blind person is able to recognize someone by his footsteps, similarly, the wise should recognize what is being said here.
23. One who composes poetry does so according to how he perceives things. However, one should verify what has been said in one's own experience.
24. Lord Brahma has created all, but who has created Brahma? Lord Vishnu is the sustainer of the world, but who sustains Lord Vishnu?
25. Lord Shiva is the destroyer of the world, but who is the destroyer of Lord Shiva? One should know who it is who is the controller of time.
26. If this thought is not understood through deep thought and inquiry (vichara), then there is only the darkness of ignorance. Therefore, one should investigate using the power of discrimination (viveka).
27. The universe has come to be quite naturally, and although we have imagined it to be like an individual human body, this has not actually ever come to be our actual experience.
28. When looking at the experience of the universe many doubts arise. The listeners should understand that all of these doubts are definitely born from imagination.
29. Who can bring forth such speculation that the construction of the universe is like that of a physical body? In the universe there are so many various objects, how can they all be in a single body?
30. There are millions of beings, millions of holy places, and millions of mantras that can be found in the universe. Where are they found in the human body?

31. It is said in Hindu mythology that there are three hundred and thirty-million gods, eighty-eight thousand sages, and ninety-million wrathful deities. How can one think of all these in one body?
32. It is said that there are five hundred and sixty-million goddesses, billions of individual beings, and eight million four hundred thousand (8.4 million) various species populating the universe. Where are they to be found in one body?
33. All of the objects that have been created in the universe are separate according to their various distinctions. How can all of these be accounted for and explained to be one body?
34. There are many medicinal herbs, many different fruits and varieties of juices, and many types of seeds and grains. How can all of these be explained to be in one body?
35. There is no end to telling about these types of descriptions, therefore one should not speak unnecessarily. If whatever is said cannot be experienced it is basically shameful to talk about it.
36. If whatever is spoken about cannot be experienced, it is just meaningless talk. Therefore, there is no reason for indulging in such imaginary speculation.
37. The five elements which are present in the universe are the same five elements that are present in the body. One should see this for oneself and get the actual experience of it in the moment.
38. The universe is made up of five elements and the body is made up of five elements. Whatever is said other than this is mere conjecture.
39. Whatever is spoken about out of imagination must be given up like vomit. Only that which comes from one's own experience is speech born of conviction.
40. The fact that whatever is in the body is also that which is in the universe can be actually experienced. The flurry of activity of the five elements can easily be seen in both places.
41. Therefore, to say that whatever is in the universe is in the body is all conjecture. Now, I shall explain the truly satisfying answer to all of this.

Thus in Shri Dasbodh, a dialogue between the Guru and disciple, Sub-Chapter 5 of Chapter 9, named "Removing Guesswork" is concluded.

Chapter: 9, Sub-Chapter: 6

Explanation of Attributes and Forms

|| ShriRam ||

1. Brahman can be thought of as being formless like the sky (space). Similarly, like the wind that appears in the formless sky, the Primal Illusion (Moolamaya) appears as the first modification in the formless Brahman.
2. This has been stated previously in Dasbodh (chapter seven) and explained clearly in the chapter on Knowledge (chapter eight) where the five elements have been shown to be contained in the Primal Illusion.

3. The listeners should understand that the quality of knowledge (Janiva; awareness or consciousness, percipience) is the sattvaguna, the quality of knowledge mixed with ignorance is the rajoguna, and the quality of ignorance is the tamoguna.
4. You may ask, "What is this knowledge that is there?" Listen now to the explanation about what this means. For the human being there is what is called the Great Casual Body (Mahakarana Deha) which is the state of Beingness that is the witness of all.
5. Similarly, the Primal Illusion is the Great Causal Body of the universe. Therefore, the quality of knowledge or awareness naturally resides there.
6. The three attributes (gunas) reside latent and unmanifest within the Primal Illusion. Then with some stirring of the expressive power of the gunas, the three attributes become manifest, intermixed with each other. The wise should understand this through minute observation.
7. Similar to the grasses of grain which are first closed and then open up to release the seeds is the play of the Primal Illusion and how it gives rise to the expression of the three gunas.
8. The Primal Illusion is in the form of wind. Listen to how the stirring of the expression of the gunas gives rise to form. Even a small modification arising in the gunas is called the stirring, or the expressive power of the gunas (gunakshobhini).
9. There in that expression, the knowledge (sattva), the combination of knowledge and ignorance (rajas), and ignorance (tamas) become manifest, all intermingled with one another to form the very nature of the universe from where the primordial word AUM arose.
10. The quality of the word is that of space. This is the meaning of the statement about that which is in the universe is in the body. From the original word (OM) the words of the *Vedas* and other scriptures became formed.
11. The five elements and the three gunas are all only of the nature of the changing modifications of wind. Even the play of knowledge and ignorance are formed only from wind.
12. Without wind, how can knowledge exist? And without knowledge, how can ignorance exist? Both knowledge and ignorance exist solely because of wind.
13. Where there is no movement, how can there be the attribute of knowledge? Therefore, understand that the essence of the quality of knowing is wind.
14. It can be said that one thing has originated in another, and that this coming forth can be observed. However, the basic true nature of the Primal Illusion appears originally as the three gunas and five elements indistinguishably intermingled together.
15. Like this, all of these are originally an intermingled mixture, and then they become apparent one by one in sequence. Thus, it can also be said to be true that one originates and comes forth from another.
16. It has already been mentioned that the intermingled mixture containing all of that is wind. From that wind, came the formation of fire (light). When looking minutely, fire can also seen to be in the form of a mixture.
17. From fire came water which is also in the form of a mixture. From water came earth which is also is in the form of a mixture.
18. Here the listener raises a doubt. "Where is knowledge seen in the elements? We have never heard that it has ever been said before that the elements have knowledge."

19. Knowledge is inherently of the nature of movement, which is itself the sign of wind. It has already been explained that all attributes are contained within wind alone.
20. Therefore all the elements function with a combination of knowledge and ignorance. Thus it is shown that there is knowledge within the elements.
21. This is readily apparent in some places, and not so evident in other places, yet it does exist in all of the elements. If one observes with sharp intellect one can see both its gross and subtle presence.
22. The five elements have assumed their respective forms and are intermingled together. When looking at them, some of their aspects appear more gross and some are more subtle.
23. When the wind is still, it is not felt. Like that, knowledge is not always obviously apparent in the elements. Even though it is not seen, it is still there, in the forms of the elements.
24. For example, in the same way that the fire that is inherently hidden in wood, and the stillness of the wind are not readily seen, knowledge is not so obviously apparent in the elements.
25. The elements appear to be different, but upon close observation they are felt to be one. One should very cleverly recognize and experience this for oneself.
26. From Brahman arises the Primal Illusion (Moolamaya), and from this Primal Illusion arises the "Illusion of Attributes" (GunaMaya). And it is from this Illusion of Attributes, that the attributes (gunas) are born.
27. From the three gunas, the elements come into their manifest and identifiable state. The various forms of the elements has been explained previously.
28. At this point the listener raised a doubt. "It is not reasonable to say that space has been formed from out of the gunas. This could never happen. And how can you conceive that space has come from the attribute of sound?"
29. When explaining one thing, something else is imagined and confusion is unnecessarily created. Who can make such a foolish person understand what is being said?
30. When he is given teaching, he cannot understand. Even with detailed explanation he does not comprehend. Even with the use of may similes such a dull-minded person cannot understand what has been said.
31. It has been explained how one element is a greater element than another, but what is it that is there beyond and independent of the elements?
32. Using the power of discrimination, see what remains beyond the Primal Illusion that contains the five elements. The only thing that is beyond the Primal Illusion is Attributeless Brahman (Nirguna Brahman).
33. The Primal Illusion appeared in Brahman. Upon minutely examining the play of its activities, it is clearly seen to consist only of the five elements and the three gunas.
34. Four of the elements are subject to modifications while space is unchanging without any modification. Space is considered an element because it has properties and is like a covering or veil on Brahman.
35. The Consciousness in a body is called the individual self or jiva, and that same Consciousness in the universe is called the cosmic self, or Shiva. In the same way, space is an element, and it is also all-pervading.
36. Space is subtle yet it can be seen to have the appearance of certain properties. Therefore, space is considered to be in the form of an element.

37. Space has the property of being space that is vast, or empty, or void. No such properties exist for Parabrahman, the Absolute Reality. Only that space which is without any properties is Brahman itself.
38. Knowledge, ignorance, and the mixture knowing and not-knowing, are the identifiable signs of the three gunas. Now the three gunas have been explained and their forms have been revealed.
39. Creation (Prakriti) has spread out everywhere. That which is only One has become many things which are all subject to change. How can it be measured?
40. By mixing black and white one gets a grey color. When mixing blue and yellow one gets the color green.
41. Like that, colors of many varieties are mixed and changes take place. In much the same way, all of the visible appearances are constantly going through changes.
42. In the case of water, it takes on the appearance of many colors, and ripples constantly appear on it one after the other. The speed at which these changes that we see take place cannot be described in words.
43. Just as the modifications of the one water element appear to be unlimited, similarly, all of the five elements expand into the modifications that make up the 8.4 million species.
44. Water is the basis or seed from where all bodies come. All the people, insects, ants, and all the wild animals have come from water.
45. Blood and semen are made up of water, and from that water the body is formed. Even the nails, teeth and bones are basically made from that water.
46. There are tiny thread-like strands at the tips of the roots of trees which are filled up with water. That water rises up to expand throughout the entire tree.
47. The mango trees come to blossom because of water, and all other trees flower and bear fruit in due course because of water.
48. If one breaks open the trunk of a mango tree, or if one breaks apart the branches, there are no mangoes or fruit seen inside. All that is found is only wet bark.
49. If one looks from the roots all the way up to the top of the tree there is no fruit to be found within the tree. The wise understand that the fruit is basically a form of water.
50. It is only when water reaches to the tips of the branches that the tree bears blossoms. In this way it can be seen how one thing comes from another.
51. So many differences are there in the leaves, flowers, and fruits. How many descriptions and explanations should be given? Only by looking with subtle vision does one come to understand what has been said.
52. How can one tell about all of the modifications that go on in the universe from moment to moment? From out of that which is One come so many various colors and forms.
53. There is so much activity that is going on with the three gunas and the five elements. Looking at all of this activity we see many changes in many various forms. How much of this can possibly be described?
54. By using the power of discrimination, creation has to be thrown off and discarded with a sense of tranquil ease. Then, one becomes one with, and unflinchingly devoted to, the Supreme Self, Paramatman.

Thus in Shri Dasbodh, a dialogue between the Guru and disciple, Sub-Chapter 6 of Chapter 9, named "Explanation of Attributes and Forms" is concluded.

Chapter: 9, Sub- Chapter: 7

Removal of Doubts

|| ShriRam ||

1. The listener said, "First there is the gross body, then because of it, there is the inner-mind (antahkarana) with its five aspects (antahkarana, manas, chitta, buddhi, ahankara). It is because of the gross body that understanding and discrimination are possible.
2. Similarly, without the created universe, there is no knowledge of the Primal Illusion. All functioning is carried out only through the medium of the gross.
3. If there were no creation of the gross body, where would there be any place for the inner-mind to reside?" The listener made a query like this. Please listen now to the answer.
4. There are silk worms and other worms with shells, and other creatures both large and small that make their houses on the exterior of their body according to their capacity.
5. There are conchs, and snails, and many other creatures with hard shells on their backs. One must investigate and think about whether the creatures or the houses were formed first.
6. The creatures came first, and then they created the houses. This is the direct experience that is not really required to be stated.
7. Similarly, understand that first comes the subtle, and *then* the gross is created. With this simple simile, the query of the listener has been answered.
8. Then the listener said, "May I ask a few more questions that I have remembered? Please explain to me about the discrimination between birth and death.
9. Who is put into birth, and who takes the birth once again after death? What is this experience and how does it happen?
10. It is said that Lord Brahma creates the birth, that Lord Vishnu is the sustainer and protector of life, and that Lord Shiva destroys everything.
11. This is what is traditionally said, but this statement falls short of understanding the actual experience. If one tries to get the experience of this, it does not happen.
12. Who created Lord Brahma? Who sustains Lord Vishnu? Who destroys Lord Shiva at the time of the final destruction?
13. This is all a part of the play of creation which is of the nature of Illusion. How can we say that the doer is the attributeless God, as He is still, without any modifications.
14. If we say that Illusion is what gives birth to things, that would be to say that it has expanded by itself. However, upon investigation, we come to know that whatever appears is not eternal.
15. So now, who is it that is born, and how is he recognized? What is meant by what is said about the signs of the accumulation of past deeds (karma)? That also must be explained.
16. What is the meaning of what is said about the nature merits and sins? Also, who is the one who raises these questions, using these words? Who is the doer here?
17. I cannot come to any conclusion about these things. It is said that desire takes the birth, but this is not a visible thing that can be seen, nor it is possible to hold.

18. The fivefold aspects of the inner-mind have an endless variety of attitudes and tendencies such as desire, lust, imagination, intentions, feelings, intellect, etc.
19. This is all the mechanical functioning of knowledge, and knowledge itself basically only means memory. So how has memory tied itself to a birth?
20. The body is created out of the five elements, of which, the wind is the mover of all, and "knowing" is the fundamental natural disposition of the mind.
21. It has happened naturally that the five elements are all intermingled. So who has given birth to whom, and in what way?
22. Even having looked into all of this, it is still not apparent that there is any birth or any being that has become born or that comes back to life again.
23. If there is no birth to anyone, then what does keeping the company of saints do?" This is the line of questioning being put forth by the listeners.
24. Originally, there is neither memory nor forgetting, and then at some point in-between, some remembrance arises. Understand that the inner-mind is the seat of consciousness (being conscious).
25. The sense of being conscious is that remembrance, while losing the sense of being conscious is the lack of memory, and when remembrance is lost is when beings die.
26. Having lost both memory and forgetfulness, death comes to the body, so who is there that can be later put into birth, and by whom?
27. Therefore, it follows that there is no birth, and no suffering after death can be seen either. All is only unnecessary imagination that becomes strengthened.
28. It also follows that there is no rebirth for anyone. Those who are dead do not come back and get born again.
29. Dried wood does not become green again, a fallen fruit does not become attached again. In the same way, a fallen body does not come back to birth again.
30. When an earthen pot is broken, it stays broken forever. Similarly, a human being is not born again.
31. Whether one is knowledgeable or ignorant does not matter. Both are the same and equal." Speaking like this, the doubts of the listeners became stronger.
32. The speaker says, "Oh listeners! Don't engage in all of these opinions. When there are doubts, use the power of discrimination to see clearly.
33. It does not happen that without effort work gets done, or that without meals hunger is satisfied, or that without Knowledge one becomes liberated.
34. When one has had his meal he may feel that other people have also satisfied their hunger, but this is not the case. They all must have their own meals.
35. One who knows how to swim will float and one who does not know how to swim will drown. Who can have any doubt about that?
36. Similarly, only those with Self-Knowledge cross beyond the ocean of this world, and only one whose bondage is broken is liberated.
37. One who becomes free says that there is no bondage, but actually many people are in bondage. Just how it is that those who are in bondage can become content is the point that should be seen by the listeners.
38. One who does not feel the suffering that others are experiencing feels indifferent to their sorrow. Understand that the experience of one who is liberated is similar to this.
39. The one who has Self-Knowledge, having reflected upon the various elements and the fundamental Reality, has gained complete contentment.

40. Only with Self-Knowledge does one escape the cycle of birth and death. It is not correct to say that this is the case for everyone, regardless of whether or not they have Self-Knowledge. What then would be the purpose of the *Vedas*, scriptures of spiritual science (*Shastras*), and mythological stories (*Puranas*)?
41. The thoughts and statements in the *Vedas* and other scriptures are said by people of "Great Experience," but all of the people on the earth do not accept what is said there.
42. If everything said there is considered to be false, then what authority is one to go by? Only one with actual Self-Knowledge is liberated.
43. The statement that everyone is liberated is a statement that can only be made by those with Self-Knowledge. Without Self-Knowledge, there is no liberation. This is certain.
44. When one gains Self-Knowledge, the visible world is known to be false. However, all others still feel affected by appearances.
45. Now this question has been answered. One who is Knowledgeable has become liberated with Self-Knowledge, while the ignorant one remains bound by his own imagination.
46. One should not equate ignorance (Ajnana) with Supreme Knowledge (Vijnana), bondage with liberation, or conjecture with conviction.
47. There is not really anything such thing as bondage, yet it has affected everybody. There is no remedy to this situation without Self-Realization.
48. First see this surprising thing of how something that does not exist affects someone. When that bondage, which is unreal, is not understood to be false one feels bound.
49. It is an incorrect view to think that one can accomplish liberation with only simple faith. Liberation is immediately at hand if one sees clearly and understands by using the power of discrimination.
50. In order for one to become free, first he must have Knowledge (Jnana). With Knowledge, one quite naturally is the knower of all, like the sky.
51. Not knowing anything is ignorance (Ajnana), knowing everything is Knowledge (Jnana), and when even Knowledge is left behind, there is the Supreme Knowledge (Vijnana) of one's Self.
52. One who has consumed immortal nectar and becomes immortal inquires into how people could die. Similarly, one who uses proper discrimination asks how can there be birth for someone in bondage.
53. One who has some knowledge asks, "How can a ghost affect you?," and a person who has not been affected by poison asks "How can poison possibly affect you?
54. First understand what it is like to be an ignorant person, and then it is not required to ask what it is like. Aside from the understanding that you have gained using the power of discrimination, understand what it is like to see through the eyes of an ignorant person.
55. The one who is awake sees someone who is babbling in his sleep and wants to know why is he acting like that. If he truly wants to understand that experience he must go to sleep himself.
56. The disposition of the knowledgeable person is not like the ignorant person who is entangled in the visible world. The experience of the one who is hungry is not the same as that of one whose hunger has been satisfied.

57. With this explanation, the doubts have been cleared. Liberation only happens for one who gains Knowledge, and by seeing clearly using the power of discrimination one arrives at Self-Realization within.

Thus in Shri Dasbodh, a dialogue between the Guru and disciple, Sub-Chapter 7 of Chapter 9, named "Removal of Doubts" is concluded.

Chapter: 9, Sub- Chapter: 8

The End of the Body

|| ShriRam ||

1. "The one who is Knowledgeable (the Jnani) has been liberated due to Knowledge (Jnana), but how is there rebirth for the one in bondage, and what is it that is born after the end of the body?
2. When the person in bondage dies, nothing remains there. There is even a loss of awareness (janiva) at the time of death."
3. This is the doubt that was raised by the listeners. Listen to its answer. The speaker says, "Please do not become restless and inattentive at this time."
4. The five vital energies (pranas) leave their places in the body. The pranas and lingering desires intermingle together as they leave the body.
5. The latent desires (vasanas) leave the body like the wind. Remaining for some time in a form like that of wind, the desire takes a birth according to the intention.
6. Many beings die, and because of their desires those beings come back again. If their death was caused by some damage to the body, they may be born with some injury to their hands and legs.
7. For example, when someone gets snakebite and goes into some unconscious state he is desireless for some time, and then when the effects of the bite disappear after a few days and he becomes conscious again, the desires also come back again.
8. Many fall down as dead bodies and by some means or another are made alive again and brought back from the house of the God of Death.
9. There are tales of many who in the past have been cursed and were turned into some other form of body, and then when the curse was lifted, they reverted back to their original body.
10. Many have taken numerous births, and many are known to have even entered in the body of another. There are countless cases like this.
11. The prana leaves the body like wind being exhaled, and this form of wind mixed together with the momentum of desires is what takes a birth.
12. There are many various attitudes of the mind, and in these attitudes is where desire is born. When looking, this is not seen, but still it is there.
13. Understand that desire is tied to the sense of being conscious, or aware. This consciousness is tied like a fiber to the Primal Illusion, and is intermixed in it in the form of a cause or motive.
14. The cause is present in the universe, and it functions in the body in the form of actions. This is not possible to understand through guesswork.

15. But it is there in very subtle form, like as is the case with the true nature of wind. All of the gods as well as all beings in creation are only in the form of wind.
16. The wind undergoes many modifications. Even when looking for it, the wind cannot be seen. Similarly, the desires of the conscious state are present at a subtle level.
17. The three gunas and five elements are intermixed in the wind. This should not be considered false because one cannot see them.
18. Wind moves about spontaneously, but still we can come to know pleasant aromas and offensive smells it carries, and it can be seen that hot things gets cooled, and that hot living beings are pacified by the wind.
19. Because of the wind, the clouds and even the stars in the heavens move. All of the functions of creation happen because of wind.
20. It is only because of some form of wind that some deities or spirits can enter the body, and only by the power of wind that dead bodies can become alive again.
21. It is only because of the power of wind that a spirit possessing someone will be dispelled, or that some hidden treasure might be found, or that someone caught up in difficulties is relieved.
22. The force of the wind cannot speak independently. Only when it fills a body does a person move and bend. Many beings have taken birth because desire in the wind.
23. Like this, are the modifications of wind. Its expanse cannot be understood. Everything animate and inanimate in the entire universe exists because of wind.
24. Wind in its static form supports the creation. Wind in its restless form creates the motion of the universe. If you do not understand, inquire into this and think about it deeply. Then you will understand.
25. From the beginning until the end, it is wind alone that does everything. If there is anything other than wind that has such capacity, I ask a clever person to explain it to me.
26. The Primal Illusion is in the form of consciousness, or awareness. This consciousness is in many beings in the universe in its manifest state. It functions in the universe when it is revealed as well as when it is concealed and unmanifest.
27. It conceals itself somewhere, and then reveals itself somewhere else, much like water that springs up and then vanishes and then comes flowing back again from the earth.
28. Similarly, the wind is like this consciousness. It arises and vanishes continuously. Some times it is moving and sometimes it is still, and sometimes it unnecessarily makes noise.
29. When the wind goes away from the body, the hands and feet shrivel up, and when the wind moves fire it burns up the crops ready to be harvested.
30. Many diseases are caused by different types of wind causing pain and misery on the earth. Even the lightning crashes loudly in the sky because of the wind.
31. The various musical moods are played because of the wind. One can definitely recognize and identify them. It can also be recognized that certain lamps get lit, and even the clouds give rain because of these musical moods caused by the wind.
32. Because of the power of the moving wind, people get hypnotized by the spoken word. Because of wind wounds get dried up, and it is only because of the wind that mantras are effective.
33. With the power of wind in mantras, gods can be called to manifest, spirits can be dispelled, and magic tricks and spells can be performed.

34. Because of the power of the wind, the hypnotic tricks of demons cannot be understood, even by the gods. Many strange things occur, such as a person becoming paralyzed or hypnotized, all by the power of the wind.
35. Because of the wind, a person in good condition can be made to go mad, and a mad person can be brought back to normal. There are so many modifications of the wind, how many can be told?
36. By the power of the wind in mantras wars can be conducted by the gods, and even sages become proud. Who knows all of the greatness of the power of mantras?
37. By the power of the wind in mantras birds can be made to fall dead, rats and wild animals can be bound, great snakes can be made to remain still, and one may gain great sums of money.
38. Now, let this be enough of this discussion. The listener's question about how the birth of an ignorant person comes to be experienced has been answered.

Thus in Shri Dasbodh, a dialogue between the Guru and disciple, Sub-Chapter 8 of Chapter 9, named "The End of the Body," is concluded.

Chapter: 9, Sub- Chapter: 9

Removal of Doubt

|| ShriRam ||

1. Brahman cannot be avoided, cannot be pushed aside, and does not subside.
2. Brahman cannot be broken, cannot be cut, and cannot be pushed away even if one tries.
3. Brahman is continuous, it cannot be divided into parts. In Brahman there is no other thing. However, the question arises as to how the universe has appeared in it.
4. How have the mountains, stones, boulders, peaks, many various places, and even the structure of the earth itself, appeared in Parabrahman, the Absolute Reality?
5. Earth is in Brahman, and Brahman is in the earth. When looking into this, each one is clearly seen in the other.
6. The earth has made its expanse in Brahman, and in penetrating Brahman, the earth is also penetrated by Brahman. When enquiring into this, it can actually be seen.
7. To say that Brahman has penetrated the universe appears to be correct, but to say that the universe has penetrated Brahman does not sound proper.
8. Even if one says that the universe has not penetrated Brahman, it is still there quite naturally, in Brahman. This experience is seen by everyone.
9. The listeners have put forth the objection that how this has happened must be explained, and that some inquiry and deep thought must be given to this riddle.
10. Here some doubtful thoughts have been expressed. Now, please listen to the answer in silence with alertness.
11. If we say that the universe is not there, it still has an appearance, and if it appears, it is certain that it will be destroyed. Now the listeners are requested to listen and understand this.
12. At this the listeners became excited and said, "We are listening to you attentively. Please tell us the right answer according to this occasion."

13. When a lamp is lit in the sky, it does not happen that the lamp somehow makes the sky move aside. This can easily be seen by the listeners.
14. Even water, light, and wind all together cannot move the sky aside. The sky is dense and spread out everywhere, how can it be moved?
15. And even though the earth has become solid and penetrates the sky, the sky still remains, permeating everywhere, even through the interior of the earth.
16. The actual experience of the situation is that whatever becomes gross eventually gets destroyed, but the space remains as it is and does not get disturbed.
17. When seen as being separate, it is called the sky, when it seen as naturally not being separate, space is called Brahman.
18. Space does not move. Its distinctive quality of being space is not easily understood. Understand that if there seems to be any appearance attributed to Brahman it is actually the space element.
19. Space appears to be like Attributeless Brahman, but if it is imaginable or is known by some inference, it is the space element and is conceptual.
20. If it appears to the imagination, or is conceptual, understand that to be the space element. Parabrahman is void of any appearance or modification, and is incapable of being represented by any simile or being comprehended by any conceptual modification.
21. Space resides among the five elements, thus it is called space. While it is only a small fraction of Brahman that is within the elements, space itself is nothing but Brahman.
22. The four elements of wind, fire, water, and earth all take form and then vanish. How can they be called changeless, or be said to have really affected space?
23. When earth dissolves, water remains, and when water dries up, light remains, and when light is extinguished, wind remains, and then, even the wind disappears.
24. That which is false comes and goes, and this occurrence makes it seem like that which is True gets destroyed. How can it ever be experienced that what is True gets destroyed?
25. That which is seen appears to be real because of delusion. If examined thoughtfully, what is there? How can this world that is rooted in delusion be called True?
26. When searching through this delusion, it is seen that nothing is there. Who can say that anything has differentiated itself from anything else? Saying that the Illusion has differentiated itself from Brahman, is basically only false delusion.
27. When the form of Illusion is known to be false one may say that it is different from Brahman. However, whatever is basically false can only create something that is false.
28. No one stands to lose anything by saying that what is false has done many things. However, the wise understand that even though they say that the false done has done many things, all of it is not True.
29. Everything that is visible is like a tiny poppy seed in the ocean of Parabrahman. Understanding within increases according to your intellect.
30. If the intellect is expanded, it becomes large enough to encompass all of space. Seeing in this way, the entire universe appears small like the fruit from a wood-apple tree.
31. If one expands one's state larger than that, the universe appears like a small berry. Taking the form of Brahman, there is no universe at all.

32. When one becomes expansive beyond all limit through the power of discrimination, the universe seems smaller than the seed of a banyan tree.
33. The more expansive one becomes, the smaller the universe appears to be. Being complete in oneself, there remains nothing to be seen.
34. When due to delusion one becomes small and considers oneself to be the body, then how can he be more expansive than the universe?
35. One should enlarge one's state so much that it is spread out to such an extent that no personal state exists. Then the completeness of Brahman permeates everywhere on all sides.
36. If you can imagine taking a small thing like a little bit of gold and spreading it out over the entire universe to cover everywhere, visualizing that principle is similar to what is being said about making oneself more expansive.
37. When the Reality engulfs the small state of mind, the small state of mind breaks apart and dissolves. Then the Self without attributes alone remains, as it is.
38. Now your doubts should have been cleared. The listeners should not hold on to any doubt. If there is still some doubt remaining, then look clearly with the power of discrimination.
39. Doubts are cleared with discrimination, and with discrimination one gains contentment. With discrimination there is self-surrender and liberation.
40. Leaving behind the notion of liberation, with discrimination one sets aside the primary premise presented in the doctrines and statements of the *Vedas*, and in the "final conclusion" the Self is Self-evident. No other proof is required.
41. These answers emanate out of experience. Investigate and give deep thought to what is Essence and what is non-essential. With persistent meditation and reflection, one arrives at the revelation of the Self.

Thus in Shri Dasbodh, a dialogue between the Guru and disciple, Sub-Chapter 9 of Chapter 9, named "Removal of Doubt" is concluded.

Chapter: 9, Sub-Chapter: 10

The State of the Self

|| ShriRam ||

1. If there is an image of God in the temple and there is crow sitting on top of the temple, one would never say that the crow is greater than God.
2. If there is a meeting being held in the king's court and a monkey climbs up on the top of a pillar, the monkey would not be considered superior or wiser than the attendees of the assembly.
3. The brahmin priests go to have their bath and then leave while a crane continues to stand there in the water, yet one would not say that the crane is better than the brahmins.
4. Among the brahmins, some are more disciplined in their behavior and routine than others, and while a dog may sit still and behave nicely, it cannot be said that the dog is better than the brahmins.
5. A brahmin may not have the same power to concentrate on an object like a cat that is focusing on a target of prey, but who will say that a cat is more special than the brahmin?
6. A brahmin notices differences and may make distinctions while a fly will land on anything without making any distinctions, but it will never happen that the fly will realize Self-Knowledge.
7. Someone who is poor or of low standing may wear expensive and proper clothing, while one who is Self-realized may sit with little or no clothing, but his status is still recognized by those who are wise.
8. Someone may outwardly makes a public display or big show about their spiritual accomplishments, but all of that is just carrying on in the world. What is required here is inner accomplishment.
9. A person may earn a good name and fame yet not be alert within. One who misses finding God is like someone who commits suicide.
10. Those who worship various gods attain the realm of the gods, those who worship ancestors attain the realm of ancestors, and those who worship ghosts will attain their realm.
11. The way in which one worships determines the abode that they will attain. When one worships the Attributeless (Nirguna), one becomes attributeless oneself.
12. How does one worship the Attributeless? One must be one-pointed and completely without attributes oneself. One who is completely without attributes without allowing for anything "other" is truly blessed.
13. The ultimate accomplishment is that one should realize God. One should use the power of discrimination to see that this is one's own True Self.
14. When investigating and thinking deeply it is seen that God is formless, and whatever one calls oneself is illusory. With the firm determination of Soham, "I am He," one becomes established in this realization.
15. Speculation and guesswork is not needed now. Reality is as it is, in its place, the place of Reality. There is no feeling of being limited to a body that can be found.

16. For the one who is accomplished (the Siddha), there is no longer any need do to any spiritual practice. To say that there is, is only imagination. For the one who is liberated there is no such thing as bondage.
17. Anything that was to be achieved with spiritual practices is known to be already naturally present within oneself. That which was being called by the term "aspirant" no longer exists.
18. If a potter is granted a kingdom, why should he have any reason to look after the donkeys (to carry the pots) any longer? Why should he feel inclined to continue on with the business of being a potter?
19. Similarly, when everything that is to be accomplished has been accomplished using various remedies and spiritual practice, what is the need for spiritual practice any longer?
20. What more does one need to accomplish, and what fruit does one get from spiritual practice once one has realized oneself to be Reality? For what reason would one wander needlessly down the path of some particular spiritual practice?
21. The body is made up of five elements, and the individual being is but a small fraction of Brahman. Realize your unwavering oneness with the Supreme Self, Paramatman, and be That.
22. When looking superficially the sense of "I" is seen. When looking into it, there is nothing to be found. By analyzing the elements and observing how they disappear one into another it is seen that only the pure Self remains.
23. The Self exists in its own Self Form (Swaroopa). The individual also exists as the individual self, and Illusion exists spread out everywhere as Illusion.
24. In this way, everything exists, and one also exists oneself. However, only the one who investigates and searches out the Reality in everything can be called the Jnani who has Self-Knowledge.
25. If one knows about everything, but does not know oneself, this type of knowledge is one-sided knowledge in the form of attitudes, or states of mind (vritti).
26. When that knowledge is seen to be only in the form of attitudes or states of mind, it is seen to be nothing. Everything in manifestation is subject to change and is destined to disappear entirely.
27. That which remains is That which is without any attributes. Analyzing this deeply and realizing that this is oneself, is the sign of Supreme Truth which is beyond comprehension.
28. With the power of discrimination one must see that one is not different from Reality itself. One is already That which one is striving to attain.
29. If one who was a beggar becomes a king, he then behaves in the manner of a king. He only behaves like a beggar when he is a beggar.
30. There are many explanations regarding the *Vedas* and the many various scriptures and mythological books. The "accomplished" (Siddhas) and "knowledgeable" (Jnanis) have made many efforts to realize their meaning.
31. When one has investigated deeply into what is Essence and what is non-essence, and has realized oneself to be of the nature of Brahman, the question does not arise about whether or not to do any appropriate or inappropriate thing.
32. A peasant becomes afraid because of the orders of the king, but when becoming king himself, the fear disappears along with his poverty.
33. How is it that the *Vedas* will behave according to their own dictates? How will the *Shastras* study the sciences of the scriptures? How can a pilgrimage go to visit itself?

34. How will the nectar of immortality drink itself? How can the endless see endlessness, and how does God strive to become God? How can this happen?
35. How can tranquility give up the untranquil? How can the attributeless ever break attributelessness? How can one's True Nature ever get lost from itself?
36. How can eye medication be applied to eye medication? How can money earn money? How can light experience itself?
37. How can the spiritual practices practice themselves? How can the object of contemplation contemplate itself? And how can no-mind control the mind?

Thus in Shri Dasbodh, a dialogue between the Guru and disciple, Sub-Chapter 10 of Chapter 9, named "The State of the Self" is concluded.

Chapter 10. The Universal Flame

Chapter: 10, Sub-Chapter: 1

The Oneness of the Inner-Mind

|| ShriRam ||

1. "Is the inner-mind (antahkarana) of all one, or is it different for everyone? Please explain this to me convincingly."
2. The listener asked like this as to whether the inner-mind is one, or if it is different for all. The listeners are now requested to listen to the reply.
3. The inner-mind of everyone is one. Using the power of discrimination one gains the experience of this, and by leaving doubt behind one gains understanding with conviction. The answer has now been given to you.
4. The listener said to the speaker, "If the inner-mind is one for everybody, then why does one person not agree with the other? What is the reason for this?
5. If it is one, then why when eating food, when one person is satisfied all are not satisfied, or when one person becomes peaceful why don't all become peaceful, and when one person dies, why don't all die?
6. Why does it happen that when one person is happy, another is sorrowful? How can one understand how to identify the oneness of the inner-mind?
7. People have different feelings and emotions and one person does not agree with another, therefore this oneness cannot be imagined.
8. If the inner-mind is one, then one person should always be able to understand the other, and one person would not be able to hide and keep secrets from another.
9. Therefore, one cannot arrive at the conclusion that the inner-mind is one. What is the reason why people get into opposition with each other?
10. If a snake comes to bite someone, that person runs away in fear. If the inner-mind is one, then such enmity should not exist."
11. Like this the listener expressed his doubts. The speaker said, "Don't become restless now, but remain alert and listen to the explanation."
12. Inner-Mind means knowledge (which is consciousness, or awareness). Knowledge is of the nature of "knowing," or being aware (being conscious), and in this knowing there is the instinct for the protection of the body.
13. The snake, being conscious, comes to bite, and the person, being conscious, knowingly runs away. See that it is knowledge that is functioning on both sides.
14. If you look to the functioning of knowledge, you will see that it is the inner-mind that is functioning on both sides. If you think this over, you will have the experience of this in the form of knowledge.
15. The inner-mind of everyone is one in the form of knowledge. Thus it is true for all living beings, that the quality of knowing, or being aware, is one.
16. It is with the eyes that everyone sees, it is with the tongue that everyone tastes, and the functions of listening, touch, and smell are also common in the same way to all.
17. All of the animals, birds, worms, ants, and other living beings in the world have this faculty of knowledge, or awareness, which is the same.
18. The fact that water is cold for everyone, and that fire is hot for everyone is the faculty of the knowledge of the inner-mind alone.

19. The many different likes and dislikes are all according to the various dispositions of different bodies, but the knowledge of sensations are because of the functioning of the knowledge of the inner-mind.
20. The inner-mind of all is one, this is definitely confirmed. The wonder of this can be seen everywhere.
21. Now that this doubt has been cleared there should be no more speculation about the matter. All that is known is known by the one inner-mind.
22. It is through knowledge that all beings take their food, that they know to hide in fear, and know to run away.
23. From worms and ants to Lord Brahma and others, all have the same one inner-mind. Understand the marvelous nature of this fact in your own experience.
24. Large or small, fire is fire, and whether it is in small or large quantities, water is water. This knowing that something is less or more is the common functioning of the knowledge of the inner-mind.
25. However, the degree of knowledge may vary. In some places it is less, in some places it is more, but the basic quality the nature of knowledge is the same. No living being exists without this quality of knowledge (the sattvaguna).
26. Knowledge means inner-mind. Know that the inner-mind is but a fraction of the Consciousness that is "the sustainer of creation," which is called Lord Vishnu. It is with this knowledge that is the inner-mind, that Lord Vishnu protects living beings.
27. Without knowledge, beings get destroyed. The lack of knowledge is the quality of ignorance which is called the tamas quality (the tamoguna). This is called the functioning of Lord Shiva (Rudra), the quality of destruction as the tamoguna.
28. The mixture of knowledge and ignorance is the nature of the rajas quality (the rajoguna). It is this mixture of knowledge and ignorance that causes living beings to take birth.
29. Knowledge begets happiness, and ignorance begets sorrow. Both happiness and sorrow are unavoidable after taking birth.
30. Understand that the intellect, which is partly knowing and partly not knowing, is called the functioning of Lord Brahma, the creator, in the body. The creator of the gross body is the rajoguna, or Lord Brahma.
31. Like this is the creation, preservation, and destruction. I have explained this according to the occasion in this discourse. However, what has been said is something that one must confirm for oneself in one's own experience.

Thus in Shri Dasbodh, a dialogue between the Guru and disciple, Sub-Chapter 1 of Chapter 10, named " The Oneness of the Inner-Mind" is concluded.

Chapter: 10, Sub-Chapter: 2

Doubt About the Body

|| ShriRam ||

1. The listener said, "The speaker has put forward thoughts about Lord Vishnu, Lord Brahma, and Lord Shiva, but in actual life they are not seen and seem to be absent.
2. The processes of creation, preservation, and destruction are said to be carried on by Brahma, Vishnu, and Shiva, but when thinking about them and trying to see them, they are not actually experienced.
3. Brahma the creator is said to have four faces, but there is no experience of this for the body. Vishnu the sustainer is said to have four arms, yet this is also is known only by hearing about him.
4. It is said that Shiva is the destroyer, but how is this to be experienced? In the ancient mythological books (*Puranas*) the greatness of Shiva in the form of the Lingam is spoken about quite differently.
5. Who is the creator of the Primal Illusion (Moolamaya)? This must be understood. The appearance of the forms of the three gods has come after the Primal Illusion.
6. The Primal Illusion is the mother of creation. From her arises the stirring or arousal of the attributes (the gunas). From this arousal of the attributes (gunakshobhini), comes the birth of the three gods (with their qualities of creation, preservation, and destruction).
7. It is said to be like this by the writers of the ancient scriptures and by people who are scholarly, but when asked how to gain the experience of this, they mostly just get irritated.
8. Therefore, one cannot ask them, and the experience cannot be gained from them. Without experience, various efforts only become tiresome and make one weary.
9. For example, if one calls himself a doctor, but does not have any actual experience or knowledge, and engages in various medical activities, he is merely a fool who gets into trouble.
10. The thought here is similar. One has to make a determination and gain experience. Without having actual experience there is darkness and ignorance on both the side of the guru and of the disciple.
11. How can any blame be put on the so-called 'wise' people? What they say is correct, but we kindly ask the speaker to please give us the proper explanation.
12. If we say that Illusion is made by the three gods, the fact is that the forms of the gods are themselves found only in Illusion. If we say that Illusion is made by Illusion, that implies that there is some second Illusion.
13. If we say that the elements created Illusion, we can see that the elements are only present in Illusion, and part of it. If we say that Illusion is created by Parabrahman, the Absolute Reality, this cannot be true, because by definition there is no doing in Parabrahman.
14. If we say that Illusion is true, then Brahman must somehow be involved in the activity of Illusion as the doer, and if Illusion is said to be untrue, then where is there any question of any doership?

15. Now all of this must be explained so that experience can be gained, and the mind will be satisfied. Something such as this must be explained through the benevolent teaching of the Sadguru.
16. The *Vedas* cannot exist without words, words cannot exist without the body, and bodies cannot be created without other bodies.
17. Among all bodies, the human body is best, and among human bodies, the body of a brahmin priest, who is an authority on the study of the *Vedas*, is considered superior.
18. So, the question is, from where have the *Vedas* come, and what are all of the various bodies made up of? Furthermore, how have the three gods appeared? How has all of this happened?
19. Like this, the doubts of the listeners were strengthened. Therefore, answers that offer satisfaction must be given. The speaker says, "Please listen now with alert attention."
20. If one tries to observe and gain experience of all this, much confusion arises, and everything seems upside down. Thinking about these things from one moment to the next, one indulges in guesswork and speculation and a lot of time gets wasted.
21. People have many different ways of thinking and many various opinions, and the scriptures give various different assertions as well. Therefore there is no uniformity of experience, and it is difficult to determine the Truth.
22. If we try to hold on only to the authority of the scriptures, even then such confusion cannot be escaped. And if one tries to resolve this confusion by oneself, the differences and dissension among the scriptures becomes more evident.
23. Now the problem arises as to how to explain the knowledge that is stated in the scriptures and gain actual experience. This is done by first explaining the "primary premise" that is given in the *Vedas*, as well as to move beyond that, and explain the "final conclusion," or siddhanta, in such a way that both the wise and the dull-minded will understand.
24. According to the scriptures, the "primary premise" presented in the *Vedas* is to be given, and then later on, that primary premise is revealed to not really be true. Understanding this, there should be no criticism of the contradictions that are seen.
25. Nevertheless, some explanation should be given so that one protects and appreciates what is said in the scriptures. The listeners are now respectfully asked to attentively listen to what is said while utilizing the power of discrimination.

Thus in Shri Dasbodh, a dialogue between the Guru and disciple, Sub-Chapter 2 of Chapter 10, named "Doubt About the Body" is concluded.

Chapter: 10, Sub-Chapter: 3

Clearing Doubts About the Body

|| ShriRam ||

1. The space that is without any distinguishing properties is itself Brahman which is imperceptible. In that imperceptible Brahman, the Primal Illusion (Moolamaya) appeared.
2. Know that the main attribute of the Primal Illusion is the form of wind (vayu), and that the five elements and the three gunas are all contained within that wind.
3. The wind (air element) that has emanated from the space (sky) is called the "Wind God." The fire (light) which has emanated from wind is called the "Fire God."
4. The water that has emanated from fire is the form of Lord Narayana. From water, arose the earth, which contained many seeds.
5. Within the earth there are many stones, some of which are used to create symbols representing God. Many people have experienced the existence of God because of their worship of these symbols made from stone.
6. Many people in the world also experience the existence of God because of their worship of symbols made from wood and earth, etc. All of this is due only to the existence of the one God, that is wind.
7. In different places there are many entities that are considered gods, messengers of gods, and various spirits and deities with different powers that are given different names according to the region.
8. There are many gods given masculine names, and there are numerous spirits and deities that are given neutral names.
9. There are innumerable male gods and female goddesses, deities, and spirits on the earth, but these can all be said to only exist within the form of the wind.
10. They always remain only in the form of wind, but according to various situations they may assume bodies and conceal themselves, or they may reveal themselves to all.
11. They move around in the form of wind. Also there in the wind is the "Light of the Universe" which takes many different forms such as knowledge, desires, habits and various states of mind.
12. Wind arose in space and became divided into two forms. The listeners must be alert and think this over carefully.
13. One form is wind, which is known by all, and the second is the form of the "Light of the Universe." There are an endless number of idols in the form of various gods and goddesses that symbolize this light which illumines the world.
14. Wind has undergone many modifications, but it became divided into two main forms. Now, listen and give some thought to the form that is light.
15. Light emanated from wind, which also divided into two forms, which are hot and cold light. Listen to the description of the two forms of light.
16. From the light that is hot, the sun was formed, as well as the fire that consumes everything, and electrical energy, such as lightening.
17. From the light that is cool, water, nectar, the moon and stars, and all cool things were formed. Now, the listeners are asked to remain attentive.
18. The light element has undergone various modifications in many ways, but only two have been described. Similarly, water has divided into two forms and is explained

here basically only in these two forms, which are the forms of simple water and that of nectar[50].

19. Now, give some thought to the element of earth. Stones and mud are considered to be the common form of earth, and gold, precious gems, and the philosopher's stone are considered to be the second form.
20. Many varieties of stones come from the earth. Upon examination and careful thought, one is able to determine which are true gems and which are false.
21. The main question that still remains is, "From where, is it that living beings have come into existence?" The listeners are asked to keep their state of mind alert, and to listen attentively.

Thus in Shri Dasbodh, a dialogue between the Guru and disciple, Sub-Chapter 3 of Chapter 10, named "Clearing Doubts About the Body" ends.

Chapter: 10, Sub-Chapter: 4

Description of the Seed

|| ShriRam ||

1. Now if we look into the process of creation, we see that human beings are born from human beings, and animals are born from animals. This is clearly evident.
2. All of the bodies of creatures that fly, that move on land, and the wild beasts and aquatic animals of all species, are all produced only from bodies.
3. To ask for proof of what is evident, or to speculate about that which one is certain about, is like taking the wrong path while seeing the correct one.
4. Bodies with defects are formed from bodies that have those defects inherent in them, but they are still called bodies. Without bodies, procreation does not take place.
5. But still, how does this procreation take place? Who makes this happen and out of what? And what of the one who created him? Who is the creator of the creator?
6. If we try to look into the matter in this way, the explanation becomes too lengthy. Basically, the question is, "How has the body been created, what is it made of, and who created it?"
7. This is the previous doubt that remains which has not been cleared. Now, listen to the answer and do not continue on with imagination after gaining actual experience.
8. The experience is itself the proof, yet the fool feels that experience is not proof. Know that the one who accepts what is being said gains experience through words.
9. The Primal Illusion appeared in Brahman, and is called the eightfold creation. The Primal Illusion consists of the intermingling of the three gunas and the five elements.
10. The Primal Illusion is in the form of wind, which is also in the form of knowledge (or awareness). Desire is present there in that knowledge, but it is not something that can be attributed to Brahman.

---

[50]The five types of nectar are classically considered to be milk, curds, clarified butter, honey, sugar

11. Even if desire is said to be imagined as being in Brahman, such words are meaningless, because the Self is attributeless and exists beyond words.
12. The attributeless Self is the reality that is Brahman. Whatever names are given to it are only delusion. Even if some names are given to it in reverence, they do not really apply to Brahman.
13. Even if one persists in trying to apply a name to it, it is useless. It is like trying to break the sky by throwing a stone at it, or spitting at it.
14. Brahman is without modification. Even if one were to try to apply modifications to it, modifications get destroyed while Brahman remains as it is, always without any modification.
15. Now, listen to the words of experience, and with understanding gain conviction. Only then will one have success in gaining experience.
16. The Illusion that is in Brahman is in the form of wind. That wind is the knowledge that is God (Ishwara), and only He is the "God of gods."
17. This same God gave rise to attributes, which became differentiated as three distinct attributes (the three gunas). Brahma, Vishnu and Shiva are born from these three attributes.
18. Sattva, Rajas, and Tamas are these three attributes. The nature of these has previously been explained in sequence.
19. Vishnu is full with knowledge (awareness; sattva guna), the four-faced Brahma is a mixture of knowledge and ignorance (rajas guna), and the five faced Shiva is ignorance (not-knowing; tamas guna). All of this is very basic.
20. The three gunas are intermingled with each other. How can they be separated? When there appears to be variation in their proportions it needs to be explained.
21. Originally, Vishnu was present in the wind, and his form is basically only the form of wind. Later on he took a bodily form which has four arms.
22. Similarly, Brahma and Shiva were residing only in the wind, and after some time they took bodily forms, and can become visible and invisible in an instant.
23. There are some human beings that can appear and disappear in an instant. If there are humans who can do this, then why not the Gods who are much more powerful than humans?
24. Gods, goddess, and various spirits and deities all have powers in varying degrees. In the same way, demons also possess some power.
25. For example, there are some categories of spirits that can move around and make sounds, and even make pieces of fruit or dates fall suddenly.
26. Even if all of this is taken to be false, it has been seen to happen by many people in the world who know it in their own experience.
27. Human beings hold a physical form, and some even have the power to enter into the body of another person. Why then would the Supreme Self, Paramatman, not have the power to be able to hold a physical form?
28. Therefore, know that Brahma, Vishnu, and Shiva were holding bodies in the form of wind, and later they proliferated in the forms of their children and grandchildren.
29. Within their minds, the gods imagined women, and from that imagination the bodies of women were created. However, no offspring were then created by them at that time.
30. By their will, the gods imagined sons and they were created according to the various situations. In this way the gods Vishnu and Shiva executed their will.

31. Later on, the visible world containing all living beings was imagined by Brahma and was created according to his wish.
32. He imagined various types of animals and created them according to his wish. Many living beings were born from the coming together of male and female and emerged from eggs, or from the womb.
33. Some creatures were created from the combination of water and heat, and there are some living beings that come out of the wind and are suddenly born from seeds.
34. Human beings have some knowledge of magic, demons have some knowledge of hypnosis, and Brahma has the knowledge of how to create the world.
35. Human beings have this power to some extent, demons have more power than human beings, and even more than that is the special power of Brahma for creating the world.
36. Both knowledgeable and ignorant beings were created. Reciting the knowledge contained in the *Vedas*, beings were given a path in life. This is all the work of Brahma.
37. Then, from physical bodies more bodies were created, and the visible world expanded with many modifications. All bodies were created in this way.
38. Here the doubt has been cleared about how the visible world expanded out all over. Upon investigation and thinking it can be experienced and seen in this sequence.
39. Like this the visible world was created, and later on was protected by Vishnu. This should also be analyzed and seen by the listeners.
40. All living beings that are created are protected in their original form of beingness. It should be seen that only the many types of bodies, including the bodies of the evil-minded, get destroyed, and not their being.
41. Many incarnations of Vishnu have taken birth in bodies for the destruction of evil and the establishment of righteousness.
42. It should be understood that those people who establish righteousness are the incarnation of Vishnu, and it is non-devotional evil-minded people who are classified as demons.
43. Creatures that are born are destroyed because of ignorance. The basic nature of destruction is like this.
44. When the destructive quality of ignorance is active in the body, that is the time that the world of the living being gets destroyed. Ultimately the entire universe will get burned up at the time of the final destruction.
45. Thus, the thoughts about creation, protection, and destruction, are described like this. The listeners should remain alert, giving their attention to what is being said.
46. Total destruction will take place at the time of the final dissolution. I shall tell about this later on. Know that the one who can recognize the five types of dissolution is the true Knowledgeable One, a Jnani.

Thus in Shri Dasbodh, a dialogue between the Guru and disciple, Sub-Chapter 4 of Chapter 10, named "Description of the Seed" is concluded.

Chapter: 10, Sub-Chapter: 5

The Five Dissolutions

|| ShriRam ||

1. Listen to the signs of dissolution. Know that for the body there are two types of dissolution. One is deep sleep and one is death at the time of the end the body.
2. The listeners should know that when the three deities, Brahma, Vishnu, and Shiva go to sleep, that is what is called the dissolution of the universe through sleep.
3. And know that when the three deities come to an end, that the universe will also come to an end. That time is called the dissolution of Brahma.
4. Two dissolutions are for the body and two are for the universe. In all, there are four dissolutions in the universe. Know that the fifth dissolution is the dissolution which occurs due to the power of discrimination.
5. These are the five dissolutions which have been mentioned in sequence. Now they will be explained so that you may gain experiential understanding.
6. When a living being goes to sleep, at that time the activities in the waking state cease to exist, and suddenly there is either deep sleep or dreams.
7. When the world of the waking state ceases to exist it is called dissolution by sleep. Now, listen to the explanation of the dissolution of death that happens at the time of the end of the body.
8. When diseases grow strong or if some calamity befalls the body, the five vital energies (pranas) give up their functioning and leave their places in the body.
9. At that time, along with the five vital winds, the mind also goes out of the body, leaving it lifeless. There is no need for any speculation about this second type of dissolution.
10. The third dissolution is called the sleep of Brahma. This is when the physical world and the activities of all living beings come to an end.
11. At that time, the subtle bodies of living beings merge into the form of the wind. Then, after the lapse of a long period of time, Brahma again becomes awakened.
12. Once again, the visible world is recreated and living beings are brought to life and scattered throughout the world. Then, after a long period of time, when the entire life cycle of Brahma comes to an end, that is called the dissolution of Brahma.
13. In that dissolution there is no rain for one hundred years, and all living beings die. The earth becomes parched and unstable and begins to break apart into an unlimited number of pieces.
14. The sun puts out twelve times its usual heat and the earth begins to burn in its fire. When the fire reaches deep into the netherworld, the divine serpent Shesha begins vomiting out its poison.
15. Then, when space becomes filled with the flames of the sun, and from underneath the serpent Shesha is spewing out is venomous poison, the Earth cannot escape the burning from both sides.
16. The intensity of the sun's heat continues increasing, there is loud chaotic commotion in all directions, and the great Mount Meru begins crumbling on all sides making a terrible noise.
17. Even the kingdoms and abodes of the gods get incinerated.
18. Finally, Mount Meru, which is the center of the universe, collapses and its greatness is lost, and the host of gods are whisked around in a great whirling of the wind.

19. When the earth has been burned to ashes, hard rain pours down like water coming from an elephant's trunk, and the earth gets dissolved in a brief moment.
20. The earth disappears and only water remains. Then the water gets dried up by fire. All of the fire in the universe merges together and completely consumes everything.
21. The great ocean of fire, the fire of the third eye of Shiva, and the fire from the sun and lightening, all come together and totally engulf all of the seven coverings of creation.
22. Like this, all fire from everywhere unites, and in that fire the gods give up their various forms and merge back into their original form that is wind.
23. Then, with great force the wind extinguishes even the "Light of the Universe." The wind then moves around uncontrolled in the expanse of Parabrahman.
24. And then, like smoke that disappears into space, similarly, the wind will disappear. Like this, in sequence, the smaller element dissolves into the greater one.
25. Understand, that when the wind dissolves, the subtle elements and the three attributes also dissolve, and even God, Ishwara, gives up his place and recedes into the attributeless.
26. There, only Supreme Knowledge remains. The Universal Light is extinguished and only pure Essence remains as its True Form (Swaroopa).
27. Anything that has a name is because of the attributes of manifestation (Prakriti). When manifestation is absent, how can one say anything or speak of names?
28. When manifestation exists, one should use the power of discrimination to put it aside. This is called the dissolution through discrimination. Now, all five types of dissolution have been explained to you in a nice way.

Thus in Shri Dasbodh, a dialogue between the Guru and disciple, Sub-Chapter 5 of Chapter 10, named "The Five Dissolutions" is concluded.

Chapter: 10, Sub-Chapter: 6

Explanation of Delusion

|| ShriRam ||

1. The processes of creation, preservation, and destruction have previously been explained. The Supreme Self, Paramatman, is attributeless and formless. It is as it is.
2. The processes of becoming, existing, and disappearing have no relation to Paramatman. It exists before, during, and after all appearances.
3. The Absolute Reality, Parabrahman, alone exists eternally. In it, there is the appearance of this Illusion that gets destroyed after a period of time.
4. Creation, sustenance, and destruction appear to be going on continuously, however, at the end of the epoch all of this activity will come to an end.
5. One who utilizes the power of discrimination knows this already, because he has investigated and seen what is Essence and what is non-essence.
6. When there are many people who are living under delusion and there is one among them who has realized his True Form, he is not respected. But what can he do? There are very few people in the world who are truly realized.

7. Some description of one who is realized will be now be given. Those great people who are realized are devoid of any delusion, mistaken concepts, or mistaken ways of seeing.
8. One who is free of delusion can be recognized with your mind. Now, listen to the explanation about delusion.
9. The one Absolute Reality is pervasive everywhere, and never undergoes any modification. Whatever appears is different from "That," and is of the nature and form of delusion.
10. Those things that have been described as coming to an end at the time of the final dissolution, the three attributes and five elements, are all in the form of delusion.
11. The notions of "you" and "me" are delusion, worship is delusion, and to project any concepts or feelings about God is also delusion. This is definite.
12. Taking this world appearance to be true is delusion. Only the one who inquires deeply into all of this, and into one's Self Form (Swaroopa), is truly blessed.
13. Now the nature of delusion will be made clear to the listeners by using the help of examples to explain.
14. If someone is roaming about in a far off country and loses track of the direction he wishes to go, or if someone fails to recognize those near and dear to them, this is called delusion.
15. If someone is under the influence of some intoxicant and is affected by double-vision or hallucinations, or if someone feels that they are being haunted by ghosts or spirits, that is called delusion.
16. In a folk play, if one is fooled by men playing the parts of women, or if one witnesses magic tricks that cause doubts in the mind, this is called delusion.
17. If someone forgets the hiding place of some treasure, or gets lost while walking on a path, or gets confused and turned around in a big city, this is called delusion.
18. If someone thinks that some object that is in their possession has become lost and therefore becomes worried, or if someone forgets to do something, this is called delusion.
19. If some objects are forgotten, or if something that has been learned cannot be remembered, or if someone gets scared because of a fearful dream, this is called delusion.
20. If someone hears of some bad indications, or an ill-omen, or false news, and the mind becomes worried, or if someone gets startled upon seeing some object, this is called delusion.
21. If someone sees some trees or a log of wood and feels in the mind that it is a ghost, this is called delusion..
22. If someone mistakes water for a glass floor and steps on it and falls in the water, or if someone sees a gathering in a mirror and thinks it to be true, or takes a door going in the wrong direction, this is called delusion.
23. If something is felt to be something else, or if something heard is misunderstood, or if something appears to be something else, this is called delusion.
24. If someone believes that something that is given in charity in this life will be received back in the next life, or if a dead man is thought to have come for food, this is called delusion.
25. If someone thinks that the benefits from good deeds done in this life will be reaped in the next life, or if someone gets enamored by another person's name, this is called delusion.

26. If a dead person comes to someone in the dream and asks for something, and that occupies the mind continuously, this is called delusion.
27. To say that everything is unreal but at the same time to crave after material power, or to become caught up in keeping a good name and seeking personal glory, this is called delusion.
28. If someone has a distaste for spiritual knowledge because of orthodox views, or if someone deliberately strays away from the path of knowledge, or behaves in a manner which displays no self control or discipline, this is called delusion.
29. When someone has pride about their body, their actions, caste, family lineage, knowledge, or in being liberated, this is called delusion.
30. When someone does not understand the difference between justice and injustice, or when someone blows up in anger for no reason, this is called delusion.
31. When someone cannot remember anything about the past, does not give any thought to the future, and is continuously doubting and guessing about everything, this is called delusion.
32. When someone takes medicine without observing the effects, or observes some dietary restrictions without any experiential knowledge, this is called delusion.
33. When someone conducts many experiments without looking for any appreciable results, or does yogic practices without any knowledge of yoga, or is obsessed with enjoying pleasures with the physical body, this is called delusion.
34. When someone holds on to the superstitious stories about Lord Brahma writing our destiny and a goddess reading it and deciphering it, this is called delusion.
35. Delusion has been greatly expanded and spread out among ignorant people. A brief description has now been given here for the purpose of understanding.
36. The nature of the world is in the form of delusion. How much more needs to be told about it? Other than the Attributeless (Nirguna) Brahman, everything else is the form of delusion.
37. It is said by many people that the Jnani has no worldly life, and that a Jnani can perform miracles even after the death of his body. This is all delusion.
38. Here the listener raises the doubt asking, "If one worships at the memorial shrine (samadhi) of a Jnani, is there some beneficial experience to be gained or not?
39. It has been seen that even after the incarnations of Jnanis has ended, their "power" still seems to continue on. Can it then be said that they are bound to the world because of lingering desires?"
40. This was the doubt that arose in the listener which must be cleared by the power of the speaker. Here the explanation about delusion is completed.

Thus in Shri Dasbodh, a dialogue between the Guru and disciple, Sub-Chapter 6 of Chapter 10, named "Explanation About Delusion" is concluded.

Chapter: 10, Sub-Chapter: 7

Worship of God with Attributes

|| ShriRam ||

1. Saints and Jnanis who are incarnations of God have become liberated through their discrimination and investigation into Essence and non-essence. How does their "power" work?
2. This was the doubt of the listener that was raised as a good question. The speaker responded, "Please remain alert and listen to the answer."
3. The Jnanis have become liberated in their life, and their power continues to be evident after the passing away of their body, but it is not true that they come back because of lingering desires.
4. People experience miracles and they consider them to be true. However, one must inquire and think deeply about this in order to see clearly.
5. When alive, so many miracles were taking place amongst the people around the Jnani that one does not even know how many such things have occurred. One must inquire into this in order to verify directly what this phenomenon is.
6. Even though the Jnani does not come back after leaving his body, he is actually seen by people to be present at some place or other. What can be said about such a miracle?
7. This happens according the to the faith of the people. God is seen to be real according to one's devotion and faith. Imagining otherwise is useless wrong thinking.
8. Something that is liked is seen in a dream, but from where has that thing come? It can be said that it was because it was remembered that something was seen.
9. Imagination is like this. Many various objects appear in a dream, but those actual objects do not really travel to that dream place. In addition to this, many objects appear in a dream even though they are not remembered.
10. Here the doubt has been cleared away. Do not imagine rebirth for the Jnani. If you still do not understand, then look and see with proper discrimination.
11. The Jnanis became liberated while alive, but their power continues on even after the passing of their body because of the virtuous lives that they led.
12. For this reason, tread on the path of virtue, support the worship of God, and do not give up justice by going down the path of injustice.
13. Continue with devotional practices, visit pilgrimage places, and enhance your power with the strength of your detachment.
14. When one's determination is fixed upon the realization of Reality, one's power increases on the path of Knowledge (Jnana). Do not do anything that takes away from your sense of Oneness.
15. One must have devotion somewhere, whether in one's Master or in the one God. Without devotion, everything is in vain.
16. If upon having gained knowledge of That which is without attributes, one ignores That which has attributes, such a "knowledgeable one" looses out on both sides.
17. For such a one there is no Devotion (Bhakti) and no Knowledge (Jnana), but only pride that takes over in between. Therefore, don't give up chanting and repeating the Lord's name in meditation.

18. Even though one may be knowledgeable, by giving up the worship of God with attributes, one becomes unsuccessful in realizing Brahman, so don't give up the worship of God with attributes.
19. Worship without any desire in the intellect has no equal in all the three worlds. Desireless worship without any expectations cannot happen without strong power.
20. With desire, one gains various fruits, however when one worships without any desire or expectation, the devotee is one with God. Gaining some fruit and being God are two very different things.
21. There are many fruits that God can give, but worship with the desire for some fruit distances one from God. Therefore, worship God without any expectation or desire.
22. The fruit of worship without expectation is beyond measure. With it, one's power increases beyond any limit. The ordinary fruits coming from the satisfaction of desires cannot compare.
23. With desireless devotion, whatever may be going on in the mind, God is doing as oneself. One does not need to ask God as a separate entity for anything at any time.
24. When the power of the devotee and God are one, even death is powerless. In that power, anything else is less significant than an insect.
25. Therefore, the "Knowledge of Brahman" combined with "Desireless Devotion" is supreme. Even all of the three worlds combined fall short in comparison.
26. Here the brilliance of the intellect is at its pinnacle, and one's glory, fame, and success are immeasurable.
27. Many people are attracted to where explanations and investigation into one's True Form, and the explanations about God are taking place.
28. Where there is one who is not corrupt, his Self-Realization cannot be concealed. The satisfaction of true conviction is never disrupted.
29. Inquire into what is Essence and what is non-essence, and always look to see what is justice, and what is injustice. The higher intellect is a great gift of God which can provide great understanding.
30. When the devotee remains singularly one with God, God gives that devotee his own intellect. Pay attention to this statement that has been made by God in the Bhagavad Gita. "I gave devotees intelligence of Oneness by which they may come to me."
31. The worship of God with attributes combined with the extraordinary "Knowledge of Brahman," gives the experience of contentment that is very rare in this world.

Thus in Shri Dasbodh, a dialogue between the Guru and disciple, Sub-Chapter 7 of Chapter 10, named "The Worship of God with Attributes" is concluded.

Chapter: 10, Sub-Chapter: 8

Explanation of Actual Experience

|| ShriRam ||

1. Listen to the description of experience. Those who see with actual experience are wise, while others, without any actual experience, are unfortunate and foolish.

2. There are many types of gems and coins. If one accepts them without first examining them properly, then there will be a loss. If one cannot get the experience of what is being taught, then he should not sit and listen to what is being explained.
3. Things such as horses and weapons must first be seen and used, and found to be good by properly examining them. Only then, after becoming knowledgeable should one accept them.
4. Test the seeds to make sure that they sprout, and then buy them. Similarly, one should listen to explanations only if actual experience can be gained from what is being said.
5. Only if it is first proven in the experience of other people that some medicine results in a healthy condition of the body, should one consume that medicine without hesitation.
6. If a medicine is taken without that is not a proven remedy, then one's health will become disturbed. Similarly, to do some action based solely upon guesswork and conjecture is foolish.
7. If one does not have any experience with gold asks to have some ornaments made without properly examining the quality, later on he will come to know that he was cheated very easily.
8. Without investigating and checking to see whether or not some work that is to be undertaken can be accomplished, the work may not get completed, and may even put one's life in danger.
9. Therefore a sensible person should not undertake any activity using only guesswork and imagination. This will surely only bring about negative, rather than positive results.
10. One would not purchase a buffalo seen sitting mostly submerged in water. This would not be a good use of one's intellect. Without conducting a thorough examination one will surely suffer a loss.
11. How many people have heard of buying a house based only on the assurance of another? One must investigate properly because cheaters will certainly take advantage of you if given the chance.
12. To buy food and clothing without proper examination can be life-threatening. To have trust in someone who is not trustworthy is foolish.
13. If you keep the company of thieves, you are sure to meet with disaster. Find out who is a thief or a double-crosser and avoid such people.
14. There are some people who are making brass look like gold, others who are making counterfeit money and fake coins, and many other types of deceivers. These people should be found out and avoided.
15. Some people who are bankrupt put on a big show to make themselves appear to be wealthy. If one puts their faith in such a false show, there is sure to be humiliation to follow.
16. In the same way, without the actual experience of Knowledge (Jnana) there is no contentment. Many have met with loss by going only on guesswork and conjecture.
17. By following advice to repeat certain mantras or concentrate on geometrical diagrams (yantras) many ignorant beings have become entangled in Illusion. This is similar to treating a sick person by covering him with cloth and killing him with it.
18. If a doctor who is lacking in knowledge treats a child and the child dies, what is there that anyone else can do?

19. If one who is suffering from pain feels too shy to say anything when the doctor asks him to tell what the problem is, then that person is effectively killing himself.
20. If one who is ignorant considers himself to be superior to one who has Self-Knowledge, he remains in ignorance because of pride. It can easily be seen who has suffered a loss in that case.
21. It is better when one experiences for oneself how accumulated sins get annihilated and how one escapes the sufferings of birth.
22. It is better when one recognizes one's own status as the one Supreme God and realizes one's own Self-identity.
23. It is better to recognize who has made the universe, how and what it is constructed of, and who is the main doer.
24. If one only goes on guesswork and imagination, then whatever spiritual practices have been done have only been done in vain, and the person gets drowned in doubt without gaining any actual experience.
25. This is the key to spiritual life. Understand that one who says that spiritual life is false, is considered the worst among men, and the one who considers spiritual life to be inferior to worldly life is even lower in human evolution.
26. Here the limit of what can be said with speech has been reached. The ignorant person cannot know Paramatman. Know that no false statement has been made here to you.
27. The greatness of my effort here is to impart only true Knowledge. If I say something that is not true, surely some blame will be attributed to God.
28. Therefore, I speak only the truth. Recognize the true doer, and find out the origin of Illusion at the root.
29. Some further explanation will be given again to validate what has already been said. The listeners are requested to keep their inner-mind alert while remaining attentive.
30. When subtle explanations are given, whatever has been said previously must be repeated so that the listeners will understand correctly.
31. When having gained understanding from direct experience, the traditional presentation of the teaching seems to have become meaningless. Therefore great care must be taken with regard to what is said.
32. If one's speech is only along the lines of traditional ideas of teaching, then the satisfaction of the experience is not gained, and if we protect only the satisfaction of actual experience, then the traditional ideas become meaningless.
33. In this way there is a dilemma on both sides. Therefore, I must say again what has been previously explained. Taking care to respect both opinions, I shall show how this riddle is resolved.
34. Keeping intact both the traditional teachings on one side, and the proof of actual experience on the other side, I shall give further explanation. The listeners who are wise should listen closely and reflect on the explanation that follows next.

Thus in Shri Dasbodh, a dialogue between the Guru and disciple, Sub-Chapter 8 of Chapter 10, named "Explanation of Actual Experience" is concluded.

Chapter: 10, Sub-Chapter: 9

Primordial Existence and Manifestation

|| ShriRam ||

1. Just like wind was created in space, in the same way, the Primal Illusion (Moolamaya) was created in Brahman. Being of the nature of wind, the Primal Illusion is made up of the three gunas and the five elements.
2. A mighty tree exists contained within the seed of the Banyan tree, but upon breaking open the seed, the tree cannot be seen there. From one seed a great many trees can come to be.
3. Similarly, the Primal Illusion is in the form of a seed, and the entire expanse of Illusion has come from there. Its true nature can be seen if one takes up proper investigation.
4. Two different things can be seen in one's actual experience if one looks using the power of discrimination. There is stillness, and there is a state of movement or restlessness, which is the wind itself.
5. Contained within that wind is Pure Consciousness, which is the source of the Life-Energy that is the "Light of the Universe." That Pure Consciousness in combination with the motion of wind is called the "Primal Illusion."
6. Sarita is the word for river, which is a feminine gender word that reminds us of a woman, but if we look at the river, all that is seen there is water. Oh thoughtful people, understand that the Primal Illusion is like that.
7. Wind, and Pure Consciousness, the "Light of the Universe," conjoined together are called the Primal Illusion. The words "Prakriti" (Primordial Female, the Energy of Manifestation) and "Purusha" (Primordial Male, Pure Consciousness) are names that are given to it.
8. The wind is called Prakriti or the "Energy of Manifestation," and Purusha is called the "Light of the Universe." Shiva and Shakti are other names given to this combination.
9. The special quality of Pure Consciousness in the wind is Purusha, which is conjoined with the Life-Energy of Manifestation, that is Prakriti. Some faith is required initially to understand the meaning of this statement.
10. People use the terms "Power" or Shakti, for wind, and "God" for Consciousness, and refer to this combination as half man and half woman.
11. The quality of Consciousness that is in the wind is what is described by the term God. It is from that Consciousness that the three gunas become manifest.
12. Foremost among those three gunas is the Sattva guna, which is the quality of "objectless Consciousness," or awareness in living beings. Lord Vishnu is the embodiment of this Sattva quality.
13. In the *Bhagavad Gita* it is told that the world is sustained by a fraction of His Consciousness. Those who look, and inquire into this, understand, even though they are engaged in the visible world.
14. It is this one Consciousness, or "knowingness," that is dispersed around in all living beings, and being of the nature of awareness, it protects all bodies everywhere.
15. The name of it is the "Light of the Universe" and all living beings are alive because of this Universal Light. The actual experience of it is evident and can be seen directly for oneself.

16. It is this Consciousness that animates the bodies of the birds, wild animals, insects, ants, and all other living beings in the world.
17. It is with this Consciousness that all creatures knowingly run away to save their lives, and that they knowingly hide and conceal themselves.
18. Because this Consciousness protects all life in the universe it is called the Universal Light. If this Consciousness leaves the body, the living being will die right then and there.
19. First there is the basic Consciousness, and then some changes occur in its form and like the spray of water with an endless number of droplets, it gets expanded spreading out the display of Consciousness everywhere.
20. Similarly, the various gods, goddesses, deities, and ghosts move about in nature with their respective strengths and power, and should not be considered to be non-existent.
21. They wander around in the form of wind. They change their forms with their own wish and affect the ignorant people who are under the delusion of imagination.
22. However, those who are knowledgeable are not under the sway of imagination and are not affected. Therefore, one should gain Self-Knowledge through study and spiritual practice.
23. By gaining Self-Knowledge through study and spiritual practice all of the bondage of the fruits of actions (karma) is broken. This is proven with actual experience. There is no doubt about this.
24. It has never happened that the bondage of karma has been released without Self-Knowledge. Likewise, it cannot happen that one can gain Self-Knowledge without the instruction of a Sadguru.
25. Therefore, one should seek out a Sadguru, as well as seek out and keep the company of virtuous and Self-realized people. One's mind and attention should be utilized to inquire within and reflect upon the explanations about Reality.
26. By analyzing the elements and dissolving one element into another, one remains singularly alone in oneself, and in this way, one's life is spontaneously fulfilled.
27. Whatever is done without giving proper thought to it, is useless, and only goes waste. Therefore one must first be thoughtful before acting.
28. One who investigates and sees clearly with thoughtfulness is a true human being, while one who does not investigate and see clearly is only an animal. Statements such as this are said by God in many various places.
29. In order to arrive at the proof of the Final Reality one must first analyze and reflect on the primary premise presented in the *Vedas*. However, for a sincere aspirant, Self-Realization can come by only listening to explanations.
30. By listening, reflecting, and verification in one's own experience (shravana, manana, and nididhyasana) one gains confidence and surety. This is the direct path to Self-Realization which does not require strenuous effort.

Thus in Shri Dasbodh, a dialogue between the Guru and disciple, Sub-Chapter 9 of Chapter 10, named "Primordial Existence (Purusha) and Manifestation (Prakriti)" is concluded.

Chapter: 10, Sub-Chapter: 10

The Moving and the Unmoving

|| ShriRam ||

1. Brahman is empty like the sky. It is limitless and expansive, attributeless, pure, and eternally still like space.
2. It is called Paramatman, the Supreme Self. It is not possible to know all of the names that it has been given. Understand that it is as it is, at the beginning and at the end of everything.
3. It is expansive and spread out everywhere like open space. It has no appearance and it is imperceptible. It is as it is.
4. It exists everywhere in all directions, as well as in the netherworld. It does not end at the limit of space, or even at the end of an era. It always continues to exist.
5. Like this, it is That which is unmoving. In that stillness there arises the appearance of movement. This movement has many names and is evident in three different ways.
6. Not being visible, different names are given to it. Because it is not seen, some descriptions of it must be given, and so it can be understood, it is called by many various names.
7. It is called the Primal Illusion (Moolamaya), Original Creation (Moola Prakriti), and Original Being (Moola Purusha). It is also called Shiva-Shakti as well as many other names.
8. However, whatever the names are that are given to it, primarily it must be recognized first. Without actual experience how can one say anything about it?
9. Without having ascertained its form, nature, and relative associations properly, one should not get carried away with its names. Without actual experience there is only confusion and imagined knowledge about it.
10. In the unmoving sky there is a restless wind that makes various sounds with its motion, but there is a difference between the sky and the wind.
11. In the same way, the Absolute Reality is still, and in it the restless Illusion (Maya), which is delusion itself, appears, whirling around. Now the confusion and bewilderment of this whirling Illusion will be shown.
12. Just as the wind moves in the sky, in the same way there is movement in the unmoving. The indication of this stirring of movement is the arising of desire in the form of an inspiration or subtle assertion.
13. The sense of "I Am" is itself Knowledge or Consciousness, and is what is called the Primal Illusion. This is also called the Great Causal Body of the universe.
14. This "Great Illusion" (Mahamaya) is called the Original Creation (Moola Prakriti), the Primal Illusion. It is unaffected by the Casual Body that is ignorance, the Subtle Body that is the intelligence in the universe, or the Gross Body that is the manifest gross form of the universe.
15. This is the classical presentation of the five parts of the whole according to the scriptures. These are known as the four bodies of God that are the coverings on the Absolute Reality. Therefore, it is said that Consciousness is the Primal Illusion.
16. Masculine names that are given to this one principle are Supreme Self (Paramatman), Supreme Lord (Parameshwar), Lord above All (Paresh), Dense

Knowledge (Jnanaghana), Lord of the World (Jagadisha), and Self of the World (Jagadatma).

17. It is the Form of Power (Sattarupa), the Form of Knowledge (Jnanarupa), The Form of Illumination (Prakasharupa), the Form of Light (Jyotirupa), the Form of the Cause (Karanarupa), and the Form of Consciousness (Chidrupa) that is pure, subtle and unattached.

18. It is called the Self (Atma), the Inner-Self (Antaratma), the Universal Self (Vishvatma), the Seer (Drashta), the Witness (Sakshi), the Self of All (Sarvatama), the Knower of the Field (Kshetrajnana), the Self as Shiva (Shivatma), the Self as the individual (Jivatma), the One in the body (Dehi), and the One who is perpetually the same (Kutashta).

19. It is called the Self that is the Lord of the Gods (Indratma), the Self that is Brahman (Brahmatma), The Self that is Shiva and Vishnu (Hariharaatma), the Self that is the God of Death (Yamatama), the Self that is Religion (Dharmatma), the Self that withdraws into peace (Nairutyatma), the Self that is the deities of water, wind, and wealth (Varuna-Vayu-Kuberatma), and the One who is the support of the sages, gods and ascetics (Rishi-Deva-Muni-Dharta).

20. It is the one Self that is within the various groups of celestial singers, scholars, and musicians. It is the Self that is the inner-mind of all.

21. It is the Inner-Self that governs the moon, the sun, the constellations, the various lands, the clouds, the twenty-one heavens, and the seven hells.

22. The hidden vine of the Primal Illusion has spread itself out everywhere. Many examples of its masculine names have been given, and now the listeners are asked to listen to some of its feminine names.

23. The Primal Illusion (Moolamaya), the Goddess of the World (Jagadishwari), Supreme Knowledge (Paramavidya), the Supreme Goddess (Parameshwari), the Goddess that pervades the world (Vishvavanda), the Goddess of the Universe (Vishveshvari), the Mother of the Three Worlds (Trailokyajanani).

24. The Hidden Cause (Antarhetu), the Hidden Aspect (Antarkala), the Womb of Silence (Maunyagarbha), the Lustre of Intelligence (Janivakala), the Most Active (Chapala), the Universal Light (Jagajyoti), the Blooming of Life (Jivanakala), the most subtle sound within (the first stage of speech, or Para Speech), the sound at the heart (the second stage of speech, or Pashyanti Speech), and the soft whisper of recognizable sound (the third stage of speech, or Madhyama Speech).

25. It is also called ingenuity, intellect, remembrance, awareness, various inspirations, and that which reveals and displays the past, present, and future to the intellect.

26. It is the knower of the waking, dream, and deep sleep states, and it is the ever constant knowingness of the fourth state (Turya). It is the knower of pleasure and sorrow, respect and insult. It is the knower of everything.

27. It is extremely cruel yet benevolent. It is extremely tender and affectionate, as well as extremely passionate and greedy beyond limits.

28. It is the bestower of peace, forgiveness, detachment, devotion, Self-Knowledge, the final liberation of complete union with the Self, the power of inquiry, and the effortless "natural state."

29. Previously the masculine names were given, and then the feminine names were stated. Now, the listeners are asked to listen to the names of the neuter gender of the ever-changing Illusion.

30. It is called knowing, the inner-mind, listening, reflecting, Life-Energy, and the Life that comes and goes. See this while remaining alert and composed.

31. It is the knower of both the sense of "me" and of "you." It is the Knowledge that is the knower of all. It is the knower of the state of the individual, the state of Shiva, the state of God, and the state of desirelessness.
32. There many names such as these, but it is all only one Universal Light. Those who inquire deeply know that it is the one Self that is the knower of everything.
33. Whether it is called the Self, the Universal Light, or the "knower of all," know that all three of these names indicate only One, alone. Understand that it is the inner-mind that is itself the living proof of existence.
34. There are innumerable names of masculine, feminine, and neutral gender that are used, but how can the vast structure of creation be described?
35. The Inner-Self is One and it moves the many, from ants right up through Brahma and the other gods.
36. Understand now to some extent how the Inner-Self is present and how it reveals many kinds of diverse activities.
37. It can be understood but cannot be seen. It comes to be experienced but it does not have an appearance. It is in the body but it does not reside in one place.
38. It fills the sky intensively. When seeing a lake, it is seen spread out all over its surface. It becomes an object yet it remains spread out in all directions.
39. Seeing an object it becomes like that object, and it changes faster than the wind.
40. It sees through many eyes, it tastes through many tongues, and it identifies many things with the mind.
41. It occupies the ears and is the hearer of sounds, it smells scents with the nose, and it knows the sensations of hot and cold as well as other sensations with the skin.
42. Like this, it knows the inner play of all the activities of Consciousness. It dwells within all things, but remains different from them. He alone knows and sees his own wonderful play.
43. It is not male or female, nor a young boy, nor a young girl. It holds the body that is without gender, yet it is not impotent.
44. It is the mover of all bodies. It does everything but is a non-doer. It is the knower of the field, it is resident in the body, and is the holder of the body, all the while uniformly permeating everywhere.
45. In this world there are two types of "being." One is called destructible and one is indestructible. All living creatures are destructible, and That which permeates everything is indestructible.
46. That primary Being is quite different, as it is without the motion of the five elements, untainted, and unseen. That Supreme Self, Paramatman, is alone and without any modification.
47. Having thrown off all four bodies the aspirant resides beyond any body. Understand that the devotee that is bodiless is the true devotee.
48. Here the question arises, that when all of the bodies have been given up, where can the Inner-Self remain when the changing forms no longer have any place in the unchanging Self.
49. The unmoving Absolute Reality, Parabrahman, is One. Understand that the restless movement is illusory. This actual experience and conviction of this can be gained using the power of discrimination.
50. Here, a great amount of discussion is not required. One is moving and one is unmoving. The Knowledgeable (Jnanis) easily recognize what is Eternal.

51. Give up what is insubstantial and accept and embrace the true substance. Through inquiry into what is Essence and what is non-essence the Jnani always sees what is ephemeral and what is Eternal.
52. Where Knowledge (Jnana) becomes the Supreme Knowledge (Vijnana) of the Self, and where the mind becomes no-mind, how can there be any unsteadiness in the Self?
53. All of this is not something that can be understood with secondhand knowledge. This must be known in one's own experience. To make many efforts without gaining any actual experience is to make a mistake.
54. There is no virtue greater than Truth, and no mistake greater than untruth. Without actual experience there is no contentment.
55. Truth means one's True Form (Swaroopa), and what is untrue is Illusion, this is a proven fact. Here the true nature of virtue and error which are often called merit and sin have been described.
56. When the mistaken visible disappears, the virtue that is the Absolute Reality remains. Being one's Self alone, one is beyond all names.
57. One is the self-evident Reality oneself. The body has no significance here, and the mountain of error is automatically burned up.
58. Otherwise, without the Knowledge of Brahman, all spiritual practices are useless and tiresome, and the mountain of error does not get washed away.
59. The body is made from error and mistaken concepts, and from there much more error is generated. What can any superficial treatment such as many various spiritual practices do when the disease is in the mind?
60. One can shave off all of the hair on the head, go to many pilgrimage places, do many types of strict penance and torture the body with strict discipline in many places.
61. One can anoint the body with many different kinds of soil, or burn it with hot coins, or even peel off the skin, but it still does not get purified.
62. One can eat cakes of cowdung, or drinks jars of cow urine, or wear different rosaries made from rudraksha seeds or wooden beads.
63. One can even wear religious garments, yet still the error is present in the mind. For the burning up of all this error, Self-Knowledge is required.
64. The greatness of Self-Knowledge is millions of times more important than any spiritual vows, charities, yogic practices, or visiting places of pilgrimage.
65. There is no limit to the virtue of one who always sees with Self-Knowledge, because the affliction of error has vanished.
66. The *Vedas* and other scriptures have described the true nature of the Truth, and that itself is the form of the Jnani whose virtue is immeasurable, and whose good deeds are without limit.
67. This a matter of actual experience. Experience should be gained with Self-vision. One should not remain sorrowful because of a lack of actual experience.
68. Oh, you people who want actual experience, know that without gaining actual experience, life is full of sorrow. Remain determined to gain experience with the blessing of Lord Rama.

Thus in Shri Dasbodh, a dialogue between the Guru and disciple, Sub-Chapter 10 of Chapter 10, named "The Moving and the Unmoving" is concluded.

Chapter 11. Bhima Dashaka

Chapter: 11, Sub-Chapter: 1

Explanation of the Final Conclusion

|| ShriRam ||

1. Wind arises in space. This can be experienced. Now, listen with alertness to how fire is formed from the wind.
2. The friction of the wind moving quickly has a quality of hardness. From that friction, fire (light) gets created. And, it is from the quality of softness in the wind that is moving slowly that cool water is created.
3. Earth is formed from water. Know that the earth is in the form of many seeds, and that many things are naturally created from seeds.
4. The visible world originates from a concept, which is imagination. This imagination is the Primal Illusion from where the bodies of the three gods have been formed.
5. The moving, which is mere imagination, appears in That which is unmoving. The root of the eightfold manifestation (Prakriti) is in the form of imagination, a concept.
6. The eightfold manifestation is conceptual. It is all the form of imagination. Understand that the origin of the eightfold manifestation is like this from the beginning.
7. Understand that the five elements and three gunas together make eight, therefore it is called the "eight-fold" manifestation.
8. Originally it existed only in the form of imagination, and then later on it proliferated as gross manifest creation in the form of the universe.
9. Originally, the Primal Illusion appeared first, and then the formation of the three gunas appeared as Illusion with attributes. Afterwards, when Illusion became manifest in its gross inert form due to ignorance, it appeared as the form of the visible universe.
10. Later on, the four types of created beings came into existence proliferating with the four types of speech. Many varieties of species have come into being with many different forms.
11. Creation came to be like this. Now, listen to the explanation of the destruction, which was described in detail in the previous chapter.
12. However, now I will describe the destruction in a condensed form. The listeners are asked to focus their thinking and listen to what is being said here.
13. After a hundred years of drought, the world with all of its living beings will dry up. This is the description of the final destruction that is given in the scriptures.[51]
14. The heat of the sun will be twelve times hotter and the earth will turn into ashes. Afterwards, the ash will be dissolved into water.
15. Fire will dry up all of the water, and then the fire will be extinguished by the wind. The wind will then dissipate into the formlessness that is as it is.

---

[51] Shri Siddharameshwar Maharaj has given a very nice commentary on symbolic meaning of this in the book "Master of Self-Realization."

16. Like this, the destruction of the visible world will take place as has been described previously in detail. With the passing away of Illusion only the True Form of Reality remains.
17. There, the fiction of the individual (Jiva) and God (Shiva), and the physical body and the universal body disappear entirely, and the commotion of ignorance that is Illusion gets dissolved.
18. This is the destruction of the universe through discrimination that has been told to you. Therefore it is called the dissolution by discrimination. Only the one who uses the power of discrimination can understand. The foolish person will not understand what has been said.
19. When examining the entirety of creation, two things are found. One is moving, and one is unmoving. The doer or the cause of the moving is the movement itself in the form of motion.
20. That doer who exists in all bodies, and who is the initiator of all activity, is called the non-doer even though doing everything.
21. Regardless of whether one is rich or poor, or one is Lord Brahma or one of the other gods, it is the Self alone that is the One which moves all bodies and functions through the organs of action.
22. It is called the Supreme Self, Paramatman. Know that it is the doer of all but that it will also perish. This must be seen in one's own actual experience by using the power of discrimination.
23. It is the one that barks in the dog, that squeals in the pigs, and that brays obstinately in the body of the donkey.
24. Many bodies are seen by people, but the one who utilizes the power of discrimination sees the Inner-Self of all bodies. Thus, the knowledgeable see all things with the vision of equality.
25. While seeing the many various bodies, their appearance is different, but the inner oneness of all living beings is the same, and all see with the one inner-mind.
26. Many living beings have been created, but it is one light that is the Life in all. That is the "Light of Knowledge." It is the "Light of Consciousness" that is called the "Universal Light."
27. With ears it knows many words, with the skin it knows cold and hot, and with the eyes it sees and knows many objects.
28. It knows taste through all tongues, knows various smells through all noses, and through the organs of action it knows all actions.
29. Its form being subtle, it protects the gross. It is the perceiver of many pleasures and sorrows so it is called the "inner-witness," and the Inner-Self.
30. It is called by many names such as the Self, the Inner-Self, the Universal Self, Life-Energy, the Self in All, the Subtle Self, the Individual Self, the Self as God, the Supreme Self, the Seer, the Witness, and the Form of Complete Power
31. Only those with inferior intellect call that which is prone to change, which is constantly changing, and which is the cause of many changes, as the Reality.
32. Everything looks similar to them so they put everything into one category. This is due to the illusory nature of the moving.
33. The ever-changing Illusion is illusory and restless. The unmoving Absolute Reality, Parabrahman, is different from this and is the one true thing. For this reason one must use the power of discrimination to know the difference between the Eternal and the ephemeral.

34. The property of Life that leaves the body is the vital energy (prana). The property of Life that does not know is ignorance. The property of Life that is born takes birth because of desires.
35. That property of Life which is the part of Brahman that is present in the living being and is united with the totality of Brahman, is where the concepts of bodies and the universe dissolves. Here, the distinguishing attributes of the four properties of Life have been described.
36. Let all of this be as it is. Know that all that is moving will vanish, and That which is unmoving will remain still and unchanging from the beginning through the end.
37. Reality is always the same at the beginning, in the middle, and at the end. It is without modification, attributeless, untainted by anything, unattached to anything, and uninvolved in worldly affairs.
38. With the throwing off of all coverings, the individual self (Jiva) and God (Shiva) become one. When observing minutely it is seen that these coverings are not really there.
39. Whatever is known is Knowledge (Jnana), but that Knowledge gets transformed into Supreme Knowledge (Vijnana) with experience. How can that which is "no-mind" be recognized by the mind?
40. The attitudes or states of mind cannot understand that which is not a state of mind, and that which has attributes cannot become attributeless. The saints help aspirants go beyond attributes with the power of discrimination.
41. First, listen to explanations (shravana), and then reflect upon the Essence (manana). With reflection one can understand what is Essence and what is non-essence. Then, with verification in your own experience (nididhyasana) comes the realization (sakshatkara) of the unattached aloneness of the Reality.
42. Attributeless Oneness is itself the final liberation of complete union. Now, enough of this talk about that which is to be understood through the use of words.
43. Keep your attention on "That" which cannot be described. In the Final Conclusion (Siddhanta), where is there any place for the primary premise set forth in the *Vedas*? How can That which is beyond the senses become evident? It exists, but it is not visible.
44. Even though the coverings of Maya may be present, one can still remain in the effortless natural transcendence of Sahaja Samadhi. By listening, the intellect can be transformed so that it becomes doubtless.

Thus in Shri Dasbodh, a dialogue between the Guru and disciple, Sub-Chapter 1 of Chapter 11, named "Explanation of the Final Conclusion" is concluded.

Chapter: 11, Sub-Chapter: 2

The Four Types of Gods

|| ShriRam ||
1. There is one thing that is unmoving and one that moving. Everything that has an appearance is entangled in the moving while That which is unmoving is still, remaining always just as it is.

2. The one who sees the unmoving using the power of discrimination is one among hundreds of thousands. Becoming fixed in the stillness of the unmoving, such a one is the unmoving itself.
3. Many people speak about That which is eternally unmoving, yet still run after the movement of Illusion. There are very few who escape from the wheel of the moving Illusion.
4. Movement is born in the movement of Illusion, and the movement grows only there in that movement. The entirety of life occurs within this movement.
5. The universe is entirely contained within this movement. Whatever happens takes place in movement. Who is there who gives up the moving and resides in the unmoving?
6. That which is moving never becomes still, and the unmoving never moves. People can understand this by using discrimination with regard to what is Eternal and what is ephemeral.
7. Because of some small doubts, something may be known, while some things are not fully known, something may be understood, while some things are not fully understood, and something may be realized, yet one's realization is not complete.
8. Doubt, guesswork, delusion and all efforts occur in the moving. There is no place for any of these in the unmoving. This secret must be understood.
9. All that is moving is Illusion, and whatever is illusory gets destroyed regardless of whether it is said to be small or very large.
10. The Illusion is spread out everywhere in the eightfold manifestation as many strange modifications and countless forms.
11. There are many things that have been created that undergo modifications, there are many beings, both small and large, and there are a great many objects and many different forms.
12. Whatever is prone to modification has been modified. The subtle has assumed material form, and that gross form has spread out and seems to be limitless.
13. Afterwards, many bodies were created and many names and titles were given to them through the use of language, and through words objects became recognizable.
14. Afterwards, many customs, traditions and practices were initiated, each one being different from the other. Then, all of the people started behaving according to their various common traditions and customs.
15. All bodies, small and large, were created out of the eightfold creation, and then they began behaving in their own ways.
16. Many opinions and sects were created, many false doctrines proliferated, and many types of rebellions and diversifications of opinion occurred.
17. People continued living according to the traditions to which they were accustomed as there was no one who could uplift them.
18. The whole Earth became chaotic with one person claiming to be more superior than the other. Nobody knew who was true and who was false.
19. The conduct of the people became varied and confused. People were abandoning their moral values for the sake of making a living, and everyone was putting on an outward show, puffed up with pride.
20. Gods became innumerable, and people professed the importance of their particular god. People made up fictitious stories about their gods and even the worship of spirits and ghosts became popular.

21. No one was able to identify or understand the true nature of God. There was no agreement among anybody, and no one listened to anyone else. Everywhere there was uncontrollable disagreement.
22. In this way, the capacity for people to think clearly became corrupted, and nobody was able to distinguish the Essence from non-essence, and no one was able to discern what was superior and what was inferior.
23. The sacred scriptures were put up for sale in the marketplace and there was confusion about the existence of many gods. People were making vows and worshipping for the gratification of desires.
24. Like this, everything became spoiled. The people were deprived of the knowledge of what is true and what is untrue, there was anarchy due to a lack of leadership.
25. Due to the confusion of so many various opinions, nobody respected anyone else. Everyone was caught up in their own opinion, thinking it to be superior.
26. When one takes pride in that which is not true, there is a downfall. Therefore, knowledgeable people search in earnest for the truth.
27. People say all kinds of things about God, but for a knowledgeable person the truth is as easy to recognize as one's own palm. Listen alertly now with discrimination.
28. Listen alertly to the description of the paths that people follow, and gods that people worship, in order to gain actual experience.
29. There are many idols made out of earth, metal, stones and other things. It is common that most people worship an idol as God.
30. Some people listen to the stories and biographies about incarnations of gods, while some continuously do chanting and meditation as a form of worship.
31. Some consider the Inner-Self which functions as the Self in the universe to be God. This Self that is the all-knowing seer, or witness, is considered to be God.
32. And some worship That which is stainless and still. Never moving, and being one with That, they are Reality itself.
33. One type of God is seen in many idols. The second is the greatness of many incarnations. The third is the Inner-Self, and the fourth is changeless Brahman.
34. Like this, are the four types of gods in the universe which exist naturally. There is none other than these anywhere.
35. All consider God to be only One, and the witness of everything. However, one must understand the nature of the eightfold manifestation that is being witnessed.
36. Any god in creation is of the nature of creation and is illusory. Those with the greatest experience understand what is beyond the world by utilizing the power of discrimination.
37. One who meditates on That which is alone pure, becomes purity itself. Understand that one becomes what one worships.
38. Just as the Royal Swan can separate milk from water, those with the greatest experience are able to separate Essence from non-essence.
39. Oh dear one, please understand that the one who meditates on the moving will be of the nature of movement, and the one who worships the unmoving will become the unmoving itself.
40. Move along with the creation, but inwardly be identified with That which is eternally unmoving. Abide as the truth of your True Form inwardly, but outwardly behave like other people according to social norms.

Thus in Shri Dasbodh, a dialogue between the Guru and disciple, Sub-Chapter 2 of Chapter 11, named "The Four Types of Gods" is concluded.

Chapter: 11, Sub-Chapter: 3

The Teaching

|| ShriRam ||

1. At the end of many births, one suddenly gets a human body. Here one should live a good life with a sense of morality and justice.
2. One should carry out the duties of family life properly, as well as take care in using discrimination in spiritual life, so there is satisfaction in both worlds.
3. In a hundred years of desired life, the childhood is spent without knowing anything, and the youth is spent pursuing sensual pleasures.
4. In old age one must suffer many diseases that are the fruits of a lifetime of actions, so where is there any time left for communion with God?
5. There are many troubles in life that come from various authorities and destiny. One has many worries about food, clothing and affection for the body, and then all of a sudden the life is over.
6. People die and disappear all of the time. This is commonly experienced with the passing away of the elderly. Knowing that death is certain, why does one feel secure about oneself?
7. The house is on fire, yet one sleeps comfortably inside. How can such a person be called wise when he is basically committing suicide?
8. When the path of virtue is totally lost and there is an abundant accumulation of wrongful deeds, the suffering in death will be very harsh.
9. Do not be like this. Behave thoughtfully with proper discrimination and be successful in both worldly life and in the spiritual life.
10. The fruits of laziness are evident. One yawns and falls asleep. This gives some pleasure to lazy people, and they enjoy this type of happiness.
11. However, if one does some hard work in the beginning, afterwards they become comfortable and enjoy good meals because of their efforts.
12. Laziness causes depression and brings about loss. It hampers one's efforts, brings bad luck, and makes one show one's negative qualities.
13. Therefore, do not be lazy, and only then will you be prosperous, gaining satisfaction in worldly life and in spiritual life.
14. Keeping your awareness alert for a moment, listen to the explanation about what efforts one should make.
15. Wake up early in the morning and do some reading or reflecting on what has been learned by heart, and remember God according to your capacity.
16. Then, appropriately keeping to yourself, proceed with your morning routine of going to the toilet, cleansing the body and mouth, and drinking some clean water.
17. After washing the body and cleaning the mouth, proceed with a daily routine of worshipping God in some way that suits you, and offer some food to God.
18. Eat some food or fruit and then attend to the duties of your family life. Speak with kind words, keeping all of the people around you happy.
19. Be alert and attentive in whatever occupation you are engaged in doing. With carelessness, even a small child can make a fool of you.
20. You can experience for yourself how one suffers when one gets deceived, or forgets or loses things, and how one feels upset when recognizing one's mistakes.

21. Therefore, be alert and have your mind focused on your work. Then, afterwards when dining, you will feel relaxed and will be able to enjoy your meal.
22. After dinner, read something, or reflect on something learned by heart, or have some nice conversation with others. Then, take some time alone to read from some good books.
23. In this way, a person becomes wise. Otherwise he remains foolish, and merely looks on as others are enjoying nice meals.
24. Listen to the description of a fortunate person. He is one who does not allow even a moment to go waste, and who gains appropriate knowledge of worldly matters.
25. He earns something first, and then he has his meals. He puts the body to good use in various ways by helping other people with their difficulties, and in solving their problems.
26. He spends time engaged in spiritual discourses talking about God, and giving explanations. He does not waste even a moment in either worldly life or spiritual life.
27. One who is alert like this on both sides does not experience grief. With discrimination he breaks the connection of bodily misidentification.
28. His conduct and conviction is, "Whatever exists belongs to God." It is in this way that the root of misery is broken.
29. For success in leading the family life one needs wealth, and for success in the spiritual life one must have the knowledge of the five elements and understanding of the meaning of the "great statements" (Mahavakyas) contained in the *Vedas*.
30. Through proper action, worship, and knowledge one remains content in life. Please listen further to the means for leading a spiritual life.

Thus in Shri Dasbodh, a dialogue between the Guru and disciple, Sub-Chapter 3 of Chapter 11, named "The Teaching" is concluded.

Chapter: 11, Sub-Chapter: 4

Discrimination of Essence

|| ShriRam ||

1. Brahman means That which is formless. It can be thought of as being similar to the sky, as there is no modification or change in it. That which is changeless is Brahman.
2. Brahman means unmoving, or still. The Inner-Self is moving and it is called the seer or the witness.
3. That Inner-Self means God, and his nature is movement. He sustains all living beings and resides within them.
4. Aside from living things, all other objects are inanimate. Without the Self, the body is useless, while with it, the pinnacle of spiritual life can be attained.
5. All of the different paths such as the path of actions, the path of worship, the path of knowledge, the path of the final conclusion, the path of engagement, and the path of withdrawal are all the work of God.

6. Without the moving, the unmoving cannot be understood. The moving never becomes the unmoving. This can be seen by inquiry and thoughtful consideration.
7. The intellect gets left behind at the borderline of the moving and the unmoving. Therefore, the path of rituals and action is of a much lower order than that discrimination.
8. God is the root of all, but for God there is neither a root nor a tip. The Absolute Reality, Parabrahman is unmoving and changeless.
9. One who says that the ever-changing and the changeless are the same is lacks discernment. With thoughtful inquiry, this notion becomes dispelled in no time.
10. The basis for spiritual life lies in the proper analysis of the five elements and understanding the meaning of the four Mahavakyas ("Only Brahman Exists"). This should be deeply considered again and again.
11. The first body is the gross body, and the eighth body is the Primal Illusion. With the dissolution of all eight bodies, how can there be any change or modification?
12. That which is ever-changing appears to be real, like some sort of magic trick. Some understand it like this, and some think it to be real.
13. That which is changeless is different from the processes of creation, sustaining, and destruction. To understand this, one must inquire into what is Essence and what is non-essence.
14. When Essence and non-essence are considered to be one, it only shows a lack of utilization of the power of discrimination. Those who do not know to differentiate the two are mistaken and unfortunate.
15. The one who has spread itself out everywhere is called the Inner-Self. It has many modifications and is ever-changing. It is not the changeless.
16. This is evident and can be seen in one's own experience, but that which gets destroyed and That which remains is still not understood.
17. That which is incessantly appearing, disappears. That which is constantly being destroyed is being experienced directly by all people.
18. Some cry about it, some get annoyed, and some go wild grabbing at the neck of another person. They fight with each other like people who are starving from famine.
19. People behave without any sense of justice or morality saying that everything is real, because they lack discrimination.
20. In life they know to leave the stones and take the gold, and to eat the food and leave the soil, yet they foolishly say that everything is Essence.
21. Therefore, give some thought to this, and stay on the path of Truth. Gain the benefit of understanding by using discrimination.
22. If one says that a pebble and a precious stone are of the same value, where is there any place for examination? Therefore, wisely examine everything.
23. Where there is a lack of examination, it is like giving and receiving blows. Acting as if all things are the same is foolishness.
24. Whatever is worth accepting should be accepted, and whatever is not acceptable should be given up. Recognition of what is of a higher or lower caliber is what is called Knowledge.
25. Of all those who come to have a life, some gain the benefit of becoming immortal, while others are unfortunate and get deceived. They lose the very wealth of human life.

26. The knowledgeable do not do this. After examination, the Essence is kept and non-essence is abandoned like vomit.
27. Consuming that which is vomited is the description of what a dog does. What would a true Knower of Brahman be doing acting like that?
28. Whatever deeds have been done in the past, one experiences the fruits accordingly. The repetition of activities creates habits that are not abandoned easily.
29. Some eat good quality food while others eat any kind of dirty food as they pridefully talk about the greatness of their ancestors.
30. Let this be as it is. Without utilizing the power of discrimination such speech is merely tiring. Therefore, some of you must continue to listen and reflect upon the explanations that have been given.

Thus in Shri Dasbodh, a dialogue between the Guru and disciple, Sub-Chapter 4 of Chapter 11, named "Discrimination of Essence" is concluded.

Chapter: 11, Sub-Chapter: 5

Discourse on Politics

|| ShriRam ||

1. Actions must be done, meditation must be undertaken, and what has already been explained must be explained again and again.
2. That is what is happening here. Whatever has been said previously must be repeated. If one becomes disturbed, it must be remedied so there is contentment again.
3. The purpose of these discourses is to unify the followers of this path, and so that devotional feelings might arise in other people.
4. Most important are the explanations and narrations about God. After that, importance should be given to politics. Thirdly, one should be attentive in all matters.
5. Fourth, there should be the utmost perseverance in clearing away all arguments and misconceptions that others may have, and the injustices or offenses that have been committed by someone, whether small or large, should be forgiven.
6. Understand the minds of others while remaining disinterested, but don't distance yourself from morality and justice.
7. With indirect signs and indications one should be able to attract the attention of the people in order to instruct and give knowledge tactfully. At the same time one should look after one's family life to the best of one's ability.
8. The situations in one's worldly affairs should be recognized and handled calmly and courageously without allowing oneself to become entangled in them too much.
9. The work activities should progress, but one should not get too caught up in them. In the beginning, one must accept low positions and recognize the limits of one's own knowledge.
10. When seeing the faults of others, they should not be openly revealed. Do not continuously speak about the bad qualities of others. If an evil-minded person is found, act with kindness towards them, and then leave their company.

11. One should not be eccentric in one's behavior. Try to suggest many solutions to difficult problems, and put forth great efforts to do the work that needs to be done in order to solve them.
12. Special gatherings should be supported and maintained, and one should not allow the public gathering to be disrupted. No one should be allowed to enter into excessive arguments.
13. One should understand the wellbeing and interests of others, and bear a lot of suffering imposed by others. If you are unable to bear it, then go away from there to some other place instead.
14. Understand the sorrow of others, and after listening, be supportive and share their sorrow with them. Bear both the good and the bad with the members of the gathering.
15. A great many things should be learned by heart. Try to always be close to others with thoughtfulness, benevolence and kindness.
16. Being peaceful, help others to be peaceful, giving up eccentricity, help others to give it up, and by doing many activities yourself, inspire others to action as well.
17. If some punishment needs to be done to someone, it should not be shown publicly by speaking about it openly. If someone needs to be taught a lesson, it should be made to happen indirectly through others.
18. One who does not bear the sorrow of many others will not attract many people to gather together with him. However, one should not bear the sorrow of others out of proportion because one will lose one's own importance.
19. One should undertake many political activities without allowing them to be known. However, one should not have their mind set on creating trouble for others.
20. Examine people well and know whom to keep away from. Cleverly remove the pride from others with diplomacy, and work to bring people together who have become distant from each other.
21. Keep away from quarrelsome people. Don't speak your mind to someone who is fearful or timid. If you are required to meet with them, go away from them as soon as you can.
22. Let the politics be played like this. It is not possible to tell you how to act in all situations. If the mind is alert and clear, you will know the correct political actions.
23. When someone who is unworthy sits in a high position he should be removed from there. People who are of a battling nature should be left aside. How can all of the various strategies of administration be described?
24. It is difficult to find such a genuine person in politics even after searching high and low. When people want to praise him, he avoids the situation. Even if prosperity comes to him, he does not have any desire for it.
25. Giving support and protection to one person and not doing anything for another is not a sign of wisdom.
26. If someone does not agree with justice, and does not want to accept what is beneficial, there is no working with such a person and they should be avoided.
27. The listeners have raised some doubts even after knowing, therefore what was said previously has been repeated again. The listeners are asked to please forgive any shortcomings in the explanation.

Thus in Shri Dasbodh, a dialogue between the Guru and disciple, Sub-Chapter 5 of Chapter 11, named "Discourse on Politics" is concluded.

Chapter: 11, Sub-Chapter: 6

Signs of a Spiritual Leader

|| ShriRam ||

1. Write cleanly and legibly. After writing, find and correct any grammatical mistakes. After correcting, re-read again making sure that there are no mistakes.
2. The characters should be written properly and the style of handwriting should be consistent. Stories being told should be made interesting by using colorful imagery.
3. The difficulty lies in the fact that what is known cannot be expressed in words, yet without proper expression nothing can be understood.
4. One should be able to narrate stories about God and give correct explanations. One should be able to know how to act appropriately with regard to politics and in everyday life.
5. One should know how to ask the right questions, and how to give explanations of meanings that please and satisfy everyone.
6. Such a man understands indications and has foresight of things to come. With alertness, the power of reasoning becomes strengthened, and many things are understood properly by persistently thinking them over.
7. One who understands like this is a "great spiritual leader" (Mahanta) who is intelligent. Apart from one such as this, all others will perish.
8. He understands the importance of timing, knows how to compose essays and poetry, and when to use important statements from various texts in the appropriate situations. He knows how to use tactful words in meetings.
9. He is eager to be in solitude, he learns the important things by heart, and he goes into the deeper hidden meanings of texts.
10. One who learns first and then teaches attains a high position and is able to free people from their difficulties with the power of discrimination.
11. His writing, reading, and speech is beautiful, and he walks gracefully. He shows Devotion, Knowledge, and Desirelessness by his example.
12. He likes to make efforts, and boldly handles situations successfully. He faces situations courageously and does not hide himself.
13. He knows how to behave in difficult situations. He knows to adapt to complex circumstances while keeping aloof and not becoming entangled by them.
14. Just as the Inner-Self is in all places but is invisible, his presence is felt in all places even though he is not anywhere to be seen.
15. There is nothing other than his existence, but if we go look for him, he cannot be seen. Without being seen, he directs the activities of all living beings.
16. He makes many people wise in various ways, and he explains many streams of subtle and gross knowledge.
17. Those who become wise because of him naturally become supportive and loyal to him. Such is the greatness of his wisdom.
18. He knows how to maintain justice and morality, and he does not let any injustice be done by himself or by others. He knows how to remedy difficult situations.
19. Such a person is worthy of being supported, and is himself the support of many people. Ramdas says that you should take up these good qualities of Lord Rama.

Thus in Shri Dasbodh, a dialogue between the Guru and disciple, Sub-Chapter 6 of Chapter 11, named "Signs of a Spiritual Leader" is concluded.

Chapter: 11, Sub-Chapter: 7

The Ever-Changing River

|| ShriRam ||

1. There is an ever-changing river, the hidden Ganga (the Primal Illusion). Simply by remembering it, the world becomes purified. This can be seen in one's actual experience, as it is not false.
2. It began moving in the unmoving stillness (Parabrahman). It moves downward with force, flowing continuously, yet it is not seen by anyone.
3. It has many bends, turns, whirlpools, bubbles, ripples, springs, and waves, and its flow gets split off in many directions.
4. There are places where it begins to dry out, and places where it flows intensively, and it has many streams, waterfalls and crosscurrents. In some places this restless water is narrow, some places shallow, and some places it is broad.
5. It has foam, it ebbs and swells, and in some places it runs uncontrolled. This water sprinkles around countless drops and small particles beyond measure.
6. There many things that get carried away in its torrents and cascades. There are many pebbles, stones, boulders and islands in its path, but the water flows around them.
7. The softest soil breaks apart and gets carried away. The hard parts remain where they are. Many such things like this can be seen in the world.
8. Some get carried away by the water, some are engulfed by whirlpools, and some become entangled in narrow bends getting dragged downwards.
9. Some are beaten down when hitting on the rocks, some get crushed, and many become swollen and filled with water. (The various states of beings in Illusion.)
10. Some select few are strong and swim to the origin of the river. With the glimpse of the river's origin, they became purified and obtained the greatness of that sacred form.
11. The abodes of Brahma, Vishnu, and Shiva, and the abodes of all the other gods of the universe are all seen together in that flow when one has seen upstream of that sacred river Ganga.
12. There is no other water which is as pure and as ever-changing as that water. That water is the form of the one who pervades all, Lord Narayana, himself.
13. That great river flows in space, and it pervades everywhere, at all times. It permeates the heavens, the earth, and the netherworlds.
14. Up and down and in all directions, its water encircles everything. The knowledgeable know that it is the "Lord of the World."
15. It fills an endless number of vessels. It runs through everything, and is used in many things and in many beings for worldly life.
16. In one form it is bitter, in another it is sweet. In some things it is spicy, in some it is pungent, and in some it is salty.
17. Whatever it mixes with, it becomes unified with, and of the same substance. In deep places, it fills their depths.
18. It is the poison in poison, and it is the nectar in nectar. It is the fragrance in the fragrant smell, and the odor in foul odor.

19. It is intermixed with good and bad qualities and assimilates itself as those qualities. The greatness of that water cannot be understood without that water itself.
20. That water flows beyond any boundaries and one cannot understand whether it is a river or a lake. Many people have chosen to live only in this water (Illusion) and have remained there.
21. Those who went beyond this water to its origin turned back from there to see that the water had dried up and nothing was there.
22. The realized one who is void of any states of mind or attitudes, sees this through thorough inquiry and deep thinking. Ramdas, the servant of God asks, "How many times shall I tell you again and again?"

Thus in Shri Dasbodh, a dialogue between the Guru and disciple, Sub-Chapter 7 of Chapter 11, named "The Ever-Changing River' is concluded.

Chapter: 11, Sub-Chapter: 8

The Inner-Self

|| ShriRam ||

1. First we must pay respect to the doer of all, the one who is the supporter of all the gods. His praises must be sung first.
2. No activities can happen without him. Even a fallen leaf cannot move. All of the three worlds move because of him.
3. It is the Inner-Self (Antaratman) that is the Self of all. He is the Self of the gods, demons and human beings. He is the origin of the four streams of beings, and the four types of speech.
4. It is He alone who resides in all beings and conducts their lives in various ways according to circumstances. How many of his activities in creation can be told?
5. Such is the one who is the hidden God. He is called God, or Ishwara. It is because of him that people can revel in the greatest of glories.
6. One who recognizes God becomes that "Universal God" oneself. Being God oneself, who is there to care about absorption in the state of samadhi, or the effortless sahaja state?
7. Only when analyzing the entire expanse of the three worlds (waking, dreaming, and deep sleep) will the secret become known, and will the great windfall of Knowledge be gained suddenly without any strenuous efforts.
8. Who has really seen and analyzed the Inner-Self like this? Many see and understand only a little of him, and with that little knowledge remain satisfied.
9. Oh listener! Whatever has been seen must be seen again and again. Hear the same explanations again and again. Read what has already been read again and again.
10. However much one sees of the Inner-Self is according to the condition of the one who sees. One can only tell what has been seen and observed according to the extent of one's utilization of the power of discrimination.
11. Much has been observed and seen of the Inner-Self but that is not sufficient to be able to describe him. What capacity does a small embodied being have to understand him?

12. That which is complete in itself cannot be understood by the limited individual if the analysis has not been continuous and uninterrupted. Only by continuous analysis and reflection on the explanations will one remain completely non-separate from God.
13. Only one who is not separate from God can be called a devotee. Otherwise, one is only tiring oneself with unnecessary efforts.
14. It is like visiting a house without meeting its owner, or like going to some kingdom without meeting the king.
15. It's a great wonder that human beings enjoy sensual pleasures and show off with the body, but they miss knowing who it is that sustains the body.
16. Like this, people don't use discrimination even though they say that they do. But this is alright, as people do according to their capacity.
17. The foolish don't know how to control the mind. Therefore, be wise. Know however, that even some who have become wise have also experienced downfall.
18. Just like a person who has forgotten a treasure that is being kept within the house goes searching for it from door to door outside, the same thing happens to the ignorant person who does not understand God.
19. What worldly person is able to meditate on God? When the attention is directed to the visible world delightfully, how will one come to know God?
20. Innumerable beings in various forms and with various types of speech have proliferated throughout the universe. They can even be found living in the earth and in stones.
21. The Inner-Self pervades all places and assumes many forms. He is One among many. He is both hidden and revealed in many places.
22. The moving can never become the one that is unmoving. This can only be understood in one's actual experience. The ever-changing Illusion cannot become the changeless Absolute Reality.
23. When the elements are dissolved one into another, body-consciousness falls away, and the pure untainted all-pervading stillness is as it is.
24. To find out who one is, and from where and how one has come to be, is the path of discrimination. One who does not have a keen intellect will not understand.
25. The wise will utilize the power of discrimination and cross the difficulties of worldly life. With devotion to God, all of one's family is uplifted.

Thus in Shri Dasbodh, a dialogue between the Guru and disciple, Sub-Chapter 8 of Chapter 11, named "The Inner-Self" is concluded.

Chapter: 11, Sub-Chapter: 9

The Teaching

|| ShriRam ||

1. First, one must act according to the situation. One's activities must be carried out correctly. If there is some shortcoming, then an unpleasant situation will occur.
2. Therefore, proceed with activities that have been started. Some will work out well, and sometimes difficulties will arise. No matter what may happen, remember God, Lord Vishnu.

3. Naturally, the question arises, "What is this God Vishnu?" One should give some thought to this question and see for oneself. It is said that before performing religious rituals one should remember the twenty-four names of God.
4. He has twenty-four names, he has a thousand names, he has an endless number of names, and yet he is nameless. One must recognize within how he is, by utilizing the power of discrimination.
5. A brahmin priest worships God in the form of an idol after having his bath and performing his prayer ritual.
6. People worship many gods, and many idols and images with love, but what is the image of Paramatman, the Supreme Self? What is He?
7. One must first recognize God, and *then* worship him, much like how an officer or master is honored after recognizing his status.
8. In the same way, properly recognize that the Supreme Self is God through inquiry and deep thinking. Only then can one cross beyond the sea of Illusion.
9. Idols and images are worshipped, but it is in the body that the Inner-Self is awakened. It is the appearance of the body that comes and goes that is the abode of the incarnations of God.
10. However, those incarnations always remain in their true form which is of the nature of Universal Light. This is called the Sattva Guna, the quality of purity that is the brilliance of Knowledge (Consciousness).
11. Within the brilliance of that Consciousness, there exist countless gods. This can be seen and verified in one's own experience.
12. God (Isha) resides in the town (Pura) of the body and is therefore called Purusha, or Beingness. In the same way, God resides in the universe and should be recognized as the Lord of the Universe.
13. In the universe, he is in the form of Consciousness residing and functioning within all bodies. Recognize Lord Vishnu as the inner-mind of all in this way.
14. Lord Vishnu exists within the universe as well as within all living beings. He is the doer as well as the experiencer of all activity. The wise recognize him as the Inner-Self.
15. It is he who listens, sees, smells, tastes, understands, and inquires. It is he who recognizes everything, and who is able to identify friends and strangers.
16. The Inner-Self of the entire universe is only one, but because of holding on to pride for the body, the bodily identification creates a hindrance that is the habit of thinking oneself to be a separate individual,.
17. It is he that is born, grows, dies, and kills, like waves that arise and fall one after another in an ever-changing sea that is the appearance and dissolution of the three worlds.
18. It is he alone who exists and directs the three worlds. Therefore, he is called the "Lord of the Three Worlds." This must be seen and experienced for oneself using the power of discrimination.
19. The Inner-Self is described as being like this, and he also exists within the five elements. Moreover, deep consideration must be given to the four Great Statements (Mahavakyas) from the *Vedas*.
20. First, see the one who occupies the body, then see the one who resides in the universe. Having realized that, afterwards, the Absolute Reality, can be attained.

21. Having given deep thought to Parabrahman, one can determine what is Essence and what is non-essence, and one becomes unmistakably convinced that all that is moving is destined to disappear.
22. Understand that all that has a creation, existence, and destruction is not the same as the untainted Reality. It is here that Knowledge (Jnana) turns into Supreme Knowledge (Vijnana).
23. The eight bodies appearing in time and space and should be understood and thrown off. What remains is pure untainted Brahman.
24. With thorough investigation and deep thought one becomes singularly unified with Brahman without the experience of any separate observer. See that this is also a state which must be dissolved, and become stateless.
25. Here, what remains is not possible to be indicated with words. The indication as well as that which is being indicated are given up and any remnant of any state disappears.

Thus in Shri Dasbodh, a dialogue between the Guru and disciple, Sub-Chapter 9 of Chapter 11, named "The Teaching" is concluded.

Chapter: 11, Sub-Chapter: 10

Desireless Behavior

|| ShriRam ||

1. A foolish person has a limited perspective, but the wise one sees everything with a wide perspective, and enjoys many pleasures in many ways.
2. The Inner-Self and the spiritual leader (Mahanta) are the same. He will never become petty or limited. He is unconfined and vast like space, and all-knowing. He is a renowned yogi. (One who abides without distinction as Oneness.)
3. He is the principle doer and enjoyer who is the power that works everywhere on the earth. Only the knowledgeable are able to recognize him.
4. The spiritual leader is like this. He has searched through everything and held to the Essence. If we try to see him, he is not easily located.
5. He is well known in the form of fame. Large and small alike know him. If we look at his outer garments, not even one of them is permanent.
6. His fame can never become diminished. Many people do not understand him when they see him, or why he behaves as he does.
7. He takes no pleasure in adorning himself with expensive clothing. He is adorned with the adornment of fame and having a good name. He does not waste even a single moment without being engaged in some productive activity.
8. He is constantly leaving the company of acquaintances and moving on to make new acquaintances. People look to see into his mind, but no desire is seen in him.
9. He does not look at anybody with interest for a long time, and he does not talk with anyone for a long time. He does not stay in any one place for long, and he is constantly getting up and going away.
10. He does not tell where he is going, and the places he does mention, he does not go to. He does not allow any conjecture or imagination as to his own inner state.

11. Whatever opinions that people form about him, he proves them wrong, whatever people imagine about him gets turned upside down, and he easily disproves faulty logic that people present to him.
12. He has no respect for those things that people look to with great respect, and he is disinterested in the things that people are always eager and hungry to obtain.
13. Thus, he can't be imagined with imagination, nor can he be conceived of with logical ideas. Any ideas or feelings that people have as to how he is are incorrect. He is the "Master of Yoga" (Yogeshwar).
14. Like this, his mind cannot be located. He cannot be found in one physical location, but when it comes to spiritual discourse and praising God, he does not stop, even for a moment.
15. Whatever people imagine and conceive about him is proven incorrect, and in this way he exposes the errors in the concepts and states of minds of the listeners. Such is the Master of Yoga.
16. Many people seek him out and he is appreciated by many who understand the great work that he has accomplished.
17. He constantly seeks solitude going off on his own to study, and he makes worthwhile use of his time in service of other people.
18. He develops the best qualities and teaches them to others. He gathers groups of people together, but does so discretely.
19. He is continuously occupied with the work of inspiring people to worship God. When people come to understand his worth, they have a desire to follow him.
20. First, the hard work must be completed, and only then are the returns forthcoming. Without putting in any effort, there is no fruit. One who does not put in any spiritual effort lives life to just feed the body.
21. Seek out many people and understand their capacity. After understanding, then one can consciously keep them near or leave them.
22. Work gets done according to one's capacity. If one does not have the proper capability, then the work that gets done goes to waste. Knowingly look into the minds of the people and understand their capabilities in various ways.
23. Entrust the person with work according to their capacity. Only when seeing someone's hard work and capabilities can one have confidence in them, but one should always make sure to maintain one's own position of respect and prominence.
24. This is told from actual experience. I have done first and then talked about it. Anyone who agrees with this will accept it.
25. A capable spiritual leader will develop others to be like him. By training others with proper thinking and intellect, he makes them Knowledgeable (Jnanis) and then sends them out to many places.

Thus in Shri Dasbodh, a dialogue between the Guru and disciple, Sub-Chapter 10 of Chapter 11, named "Desireless Behavior" is concluded.

Chapter 12. Discrimination and Desirelessness

Chapter: 12, Sub-Chapter: 1

Description of Purity

|| ShriRam ||

1. First, take care of the duties of worldly life, then take up the spiritual life using the power of discrimination. The wise will not be lazy about taking care of both aspects of life.
2. If you neglect the worldly life and only follow the spiritual life, you will create suffering for yourself. If you take care of the worldly life along with the spiritual life, then you can be said to be wise.
3. If one completely gives up the worldly life for spiritual life, then he cannot even get food for his meals. How can such a destitute person have any success in spiritual life?
4. If spiritual life is forsaken and one only pursues worldly life, then there will suffering at the time of death. With no spiritual life you will be extremely miserable at the end of your life when death comes.
5. If one does not carry out the work assigned by the boss but only sits lazily at home, the boss will punish him and this will be seen by others.
6. In such a situation one loses his reputation and people cruelly make fun of him. In this way, the living being creates great suffering and sorrow during one's life.
7. The same principle applies with regard to what happens at the end of one's life. Therefore, you must have devotion to God and gain actual experience of your own divine True Form (Swaroopa).
8. Understand that one who is liberated while still leading a worldly life is a true yogi. He continuously sees clearly and gives thought to what is proper and what is inappropriate.
9. One who is alert in worldly life can easily understand what will make the spiritual life successful. One who has no capacity to function appropriately in worldly life will also not be successful in spiritual life.
10. Therefore, take care, and be alert in both worldly life and in spiritual life. If you fail to do this, you will suffer many sorrows.
11. Even worms and insects look carefully when stepping from one leaf to another. All living beings in the world move about using some sense of discernment and discrimination. What then can be said about human beings who live their lives wandering about in delusion?
12. Therefore, you must have foresight and be continuously analyzing situations trying to surmise what might happen in the future and make efforts to bring about good solutions.
13. One who remains alert is happy, and one who is careless becomes unhappy. The evidence of this basic worldly thinking is seen everywhere in daily life.
14. One who is alert and attentive in all things is truly blessed with greatness. He alone remains content among the people.
15. One who becomes lazy and does not do any analytical thinking suddenly falls into calamity without having any time to get the situation under control.

16. Therefore, people who exercise foresight and thoughtful analysis should be observed. Because of the example set by such people others become wise.
17. Recognize those who are truly wise and adopt the qualities of virtuous people, and drop those vices which are observed in others.
18. Examine all whom you come into contact with and don't keep the company of everyone you meet. Don't cause any hurt in anyone's mind while silently making observations about the people you meet.
19. The thoughtful person looks similar to all other people. However, he is thoughtful and discerning, and is able to observe those who are useful and industrious, and those who have some shortcomings.
20. He knowingly observes and accepts everyone. This is his extraordinary quality. He knows how to respect all appropriately.

Thus in Shri Dasbodh, a dialogue between the Guru and disciple, Sub-Chapter 1 of Chapter 12, named "Description of Purity" is concluded.

Chapter: 12, Sub-Chapter: 2

Explanation of Direct Experience

|| ShriRam ||

1. Oh, you men and women who are living a worldly life, please listen in an impartial manner with a clear and focused mind and see the inner meaning of what is being explained.
2. What does your desire say? What does your imagination conceive? Many ripples of various kinds arise in many ways within the mind.
3. Desire is such that one should eat only good food, have fine meals, have good clothing to wear, and that everything should be in accordance with one's liking.
4. The mind is constantly thinking like this, and yet, nothing happens according to its liking. One always wants something good to happen, and suddenly something bad happens.
5. Some people are happy, and some are miserable. This is the direct experience of what can be seen happening everywhere in the world. In the end, when suffering comes, people put the label of destiny on it.
6. Because one does not make the proper effort, whatever is done does not bring successful return, and meanwhile, one does not recognize one's own faults.
7. How can one who does not know oneself know others? Giving up the sense of justice and morality, people become pitiable.
8. People do not understand the minds of others and do not behave according to what other people want, and because of foolishness many disputes arise among people.
9. When quarreling increases, people become more troubled by each other. Without making any proper effort everything merely becomes tiring in the end.
10. Don't act like this. Observe many people, and understand people as they are, in an appropriate manner.

11. Examine the words used by another, and examine and verify the inner experience of others. How can one who is of dull intellect and who is without insight be able to know the mind-set of others?
12. What is mainly seen among worldly people are the signs of criticizing others with words and defending one's own views.
13. To be considered praiseworthy by the people one must bear a lot of sufferings imposed by others. If you do not bear them, the mind naturally becomes irritated.
14. Wherever is not agreeable to oneself, do not stay there. However, you should not leave broken relationships remaining behind.
15. All people small and large respect one who speaks truthfully and behaves accordingly. Such a one naturally sees and knows justice and injustice.
16. As the common people cannot understand, the thoughtful ones must pardon them. One who does not pardon them, becomes like them.
17. Until the sandalwood is rubbed its fragrance cannot be known, and any similar looking tree might be mistaken for a sandalwood tree.
18. As long as your best qualities are not revealed and understood by people, how can they understand you? When seeing your best qualities people are pleased in their minds.
19. When people feel inwardly pleased, there is love and friendship for you among the people, and the people of the world will be drawn towards you.
20. When you make God in the form of the people pleased, there is nothing felt to be lacking in oneself. However, it is difficult to please everyone.
21. Whatever is sown grows accordingly. Whatever is borrowed, one must return. If we expose someone's secrets, it hurts that person's mind.
22. Good actions that are done in one's worldly affairs increase the love of the people. One's approach toward others is reflected in the response one that receives.
23. All of this resides within oneself, so we cannot blame other people. One must teach their own mind, from moment to moment.
24. If one meets with a cruel and hurtful person, and the patience to pardon him sinks too low, then the aspirant should leave that place quietly without speaking.
25. People know how to evaluate many things but they don't know how to gauge the inner experience of the mind of others. Beings that don't understand this become unfortunate, there is no doubt about it.
26. Knowing that death will come to you, remember to behave benevolently towards others. It is very difficult to always show kindness and proper discrimination.
27. Consider all as equal, whether they are great or small, or considered as one's own. Showing increasing closeness and affection towards others is helpful in life.
28. When doing good things for others, good things happen for you. This is actually experienced by people. Now, what more should I tell, and to whom?
29. Listen to discourses and explanations about God. Conduct political activities with appropriate benevolence. Without seeing situations clearly, all goes in vain.
30. Even if one has gained great knowledge, if one does not know how to act appropriately according to the situation, there is a lack of respect for that knowledge.

Thus in Shri Dasbodh, a dialogue between the Guru and disciple, Sub-Chapter 2 of Chapter 12, named "Explanation of Direct Experience" is concluded.

Chapter: 12, Sub-Chapter: 3

Signs of a Devotee

|| ShriRam ||

1. There are many people in the world, see them with discrimination. See correctly what is of this world and That which is not of the world.
2. For being successful in worldly life, keep the company of one who knows about worldly affairs. To be successful in the spiritual world, one must ask a true master, a Sadguru.
3. It's natural that one does not know what to ask the Sadguru. The aspirant should ask him two things.
4. What are these two things? Ask first, "Who is God?" and then "Who am I?" The explanation about these two things should be reflected upon again and again.
5. First, find out the principle God, and then the devotee must understand who one is oneself. Then the analysis of the five elements and the inner meaning of the four great vedic statements (Mahavakyas) must be understood.
6. The fruit of this is the recognition of the eternal unmoving stillness, and one finds out for oneself the answer to "Who am I?"
7. When considering the thought of Essence and what is not essential, it is seen that there is nothing that is permanent in this world. The one God that is the original cause of all must first be recognized.
8. The unmoving, the moving, and the inanimate are all the play of Illusion. Reality, being the source of all this, does not become diminished by any of it.
9. One should seek out the recognition of Parabrahman and explore the entirety of the three worlds by using the power of discrimination. One who skillfully investigates cuts down all that is illusory through thorough examination.
10. That which is untrue should be given up and the True should be accepted. One who investigates skillfully examines the entirety of Illusion and understands that all forms are illusory.
11. Illusion is made up of five elements, is false, and will disappear. The physical body, the universe, and the eightfold manifestation (Prakriti) are all perishable.
12. Whatever appears will be destroyed, whatever is born will perish, and whatever has been constructed will be demolished. That is the nature of Illusion.
13. Whatever expands will break, and whatever comes, goes away. One element is dissolved into another with the dissolution of creation.
14. The physical body that is currently being held will get destroyed. This is the direct experience of all. Without human beings how can there be any semen or procreation?
15. Without food how can seminal fluid exist, and if there are no plants how can any food exist? How can plants have life if the earth does not exist?
16. If water is absent, the earth cannot exist. Without light, water cannot exist. Without wind, light cannot exist. Understand like this.
17. Wind cannot exist without the Inner-Self. How can the Inner-Self exist without the arising of modification? How can there be any modification in the changeless? See how there is no change in the changeless.
18. There is no earth, water, light, wind, Inner-Self, or any other kind of modification in the Absolute Reality, Parabrahman.

19. Changelessness and attributelessness are the signs of Brahman. The eight-fold visible creation is completely destructible.
20. When we look, we understand that everything that appears perishes, and that even though it had an appearance it never really existed. With discrimination between the real and unreal one gains contentment.
21. By using the power of discrimination and with inquiry the mind comes to know what is Eternal and what is ephemeral, and because of this, the understanding as to what is True becomes firm.
22. The eternal God is attributeless. When one is inwardly convinced of this, it is a sign that one knows God. Next, one must come to know "Who am I?"
23. In order to know "Who am I?," one must search through all of the various elements of the body. Examining in this way, one comes to know that the feelings of "you" and "me" are only mental attitudes, or states of mind.
24. When the entire body is searched, the sense of "I-ness" cannot be found. The entire duality of "you" and "me" dissolves along with elements, one into another.
25. The search reveals that whatever is visible is going to disappear, one element dissolving into another. At that point, how can any duality remain? Only the original principle, Reality remains.
26. Understand the analysis of the five elements and the principle elements making up the body. Understand the inner meaning of the four Mahavakyas of the *Vedas* regarding Reality (Brahman), and surrender yourself with complete detachment.
27. When searching to the root of God and the devotee, it is seen that all is the attributeless Self alone, without any separate identity or label.
28. By using the power of discrimination the sense of a separate "I" disappears along with any sense of distinctions, and one recedes into the "stateless state" which is no-mind.
29. Knowledge (Jnana) has merged into Supreme Knowledge (Vijnana), and the object of mediation and the meditation have become one. The entirety of all that is seen to have cause and effect is discarded with clear seeing.
30. One escapes the cycle of birth and death, and all accumulated deeds disappear along with the sufferings associated with death.
31. All bondage is entirely broken. Through the utilization of discrimination and inquiry one attains liberation, and it is felt that one's life has been entirely fulfilled.
32. Many doubts get cleared, and many dangers are warded off. With the Knowledge gained through the power of discrimination, many people become purified.
33. The servants of the saints who uplift the downtrodden also purify the world. This is experienced in the minds of many people.

Thus in Shri Dasbodh, a dialogue between the Guru and disciple, Sub-Chapter 3 of Chapter 12, named "Signs of a Devotee" is concluded.

Chapter: 12, Sub-Chapter: 4

Discrimination and Detachment

|| ShriRam ||

1. In the same way that if a great fortune is as good as useless if it comes into someone's hands who does not know how to enjoy it, if one has detachment but does not utilize discrimination, that detachment is also useless.
2. There are many conflicts, pains and troubles in the family life that make one sorrowful. When one hears about this and sees for oneself, it brings about detachment.
3. There are many pressures, calamities, and problems in worldly life. So much so that one may even leave his family and go to another country.
4. He then becomes freed from his worries and escapes from his dependence on others, like a person who becomes relieved from the pains of disease.
5. But such a person should not then become lacking in self control and act in a destructive, corrupt, and mischievous manner, like some animal who roams around out of control.
6. If one is detached without proper discernment, then this lack of clear thinking will cause many problems, and both the worldly life and the spiritual life become useless.
7. If one does not have a worldly life or a spiritual life, then the entire life itself becomes meaningless. Without proper discrimination many problems are created in life.
8. In the case of someone who babbles on about Knowledge but is not free of desires, it is like someone who is locked up in prison while talking about his courageous accomplishments.
9. Knowledge without desirelessness gives rise to vain pride. Such a person becomes distressed and agitated because of greed and hypocrisy.
10. Such a person gets annoyed because of his selfishness like a dog that barks when it is tied down. Because of pride, he cannot bear to see others who have superior qualities or understanding.
11. Thus, having one without the other gives rise to unnecessary grief. Now, listen to the benefit of having the combination of both detachment and discrimination.
12. With discrimination one becomes liberated within. With desirelessness one breaks the bonds of worldly life. Such a yogi who is without attachment is free inwardly and outwardly.
13. With his mouth he speaks of Knowledge and all of his actions reflect that Knowledge accordingly. Seeing his example, even pure and virtuous people are amazed.
14. He has no interest in the three worlds. The state of desirelessness is fully established in him. There is no limit to his kind efforts and thoughtfulness.
15. Such a person enjoys devotional music and singing God's praises and telling stories of God.
16. He sets people on the right path and causes discrimination to arises within. The content of his speech is based in Self-experience.
17. On the righteous path he becomes one with the people in the world, and this pleases the Lord of the Universe. He understands propriety in various situations.

18. With desirelessness, he is disinterested in worldly life and is immersed in the actual experience of the Knowledge of Brahman. He practices appropriate rituals of worship and sings the praises of God in a virtuous way.
19. Desirelessness together with the discrimination is like this. Empty detachment is merely repression, and the word knowledge by itself is merely felt to be boring.
20. Therefore discrimination and desirelessness together should be understood to be the sign of great fortune. Ramdas says that the sages understand this properly.

Thus in Shri Dasbodh, a dialogue between the Guru and disciple, Sub-Chapter 4 of Chapter 12, named "Discrimination and Detachment" is concluded.

Chapter: 12, Sub-Chapter: 5

Self-Surrender

|| ShriRam ||

1. A line is curved and shaped to make the letters of the alphabet. The letters of the alphabet form words and the words are put together to make poetry, prose, and essays.
2. There are many books of spiritual science, the *Vedas*, mythological books, many poems, explanations, and translations of many texts. There are so many texts it is not possible to name them all.
3. There are many sages with many opinions. It can easily be seen that there are innumerable languages and texts to be found everywhere. What opinion is missing in written literature?
4. There are many sub-divisions of the *Upanishads*, of various texts compiled by sages, various religious texts, many types of poetic forms, and various standards of writing with many different names.
5. There are many types of songs, many verses, many types of meter, many ballads, many short verses, many poems, all with many names to identify them.
6. There are various types of singing with drums and string instruments. There are many types of songs of narrations, songs for different occasions, festive songs, and folk songs.
7. There are many types of musical sounds, loud acclamations, the sounds of bells and cymbals with rhythmic tunes, and many forms of speech. There are many differences in types of sound, music and speech that can be heard.
8. There is the Para speech which is the subtlest sound in the form of an inspiration, the Pashyanti speech which is the subtle inner sound beginning to take form at level of the heart, the Madhyama speech at the throat where words take the form of a soft whisper, and the Vaikhari speech where the tongue pronounces many word jewels.
9. There is the three and a half syllables of the AUM from which the letters and sounds of the alphabet come forth.
10. There are many differences in the moods of music, many different forms of dancing, musical rhythms, melodies, and different interpretations of philosophical knowledge and analysis.

11. Understand that among all of the principle elements, the main element is pure Sattva. The half crescent mark in the OM symbol (ॐ) is representative of the great original element that the Primal Illusion.
12. The small and large elements together make up the eight bodies as well as the eight-fold manifest world appearance that is of the nature of wind which disappears.
13. When the wind disappears there is only empty sky. In the same way, only the solid Parabrahman remains when the eight bodies are thrown off.
14. There is the creation and destruction of the universe and the physical body (each consisting of four bodies, eight in all), but Pure Brahman is seen to be different from these when looking into what is Eternal and what is ephemeral.
15. Objects are inert, the Self is moving, and Pure Brahman is still and unmoving. When this is analyzed and clearly understood, the inert and the moving are immediately dissolved into the one form of Brahman.
16. On the level of the inanimate, the gross or objective aspect of self-surrender is knowing that all objects, the mind, the body, one's speech, and everything referred to as "me" or "mine," belongs entirely to God.
17. At the level of the moving, the Lord of the Universe is the doer of all that is moving and changing. All living beings are but a fraction of him. All is his, and all is only him. There is no trace of "me" in him.
18. The description of self-surrender that is the surrender of everything that is moving has now been told. There is no place where God who is the doer of everything does not exist.
19. That which is of the nature of change and motion is insubstantial like the form of a dream. At the level of the unmoving, the unmoving God is formless. Understand that the third aspect of self-surrender relates to this.
20. Where there is no trace of movement, how can any initial sense of "I" arise? Self-surrender that is of the nature of the unmoving is revealed through the power of discrimination like this.
21. In all three modes of self-surrender, the sense of oneself as a separate individual is not there. There is no sense of "other." When one does not exist oneself, there is no sense of "I" to be found anywhere.
22. By seeing again and again, one comes to the eventual conclusion of knowing and understanding. Once one's seeing is complete, one becomes calm and silent and even speech comes to an end.

Thus in Shri Dasbodh, a dialogue between the Guru and disciple, Sub-Chapter 5 of Chapter 12, named "Self-Surrender" is concluded.

Chapter: 12, Sub-Chapter: 6

The Sequence of Creation

|| ShriRam ||

1. Brahman is pure, unmoving, eternal untainted Essence without any blemish. Like the sky, it is clear pure vast empty space.
2. It does not do anything and it does not hold or retain anything. It has no birth, no death, no knowing, and no not knowing. It is beyond the void that is nothingness (sunyata).
3. It does not get created nor destroyed. It does not come into being nor does it disappear. It is beyond Illusion, free of any ignorance or imperfection, and it is limitless.
4. In that Brahman there arose an inspiration or desire that is called God with six qualities (Knowledge, Omnipresence, Energy, Power, Life, and Brilliance), and is also called God that is the half male and half female principles.
5. It is called the God of all, the knower of all, the witness, the seer, the fullness of Knowledge, God which is beyond everything, the Supreme Self, the Life-Energy of the universe, and the primal Beingness.
6. That Primal Illusion is richly endowed with many attributes and faces downward producing an arousal or stirring of the gunas. The three gunas (rajas, tamas, sattva) have been created from this excitation in the Primal Illusion.
7. Later, Lord Vishnu who is the of the nature of Knowledge (Consciousness) and the sattva guna, and who protects and sustains the three worlds, was created.
8. Understand that afterwards came Lord Brahma, who is the combination of knowledge and ignorance. It is from rajas guna that the three worlds were created.
9. Later, came Lord Shiva who is of the nature of ignorance (tamas) and is the reason for the destruction of everything. The doing of all of this activity (creation, preservation, and destruction) has come from the Primal Illusion itself.
10. Afterwards, from there, the forms of the five elements appeared. Like this, the eightfold visible manifestation emerged from the Primal Illusion.
11. When movement occurred in the unmoving, that itself is the description of the wind (vayu). The five elements and the three gunas in their most subtle form is called the eight-fold creation.
12. Space (sky) means the Inner-Self. Its greatness must be seen with direct experience. From that space, wind has come into being.
13. Listen now to how that wind flows in two streams, one is hot and one is cool. From the cool stream of wind the moon and stars came into being.
14. From the hot stream of wind came fire, the sun, lightening, and more. Understand that the hot and cool wind intermingled together are the form of light.
15. From that light came water. When water became condensed and solidified, earth was formed. Later, innumerable plants and trees came into being.
16. From the plants came many medicinal juices, many seeds, many juices for drinking, and the 8.4 million species of living beings that came into existence on the earth.
17. In this way, the universe was created. One must investigate this and deeply think about it for oneself in the mind. Without actual experience one is left to depend upon guesswork and speculation.

18. The creation and destruction of the universe takes place like this. This is called the inquiry into the Eternal and the ephemeral.
19. In the same way that everything has come into being one thing from another, everything will disappear and return in the same way. In this way, everything gets destroyed at the time of the final dissolution.
20. The wise people give thoughtful consideration to That which is pristine and eternally existing at the beginning, throughout the duration, and after the end of everything.
21. Many forms come into being and yet none of them is permanently sustained. For this reason, there must be some investigation into what is Eternal and what is ephemeral.
22. Everywhere people talk of the greatness of the seer that is the witness or Inner-Self. However, one must with see with one's own actual experience what this all-seeing state actually is.
23. From the beginning up to the end, everything is completely only Illusion, and all of the many streams of knowledge, arts, and skills are contained within it.
24. One who gives up all attachments will arrive at the ultimate realization and understand that all is Illusion. For the one who is completely entangled in attachments, who can rescue him?
25. How can That which can only be directly experienced through the power of discrimination ever be understood through delusional guesswork and speculation? It is only through the investigation into the Eternal and ephemeral that clearly reveals Illusion that one can attain the realization of Brahman.
26. Understand that the "Great Causal Body" of the universe is the Primal Illusion. Those who say that the incomplete is the complete Brahman do not properly utilize the power of discrimination.
27. There are many people in this creation. Some enjoy the king's throne, and some are fascinated with the expanse of Illusion. Understand this and have the direct experience right now.
28. There are many people who consider themselves great. However, it is only those who use the power of discrimination that truly understand the nature of everything.
29. Like this is the position of those who inquire into Reality. Therefore, inquiry and deep thought is required. Do not become spoiled and get carried away by the speech of worldly people.
30. Do not merely hold on to the confirmations of knowledge contained in books. What then would be the purpose of finding a Sadguru? One must gain understanding by means of one's own direct experience.
31. Understand that the one who gets swept away with the opinions of many people surely gets deceived. When there is not only one boss but many, who does one ask for payment?

Thus in Shri Dasbodh, a dialogue between the Guru and disciple, Sub-Chapter 6 of Chapter 12, named "The Sequence of Creation" is concluded.

Chapter: 12, Sub-Chapter: 7

Renunciation of Sense Objects

|| ShriRam ||

1. The listener says, "Most people get bored with harsh talk about propriety and virtue. It is not advisable to take food when there is the sensation of vomiting. (Meaning that one should not continue to listen with a mind that is rejecting what is being said.)
2. Many people criticize the sense objects yet continue to enjoy them. The body does not continue to function when giving up sense objects entirely.
3. When one speaks in one way and behaves in a contradictory manner, such a person is said to have a low level of discretion and sense of propriety. People laugh at this type of behavior.
4. There are many statements made in many various places that say unless sense objects are given up, one cannot attain the fulfillment of spiritual life. One must understand the meaning of this for oneself.
5. Is it the case that worldly people take meals and those living a spiritual life must constantly be fasting? Both appear to be the same with regard to the enjoyment of sense objects.
6. Who has completely given up sense objects while the body is living? The revered teacher is requested to please explain this.
7. If it is said that one must entirely give up all sensual pleasures before one can live a spiritual life, statements such as this only create confusion."
8. The listener put forth the question in this way. The speaker then replied, "Please become alert and concentrate your mind on this subject."
9. The culmination of spiritual life is only realized if one gives up everything by being desireless. It is only by abandoning the worldly life and all attachments that complete spiritual fulfillment is attained.
10. In the past, many Jnanis have come and gone. They made many strenuous efforts and then went on to become famous in the world.
11. Many have merely passed away living their lives filled with envy, while others died constantly crying for food. So many lives have been wasted only for the sake of filling the belly.
12. Basically, if a person has no desirelessness, no knowledge based on experience, and no virtuous behavior, how can there be any real devotion?
13. Such people call themselves virtuous, but upon examination, it is seen that what they say is only based upon speculation and guesswork.
14. For those who do not see the error in their ways and change their minds and conduct accordingly, it is an indication of errors and mistakes made in the past. From moment to moment, such people feel envious seeing the success of others.
15. This feeling of "If I don't get to have something, then you should not be able to have it either," is known by all. One who does not get enough to eat, cannot tolerate seeing someone else who gets enough food. This can be seen everywhere.
16. Fortunate people are criticized by unfortunate people, and thieves get irritated when seeing those who are virtuous.
17. There is no fortune greater than desirelessness. Not being desireless is the greatest misfortune. Without being desireless, there is no ultimate fulfillment in spiritual life.

18. Know that the one who has gained Knowledge from actual experience, who has become detached with the power of discrimination, and who has renounced everything is a great yogi, a godly person.
19. Having given up the eight spiritual powers of accomplishment (siddhis), and having been initiated on the path of yoga, even the great god Shiva (Mahadeva) goes from house to house asking for alms.
20. How can one who merely wears the garments of a monk, but who has no actual experience equate himself with God? The two cannot be compared.
21. People seek out the one who is disinterested in worldly life and who utilizes the power of discrimination, while those who are greedy and foolish live a pitiful life like that of a pauper.
22. Those who have turned away from inquiry and thoughtfulness, who have a corrupt sense of moral conduct, and who have forgotten to use the power of discrimination are greedy for sensual pleasures.
23. They do not worship God, nor enjoy chanting God's name, and because of this they cannot bear to be around virtuous people.
24. By being desireless one does not become corrupt, nor does one give up Knowledge (Jnana) and Devotion (Bhakti). Although such a one is well versed, he does not get into arguments. Such a desireless person as this is very rare.
25. Just as it can be seen that putting in hard work in the fields brings in a good crop, and that high quality goods get sold out immediately, similarly, many people are attracted to the feet of those who are knowledgeable.
26. Others only become completely fatigued and useless because of their unreasonable hopes and desires. Because of their greed, their knowledge becomes confused.
27. Give up the strong attachment to sense objects and understand the pure cause and effect (that which is essential to sustain life). Recognize the signs of abandoning attachment to sense objects to be like this.
28. Everything is only God, and God is the only doer. Manifestation does not have any place to exist. Only those who utilize the power of discrimination understand this with discrimination.
29. One who is courageous in difficult situations is respected by the young and old alike. How can someone who is a hard worker be considered to be the same as someone who is lazy?
30. One who is wise understands what is to be given up and what is not to be given up. He acts in accordance with his speech and has correct understanding about the physical body and the universe.
31. One who is like this understands everything and is fully endowed with the best qualities. The fulfillment of life comes naturally for him.

Thus in Shri Dasbodh, a dialogue between the Guru and disciple, Sub-Chapter 7 of Chapter 12, named "Renunciation of Sense Objects" is concluded.

Chapter: 12, Sub-Chapter: 8

The Form of Time

|| ShriRam ||

1. The "Lord of the Universe" is the Primal Illusion. Later, from that the eight-fold manifestation expanded and the structure of the universe took form.
2. When all is not there, only pure formlessness exists like space, without any form. Time does not exist there.
3. With the expanse of the covering of Illusion, the concept of time came into existence. Other than in Illusion, there is no place that can be seen for time to exist.
4. There are only two things, one is movement and the other is stillness. When the moving is there, then there is the concept of time. Where is time apart from movement?
5. Space has some distance or interval contained within it. Space has some lapse or duration of time, as well as "from" and "between" in it. Know that this duration or interval in space is time.
6. Because of the sun, there is the knowledge of duration where the counting of one moment to the next, and everything from a single second until the end of an eon, is comprehended.
7. In this way, seconds, minutes, hours, days, day and night, a fortnight, a month, six months, a year, and an eon come to be known.
8. The counting of epochs (yugas), as well as the various life spans of the gods that are described in ancient scriptures, go on like this on the earth.
9. The activities of the three gods (the three gunas) takes place in a subtle manner, and if some inconsistency in the order of things is imagined to be occurring, people become concerned.
10. The intermixture of three gunas cannot be separated. The entire structure of the universe has taken place in that mixture from beginning to end. How can it be said the one is superior or inferior?
11. Let this be as it is. These matters are understood by the knowledgeable. The ignorant person only unnecessarily becomes entangled in delusion. These hidden things are known in actual experience with Knowledge.
12. The time of the generation of creation, the time of expansion of creation, the time of sustenance, and the time of destruction of creation, are the form of the duration of time, from beginning to end.
13. The name of any particular period of time is given according to what occurs during that time span. If this is not properly understood, then please listen further.
14. The rainy season, the winter season, the hot season, the time of contentment, the pleasurable and sorrowful times, and times of enjoyment are all experienced.
15. Morning time, afternoon, evening time, spring time, auspicious time, and difficult times are all understood by people.
16. The time of birth, the time of childhood, the time of youth, the time of old age, the time of death, and fortunate times are all forms of time.
17. Plentiful time, time of famine, non-auspicious and auspicious times, all of these times together make up what is called time.

18. When there is one thing, but it is felt to be something else, this is called the lack of discrimination. People who are continuously engaged in many worldly activities understand only on the level of being engaged in those activities.
19. When the mind is continuously engaged in worldly activity, it is directed downward (into objectivity). When the mind is withdrawn away from all worldly engagement (away from objectivity), there is upliftment. The pleasure of this upliftment is known to those who utilize the power of discrimination.
20. Those who utilize the power of discrimination to see from where the formation of the universe originated, and who look into this again and again, attain that original status of Brahman.
21. Being in the worldly life while seeing one's divine True Form, one attains this state of Brahman and stays among the people according to destiny and past deeds.
22. The root of all is only One. Some know it and some are unaware. By using the power of discrimination one can attain the culmination of spiritual life immediately.
23. Only then does one's life become worthwhile. The wise see both the worldly life and the spiritual life clearly. The most important primary thing is that one must see using the power of discrimination.
24. Understand that those people who do not use discrimination are like animals. How can one attain the culmination of spiritual life by listening to their speech?
25. Let that be as it is, it does not affect us. Whatever they have done, they will reap the fruit accordingly. Whatever has been sown is what has grown and is what is being experienced now.
26. In the future as well, whatever one does, the fruits are received accordingly. One who has devotion attains God. When God and devotee are united, contentment proliferates.
27. Those who died without praising God have uselessly come and gone. Even some who were wise were mesmerized by the things in Illusion and forgot their True Form. What can one say about them?
28. Whatever is here in this world remains here. This is the experience of everyone. Tell me what does anyone take away with them in the end?
29. Be disinterested in worldly things. See everything with composure and ease using the power of discrimination. In this way, the Lord of the Universe who is very rarely realized, can be realized.
30. There is nothing as great as realizing the Lord of the Universe. When one carries out one's worldly affairs in a detached manner that is appropriate to various situations, one can live a life of contentment.
31. In the past, there were many people like King Janaka who led a life of contentment while ruling their kingdoms. Even today, there are virtuous people like this.
32. If death comes to a king and the king offers to pay millions or billions of rupees, he will still not be exempt from death.
33. Life is like this. It is always at the mercy of others and of death. In life there are many pains and sufferings, and many grievances and worries. There are so many that it is not possible to tell all of them.
34. In this marketplace of worldly life that is going on, one should look for the profit of realizing God. It is only by realizing God that one gets relief from the sufferings of life.

Thus in Shri Dasbodh, a dialogue between the Guru and disciple, Sub-Chapter 8 of Chapter 12, named "The Form of Time" is concluded.

Chapter: 12, Sub-Chapter: 9

The Teaching About Effort

|| ShriRam ||

1. The listener said "Suppose that there is someone who is weak, who has no proper mode of conduct, who is financially unstable, lazy, gluttonous, deeply in debt, foolish about everything, whose life is completely in disorder, and who has nothing.
2. He has nothing to eat and no good meals, nothing to wear or drape around his body, no bed, no cover, not even a small hut to live in, he is so unfortunate.
3. He does not have any near or distant relatives, no well-wishers, no friends or acquaintances anywhere. He is like a stranger without any support.
4. What should he do? What hope should he hold onto in life? Should he survive or die, and in which way?"
5. Someone asked this question, and the speaker will give the reply. Now, the listeners are requested to remain alert while listening.
6. Any work, whether small or large cannot be accomplished without actually doing the work. If there is someone who is unfortunate and wishes to become fortunate, remain alert and listen to what is being said.
7. If there is no alertness within, and no efforts are made, how can there be any talk of happiness and contentment?
8. Therefore, give up laziness. Make earnest efforts with perseverance and break the presence of depression from the mind forcefully.
9. Get up early in the morning and worship God. Remember and reflect regularly upon whatever has been learned by heart.
10. Go over what you have learned already to make it fresh, and learn by heart some more in addition. Keep firm with regular discipline, and do not engage in meaningless babble.
11. Go to a distant place for morning bath and toilet. Come back clean and bring something back with you. Don't return empty handed. (This is saying not to be lazy, and to make oneself useful in the village life.)
12. The washed clothes should be wrung out and hung up for drying, and some worship of God should be done according to what is customary or appropriate.
13. Then, have some fruit to eat and afterwards tend to your business or occupation, taking care when dealing with those who are close to you, as well as with strangers.
14. Write nicely and read clearly and smoothly. The inner meaning of the words should be understood with proper analysis and consideration.
15. When asking questions, they should be exact and appropriate to the situation. When giving answers, the explanation should be thorough. To speak about something without experience is a mistake.
16. Remain alert, and behave morally, accomplishing works that please many people.
17. Try to satisfy those who come calling to meet with you. The explanations about God should be given, and you should act in a manner which is appropriate according to the situation.
18. When speaking, the style and expressions should be clear in meaning, and interpretations and themes should be used for clarification. Prose and poetry examples that are used should be clear and relevant.

19. Make use of music, the playing of instruments, dancing with joy, and hand movements to make statements and to entertain the crowd. Use short stories and various poetic styles during the narrations.
20. Keep in mind the satisfaction of many people and speak about that which is agreeable to the majority. Contradictions and points of contention should not be brought into the narration.
21. Don't speak in such a way that is boring to the people. Speak in a manner which will touch their hearts. In that way, people will naturally speak about you with praise.
22. Experiment with the combination of Devotion (Bhakti), Knowledge (Jnana) and Detachment (Vairagya) in your spiritual practice. With proper reflection you can cure the sickness of worldliness.
23. One's behavior in life should be in accordance with one's speech. In this way, one naturally acquires the qualities of leadership.
24. Having yogic knowledge without any sense of propriety is a sign of the disease of selfish desires. People in the company of such a person will surely suffer from misfortune.
25. Do not do anything that will cause other people trouble. A great leader contemplates on the all-powerful Lord Rama in the heart.
26. People like the one who has a detached attitude. Give explanations and narrations about God and spread the word of Rama throughout the universe and beyond.
27. When there is a great leader present whose presence is accompanied by music and singing, how can the gathering fall short of glory? People will cluster around him like the stars in the galaxies in the sky.
28. Where there is a lack of higher intellect, everything is disorganized. Without intellect how can there be any wisdom?
29. Making use of higher intellect, understand the Reality. Become more vast than the universe by way of your understanding. How can anyone bring in faulty pettiness there?
30. Here the doubt is removed, the intellect begins making efforts, and some good hope increases within the mind.

Thus in Shri Dasbodh, a dialogue between the Guru and disciple, Sub-Chapter 9 of Chapter 12, named "The Teaching About Effort" is concluded.

Chapter: 12, Sub-Chapter: 10

Narration About the Best Person

|| ShriRam ||

1. One should eat to satisfy one's hunger and whatever food is left over should be distributed. Letting food go to waste is not proper.
2. The same applies when one gets satisfied with Knowledge. The Knowledge must be spoken about to the people. One who can swim should not allow a drowning person to drown.
3. One must develop the best qualities in oneself first, and then speak about those qualities to many people. One who speaks without first practicing speaks falsely.

4. Do your morning bathing, some routine of worship, meditate on and chant the name of God, and listen to stories and explanations about God.
5. Use the body for helping others. Be useful in helping the work of many people to get accomplished, and help to ensure that nobody suffers from any shortages.
6. Understand the troubles and oppression of others and do what you can to help them. Speak in a soft manner to everyone.
7. Empathize with the sorrow and grief of others as well as sharing in their joy and happiness. Bring people together in friendliness with good and kind words.
8. Pardon the mistakes and faults of many people and help them to do their work and accomplish their goals. Bring strangers near and make them feel welcome.
9. Understand the minds of others and behave appropriately. Examine and appreciate people in many various ways.
10. Speak precisely and to the point, and give prompt replies to questions. Maintain a forgiving nature and don't become angry with others.
11. Give up laziness entirely making many kinds of efforts. Don't speak with envy or be jealous of anyone.
12. Offer the best things to others. Speak carefully, wisely selecting your words, and be attentive to leading the family life with care.
13. Remember that one day the body is going to die and be consistent in your devotion to God. In this way your fame will live on after the body is gone.
14. One who lives in a disciplined manner becomes known to many people and is well respected. Such a person does not feel that there is anything lacking.
15. A person with such special and best qualities as these, is called a great person. The Lord of the Universe is pleased with the worship of such a person.
16. Even if people insult and humiliate him, he does not allow his peace to become disturbed. Such a person who can get along even with villainous people is truly a blessed sage.
17. One who is adorned with the best qualities and is radiant with Knowledge and desirelessness is considered to be a great person on this earth.
18. Do hard work yourself and tolerate the faults and suffering of many people. With your hard work, you will leave behind fame in many ways.
19. If you only run after fame, there will not be happiness in life, and if you only run after pleasures, there will be no fame. Without proper thoughtfulness, there is no satisfaction to be found anywhere.
20. Do not hurt the feelings or minds of others. Mistakes should not be committed with regard to this. One who is forgiving does not lose the admiration of others.
21. Work should be carried out without discrimination as to whether it is one's own or someone else's work. It is not proper to try to escape or avoid following through on one's own duties.
22. Saying nice things makes others feel happy, this is experienced by everyone. Speak to others as you would like to be spoken to.
23. Harsh words make other feel bad, this is also experienced by everyone. So, there is no excuse for speaking harshly to others.
24. If you pinch yourself you feel the pain of it. Understand from your own experience that others feel pain as well, and care about the pain of others.
25. Speech that is hurtful and causes pain to others is immoral, and at times my cause injury to oneself as well.

26. For whatever is sown, the crop grows accordingly. For whatever is spoken, the reply also comes back accordingly. For what reason then should anyone speak in a harsh manner?
27. Make many people happy with the wealth and substance of your own Being. To give people trouble is to act in a demon-like manner.
28. Hypocrisy, disrespect, pride, anger, and harsh speech are signs of ignorance that are described in the *Bhagavad Gita*.
29. Many people move about looking for one who is adorned with the best qualities. Such a person is alone considered to be the "greatest person."
30. Having knowledge without the corresponding appropriate behavior is comparable to the vomit of a dog. Good people never even pay attention to it.
31. People seek out a great person that has heartfelt devotion and upholds the best qualities with respect.
32. Such a one with the greatest of experience should organize a group of devotional people and commune in oneness with the God of gods.
33. If such a one dies suddenly, who will carry on the devotional practices and worship? For this reason, involve many people in devotional worship.
34. My own resolution is such as not to ask for anything from the disciple, but only to ask him to continue to worship God after my passing.
35. For this reason there should be a group of devotees and regular festivals of devotional activity so that devotees will continue to be in communion with the God of gods.
36. To organize gatherings of devotees two main qualities are required. The listeners are asked to listen with alertness of mind.
37. The first quality is that one must have the power to teach in such a clear manner as to make many people turn towards devotion. The second quality is that one must be able to please others and win over the hearts and minds of many people.
38. The best qualities have now been described, and one who has them is recognized as someone who is authoritative. The power of such a great person's spiritual instruction continues on long after his passing away.
39. One whose behavior is in accordance with his speech, and who does himself what he tells others to do, is respected by the people, and they consider what he says to be true.
40. People will not follow and accept what they do not feel is acceptable. Everyone is alone with oneself among so many people in the world.
41. Therefore, be with people and bring people along with you, teaching them step by step, gradually taking them to the end with discrimination.
42. However, this work is only for a patient and thoughtful person who uses the power of discrimination. Only he can do it correctly. Others are confused with delusion and will begin to quarrel among themselves.
43. One who quarrels with many people will find himself alone, like a leader without an army. Therefore, it is important to please many people.

Thus in Shri Dasbodh, a dialogue between the Guru and disciple, Sub-Chapter 1 of Chapter 12, named "Explanation About the Best Person" is concluded.

Chapter 13. Name and Form

Chapter: 13, Sub-Chapter: 1

Discrimination of Self and Non-Self

|| ShriRam ||

1. One must must discern the difference between Self and non-self using discrimination. Analyze this properly and firmly retain the understanding of this analysis in your being.
2. Analyze what is Self and what is non-self. The explanation of this will now be given. Please listen attentively.
3. The four categories of living things, the four types of speech, and the 8.4 million species of living beings as described in the ancient mythological books (*Puranas*) are in existence now.
4. There are many types of bodies that are seen in the universe. Who is the Self in them? This must be determined with certainty.
5. It is the Self that sees through the eyes, listens through the ears, and tastes with the tongue. This is evident right now.
6. The Self smells through the nose, touches with the body, speaks with the voice, and understands the words.
7. Alert and moving, the Self is active everywhere. It is the Self alone that is the activity of the sense organs.
8. It is the Self that moves the legs, moves the hands, raises and lowers the eyebrows, and blinks the eyes, and it is the Self that speaks, giving indications about itself.
9. It is the Self alone that is courageous or shy, and that scratches, coughs, vomits, spits, drinks and eats.
10. It is the Self the controls the body. It makes the body expel urine and feces. It is the Self that establishes mental states and dispositions as well as exists without mental states and activity. It is the Self alone that both explains and interprets.
11. It is the Self that listens, sees, smells, tastes and recognizes many things, as well as feels contentment and fear.
12. It is the Self that knows happiness, humor, boredom, worry, the body, and the identification with body, which is like a fleeting shadow. It is the Self alone that suffers the many various ailments that afflict living beings.
13. It is the Self that holds a liking for objects, and that acts in good ways and bad ways among the people. It is the Self that protects one's own possessions and people and beats or kills others who are not one's own.
14. When there is war, it is the Self that acts through all of the bodies on both sides, killing and being killed.
15. It is the Self that comes, goes, resides, and acts in all bodies, and it is the Self alone that laughs, cries, repents, and becomes powerful or unfortunate, depending on one's affairs and corresponding activities.
16. It is the Self alone that is cowardly, strong, educated, bold, just, and arrogant.
17. It is the Self that is patient and courageous, generous as well as miserly, stupid as well as clever, and out of control as well as tolerant.

18. It is the Self that is joyful in both knowledge and ignorance, and that pervades everywhere.
19. It is the Self that sleeps, wakes up, sits, walks, runs, makes others run, swings, carries weight, and establishes relationships with relatives and friends.
20. It is the Self that reads religious texts and explains their meanings. It keeps the beat, carries the rhythm, and begins to sing. And it is the Self alone that indulges in arguments unnecessarily.
21. If the Self is not active in the body, then that body is but a dead corpse in this world of animate and inanimate things. It is in connection with the body that the Self does all things.
22. If the body is without the Self, or the Self is without the body, both are basically of no use. Therefore the union of the body with the Self has come into existence.
23. The body is ephemeral and the Self is eternal. This is seen by utilizing the subtle activity of discriminating between what is Eternal and what is ephemeral. This is understood by the Jnanis.
24. The one who possesses or wields the body is called the jiva, or individual. The one who possesses the universal body is called the "Light of the Universe," or Shiva. It is the Self, the Supreme Lord (Ishwara), that wields all four bodies of the jiva and the four bodies of Shiva.
25. That one God, Ishwara, is beyond the three gunas, and is in the primal form of God that is half masculine and half feminine. From there the entire expanse of the visible world has come into existence.
26. Careful investigation and clear seeing is required here. There is nothing that can really be considered to be masculine or feminine, only something that is in the form of subtle movement is actually experienced.
27. From the beginning to the end, from Brahma and the other gods to the ant and human beings, this Self, Ishwara, is the wielder of all bodies. The wise understand this by utilizing the power of discrimination to discern the Eternal from the ephemeral.
28. That which is gross (the body and physical world) disappears quickly while that which is subtle (Consciousness) has a longer lasting duration. However, there is an even more subtle discrimination between the ephemeral and Eternal which will be explained later on.
29. Going beyond the gross and the subtle bodies, the causal and the great causal bodies (the four bodies of the jiva) must be left behind. Going further, the gross visible world and the subtle body of the universe must also be dissolved with the power of discrimination.
30. Beyond that, after leaving behind the causal body of the universe, one's state becomes established in the fourth body of the universe which is the Primal Illusion. In order to become withdrawn from that state, to become stateless, please listen to the explanation that follows.
31. The discernment between the Self and non-self has now been explained, and the Self, as movement, or the active principle, has been experienced. In the next sub-chapter, the investigation into Essence and non-essence (Saraasara) will be explained.

Thus in Shri Dasbodh, a dialogue between the Guru and disciple, Sub-Chapter 1 of Chapter 13, named "Discrimination Between Self and Non-Self" is concluded.

Chapter: 13, Sub-Chapter: 2

Explanation of Essence and Non-Essence

|| ShriRam ||

1. Listen to the explanation about the discrimination between Essence and non-essence. In this vast expanse of the structure of the universal appearance one must thoughtfully recognize what is Essence and what is non-essence using the power of discrimination.
2. Whatever is visible will be destroyed, and whatever comes will go. That which is truly substantial is eternally present, and is Essence.
3. Previously, the discrimination between the Self and non-self was explained. Upon recognizing the non-self, it must be given up. What remains is the Self, the knower that is tied to the fundamental Primal Illusion.
4. It is important that the listeners see properly through the investigation into Essence and non-essence that this root identity which remains is still a state (vritti) which should should disappear into statelessness (nivritti).
5. The discrimination between the permanent and impermanent has been done, and the Self that is permanent has been determined. However, in that, there still persists a subtle concept of being formless.
6. That notion is itself a subtle movement, while That which is attributeless is unmoving. Here, by investigation into Essence and non-essence it is seen that whatever is moving has a coming and a going.
7. See with certainty that whatever moves is the moving, and That which does not move is the unmoving. The moving appears and disappears in That which is eternally unmoving.
8. Knowledge and devotion to God are one. The people of the world are uplifted by the adoration of God.
9. See that God is the seer, the witness, the fullness of Knowledge, and the power that is the Life-Energy. God is Knowledge itself.
10. That Knowledge (Jnana) gets transformed into Supreme Knowledge (Vijnana). If you search for opinions, you will find many. All of those opinions are of the nature of movement and are destined to disappear.
11. If one has any doubt in the mind as to whether or not the perishable is destined to be destroyed, then that person is not authoritative in Self-Knowledge.
12. If one has a firm conviction regarding the Eternal and ephemeral yet still continues to harbor doubts, it is said that such a one is swept away in the great mirage of Illusion.
13. That which is Eternal is indestructible and all-pervasive, spread out everywhere. It is changeless, and in it there is no place for any desire or any doubt about its Reality.
14. That dense Reality is unmoving, steady and uninterrupted, from the beginning, throughout the duration, and at the end of everything. It is eternally as it is.
15. Upon consideration it can be compared to the sky, but it is more dense and subtle than the sky. It is unseen and never tainted by anything, and it is never in contact with the world.

16. The distinction between seeing with the physical eyes and with the eye of Knowledge is a primary premise contained in the *Vedas*, however That which is without attributes is imperceptible and cannot be seen.
17. Without giving up all identification and the attachment to everything, the Absolute Reality cannot be realized. Only by giving up all attachment is the essence of silence seen.
18. Everything that passes away entirely passes away, and everything that is moving disappears. What remains is the unmoving Parabrahman that is the Essence.
19. The eighth body is the Primal Illusion (Moolamaya). The sages benevolently tell us to reject the eight bodies and let them pass away.
20. The meaning behind the statements "Soham" (I am He), "Hansa" (He is I), and "Tatvamasi" (You are That) is that you are Brahman. With investigation and subtle thoughtfulness one easily arrives at That state.
21. In this way, by investigation into Essence and non-essence, the aspirant becomes void of all states and remains as Brahman.
22. That attributeless Parabrahman never gets hot or cold, bright or dark, or polluted or clarified.
23. That which cannot be seen or perceived, is not born or destroyed, and does not come and go, is Parabrahman.
24. That which never gets wet and never dries up, and which cannot be diminished or taken away by anyone is Parabrahman.
25. Blessed is the sage who is established as that formlessness which is facing in all directions, and to where all visible appearances disappear.
26. Recognize that only the one who is stateless, and beyond all concepts and imagination, is the true tranquil saint (santa). Other than that, everything else is all tempestuous mind (asanta) in the form of delusion.
27. Only one who has given up the false and accepted the True can be called one who has investigated thoroughly and completely. Give up non-essence (all transient appearances) and accept the Essence that is Parabrahman.
28. As one's knowing becomes more and more subtle, one's knowledge becomes united in one's own true state which is one with formlessness. The devotion of self-surrender is like this.
29. Devotion and liberation must be spoken about using words, but one must arrive at the meaning of what is being indicated and become one with it by using proper analysis. With proper analysis, even the intention or desire for liberation disappears, and there is only the Oneness of the Self.
30. Being, Pure Awareness, and Oneness are all one's own form. When all of the elements, which are non-essence, have been left to disappear, what remains is Essence and there is the realization that one's true identity is formless.

Thus in Shri Dasbodh, a dialogue between the Guru and disciple, Sub-Chapter 4 of Chapter 13, named "Explanation of Essence and Non-essence" is concluded.

Chapter: 13, Sub-Chapter: 3

Explanation of Creation

|| ShriRam ||

1. Brahman is dense and empty at the same time. It is more expansive than space. It is pure and unmoving without any modification.
2. Brahman remained like this for a long time, then the creation of the world arose. Listen with alertness to the root of the world.
3. In the unmoving Parabrahman there arose a desire which is of the nature of movement. That alone is what is called the "Primal God" (Adinarayana).
4. The "Lord of the Universe" (Jagadishwara) is the Primal Illusion (Moolamaya) itself. He is also called "God with Six Qualities." Investigate thoughtfully and see that this is the eightfold creation.
5. After that, there arises the turbulence of the subtle gunas (gunakshobini), and from that the three gunas (rajas, tamas, sattva) took tangible form. Understand that AUM (OM) also originates from there.
6. The three sounds A, U, and M together form the AUM, and from there the expanse of the five elements has spread out everywhere.
7. The Inner-Self is called space, and in it, arose the wind. From the wind, light was created.
8. From the friction of the streams of wind, the heat of light (fire) created the sun.
9. From the coolness of the streams of wind, water was created. When that water became condensed and solid, earth was created.
10. Contained within the earth are an endless number of seeds, and when earth and water came together many sprouts were germinated.
11. On the earth there are many vines with leaves and flowers of many colors, and from them came the various fruits with many different flavors and smells.
12. From these leaves, flowers, fruits, and roots of many colors, tastes and flavors, came many juices and grains and various types of food.
13. From this food, semen was created, and from semen living beings were created. This is the observable experience of creation.
14. The four streams of species of living beings are born from eggs, the womb, a combination of heat and moisture, and seeds, but all have their origin in water and earth. This is the wondrous play of creation.
15. In this creation there are the four categories of living beings, the four types of speech, the 8.4 million species, the three worlds, the individual body, and the universal body.
16. The visible creation is the eightfold manifestation (three gunas and five elements), and all living beings are born from water. If there is no water, all living beings will die.
17. This talk is not based on imagination. One can gain the actual experience of this. Moreover, this is supported by statements in the *Vedas*, ancient scriptures (*Shastras*), and mythological books (*Puranas*). Gain the experience of this for yourself.
18. That which cannot be verified in one's own experience is merely speculation and guesswork, and should not be accepted. Without verification in actual experience, people do not function properly in life.

19. Whether one is on the path of activity, or the path of withdrawal from activity in life, there must be actual experience. Without experience, there is a lack proper discrimination and one is left only with guesswork and imagination.
20. Like this, the investigation into the functioning of the visible world is told in short. Now, listen to the process of the destruction of the visible expanse of creation.
21. From the beginning until the end, it is only the Self, Lord Rama, that does everything. It is also He who gives the correct explanations.
22. In the next sub-chapter the destruction is explained. The listeners are asked to listen attentively. This sub-chapter is completed here.

Thus in Shri Dasbodh, a dialogue between the Guru and disciple, Sub-Chapter 3 of Chapter 13, named "Explanation of Creation" is concluded.

Chapter: 13, Sub-Chapter: 4

The Dissolution

|| ShriRam ||

1. The earth and the five elements will come to an end at the final dissolution of the epoch (kalpa). This is the description that is elaborately explained in ancient scriptures.
2. There will be a lack of rain for a hundred years and creation will be burned up. The mountains and the surface of the land will be broken and cracked.
3. The sun will blaze twelve times brighter, and from its rays, flames will emerge that will scorch the earth for a hundred years.
4. The earth will become red hot. The flames will burn the divine serpent Shesha, and in his torment from being scorched he will vomit poison everywhere.
5. From that poison great flames will emanate which will burn the netherworlds and turn them to ashes.
6. Then the five elements will become greatly agitated and destructive winds of annihilation will spread the destructive fire, engulfing everything in all directions.
7. Then, the eleven destructive forces are whipped up into a furious frenzy and the fire from the twelve times increase of brightness of the sun will scorch everything entirely to destruction.
8. The wind and lightening will lash down and the hardness of the earth will crumble and get spread out in all directions.
9. Where will the great mountain Meru be, and who will care for whom? The sun, moon, and the stars all turn into dust.
10. The earth turns into powder and is consumed in the blazing fire, and the universe gets engulfed in an instant like it was in a huge furnace.
11. After the incineration, ashes are spread everywhere, and then in a great deluge, the earth becomes dissolved in water.
12. In the same way that baked lime dissolves in water, the earth will have no stability to hold itself together and the powdered ash will become dissolved in the water.
13. The forms of the serpent, tortoise and bear all disappear, and with them the support of the earth vanishes. Losing its hardness it becomes one with the water.

14. Then, huge clouds of destruction come together making a horrendous uproar of sound and violent thunder. Lightening strikes continuously with tremendous noise.
15. Hailstones, huge like mountains, fall down, and the wind is so powerful that even those mountains are blown away. The pitch-black darkness is so thick that there is no simile that can be used.
16. The ocean and the rivers merge into one and appear as if pouring down from the sky. The combining of all the waters is so great that the deluge of water covers everywhere.
17. Huge fish, tortoises and serpents as big as mountains fall everywhere and with a huge roar, all of the water gets mixed together.
18. The seven seas disappear into the surrounding oceans, and the oceans open up their boundaries overflowing with water everywhere. Then, the great blaze of fire becomes extremely turbulent and flares up in all directions.
19. The entire universe becomes like a great burning sphere of fire that burns up all of the water. It is truly a wondrous thing to see such a thing happen to the water.
20. With that, the water becomes completely evaporated, and the fire becomes unimaginably disastrous. Then, the fire gets extinguished by the great tempest of destructive wind.
21. Like a lamp that is extinguished with the movement of air, in the same way, the destructive fire is extinguished by the wind. Then the wind becomes so vast, it is beyond all imagination.
22. The wind is enormous, but it gets swallowed up and is dissipated into limitless empty space. The vast expanse of the five elements has come to an end.
23. The vast manifest creation and the Primal Illusion forget themselves thus dissolving the Great Causal Body. There is no place for even a tiny speck of anything to remain.
24. The visible universe disappears by this great dissolution. All that is inert as well as all that moves disappears. What remains is only the indestructible Absolute Reality, Parabrahman.

Thus in Shri Dasbodh, a dialogue between the Guru and disciple, Sub-Chapter 4 of Chapter 13, named "The Dissolution" is concluded.

Chapter: 13, Sub-Chapter: 5

A Story

|| ShriRam ||

1. Two people were moving around the world without any attachment to anything. To pass the time, one of them began to tell a story.
2. The listener says to the speaker, "Please tell a good story." The speaker said to the listener, "Please listen attentively."
3. There was a man and a woman who loved each other so much that they were only One and there was no difference between them. (Purusha and Prakriti.)

4. After some time passed, it happened that a son was born to them. He was a very good son and he was always engaged in doing all kinds of activities. (The son is Vishnu.)
5. After some time, a son was born to him. This son was much more active than his father. He was more ambitious and active than his father, but was half as wise. (The grandson is Brahma.)
6. This grandson was constantly busy and occupied in activity. He gave birth to many daughters and sons and produced many offspring in various ways.
7. His eldest son, the great grandson, was ignorant and angry. If anybody made a mistake, he would kill them. (Great grandson is Rudra; destructive aspect of Shiva.)
8. The original father sat quietly inactive (Purusha), while his son (Vishnu) was very active. This son was all-knowing and very good natured.
9. The grandson (Brahma) had half of the knowledge of his father. The great grandson (Shiva) did not know anything at all. He was extremely hot tempered, and would bring about destruction as a result of even the smallest mistake.
10. The son (Vishnu) protects everyone. The grandson (Brahma) continuously adds to the number of people, and the great grandson (Shiva) destroys suddenly if any mistake is made.
11. The family (8.4 million species of living beings) proliferated greatly and became very expansive. In this way, a lot of time passed away happily.
12. The family expanded to such an extent that it could not be measured. As time passed, no one in the family respected the elders (the grandfather and grandmother, and the father, son, and grandson.), and there was a lot of doubt and suspicion in the minds of everyone.
13. There were many family disputes and as a result there was a great deal of destruction taking place. Anarchy took over, and there was disagreement and a falling out among all of the elders.
14. Due to excessive ignorance everywhere, everyone was destroyed.
15. The father, son, grandson and great grandson were all annihilated. Nothing remained of the daughters and sons, and their intentions and life stories all became totally extinct.
16. The one who understands this story is sure to be liberated from the birth cycle, and both the listener and the speaker become blessed by the experience.
17. This is truly an unsurpassed story which takes place many times. After the narration of the story, both the speaker and the listener became silent.
18. Now that this story is over it should be explained in such a way that its meaning makes an impression within your mind.
19. What has been remembered has been told. If there are some errors or gaps, the listeners are asked to pardon any shortcomings.
20. Ramdas says that this story goes on forever. Those who listen to it using proper discrimination will uplift the world.
21. The explanation of the signs of the upliftment of the world must now be given. The discourse that indicates selecting the Essence is what uplifts the world.
22. By such discourse, the explanation of experience should be understood, and many puzzling questions about Reality should be resolved. As one's understanding becomes greater and greater, one become doubtless.
23. Upon analyzing the eight bodies, one naturally becomes free of doubt. By continuously listening to explanations one remains content.

24. Where there is confusion about the various principles (mainly the five elements, the three gunas, the elements of the subtle body, etc.) how can there be contentment and peace? For this reason, one should stay away from the confusion of various arguments.
25. One must minutely analyze subtle dialogue. The listeners are asked to listen attentively to the summary of the teaching in the next sub-chapter.

Thus in Shri Dasbodh, a dialogue between the Guru and disciple, Sub-Chapter 5 of Chapter 13, named "A Story" is concluded.

Chapter: 13, Sub-Chapter: 6

Summary of the Teaching

|| ShriRam ||

1. Learn the names of the five elements by heart, and then gain an understanding of their forms by direct experience.
2. Analyze them and discover what is Eternal and what is ephemeral. This analysis must be done through observation and understood in one's actual experience.
3. The investigation into the five elements is done by understanding their names and forms, and sifting the Essence from the non-essential. This is being told to you with a firm purpose. Please listen attentively.
4. Earth, Water, Light (Fire), Air (Wind), and Sky (Space) are the names that are commonly used for the five elements. Now, listen to the description of their forms with confidence.
5. Earth means the earth that supports us. Water means the water we drink, water from rain, rivers, seas, etc. Light means fire, the sun, and all luminous objects.
6. Air means the wind. Sky means vast empty space. Now, inquire into your own mind as to what is permanent.
7. Just as one can know the condition of the entire pot of rice by testing just one cooked grain, similarly, with a small amount of experience a great deal can be understood.
8. With regard to earth, many things get constructed and destroyed. It is the actual experience of everyone that many structures are created and then disappear in the visible world.
9. Therefore, it can be seen that whatever gets constructed gets destroyed. It can also be seen that water gets dried up, light appears and disappears, and the movement of the wind becomes still.
10. It can also be seen that space is only a name, and that upon investigation, the name does not remain. Thus, it can be recognized that whatever is made up of the five elements will not remain permanently.
11. The entire expanse of the five elements is such that it is definite that it will all perish. Understand that only the formless Self is eternal and real.
12. That Self cannot be comprehended by anybody. Without Knowledge (Jnana) it cannot be realized. Therefore, ask the saints about it.

13. When asking the saints, they say that it is indestructible. One cannot speak of birth and death in regard to the Self.
14. Forms appear in the formless, and the formless appears in the forms. The formless and forms can be recognized using the power of discrimination.
15. Understand that the formless is Eternal and forms are ephemeral. This is called the investigation into the Eternal and the ephemeral.
16. The non-essential appears in the Essence, and the Essence is in the non-essential. Investigate the difference between Essence and the non-essential and see the results of this type of investigation.
17. All that is made up of five elements is illusory, but they appear in a myriad of forms. The Self is the only one thing that exists permeating everything.
18. Sky (space) is present in all of the other four elements. In the same way, the Reality is present permeating the sky. Observing minutely, it can be seen that the sky and Reality are inseparable.
19. Sky is known as sky because it has attributes, or certain properties (which are destructible). Without those attributes there is no appearance of sky as such. That which has no appearance is indestructible.
20. Now, let this analysis be enough. That which does not get destroyed must be discerned and seen with thoughtful investigation.
21. The Supreme Self, Paramatman, is formless. This is understood through investigation into Essence. This must be seen for oneself.
22. When the body comes to an end, the wind element leaves it. This can be understood to be true right now by trying to hold your breath.
23. When the breathing is finished, the body falls dead and is called a corpse which has no capacity to do anything.
24. Without the body, the wind cannot do any actions, and without the wind the body cannot perform any functions. With thoughtfulness it can be seen that either one cannot do anything without the other.
25. With the common way of seeing, there is the appearance of what we call the human body. By utilizing proper thought, it is seen that there is nothing really making up a body. Recognize this to be the sign of non-dual devotion.
26. If one says that "I am the doer," then everything should happen according to one's desire, but everything does not happen according to our desires. This being the case, it is proven that the statement "I am the doer" is false.
27. If oneself is not the doer, then who is the enjoyer? This can only be understood by correct thoughtfulness. Without thoughtfulness this will not be known.
28. Thoughtfulness and thoughtlessness are like light and darkness. That which is changing is not the same as the changeless.
29. Where there is no thoughtful analysis, understanding is not possible. The Truth cannot be know through guesswork and speculation.
30. That which is understood through direct experience is correct. Without actual experience one cannot have correct understanding. How can one who is blind from birth evaluate the value of various gemstones?
31. Therefore, blessed is the knowledgeable person who is one with the attributeless. Such a one is recognized by his self-surrender and is truly regarded as "Supreme Being" (ParamaPurusha) itself.

Thus in Shri Dasbodh, a dialogue between the Guru and disciple, Sub-Chapter 6 of Chapter 13, named "Summary of the Teaching" is concluded.

Chapter: 13, Sub-Chapter: 7

Explanation of Experience

|| ShriRam ||

1. The simile of the sky is used for That which is pure, still, and which has no appearance. Sky means expansive space which pervades everywhere.
2. First there is space, and then comes the object. Seeing with experience means seeing correctly. Without actual experience, nothing is understood correctly.
3. Brahman means that which is unmoving. Self (Atman) means that which is moving. This can be understood by using the simile of the wind.
4. The simile of the space in a pot is used for Brahman, and the simile for the reflection of an object on the water in the pot is used for the Self. When thinking this over, it can be seen that the two are very different.
5. The past means that which has already happened. Whatever has happened is over. Understand that movement comes and goes like this.
6. Ignorance is inert like camphor, and the Self is moving like fire. Both the camphor and the fire disappear when the burning is exhausted.
7. Brahman, like the sky is unmoving. The Self, like the wind, is moving. Upon examination it can be seen whether this is true or false.
8. The gross inert objects are many, but the Self is one. This is seen with the discrimination between the Self and non-self. One who moves everything in the universe is called the "Lord of the Universe" (Jagadisha).
9. The Self kindles the movement of the gross inanimate objects. The one that dwells in all is the Self. The Self together with the "all" is of the nature of moment. It is not the unmoving.
10. Parabrahman is still and unmoving and in it there is no visible Illusion. That pure Brahman is as it is, without Illusion.
11. First, one must discriminate between Self and non-self. Then must follow the investigation into Essence and non-essence. With investigation and subtle thought the visible creation is dissolved.
12. With thought the visible creation gets dissolved, and visible beings disappear. The Inner-Self merges with the attributeless by listening to spiritual discourses.
13. If the attention is directed towards the subtle Inner-Self, the Self is known to be subtle. If the focus is downward towards the gross world, the Self is thought to be in and of the world.
14. The Self becomes like whatever is given significance or meaning, and goes where it is directed. With speculation and guesswork one becomes filled with doubts.
15. If one gives no significance to doubts, then the Self becomes doubtless, and if one gives significance to doubts, then the Self is doubtful.
16. For example, if the speaker's speech is rich with meaning and subtle significance, the listener's mind becomes one with its meaning. If the speech is frivolous, everything becomes frivolous.
17. It is similar to the chameleon that changes its color according to its environment. Seeing this, select the best path, and hold to it.
18. If one goes on talking about the best food, the mind takes the form of that food. If one goes on describing the beauty of a woman then the mind gets seated there.

19. The descriptions of objects can be told in many ways. One must have correct inward realization as to whether they really exist or not.
20. Whatever is seen and heard, that image gets firmly fixed in the mind. The wise examine and verify what is beneficial and what is not.
21. Therefore, giving up everything, search out the one God. Only then does the "essential thing" come to be known to some extent.
22. God has created many pleasures, but focusing on them, people have forgotten God and continue on like that their entire life.
23. God has said, "Drop everything and seek Me." But people have not accepted these words of God.
24. Therefore they suffer from many sorrows and are always troubled. There is desire for happiness in the mind, but it cannot be obtained.
25. The ignorant ones miss the one God who is the source of happiness. Constantly seeking happiness externally, they die, suffering from life's sorrows.
26. The wise do not carry on like this. They do what provides true happiness by searching for God beyond the appearance of the universe.
27. When one reaches the one main God, nothing is lacking in him. Foolish people give up utilizing the power of discrimination.
28. The fruit of discernment and thoughtfulness is happiness, while the fruit of thoughtlessness is sorrow. Selecting between these two, one should do what is beneficial for oneself.
29. Recognize who is the doer. This is called thoughtfulness. Giving up the utilization of the power of discrimination one becomes sorrowful.
30. Now, let this be enough of this talk. Recognize the doer. The wise one will not miss what is good for oneself.

Thus in Shri Dasbodh, a dialogue between the Guru and disciple, Sub-Chapter 7 of Chapter 13, named "Explanation of Experience" is concluded.

Chapter: 13, Sub-Chapter: 8

Explanation of the Doer

|| ShriRam ||

1. The listener asks the speaker, "Who is the doer? Who created the visible world and the universe? Please give a definitive answer."
2. Then many knowledgeable people in the gathering began speaking one after another. The listeners are respectfully asked to listen to what they had to say.
3. Some said, "God is the doer," and some said, "Who is God?" Then everyone went on expressing their own opinion.
4. Everyone considered their own beliefs to be superior, and according to their own feelings they expressed their opinions as to what beliefs were the best, medium, or lowly.

(Note: Stanzas 5 through 17 list various Hindu Gods as being the doer according to various opinions.)

5. Some say that Lord Ganesha is the doer and some say that the Goddess Saraswati does everything.
6. Some say that the doer is God Bhairav. Some say it is Khanderav, some say it is God Beeradev, and some say Goddess Bhagwati.
7. Some say it is Lord Narasimha, some say it is Banashankari, and some say it is Lord Narayana who does everything.
8. Some say it is Lord Rama who is the doer. Some say it is Lord Krishna, and some say it is the God Keshavaraj who is the doer.
9. Some say that it is Panduranga (Vithalla), some say it is Shrirang (Lord Krishna), and some say it is the God of Spirits who does everything.
10. Some say that it is the spirit of a brahmin who is the doer. Some say it is the Sun that is the doer, and some say it is Fire that is the doer of everything.
11. Some say it is the Goddess Laxmi, the goddess of wealth, who does everything. Some say it is Hanuman, and some say it is the Earth that does all.
12. Some way it is the Goddess Tukai, some say Yemai, and some say it is Satvai who does everything.
13. Some say that Bhargava is the doer, some say its Wamana (incarnation of Vishnu) who is the doer, and some say that Paramatman, the Supreme Self is alone the doer of everything.
14. Some say it is Viranna, some say it is Basvanna, and some say it is Revanna who is the doer of everything.
15. Some say it is Ravalya, some say it is Kartika, and some say it is Lord Venkatesha who is the doer of all.
16. Some say that the Guru is the doer, some say that Lord Dattatraya is the doer, and some say it is the Vodhya Jaganath who does everything.
17. Some say that Lord Brahma is the doer, some say that Lord Vishnu is the doer, and some say that it is Lord Shiva that is definitely the doer.
18. Some say it is the rain that is the doer, while some way that it is the wind. Some say that the doer is the attributeless God, who is a non-doer, doing everything.
19. Some say that it is the power of Illusion that does everything. Some way it is the individual (Jiva), and some say that everything is done by destiny.
20. Some say that it is one's own efforts and the nature of the mind that does everything, and some say, "Who knows who is the doer?"
21. Like this are some of the various thoughts about the doer. It is like a marketplace filled with many varieties of answers. Now, whose answer is to be considered correct?
22. Whatever God people believe in, they call that God the doer. Like this, the confusion among people never gets diminished.
23. Their minds have formed conclusions and they hold onto them because of pride and never investigate to see what is really true.
24. There are many opinions of many people, but these must be kept aside entirely, otherwise the circus of opinions will overwhelm you and confusion remains. The thought regarding the investigation into the doer will now be given.
25. The listeners are asked to remain alert. Speculation as to who the doer is should definitely be broken. The knowledgeable consider only the understanding that comes through experience to be proof.
26. Whatever is done by the doer all happens after him. Nothing done can be found to exist before the doer.

27. Whatever has been done comes out of the five elements. Even gods like Brahma and others are made up only of the five elements. It is not possible that anything that is made up of the five elements can make the five elements.
28. Separate the five elements and set them aside, and then recognize the doer. The five elements are naturally contained within the doer.
29. That which is attributeless is different from the five elements. There is no doership in it. Who can attach the quality of change to That which is changeless?
30. Activity does not happen in That which is without attributes (nirguna), and attributes (saguna) are included in what has already been created. Now, look with subtle observation to see who the doer is.
31. Who is the doer of this false appearance? Asking this question is not appropriate. Therefore, it is only proper to say that whatever has happened has come up naturally (because of ignorance).
32. Brahman is both with attributes (saguna), and without attributes (nirguna). To what should doership be attached? Analyze the explanation of this and see for yourself.
33. If we say that Brahman with attributes has made the attributes, that is saying that attributes were already created previously, and it is not correct to say that Brahman without attributes is the doer.
34. Here, no doer can be seen. Therefore, on the basis of this experience, one comes to the conclusion that the visible is unreal.
35. If whatever is done is all false, to then talk about who the doer is, is meaningless. The speaker says that this must be seen using the power of discrimination.
36. Seeing this clearly, one gains the experience. Why then would one become confused when this certainty is in one's inner experience?
37. Now, enough of this talk. Only one who uses the power of discrimination will understand what is being spoken about. The primary premise of the *Vedas* must be discarded because what is being indicated here cannot be described with words.
38. At that time, the listener asked the question, "Who is the enjoyer and the sufferer in the body?" The explanation of this will follow in the next sub-chapter.

Thus in Shri Dasbodh, a dialogue between the Guru and disciple, Sub-Chapter 8 of Chapter 13, named "Explanation of the Doer" is concluded.

Chapter: 13, Sub-Chapter: 9

Explanation of the Self

|| ShriRam ||

1. Because of the body, the Self experiences the disturbance of sorrows. The Self lives in association with the body. This is clearly evident.
2. If the body does not eat food, then the Self does not remain with the body. Without the Self there is no Life-Energy in the body.
3. If these are separated from one another, they become useless. Any work that gets accomplished happens because of the two being together.

4. The body by itself has no Life-Energy, and the Self without the body has no capacity to lift any object. One's hunger cannot be satisfied with meals taken in a dream.
5. The Self enters in the dream state while continuing to reside in the body. See the wonder that even while one is asleep, the scratching of the body still happens.
6. The body grows with nutritious food, and with the growth of the body, the thinking capacity grows. Later in life, both become diminished due to old age.
7. The body consumes intoxicating substances, and through its association with the body the Self forgets itself. Forgetting itself, the Self loses its sense of freedom and understanding of what is correct.
8. When the body takes poison, the Self leaves the body in due course. The Self experiences the growth and destruction of the body. This is certain.
9. Because of the identification with the body, the Self experiences growth and destruction, coming and going, and suffering in many various ways.
10. An anthill has hollow tunnels which are passageways for the ants to move around. Understand that the body is similar to this.
11. In the body there is an array of veins and arteries. These blood vessels are hollow tunnels. All throughout the body, it is full of these small and large blood vessels.
12. The living being takes food and water that becomes nutritious fluid which is circulated throughout the body by the wind in the form of the vital breath (prana).
13. Life flows through the veins, and in this way, the wind plays in life. Understand that the Self moves around like the wind.
14. The body has the sensation of thirst. It is the Self that understands this and directs the body to get up, and moves it to walk to the water.
15. The Self makes the body talk and ask for water with words. In this way it can be seen that the Self directs the body to move according to the situation.
16. The Self understands when the body is hungry, and moves it to get up and get food. If it doesn't get food the Self speaks harsh words to others because of hunger.
17. In the body of women the Self says, "I have finished my duties and have changed into suitable clothing for dinner," as it gives strength to the legs and makes the body walk quickly to the dining room.
18. The Self makes the body sit with a plate for meals, and it sees the meal with the eyes and is content. It then proceeds to direct the body to commence eating the meal.
19. Through the hands, the Self lifts the food, and opening wide, it puts the food in the mouth. With the teeth, the Self chews the food again and again as needed.
20. The Self plays in the tongue and gets the nice taste of the food. If there is some piece of hair, or some small twig or stone, the Self moves the body to immediately spit it out.
21. If the food is bland, the Self asks for salt and directs the body to look at the wife angrily speaking harsh words.
22. When tasting sweet things the Self feels happy, and if the food is not sweet, there is the recognition of a feeling of sorrow. When something tastes unpleasant, it is recognized within by the Self.
23. The Self has a liking for tasting many varieties of food, and it selects foods with various flavors. When tasting something spicy or pungent, it moves the body to shake the head and cough.

24. If there is too much pepper put in the food, the Self speaks harsh words of disapproval with the tongue.
25. If the body eats too many sweets prepared in ghee (clarified butter), the Self directs the body to lift a glass and leisurely drink a lot of water.
26. The one who experiences joy and sorrow in the body is the Self. Upon investigation it is seen that without the Self, the body becomes a useless dead corpse.
27. There are an endless number of attitudes of the mind. It is the Self that understands all of those states of mind. In all the three worlds it is the Self that is present within all living beings.
28. In the world, which is the residence of man, the Self is called the "Self of the World" (Jagadatma). In the vast expansive universe, the Self is called the "Universal Self" (Vishvatma). This Self is the Self within all (Sarvatma), which moves all of the many myriad forms.
29. It is the Self that smells, tastes, listens, sees, and recognizes the difference between soft and hard. It is the Self that immediately comes to know what is hot and what is cold.
30. With alertness and interest the Self does many activities, and it is the cleverness of the Self that recognizes cleverness in other people.
31. Aromas are carried along by the wind, but those smells dissipate in due course. And the wind brings in a lot of dust which also goes away.
32. The hot and cold, as well as nice fragrances and stench all ride on the wind. But all of these remain only for a short time and then disappear.
33. Diseases are also carried along by the wind. The spirits move around with the wind, and smoke and fog is carried by the wind.
34. Nothing stays with the wind forever, just as the wind is not sustained in the Self forever. Understand that the swiftness of the Self is much greater than that of the wind.
35. Wind can be blocked by hard substances while the Self permeates all hard substances. If we investigate, it can be seen that the Self cannot be pierced by anything.
36. The wind makes a roaring sound, and the Self does not make any noise. However, one who properly investigates silence can see and understand.
37. When the body is made healthy the Self experiences that, and feels content because of the connection with the body.
38. Many things can be done outside of the body, but the Self does not feel affected by such things. Its desires are satisfied only through the medium of the body.
39. The description of the relationship of the Self with the body has been given in many ways. Without the body, the Self is hindered in its ability to experience.
40. When the Self and the body are united, many things can happen. If the Self is separated from the body, nothing can happen. With the union of the body and the Self, one can know everything about the three worlds by utilizing the power of discrimination.

Thus in Shri Dasbodh, a dialogue between the Guru and disciple, Sub-Chapter 9 of Chapter 13, named "Explanation of the Self" is concluded.

Chapter: 13, Sub-Chapter: 10

The Teaching

|| ShriRam ||

1. There are many types of garlands. There are garlands of leaves, flowers, fruits, seeds and shells that are all held together by thread.
2. There are garlands of crystals, coins, wooden beads, fragrant pastes, gems, knitted work, and long decorative threads of symbolic stones.
3. All of these are held together by the thread. If the thread is not there everything becomes disorganized. Similarly, the Self is interwoven in all beings, but even this simile is not entirely appropriate.
4. The beads are all connected together with the thread. The thread runs through the middle of the beads, but the Self permeates everywhere. This must been seen for oneself.
5. The Self naturally has the quality of being swift. Thread does not know how to animate motion with Life-Energy. Therefore the comparison of the Self with thread does not fit and is not really appropriate.
6. There is water present in many types of vines, and the sugarcane is filled with sweet juice, however, the juice and the fibrous chaff are not the same.
7. The Self is in the body, but the body is not the Self (Atman). Beyond the Self is the Supreme Self, Paramatman. No simile can be given for that unseen Supreme Self.
8. From the king to the pauper there are many types of human beings. How can one put them all into one category and consider them to be the same in their status?
9. There are gods, demons, human beings, lowly people, lower species, villainous beings, and virtuous beings of many varieties.
10. The entire world functions with but a small fraction of the Almighty God. However, each being has different capacity. In the company of one you may become liberated, and with another, be in hell.
11. Sugar and soil are both forms of earth, yet we cannot eat soil. Poison is a form of water, but it is not water for drinking.
12. The Inner-Self is within both the virtuous person and the non-virtuous person, yet the difference between the sage and a hypocrite should not go unnoticed.
13. It is true that the Inner-Self is one, but in practical life, one does not associate with lowly people. How can scholars and mischievous boys be considered to be the same?
14. How can the human beings and donkeys, or royal swans and chickens, or kings and monkeys be considered to be the same?
15. The water of the Ganges, the water from a pond, and the waste water from the gutter are all water, but one cannot drink even a little bit of filthy water.
16. Therefore, behave in a morally pure manner, and on top of that have purity of intellect. Be detached and intelligent.
17. If a coward is given more prominence than a courageous man there will be terrible catastrophe during a time of battle. What will be the outcome if one serves a pauper rather than a rich man?

18. Many things are made from the one water element, but one must look carefully before consuming any liquid concoction. If all liquids were considered to be the same, that would be foolish.
19. Food is formed out of water, and vomit is made out of food, but one cannot make meals of vomit.
20. Similarly, one should give up and forget that which is of a lowly nature, and adopt that which is praiseworthy and hold it dear in the heart. In this way, one should fill the entire earth with one's good name and fame.
21. The best things are liked by the best people, and lowly people do not like them. Therefore, God has made such people unfortunate.
22. Give up negative qualities and keep the best qualities, such as listening to explanations about God and meaningful mythological stories, behaving with good moral conduct, and upholding justice.
23. Conducting oneself with proper discrete behavior, keep all people pleased. Step by step, continue to make them virtuous.
24. Walk with the speed of a child, and speak to the people as if they have the mind of a child and teach them slowly step by step.
25. The most important thing is to please the minds of everyone. This is a sign of true wisdom. Only the wise one knows the ways to please the minds of all. Other people act foolishly.
26. Never say to a foolish person that he is foolish, and do not speak about secrets at any time. Only then does success come to one who is desireless.
27. There are many places and many situations that occur. Outwardly, knowingly act appropriately according to whatever is required to be done. Inwardly, become one with all living beings.
28. If you keep the minds of others pleased, there is naturally a mutual relationship and sense of unity with others. If you hurt the minds of another, then the relationship becomes spoiled.
29. For this reason, one who keeps the minds of others pleased is truly a great spiritual leader (Mahanta). Many people are naturally attracted to such a person.

Thus in Shri Dasbodh, a dialogue between the Guru and disciple, Sub-Chapter 10 of Chapter 13, named "The Teaching" is concluded.

Chapter 14. Constant Meditation

Chapter: 14, Sub-Chapter: 1

Description of Desirelessness

|| ShriRam ||

1. Listen to the teaching about the desireless person, and the tact, intellect and wisdom with which one will always remain content.
2. My simple speech is like an easy mantra that comes from experience and is sure to bring definite results, like a simple medicine.
3. The sharp listeners should consume the strong medicine of my words. With proper effort all negative qualities disappear, and one immediately acquires the best qualities.
4. First, one is cautioned not to take up the difficult task of becoming desireless as it is not for everyone, but if you do, then it shouldn't be given up. If you do give it up, then it is best not to remain in the company of your acquaintances and those people whom know you.
5. Do not keep your eyes constantly looking at women developing a taste and a liking for them in the mind. If your resolve in this does not remain firm, do not stay in those situations and show your face to those people.
6. Do not stay in one place and be under the pressure of obligations to others. Do not look greedily at another's money or woman.
7. Do not swerve from the path of good conduct. Do not take any money offered to you, and try to ensure that no words of blame come to fall on you.
8. However, do not be ashamed to take alms that are offered, but do not accept more than is needed. Do not disclose your identity immediately when asked.
9. Wear proper and clean clothes, not dirty tattered ones. Do not crave eating sweet food. Do not be obstinate or opinionated, and behave appropriately according to the circumstances of the situation.
10. Do not let the mind pine for indulging in sensual pleasures. Do not be troubled with the body's pains and ailments. Do not hold on to great hopes for the future or the desire to live a long life.
11. Do not allow your detachment from the world wane. Do not allow the strength of your courage to falter. With the strength of the power of discrimination do not allow your Knowledge to become dull or rusty.
12. Do not give up praising God with great feeling. Do not give up continuous internal meditation. Do not break the thread of love for the form of God with attributes.
13. Do not hold on to worries in the mind. Do not consider hard work to be sorrowful or distressing. Do not give up your courage in difficult and trying times.
14. Do not feel disheartened when being disrespected or dishonored. Do not feel injured when being badly insulted. If someone constantly derides you with harsh criticism, do not take it to heart, whatever the case may be.
15. Do not worry about or feel any fear of what other people might think of you. If someone tries to ridicule you, do not feel any shame. When someone tries to offend you, do not get offended, simply remain unconcerned and desireless.

16. Do not leave the path of righteousness, and do not argue with villainous people. Do not associate with lowly and evil-minded people.
17. Do not be hot tempered, and if someone tries to provoke you into a quarrel, do not quarrel with them. If someone tries to cause you trouble, do not give up your peaceful state and become disturbed.
18. Do not laugh if you are provoked by vulgar speech. Do not be instigated to speak negatively. Do not harass or torment others from one moment to the next.
19. Do not always wear clothing and adornments of the same style. Move around and do not stay in one place all the time.
20. Do not develop too much intimacy with anyone. Do not delight in taking gifts. Do not sit in meetings longer than necessary.
21. Do not be a slave of physical habits. Do not become reliant on anyone. Do not become stuck in fixed patterns of habit.
22. Do not abandon your daily duties, or your studies and spiritual practice. Do not become dependent on anyone or anything.
23. Do not give up your independence and freedom. Remain without putting any expectations on anyone, and do not become dependent upon others all the time.
24. Do not look at the prosperity of others longing for it. Do not become attached to the pleasure of obtaining possessions. Do not allow the solitude of being alone in your True Form be broken.
25. Do not run around behaving in an uncontrolled manner, and do not be concerned with what other people think about you. Do not become attached to anything at anytime.
26. Do not allow the tradition of your lineage to be broken, and do not allow your connection with it to be lost. Do not leave the path of Knowledge (Jnana) at anytime.
27. Do not give up the path of action, and at the same time do not allow your detachment from action to falter. Do not discontinue spiritual practice or praising God, even for a short time.
28. Do not engage in excessive argument or harbor immoral intentions within. Do not become full of anger or behave improperly.
29. Do not give advice to one who never listens, do not speak about boring things, and do not stay in one place for too long.
30. Do not get involved in too many things, and if you do become involved with something, do not become attached to it and cling to it. Carry out your involvement without becoming entangled in attachments.
31. Do not consider yourself to be superior, and do not be adamant about your importance. Do not desire or expect to be honored from anyone, at any place.
32. Never give up your simplicity or puff yourself up as being great. Do not be attached to any pride about yourself.
33. Do not give advice without proper authority, or force spiritual teaching on anyone whose ears are not open to hear about the spiritual path.
34. Do not give up desirelessness even though it may be hard for you, and do not give up studying diligently. Do not take a harsh stance against anyone.
35. Do not speak harsh words or give difficult tasks to others. Do not give up your patience and encouragement towards others.

36. Do not become attached to anything, and do not speak of doing something without actually doing it. Do not make many demands on disciples for long periods of time.
37. Do not speak arrogantly. Do not constantly be dwelling on the sense organs and their pleasures. Do not get involved with occult powers and take liberties in using them.
38. Do not feel ashamed to do lowly tasks. Do not become intoxicated with riches, and do not get angry because of pride.
39. Do not get puffed up because of some high position or rank. Do not abandon justice and morality, and do not engage in inappropriate behavior.
40. Do not speak without being properly informed or make decisions based upon speculation and imagination. If anyone gives you good advice or criticism, do not foolishly feel hurt or sorrowful.
41. Always remain alert and take a comprehensive view of things. Do not take pleasure in laziness.
42. Do not harbor any doubts in the mind. Do not issue commands out of selfishness, and if some orders must be given, do not give them with selfish intent, placing yourself before others.
43. Do not speak without proper occasion Do not sing the praises of something without having knowledge of it. Do not neglect thoughtfulness by going down the path thoughtlessness.
44. Do not give up helping others, and do not cause harm to others. Do not create doubts in anyone.
45. Do not abandon the understanding that there are things you don't know. Do not move around from place to place giving explanations about God or singing his praises for money.
46. Do not say things that will create doubts. Do not hold on to many firm beliefs. Do not make comments on a book without having the ability to explain what it says.
47. Do not knowingly ask questions with an air of being clever. Do not show pride to anyone by saying that you will give the explanation.
48. Do not have pride in Knowledge. Don't harass anyone unnecessarily or get into many disagreements with anyone.
49. Do not have any attachment to selfish intellect. Do not get involved in too many activities. Do not become a worker in the political field.
50. Do not become overly obligated to anybody. Do not ask for large amounts of alms or charity. Do not advertise your spiritual lineage for the purpose of acquiring alms.
51. Do not act as a middleman in arranging marriages. Do not become a mediator in disputes. Do not become attached to the responsibilities of being a householder.
52. Do not visit a place where there is a big commotion of family life going on. Do not eat unhealthy food. Do not bring a guest when invited to visit someone or have a meal somewhere.
53. There are many rituals and ceremonies performed at the time of someone's death, and various rituals that are performed on death anniversaries. There are ceremonies to ward off the negative effects of the stars, rituals for peace, rituals to celebrate pregnancy and the naming ceremony, and ceremonies for meals after having fasted for many days. There are special meals offered after the completion of vows, and ceremonies for making spiritual offerings.

54. Being desireless, do not go to such events. Do not eat food from there, or go there and act foolishly.
55. Do not go to wedding ceremonies. Do not go around singing the praises of God and giving explanations asking for money to make your living.
56. Do not give up asking for your own alms, but do not depend upon that and make a schedule for eating food at a particular person's house. A desireless person does not go on a pilgrimage at the cost of others.
57. Do not do good actions or become a priest for the purpose of making money. A desireless person does not accept a reward for doing what is right even if it is offered to him.
58. Do not make a monastery anywhere. Even if it is done, do not cling to it. A desireless person does not become the head of the monastery and take up residence there.
59. Being desireless, do everything without getting entangled in it. Promote the path of devotion with the mutual co-operation of others amongst themselves, with your own involvement barely being noticed.
60. Do not remain in a state of not making any efforts towards any work. Do not even look at laziness. As long as there is body, do not become distanced from spiritual worship.
61. Do not get involved in or attached to the causative and operational activities of the body. Do not leave the path of devotion carelessly or apathetically.
62. Do not get involved in an excessive amount of worldly activity, while at the same time do not give up all activity. Do not give up the devotion to God with attributes, but do not worship God with a false sense of separation.
63. Do not run after things for a long time. Do not stay in one place for many years. Do not do engage in excessive hard work, but do not be fraudulently exempt.
64. Do not talk too much, but do not remain always without talking, as that is of no use. Do not eat too much food, but do not fast too much.
65. Do not sleep too much, yet do not go without enough sleep. Do not cling to too much discipline, but don't be undisciplined.
66. Do not stay in a crowded place with many people, yet do not spend too much time retreating to the forest. Do not pamper your body too much, but conversely do not intentionally kill the body.
67. Do not keep the company of many people, and never give up keeping the company of saints. Performing too many rituals and rites is of no use, but improper behavior is equally wrong.
68. Do not become too famous, yet do not become dependent on other people. Too much love and affection is of no use, but being heartless is no good.
69. Do not harbor many doubts. The path of unbridled liberty is of no use. Do not get into excessive spiritual practices, however, remaining without any spiritual activity at all is not proper.
70. Do not enjoy and cherish sensual pleasures too much, but you can't completely abandon sensory experience. Do not be too attached to the body, yet giving it too much trouble is also not right.
71. Do not become addicted to many types of experience, but to have no experience is not useful. Do not talk too much about your inner experience, but to keep totally silent is also not proper.

72. Do not be continuously fascinated with the activity of the mind, but being totally thoughtless is of no use. Do not try to see Reality, but it is not correct to go without seeing it.
73. Reality is beyond the mind and intellect, but without the intellect, there is only the darkness of ignorance. Forget the sense of individual consciousness that is only false ignorance.
74. Do not hold on to the feeling of being knowledgeable, yet to not have any knowledge is of no use at all. Do not try to conceive of That which inconceivable, but to not try to conceive of it is also not correct.
75. Constant remembrance of lingering memories of the visible world is not useful, but completely forgetting the worldly existence is also not correct. Do not indulge in meaningless discussions, but there must be some discussion.
76. Making divisions in the world is not useful, but inter-mixing the castes is not proper. Do not forget your own own duties and role in life (dharma), but do not take pride in it.
77. Do not speak about having many hopes, and do not act without proper discrimination. Do not allow your peace and contentment to be disturbed in any way.
78. Do not write a book that has many errors, but to not write a book is of no use. Do not make many mistakes when reading, yet to go without reading is no good.
79. Being desireless, do not avoid speaking when necessary, and if anyone raises any objections while you are talking, do not get into an argument. Never ridicule or dishonor a listener.
80. If you consistently abide by this teaching faithfully, you will gain contentment and tranquility, as well as acquire the qualities of a spiritual leader without expecting it.

Thus in Shri Dasbodh, a dialogue between the Guru and disciple, Sub-Chapter 1 of Chapter 14, named "The Description of Desirelessness" is concluded.

Chapter: 14, Sub-Chapter: 2

Explanation of Taking Alms

|| ShriRam ||

1. The main practice of a brahmin (priest) is to ask for alms and offer everything to God. The importance and significance of this tradition must be maintained.
2. It is said that one who gets his meals by asking for alms eats as if he has not eaten anything. He remains unaffected by the effects associated with possessing anything.
3. Whether a person is virtuous or not, when one asks for alms and takes his meals in that way, it is like consuming nectar everyday.
4. Such is the significance of the tradition of asking for alms. Begging for alms is acceptable to God. God's greatness is beyond imagination, yet he also asks for alms.
5. Lord Dattatraya, the sage Gorakshanath, and others who were accomplished like them, also asked for alms from the people. By asking for alms the quality of desirelessness is made apparent.
6. One who eats regularly at someone's house on certain days of the week becomes dependent. In the same way, if he takes his meals at one particular house everyday there is no freedom for him.
7. If grains are collected only once every eight days and he stores them to eat throughout the week, this routine soon becomes tiresome, and the person misses out on the newness of every day.
8. Everyday, new and different places should be visited. Only then is asking for alms appreciated and admired by the people.
9. One who is accustomed to the practice of asking for alms does not feel like a stranger at any place. Wherever he goes, that place feels like his own home town.
10. One should not grumble while asking, or feel ashamed to ask for alms. Do not get tired of asking, but keep moving continuously from place to place.
11. When people see someone asking for alms and speaking the praises of God, miracles happen and the people are filled with wonder.
12. Accepting alms is like a wish-fulfilling cow whose milk is not ordinary. The one who rejects begging for alms is unfortunate, even though he may be a monk.
13. Many new acquaintances are made and false beliefs are removed by begging for alms. Although asking for alms seems to be very trivial, all beings see the benefit of giving in charity.
14. Accepting alms means being in a fearless state. By asking for alms one reveals the greatness of humility. One gains freedom and unity with God by accepting alms.
15. There is no hindrance or bondage in begging for alms. One who lives on the alms received is always free. In begging for alms some of the day's time is well spent.
16. Asking for alms is like a divine vine which is always blossoming with fruit. In hard times it proves to be fruitful for the one who begs without the ego associated with being shy or ashamed.
17. There are many countries on the earth, and if one roams around them asking for alms, one will not die of hunger, and he does not become a burden to the people of any one place.

18. The occupations of raising cattle, trading, and farming are respectable ways of living, but begging for alms is more respectable. Therefore, one should not disrespect the bag or bowl at anytime.
19. There is no greater detachment than asking for alms. There is no fortune greater than having such detachment. Not having detachment is being attached to one place, and this is unfortunate.
20. If some small amount of alms is given, be content with that little amount. If a large amount is offered by a householder accept only one handful.
21. Asking for alms should be done joyfully with soft speech and a pleasant demeanor. These are some of the signs of a desireless person.
22. Such is the description of one who begs for alms. I have told them to you in short according to my capacity. Begging for alms wards off problems from calamities which may come in the future.

Thus in Shri Dasbodh, a dialogue between the Guru and disciple, Sub-Chapter 2 of Chapter 14, named "Explanation of Taking Alms" is concluded.

Chapter: 14, Sub-Chapter: 3

The Art of Poetry

|| ShriRam ||

1. Poetry is like a garland of flowers made of meaningful words that have a special fragrance. Like the bees that enjoy the flowers, the saints remain joyful hearing meaningful words.
2. Such a garland is threaded by the inner-mind, then laid as an offering of worship at the feet of Rama, and the continuous sound of AUM (OM) resounds without interruption.
3. Poetry should be composed for the sake of helping others. I will now tell the signs of such poetry.
4. Poetic skill should be developed so that the poetry that is composed draws the listener towards devotion for God, and inspires an increased sense of detachment.
5. If there is only word knowledge without the experience gained from spiritual practice, it will not be considered acceptable by virtuous and wise people. Therefore, please God first by abandoning the attachment to worldliness and objectivity.
6. When God is pleased like this, all of one's speech becomes praiseworthy. Such speech is a called inspired and is a blessing to mankind.
7. There are three types of writings. The first is spontaneous which occurs effortlessly without forethought. The second is based upon memory and what one has learned in the past. The third type of poetry inspired by the blessings of God. These are the three main types of poetry that are being spoken about. Now, I shall briefly describe them.
8. Spontaneous means that whatever surges up and comes into one's mind is boldly expressed in the composition. This is called spontaneous writing.

9. Learned writing is when one recites what one has learned by heart. This type of writing is a product of what one has seen in many texts and is an imitation of that style.
10. When poetry is composed very quickly on the spot describing whatever is seen with the eyes, yet is done without devotion, is called spontaneous writing.
11. The poems that are sensual, romantic, passionate, amorous, courageous, humorous, jovial, as well as poems about repentance and appreciation, and many other varieties all fall under the name of spontaneous poetry.
12. With this type of poetry, the mind becomes passionate towards objects, and this is reflected in the words being used. With this type of spontaneous writing there is no possibility of going beyond the worldly life.
13. If one writes poetry to make a living, and compositions are made in praise of various people, that is a type of spontaneous poetry.
14. Poetry should not just be a crude expression about appearances. Poetry should not take a lot of effort, nor should it be arrogant and heretical.
15. Poetry should not contain arguments, or contradiction of moods, or become boring because of a lack of examples.
16. Poetry should not ramble on or be frivolous, and it should not be harsh towards others.
17. A poetry composition should not be of low quality, and there should not be repetition of what has already been said. Proper poetry should follow the accepted styles and the author's name should be mentioned at the end.
18. Poetry should have authority in knowledge, logic, and an artistic sense with proper wording about Devotion (Bhakti), Knowledge (Jnana), and Detachment (Vairagya).
19. Understand that poetry that is without devotion is the dullest expression of the opinion of the intellect. Speech that is without delight and joy is only boring.
20. The composition that is written without devotion is like a big joke. Without any delight in God, how can meaningful dialogue take place?
21. This is enough now about the characteristics of spontaneous writing. It is written out of the madness of attachment and pride. Now, I shall tell about inspired poetry that is a blessing.
22. It begins to make one feel that prosperity, woman, and wealth want to make him vomit, and he begins to turn his attention inward towards the contemplation of God.
23. For one who has appreciation for God from moment to moment, it makes his fondness for singing the praises of God increase.
24. It inspires one to not let go of devotion and praising God for even a moment. It immerses one's awareness in the richness and color of devotion at all times.
25. When God dwells peacefully within, whatever is naturally spoken about is the explanation of Brahman.
26. When God dwells within, one has a liking for devotion to be enhanced. Such a one does not speak of anything else other than devotion to God.
27. When one develops the habit of delighting in God within, one's words and speech reflect that appreciation. With a deep feeling of compassion one gives the explanations about God, and dances and sings God's praises out of overwhelming love.
28. When the mind becomes filled with God, there is no remembrance or impression of body awareness. Doubts and feelings of shame become shy and run off far away.

29. Such a one is immersed in the splendor of divine love, and is energized with intoxicating devotion. The feeling of being a separate individual gets crushed underfoot.
30. Such a one continues to sing and dance free of doubt and hesitation. How can he see any other people around him when his vision remains filled only with God?
31. Like this, he is immersed in God, and does not require anything else. Out of his own wish and inspiration, he begins to describe the delight in meditation, and the greatness and glory of God.
32. There are many representations and images symbolizing the greatness and glory of God. Compared to that, praising the greatness and fame of human beings is petty and insignificant.
33. Let this be as it is. A devotee of God who is detached from worldly life is considered by the sages to be liberated.
34. The poetry that comes from the deep appreciation of devotion is called poetry that is inspired by the blessings of God. Such a one effortlessly speaks about what is revealed through the power of discrimination.
35. Listen to the signs of good poetry. The explanation will be given in such a way that the inner-mind of the listeners will be pacified.
36. Poetry should be clear, simple and direct, with various thoughts presented in proper sequence for clarity.
37. Poetry should have devotional content and be full of deep meaning, and free of egotism.
38. Poetry should depict the glory of God in pleasing and sweet ways. It should be full of content in the glory of God.
39. The poetry should be simple, brief and easy in compositional style and meter.
40. The poetry should be soft, melodious, appeasing, grand, marvelous, wide in perspective, proper in composition, interesting, and filled with the sweetness of devotion.
41. Poetry should use beautiful words, sentences and phrases with clever constructions, and skill in using various types of meters and incorporating many types of expressions.
42. This type of poetry should be skillful in many ways of explaining to the intellect, should have artistic construction, and should show an extraordinary skill in substantiating main principles with the utilization of many easy examples written in poetic style.
43. This poetry should have many examples from various literary works, and give logical explanations with details and particulars. It should include reference to stories and episodes to help explain the primary premise that is presented in the *Vedas* as well as present the principle of the "final conclusion" (siddhanta).
44. It uses various ways to express scholastic knowledge with many intellectual expressions full of inspiration, and addresses common suppositions with courage. This is what is called good poetry.
45. It addresses all doubts, objections, and skepticism with the support of examples from many poems. It is supported by spiritual science and it breaks down all doubts to their dissolution with determination.
46. This poetry addresses various situations and their associated concepts, gives explanations about yoga, and discusses the principle elements as well as Essence in many ways. This is what is called good poetry.

47. It explains many types of spiritual practice, the repetition of mantra, the significance of austerities and pilgrimages, and clears many doubts.
48. This poetry inspires a turning away from worldliness where one feels ashamed to be entangled in worldly matters, and gives rise to Knowledge.
49. This poetry strengthens Knowledge, dispels attitudes and states of mind, and properly explains the path of devotion.
50. With this poetry, the body-consciousness is snapped off, the ocean of worldliness dries up, and God is revealed.
51. With this poetry one gains rightmindedness, and this poetry has the power to destroy heretical opinions by arousing the power of discrimination.
52. Through this poetry, the Supreme Reality is revealed, Illusion disappears, and all distinctions are destroyed.
53. With this poetry one becomes content. It breaks the bondage of worldly life and is respected by the wise.
54. This is the description of good poetry. It is difficult to tell everything about it, but it has been explained to some extent for the purpose of understanding.

Thus in Shri Dasbodh, a dialogue between the Guru and disciple, Sub-Chapter 3 of Chapter 14, named "Explanation of Poetry" is concluded.

Chapter: 14, Sub-Chapter: 4

Narration About Praising God

|| ShriRam ||

1. In this Kali yuga there should be continual explanations about God. The expressions should be delicate and skillful, avoiding difficult, harsh, and unpleasant words.
2. The noise of chatter must be stopped and put aside, and do not get engaged in arguing with argumentative people. Do not make your mind turbulent with ideas of true and false.
3. One should not praise God proudly, or ever tire of singing his praises (in kirtan). When talking, one should not delve into delicate subjects, but instead focus on positive qualities.
4. Coughing and making distracting noises and causing disruptions while the praising of God is going on is not proper.
5. Speak about the many names of God and give explanations about God with attributes. Give many narrations about the wondrous greatness and glory of God.
6. Avoid speaking in a way that instigates derogatory and vulgar exclamations of disagreement among the people. Speak in such a way that does not use hurtful or disrespectful words.
7. Do not single anyone out with heavy criticism. Do not harass anyone by teasing them, and do not cause trouble for someone because they harassed you.
8. One should not simply passively patronize everyone saying "yes, yes, yes" to everything. One who is alert and awake becomes purified by listening to the

narrations about God. With meditation and repetition of God's name, the one God that resides in the hearts of all beings is pleased.

9. One's speech should make the gathering swell with devotional feelings, and one's brilliance should be attractive, seen shining from afar so all living beings are drawn near.
10. The wise person speaks in such a way that people don't need to be called again and again to come and listen. There is no need to take any action to plead with anyone to come because people eagerly come to listen without any invitation.
11. One should not continue on with speech that is irritating to people, or continue speaking when people are not listening to what is being said. Do not keep chattering on, thus making your speech boring.
12. Do not keep the company of stubborn people who are rigid and outspoken. One should not just continue prattling on with tiresome speech, and it should be well understood that meditation does not become established when there is any kind of outward show going on.
13. One's mind should not be constantly unsteady causing one to be afraid of speaking. Constant wavering in the mind while talking is of no use. And if you are uncertain about something, do not be obstinate in making a mistake.
14. Some people simply carry on clumsily with rituals and dancing, while others sit in one spot on a big mound and don't move. All of this is only tiring.
15. Speak in various methodical and cultured ways. Use humble speech to extol the many qualities of God. One's singing should be precise, melodious and proper.
16. Use percussion instruments and stringed instruments to accompany your singing. Sing rhythmic compositions accompanied with musical instruments so that even opinionated people become engrossed with their bodies and minds.
17. Sing the Lord's praises with high pitched voices coming together, and the feet of the devotees dancing ecstatically in divine love.
18. Singing the praises of God should be done in such a way that the alert and astute devotees become overwhelmed by the narration and divine song that resounds rhythmically, filling the entire atmosphere both inwardly and outwardly.
19. The singing of God's praises should be such that if some clever and crafty person comes rushing in with the intent to disrupt, he becomes subdued by the atmosphere and his intentions get spoiled, and everyone rejoices totally in God's splendor.
20. There are many powerful verses spoken that people enjoy with great appreciation. Such speech is articulate and precise, and attracts learned people to come to such gatherings.
21. With such praise, one's negative tendencies run away and disappear, and virtue is revealed outwardly. People come back again and again because they develop a liking for it within.
22. This praise does not include any useless, unworthy, or deceptive talk, or any kind of meaningless acrobatics or unnecessary body movements. It is free of dull useless words and harsh criticism.
23. This type of narration is praised by the people and addressed respectfully by them. People seek out the narrator and persuade him to speak again and again.
24. Such a speaker is known as a good pious person among the people. Because of his devotional feelings he stands out from the crowd. He is admired by others because of his kind and helping nature.

25. If you agree, then keep what has been said in the mind. Do not become intoxicated with affection for yourself. Many people remain intoxicated with pride and always go around chanting "I, I, I."
26. Some people persist and carry on asking others, "When will I be called to come and lead the kirtan?" For the good speaker who has previously been described, no such invitation is required.
27. His praise (kirtan) is rich and interesting, expressing many moods with melodious music. Those who are expert in selecting that which is most valuable run after it.
28. Such praise brings about overwhelming joy that brings tears to the eyes of the listeners. Their minds are filled with joy. Crowds of people are drawn in because of their appreciation for such speech.
29. Such praise does not contain any absurd statements or vulgar thoughts. Such a speaker's speech brings peace to the people.
30. He teaches discrimination of Essence and non-essence to all. With the utilization of literature and music, virtuous people feel better.
31. When one understands what is true and what is false, agitation and dissatisfaction end. When it is known to be false, the unreal disappears.
32. It is very difficult to find the truly wise who are capable of explaining the meaning of scriptures. Without them, the meaning of the *Vedas* cannot be understood. Their words cannot be equated to the sweet words of a parrot who cannot stop chattering.
33. One who gets contentment from amusing people with speech gets enticed by the approval and praises from others. He does not get any benefits from doing this in life, nor does he go beyond the world appearance.
34. Put your attention on That which cannot be seen with the eyes and cannot be conceived in the mind. Going beyond the body-consciousness, become absorbed in Reality by the most direct path, the "Bird's Way" (Vihangam Marg).
35. The Inner-Self that dwells in the body is subject to agitation. One who pacifies this agitation and helps others feel peaceful is truly blessed. It is the one Self that gets agitated as well as pacified that resides within everyone.

Thus in Shri Dasbodh, a dialogue between the Guru and disciple, Sub-Chapter 4 of Chapter 14, named "Narration About Praising God" is concluded.

Chapter: 14, Sub-Chapter: 5

Narration About God (Lord Vishnu)

|| ShriRam ||
1. Previously the listeners have asked for the narration about the description of God (Hari; Vishnu). The wise are asked to remain attentive while listening.
2. Listen to how the explanations about God should be full of splendor and excellence so that all are showered with Lord Rama's blessings.
3. If gold were to have a fragrance, or sugar-cane were to bear fruit it would be something extraordinary.

4. Similarly, if a servant of God is desireless, knowledgeable, and a loving devotee who is also a scholar that never engages in argument, this is also extraordinary.
5. If one has knowledge of the musical moods, rhythms, knowledge of all the arts, has the Knowledge of Brahman, and dwells among the people without pride, this is also extraordinary.
6. Such a one has no jealousy, is liked by the virtuous, understands the four facets of the mind, and remains absorbed in inner contemplation.
7. God is present at various birth anniversaries, pilgrimage places, and many auspicious ceremonies in the form of power.
8. How can those unfortunate people who do not honor, respect, or visit pilgrimage places and call them false only because of word knowledge, meet God?
9. If one has a skeptical mind, That which is without attributes is lost, and if one has the Knowledge of Brahman, but loses God with attributes because of pride, there is loss on both the sides.
10. If there is an image of God with form present, and one begins narrating the description of the formless while emphatically denying the presence of God with attributes, such a one is a learned fool.
11. The narration about God should not be given in such a way that the listeners begin doubting both paths. Now, listen to the narration about the description of God.
12. If there is an image of God with attributes, give a narration that is full of devotional feeling. Praise the compassion and mercy of God, sing the names of God in an uplifting way, and describe the glory and greatness of God.
13. By singing the praises of God and giving the explanations about God in a natural way, everyone becomes filled with happiness and divine love.
14. The sign of good explanation is that one does not speak of That which is without attributes while describing God with attributes, and the faults and virtues of others are not spoken of at any time.
15. Describe the glory and greatness of God in various ways. Give the narration about God with attributes with devotional feelings.
16. Do not give up the narration about God because of shyness about what people will think, and do not give explanations out of desire for acquiring money. Taking enjoyment in singing the praises of God, give new and interesting explanations.
17. Remain humble in the forum where explanations about God are being given. Being free of doubt, bow down to God, dance with joy, and sing the names of God clapping your hands.
18. Do not praise one person in front of another, or speak of one deity while in the temple of another. If one gives explanations like this it will be awkward and confusing. Therefore, be clear about what is proper to say at a particular place.
19. If there is no image of God with attributes present, and the listeners that are sitting to hear the discourse are saintly or virtuous people, then the explanation of non-duality should definitely be given.
20. If there is no image of God, nor any virtuous people sitting to listen to the narration, but the audience is comprised of devotional people, then the narration should be about detachment and changing one's worldly ways.
21. If the narration contains explanations about various moods such as courage, devotion, etc., the descriptions of the beauty and attractiveness of women should be avoided.

22. If the beauty of women is described, the listeners become distracted and their minds become attracted to the objects of the senses.
23. Therefore, speaking about that which is distracting to the spiritual aspirant should be avoided. When listening to such descriptions the mind of the aspirant becomes fixated on the meditation about women.
24. If one meditates upon the beauty and charms of women, the mind takes on the image of the woman and becomes desirous of sexual pleasure. How can one meditate on God in such a situation?
25. If one feels happy by hearing the descriptions of the charms and beauty of women, understand that he is considered to have strayed away from God.
26. Even if the listener's interest in God wanes, but there is strength of devotional feelings in the explanations about God, in a moment one's interest can become reestablished by meditating on the Supreme Self, Paramatman.
27. When the mind is absorbed in meditation on God how can one be aware of other people? When one who is free of doubt and hesitation gives explanations about God, the splendor and excellence of the narration becomes great beyond all bounds.
28. One who has the knowledge of musical moods, rhythms, and vocal intonations knows how to give explanations full of meaning in an easily comprehensible manner.
29. There are many languages and many skillful ways to give narrations. One may even have a sweet voice like that of a nightingale, but the path of devotion is quite different from all of this. This is only understood by devotees.
30. Devotees meditate on God alone. They do not know anything other than God, similar to an artist whose mind is filled only with his art.
31. Any art which excludes God cannot be considered good art. Art that excludes God only leads one astray and creates a sense of separation from God.
32. Many various art forms come between oneself and God, like a snake coiled around a sandalwood tree, or a buried treasure that is protected by someone.
33. If one leaves aside God who is the knower of all, and becomes engrossed in musical melodies, this is truly an obstacle to realizing God.
34. When one's mind becomes engrossed in music, how will one be able to contemplate on God? It is like a thief who forcefully takes a person away and makes him an accepting servant.
35. When it comes to having a glimpse of God, the knowledge of music is a hindrance that holds the attention of the mind as it gets carried away by focusing on notes and melodies.
36. The art holds the attention of the artist similar to when a person goes to meet a king in his court and then is forcibly held there and made to become a servant.
37. One who keeps the mind focused on God while giving narrations about God is truly blessed in this world appearance.
38. For such a one who is interested in the explanations about God, and in whom there is always a liking for God, he becomes united with God.
39. The devotee of God eagerly gives up everything, and leaves laziness and sleep behind to go to the places where the narration about God is taking place.
40. The one who takes up many types of work in the house of a devotee and helps the devotee in every possible way in his devotion,

41. Is called a true servant of God because of his full faith in the name of God. At this point, this sub-chapter is completed.

Thus in Shri Dasbodh, a dialogue between the Guru and disciple, Sub-Chapter 5 of Chapter 14, named "Narration About God" is concluded.

Chapter: 14, Sub-Chapter: 6

Description of Discernment

|| ShriRam ||

1. A beautiful appearance cannot be acquired through study. Each person is born with their own natural qualities that cannot be altered. Therefore, one should at least try to make some effort master those qualities that can be developed.
2. A black skinned person cannot become fair skinned, the various marks on the body cannot be removed by any means, and one who is born mute cannot get his speech back, as these are inherent qualities for such people.
3. One who is blind cannot see, one who is deaf cannot hear, and one who is lame cannot use his limbs. These are inherent qualities.
4. How many such types of physical deformities should be told? The inherent qualities and beauty of a form do not change.
5. Bad habits can be given up and they will disappear. The best qualities can be developed with study and practice. The wise give up wrong knowledge and gain true Knowledge.
6. Foolishness disappears if given up. Wisdom can be acquired through learning. Everything can be understood if one puts in effort and takes care in how one conducts one's affairs.
7. Recognition and respect are liked by all beings, and yet there is still a neglect of making right efforts to gain them. Without proper discernment one does not gain higher status.
8. When this type of actual experience comes to one's mind, why not do something for your own good? One who is progressing on the right path is respected by both the common people as well as by saintly people.
9. The body is dressed up and adorned properly but that is useless without proper discernment. It is like a mad person who has no virtues putting on a show.
10. One should be adorned with discernment and the understanding of many things in many ways. Then, prosperity will be enjoyed in due course.
11. If one does not make any efforts to learn or to do any hard physical work, the best qualities are not imbibed, and one is prone to becoming angry very quickly.
12. As you do to others, you get back in return. If one causes troubles for others, one receives a lot of trouble from others.
13. One who behaves in a just manner is wise. One who is unjust becomes a lowly person. There are many signs of discernment and intelligence that are known to the wise.
14. That which is respected by many becomes accepted by many others. That which is not accepted becomes useless and is universally criticized.

15. People may act favorably toward you, or they may be entirely against you, therefore act in such a way that brings about the most satisfaction to various situations.
16. By satisfaction, more satisfaction is spread to others, by friendliness, more friendships develop, and by breaking off relations, even good friendships can be broken in a moment.
17. People say "What are you doing? Why are you behaving that way?," and one hears these comments, yet still does not learn and clear away incorrect activity.
18. Discernment is an adornment of one's consciousness, like beautiful clothes are an adornment for the body. See which one is superior between the two.
19. What benefit do people receive if the body is outwardly decorated? However, with the adornment of wisdom, many people are protected in many ways.
20. People desire to eat good food, share good meals, to wear good clothes to adorn themselves, and that others should say good things about them.
21. Work hard for others with the body and mind and you will receive respect from the people. However, if you only sit idly by imagining, troubles will surely come afterwards.
22. When some work is not getting done and someone comes along and completes it properly, people are naturally drawn to the person who gets things done.
23. Therefore, work to make others happy, which will also please yourself. If one gives trouble to others, one only makes more trouble for oneself.
24. This principle is clearly evident but unless one sees properly, it is of no use. To realize this is the solution to dealing with all beings.
25. Those who understand this and act in the world accordingly are the people of great fortune. All others can be considered to be unfortunate.
26. According to the extent of one's activities, likewise is one's prosperity. One's prosperity is in accordance with one's conduct. This principle is evident and should be properly understood.
27. Laziness hinders the completion of undertakings, but with hard work, things happen in due course. If one cannot understand what is readily apparent, how can he be called wise?
28. With friendship activities get accomplished, and with enmity things get broken and death occurs. Recognize for yourself if what is being said is true or false.
29. If one doesn't know to how make oneself wise, he cannot understand what is in his own best interest. Such a person does not not know to protect friendships among people, and creates many enemies.
30. People such as this are called ignorant. Who can get any satisfaction in dealings with them?
31. If one is all alone and is always quarreling with everyone in the world, how can he become successful with other people?
32. Let many people speak of you and remember you for your good qualities. Explain the best qualities to the people.
33. Make people wise and uplift the downfallen. Increase devotion to God in the world.

Thus in Shri Dasbodh, a dialogue between the Guru and disciple, Sub-Chapter 6 of Chapter 14, named "Description of Discernment" is concluded.

- - - - - - - - - - - - - - - - -

Chapter: 14, Sub-Chapter: 7

The State of Present Times

|| ShriRam ||

1. There are many manners of dress and the different ways of life (ashramas[52]). However, of all the different ways of life, the principle way where people find rest and relief in the three worlds is the householder's life.
2. Gods, sages, monks, yogis, ascetics, renunciates, ancestors, and all types of guests and visitors all come from households.
3. They are all born in the householder's homes, even though they may have forsaken that way of life, their presence persists there because of their name.
4. For this reason the householder's life is considered best of all, however, one must know one's own disposition (swadharma) and have compassion for all ways of life.
5. In the virtuous household, the six types virtuous activities[53] are upheld, and people are spoken to with sweet sounding words.
6. The virtuous householder is disciplined in these six activities that have been presented in the scriptures. Especially divine is to follow the path of devotion.
7. Such a householder practices repetition of mantra, observes religious vows, and is diligent in making spiritual effort. For him, there is nothing more important than the Lord of the Universe.
8. His body, speech, life and breath is dedicated to God, and his mind delights in singing God's praises.
9. Such a devotee of God is especially detached within. By giving up attachments to family life for the sake of God, he becomes liberated.
10. Understand that the greatest fortune is to be inwardly detached, and that there is no greater misfortune than being attached to worldly things.
11. Even kings have given up their kingdoms and become wanderers for the sake of realizing God, and then gone on to become famous because of their achievements.
12. Such one who is a great yogi with inner experience and thoughtfulness, can help other living beings because of his understanding of their inner experience.
13. Such a one has an attitude of detachment in the worldly life, and above that he has Self-Knowledge. Simply by having a glimpse of such a person people become content.
14. Such a one is a means of salvation for many people, but he is not easily accessible to everyone. His heart is always filled with God's radiance.
15. He may appear restless to people, but he is very alert, and his thoughts are always on God.
16. He is either worshipping an image of God, absorbed in contemplation on the Self, or he is listening to and studying spiritual discourses and reflecting on their meaning.
17. Only if one has accumulated a great amount of virtue does one get the chance to meet such a person.

---

[52] Brahmacharyashram is the bachelors life studying with a Guru, Gruhasthashram is the householders life, Vanaprasthashram is retiring after the householders life, and Sanyasashram is renouncing the worldly life
[53] The six virtuous activities are: studying, teaching, making offerings, helping others make offerings, giving of alms, and accepting donations.

18. Knowledge without actual experience is only imagination and conjecture. With such knowledge, how can there be any success in spiritual practice for living beings?
19. For this reason, direct experience is very important. Without experience, knowledge is useless and one cannot gain realization. The wise understand that without actual experience, a remedy becomes a calamity.
20. If a person foolishly gives up worldly life, he will only die with suffering and hardships. He loses both in worldly life as well as the spiritual life.
21. If one leaves his home and goes away in anger and then dies after having arguments with many people, he has only been a source of trouble and suffering to others and himself.
22. If such a person who is ignorant leaves his home and other people begin keeping his company for advice, both the teacher and the disciple remain ignorant.
23. If a person is full of desire and behaves in immoral ways, even if he goes to other countries, he still continues his immoral behavior there among the people in those places.
24. If there is not enough to eat at home, and one becomes miserable and goes away and takes to a life of thievery, he will only be beaten in those places where he is caught stealing.
25. However, if one realizes the unreality of worldly life, and then leaves his home, he is able to make others knowledgeable like himself.
26. By keeping the good company of such a person, many people find salvation while others will only suffer downfall when keeping the company of the ignorant person. See that for this reason, you should take care to keep good company.
27. Where there is no utilization of the power of discrimination and proper examination, how can there be initiation into Self-Knowledge? For such a person, it is like one who goes from one house to another asking for alms and not receiving anything anywhere.
28. One who understands the minds of others knows how to behave properly according to any given place, time, and situation. What can be lacking for such a person?
29. If a person of low character and conduct becomes a guru, it is certain that the conduct of those around him becomes lowly as well. In such a situation, who will care for the knowledge of the *Vedas* and scriptures, or the "Knowers of Brahman"?
30. The authority of the discourse and thinking about the Knowledge of Brahman, is present only with the Knowers of Brahman. Therefore it is said that only a Knower of Brahman is a true guru for all castes of people.
31. Many who call themselves brahmins have deviated from pure intellect, abandoned good conduct, and become morally corrupt. Giving up the high status of being a guru they only become a disciple of their disciples.
32. Among these so called brahmins, many begin to worship some lower deities and various spirits, or they convert to some other religion according to their desire.
33. Such is the conduct in the present age (Kali yuga) where people act according to habitual patterns without any thoughtfulness. As the age progresses even marriages between castes will take place.
34. When a person of low character takes on the status of being a guru, it only serves to increase his own sense of importance. Such lowly people only do dishonor to the real Knowers of Brahman.

35. Such so-called brahmins do not have true understanding, nor have they attained any elevated state. In their case, false pride and foolishness has not been abandoned.
36. In these times, Muslim warriors have taken away the kingdom[54], and the status of guru has been taken up by unworthy people. Because of this, the people lose both in worldly life and in spiritual life.
37. Because of politics and envy, the high status of the true Brahmins (Knowers of Brahman) has been ruined. The lowly so-called "brahmins" have strayed from God and accordingly are considered to be cursed.
38. I say with great sorrow that the high status of being a Brahmin has passed away because of in-fighting and the blind following of religious practices that have left negative effects all around us.
39. Can you see what these so-called brahmins are doing in present times? Their state is such that they cannot even get enough food to eat. Have you not seen this for yourselves?
40. It is best not to blame those elders who have come before. It should be understood that this is the misfortune of these present day brahmins. I have naturally spoken about this because of the state of affairs of the present times. The listeners are asked to pardon my harsh words.

Thus in Shri Dasbodh, a dialogue between the Guru and disciple, Sub-Chapter 7 of Chapter 14, named "The State of Present Times" is concluded.

Chapter: 14, Sub-Chapter: 8

Uninterrupted Meditation

|| ShriRam ||

1. What has happened in the past is over and gone. Now, at the very least, the true Brahmins must make themselves wise.
2. Worship of God should be done with pure hands (purity of character). In that way, good fortune comes to all. The foolish who are not devotees suffer from poverty.
3. First, God must be recognized. Then, becoming one with him, worship him with single-pointed devotion and uninterrupted meditation.
4. The one among all who has the best qualities, is called the best of all. By utilizing the power of discrimination to discern Self from non-self, one comes to know God.
5. The Self is the knower of the body and the inner-witness that sees everything and knowledgeably recognizes all objects.
6. The Self resides in all bodies and functions through the sense organs. The Self is experienced in one's actual experience by all living beings.
7. The inner Universal Self resides in all living beings. Therefore, take care not to hurt the minds of all people. The Self is everything, both the giver and the enjoyer.

---

[54] In the time of Samartha Ramdas, the country was in great turmoil because of Muslim invaders and a decline in social values.

8. God abides in the universal mind. It is He that is one's own mind, and that which is seen in all living beings in the three worlds.
9. He is the original "one seer" that is distributed in all the various manifest bodies and distinct and separate forms.
10. He appears to have many separate bodily forms, but he is singularly alone within all. All activities such as talking and walking happen only because of him.
11. It is he alone who is one's own Self *and* the Self of all others. He is in all beings including birds, animals, wild beasts, worms, ants. He is in all beings with physical bodies.
12. He is in all living beings that move about in the sky, on the land, in the forests, and in the water. He is life itself, in so many ways. How much can be told about his expansive existence in all the four categories of beings?
13. It is he that is active as the consciousness of all. This can be seen by direct experience. He is always present within us all.
14. Recognize that the Self of the Universe permeates all form. Seeing this, all beings are known to be unified, and one pleases all beings knowing that they are all only oneself.
15. The responsibility rests with oneself to please everyone. Whatever good one does with the body is enjoyed by the Self.
16. God resides even in evil-minded beings. It is only his nature that is revealed as being arrogant and violent. Just as in the case of when the king becomes angry, we never argue with him, in the same way, we should not quarrel with arrogant people.
17. In some situations it is necessary to leave a place. Afterwards, one should reflect on the situation with discerning wisdom. By utilizing such discriminative intellect you will be respected as a saintly person among the people.
18. The differences that appear in the Self are in relation to the body only. It is like how water is always water but tastes different when various herbs or plants are added to it.
19. Poison and nectar both exist, but their basic nature of being water does not change. In the same way, see that the Self is the witness in all.
20. One who is firmly seated in the Self within is special in his inner state. He recognizes the Lord of the Universe in the world.
21. God is in all bodies. He is the eye that sees the eyes, and the mind that liberates the mind.
22. Without him, no activity gets accomplished. Everything happens because of his doing. It is because of him that human beings come to know their unity with him through the power of discrimination.
23. Whatever actions take place in the waking state happen because of connection with him. Whatever happens in the dream is also because of the same connection.
24. The sign of uninterrupted meditation is the sign of uninterrupted remembrance of God. In this knowingness, the explanations about God happen spontaneously.
25. Giving up what is effortless and natural, people make troublesome efforts to focus on some particular thing. Such people stray away from the Self and hold to meditating on what is not the Self.
26. However, when trying to hold on to what is not the Self, it cannot be held onto. Many things appear in the mind and cause unnecessarily trouble, making the mind uneasy and anxious.

27. When one makes effort to meditate upon an image of God, instead of that image, something else is seen. It is surprising how what should not appear, appears in front of the mind's eye.
28. One must analyze and properly decide if meditation should be on God or on the temple of God.
29. The body is the temple, and the Self is God. See where your devotion should be focused. Recognizing God, one's devotion should be focused there.
30. Meditate with strong inner conviction. The traditional types of meditation are not like this. Meditation without actual experience of the Self is useless and is only meditation on imagination.
31. With meditation on imagination, imagination and speculation only increase. Holding on to imagination only disrupts true meditation. The unfortunate ignorant people cause unnecessary trouble for themselves by meditating on gross objects.
32. When one imagines God to be a physical body, many doubts and wrong ideas about enjoying versus renouncing things, and about how to face difficulties arise because of the association with the body.
33. When such things are focused upon, delusional thinking occurs in the mind, just like many strange things that appear in one's dreams.
34. Whatever is seen by such a person is not understood and cannot be satisfactorily explained. Such an aspirant only becomes inwardly disturbed.
35. When meditation is done correctly, it is clearly evident in one's own mind. Such meditation does not leave room for any doubt to appear in the mind.
36. Meditation where the mind is only made to concentrate is useless. Such meditation is interrupted because of the restless mind. Who can get anything worthwhile in that kind of meditation?
37. If one is constantly meditating but is not receiving any benefit, understand that that type of meditation is not correct meditation. Consider the meaning of this carefully.
38. Understand that the one meditating and the object of meditation are one. Recognize that they are not two.
39. The state of Oneness is what is natural. The aspirant goes on searching, but does not see this. The Jnani sees correctly and remains content.
40. Like this, with actual experience one remains content. Without experience, people hold to delusional traditions and remain affected by such delusion.
41. Holding on to such traditional approaches to mediation is an error. Common people do not understand the difference between correct and incorrect meditation.
42. Such people merely spread false information and give bad advice. However, if all of this is keenly considered by the mind, one easily recognizes in the end that such ideas are entirely false.
43. If someone is meditating on some image or idol, someone else gives him the advice, "You are putting a crown on that idol. Remove the crown and put a garland of flowers instead. That is better."
44. There is no drought of such ideas in the mind. Soon the garland will be imagined to be too short. Understand that in this case, both the listener and the speaker are fools.
45. The aspirant is not really required to go to any such trouble. One does not need to make a garland of thread and flowers and then imagine that somehow the garland is too short. What is the meaning in all of this nonsense?

46. Such people do not have sharp intellect and are basically dull-minded fools. Who wants to argue with such fools?
47. There are some people who establish some sort of spiritual path and build up a tradition around it. Such a person then gathers followers around him who practice his newly formed tradition and takes great pride in it.
48. Taking pride in spiritual practice without having any actual experience is like keeping sick patients in the dark and slowly killing them. If a practice is based only upon imagination and speculation, how can there ever be any Self-Knowledge?
49. Give up all pride and gain actual experience by utilizing the power of discrimination. The primary premise of the *Vedas* regarding the false nature of Illusion should be proven with the strength of the power of discrimination.

Thus in Shri Dasbodh, a dialogue between the Guru and disciple, Sub-Chapter 8 of Chapter 14, named "Uninterrupted Meditation" is concluded.

Chapter: 14, Sub-Chapter: 9

Explanation of the Eternal Reality

|| ShriRam ||

1. We have seen the wonder of the physical body and seen with discrimination what is Self and what is non-self. The body is not the Self, and it is the Self alone that does everything.
2. It is said that the Self is one without a second, and this can be experienced through the power of discrimination. Now, the composition of the universe must be understood.
3. At the level of the body, one must discern between Self and non-self, while at the level of the universe, one must investigate what is Essence and what is non-essence. This should be considered again and again until the understanding becomes firm.
4. The physical body is the result of the universe, which is its cause. This needs to be clearly understood, so more explanation will be given.
5. Non-essence means that which is destructible. Essence means that which is Eternal. Whatever comes to an end is not the Essence.
6. Earth is formed from water, but afterwards dissolves back into water. Water is formed out of light.
7. Water gets engulfed and becomes completely evaporated by that great light. Afterwards, only light remains everywhere.
8. Light is formed from wind, and is extinguished by wind. Having extinguished the light, only wind remains.
9. The wind emanates from sky, and then dissolves back into from where it has come. Such is the final dissolution of the universe, as described in the *Vedas* and other scriptures.
10. Then, Illusion with attributes (Gunamaya), and the Primal Illusion that is without attributes (Moolamaya) dissipate in Parabrahman, the Absolute Reality. In order to Realize Parabrahman, the utilization of the power of discrimination is required.

11. When all attachments come to an end, the visible world is not present and only Brahman without attributes singularly exists everywhere.
12. Even if the final dissolution takes place many times, Brahman still does not get destroyed. the Eternal is recognized by giving up Illusion.
13. The Inner-Self is God with attributes. One can attain the realization of That which is without attributes through the worship of God with attributes. With the knowledge of That which is without attributes, Supreme Knowledge (Vijnana) is gained.
14. That which is pure and beyond imagination is never tainted by any blemish of Illusion. All that is visible has an appearance and subsequent disappearance, and is false.
15. That which has an appearance and disappearance can be experienced. That which has no appearance or disappearance can only be recognized with discrimination.
16. In this universal appearance there is knowledge, ignorance, and wrong knowledge. When all three disappear, that is Supreme Knowledge, Vijnana.
17. One should understand the principles presented in Vedanta and Siddhanta and should verify what is presented there. It is only in one's own actual experience that one finds the changeless Reality that is spread out everywhere.
18. Seeing with the eye of Knowledge, remain as the oneness of Reality. Understand that this is what is called self-surrender.
19. The visible world appears to one's sight and is conceived of in one's mind. That which is beyond the visible appearances is the indestructible Absolute Reality, Parabrahman.
20. If one tries to see Parabrahman, it seems to be far away even though it is within as well as outside of everything. As it has no end, how can anyone make any comparisons to That which is endless?
21. Whatever is moving does not become still, and That which is unmoving never moves, just as clouds come and go while there is no movement for the sky.
22. That which is constantly changing grows and gets destroyed. How can it be Eternal? At the time of the final destruction everything gets destroyed.
23. Those who are inwardly deluded due to the deceptive power of Illusion cannot understand the nature of this great wheel of the universe.
24. If you are hesitant, no transaction can take place. If one does not inquire into the nature of Reality, the final conclusion (siddhanta) cannot be understood. If one remains hesitant in this way, God remains unknown in one's consciousness.
25. For example, if a medicine that a doctor prescribes does not give any experience of relief but the patient is hesitant to say anything, the patient will most certainly not survive.
26. One who recognizes the king will not call any other man king, and one who recognizes God becomes God.
27. How can one who is hesitant to say that false things are false, speak the truth? Seeing this clearly, everything becomes clear.
28. Hesitation exits only within the boundaries of Illusion, while Parabrahman is beyond illusion. However, Parabrahman is always both beyond, as well as within the boundaries of Illusion.
29. Holding on to the false because of the hesitation to inquire into Reality, one does many absurd things in his delusion. This is not the sign of one who utilizes the power of discrimination.

30. All that is false should be entirely given up, and Reality should be recognized in one's own experience. Drop Illusion and realize Parabrahman.
31. The description of Illusion will be explained next. Listen to the explanation with an attentive and tranquil state of mind.

Thus in Shri Dasbodh, a dialogue between the Guru and disciple, Sub-Chapter 9 of Chapter 14, named "Explanation of the Eternal Reality" is concluded.

Chapter: 14, Sub-Chapter: 10

Explanation of Illusion

|| ShriRam ||

1. Illusion appears and then gets destroyed. Reality has no appearance and never gets destroyed. Illusion is felt to be true, but never becomes true.
2. The destitute person lies idle on his back and imagines many things, but nothing ever comes of it. Illusion is like that.
3. In a dream, the prosperity of wealth, and the enjoyment women and many activities are felt to be true for a moment, but it is all false. The same is true of Illusion.
4. In the sky, the cloud formations take the appearance of many various forms and even look like many glorious cities and towns that change in many ways. Illusion is just like that.
5. A con-artist plays many tricks pretending to be wealthy, and when he speaks of his wealth, it seems to be real, but in actual experience, it is not true. The same is true about Illusion.
6. On a special day of the Hindu calendar which is the day of sharing gold, it is customary to take leaves with little thorns from a tree and this is considered to be like looting gold. But it is all not true, just like Illusion.
7. People observe grand ceremonies on the death anniversaries of a dead person, or adorn a woman who will burn herself on her husband's funeral pyre, and they all go and cry at the cremation grounds. Illusion is like this.
8. A prostitute, a string tied around a pregnant woman for the safety of the baby, and a name given to someone are all called Laxmi, but this is all false like the nature of Illusion.
9. A girl who becomes a widow in her childhood is given a name meaning "eternal spouse" and someone who begs from house to house is named after the God of Wealth, but this is all false, the same as Illusion.
10. An actor plays the ten incarnations of Lord Krishna in a drama, but is a beggar in real life, and a dry river is given a name meaning "full of water." Illusion is like this.
11. A fraud plays the part of a king in front of the villagers and carries himself with the expressions of a great king, but it is all false. Illusion is the same as this.
12. In the house there is an idol of the Goddess of Abundant Food, but there is no food in the house. A woman is named after Saraswati, the Goddess of Learning,

but she does not learn anything, and only prepares cowdung cakes[55]. Illusion is like this.
13. A dog is named Tiger, a son is named Indra (King of the Gods), and an ugly woman is said to be beautiful. Illusion is the same as this.
14. A fool is called a master of the arts, a donkey brays and it is called a nightingale's song, or a blind woman is said to have good vision. Illusion is like this.
15. A person born into a low caste is given the name of a holy plant. A woman shoemaker is named after the holy city of Kashi, and a lowly untouchable woman is given the name of the holy river Ganges. Illusion is like this.
16. If the shadow becomes merged into the darkness, it is imagined that there is something there. Illusion is the same as this.
17. When one's earlobes, fingers, joints, or palms are held up to the light, they give off the appearance of being red in color. This is just like Illusion.
18. When seeing an orange robe it looks to the mind like a burning fire, but upon investigation it is seen to be untrue, just like Illusion.
19. If we put our feet in water they appear to be distorted and short, long, thin, crooked, etc. What is seen in the water is false. Illusion deceives in the same way.
20. When someone is having a seizure, the earth looks like it is crumbling down. Someone who is jaundiced appears to be yellow, and someone with a high fever experiences hallucinations. Illusion is the same as this.
21. When there is some change in an object, it appears to be something else, but it is always only the same object that has simply undergone some kind of change. This is the same for Illusion.

Thus in Shri Dasbodh, a dialogue between the Guru and disciple, Sub-Chapter 10 of Chapter 14, named "Explanation of Illusion" is concluded.

---

[55]In rural India, cowdung is mixed with straw and made into flat round cakes and used as a source of fuel for cooking fires.

Chapter 15. Chapter on the Self

Chapter: 15, Sub-Chapter: 1

The Signs of Wisdom

|| ShriRam ||

1. Bodies are made of bone and flesh, and in them resides the living God that experiences many changes, and who is the knower of those changes.
2. He is the knower of what is solid and what is hollow in life, and who understands what should be taken and what should not be taken.
3. Some people ask repeatedly to receive certain things, while others give without asking for anything. Each person must recognize what is virtuous for oneself, in one's own experience.
4. Pour your life into the life of others, merge yourself with the Self in others, and try again and again to discover the inner core of the minds of others.
5. For example, if the "sacred thread" is loosely braided, the threads that it is comprised of get all tangled up, but if it is braided correctly, it retains its proper appearance.
6. Similarly, one's mind is joined and intermingled tightly with the mind of another with the help of the power of discrimination. If this tight intermingling is not there, imagination and speculation run rampant.
7. Imagination and speculation only generate more imagination and speculation, and because of hesitation, the success of one's work gets derailed. For this reason, one must first see clearly and gain direct experience.
8. If one does not understand what is going on for others, it is difficult to know their minds. If this is the case, how can one expect to win over the hearts and minds of others?
9. People try to win over the minds of others without a clear comprehension of what is going on for them. Trying to win over the minds of others with an incomplete knowledge of their situation, their attempts only fall short at every step.
10. The Lord of the Universe is the Inner-Self of all, so what is the case for using some deceptive means of persuasion on anyone? One who gives explanations with the support of the power of discrimination is truly the most excellent person.
11. Such an excellent person completes his tasks with superior quality. Those who act deceitfully perform an inferior type of work. According to one's actions, living beings either bring ruin upon themselves or bring about their own welfare.
12. A noble person treads on the path of virtue, while deceitful people tread on the path of deception. The ignorant person foolishly gets cheated by his petty concern for small gains.
13. The fool thinks that he is wise, but he is really a pitiful fool. Only one who is wise understands the signs of wisdom.
14. Only the one who becomes consciously merged with the Universal Self becomes that Universal Self. What can be lacking then for him, either in worldly life or in spiritual life?

15. The intellect is a gift from God. What is a human being without the intellect? He is like a king who has abandoned his kingdom and roams about begging for alms like a pauper.
16. People generally like the life and environment that they create for themselves and because of their pride for these things, they become entangled in Illusion. This can be seen everywhere.
17. Everyone thinks, "We are great, we are beautiful, we are the smartest people on earth."
18. When one thinks this over, it is clear that nobody thinks of oneself as being insignificant or inferior. Those who are knowledgeable understand that everyone everywhere thinks like this.
19. Because of pride about oneself, people live their lives imagining themselves to be special. This must be seen using proper discernment.
20. To take pride in what is untrue, and to give up what is True is the sign of foolishness.
21. Understand that pride in the True is not pride in the untrue, and that justice and injustice can never be the same.
22. Justice means That which is eternal, and injustice means that which is ephemeral. Similarly, how can being disciplined and being undisciplined be the same?
23. Some people enjoy their good fortune openly, while thieves run away. The greatness of some is plainly evident, while the greatness of others is difficult to see.
24. Actions that are done immorally and thoughtlessly cause many troubles. Therefore, seek out those who are wise and intelligent.
25. One meets many crafty people in the world, but the wise know how to handle such people. The tricks and deception of such people do not work on a wise person.
26. For this reason, one should make friends with prominent people who exhibit leadership qualities. With their support it is possible to manage others and have influence among many common people.
27. Those who are wise are liked by others who are wise. Wisdom is appreciated by the wise while fools carry on without accomplishing anything.
28. Wisdom is understood by the wise, and in that wisdom there is a meeting of the minds. However, it is best if their activities are carried out discretely.
29. When you win over the mind of a powerful person, many common people as well as virtuous people will seek you out for advice.
30. Through acquaintances meet new people. With your intellect enlighten the intellect of others. With justice and morality overcome the resistance of non-believers.
31. Dress in a simple and ordinary fashion, but inwardly maintain and develop many good skills and qualities. Be careful not to break the affection that others feel towards you.
32. One who is desireless, having an attitude that is always new and fresh, who has the Knowledge of Brahman and who is recognized and known to be a virtuous man, is very rare in this world.
33. Such a person knows many subjects by heart, and can easily pacify the minds of all. After staying somewhere for a short time, he does not remain only in one place and moves on.
34. If such a person only stays in one place, his undertakings become negatively affected. Therefore, he meets with many people and tends to the needs of all those whom he comes into contact with.

35. People remember such a person and want to meet with him again and again. These are the signs of wisdom and of the best qualities in a person, with which human beings become content.

Thus in Shri Dasbodh, a dialogue between the Guru and disciple, Sub-Chapter 1 of Chapter 15, named "The Signs of Wisdom" is concluded.

Chapter: 15, Sub-Chapter: 2

Detachment from Worldly Life

|| ShriRam ||

1. The whole world is crowded with innumerable human bodies large and small that constantly experience many mental modifications.
2. There are as many different dispositions among people as there are bodies, and none stay the same from the beginning to the end of their lives. It can be seen that nothing remains constant for anyone.
3. Many people have been taken away and forcibly converted to Islam, many have come under Portuguese rule, and many have been put into confinement because of language differences.
4. Maharashtra province has become greatly diminished in size, many people have become entangled in politics, and many have become so involved with worldy affairs that they do not even have time to take meals.
5. Many have become involved in the business of war and are intoxicated with it to such an extent that day and night they are discussing only that.
6. Businessmen have become so involved in business that they have no time for anything else. Everyone has become obsessed with only thinking about earning money in life.
7. There are many differing opinions regarding various philosophies, and many sectarian and contrary beliefs and teachings have proliferated all over the earth.
8. There are many followers of Shiva and many followers of Vishnu that have been carried away by the various teachings of the many different sects to such an extent that it has caused great confusion for everyone.
9. Many people have become devotees of passion and sexual gratification. Who among them bothers to look and see what is proper and what is improper?
10. In all of this commotion, confusion continues increasing among the followers of the various sects to such an extent that their teachings cannot be tolerated by those who are followers of the *Vedas*.
11. In all of the confusion many people have become attracted to singing the praises of God, but who among them actually gains the Knowledge of Brahman?
12. For these reasons true Knowledge (Jnana) is very rare, and it is not easy to become virtuous in this world. However, for one who inquires into his true nature, everything is easily known.
13. It is very difficult for one to express in words what is understood through inquiry. When trying to express it, the limitations of speech often act as a hindrance rather than a help.

14. In trying to express that understanding, the one with a sharp intellect will not let a single opportunity slip by. A person who is wise, logical, and intelligent is liked by all.
15. Such a person knows many things by heart and is easily able to utilize appropriate quotes and examples whenever needed, and provides a straight path with the power of his Knowledge.
16. The power of such a one uses many means to awaken others. He knows the inner-mind of all, and after hearing him speak, people develop a longing to listen to him again.
17. Such a person understands many various opinions and is able to remove differences in opinion by speaking from direct experience, He knows how to guide aspirants properly in giving up useless practices and beliefs.
18. His statements are appropriate and penetrating. He always sees the circumstances of various situations and is able to walk away from a situation unconcerned with a disinterested attitude.
19. Such a person speaks from direct experience and then freely gets up and moves on without attachment. Listeners begin to develop an interest in what he says. Leaving behind many types of spiritual practice, they take refuge in his guidance.
20. He cannot be found anywhere or be located at any particular place. His attire and appearance is that of a simple and humble person.
21. He accomplishes many things in secrecy but his nature is such that he comes across as a meek person and does not take the credit. He is beyond the limitations of success, fame or courage.
22. He motivates people at various places to take up devotion and singing the praises of God while remaining aloof. He is not touched by the envy and jealousy that entangles others.
23. He goes to stay at his own place where he is not seen by others, all the while remaining devoted to caring for everyone.
24. He is disciplined to be able to live in difficult places among difficult people, and he is much sought after by the people of the world.
25. Such a person is not troubled by anyone, and it is not possible to guess even a little bit about him. He gets people to work together and has them take part in the relevant politics.
26. He increases the number of people gathering together beyond measure, with his power on earth that works in hidden ways.
27. People are attracted to him and gather around him, coming from many places. He spreads the disposition of spirituality to people everywhere.
28. He spreads the enthusiasm for worship and devotion, and his greatness increases from place to place. With his experience of the Self he can free many people.
29. Like this, he has many skillful means of helping people to become wise, and everywhere he goes people gain the experience of the Self.
30. Be well known before passing away so that your coming into this world is made worthwhile, says Ramdas. I have spoken about this in a natural way to indicate this to you.

Thus in Shri Dasbodh, a dialogue between the Guru and disciple, Sub-Chapter 2 of Chapter 15, named "Detachment from Worldly Life" is concluded.

Chapter: 15, Sub-Chapter: 3

The Greatness of the Inner-Self

|| ShriRam ||
1. At its root, the expanse of the universe is entirely made up of the five elements. The common thread in the universe is the Inner-Self that is the witness which sees all and is the form of Reality.
2. On one side is a crowded army of objects and on the other side is the King (Inner-Self) sitting high on his throne. Understand the meaning of this within.
3. The body is made up of bones and flesh. Understand that the King is the root of the visible world in the form of the original element.
4. Everything is made entirely of the five elements and functions only due to the power of the King that is the awareness beyond the elements.
5. Many have become free using the power of discrimination and have thereby come to be called incarnations of God (Avatars). The sage Manu and others became great in this way.
6. Those with expansive awareness are truly fortunate, while those with narrow awareness remain unfortunate.
7. Those who engage in intelligent activity and who courageously endure hardships become fortunate in no time.
8. Those who live like foolish people do not understand, while those who use the power of discrimination understand everything.
9. Greatness and the lack of greatness depend upon the intellect, but ordinary people do not understand this. They say that only those who are elders are great.
10. Even if a king is young, the elderly people must bow to him. One must understand how the wondrous power of discrimination works.
11. The knowledge of ordinary people is born of imagination and speculation, and accordingly they only follow the path of traditional customs.
12. But to whom should we say that their beliefs are not true? The common people do not understand, so how much should be said to them?
13. If a young person rises up and attains a higher state, people detest him. Therefore, an accomplished person should keep away from those people he had close association with before he gained understanding.
14. They do not understand the exact meaning of his statements, nor the significance of political correctness. They unnecessarily hold on to foolish notions.
15. One who does not understand correctly cannot say what is correct. Just because a person is younger, no one cares about his greatness.
16. If a young person says something wise, those who are older than him do not respect him, saying that he is young and not modest. Those who speak like this are not wise.
17. One who is older, but does not have any good qualities has no real authority. Authority that comes from actual experience is real greatness.
18. However, one should still show to respect their elders, and the elders should understand how to behave as an elder deserving of respect. If they do not understand this, they only suffer in their old age.

19. The Inner-Self is the true elder. When it is awakened, there is greatness. This is clearly evident but there are no words to explain it.
20. Therefore, wisdom must be gained with the power of discrimination. If wisdom is not gained through discrimination, one is not looked upon with respect in society.
21. If respect and credibility are lost, what has been accomplished with one's life? Such a person puts himself in a sorry state.
22. Men and women of all types abuse such a person saying that he has become sidetracked. Like this, such a person gets stuck in foolishness.
23. Nobody should live such a life. Make your life worthwhile. If this is not understood, then various texts should be consulted.
24. There is always demand for a wise person while one who is foolish is sent away. If one wants to be successful, he must first become wise.
25. Obtaining this wisdom, one must endure many difficult people, however, know that the best use of one's life is to gain wisdom.
26. Understand that the person who has become wise is respected by many people. How can there be anything lacking for such a person?
27. One who does not tend to one's own good in this life is considered to be one who commits suicide. There is no one who is more foolish than such a person.
28. Such a person undergoes many hardships in the life of a householder and ends up on the receiving end of many people's anger. One who is wise among people does not live like this.
29. I have spoken about this to you aspirants in a natural manner. If you agree with what has been said, happily take what has been offered. If you disagree, then leave it aside.
30. You listeners are extremely attentive and capable of giving your attention to the inconceivable, so you easily understand that what has been said just now is very ordinary and obvious.

Thus in Shri Dasbodh, a dialogue between the Guru and disciple, Sub-Chapter 3 of Chapter 15, named "The Greatness of the Inner-Self" is concluded.

Chapter: 15, Sub-Chapter: 4

Eternal Brahman

|| ShriRam ||

1. Trees are formed from the earth, and from trees we get wood. When the wood is burned it then returns back to earth.
2. Many types of vines that have many various parts such as branches, leaves, flowers, and fruits all come from the earth. Afterwards, when they dry and decompose, they return back to the earth again.
3. There are many foods that human beings eat for their meals that are prepared from various different grains. Afterwards, the food returns back to the earth as feces or vomit.
4. Many birds eat the various grains and in the same way, it becomes waste matter afterwards which then dries up and returns to the earth.

5. When the human body dies it is eaten by worms, or it is turned to ash when burned, and then it returns to the soil. A great many bodies have fallen and returned to the earth in these ways.
6. Many types of grass and plant matter have decayed and returned to the soil. Even the worms return to the earth after dying.
7. There are unlimited objects that have proliferated on the earth, how much can be told of their expanse? Other than the earth, what resting place is there for them?
8. Trees, leaves, and the grass are eaten by animals and become dung, manure, urine and ash which all get mixed together and once again return to the earth.
9. Whatever is created has a duration and gets destroyed. Everything returns back to the earth. Everything that gets created gets destroyed and again becomes earth.
10. There is a great abundance of seeds that grow up to touch the sky only to eventually merge back with the earth and disappear.
11. Many metals are buried in the earth by people and after many days they are turned into soil. Even the fate of gold is like this.
12. Gold as well as stones are formed out of the soil, but when exposed to great heat, they are merged back into the earth again.
13. Gold thread is made out of gold and then goes on to decay, and even the gold that has become molten liquid dissolves back into the earth in the end.
14. Metal is formed from the earth. After having been melted in fire, the molten metal again becomes solidified and returns back into the earth.
15. Water from different places releases various smells and odors. The presence of earth is revealed even there as day by day the water dries up, leaving only earth behind.
16. Many leaves, flowers, and fruits grow and are eaten by many living beings. After dying, all of these beings return back into the same earth from which they emerged.
17. Everything that has been formed has the earth as its support. So it happens that all living beings that assume form pass away and in the end return back to the earth.
18. How much more should be told about this? Utilizing the power of discrimination everything is understood. With discrimination the creation and dissolution of the universe is understood.
19. When water evaporates, only earth remains, and when the earth is burned and turned into ash, the ash dissolves back into water again.
20. Water is formed from light, and later becomes dried up by the heat of the light. Light is formed from the wind, and afterwards is absorbed back into the wind.
21. Wind was created in the sky, and afterwards dissolves back into the sky. One must see for oneself these processes of creation and dissolution in the universe.
22. From wherever anything is created, it returns to that same place when it is destroyed. All of the five elements are destroyed in this way.
23. The elements have been created and then get destroyed. After the elements disappear only the eternal Absolute Reality, Parabrahman, remains.
24. So long as Parabrahman is not realized, the cycle of birth and death can't be escaped, and one is destined to be born into the streams of the four types of living beings.
25. The origin of gross manifestation is the moving, and the root of the moving is the still unmoving Reality that has no beginning or end. One must see this for oneself.

26. The primary premise as presented in the *Vedas* indicates that Illusion has emanated from Reality, while the "final conclusion" (siddhanta) negates the existence of Illusion. That which exists beyond both perspectives is Parabrahman.
27. This must be understood in one's own experience. Through investigation and thoughtfulness, the indications about Parabrahman are realized. Without such investigation and thoughtfulness one only becomes exhausted with foolish nonsense.
28. If a knowledgeable person gets caught up in attachments, how can he realize the unmoving Parabrahman when he is unnecessarily involved in the commotion of Illusion?
29. A wise and discerning person comes to the conclusion that when Illusion is completely destroyed there is nothing that remains.
30. When nothing remains after the dissolution of Illusion, this is what is called self-surrender. How can Supreme Knowledge (Vijnana) be realized when even words and their meanings do not exist?
31. One who is attached to what people say only gets lost in opinions and imagination. Therefore, the aspirant must see again and again with direct experience.

Thus in Shri Dasbodh, a dialogue between the Guru and disciple, Sub-Chapter 4 of Chapter 15, named "Eternal Brahman" is concluded.

Chapter: 15, Sub-Chapter: 5

Explanation of the Moving

|| ShriRam ||

1. The three gunas are the functioning of the combination of the formless (Purusha; primordial male principle) and the active eight-fold creation (Prakriti; primordial female principle). In the vacillation that is the activity of these two, the eternal unqualified Reality that is neither masculine or feminine is forgotten.
2. The great-grandfather (Purusha) is obscured by the grandfather (Vishnu), and the father (Brahma) is killed by the son (Shiva) with his activity. In all of this, the four of them have lost track of the King (Parabrahman).

(Editors note - Here Samartha Ramdas is being very poetic in his imagery and usage of words. The meaning of this symbolism can be gleaned by thinking about this stanza in different ways. The great-grandfather can be said to be Purusha or Moolamaya (Maya prior to the appearance of the gunas), the grandfather is Vishnu or Consciousness (or Sattva Guna), the father is Brahma or the Creator (Rajas), and the son is Ignorance or the objective world (Tamas) which has lost track of its origin. The main point is basically that what is more subtle is obscured by the less subtle, and that the original still Essence (the King) is forgotten in all of this activity.)

3. God is alone, hidden inside the temple. If we worship the temple, the worship reaches him. In the same way, worship that is done in creation reaches him.

4. Two names (Purusha and Prakriti) are given to the one Supreme Self. People have imagined this, but if we use the power of discrimination, it can be seen in actual experience that these are but two names for that which is only One.
5. The Reality is neither masculine nor feminine. This has only been imagined by people. When properly investigated, it is seen that nothing like this exists.
6. In the Marathi language, the word for river is feminine and the word for stream is masculine. These words are used like this by everyone. However, if some thought is given to this, it can be seen that water is only one, and that there are no male or female bodies that can be found with regard to water.
7. One does not know one's Self and when trying to see it, it cannot be perceived. If one tries to see with the aid of something else, it cannot be seen because there is no apparent unity in the vast expanse of things.
8. The one Self alone has assumed many forms and alone pervades all forms, yet it cannot bear its own commotion.
9. The Self, being one, appears as many. Even though the Self appears as many forms, it is One, alone. This strange phenomenon is evident in all living beings.
10. Water resides in all the various types of vines, even though the water is not evident by looking at the forms of the vines. Without water the vines cannot survive.
11. In amongst a group of trees and plants there is some water contained there that they all share, but each tree grows separately. There are also many types of plants that grow in the sky taking their moisture from the air.
12. They grow apart from the ground, but they do not become dried up. In fact, they grow strong in their respective places.
13. The trees move because of the presence of God in them. If the life quality of God was not there, they would become dry wood. This is easily seen. It is not difficult to understand.
14. There are some plants that grow on trees high in the sky. Their roots do not penetrate the earth at any time.
15. When plants and trees decay they form green manure for other trees which feeds the cycle of growth and decay everyday. Some speakers are like trees that spread their words out like branches with many leaves inspiring thoughtfulness and analysis.
16. What has happened in the universe has already happened and people try to explain it using their imagination, while one who is knowledgeable and wise understands everything beyond the words.
17. Some have understood but have no conviction or realization. Some have conviction, but do not have knowledge. Without actual experience everything is only based upon imagination and speculation.
18. One must see for oneself and understand That which is the most superior of all. If you realize this, you find only your own Self in the universe.
19. Those with inner understanding and conviction are of a high caliber, while those who make an outward show are in a backwards state. How can fools know what the wise understand?
20. If one pleases the minds of others, even strangers will praise him. However if people's minds are not pleased, even a good meal will not make them happy.
21. It can easily be seen that things actually happen like this. Keep your attention on That which is beyond concepts. If one who is alert meets another who is also alert, both people feel content.

22. If there is a merging of the two minds, the unseen is seen and there is a crossing over of the revolving cycle of the transient world appearance and one knows oneself to be beyond it.
23. Once the unseen is seen, it is known to be very close within oneself. It can never be seen with the physical eyes.
24. In all of the many bodies there is movement and continuous activity. Parabrahman, the Absolute Reality, is eternally unmoving, permeating everywhere.
25. That which is moving moves from one place to another. When it moves from a place it ceases to be in that place. Thus, the moving can never be present everywhere at all times.
26. The moving does not know the entirety of the moving, nor can it comprehend its expanse. Thus, how then can it ever experience the limitless unmoving Reality?
27. Fireworks move across the sky, but can never reach beyond the sky, as their nature is to be extinguished there in the sky.
28. Similarly, the nature of the mind is to function on the side of the moving, so how can it ever it recognize the Reality? Not being able to recognize the attributeless, it is unsuccessful in knowing the Reality and says that everything is Brahman.
29. When there is no investigation into Essence and non-essence, there only the darkness of ignorance. As with an ignorant child, the True is not recognized and the false is taken to be real.
30. The five elements arise from the Great Causal Body of the universe (Moolamaya). However, the interpretation of the "Great Statements" (Mahavakyas) is different from this. (They say that "Only Brahman Exists.")
31. Understand that God is the greatest element, which is the great principle of Consciousness. This is the pinnacle of aspiration, as all spiritual endeavor and worship ends there.
32. Action (karma), worship (upasana), and Knowledge (Jnana) comprise the three divisions, or prescribed paths found in the *Vedas*. However, with the realization of Parabrahman, Knowledge (Jnana) dissolves away into Supreme Knowledge (Vijnana).

Thus in Shri Dasbodh, a dialogue between the Guru and disciple, Sub-Chapter 5 of Chapter 15, named "Explanation of the Moving" is concluded.

Chapter: 15, Sub-Chapter: 6

Description of Wisdom

|| ShriRam ||

1. From a yellow seed, black ink is created, and from the writing formed by that ink knowledge has proliferated on the earth. Without the writing formed by that ink, knowledge cannot be obtained.
2. The ink is so ordinary in nature, yet it can preserve and store knowledge. Both the best and the lowest qualities of living beings are described in texts because of it.
3. A reed of wood is sharpened and split at the tip to make a writing instrument. Then the pen and ink come together to perform the act of writing.

4. When the paper and the pen come together with the black ink transferring between them, words are written and the worthwhile accomplishment of spreading knowledge is made possible in this world.
5. With analysis and thought about what is written even fools can become wise. In this way, the experience of Truth and the realization of That which is beyond this world can be obtained.
6. That which is agreeable to everyone is what becomes common knowledge. However, the wise do not accept this common knowledge to be true.
7. Different lines that are written are considered to be best, mediocre, and bad, and with some lines, their merit or lack or merit is not apparent. The experience of these four types of lines is different for different people.
8. Those who talk about the greatness of the past fourteen generations of their ancestors may be wise or stupid, who knows? What is important is that the listener must see what needs to be done for oneself.
9. The lines that are written disappear and are gone, but what is written about should be experienced for oneself. This aspect of understanding should not be neglected.
10. One who entertains all sorts of opinions of many people only gets lost in guesswork and imagination, and is deprived of the definite conviction of what is true.
11. Go ahead and listen to what many people have to say, but use the power of discrimination and see for yourself, in your own experience, what is true and what is false.
12. Do not openly contradict anyone, but understand what will be hurtful or helpful to another so that he might get the experience himself. What is the use of a lot of unnecessary talk?
13. Even if a person is stubborn and immature, he should still be respected. In this way many people will pleased in their minds.
14. If someone's mind is twisted and perplexed by a problem and he keeps turning it around backwards and forwards, the problem only becomes multiplied many times. How can one say someone is wise who does not know how to pacify the mind of another?
15. Only if one can make foolish people wise does his life become praiseworthy. To unnecessarily be involved in arguments is foolishness.
16. Meet and mingle with others, and with a humble and kind approach, win them over and change their understanding, and as a strategy then retreat. Using proper discretion and thoughtfulness do not let them know anything of your intentions.
17. To do this, walk and talk according to the disposition of others, and join with them in their way of life.
18. One who cares for the benefit of others does not engage in argumentative behavior. Little by little, from his experience he gives explanations to others that provides understanding in their minds.
19. First the mind of another should be won over so that he accepts you. Then, slowly provide solutions to his concerns that help him to understand, and by using various means, take him beyond the world.
20. When one stubborn person meets another, only confusion ensues. Where constant bickering is going on there is no room for wisdom.
21. Many people go on unnecessarily chattering, but actual accomplishment is difficult. To win over another's mind and take them beyond the world is not easy.

22. One must bear the brunt of the stream of abusive and mean words in order for others to change their minds and see things differently.
23. Speak only after understanding the situation, but do not present an attitude of having superior knowledge. Wherever you go, maintain a kind and modest demeanor.
24. When asking for alms, visit both nice towns as well as poor villages and observe many households. Study and evaluate common people as well as renowned people, and then move on.
25. In most places you find something of value. Make friends among the people and develop good relationships with those who are virtuous and clear-minded. By sitting around idly you cannot accomplish anything. Move from one place to another giving explanations.
26. Be alert and understand everything well before giving information to others. If there is some place you wish to go, use proper discernment first to understand the level of receptivity among the people before going there.
27. One should have a good understanding of many subjects by heart so the minds of everyone can be pacified. Write books and give them to others. Show benevolence towards others beyond limit.
28. Give others what they need, and by that giving you will become well-liked and accepted by all.
29. One who is accepted and respected by everyone cannot be said to be an ordinary person. Many people are wholeheartedly appreciative of such a person.
30. Such are the signs of wisdom. With wisdom one can win over the entire world. There is never anything lacking for such a person, wherever he may go.

Thus in Shri Dasbodh, a dialogue between the Guru and disciple, Sub-Chapter 6 of Chapter 15, named "Description of Wisdom" is concluded.

Chapter: 15, Sub-Chapter: 7

Explanation of Above and Below

|| ShriRam ||

1. It is the Primal Illusion (Moolamaya) alone that is root of many modifications. It is the subtlest form of movement which occurs in the unmoving stillness.
2. The Primal Illusion is of the nature of awareness that is the original root desire, the original determination (concept). It is God that is identifiable as being endowed with six pure qualities[56].
3. It is called various names such as Purusha/Prakriti, Shiva/Shakti, half masculine/half feminine, etc. However, the Primal Illusion is the root of all this and is the "Light of the Universe."
4. This original desire or movement in the Primal Illusion is of the nature of wind. The three gunas and the five elements arise from this wind.

---

[56] In Vedic cosmology the six pure qualities of God are considered to be Jnana (Knowledge/Consciousness), Aishvarya (Omnipresence), Shakti (Energy), Bala (Strength/Power), Virya (Vitality/Life), and Tejas (Brilliance).

5. For example, if we look at a vine, its roots are deep in the earth and the leaves, flowers and fruits spring forth out from the roots.
6. In addition to these there are many colors, shapes, changes, and varieties of tastes that come forth from within the roots.
7. If the root is broken open, none of this can be seen inside. It is all only found once the root begins to grow day by day.
8. In the case of the manifest universe, the vine can be thought of as starting out beginning to grow high up on a cliff with the roots moving forcibly downwards, expanding as it stretches out as the visible world.
9. Like this, the five elements and the three gunas have their origin in the Primal Illusion. The understanding of this must be confirmed in actual experience.
10. This vine grows continuously and is adorned with many changes and modifications which in turn create many more changes and modifications.
11. This vine of manifest creation sprouts many branches and stems from which grow an endless number of offshoots.
12. Many fruits fall and then more grow to replace them. This process of coming and going is happening continuously.
13. Some offshoots get dried up and more sprout up in their place. Like this so many appearances have come and gone.
14. Leaves fall off and new ones sprout. The same is also true for the flowers and fruits. In this process, innumerable beings come and go in this world appearance.
15. Sometimes the entire vine gets entirely burnt up, and then a new one sprouts forth again. The meaning of this should be investigated and understood in one's own experience.
16. When the root is dug up and taken out with Knowledge based in direct experience it is completely uprooted and stops growing entirely.
17. The seed is present in the beginning and at the end. It is also present in essence in-between in the form of water. Like this, its nature is spontaneously spread out everywhere.
18. It is from the root that is created from the seed that all things come to be known. The essence, which is the seed, is effortlessly present there in all of the parts.
19. Things disappear and appear and disappear again in the repetitive cycle of experience. Only the one with Self-Knowledge is not part of this cycle.
20. Even though we say that the Jnani is not part of this cycle, this is something that is required to be understood inwardly. How can ordinary people understand it?
21. All activities are done by the strength of the Inner-Self, yet it is invisible and is not known. How are the poor people to know it if it cannot be seen?
22. Enjoyment of sense pleasures takes place only because of the Inner-Self. Nothing can happen without it. To know the Self, one must give up the gross and rest in the subtle.
23. That which is our own mind is one with the universal mind. Due to the many changes of the different bodies, that which is One seems to have become many.
24. The pain in one finger is not known by another finger. The same principle applies to the hands, feet and various other organs.
25. If one body part does not know the experience of another body part, how can one's mind understand the experience in the minds of others? It is like this that the minds of others are not known.

26. Many different plants grow and appear due to the presence of water, which is only one. When a part of a plant is broken off it gets disconnected from the water and dries up while the remaining parts of the plant remain fresh and blooming.
27. Understand with this simile how the Self has become differentiated. On the relative level one person does not have the same experience of another, but for the Self who is the knower, there is no difference.
28. The appearance of differences in the Self is only because of the differences in the varieties of bodies. This is understood by those who are knowledgeable.
29. The wise look, listen, and understand by examining the mind. They inwardly understand everything quietly and secretly.
30. Such people protects and care for many people, and are able to understand their minds. In their wisdom they understand everything.
31. All living beings try to first see what is in the mind of another before they put their trust in them.
32. Forgetfulness follows remembrance. This is directly experienced by everyone. Often it happens that one loses something that has been put away somewhere.
33. Sometimes what has been said by oneself previously cannot be remembered. An endless number of concepts arise in the mind, how can they all be remembered?
34. Like this, the wheel of movement revolves. It is straight in some places and crooked in other places. One is the "King of Gods" through remembrance, or a beggar through forgetfulness.
35. Remembrance of the Self is to be God, and forgetfulness of the Self is to be a demon. The combination of remembrance and forgetfulness is to be a human.
36. Therefore, understand the effects of these two qualities of remembrance and forgetfulness. One is to be like God, and the other is to be like a demon. Understand this through actual experience in the mind by utilizing the power of discrimination.
37. Use discrimination to understand the power of discrimination. Recognize the Self with the Self. It is like seeing your own eyes by looking at them in the mirror.
38. The gross only comes into contact with the gross, and the subtle can only be understood through the subtle. The subtle indications about the Self can only be known subtly by the Self.
39. Thought is understood with thought, and mind is understood with mind. The minds of other's are known by becoming one with them.
40. In the wholeness of remembrance there is forgetfulness. This is where the concept of differentiation comes in. This is a lop-sided perspective that can never become complete.
41. As learning continues, what has been learned in the past is forgotten. It is like a light in front and darkness behind. As new things are remembered, the things of the past are forgotten.
42. Understand that the fourth body (Turya; Consciousness) is the remembrance of the Self, and that deep sleep is forgetfulness. Know that both of these states are present in the body right now.

Thus in Shri Dasbodh, a dialogue between the Guru and disciple, Sub-Chapter 7 of Chapter 15, named "Explanation of Above and Below" is concluded.

Chapter: 15, Sub-Chapter: 8

Explanation About Microscopic Creatures

|| ShriRam ||

1. There are many microorganisms and tiny creatures that are very small, and their life is very short. Accordingly, their intellect and capacity in life is also very small.
2. There are many such miniscule creatures that cannot be seen by the naked eye. The five facets of the inner-mind (thoughts, mind, intellect, sense of "I am," and consciousness) are also present in these organisms.
3. Their knowledge is very limited, as are the objects of their sense organs. Who bothers to analyze the details of their experience?
4. For them, an ant is very huge, in the same way an elephant is for humans. It is said that a stream of urine is like a great flood for an ant.
5. There are many bodies in this universe both large and small, and the Self that is the Life-Energy resides in all of them.
6. There are a great many such microorganisms that occupy the vast expanse of the universe. One who investigates can easily observe this.
7. There are as many types of microorganisms as there are stars in the sky. To them human beings appear huge like mountains, and for them, their lives seem to have a long duration.
8. Just as there are small and large birds, there are also small and large snakes and fish as well.
9. There are creatures from the size of an ant to larger creatures, and there are even much more vastly larger creatures. With observation, the nature of the minds of these creatures can come to be known.
10. In the great variety of creatures, there are many colors and varieties of life. Some are beautifully colorful and some are without any color at all. How many of them can be described?
11. God has created many creatures. Some have soft and delicate bodies, some have very hard bodies, and some have bodies that shine like gold.
12. There are many differences in their bodies, types of food, communication, and other qualities, but they all have the same undifferentiated Life within.
13. There are some creatures that are troublesome, and some are even deadly. When observing, it can be seen that there are innumerable species of creatures, some being very rare.
14. Who has investigated and categorized all of the varieties of living creatures? Humans see very few of these creatures as we are limited to the scope of our own perception of the universe.
15. There are nine continents and seven seas on this earth. Who among men sees the cosmic water beyond the universe?
16. There are many huge beings which exist in that water. Who can know the states of such beings?
17. Where there is water, there is life. This is the nature of creation. If one looks into this, it can be seen that the expanse of creation is very vast.
18. Inside the crust of the earth there can be found various forms of water, and in these waters there are many varieties of bodies small and large. Who knows all of them?

19. Some beings that live high in the sky have not been seen on the earth. After getting their wings, they fly high above the earth.
20. There are many living beings in the air and on the land, and many that live in the forest and in the sea. Of the 8.4 million varieties of species, who can know them all?
21. With the exception of in the scorching fire, there are living species that can be found everywhere. There are even beings that are formed out of imagination. Who can know them all?
22. Some beings are formed using different powers, and some are formed from spells and have bodies that are cursed.
23. There are some bodies formed by magic, some by demonic powers, and some that are formed by the gods in various ways.
24. Some bodies are formed out of anger, some out of penance, and some that are formed by the removal of a curse.
25. Such is the myriad variety of creatures created by God. How much of all this can be explained? A great many strange things happen because of Illusion.
26. Many strange and incomprehensible beings have been created which are neither seen nor heard by anyone. Such a strange play of creation should be understood to happen in Illusion.
27. Very little is known about such things by people who only learn enough knowledge as is needed to make a living, and who unnecessarily take pride in calling themselves knowledgeable.
28. It is the Inner-Self alone that is knowledgeable. The Self permeates everything. Who has the intellect to know its greatness?
29. The seven sheaths of the universe are the same as the seven sheaths associated with the body (the five elements, the ego or ignorance, and Chaitanya or the Self). Within the body there exist many living beings as well.
30. When a person does not even understand one's own body, how can he understand everything else? People become puffed up with pride having gained only a little knowledge.
31. For beings that are as small as atoms and molecules, humans are huge beings. Our lives are gigantic compared to their lives.
32. Their behavior and the laws governing their lives are many and various according to the species. Who understands all of these things?
33. So wondrous is the creation of God that one cannot imagine it with the mind. It is the vain imagining of the ego that makes the mistake of thinking it knows everything.
34. Giving up the ego, reflect upon the many creations of God. See that in the vast expanse of creation the life of a human being is short and insignificant.
35. The human life is very short and the body is mortal. Yet, because of pride people cry for the body in vain not knowing that it will surely die in a short time.
36. The body is conceived in a dirty place and begins to grow in dirty fluids. By whose account can it be said to be great?
37. This body is a dirty thing and is prone to destruction in a moment's time, yet people are continuously engaged in worrying about it and its ailments. Without thinking, people foolishly call it a great thing.

38. The body is an illusion that lasts only for a short time. From beginning to end it is a cause of pain and suffering, yet people clothe it and decorate it, trying to show off its greatness in vain.
39. Even though the body is clothed, it still becomes exposed at the time of death and creates a terrible stench. One who has gained understanding through the power of discrimination is truly one who is blessed.
40. What value is there in going around arguing uselessly? It is better to break the egotistical pride associated with the body. The best use of life is to know God using the power of discrimination.

Thus in Shri Dasbodh, a dialogue between the Guru and disciple, Sub-Chapter 8 of Chapter 15, named "Explanation About Microscopic Creatures" is concluded.

Chapter: 15, Sub-Chapter: 9

The Creation of the Body

|| ShriRam ||

1. All of the four categories of beings grow because of the presence of water. Because of water, innumerable beings come and go.
2. The body is formed from the five elements in combination with the Inner-Self. If we seek out the origin of all bodies, we find water.
3. Just as sweat comes out of the body, similarly, semen comes out of the body and mixes with other fluids and blood to form bodies.
4. Blood and semen together with the fluids from food all come together to form the mold of the body which then begins to slowly grow and take shape.
5. As it begins to grow, it increases in size. From soft fluids the solid structure of the body was formed. Later on, the water in the form of bodily fluids spread throughout the various body parts.
6. When the bodily form becomes fully developed, it comes out from the mother and begins to cry. This is how it happens for all people.
7. As the body grows, wrong thinking also begins to grow. Every part of the body begins to grow from conception. As the body develops, the body parts change and continue to grow in front of our eyes.
8. Later, as the bodies become bigger day by day, many thoughts begin to appear in a variety of ways.
9. Just as a seed develops into a piece fruit, the same principle applies for the body as well. By listening and hearing many different things, the process of learning and recognition develops accordingly.
10. Seeds sprout because of water. Without water, the seeds dry up and blow away. Only if water and soil are both present will the seed begin to grow.
11. When both soil and water are present the seed gets wet and sprouts easily. As the plant continues to grow it brings great joy.
12. The roots begin to move down deep in the earth and the shoots reach upwards and move in the wind. As the plant grows, the shoots and the roots continue to move in opposite directions away from the seed.

13. The roots grow underground, and the tips of the plant continue to move upwards in the sky. After some time, the trees become laden with many leaves, flowers and fruits.
14. Prior to fruit are the flowers, prior to flowers are the leaves and, and in sequence, prior to leaves there is only wood.
15. Prior to wood are the tender roots, and before the fragile roots there is water. When the water becomes dried and condensed, earth is formed.
16. This is the actual experience in nature. Prior to all things is the world, and prior to the world is God in the form of water.
17. Prior to that is God in the form of fire, and prior to that is God in the form of wind. Prior to wind is the Inner-Self in its own nature.
18. The Inner-Self is prior to everything. One who does not know it is considered to be one who is fallen. This means that one has missed the Self and lives life as being apart from it.
19. The Self is what is most near, yet people miss it. They have not acquired a fondness for experiencing it. Without knowing God in this life, people are unnecessarily taking birth and merely passing away.
20. God is prior to everything. By becoming one with him, the nature of one's disposition begins to change.
21. The devotee of God never ceases meditating on the Self. While walking and talking such a devotee does not stray from his contemplation.
22. That which is created by one's ancestors can easily be seen, but how much can be seen of all that the Self has done?
23. The one who is fully conscious of the Self is the truly fortunate person. One who is only partially conscious of the Self is less fortunate.
24. When one is continually conscious of Lord Narayana in the mind, the Goddess of Prosperity (Laxmi) is always with him.
25. God permeates everywhere in the world, and accordingly, should be worshipped. By serving him in everyone, the Self becomes satisfied.
26. In worshipping him in everyone, he is seen to be everywhere in the world. If he is not known and if his activity is not examined, his presence is not appreciated.
27. The play of God is only understood by God. No one else sees his play. When seeing correctly, you see that you are one with God.
28. Worship him in all places, because there is no place where the Inner-Self does not exist. Everywhere it is only the Self, Lord Rama, who does everything.
29. Such is my worship, the greatness of which cannot be imagined. Such worship takes one beyond the visible world.
30. Actions take place because of God, worship takes place because of God, and people become knowledgeable only because of the existence of God.
31. Many various scriptures and opinions are spoken by God alone. All actions whether disciplined or undisciplined, proper or improper, happen according to the law of action (karma).
32. It is God who does everything. In all of this activity of God, one takes as much as one can according to one's capacity.
33. According to the primary premise of the *Vedas* it is stated that one must understand the transient nature of the appearance and disappearance of the universe. In the next sub-chapter, the "final conclusion" (siddhanta) will be explained.

34. Vedanta (the end section of the *Upanishads*), siddhanta (the final conclusion), and dhadanta (self-experience), must be understood with correct understanding, and experienced with certainty. Leaving behind the creation consisting of the five elements, the meaning of the great statement "I Am Brahman" (Aham Brahmasmi) is correctly understood.

Thus in Shri Dasbodh, a dialogue between the Guru and disciple, Sub-Chapter 9 of Chapter 15, named "The Creation of the Body" is concluded.

Chapter: 15, Sub-Chapter: 10

Explanation of the Final Conclusion

|| ShriRam ||

1. In the sky many things come and go, but the sky remains unaffected. In the unmoving stillness of the sky there are many things that move. This fundamental principle is easily observed.
2. When there is darkness, the sky appears black. The same sky appears yellow when seeing the sun's rays.
3. In the winter time, the sky appears to have become cold, and in the hot weather it appears to have become dry.
4. Like this, whatever appears in the sky passes away. It has never happened that anything has remained other than the sky.
5. One with good intelligence easily understands that the sky does not come and go, and that whatever has an appearance is false.
6. The elements of water and wind are spread out everywhere, but the Self is spread out to a much greater extent. The Inner-Self is the element that permeates all of the other elements.
7. Understand within that everything that has an appearance moves, while the Self does not move. Upon proper analysis this is understood by living beings.
8. Analyzing this again and again one eventually comes to rest continuously in the Self. Once having merged in the Self, one does not become separate from it.
9. There, Knowledge (Jnana) turns into Supreme Knowledge (Vijnana), and the mind becomes no-mind. Utilizing the power of discrimination, one understands the nature of the five elements and becomes one with the Self.
10. When the Primordial Self is sought and then seen, the moving becomes still and the duality of God and devotee disappears there.
11. When saying "there," this does not mean a place. What is meant is that there is not anything objective that exists. However, something has to be said so that you may gain some understanding.
12. What is being indicated is that the power of ignorance as well as the power of Knowledge both disappear. See how this stateless state of no-mind comes to be realized.
13. Basically what is being indicated is that the dissolution of the energy of ignorance occurs when the restlessness of movement comes to rest in the peaceful still silence of the unmoving Reality.

14. The modifications and effects of the moving do not continue when movement itself disappears. It can never happen that motion can be the same as the unmoving stillness.
15. The authority of the Great Statements (Mahavakyas) rests with the true renunciate (sanyasi). Only the person who is blessed by God sees the meaning of the Mahavakyas and is able to come to the firm conclusion ("I Am Brahman") presented by them.
16. The true sanyasi is one who has completely given up the six afflictions of the mind (desire, anger, arrogance, lust, jealousy, enticement). Only those who inquire into their true nature and are deeply thoughtful can be true renunciates. One's spiritual progress is dependent upon one's spiritual practice.
17. When the Lord of the Universe is recognized, what need is there to go on speculating? Now, let this be enough. Those who are thoughtful will understand.
18. Those who are thoughtful understand and become completely unattached to anything. Those who remain full of pride for the body protect their bodily misidentification.
19. When one's attention becomes seated in the stateless state that has no focus of attention, the primary premise about the appearance and disappearance of objects presented in the *Vedas* vanishes, and the state of the inner witness disappears as well.
20. The space above and the space below are both called space. When the partition of the visible world in between is removed it is seen to be only one continuous space.
21. Space is one continuous space. It is the mind that sees with the perception of separate entities. Words cannot describe what remains with the dissolution of these entities.
22. That which is beyond words, beyond imagination, beyond the mind and intellect, and beyond the perception of the sense organs must be investigated and seen for oneself.
23. By seeing again and again we come to understand. After correct understanding comes, all that has been understood previously becomes useless. How can That which is so difficult to express in words be spoken about?
24. When the meaning and the essence of the statement "Thou Art That" is found, the individual consciousness become merged in Reality. Afterwards, someone with understanding must speak about it.
25. By searching for That which Eternal, one becomes a true Jnani. Having given up all that changes, he has become merged in the changeless.
26. Many bad dreams may be seen during sleep, but upon awakening they are all known to be false. Even if they are remembered afterwards they are still known to be false.
27. When the realization of the unmoving is confirmed, the body may remain or get destroyed due to the effects of past actions. The one who has realized the unmoving Reality is unconcerned about its fate.
28. When a seed is roasted in fire, it can no longer grow. The same thing happens to the seed of desire for the Jnani.
29. Through investigation and thoughtfulness the intellect becomes fixed in the unmoving Reality, and everything is accomplished. In this way, the intellect of all the great realized beings of the past has become fixed in the unmoving Reality.

30. The one who contemplates on the unmoving becomes the unmoving Reality. One who contemplates on the moving remains with that movement. One who contemplates only the elements merely becomes merged with the elements.
31. One who has reached the final destination cannot be affected by anything. One who has this firm inner conviction sees Illusion to be false like a magician's tricks.
32. When one comes to know through inquiry that all appearances are completely false, all fear disappears in an instant.
33. Become successful by worshipping the Self and spread devotion among the people. Realize everything within by using the power of discrimination.

Thus in Shri Dasbodh, a dialogue between the Guru and disciple, Sub-Chapter 10 of Chapter 15, named "Explanation of the Final Conclusion" is concluded.

Chapter 16. The Qualities of the Elements

Chapter: 16, Sub-Chapter: 1

In Praise of Valmiki

|| ShriRam ||

1. Blessed is the virtuous sage Valmiki, famous among sages. The three worlds have become purified because of him.
2. The whole of the Ramayana that was to occur in the future was written in advance by him, in hundreds of thousands of verses. Such a feat similar to this has not been seen nor heard of anywhere in the whole of creation.
3. Even if one prediction about the future comes true it is a very rare occurance and the people on the earth are greatly surprised.
4. Even when the incarnation of Lord Rama had not yet taken place, and there was no reference in the scriptures, Valmiki elaborately wrote the story of Rama's life.
5. The elegance of Valmiki's literary skill was so majestic that upon hearing it even Lord Shiva was greatly pleased, and he divided it into sections and spread it throughout the three worlds.
6. Such grand poetic style that was appreciated by Lord Shiva had never before been seen from any other sage. With this text, the worshippers of Rama become extremely content.
7. There have been many great sages in the past. Many of them have expressed their thoughts in poetic style, however never has a greater poet than Valmiki ever lived in the past, nor will such a great sage come in the future.
8. Valmiki did many cruel deeds early in his life, but he became pure by repeating the name of Lord Rama. By repeating Rama's name with great faith and discipline, one becomes virtuous beyond limit.
9. Even though Valmiki repeated Rama's name in reverse order, the mountains of his past wrongful deeds crumbled, and the flags of his virtue were raised in the universe. (Valmiki was a thug in his early life and was unable to repeat the holy name of Rama, so he began to repeat it in reverse order, saying "Mara, Mara," which turns into Rama, Rama when said repeatedly again and again).
10. The forest where Valmiki performed his austerities became pure and full of virtue. Through the power of the repetition of Rama's name, even dried wood began to sprout new shoots.
11. Early in his life he was a dangerous killer, and a fisherman going by the name Vali. Later in his life he became respected on earth by everyone, including learned men and sages.
12. When one turns away from all wrongful deeds in repentance, how can any wrongdoing remain? By intense spiritual practice that almost caused the death of his body, he became filled with virtue and was as if reborn.
13. He sat still in a meditation posture in one place and his body became encased in an anthill. Later in his life he became well known by the name Valmika which means "anthill".

14. Since an anthill is called valmik, the name Valmiki was appropriately suited for the sage. Seeing his rigorous penance even the greatest of the yogis and monks felt moved in their hearts.
15. He is the greatest among spiritual practitioners and the greatest among poets. He spoke in a clear and direct manner with firm conviction.
16. He is like the crown jewel of the devotees of Lord Rama. His exceptional one-pointedness of concentration and his resolve in spiritual practice inspires aspirants to remain steadfast in their faith.
17. Blessed is the great sage Valmiki, the powerful lord of poets. I salute him laying spread out in full prostration.
18. Had Valmiki not told the great story of Rama, the world would not have the Ramayana. I don't know how to adequately describe this most powerful sage.
19. He expressed and revealed the glory and fame of Rama, and thus enhanced His greatness. Devotees become greatly contented by listening to the Ramayana.
20. Many lives have become fulfilled by becoming immersed in praising Lord Rama. Many people on earth have become uplifted by what Valmiki has done.
21. There are many great devotees of Lord Rama whose grandeur is limitless. Ramdas says, "I bow at the feet of all the great devotees of Rama."

Thus in Shri Dasbodh, a dialogue between the Guru and disciple, Sub-Chapter: 1 of Chapter: 16, named "In Praise of Valmiki" is concluded.

Chapter: 16, Sub-Chapter: 2

In Praise of the Sun

|| ShriRam ||

1. Blessed is the race of kings descended from the Sun, which is the most special among ancestral successions. (Lord Rama was a descendant of this ancestry, the clan of Raghu.) The light of the Sun's radiance has spread over the earth.
2. There is a fault with the body of the moon as it wanes for fifteen days of the month, but the radiance of the Sun never becomes diminished.
3. There is no simile that can be used as a comparison to the Sun by whose light all living beings enjoy the dawn.
4. In this world there are many duties and actions which can be categorized as best, medium, or lowly. Many easy and difficult activities continue happening regularly in nature.
5. Without the light of the Sun, the *Vedas, Shastras, Puranas*, mantras and yantras, as well as bathing and other rituals, all would remain unknown.
6. Innumerable opinions and yogic practices become known, and are followed in their own ways once the Sun has risen.
7. Many worldly and spiritual activities with their causes and effects are useless and cannot be achieved without the light of day.
8. The eyes are the organs of perception of the Sun's light. Without the light of the Sun being visible to the eyes, one becomes blind to everything. Nothing can be seen to move without the Sun's light.

9. It can be argued that a blind person can write poetry, but even that happens due to the effects of the Sun. If the mind of such a poet is cold and dull, how could there be any expansion of the intellect that is required for the writing of poetry?
10. The light of the Sun gives heat, while the light of the moon is cool. If there were no heat, the body would perish.
11. Without the energy of the Sun, no activity is possible. Dear wise listeners, find this out, and see for yourselves.
12. The incarnations of the gods like Shiva and Vishnu, and the many manifestations of Shiva and Shakti all came after the sun. The Sun existed prior to them all, and still continues to exist now.
13. All beings that have come into this world have lived under the Sun, and the end of their bodies happened in the presence of the Sun.
14. The moon has emerged out of the churning of the cosmic sea in recent times. It was one among the fourteen precious gems (important things), and is known as the brother of goddess Laxmi.
15. The sun is what gives the eye of vision to the world. This is known to all creatures large and small. For this reason the Sun is considered to be the greatest of the great.
16. The Sun unceasingly traverses its path in the sky. Day after day it comes and goes, serving all beings with the power of its heat.
17. If daylight were not there, all would be in darkness, and nobody would know what is superior and what is inferior. Without daylight thieves and the creatures of the night would rule the earth.
18. What else can be compared to the Sun? It is the most brilliant thing that we know without comparison.
19. Such is the Sun that is known to all, the ancestor of Lord Rama. Its greatness is so immense that it cannot be described by human speech.
20. The ancestry of Lord Rama from which many great kings have descended is very ancient. How can their greatness be comprehended by a person of dull intellect?
21. Where the devotees of Lord Rama gather, my mind becomes engrossed in His greatness. I have become speechless trying to describe His importance.
22. In salutation to the Sun, all of one's difficulties are cleared away. Merely by looking at the Sun, one's inspiration is enhanced.

Thus in Shri Dasbodh, a dialogue between the Guru and disciple, Sub-Chapter: 2 of Chapter: 16, named "In Praise of the Sun" is concluded.

Chapter: 16, Sub-Chapter: 3

In Praise of the Earth

|| ShriRam ||

1. Blessed is the Earth, whose greatness cannot be told. All the living beings live by her support alone.
2. Even entities that live in the sky are of the nature of Earth. Living beings cannot live without a body, which is inert in nature.

3. People burn, scorch, dig, plough, burrow, and excavate her. They make her dirty with feces, urine, and vomit.
4. Whatever is rotten, putrefied, and tattered has no place except the Earth. At the time of the death of the body, it returns only to her.
5. All that is labeled as being either good or bad has no place except the Earth. There are many metals and liquids that are found in the Earth.
6. One living being kills another, but both beings have their existence only on the Earth. Where can they go if they give up the Earth?
7. There are many forts, towns, cities, and countries that can be found by traveling, and there are many gods, demons, and human beings all residing on the Earth.
8. There are many gemstones, diamonds, philosopher's stones, metals and minerals that are all hidden in the Earth. Without the Earth, they would not exist.
9. There are huge mountains like Mount Meru[57], the Himalayas, and the various other mountain ranges, which are home to many species of birds, fish, and snakes, that all exist on the Earth.
10. There are many lands across the seas, many huge pieces of broken land, and many cliffs that exist on the Earth.
11. Among those places there are numerous hidden tunnels both large and small where pitch black darkness prevails.
12. The seas and oceans covering the Earth are very vast and are filled with various fish and huge aquatic animals.
13. All of that life is supported by the wind which is dense, thick, and solid. Because of wind, the water stays contained in the seas and is unable to break away on any side.
14. That wind is firmly supported by the pride in the sense of being separate from the unmoving Reality. Who can know everything about the expanse of things on the Earth?
15. There are mines of different kinds of metals, gems, wish-fulfilling stones, wish-fulfilling trees, and reservoirs of nectar that exist on the Earth.
16. There are many islands, continents and barren lands which exist on the Earth with many creatures living on them.
17. Around Mount Meru there are many huge cliffs that cast large shadows. In the midst of those shadows there some areas that receive sunlight and are the home to many species of thick trees.
18. Close to that is the Lokaloka mountain, and other mammoth mountains such as Chandra, Dronadri and Mainak that can be seen.
19. There are many places on Earth where stores of many different kinds of hidden stones and gems lie buried under soil and ashes.
20. The Earth contains innumerable jewels. How marvelous is this place called Earth where large amounts of precious things are spread around everywhere!
21. Who is there who has visited every place on the face of the Earth? There is no simile that adequately applies to the Earth.
22. There are many plants and crops that grow in various countries, each different from one another.

---

[57]Mount Meru is a mountain of Hindu mythology that is believed to be located somewhere in northern Tibet or possibly somewhere northeast of the Indian province of Kashmir. In more modern times the names of many mountains have been changed, so the exact location and the names of surrounding mountains remain a mystery.

23. The three planes of existence, heaven, the mortal world, and the netherworld, all exist in relation to the Earth. The huge serpent Shesha lives below the netherworld as the support of the Earth.
24. There are a great many plants and crops that live on this huge Earth. Such an amazing and marvelous thing is this Earth that is the creation of the creator.
25. There are many attractive forts, castles, cities, towns and villages that are all the dwelling place of the one Lord of the Universe.
26. There were men of huge strength born on this Earth in the past who achieved great things, yet their power was never so great that they could become separate from the Earth.
27. It is improbable that there is another place in the universe as wondrous as this Earth where so many living beings and incarnations of God have appeared.
28. It is clearly evident without any need for speculation, that even in present times, a great variety of living beings exist only because of the support of the Earth.
29. Many people say that the land belongs to them, but in the end they die, and the Earth remains. So much time has passed, but the Earth remains as it is.
30. Such is the greatness of the Earth that no good simile can be given to it. The Earth is the support of all, including Lord Brahma and all of the other gods.

Thus in Shri Dasbodh, a dialogue between the Guru and disciple, Sub-Chapter: 3 of Chapter: 16, named "In Praise of the Earth" is concluded.

Chapter: 16, Sub-Chapter: 4

Explanation of Water

|| ShriRam ||

1. Now, the birth place of everyone that is the Life of all living beings, which is called the Water that is Lord Narayana (Apo-Narayana), will be described.
2. The earth is supported and surrounded by water that is the water of the seas and oceans, and the water in the clouds that flows down on the Earth as rain.
3. There are many rivers in many different countries that flow to meet the sea. Some are small, some are big, and some are sacred and revered beyond measure.
4. There are rivers that cascade down from the mountains finding their way down cliffs and through valleys, roaring with amazing intensity.
5. There are wells, ponds, lakes, and many reservoirs in various places that are filled to the brink with pure water.
6. There are many canals that have openings in the shape of a cow's mouth, many small streams, and many brooks where water trickles out from the rocks.
7. There are many small pools, springs, wells, and places where water flows out through openings in mountains and rocks. There are a great many places where water is found on the Earth.
8. There are as many streams that rush down with deadly speed as there are mountains, and there are innumerable streams and brooks that bubble out of the ground.

9. It is not possible to describe all of the water on the Earth. There are countless numbers of fountains and aqueducts that hold and carry water.
10. There are many ponds, pools, small pits, and tanks that hold water in the mountains of different countries, and many other types of containers for water.
11. There are many famous pilgrimage places with water that are considered great and auspicious holy places, and which have been described by the writers of scriptures as having limitless grandeur.
12. There are many pilgrimage sites, some with pure water, some with cool water, and some with hot springs that are found at many places.
13. There is water that has medicinal value found in many plants, fruits, flowers, roots and bulbs.
14. There are many kinds of water that are found in many different places having various compositions and qualities. Some is salty, some is poisonous, and some is sweet like nectar.
15. There is sugarcane juice, fruit juices, different varieties of milk, honey, mercury, and the liquids derived from the processing of sugar.
16. The shimmering brilliance of pearls, of many dazzling jewels, and of weapons made from metal is also called by some as being "water."
17. There are many differences in the qualities of water that can be seen in semen, blood, saliva, urine, sweat and other fluids. Upon analysis, these different qualities can easily be seen.
18. The body consists mostly of water, and the earth, moon, and planets are comprised of various forms of water.
19. There is an ocean of salt, an ocean of milk, an ocean of wine, an ocean of ghee, an ocean of curds, an ocean of sugarcane juice, and an ocean of pure water.
20. Like this, water is spread out all over from the beginning to the end of creation. It appears at one place and disappears in another.
21. Water takes on the flavor of whatever it is mixed with. In the sugarcane it has an extremely lovely sweetness.
22. The body is held together with water and it requires additional water to survive. How much can be said about its origin and expanse?
23. Water can save one's life, and water can kill. There are many types of pleasures that are enjoyed from the various forms of water. If we give thought to it, it can be seen that water is truly remarkable.
24. Water flows on the earth making various melodious sounds, and in great waterfalls it pours down with thundering force.
25. In many places there are reservoirs and huge lakes that get filled up to the brim with canals and streams flowing from them with great turbulence.
26. In many places rivers and streams flow underground that can be heard when they are running near the surface.
27. There are huge reservoirs full of water in the earth which no one has neither seen nor heard, and there are many streams that have begun flowing after lightening has struck the earth.
28. There is water hidden in many places underground, and many places where it is seen on the surface of the earth.
29. There is one river that flows through the three worlds, and there is water in clouds that rains down from the sky.

30. The root of earth is water, the root of water is fire (light), and the root of fire is wind. Like this, one element is greater than another.
31. Still greater than the elements is God. Understand, that even greater than God is Parabrahman, the Absolute Reality.

Thus in Shri Dasbodh, a dialogue between the Guru and disciple, Sub-Chapter: 4 of Chapter: 16, named "Explanation of Water" is concluded.

Chapter: 16, Sub-Chapter: 5

Explanation of Fire

|| ShriRam ||

1. Blessed is the Fire God who occupies and fills the entire universe. He is the father of Janaki (Sita), and the father-in-law of Lord Rama[58].
2. God receives all that is offered to him through his mouth which is fire. Fire is the giver of the fruits of spiritual practices to the sages, and the remover of ignorance, cold, and disease from the people of the world.
3. Although there are different castes and species of living beings, fire is very pure and is the same for all, including Brahma and the other gods.
4. All of creation functions because of fire. It keeps people satisfied (with warmth, and for cooking, bathing, etc.), and all creatures large and small are alive because of fire.
5. Because of fire, the liquid earth became solid and provided a place for people to live. Because of fire there are large lamps, small lamps, and torches scattered around the earth.
6. Because of fire, people feel hunger in the stomach, and meals become flavorful.
7. Fire occupies the entire body, and everyone survives because of its heat. Without warmth, all people would die.
8. When the heat of fire becomes diminished in the body, living beings die. This is the experience of all living beings.
9. Having the strength of fire, enemies can be defeated immediately. As long as there is fire in the body, there is life.
10. Because of fire, many medicinal preparations have been concocted, and even people stricken with leprosy have been cured in a short period of time.
11. The sun is a special manifestation of fire, but when the sun sets, fire provides light. Everywhere people accept the help of fire in the night.
12. Fire brought out from the house of even the lowliest person cannot be said to be tainted or impure. Fire retains its purity in all houses.
13. There are special places where fire is always kept lit, and many things are offered to fire. Fire becomes pleased by the things that are offered to it.
14. All beings such as gods, demons and humans move because of fire. Fire is very useful to all people.

---

[58] In the story of Ramayana, when Janaki (Sita) performed the fire sacrifice, the God of Fire appeared and said, "I accept her, she is my daughter, she is very pure."

15. Marriages and celebrations are made into grand spectacles with many types of fireworks. Many great processions that are seen on the earth are made to look more spectacular with fireworks.
16. Many sick people become healthy with warming medicines because of the heat from fire.
17. For a brahmin priest, the Sun God is everything to his mind, his body, and his life. There need not be any doubt about this.
18. Fire has many forms. Among people there is fire in the belly, and in the oceans there is fire spewing out of mountains under water. Away from the earth there is fire in the atmosphere, there is fire in the third eye of Shiva, and there is fire in the form of lightening.
19. Fire can be produced with a magnifying glass, and mirrors are used to reflect the light of fire. Fire can even be produced by the friction of rubbing two pieces of wood together.
20. Fire exists in all places. It appears with friction, and it is said that forests are incinerated with the fire from a dragon's breath.
21. Fire can be useful and destructive in many ways. However, if it is used without discretion, its benefits are wasted.
22. Everything on earth whether large or small is in some way supported by fire. God becomes satisfied with the offerings made to him by way of fire.
23. Such is the greatness of fire. Any simile used to speak of its greatness falls short. The greatness of fire is expansive beyond limit.
24. Fire makes all living beings happy, and after death, it turns the body into ashes. It consumes everything. That is its greatness. What more can be said about it?
25. At the time of the dissolution of the universe, everything gets destroyed by the great Universal Fire. Fire does not leave any object remaining.
26. People make offerings to fire in their homes, and lamps are kept burning in the temples of God and at many places of pilgrimage.
27. Many large and small lamps are used by the people to perform the waving of light (arati) before images of God, and in some cases fire is also used to test the purity of various things.
28. All the three worlds and the eightfold creation is occupied by fire. Its greatness is limitless and cannot be adequately described with words.
29. Fire is symbolically personified in the scriptures as having four horns, three legs, two heads and seven hands. The meaning of this symbolism is explained in the scriptures, but fire is not actually experienced as being a person.
30. Such is fire, which has become manifest as heat. I have described it according to my capacity. The listeners are asked to please excuse any shortcomings that might be found in what has been said.

Thus in Shri Dasbodh, a dialogue between the Guru and disciple, Sub-Chapter: 5 of Chapter: 16, named "Explanation of Fire" is concluded.

Chapter: 16, Sub-Chapter: 6

In Praise of the Wind

|| ShriRam ||

1. Blessed is the Wind God whose nature is very strange. All beings exist and are active because of wind.
2. Because of wind, breathing goes on, the study of the various streams of knowledge happens, and movement of the body is possible.
3. Moving, bending, expansion, resistance, and contraction are possible because of wind. It functions in the body as the five main types of Prana. (Prana, breath; Apana, eliminative air; Vyana, circulation; Udana, speech; and Samana, digestion).
4. It also functions in the body as the secondary kinds of Prana. (Naga, Regurgitation of food; Kurma, movement of the eyelids; Karkasha, belching; Devadatta, to bring sleep; and Dhanajayo, prana as it is leaving the body at the time of death). These are the some of many natural functions of wind that are found to exist.
5. The wind came forth in the universe, where it created the gods. From there it appeared in the body with its various attributes.
6. All of the gods in the heavenly realm, the demons of the netherworld, and the humans and great kings on earth have their strength because of wind.
7. There are many types of human bodies, and many varieties of wild animals in the forests and in the water that play joyfully.
8. It is the wind that plays in them all. Birds fly in the sky, and the flames of fire rise high because of wind.
9. Wind fills the sky with an accumulation of clouds, and then it drives them away making the sky clear again. There is nothing else that functions like the wind.
10. Wind is the power of the Self that functions in the body. There is nothing that compares to the expanse and the power of wind.
11. The armies of dense clouds that are more solid than a mountain and that benefit the people with rain, as well as the thunder and lightening, are all due to the power of wind.
12. The moon, the sun, the planets, the galaxies, and various types of cloud formations in the universe all exist because of wind.
13. The elements that are intermingled cannot be separated or pulled apart, and the complexity of their connectedness cannot be understood because of wind.
14. When the wind blows forcefully there is a downpour of hailstones, and it is the force of the wind that brings small creatures and insects to life from the rain water.
15. Just as the lotus flower is supported by its stem, the earth is supported by water, which is in turn supported by the divine serpent Shesha. It is the wind that is the support of all of this.
16. Wind is the nourishment of the divine serpent Shesha. By swallowing wind his body becomes expansive. Because of his expanse, he is able to support the weight of the Earth.
17. The body of the great tortoise (one of the ten incarnations of Vishnu) was so huge that it held the universe on his back. His huge body existed only because of the wind.
18. The great boar (another one of the ten incarnations of Vishnu) held the earth in its teeth due to the power of wind.

19. Brahma, Vishnu, Shiva, and the Lord of the Universe are all in the form of wind. With subtle discrimination and thoughtfulness one is able understand this.
20. All of the varieties of deities, the thousands of great sages and the accomplished yogis are powerful because of wind.
21. All of the angels, spirits, and ghosts exist only in the form of wind.
22. The power of ghosts and spirits is also only in the form of wind. No one knows how many such beings exist on the earth.
23. It is the power of the wind that pervades the body, the universe, and even beyond the universe. This powerful wind existed everywhere prior to the universe.
24. Like this, is the powerful wind whose son is Hanuman. Hanuman is continuously immersed in the service of Lord Rama with his body and mind.
25. It is well known that Hanuman is the son of wind, and that there is no difference between the father and the son. Hence, there is no difference between them in their power and strength.
26. Hanuman is called the "Lord of the Breath" and it is this quality that makes him so powerful. Without breath, everything becomes lifeless.
27. In ancient times, when death had approached Hanuman, the wind stopped moving and all of the gods began to suffocate.
28. So all of the gods came together and said a prayer in the praise of the wind. The wind was pleased with the prayer and revived all of the gods.
29. Hanuman is a great courageous incarnation of God. All of the other gods have been amazed to see his strength and power.
30. When the gods were imprisoned by Ravana, it was Hanuman who saw them, and he suddenly destroyed all of the demons and threw them out of Lanka (Ravana's kingdom is the realm of the senses as explained in the Ramayana).
31. He took revenge on behalf of the gods, and sought out the demons at their root and destroyed them. This was the great adventure of the "God with the Tail" that surprised everyone.
32. Ravana was seated on his throne and Hanuman went there and struck him with great blows. He withheld everything including water from the residents of Lanka.
33. Seeing his courage and bravery, the gods felt protected and supported by him. They prayed to Lord Rama and asked for his mercy.
34. Hanuman destroyed all of the demons and freed all of the gods. All living beings in the three worlds were greatly pleased with him.

Thus in Shri Dasbodh, a dialogue between the Guru and disciple, Sub-Chapter: 6 of Chapter: 6, named "In praise of Wind" is concluded.

Chapter: 16, Sub-Chapter: 7

The Great Element

|| ShriRam ||

1. The origin of earth is water, and the origin of water is fire. The root of fire is wind. This has been explained previously.
2. Now, listen to the explanation of the origin of the wind, which is the Inner-Self that is extremely restless and is present in all things.
3. The Inner-Self comes and goes but cannot be seen. It does not become steady in one place, and the grandeur of its form cannot be surmised by merely reading the *Vedas* and *Upanishads*.
4. The original inspiration arising in Brahman is the Inner-Self. Afterwards, the three gunas are formed from this great "Lord of the Universe."
5. From the intermingling of the three gunas, the five elements were formed and came into a recognizable state. The true nature of the five elements can be recognized with the power of discrimination.
6. Among them, the principle element is space (sky) which is particularly special. Everything is seen because of its illuminative light.
7. It is said that the greatest element is indicated as being Lord Vishnu. This must be seen with actual experience.
8. The five elements have been described in detail. Among those elements, the one which the others arise out of pervades everywhere. It can be seen and experienced through subtle analysis.
9. The speed of the wind cannot be compared to the speed of the Self. The speed of the Self must be experienced directly in order to be understood.
10. No action can take place without the Self. The Self cannot be seen nor found objectively. It is the hidden seer of many thoughts that come and go.
11. It occupies and supports the body as well as the universe. It plays in the form of many bodies. It is seen in the world to those who utilize the power of discrimination.
12. It is not possible or imaginable that bodies can function without the Self. It is because of the Self alone that the eightfold manifestation has taken form.
13. From beginning to end, it is the Self alone that does everything. Beyond the Self is Parabrahman, the Absolute Reality that is without any modification.
14. The Self resides in the body and stimulates the activity of the sense organs. Because of the union of the Self with the body, it experiences both pleasure and pain.
15. The universe has seven layers, and in it is the body, which also has seven layers. Of those layers, the most subtle is the Self. This is recognized through discrimination.
16. It is the Self alone that listens to words, and after understanding them makes a reply. It is the Self that knows the sensations of soft and hard, and cold and hot through the skin.
17. It is the Self that sees many objects through the eyes, and through observation and analysis of them knows in the mind what is higher and lower.
18. It is the Self alone that understands the significance of different looks such as harsh looks, sober looks, crafty looks, benevolent looks, etc.

19. It is the Self that selects, and knows the many different tastes experienced through the tongue. Whatever is known and described is spoken of only by the Self.
20. It is the Self that knows the flavors of the best food, and recognizes through the nose the fragrances of many fruits.
21. It speaks and tastes with the tongue, it gives and takes with the hands, and it comes and goes with the legs.
22. It enjoys sexual pleasure with the penis, throws out waste matter with the anus, and conceives, imagines and sees all with the mind.
23. It is the Self alone that is the doer of all activities in the three worlds, at all times. There is nothing else that can compare to its greatness.
24. There nothing other than the Self. Who can describe the greatness of the expanse and functioning of the Self, either in the past or future?
25. How could it be possible to have understanding of the *Vedas* (books of knowledge), *Shastras* (books of spiritual science), and *Puranas* (mythological books) without the Self?
26. It is the Self that recognizes proper conduct in this world, uses discrimination to recognize what is beyond this world, and makes determinations about both.
27. Many opinions, many differences, many discussions, many arguments and resolutions, and many differences and similarities are all done by the Self alone.
28. The basic principle that is the Self has alone spread out everywhere and manifest itself as many forms. The recognition of this is the fulfillment of life.
29. Writing, reading, learning things by heart, asking, telling the meanings and giving explanations, singing, the playing of musical instruments, and dancing are all performed only by the Self.
30. It is the Self alone that feels happy when experiencing many pleasures and suffers from pain and sorrow. It is the Self that occupies many bodies and leaves them in various ways.
31. The Self alone occupies all bodies and has the relationships among them. Without the Self, there can be no actor, drama, or various artistic skills.
32. It is the Self alone that assumes the multitude of forms and does many industrious works through them. Assuming many disguises, the Self is both courageous and cowardly.
33. The Self alone permeates everything and is the lone seer of all the activity of creation. What a marvel it is that the one Self has spread itself out and multiplied without the sexual intercourse of male and female.
34. In the world, females want a male, and males want a female. Such is the liking and interest for the opposite sex that provides pleasure for both.
35. The physical gross body has its origin in the subtle body. It is due to this connection of the subtle and gross bodies that the particular affairs of the world take place.
36. Without proper investigation, many people say that the soul of man and the soul of woman are different. However, the Self of all is only one. This subtle secret must be experientially understood.
37. The distinction appears because of the gross forms, but in subtle experience, everything is understood to be one. This definitely must be experienced to be understood.
38. It has never happened that procreation can take place from one woman enjoying sex with another woman. Thus, a woman inwardly has the longing for a man.

39. Outwardly the nature of a relationship is of a man with a woman, but the subtle relationship is only of the Self with itself.
40. The desire in a man is itself the female principle. Like this Prakriti is present in Purusha. However, it is in the female principle (Prakriti) that the male principle (Purusha) becomes manifest. Thus, it is correctly said that the male and female principles are one.
41. By looking to the gross body as a reference, see the universe and gain an experiential understanding of the universe. If you do not understand, then gain understanding through repeated explanation and investigation.
42. The original desire for duality is the Primal Illusion itself. From there the entire world becomes manifest. Therefore, see how both the Primal Illusion and the world have appeared.
43. Here the large task of clarification has been completed. The doubts of the listeners have been removed, and the nature of the male (Purusha) and female (Prakriti) principles have been explained.

Thus in Shri Dasbodh, a dialogue between the Guru and disciple, Sub-Chapter: 7 of Chapter: 16, named "The Great Element" is concluded.

Chapter: 16, Sub-Chapter: 8

The Self That is Lord Rama

|| ShriRam ||

1. First, we bow to Lord Ganesha, who is the embodiment of auspiciousness. Because of him, the intellect is inspired and people sing the praises of the Self.
2. Next, we bow to the Goddess of Speech (Sharada) who gives explanations about the streams of knowledge and illumines the inner consciousness.
3. Among all names, the name of Rama is supreme. By repeating the name of Rama, even Lord Shiva was able to dispel his suffering and attain peace.
4. The greatness of the name of Lord Rama is immense. Through the repetition of Rama's name day after day, one comes to know the nature and form of the One who is beyond everything and who is the God that sustains the three worlds.
5. The Self that is Rama exists everywhere. It is because of Him that people move from place to place. Without the Self, the body falls down and dies.
6. This one God exists in all gods, demons, and human beings. He is called by many names such as the individual Self (Jivatma), the Self as Shiva (Shivatma), the Supreme Self (Paramatma), the Self of the World (Jagadatma), the Universal Self (Vishvatma), the Hidden Self (Guptatma), the Inner-Self (Antaratma), and the Subtle Self (Sukshatma).
7. All paths, all walking, all talking, all of those who are on the long list of incarnations of God (avatars), and even Lord Brahma and the other gods, have come into existence only because of him.
8. The Self is known as its various forms, such as the form of sound, the form of light, the form of the witness, the form of Power, the form of Life-Energy, the "True Form" (Swaroopa), and as the form of the Seer.

9. He is known as the best person, the best courage, primordial being, the best among the kings of the Raghu clan, and the best of the best in all the three worlds.
10. Without the Self, many activities, many difficult endeavors and efforts, and many hurried actions do not happen. If the Self did not exist, no activity would exist.
11. Without the Self, the body is useless and dead. Without the Self, the body is nothing but dead inert matter.
12. One with Self-Knowledge understands in the mind and sees the presence of the Self in all people. On the earth and in all of the three worlds, there is nothing but the Self.
13. It is the Self that knows what is extremely beautiful and who is wise, and it is the Self that knows the Essence and the non-essential. Without the Self there is only darkness.
14. It is the Self that is accomplished and alert. All of the many differences, sorrows, and joys are because of the Self.
15. Whether one is a beggar or is a god like Brahma and others, it is the Self alone that moves everyone. Some see this by discrimination into what is Eternal and what is ephemeral.
16. If there is a beautiful woman in one's home, her beauty is maintained as long as the Self is there. Once the Self leaves the body, the light in the body departs.
17. The Self cannot be seen or felt. It cannot be imagined to have an outer form. All of the imaginings of the mind are due only to the Self.
18. The Self resides in the body and from that residence, it analyzes the entire universe. All of the desires and feelings are due to the Self. How many of these can be described?
19. There are an endless number of states of mind and an endless number of concepts that are had by an endless number of beings. How can the content of all their minds be enumerated?
20. There are endless number of political strategies, and good and bad types of intellect that are interpreted, understood, and not understood in various ways, all because of the Self.
21. Some people take care of others, some deceive others, some kill others, and some run and hide from others. Such is the state of enmity and commotion among beings.
22. In this world there are many who deceive one another, and there are also many devotees who help others.
23. It is the one Self that has become differentiated into an endless number of bodies, each enjoying life according to the capacity of the body. The Self actually is undifferentiated, but it gives support to many different forms.
24. In this world, a man wants a woman, and a woman wants a man. It is never seen that a wife wants a wife.
25. For the Self there is no masculine gender for men and feminine gender for women. This type of differentiation does not exist for the Self. Differentiation comes in relation to desire for sensual pleasures.
26. Each living being is interested in the food that is meant for it. If a human being is given food meant for an animal, he doesn't take any interest in it.
27. The differences in food and in physical bodies are many. Some are hidden and some are obvious. Similarly, there are many different types of joy and happiness.

28. There is water in the ocean, there is water underground. The water in the surrounding seas is gigantic and there are many bodies of animals in that water.
29. Even when we see with the subtle vision of mind, we can't know everything that there is to know about the body. How then can the entirety of the Inner-Self be surmised?
30. By investigation, and looking into the nature of the union between the body and the Self, some conclusions have been established. Yet, still there is some confusion about the interrelationship between the gross and subtle that remains.
31. To resolve this confusion, the Inner-Self has given many explanations and has spoken benevolently through the mouths of many people.

Thus in Shri Dasbodh, a dialogue between the Guru and disciple, Sub-Chapter: 8 of Chapter: 16, named "The Self that is Lord Rama" is concluded.

Chapter: 16, Sub-Chapter: 9

The Many Forms of Worship

|| ShriRam ||

1. There are many people in the world, and many types of worship and spiritual practice. According to their faith, people everywhere offer their devotion and sing the praises of God.
2. People worship their own God in various ways. The say prayers and sing in praise, and they say that their worship is of God that is without attributes.
3. The listener asked, "Please tell me your opinion. What is the significance of this kind of worship?" The speaker responded by saying "Listen now and I will tell you about the nature of worshipping God."
4. God without attributes is actually the Inner-Self that has many attributes. Understand that all of creation is but fraction of God without attributes. This must be experienced and seen for oneself.
5. Whatever is done to please all of the people reaches the one Inner-Self. However, people tend to only accept that which is presented as being authoritative and whatever is generally considered acceptable by society.
6. The listener said, "But all of that is only imagination. If we water a plant at the root, the water reaches every leaf of the plant. This is verified by direct experience in everyday life."
7. The speaker said, "If you pour a pot full of water on a plant, the water does not stay on the leaves, even for a moment. It runs off the leaves and quickly penetrates the ground down to the roots."
8. The listener then said, "This analogy is applicable for a plant, but how can a pot of water be poured on the top of a large tree? Please explain this to me."
9. The speaker said, "Even if the hands can't reach there, the rainwater that falls onto the trees goes to the roots."
10. The speaker continued, "All cannot reach the root. Without virtue, how is it possible? The mind of the sage can understand this through the power of discrimination."

11. The simile of the water that falls down on a tree is just an easy example to show where the water goes. It is not difficult to understand what happens in this example. (All worship flows to the root.)
12. Upon having this doubt cleared, the mind becomes satisfied. Now, I will explain how That which is "without attributes" is said to be "with attributes."
13. When there is restlessness (motion), and modifications (change), this is what is called with attributes, or saguna. Otherwise, That which is without attributes, or nirguna, always remains as it is, beyond all attributes.
14. This thought must be understood through the investigation into Essence and non-essence with a firm resolve in the mind. Only then can it be seen that there is no trace of any attributes.
15. It is not difficult to discern that it is the king who sits on the throne who is the actual king, and not the servant named Raja (Raja means king). Simply by thinking this over, it is easy to understand that the servant named Raja is not the king.
16. At the time of the dissolution of the universe,[59] That which remains is called nirguna, the attributeless. Everything else is in the field of Illusion.
17. There are many words and sounds that are heard in the midst of an army, in cities, at market places, and at various celebrations and festivities large and small. How do we distinguish one sound as being distinct from the others?
18. There are many sounds that are heard at various times and seasons, such as during the rainy season, in the night, etc., that are made by various creatures. How do we recognize and distinguish various distinct sounds from the whole?
19. There are many countries and places, many languages, and many opinions on the earth. There are innumerable sages with different opinions. How do we select among them?
20. When it rains, many sprouts appear in nature. There are trees and plants both large and small. How do we select and separate them?
21. There are many birds, animals, and aquatic animals with various bodies that have many different strange and unusual colors. How are they distinctly recognized?
22. This visible creation takes form, gets modified in many ways, and is spread out beyond limits. How do we select minute parts of this vast expanse?
23. In the empty space there are many clouds, small and large, that appear to take the shapes of houses and cities. How do we select particular shapes among this vast array of clouds?
24. Throughout the various times of day and night, moonshine and darkness, many types of thoughtfulness and thoughtlessness can be seen. How do we recognize them?
25. Forgetfulness and remembrance, discipline and lack of discipline, and experience and speculation are also like this.
26. Justice and injustice, as well as possibilities and impossibilities are also seen. How can one know and understand the difference between them without the proper utilization of discrimination?
27. The differences between a good worker and a useless person, between one who is courageous and a mischief maker, and between one who is virtuous and one who is not virtuous must be understood correctly.

---

[59] Here Samartha Ramdas is poetically using the double meaning of the word "KalpantaPralaya" which means the dissolution (pralaya) at the time of the end of the universe, or era (Kalpanta; Kalpa - an age or era, and Anta - the end); The second meaning is the dissolution (pralaya) of the universe that occurs when imagination or concepts come to an end (Kalpanta; Kalpa - concept, imagination, and Anta - the end).

28. The differences between wealth and bankruptcy, a gentleman and a thief, and what is true and what is false must be understood.
29. Recognize what is superior and what is inferior, and what is of the nature of confusion and what is of the nature of Truth. This can be clearly understood by investigation into Essence and non-essence.

Thus in Shri Dasbodh, a dialogue between the Guru and disciple, Sub-Chapter: 9 of Chapter: 16, named "The Many Forms of Worship" is concluded.

Chapter: 16, Sub-Chapter: 10

The Gunas and the Elements

|| ShriRam ||

1. All of the movement and activity of the universe happens because of the five elements. If the five elements were to disappear the universe would not exist.
2. The listener asks the speaker, "The significance of the five elements has been stated, but what about the three attributes (gunas)? Please explain what happens to the three gunas (rajas, tamas, and sattva)."
3. The speaker replied, "The Inner-Self is the fifth element, and the three gunas are a part of this element. Make your mind alert, and see for yourself."
4. The Sanskrit word "bhoota" means element. Element means "that which has happened." The three gunas also fall into the category of "what has happened." With this explanation the root of the doubt can be broken.
5. There is nothing apart from the five elements. Everything belongs to the five elements. Nothing is separate from them, and nothing can happen without them.
6. Wind has appeared in the Inner-Self. From the wind comes the appearance of fire, and from fire comes water. This has already been explained in detail.
7. Water was spread out everywhere and it became dried up by the heat of the Sun. Due to the presence of fire and wind, earth was formed.
8. If fire, wind, and the sun were not there, it would be cold everywhere. The heat was created in that coldness. This is the process.
9. Each element is intermingled with all of the other elements, and in that mixture of elements, the vast expanse of creation has spread out everywhere. All bodies have been formed because of this balance of the elements within each other.
10. If it was only cold everywhere, all living beings would die. If there was only heat everything would become scorched.
11. The earth became condensed by the cold and became dry by the sun's heat. In this way, God used various means for constructing the earth.
12. Thereafter, he made the rainy season which kept the earth cool. This cooling was alternated with heat, which is manifest as the winter and summer seasons.
13. In the winter season people become troubled by the cold, and the trees and other plants dry up. Therefore, when the summer season comes, there is an appreciation for the heat.
14. In those seasons also came more variety such as early morning, afternoon, evening, and night. There also came cool and warm times during the day.

15. Like this the seasons were created and organized properly in order of sequence. Because of this, the living beings everywhere have survived.
16. There are many chemicals on the earth that cause various diseases, and accordingly many medicinal herbs were also created. Through observation and analysis one can easily see the nature and order of the universe.
17. The root of the body is in the water that is in the form of blood and semen, and from that water even hard materials are formed such as the teeth and bones. The formation of many jewels in the earth can be seen to happen in the same way.
18. The basic root of everything on earth is water. Life is able to continue on because of water. If there was no water, living beings could not survive.
19. Pearls that shine like Venus as well as diamonds, rubies and sapphires all get their luminosity from water.
20. How can the greatness of one element be singled out over the others? All of the elements are intermingled together. How can one be said to be distinctively better than another?
21. Now something has been said for the mind to be able to discern and understand. Among the people there are a few who use discrimination to understand.
22. It is not possible to know everything. Even scriptures do not agree with each other. However, through speculation and guesswork one cannot gain firm conviction about anything.
23. The many qualities of God are limitless to such an extent that even the speech of the serpent with a thousand mouths (Shesha) cannot describe them. Even the rituals and instructions in the *Vedas* fall short without the grace of God.
24. The Self that is God sustains and protects everyone in the three worlds. Without Him, everything turns to dust.
25. Where the Inner-Self is not present, no activity takes place, and nothing can survive. Without Him, the beings of all the three worlds turn into corpses.
26. When the Self is not present in the body, there is no life, only death. Understand this inwardly with the power of discrimination.
27. How can understanding or discrimination take place without the Self? Therefore, it is fitting that everyone should have devotion for God.
28. When I made clear the nature of my worship, this question was raised. Therefore, the inquiry regarding God must be done.
29. Meditation and worship are the great support of the devotee. Without these, one does not have any support, and even if great efforts are made, success will not be achieved.
30. If there is no support from God, one will surely have to endure a great many hardships. Therefore, worship God again and again.
31. With worship, spiritual practice, and study, one is able to go beyond this world appearance. Ramdas says, "Hold firmly to these with faith and confidence."

Thus in Shri Dasbodh, a dialogue between the Guru and disciple, Sub-Chapter: 10 of Chapter: 16, named "The Gunas and the Elements" is concluded.

Chapter 17. Prakriti and Purusha

Chapter: 17, Sub-Chapter: 1

The Power of God

|| ShriRam ||

1. In the unmoving Brahman exists the ever-moving Self which is beyond all things. It is called the "Supreme Self" (Paramatman), as well as "Life-Energy" (Chaitanya), the "Witness" (Sakshi), the "Self as Knowledge" (JnanaAtma), and "God with Six Qualities (ShadgunaIshwara; the six qualities are Knowledge, Omnipresence, Energy, Power, Life, and Brilliance).
2. He is the God of all worlds and is therefore called "Lord of the Universe" (JagadIshwara). The expanse of the universe has spread out from him.
3. Other names that are given are ShivaShakti, the "Goddess of the Universe" (JagadIshwari), "Supreme Goddess" (ParamIshwari), the "Primal Illusion (Moolamaya), the "Lord of Attributes" (GunIshwara), and "The Stimulus of the Gunas" (Gunakshobini).
4. God is the Inner-Self that is the seer of everything, and the knower of the field of the body. It is the pure untainted "Great Principle." One who examines this is the real knowledgeable sage.
5. The "Lord of All Beings" is present in the bodies of all living beings, large and small, including the forms of Brahma, Vishnu, and Shiva.
6. He is the one who resides in the temple of the body. If devotion is not offered to him, the body gets destroyed. Thus people are devoted to him out of fear of death.
7. When people are not devoted to him they experience many troubles in life. Therefore people have developed a fondness for devotion to him.
8. Whatever was asked for, was given by him immediately. Because of this, everyone in the three worlds began to worship him.
9. The objects of the five senses are offered to him as required so that the body does not become afflicted with many ailments.
10. When the objects of the senses are not offered to the one God, he does not remain in the body, and all fortune, prosperity, and wealth are lost.
11. He does not allow anybody to know how he leaves the body. God cannot be known except by God himself.
12. To see God, the temple (body) is required. God reveals his existence through the medium of the qualities of the temple.
13. "Temples" means that there are many bodies where the "Lord of All Beings" resides. There are many bodies with endless varieties of differences.
14. Bodies are the walking and talking temples in which God resides. Understand that there are as many temples as there are bodies.
15. There are three temple bodies, those of the mythological fish, tortoise, and boar (three of the incarnations of Vishnu) that have supported the earth, which were pure, huge, and ferocious.
16. In many temples where God resides he enjoys happiness like an ocean that is filled to the brim. Yet even that happiness has a temporary duration.

17. This God is the crown jewel of the ephemeral world. Even though he cannot be seen, he is still called "The Lord."
18. When one's attention is turned towards him, everything is experienced as unified. When one's attention is turned away from him, there is multiplicity and suffering. Like this, it is said that one's inclination is to turn either upward or downward.
19. The Self that is the root of everything is gigantic and majestic yet invisible. It does not reside only in one location for even a moment.
20. Such is the unfathomable greatness of the Supreme Self. Who can know its greatness? You are yourself this Supreme God who alone understands your own divine activity (Lila).
21. Only through the discrimination between the Eternal and the ephemeral does one gain fulfillment in this worldly life and achieve success in both worldly life and in spiritual life.
22. God is continuously with the one who meditates on him day and night. There is nothing comparable to the virtue of such a devotee.
23. One who is in continuous conscious union with God is the true yogi. One who is not in conscious union with God feels a sense of separation. However, even such a one who feels separate can become unified with God through the strength of continuous meditation.
24. The greatness of virtuous people is that they guide people on the correct path. One who is a swimmer does not allow anyone to drown.
25. There are few on this earth who analyze the body and the universe, separating the gross from the subtle.
26. By continuous analysis of the nature of five elements as postulated by the *Upanishads*, the secret meaning of the "Great Statements" (Mahavakyas) of the *Vedas* is understood in one's inner-mind.
27. Blessed are those who exist in this world and utilize the power of discrimination and provide guidance through their association with others. By listening to their discourses living beings are given a means to become liberated.
28. Through the association with knowledgeable people, and by repeatedly hearing and studying good scriptures, one gains understanding and conviction. There are many benefits of keeping the company of those who have the best qualities, and the virtue of helping others is unsurpassed.
29. Those who have such great virtue and reputation are men and women of God. The passion for establishing true religion resides in them.
30. The greatest path is the investigation into Essence and non-essence, by which the world is uplifted. By renouncing all attachments, one becomes truly immortal.

Thus in Shri Dasbodh, a dialogue between the Guru and disciple, Sub-Chapter 1 of Chapter 17, named "The Power of God" is concluded.

Chapter: 17, Sub-Chapter: 2

Explanation of Shiva and Shakti

|| ShriRam ||

1. Brahman is pure and unmoving like the sky. It is alone, like formless space without any modification.
2. It is That which has no end. It is limitless, eternal, and always present. It has never not existed. Its existence is eternal.
3. Parabrahman, the Absolute Reality, is indestructible like the sky and vast cosmic space. It can never be divided or broken. It is, eternally as it is.
4. There is neither Knowledge (Jnana) nor Ignorance (Ajnana), and no remembrance nor forgetfulness in it. It exists eternally without attributes, and it is not supported by anything.
5. There is no sun, moon, nor fire in it. It is neither darkness nor light. It is alone, never mixed with anything, nor tainted by anything. It is nameless Brahman.
6. In That unmoving stillness arose movement in the form of awareness that was imagined as Life-Energy (Chaitanya). In that, the three gunas arose in equal measure which resulted in the balance of the three attributes.
7. Understand that this Primal Illusion (Moolamaya) appeared in the same way that clouds appear in the sky. Like the clouds, it appears and disappears in a fleeting moment.
8. That which appeared with its many modifications of attributes is in That which is without attributes, and is called God with six qualities. It is also called God that is half male and half female.
9. It is "Primordial Existence and Power," ShivaShakti. It is the entirety of power that is the Primal Illusion. After its appearance, many things were created in it.
10. Afterwards, from there arose the attribute of purity (sattva) which contained hidden within it the attributes of rajas and tamas. It is called the "Great Principle" (MahaTattva), and the "Stimulus of the Three Gunas" (Gunakshobini).
11. A question arises here. "If no distinctions originally existed in the Primal Illusion, how can any such thing as this half-male and half-female principle (ShivaShakti) arise? Listen attentively now to the reply with an alert mind.
12. When you examine the universe and compare it to the body, or examine the body and compare it to the universe, both the microcosm and the macrocosm can be known separately and as a whole.
13. If the idea comes to mind to break open a seed to examine it, no fruit can be found inside. However, after the seed sprouts and the tree grows tall, many pieces of fruit eventually appear.
14. Upon opening the fruit, the seed is seen inside, but when the seed is opened, no fruit can be found. This analogy is applicable in the context of looking at the body and the universe.
15. It is well known that at the level of the body there is the appearance of differences between men and women. They do not exist separately in the Primal Illusion, so how do they become different?
16. There are many ideas in the form of a seed, and in that seed, is the idea not present? This is subtle, so it is not seen immediately.

17. Desire is the root of everything that is gross. In the gross, the desire cannot be seen at first because one cannot imagine anything that is not part of the gross manifestation.
18. The visible creation is created out of imagination. This is stated in the *Vedas* and ancient scriptures. It should not be called false just because it is not immediately apparent.
19. For every birth there is a veil that is like a curtain between the individual and Reality. How can this be understood? This is a secret that is a rule in the Primal Illusion.
20. The Life of both men and women is the one Self, but it appears to be separate because of the nature and characteristics of bodies.
21. A wife does not feel a need for a wife. In this way, one begins to see the difference between the sexes. Seeing from this perspective relating to the body, the seed of the universe can be conceptually understood.
22. Both of the minds of the man and woman feel an attraction and longing for the other. Looking in this way, the nature of desire can be recognized if we look to its root.
23. The root desire arises without any differentiation. The differences appear because of the association with the body. By breaking off the association with the body (bodily attachment) the differences disappear.
24. The root cause of man and woman is in the ShivaShakti principle. When we use the body as a reference for comparison, the duality appearing as ShivaShakti can be experientially understood.
25. There are many types of attraction and desires for love that are not always shared mutually between one person and another. With keen observation one can arrive at some conclusion regarding this.
26. The mother nurtures and cares for the children. This is generally not done by the father. It is in this way that the family continues to grow.
27. The mother does not feel bored, or lazy, or grow tired of raising the children. Such affection is not seen anywhere else other than with the mother.
28. She knows how to inspire endeavors, how to inspire involvement in relating, how to increase love, and how to create affection for various objects in the family life.
29. Man has faith in the affection of the woman, and the woman gets satisfaction from the man. They are tied to each other by desire for each other.
30. God has created a thread which ties all of humanity. Human beings remain entangled in the knot of intense desire which cannot be untied.
31. Thus men and women have a great mutual affection and attraction for one another. This has originated in the Primal Illusion and can be seen directly by utilizing the power of discrimination.
32. In the Primal Illusion this desire is very subtle. Later on it becomes clearly evident. The activity of procreation continues because of the two.
33. First, the male and female principle of ShivaShakti appeared in the Primal Illusion. Later, came the existence the husband and wife. From there came the expanse of the 8.4 million species of beings.
34. The form of ShivaShakti has now been explained. The listeners are requested to apply the mind to what has been said. Understand that anything that is spoken about that is not properly explained and then analyzed is useless.

Thus in Shri Dasbodh, a dialogue between the Guru and disciple, Sub-Chapter 2 of Chapter 17, named "Explanation of Shiva and Shakti" is concluded.

Chapter: 17, Sub-Chapter: 3

The Importance of Listening

|| ShriRam ||

1. Wait! Listen first before setting this book aside. Listen attentively to what is said here.
2. The essence of listening is listening to spiritual discourses and explanations about Self-Knowledge. With concentration of the inner-mind, focus on the meaning of the explanations given in this text.
3. By listening, reflecting, and enquiring into what has been heard, gain direct experience of Self-Realization. What is spoken of here is immediate liberation. There is no talk about liberation in the future found here.
4. One must be alert while examining various gemstones or when weighing out the best quality of gold before casting it in the mold.
5. Just as how one takes care when carefully counting coins, and when evaluating various objects before accepting them, one should use discrimination and be attentive when speaking with others.
6. Likewise, when a huge offering of grain is made, it must first be cleaned properly. If uncleaned grain is offered, it is not acceptable, and God (in the form of the recipient) becomes displeased.
7. Just as one has to be very careful when discussing private affairs in secrecy, one must be much more careful when discussing the topics contained in spiritual texts.
8. There are many religious stories, narrations, parables, ballads, and important biographies of great people, but greater than these is the discussion about spiritual knowledge (adhyatma vidya).
9. What merit is gained by listening to stories from the past? It is said that merit is acquired, but that merit cannot be seen.
10. The essence of spiritual knowledge is not like that. It is of the nature of experience gained from investigation. When this type of understanding is gained, speculation and guesswork come to an end.
11. Many great beings have appeared and passed away. They all lived only for the Self. Who can describe the greatness of the Self?
12. Throughout all ages it is the one Self alone that governs the three worlds. Utilizing the power of discrimination one must see and experience the Self for oneself.
13. Many living beings have appeared, lived, and passed away. As per your request I have described their nature and behavior.
14. Where the power of the Self is not present everything becomes worthless. Without the Self, one becomes inert and helpless like a piece of wood. What can be understood in that state?

15. The superiority of Self-Knowledge is such that there is nothing else that compares to it in the entire universe. Virtuous people understand this through the power of discrimination.
16. The elements of earth, water, and light are all contained within the earth. However, the Inner-Self is the basic seed of these that always remains quite different from the elements.
17. One who goes beyond the wind with discrimination discovers the close connection of the Self.
18. Wind and space together are "Illusion with attributes" (GunaMaya), which is the Primal Illusion of the half-male and half-female principle (PrakritiPurusha). It is not easy to experience the subtlety of this.
19. Who will make the effort to understand the subtlety of the complex structure of the creation of Illusion? For the one who understands this, all doubts disappear.
20. The Primal Illusion is the fourth body (Turya; the Great Causal Body). One should realize what it is to be without this body. Blessed is the sage who remains after going beyond this body.
21. Only those who inquire and are thoughtful ascend higher and gain a higher evolution. All others, who only gain the knowledge of objects, vainly fall into spiritual poverty.
22. Objects appear to be good and attractive, but their nature is that they are destined for destruction. People who are mesmerized by them only become tarnished by worldly life and do not achieve success in spiritual life.
23. For this reason, one should give up the objective knowledge and imagination of many topics and seek the invisible Reality.
24. Greater than the eight-limbed yogic body of knowledge is the knowledge about Reality. Even greater than that is Self-Knowledge which must be experienced for oneself.
25. At the extremity of the Primal Illusion arose the original concept or desire of God, Vishnu. Through effort in spiritual practice one must embrace and experience this.
26. Then one can know the attributeless Brahman that is beyond the Primal Illusion. Its indication is that it is pure and unmoving like the Sky.
27. Prevailing everywhere, Brahman is present in all living beings. It permeates and adheres to all objects.
28. There is nothing as great as Brahman. It is more subtle than the subtlest thought. When there is the dissolution of the body and the universe one comes to know it.
29. Even though the body and the universe may still be in existence, if the dissolution is seen through the power of discrimination one begins to understand this eternal principle.
30. It is only after the elimination of all the elements, and arriving at the conclusion as to what is Essence and what is non-essence through careful consideration, that one should set aside this text, remaining content in Supreme Knowledge.

Thus in Shri Dasbodh, a dialogue between the Guru and disciple, Sub-Chapter 3 of Chapter 17, named "The Importance of Listening" is concluded.

Chapter: 17, Sub-Chapter: 4

Dissolution of Imagination

|| ShriRam ||

1. When a speaker gives spiritual discourse it is very beneficial for many people. The speaker should not become irritated when listeners ask many questions, and the consistency of the teaching should not be lost.
2. When doubts are raised by the listener, they must be cleared immediately. It should not happen that what you say contradicts your previous statements.
3. If something that is said contradicts what has been said previously, everything said appears to be absurd. In this way, one finds oneself caught in many difficult situations.
4. If a swimmer wants to save others from drowning, but cannot swim well himself, how can he save others? In such a case, the listener's doubts remain unresolved.
5. If the speaker talks about how everything gets destroyed, and with the next breath says that everything is Essence, this will only create confusion and make it very difficult for the listeners to go beyond Illusion and give it up.
6. Whatever subtle terms the speaker uses in discourse, he should be able to explain them clearly so that the listener is convinced about what is being said. Only then can the speaker be called a thoughtful person.
7. A good speaker must be able to give the explanations about Brahman, the Primal Illusion, the eightfold manifestation, ShivaShakti, God with six qualities, and the state of the equilibrium of the gunas.
8. He must be able to explain the half-male and half-female form of God, the creator and his creation, and the original subtle stirring of the gunas which gives rise to the three gunas.
9. He should be able to explain the primary premise that is presented in the *Vedas* and the extent to which it is considered to be useful. The person who can explain this and who can also explain subtle concepts in various ways is a blessed sage.
10. A good speaker does not get carried away by excessively lengthy narration repeatedly saying the same things. He is able to bring the listeners to the experience of That which cannot be conveyed in words.
11. The speaker must be careful when at one moment he says that only pure Brahman alone exists, and then says that "All is Brahman," and then in the next moment says that Brahman is the seer, the witness, and the power that moves everything.
12. If he says that the unmoving Brahman has itself become the moving visible creation, or that the moving creation is Brahman, this will in many situations only create confusion and arguments without any clear conclusion.
13. It is an error if he states that the moving and the unmoving are both only Life-Energy that appears in different forms, yet cannot explain their distinct natures.
14. In this way, he unnecessarily creates confusion in people's minds that cannot be resolved. This only results in many opinions and causes a lot of confusion.
15. If he says that Illusion is Parabrahman, and that Parabrahman is a delusion, this only reveals the delusional nature of his knowledge through his speech.
16. If he forcefully makes references to the scriptures, yet gives explanations that have no basis in experience, and is then questioned about his statements, he becomes extremely agitated in his mind.

17. One who calls himself knowledgeable and expects something in return is truly pitiful and cannot really speak the Truth. A good speaker must be able to give conclusive explanations about That which is Essence and what is non-essence.
18. The state of one who is knowledgeable but has no actual experience is like that of a doctor who praises some medicine which is not a remedy for anything.
19. Where discrimination between Essence and non-essence is not discussed, and there is no examination and inquiry into one's True Form, only the darkness of ignorance prevails in that place.
20. When one says that everything is only Brahman, where is there any place for consideration about virtuous and wrongful behavior, heaven and hell, or discrimination and lack of discrimination, when all is said to be the same?
21. In such a case, the listener is led to believe that virtue and the lack of virtue are to be considered equal, and that conviction and imagination are both only forms of the one Brahman.
22. When everything that is sweet is said to be only sugar, how can the true nature of the sweetness of sugar be selected? In the same way, when everything is said to be Brahman, how is one to understand what should be selected and what should be discarded?
23. Similarly, when Essence and non-essence are said to be one, only thoughtlessness and the lack of discrimination gets strengthened. How can there be any place for thoughtfulness and inquiry there?
24. Where the respectable and the despicable are considered the same, what can be gained from that? Those who are intoxicated with wealth, and get carried away by it, indulge in irrelevant and nonsensical talk.
25. In the same way, one who is under the delusion of ignorance gets deceived and firmly believes in his mind that everything is Brahman. To him the virtuous person and the wrongdoer are one and the same.
26. What remains to be said if such a person considers renunciation of everything to be the same as unbridled indulgence in sensual pleasures?
27. These distinctions have been created by God and no one can speak of discarding or breaking this law. A morsel of food which is meant to be put in the mouth, cannot be put in the opening of the anus.
28. The object that is appropriate to any sense organ is only fully enjoyed by that organ. This is the natural order in God's creation. This rule cannot be broken, otherwise nothing would survive.
29. All of this is the deception and delusion of Illusion. Whatever is said without actual experience is only a false argument. It is like the speech of a servant who has gone mad and just babbles on meaninglessly.
30. Listen to the explanations of the one who speaks from the Knowledge gained through actual experience. By listening to such a person Self-Realization is gained immediately.
31. Understand what is absurd and incorrect. A blind person can be recognized by the way that he walks. Whatever is said that is without real substance should discarded like vomit.

Thus in Shri Dasbodh, a dialogue between the Guru and disciple, Sub-Chapter 4 of Chapter 17, named "Dissolution of Imagination" is concluded.

Chapter: 17, Sub-Chapter: 5

The Continuous Sound of Soham

|| ShriRam ||

1. There is a repetition (japa) of twenty-one thousand breaths that are continuously being effortlessly repeated (ajapa) throughout the day. This is very easy to see.
2. The breath is continuously coming and going through the mouth and nose. This should be noticed with subtle observation.
3. At the root, it can be seen that there is only one sound (OM). In that, there are variations of high, medium, and low pitch. Of those, the base chord which can be subtly noticed to be in effortless repetition is called "ajapa."
4. The seven notes in a range or key, are sa, re, ga, ma, pa da, ni, sa, which are uttered with some effort or volition. Say the first note and watch with subtle observation.
5. The first sound "sa," arises from the place above the region of the Para speech (the navel region) and below the region of the Pashyanti speech (the heart). That is the birthplace from where these notes arise.
6. Sit alone in a quiet place and carefully observe so you can understand. See how the breath is continuously taken in and then let go.
7. Sit alone in silence and attentively observe how the appearance of the subtle sound "Soham, Soham" ("I am That, I am That") resounds.
8. This subtle sound which is not spoken is called spontaneous or effortless sound which comes to be experienced as it reverberates while not actually making any noise.
9. One who sits in silence letting this sound pass by is called a great silent sage (mouni). All of the activities of various yogic practices have this as their aim.
10. In silent solitude where does the arising of any sound occur? This sound "Soham, I am That," appears in the inner-mind.
11. The inhalation is "So" and the exhalation is "Ham." This "Soham, Soham" goes on continuously. Observe this carefully, and see that the hidden meaning is very deep.
12. None of the many living beings in the four categories of species can survive without respiration.
13. Thus, this effortless repetition goes on for all creatures. However, it is only the knowledgeable that understand. One should set aside this effortless repetition by making some effort to recognize it.
14. God is always naturally present. With some effort, God seems to scatter and disappear. Who can have faith in such a destructible God?
15. The vision of the Inner-Self of the universe spontaneously and naturally occurs with continuous meditation. All the people act according to the desire of the Self.
16. One takes in food or gathers things according to what satisfies the Self. In the same way, whatever is lost or left aside becomes an offering to him.
17. When food is taken in, it is an offering to the fire that is in the stomach. All people are obeying the orders of the Self by making food offerings through this fire.
18. The spontaneous and naturally occurring repetition of God's name, contemplation on God, movement, praise and celebration of God is all pleasing to him.
19. Understanding happens effortlessly. Doing many types of yogic practices does not result in sudden understanding.

20. One's wealth is lost and one lives in poverty when one does not know that there is great wealth hidden within one's own house. People who live in this way do not realize what they do.
21. There is great wealth in the cellar, hidden in the walls, and in the columns and beams, yet the poor unknowing person lives in poverty.
22. There amidst great wealth the person lives a miserable life of excessive poverty. What a wonder it is to see such a lack of prosperity happening in the creation of the Supreme Being, who is of the nature of "Supreme Bliss,".
23. It can be seen in life that some only look on, while some eat and enjoy the food. This can be understood through the power of discrimination. The same law applies for those who do actions in the objective world as well to those who are on the path of non-action.
24. With Narayana residing in your mind, how can there be any lack of prosperity when his wife, the Goddess of Fortune is firmly seated within you?

Thus in Shri Dasbodh, a dialogue between the Guru and disciple, Sub-Chapter 5 of Chapter 17, named "The Continuous Repetition of Soham" is concluded.

Chapter: 17, Sub-Chapter: 6

The Body and the Self

|| ShriRam ||

1. The Self resides in the body, and through it endures many joys and sorrows. In the end, it gives up the body and leaves suddenly.
2. In youth there is a lot of energy in the body and living beings enjoy many pleasures. In old age the body becomes weak and experiences a great deal of suffering.
3. Everyone feels that they would not like to die, but in old age the hands and feet become crippled and one feels like giving up on life and its many miseries.
4. Due to the association of the Self with the body, it experiences some happiness in life, but when death nears, it cries out in pain.
5. It is with this connection that the Self experiences suffering. Some people even kill others, but in the end, there is nothing left and the whole life has been lived in vain.
6. Such is the delusion that passes like two days, yet people call it Parabrahman, the Absolute Reality. They accept the many sorrows of life, and in confusion assume that it is all real.
7. In this way, all people become miserable and pass away lamenting with pain without having any satisfaction in life. Some small pleasures are enjoyed, but they are immediately followed by sorrow.
8. If you try to remember all of the suffering experienced since birth, you will see how much suffering there has been. There has been so much grief that it cannot be measured.
9. Such is the association of the Self with the body. Like this, there is an accumulation of many miseries, and the living beings, having become miserable, pass away alone.

10. All beings experience some happiness and some sorrow throughout their lives because of the connection with the body. There are many things that oppose the mind and many separations that are experienced.
11. At the time of sleep there are insects and fleas that cause discomfort in many ways, and if some chemicals are used as a remedy to get rid of them, they also cause some irritation.
12. Flies come around at mealtime, and rats and mice take away anything edible, and then cats bring trouble to those rodents.
13. There are many insects like lice, gnats, horseflies, and snakes that cause aggravation to each other, and are harassed by humans as well.
14. There are scorpions, serpents, tigers, bears, alligators, and wolves that kill humans beings, as well as human beings that are killing each another. There is not even one living being that is completely happy and content in life.
15. The 8.4 million various species in creation all devour one another. How many afflictions and ailments should be described?
16. Such is the activity of the Inner-Self. There are many living beings crowded on earth that are constantly killing each other.
17. They continuously cry, get aggravated, moan with pain, and give up their lives. Only foolish people call this Parabrahman.
18. Parabrahman never disappears and never causes sorrow for anyone. Neither praise nor criticism exist in Parabrahman.
19. If someone is abusive, all of that abuse is received by the Inner-Self alone. Through investigation, this can be experienced for oneself.
20. There is so much abusive language that is used in many ways. People call others such things as the son of an ass, the son of a prostitute, the son of a slave, the son of a bitch, the son of a rascal, the son of a dirty woman, etc. How many such abuses should be told?
21. All of this abuse does not touch Parabrahman. Even imagination does not function there. There is no knowledge of any separation of anyone in Parabrahman.
22. There are so many living beings in creation that it is not possible for all to experience greatness. Therefore God has given to each according to what is appropriate for that being.
23. There are many people that go to the market place, and they buy whatever goods are available there. Only the fortunate ones can take the best items.
24. The same thing that applies to the food and clothing that one gets also applies to the worship of God. The fortunate and wise gain the Knowledge of Brahman.
25. All people get some happiness from family life, but the common person's happiness of worldly life cannot be compared to the great pleasures that the king enjoys. How can an unfortunate person experience the same grandeur as a king?
26. However, everyone experiences many miseries in life, and in the end, at the time of death, everyone is basically in the same situation. All have enjoyed many pleasures in the past, and no one can avoid the inevitable sorrows at the time of death.
27. The hardships of sorrow cannot be tolerated, yet the breath does not leave the body. The unbearable sufferings upon the approach of death are the same for everyone.
28. Many lose various limbs and body parts and have to live in such a state. Living beings suffer in this way at the end of their lifetimes and then pass away.

29. The beauty of the form disappears and the physical strength leaves the body. Living beings suffer miserably in pain and die alone in the end.
30. The last days of life are miserable and pitiable for everyone. Such are the painful state of affairs at the time of death, which are very sorrowful.
31. People say that they enjoy life, but that they are not the enjoyer. Such talk is ridiculous. People say such things without proper consideration and clear seeing.
32. The last days of life at the time of death are truly very difficult. The life force does not leave the body easily, and at the end men become like beggars.

Thus in Shri Dasbodh, a dialogue between the Guru and disciple, Sub-Chapter 6 of Chapter 17, named "The Body and the Self" is concluded.

Chapter: 17, Sub-Chapter: 7

Life in the World

|| ShriRam ||

1. Water is basically pure. When it enters into various plants it becomes sour, pungent, or bitter according to its association with different substances.
2. Similarly, the Self is pure in its own Self-existence, yet due to its association with the body, it get filled up with pride and gets carried away in the wrong direction.
3. If it finds good association it takes on good qualities, similar to how water in sugarcane takes on the quality of sweetness, and when in association with a poisonous plant it becoming deadly to living beings.
4. There are innumerable herbs and plants. How many of their qualities can be described? In the association with many bodies, the Self takes on many qualities.
5. Among those bodies some are good and fortunate. By keeping the company of saints one becomes like the saints through the power of discrimination and gives up and leaves behind the pride for the body.
6. However, when using water as a simile, it can be seen that water becomes tainted by its associations, but with the power of discrimination, the Self is proven to never be tainted. This must be experienced and seen for oneself.
7. For the one who is truly keen to look after his own self-interest, not much needs to be told to him. Everything is understood according to each person's capacity.
8. Understand that the one who cares for one's own self-interest is his own friend, and one who damages his own self-interest is his own enemy.
9. Who can stop the one who is intent upon doing himself harm? Such a person kills himself in his isolation.
10. One who does not act according to his own best interest is considered to be one who commits suicide, and those who utilize the power of discrimination are considered blessed sages.
11. Those who are virtuous keep the company of good people while those who are without virtue keep the company of bad people. Salvation and downfall depend on the company that one keeps.
12. By keeping the company of the best people one takes care of oneself. Understand and analyze the intellect and inner experience of knowledgeable people.

13. Both the worldly life and spiritual life give happiness to those who are knowledgeable, while the one who is not knowledgeable remains ignorant due to a lack of discrimination.
14. One who is knowledgeable is a man of God while the ignorant one is like a demon. Understand which is superior between the two and take that path.
15. One who is knowledgeable is respected by all, and one who is ignorant is not. Therefore, follow the path that provides blessings and fulfillment in life.
16. By keeping the company of the industrious and wise, one becomes industrious and wise. If one keeps the company of the lazy and foolish, he will also be lazy and foolish.
17. By keeping the company of the best people one gains the fruit of contentment, while sorrow is the fruit of keeping bad company. That being the case, why would one knowingly accept sorrow while dropping the fruit of joy?
18. It is evident everywhere among the people in society that people can be seen living in both ways.
19. On one side one gets the benefits of unity with God, and on the other side there is a lack of union which results in a lack of success everywhere. Therefore, carry on your activities with the support of proper discernment.
20. When one suddenly finds oneself in a difficult situation, he makes an effort to get out of that situation. By removing oneself from such situations, one gains a great sense of contentment.
21. In keeping the company of non-virtuous people the mind gets constantly disturbed. Therefore, be thoughtful about the company you keep.
22. If one's efforts are made wisely, then there will be nothing lacking. Such a person enjoys happiness and contentment and gains acclaim from the public.
23. This is the way of behavior in nature and in the world. One who lives and sees with understanding enjoys contentment.
24. The world is full of people who are like valuable gems. By continuous reflection and thoughtfulness one gains inner understanding and experience.
25. As a rule, it happens that everyday we come across some people who are poor and some who are rich, and some people who are stupid and some who are intelligent.
26. There are some who are fortunate that pass away, and then someone new comes along and becomes fortunate. Similarly, the knowledgeable and educated appear and pass away.
27. One gets filled and another gets emptied, and then that which is emptied gets filled again. And then that which gets filled becomes empty again after some time.
28. Such is the cycle in nature. Prosperity is like a shadow at noon. It passes away slowly as one grows old with age.
29. Everyone experiences that childhood, youth and old age come to all in life. Knowing this, make your life worthwhile.
30. The body behaves in the way that it is made to act. By making efforts the work gets carried out, and results are achieved. There is no reason that one should worry unnecessarily.

Thus in Shri Dasbodh, a dialogue between the Guru and disciple, Sub-Chapter 7 of Chapter 17, named "Life in the World" is concluded.

- - - - - - - - - - - - - - - - -

Chapter: 17, Sub-Chapter: 8

Explanation of the Principle Elements

|| ShriRam ||

1. From the location of the navel arises the subtle intuition that is called the "Para" speech which is beyond the audible range of sound. Understand that the form of sound that comes next is conceived, yet still is unexpressed, and which dwells at the level of heart, is called the "Pashyanti" speech.
2. The sound that has form and is expressed as a whisper at the level of the throat is called the "Madhyama" speech, and the sound that is in the form of the expressed word is called the "Vaikhari" speech.
3. The Para speech at the position navel is the seat of the "inner-mind" (antahkarana). The explanation of the five aspects of the inner-mind will be described now.
4. Understand that the sense of remembrance that rises up effortlessly from the non-conceptual stillness is the inner-mind that is the consciousness or awareness of living beings.
5. From this remembrance of the inner-mind arises the thoughts such as, "Is something like this?" or "Is it not like this?," or "Should something be done?" or "Should nothing be done?" The arising of this type of thoughts is what is called the "mind" (mana).
6. The nature of the mind is the combination of imagination and doubt from which inferences and conclusions are drawn. Understand that from there, when a determination is made, that is the form of the "intellect" (buddhi).
7. The nature of the intellect is that it reasons and makes determinations "to do something," or "not to do something." Understand this with inward discrimination.
8. When a determination is made by the intellect and then that determination is reconsidered again and again by the mind, this is called "thinking," or thoughts (chitta). Consider the correct meaning of this.
9. When there is the subsequent holding on to the pride of doing an action and a sense that "I am definitely the doer of action," this is called the "ego" or feeling that "I am" (ahamkara).
10. These are the five aspects of the inner-mind. (consciousness or awareness, intellect, mind, thinking, and ego) These five aspects are intermingled together as one. They are differentiated according to their five distinct functions.
11. Similarly, there are five vital energies, or breaths (pranas) in the body that are differentiated according to their distinct functions. Understand that these are of the nature of the motion of the element of wind that is really only one.
12. These five aspects of wind in the body are (1) the wind that circulates throughout the body (vyana), (2) the wind at the naval region that digests food (samana), (3) the wind at the region of the throat which enables the voice (udana) (4) the eliminative wind at the anus (apana), and (5) the wind that is the breath that is present in the nose and mouth (prana). Understand this clearly.
13. The five aspects of prana have thus been described. The five sense organs of knowledge are the ears, the skin, the eyes, the tongue, and the nose.
14. The five objects of the sense organs are sound, touch, recognition of forms, taste, and smell. The five organs of action are the speech, the hands, the legs, the genitals, and the anus. These organs of action are well known.

15. The five aspects of the inner-mind, the five pranas, the five sense organs, the five organs of action, and the five objects of the sense organs, all together make up five groups with five elements in each.
16. Like this, understand that these are the twenty-five attributes that are intermingled together that make up the subtle body. Now, this mixture of the attributes of the subtle body will be explained in their relation to the five elements. Please listen attentively.
17. The inner-mind, the circulating wind, hearing, speech, and sound are of the element of space. Next, the domain of wind will be told.
18. The mind, the wind of digestion, the skin, the hands, and the sense of touch are of the element of wind. These can all be easily organized into a chart as an aid to understanding. (Refer to the table at the end of this sub-chapter.)
19. The intellect, the wind of speech, the eyes, the feet, and sight, are of the element of light. The signs of these have been indicated. One must see this for oneself with the application of concentration.
20. The faculty of thinking, the wind of elimination, the tongue, the genitals, and taste, are of the element of water. Please remain attentive as the domain of the earth element is told next.
21. The ego, the breath, the nose, the anus, and the objects that are smelled are of the element of earth. This is the way of explanation that is given according to the ancient scriptures of spiritual science (*Shastras*).
22. Thus the elements of the subtle body have been described. When this is seen with subtle observation, one becomes free of doubt. All of this will be revealed to one who applies the concentration of mind to this topic.
23. Now, the subtle body has been described. Next, the gross physical body will be explained. First, how space exists in the physical body with its five attributes will be told.
24. Desire, anger, sorrow, enticement (lust for objects), and fear are the five attributes of the element of space in the body. Next, the attributes of wind will be told.
25. Movement, turning, expansion, resistance, and contraction are the attributes of the element of wind in the physical body.
26. Hunger, thirst, laziness, sleep, and sexual intercourse are the five qualities of the element of fire in the body. Next, the attributes of water will be told.
27. Semen, blood, saliva, urine, and sweat are the five attributes of the element of water in the body. Next the attributes of earth will be told.
28. Bones, flesh, skin, nerves, and hair are the five attributes of the element of earth that are seen in the body. Thus, the description of the gross physical body has now been given.
29. Earth, Water, Fire, Wind, and Space are the five elements, each with its group of five attributes, and all are combined together to make twenty-five attributes that comprise the gross physical body.
30. The third body is called the Causal Body, which is ignorance. The fourth body is the Great Causal Body which is Knowledge. With the dissolution of all of the four bodies, what remains is Parabrahman, the Absolute.
31. With inquiry and thoughtfulness one can go beyond the four bodies, and the sense of an individual "I" along with all of these various elements dissolve in Oneness. In this self-surrender is the realization of Parabrahman.

32. Through the power of discrimination, one can escape the cycle of birth and death. This is the great achievement that can be accomplished with the human body. With devotion, the fulfillment of life becomes accomplished.
33. Thus, the description of the science of the five elements has been explained. Reflect upon it again and again, and iron can be turned to gold with this wonderful philosopher's stone.
34. However, even this simile is not entirely correct. With the philosopher's stone, one cannot create another philosopher's stone, but by surrendering to the saints and sages, one becomes a sage oneself.

Thus in Shri Dasbodh, a dialogue between the Guru and disciple, Sub-Chapter 8 of Chapter 17, named "The Explanation of the Principle Elements" is concluded.

The Twenty-Five Elements of the Subtle Body

The Five Elements	The Five Aspects of Inner-Mind	The Five Aspects of Prana	The Five Sense Organs	The Five Organs of Action	The Five Objects of The Senses
Sky / Space	Inner-Mind	Vyana	Hearing	Speech	Sound
Wind	Mind	Samana	Skin	Hands	Touch
Fire / Light	Intellect	Udana	Eyes	Feet	Forms
Water	Thinking	Apana	Tongue	Genitals	Tastes
Earth	Ego	Prana	Nose	Anus	Smells

The Twenty-Five Elements of the Gross Body

Space	Wind	Light	Water	Earth
Desire	Movement	Hunger	Semen	Bones
Anger	Turning	Thirst	Blood	Flesh
Sorrow	Expansion	Laziness	Saliva	Skin
Enticement	Resistance	Sleep	Urine	Veins
Fear	Contraction	Intercourse	Sweat	Hair

Chapter: 17, Sub-Chapter: 9

The Four Bodies

|| ShriRam ||

1. Understand that there are four bodies. They are the Gross Body, the Subtle Body, the Causal Body, and the Great Causal Body. The four bodies correspond respectively to the states of Waking, Dream, Deep Sleep, and Turya.
2. The signs of these four bodies, which are aspects of the one Self, and their relation to the body will be described now. The visible physical world that is apparent in the waking state is the sign of the Gross Body, and its place in relation to the body is in the eyes. The luminous quality of the dream state is the sign of the Subtle Body, and its place in the body is at the region of throat. The subsidence of knowledge in deep sleep is the sign of the Causal Body, and its place in relation to the body is at the heart. Self-experience in the Turya state is the sign of the Great Causal Body and its place is at the crown of the head.
3. The Gross Body enjoys visible objects, the Subtle Body enjoys the invisible objects (subtle objects such as thoughts, desires, dream objects, etc.), the Causal Body enjoys the restful bliss of ignorance, and the Great Causal Body enjoys dwelling in the higher bliss of Knowledge. These are the four kinds of enjoyments of the four bodies.
4. The syllable "A" represents the gross body, the syllable "U" represents the subtle body, the syllable "M" represents the causal body, and the half-syllable of the final nasal resonance is the crescent mark on the top of the OM symbol (ॐ) that represents the transcendental state of the great causal body. These are the signs of OM (AUM) in relation to the four bodies.
5. The Tamas quality (Tamoguna) is associated with the gross body, the Rajas quality (Rajoguna) is associated with the subtle body, the Sattva quality (Sattvaguna) is associated with the causal body, and the Pure Sattva quality (Shudha Sattvaguna) is associated with the great causal body.
6. The power of action (kriya) is associated with the gross body, the power of substance (sravya) is associated with the subtle body, the power of will (icha) is associated with the causal body, and the power of Knowledge (Jnana) is associated with the great causal body.
7. Like this, there are the thirty-two elements of the four bodies. Together with the fifty elements (twenty-five each) of the gross and subtle bodies, in all, they make eighty-two elements. In addition to these, there are two more elements that are Ignorance (ajnana) and Knowledge (Jnana).
8. Understand these elements, and know that they are illusory. Recognize that you are witness to them all and let them fall away.
9. To witness them means Knowledge. With Knowledge recognize Ignorance. With the dissolution of the body, both Knowledge and Ignorance are dissolved as well.
10. Just as there are four bodies for the living being, correspondingly, there are four bodies of the universe. These are (1) the gross manifestation (Virat), (2) the universal energy (Hiranyagarbha), (3) the unmanifest causal (Avyakrut), and (4) the Primal Illusion (Moolamaya) bodies. These are also concepts and can be dissolved with the power of discrimination and Self-Knowledge.

11. With discrimination between Self and non-self, and the investigation into Essence and non-essence, the illusory nature of the five elements is experienced.
12. Bones, flesh, skin, veins, and hair, are all of the earth element. This can be seen in the body when searching for them.
13. Semen, blood, saliva, urine, and sweat are of the water element. Understand these things that have been described.
14. Hunger, thirst, laziness, sleep, and intercourse are of the fire element. The explanation of these elements has also been given.
15. Movement, bending, expansion, resistance, and contraction are of the wind element. The listeners are asked to understand this.
16. Desire, anger, sorrow, enticement, and fear are of the space element. Without proper analysis, how can one know and understand this?
17. The gross body is made up of these twenty-five elements. Now, I shall speak about the signs of the subtle body.
18. The inner-mind (consciousness), the mind, the intellect, thinking, and the ego sense are of the element of space. Now, listen to the attributes of wind without harboring any doubt.
19. The circulating wind, the digestive wind, the faculty of wind in the speech, the eliminative wind, and the breath are of the wind element.
20. The ears, the skin, the eyes, the tongue, and the nose are of the fire element. Now, remaining alert, listen to attributes of the water element.
21. Speech, the hands, the legs, the genitals, and the anus are of the water element. Now, listen to the attributes of the earth element.
22. Sound, touch, form, taste, and smell are of the earth element. Now, the twenty-five elements of the subtle body have been explained.

Thus in Shri Dasbodh, a dialogue between the Guru and disciple, Sub-Chapter 9 of Chapter 17, named "The Four Bodies" is concluded.

Chapter: 17, Sub-Chapter: 10

Signs of a Dull-Minded Person

|| ShriRam ||

1. In the sea of cosmic water that covers the universe, there is a deity of hindrance named Hatakeshwara. Salutations are offered to him, as his extent is very great. This is what is considered the hindrance associated with the lower world.
2. However, one cannot go there with the physical body to view this deity so one must draw a conclusion about the existence of him using the power of discrimination.
3. In the mythological texts (*Puranas*) it is said that the earth is surrounded by seven seas, and that there are more lands beyond them which have steep cliffs at their outer boundaries.
4. How is it possible to cross over the seven seas? Only through the power of discrimination and by keeping the company of sages.

5. If something is not known for oneself, then it should be clarified by asking a knowledgeable person. It is not possible that the body can go somewhere with the same speed as the mind.
6. That which cannot be seen with the physical eyes must be seen with the eyes of Knowledge. Upon analyzing the structure of the universe one becomes content.
7. The earth is in the middle, in between the space above and the netherworld below. If the earth did not exist, there would only be empty space in all directions.
8. The nature of Parabrahman, the Absolute Reality, is that it is without any attributes, and it is devoid of anything called the visible Illusion.
9. What is seen with the eyes is the visible. What is seen with the mind are transient impressions (concepts, imagination, etc.), and beyond the mind there are no appearances or impressions. Understand this with the power of discrimination.
10. Only through discrimination can That which remains when the visible world and the impressions in the minds are both destroyed, be known. There are very few knowledgeable people on the earth with such subtle vision.
11. That which can be spoken is expressed in words, but the meaning which cannot be expressed in words must be understood in silence. In this way, That which is without attributes can be experienced with the help of attributes.
12. All attributes get destroyed, but That which has no attributes is indestructible. See what is beyond the gross with subtle vision.
13. That which cannot be easily seen should be understood through listening. By listening and reflecting one can know everything.
14. There are innumerable objects in the eightfold manifestation, all of which cannot be seen and known. One should not consider all of them to be equal and of the same caliber.
15. If one thinks that everything is equal, then the whole process of examination become invalid. It is like mixing many different foods together and not being able to distinguish between their various tastes.
16. Those who are dull-minded cannot understand the differences between various qualities. A fool does not understand the value of proper discrimination. He will say that discrimination and non-discrimination are the same.
17. When one does not understand what is superior and what is inferior, there can be no higher learning. How can there be liberation for the living being who only studies the multitude of gross things?
18. Only one who is mad and lacking in common sense considers everything to be equal. Such people have no proper discernment and are basically useless.
19. Such a person considers perishable things to be indestructible. What can you say to those people who are focused on gross objects?
20. God has created many differences and variations among things. The universe functions with great diversity. If the examiner is blind, how he can correctly examine things?
21. Where there is a lack of proper examination, such a person is dull-minded and has no redeeming qualities that can be considered praiseworthy.
22. When what is true and what is false are considered to be the same, where is there any place for discrimination? The sages accept the Essence and drop that which is non-essence.

23. How can the evaluation of what is best be possible for one whose vision is focused solely on the gross? How can there be any glory for the one who has not been initiated into spiritual Knowledge?
24. What good can the *Vedas*, *Shastras*, and *Puranas* do for one who goes to the toilet and in his own stupidity does not clean himself afterwards?
25. First, proceed ahead steadily with good conduct, and then develop your quality of thinking. With proper conduct and thinking one succeeds in going beyond worldly bondage.
26. How can one who has no discipline know That which is understood by those with spiritual discipline? Of what use is a blind man where even those with good vision get fooled?
27. What can be said about one who considers virtue and non-virtue, heaven and hell, and discrimination and the lack of discrimination to be the same?
28. Some people will say that nectar and poison are the same, but by ingesting poison, one loses one's life. Through wrongful deeds one becomes reviled, and through virtuous deeds one's greatness and glory spreads and gets enhanced.
29. Whether it be in worldly life or in spiritual life, if there is no common sense and proper discernment, everything is meaningless.
30. Therefore, keep to the company of saints and listen to the explanations of the meanings of sacred scriptures. Study and select the best qualities with proper effort.

Thus in Dasbodh, a guru disciple dialogue, the tenth sub-chapter named, 'The Signs of a Dull-Minded Person" is concluded.

Chapter 18. Description of Various Objects

Chapter: 18, Sub-Chapter: 1

The Description of Various Deities

|| ShriRam ||

1. Salutations to Lord Ganesha. Your greatness cannot be fathomed. It is you who gives knowledge to the intellect of the people, young and old.

(Note: In stanzas 1 through 15 Samartha Ramdas is giving praise to various manifestations of God before going on to say that they are all only aspects of the one Self.)

2. Salutations to Goddess Saraswati. From you arises the inspiration for all of the four types of speech. Very few know your true form.
3. Blessed is the four-faced Brahma who has created the universe and manifested the *Vedas* and other scriptures.
4. Blessed is Lord Vishnu who protects and sustains all living beings with just a small fraction of himself. Residing in all living beings, he cultivates and sustains life. It is Vishnu who gives knowledge and understanding to all.
5. Blessed is Lord Shiva who gives without limits. He is continuously repeating the name of Lord Rama.
6. Blessed is Lord Indra, who is the king of all the gods. How can the magnificence of his domain be described!
7. Blessed is Lord Yama, the deity of death and the upholder of religion. He is the knower of all the righteous and non-righteous ways of living beings.
8. Great is the majesty of Lord Venkatesha (a form of Vishnu who is the destroyer of sins). Many of his devotees eat food while standing as they enjoy delicious foods with great delight.
9. Blessed is the Goddess Bavashankari (goddess of orchards) to whom devotees offer many vegetable dishes. Who has the capacity to taste them all?
10. Blessed is Hanuman (son of the wind; considered an incarnation of Shiva), the monkey god with a tail like a cow who is adorned with a garland of vadas (small fried cakes made from pulse flour). When people eat these cakes after they have been offered to him, they feel satisfied.
11. Blessed is the great God Khandoba (a form of Shiva). By offerings of turmeric powder your devotees become yellow and are eager to eat the onion raita (curd salad) with thick rotis (baked flat bread).
12. Blessed is the Goddess Tuljabhavani (a form of Parvati, the wife of Shiva), who is pleased with her devotees among the people. She has so many glorious qualities, who can count them!
13. Blessed is Panduranga (a form of Krishna also called Vitthala and Vithoba), who is always in the mood for celebrations with narrations, bhajans, and many songs and stories.
14. Blessed is Kshetrapala (the defender of God). Because of him people adore God. Devotion to him with deep feeling gives the devotee the fruits of devotion without delay.

15. There are many incarnations of God, such as Lord Rama, Lord Krishna and others. Because of their greatness many people have become eager to worship God.
16. Understand that the origin of all gods, is the one Inner-Self alone. He alone is the receiver of all the enjoyments on the earth.
17. He has established himself as many Gods and has become manifest as the form of many types of power. He alone is the enjoyer of all prosperity.
18. Through investigation and thoughtfulness see that the entire expanse of the universe has spread out because of him. Many Gods and men appear and pass away. How many of them can be told?
19. Everything such as fame and blame, criticism and praise, and all the other enjoyments of everyone, are received by the Inner-Self alone.
20. Everything done by the body, and all that is enjoyed or suffered is only his enjoyment or suffering. He alone is the enjoyer, the one who renounces, and the state of detachment from both enjoyment and renunciation.
21. Living beings forget the Self because of pride. Seeing only the body, they have forgotten the primary thing, which is the Self within.
22. Oh! Who is there on this earth that sees all of the activity of the Inner-Self? It is very rare to find one who with immense virtue remains in continual awareness of the Self.
23. In that continuous awareness of the Self, all wrongful acts are completely burnt up. The Jnani who remains fixed as the Self sees and understands the meaning of this.
24. Those who are firmly seated in the Self are ferried across this world illusion while those who stray from the Self are drowned in it. They are carried away by their fascination with the objective world and appearances.

Thus in Shri Dasbodh, a dialogue between the Guru and disciple, Sub-Chapter 1 of Chapter 18, named "The Description of Various Deities" is concluded.

Chapter: 18, Sub-Chapter: 2

The Company of the Knowledgeable

|| ShriRam ||

1. Whatever has happened in ignorance has happened and passed away. Therefore, forget it all and knowingly act in a proper manner.
2. Keep the company of those who are knowledgeable and serve them. In this way you will slowly and surely develop the same good intellect as those who are knowledgeable.
3. Learn to write and read with the knowledgeable, and ask them questions about anything that you want to know.
4. Show gratitude to a knowledgeable person, and use your body to serve him. Observe and understand how the knowledgeable person thinks about many things.
5. Worship in the company of knowledgeable people, and give yourself in service to them. By listening to their explanations and narrations again and again, you will become content.

6. Learn to sing various songs, as well as how to play musical instruments and different melodies in the company of the knowledgeable.
7. Become close to the knowledgeable, and accept medical and dietary advice that they give.
8. Learn from the knowledgeable about how to examine various subjects, as well as various ways to exercise, and how to be a good swimmer.
9. Learn how to speak like the knowledgeable speak, and act according to their advice. Learn correct ways of meditation from those who are knowledgeable.
10. Learn the stories that the knowledgeable tell and understand the various strategies that they use. Analyze the ways that they use stories as a means to give explanations about everything.
11. Learn the political maneuvers and tactics that the knowledgeable use to resolve difficult issues. Learn how the knowledgeable maintain good relationships with people, and how they are able to please others.
12. Adopt the good qualities of the knowledgeable and understand how they act in various situations. Study how they are able to create waves of inspiration.
13. Understand and adopt the tireless efforts and logic that the knowledgeable utilize. Recognize and understand their methods and intentions even when they are not obvious or spoken about out loud.
14. Understand the cleverness and political skill of the knowledgeable, and continue listening to the explanations given by them.
15. Learn from the compositions and poems of the knowledgeable, and adopt their ability to speak in sweet words in the form of prose and poetry, giving kind explanations from inner experience.
16. Study the literary works of the knowledgeable, and learn the meanings and differences of the various statements that are made by them. Learn their various modes of expression and the appropriateness and timing of discussions about various subjects.
17. Understand and adopt the qualities of the knowledgeable of being intelligent, tolerant, and generous.
18. The many wise principles, ways of pre-planning, modes of analysis, and the ways that knowledgeable people utilize their minds should be understood and adopted.
19. Learn from the knowledgeable how to best utilize your time, what correct discrimination is, and what spiritual efforts will bear fruit. Observe the many good qualities of the knowledgeable and adopt them for yourself.
20. Learn about the path of devotion and the meaning of renunciation from the knowledgeable. Observe them, and learn from them how they act in all situations.
21. Gain the Knowledge of the knowledgeable, learn how they meditate, and understand their subtle indications.
22. Understand how the knowledgeable remain aloof from the world, their bodilessness, and their explanations about Brahman.
23. The Jnani is the Inner-Self. Who can describe his greatness, his Knowledge, or the magnitude of his skillfulness and good qualities?
24. By reciting the praises of the Supreme Lord, and through continuing spiritual discourse, one gains great happiness and joy.
25. Whatever is created by the Supreme God is constantly visible. The thoughtful people gain understanding of it by listening to the explanations given in spiritual discourse, and by using discrimination in analyzing their meaning again and again.

26. Whatever has been created is the creation of the Lord of the Universe. One must first learn to discern between the creation and the creator.
27. God creates people, but if one tries to see him, he cannot be seen. It is only through the power of discrimination and with proper thoughtfulness that he can be realized.
28. When continuously meditating on God, he benevolently provides for all of our needs. Therefore, be constantly engaged in thinking and speaking about God.
29. One who does not meditate on God is a non-devotee, and one who does meditate on him is a devotee. God liberates his devotees from the bondage of worldly life.
30. At the end of spiritual practice and worship, God and devotee are in constant union. Those with experience understand this fact in their own experience.

Thus in Shri Dasbodh, a dialogue between the Guru and disciple, Sub-Chapter 2 of Chapter 18, named "The Company of the Knowledgeable" is concluded.

Chapter: 18, Sub-Chapter: 3

The Teaching About Detachment

|| ShriRam ||

1. To be born with a human body is rare, and the time-span of life is short, so it should not be wasted. Ramdas says that you should carefully consider this with proper discernment.
2. If proper discrimination is not used in life, everything becomes a thoughtless endeavor. Without thoughtfulness, the human being becomes an impoverished person.
3. This comes about by one's own doing. Through laziness one becomes pitiful and destitute, and by keeping bad company one gets drowned in worldliness in a short period of time.
4. In youth, people are immature and do many foolish and destructive things, and the madness of sexual desire and passion runs rampant.
5. One who acts like a foolish and lazy young man is pitiful in all respects. Nobody gets any benefit from him. What more needs to be said?
6. Such a person does not take care of the necessary things in life, and even proper food and clothing are neglected. None of the best qualities can be found in him.
7. Such a person does not know how to speak or sit properly, and does not know how to behave appropriately in various situations. His mind and body are always diverted away from study and learning.
8. He does not read or write well, and he does not make meaningful enquiries, nor can he give good explanations. He does not practice any disciplined behavior because of his immaturity.
9. He does not understand anything for himself, and does not accept whatever he is taught. It is a foolish person who constantly speaks badly about virtuous people.
10. His way of thinking and behaving is such that he says one thing and does another. How can such a person ever lead a fulfilling spiritual life?

11. If because of some calamity in his life he changes his behavior and way of thinking, only then is there a place in his life for study and thoughtful reflection.
12. With concentration of your mind, hold steadfastly to spiritual practice. Put forth serious effort not to allow yourself to become lazy.
13. Give up all negative qualities. Study and adopt the best qualities. Learn by heart the statements contained in spiritual texts and poetry, and gain a firm understanding of their deep inner meaning.
14. Read and learn from many different poetic compositions, verses, and phrases. Observe the different poetic styles and forms of expression, so they can be used appropriately to impart knowledge according to various situations bringing about an uprising of joy in the hearts and minds of the listeners.
15. What is to be said in what situation must be realized with understanding. Why tire oneself unnecessarily doing wrong things?
16. Understand the minds of others so you can speak to them with proper respect. To simply continue on reciting whatever you have remembered without proper regard for the mind-set of others is foolish.
17. When speaking to others, be respectful and mindful of their current beliefs and spiritual practices. Be considerate of their beliefs and speak in ways that they can integrate what is being said. Studying various moods of music and rhythms can be helpful for this.
18. Make use of literature, music, and the telling of stories appropriate to the occasion so that correct understanding can be imparted. Through listening and reflecting upon what has been imparted, the listeners will progress in gaining the correct understanding of the meaning.
19. Learn many things by heart and continue to revisit what has been learned in order to refresh your memory. It is important to remember what has been said previously and to be consistent in what you say.
20. Remaining in solitude, continue to read and compare spiritual texts and discover their inner meaning. Accept and retain only what can be experientially verified.

Thus in Shri Dasbodh, a dialogue between the Guru and disciple, Sub-Chapter 3 of Chapter 18, named "The Teaching About Being Detached" is concluded.

- - - - - - - - - - - - - - - - -

Chapter: 18, Sub-Chapter: 4

The Importance of the Body

|| ShriRam ||
1. Because of the body, worship of the God of Meditation (Ganesha), and reverence for the Goddess of Knowledge (Saraswati) is possible. It is only for the body that the guru, saints, sages, and listeners are important.
2. Poetry is composed and the studying and learning of many streams of knowledge are all done for the body.
3. Many texts are written, different alphabets are developed and deciphered, and many subjects are researched all for the body.

4. The great Jnanis, accomplished ones, sages, seers, and hermits are all due to the existence of the body. Because of the body, people are able to move about visiting holy places of pilgrimage.
5. Because of the existence of the body listening can take place, the mind can reflect on what has been heard, and most importantly, the Supreme Self, Paramatman can be realized.
6. The path of action, the path of worship, and the path of knowledge all exist on the earth due to the existence of the body.
7. Those who are in union with God, the detached, those who engage in Self-inquiry, and those who make many spiritual efforts are all due to the existence of the body. It is only because of the existence of the body that the Self becomes evident.
8. It is because of the body that the worldly life and the spiritual life both become worthwhile. Without the body, everything is meaningless.
9. The repetition of chants and mantras, the making and keeping of various spiritual vows, and many types of physical austerities are all due to the existence of the body.
10. Because of the body, people become virtuous or non-virtuous, uncontrolled or disciplined.
11. Because of the body, it is possible for incarnations of the Self to appear like a person is able to wear clothing. It is only because of the existence of the body that revolutions and protests can take place.
12. The enjoyment of sensual pleasures as well as the renunciation of sensual pleasures are possible only because of the body. Due to the existence of the body people get many diseases and there are many cures.
13. The nine types devotion, the four types of liberation, many skills, and many opinions are all possible because of the body.
14. Because of the body, there are charities and donations, many secrets that are kept, and people can speak of the past actions of others.
15. There are many selfish motives, many achievements, the sense of feeling blessed, as well as the sense of futility that are all due to the existence of the body.
16. There are many arts, the sense of something being special, the sense that something is lacking, and affection for the path of devotion that are all because of the body.
17. Because of the existence of the body there are many righteous paths, spiritual practices, the elimination of bondage, and liberation through self-surrender can be attained.
18. The human body is the best among all. Lord Rama dwells in the body, and because of the body it is possible to realize that he is the Inner-Self that is present in all bodies.
19. It is because of the body that some become revered and others become reviled, and because of the body a succession of many incarnations of God have appeared and passed away.
20. Because of the body there is much confusion, delusion, and misunderstanding, and it is because of the body that those who are the best people enjoy a high status.
21. Everything gets accomplished with the body, and nothing can get done without it. When the Self leaves the body it is as if it was never there.
22. The body is like a ferry that carries one beyond the world. It is the abode of many qualities, and even precious jewels have their value because of the body.
23. Singing, music and various artistic skills are all due to the existence of the body.

24. The human body is the best fruit of the universe that is very rarely obtained. It is important to clearly understand the value of the body.
25. Many activities both great and small, and many people great and small, are known only due to the existence of the body.
26. All those who have come to be born with a body have done activities in this world and have then gone away, and many have become pure through devotion to Lord Vishnu.
27. The root of the eightfold manifest creation (consisting of the five elements and the three gunas) arose in the form of an inspiration, a movement of subtle desire. Out of that original inspiration many more desires have arisen that have become manifest in the form of the fruit called the body.
28. That original desire is Lord Vishnu, who is the root of creation, as well as of that fruit called the body. This can be seen in this moment. He is the basic element that can be discovered to exist within all bodies. This can be known with certainty.
29. From the seed, the root of the plant grows. Understand that the plant is a form of water. After the plant has grown, the seed is formed in the fruit, and in that seed is contained the origin of the root.
30. Because of the root, fruits come to be formed, and because of the fruit, the root of another plant comes to be formed. Like this, the process of the creation of the world continues on.
31. Now, let what has been said about the body be enough. How can anything that needs to be done be accomplished without the body? Utilize the body in the best way that makes life meaningful.
32. The body has come into existence because of the Self, and because of the existence of the body, the Self has a place to reside. The Self and the body function very well together, and because of their union, many activities are accomplished.
33. Whatever is done secretly is known by the Self, because all activity is only his activity.
34. The Self resides in the body, and by worshipping and taking care of the body, the Self is pleased. By troubling the body, the tranquility of the Self becomes disturbed. This is evident in the moment.
35. Without the body, worship is not possible, nor can it be enjoyed. God is present in all people, therefore the best worship of God is to please the people.
36. When thoughtfulness is expressed by a sage, the establishment of religion is possible. Such virtuous bodies of the saints and sages are alone worthy of being worshipped by others.
37. If devotional worship and praise is given to everybody in the same way, this is only a display of foolishness. What can a donkey understand if devotional worship is done to it?
38. Only those who are worthy of being worshipped are to be considered as having the right to be worshipped. However, respect should naturally be shown to all, and efforts should be made to please them. It is best to try to make sure that you do not hurt anyone's mind.
39. If the one God who resides within everyone and is present everywhere in the world is made angry, where will one have any place to live? There is no other solution to this other than to be among people and to try to please them.

40. The Supreme Lord has limitless attributes. How many of his indications can be expressed to human beings? By studying spiritual texts and listening to spiritual discourse one can gain understanding.

Thus in Shri Dasbodh, a dialogue between the Guru and disciple, Sub-Chapter 4 of Chapter 18, named "The Importance of the Body" is concluded.

Chapter: 18, Sub-Chapter: 5

The Signs of an Unfortunate Person

|| ShriRam ||

1. A measuring container measures lots of grains but does not consume any of what has been measured. Similar is the case of the living being who accumulates a great deal of knowledge but does not understand the meaning.
2. Such a person can prattle on reciting many things, but when asked about the meaning, he doesn't know. When asked about his experience, he falls into talk based upon speculation and imagination.
3. Words, like gemstones, should be examined. Look and see what is being said. If what is said is based in actual experience, then accept those words, otherwise leave them aside.
4. The experience of what remains when all that has name and form falls away is what should be pursued. To consider Essence and non-essence to be the same is foolish.
5. Should a writer be able to give a detailed explanation of what has been said, or is it enough that what has been written is merely read aloud? You should be able to see from this example what is intended to be conveyed.
6. When clear explanations cannot be given, the listeners remain confused, and if questions are asked, the speaker only becomes irritated.
7. If a speaker collects and prepares many things to say about Self-knowledge, and then speaks without having made any attempt to experience the meaning behind the words, everything that he says in front of an audience is worthless.
8. If some quantity of grain is put into the mill and the grindstone is rotated too quickly, one does not end up with finely ground flour.
9. If many pieces of food are put into the mouth in rapid succession without allowing for any time to chew, what happens when the mouth becomes full of food?
10. The sign of good speaker is that when he speaks there is not even a moment when there is a lapse of interest on the part of the listeners, and he takes care to satisfy the minds of all present.
11. He uses many subtle indications with comfort and ease, and he is able to recognize many different states and qualities of being. Recognizing them, he is able to give appropriate explanations to the listeners.
12. By easily clearing away the doubts of the listeners, they become joyful and offer their salutations to the speaker again and again.
13. When the listener's doubts are cleared they offer salutations to him, and if their doubts are not cleared, they complain and criticize him. Why should the speaker become irritated?

14. Just as gold is tested to be sure of its purity, similarly, listening and reflecting should be utilized to understand what has been said, and one must verify in one's own experience if what has been said is true.
15. If a doctor gives some medicine and it does not cure the sickness of the people, what reason does the doctor have for becoming angry with the people?
16. False statements are not valuable to anybody and people do not accept them. Therefore, one must be able to prove his conclusions with true and verifiable statements.
17. If a business is run without the knowledge of how to keep proper accounts, the operation of the business may continue on for some time without problems, but when an accountant is brought in to examine the records, he quickly finds the faults.
18. However, if all of the histories of the transactions are watched over and the accounts are kept properly, what fault will the accountant find when looking over the records?
19. If a speaker has entangled himself in many difficulties, how is it possible for him to provide good explanations? The ignorant person finds himself getting into many difficulties.
20. If someone goes to war without the strength of an army behind him, he gets totally defeated. Who is it that is to be blamed for the defeat?
21. That which can be experienced as true should be accepted with respect, while answers which are given that cannot be experientially verified should simply be considered to be empty words.
22. If we try to teach such a person, he only becomes angry, and then later gets feels tormented by his anger. If untrue statements are spoken, even when one has strong confidence in them, they are quickly detected by the people.
23. If someone gives up the truth and continues making useless false statements, there will be no shortage of criticism. The principles of justice and propriety have been established in all the three worlds by Lord Narayana.
24. If one shows disregard for justice and propriety the whole world turns against him. How long can someone continue quarreling with people and remain miserable?
25. It is never been seen nor heard of that anyone has become successful by disregarding justice and propriety, however ignorant people strongly hold to what is not true.
26. Holding onto what is not true is the definition of sin. Understand that Truth is the true nature of the Self. Everyone must select between the two for oneself.
27. All speech and movement appear to be true only in Illusion. Without Illusion how could there be any speech? For this reason, one should get to the root of wordlessness.
28. The obvious meaning of the words should first be understood, then, let the words fall away so that the hidden meaning can be understood and accepted, leaving no confusion regarding the root of wordlessness.
29. Putting aside the primary premise presented in the *Vedas* and the eightfold manifestation, direct your attention towards the Absolute Reality which is not an object of attention. Only one who is alert and who properly reflects upon this can understand what is being indicated.
30. To say that the husk and the grain are the same is a mistake. What intelligent person will throw out the juice of the sugarcane and consume the chaff instead?

31. At the level of the body, one must discern what is Eternal and what is ephemeral. At the level of the universe one must investigate into what is Essence and what is non-essence. Examine everything and accept only the Essence.
32. Because of Illusion one must use logic and reason to discriminate between Oneness and duality. If Illusion does not exist, where is there any scope for discrimination?
33. By investigating the elements and dissolving one element into another, one arrives at the realization of the meaning of the Great Statements of the *Vedas* ("Only Brahman Exists"). Through self-surrender, one gains contentment.

Thus in Shri Dasbodh, a dialogue between the Guru and disciple, Sub-Chapter 5 of Chapter 18, named "The Signs of an Unfortunate Person" is concluded.

Chapter: 18, Sub-Chapter 6

The Signs of the Best Person

|| ShriRam ||

1. The body is adorned with many clothes and a variety of ornaments, but the mind should be adorned with thoughtfulness, discernment, and unrevealed projects.
2. The body may be made to look beautiful with clothing and various ornaments, but if there is no wisdom within, there is no radiance.
3. The one who is intoxicated with himself, adamant about his opinions, speaks harshly to others, and continuously behaves pridefully, does not accept propriety and morality within.
4. Such a person who torments and causes distress to others is easily irritated, is quick to become angry, and does not adopt a respectful demeanor. He does not know how to be adaptable and harmonious in his communication or in social relationships.
5. Such mischievous and deceitful people who never make any truthful statements are the troublesome enemies of the public. Understand that such a person is said to have a demonic nature.
6. Times and situations never stay the same. If one holds rigidly to certain rules, this will not work in all times because social dynamics always continue to change.
7. Extremes should be avoided in all cases. The discerning person observes and acts appropriately according to various situations and does not adopt an obstinate attitude.
8. When one is excessively disagreeable, he makes divisions among people. Therefore, one should adopt a middle way of expression that lies between two extremes.
9. With this good approach, God is pleased. Especially pleased is the energy in the universe that is the destroyer of demons. This is understood with thoughtfulness, and then proper actions naturally follow.
10. Being ever alert, not much more advice needs to be given. However, you must come to your own conclusions.
11. There are many people around a powerful person. They should be pleased with you and respect you. Then people will have steadfast confidence in their minds.

12. There are many who reject the Truth and have become powerful charlatans. Therefore it is important to remain constantly alert.
13. God is the doer of everything, and the importance of a person who is blessed by Him is only known to a rare few.
14. Justice, propriety, thoughtfulness, discernment, the ability to act appropriately according to various situations, and to be able to know the minds of others are gifts of God.
15. To make great efforts with attentiveness, to have courage at times when it is needed, and to be able to accomplish magnificent tasks, are gifts of God.
16. To be successful, to be renowned, persevering, and to have magnificence are the best qualities that know no limits. There is no comparison for these gifts of God.
17. To have respect for God and the knowers of Brahman, to be virtuous in behavior and in one's thinking, and to always be supportive and attentive to the needs of many people, are gifts from God.
18. To be attentive to worldly life and to still be able to go beyond the worldly life while always remaining alert and ready to bear the hardships of many people, are gifts of God.
19. To be on the side of God, to take care of the knowers of Brahman, and to nurture others, are gifts of God.
20. Those who establish religion and promote virtue are the incarnations of God. They exist now, have existed in the past, and will also exist in the future. This is a gift of God.
21. One who appreciates and adopts the best qualities of sound judgement, thoughtfulness, and intelligent discernment, and who has an affinity for virtue and righteousness is a gift of God.
22. The essence of all virtues is reflection, discrimination, and investigation into one's True Form, through which, one is able to cross beyond the bondage of worldly life, achieving success both in this world and beyond it.

Thus in Shri Dasbodh, a dialogue between the Guru and disciple, Sub-Chapter 6 of Chapter 18, named "The Signs of the Best Person" is concluded.

Chapter: 18, Sub-Chapter: 7

The Nature of Ordinary People

|| ShriRam ||

1. People generally have a greedy nature. When they begin to think of God they say "deva, deva" which means give me something. (The word deva means "give," as well as "god.") People always desire something from God.
2. They do not have any devotion, but they expect their desires to be satisfied. It is like someone who does not perform any service yet asks for some salary from the boss.
3. Without hard work by people there is no fruit, no kingdom gained, nothing gets done, and there is no success.

4. It is easily experienced that by laziness work does not get done, yet people of low caliber still avoid making effort to do any work.
5. Those who bear the burden of hard work in the beginning enjoy the fruit of satisfaction afterwards, and those who take pleasure in laziness in the beginning bear the weight of sorrow later.
6. Whether in worldly life or spiritual life, the logic is the same. One must understand the value and importance of forethought.
7. Those who spend everything that they earn, or more than they earn, find themselves in difficult situations, while those who apply proper forethought to their activities are wise.
8. In the worldly life there should be some accumulation of earnings. The same principle applies to the spiritual life for going beyond the world. Without the accumulation of virtue, the life of living beings is meaningless.
9. One does not simply become free by dying. Again and again he takes birth and suffers the miseries of life. One does not save oneself, kills himself, and is said to be one who only commits suicide.
10. Who can count how many lives where someone has committed suicide? Therefore, consideration must be given as to how one can escape the cycle of birth and death.
11. Everyone says that "God does everything." However, there is a way that having the great fortune of meeting God is possible.
12. Through the power of discrimination it becomes possible for one to realize the Supreme Self, Paramatman. Seeing with the power of discrimination, discerning people find the Self.
13. When seeing God, he is known to be One, but still he appears in many forms. However, it cannot be said that these many forms are one.
14. One must understand the difference between God's creation and the one God. Without understanding this difference, people say many absurd things.
15. To show off their wisdom, they foolishly say many nonsensical things. It is like trying to satisfy one's hunger by doing something besides eating.
16. Those who put forth many efforts enjoy good fortune in life, while those who only talk about doing things remain unfortunate.
17. The signs of the misfortune of the unfortunate are easily recognized by the wise, but the signs of the wisdom of the wise cannot be known by the unfortunate.
18. When evil-mindedness is developed, how can any purity be there? Such a person considers evil-mindedness as being good intelligence.
19. How can a person who has given up purity ever be considered to be truthful? There is nothing valuable to be found where his thinking is concerned.
20. With thoughtful consideration one finds satisfaction in worldly life and beyond the world. With thoughtfulness one should discriminate between the Eternal and the ephemeral and see the truth for oneself.

Thus in Shri Dasbodh, a dialogue between the Guru and disciple, Sub-Chapter 7 of Chapter 18, named "The Nature of Ordinary People" is concluded.

Chapter: 18, Sub-Chapter: 8

Explanation of the Inner God

|| ShriRam ||

1. Brahman is formless and unmoving. The Self is of the nature of change and movement. It is what is called God by all.
2. The location of God is not fixed in one place, and God cannot be known to be in a fixed location. The one God cannot be considered to be the many gods.
3. Therefore, investigate and give thoughtful consideration to the concept of God, and discover him for yourself. Don't become confused by the existence of the many various gods.
4. Some image of God is seen at various pilgrimage places and one makes another image like it for the purpose of worship. This is a common practice that takes place on the earth.
5. The one God alone is the root of the many idols found at places of pilgrimage. You can see this and find out for yourself after searching for God at many pilgrimage places.
6. The image of God in the pilgrimage place is made out of stone. By investigating the connection of God to the image, one arrives at the root of it, and finds that the image is of an incarnation of God.
7. There have been many incarnations of God who have held a physical body, that have lived and passed away. Considered to be superior to the many incarnations of God, are Brahma, Vishnu, and Shiva.
8. The power behind these three gods is the seer who is the Inner-Self that is alone the actual doer and enjoyer of everything.
9. In age after age, and in all of the three worlds, it is He alone that does everything. The firm conviction of this is gained through discrimination, and confirmation of this can be found in the *Vedas* and other ancient scriptures.
10. The Self resides in the body and functions through it. He is God in the form of the consciousness in the body that functions in daily activity with discernment.
11. People miss the inner God, and run around to various pilgrimage places looking for him. These poor beings go to a lot of trouble because they do not know God.
12. Then, when they arrive at such places, they find only stones and water and ask themselves, "What has been achieved by unnecessarily going around to these places?"
13. One who has given some thought to this understands and holds to keeping the company of saints. Many people have found God by keeping the company of saints.
14. These are the matters to be carefully considered. Those who are thoughtful and discerning will surely understand correctly. However, those who lack discrimination remain deluded and confused without having any correct understanding.
15. The one who searches inwardly gains inner understanding, while the one who looks outwardly does not understand anything. Therefore, the wise and discerning person looks inwardly.
16. The belief or conviction that is held without the use of proper discrimination is only an opinion or a supposition. It is said that an idol is the God of a fool.

17. Through continued observation one gains understanding and arrives at the correct conclusion. Only one who utilizes the power of discrimination and sets aside the elements realizes the invisible Reality.
18. Everything that becomes manifest gets destroyed. Understand that Parabrahman, the Absolute Reality, is different from all of the commotion and chaos in the manifest universe.
19. God is movement, and Brahman is still. There is no delusion or whirling of activity in that supreme Parabrahman. With the experience and knowledge of Reality, one gets out of Illusion.
20. Whatever is foolishly done without actual experience is entirely useless. Thus, living beings die in misery being entangled in foolish activity.
21. If one does not become free of action and rituals, what is the purpose of worshipping God? Those who use proper discernment understand this effortlessly, while the foolish do not understand.
22. Through thoughtful consideration and investigation one arrives at the conclusion that only the one God exists in the universe. Through the worship of God with attributes one can realize God without attributes.
23. By looking to the root of God with attributes one easily reaches the attributeless. By giving up attachment to appearances, one becomes liberated, and becomes the true form of Reality itself.
24. Through the continuous connection with the Supreme Lord one becomes completely pure. It is chiefly through Knowledge (Jnana) that one obtains the "Supreme Knowledge" (Vijnana), which is Self-Knowledge.
25. Such is the explanation of proper discernment that should be seen clearly in the inner-mind. By listening to the explanation of the utilization of discrimination between the Eternal and the ephemeral there is upliftment among the people in the world.

Thus in Shri Dasbodh, a dialogue between the Guru and disciple, Sub-Chapter 8 of Chapter 18, named "Explanation of the Inner God" is concluded.

Chapter: 18, Sub-Chapter: 9

Explanation of Sleep

|| ShriRam ||

1. First we will offer homage to Primordial Being (Adipurusha), and then speak about the activities related to sleep, which comes easily but does not go away so easily.
2. When the body becomes affected by sleep it becomes lazy and starts yawning, and one cannot continue to sit upright.
3. Sometimes there is a sound produced by yawning, sometimes the sound of the fingers slipping away from each other can be heard, and sometimes the body droops from one side to the other.
4. For some, their eyes keep closing and opening, for some the eyes just close and they fall asleep, and some get startled and look around in all directions.

5. Some fall asleep suddenly and may even fall onto a musical instrument and break it without even being aware of it.
6. Some fall asleep sitting upright and start snoring, and some fall asleep on their back spread out leisurely.
7. Some sleep with their bodies curled up, some sleep on their sides, and some shift around on all sides.
8. Some move their hands, some swing their legs, and some clench their teeth making a grinding sound.
9. Some lose their clothes by moving around and may even begin to toss around naked on the floor. For some, their turbans get unraveled and open up, spreading out cloth and hair all over.
10. Some sleep in a disorderly position, some look like dead bodies, and some sleep with their mouths wide open with their teeth showing, looking like an awful ghost.
11. Some wake up crying out or talking, some move around in the dark, and some go to sleep on garbage.
12. Some get up and move pots from their places, some crawl around the ground moving their hands all around, and some get up and start walking around in different directions.
13. Some begin to scream in their sleep, some cry and sob, and some laugh out loud.
14. Some call out loudly, some get up and shout, and some just lie still in one place.
15. Some creep around from moment to moment, some scratch their heads, and some whimper softly.
16. Some have saliva dripping down from their mouth, some spit, and some urinate unknowingly.
17. Some fart loudly, some belch with a foul smell, and some cough loudly spraying phlegm.
18. Some pass stools in their sleep, some vomit, some cough and sneeze, and some ask for water in a sleepy voice.
19. Some get scared due to nightmares, some feel happy with pleasant dreams, and some fall into a deep sleep like a stone.
20. When dawn comes, some begin reading spiritual texts, some begin doing morning prayers, and some sing songs praising God.
21. Some awaken and immediately remember their idols of contemplation, some begin repeating mantra in solitude, and some recite passages that they have learned by heart.
22. Some start thinking about the various streams of knowledge, art, or music that they have learned, and some awaken singing popular songs.
23. When the sleep is over, people settle into the waking state and begin attending to their affairs, applying their intellect to what they are doing.
24. The knowledgeable person gives up the elements and has run away, beyond even the Turya state. Through self-surrender, he has become Brahman.

Thus in Shri Dasbodh, a dialogue between the Guru and disciple, Sub-Chapter 9 of Chapter 18, named "Explanation of Sleep" is concluded.

Chapter: 18, Sub-Chapter: 10

Negative Signs of Listeners

|| ShriRam ||

1. Sometimes when a task is undertaken some difficulty may arise, but if the time is right, the work gets done spontaneously.
2. When the work is progressing, living beings feel enthusiastic and inspired day by day.
3. It is seen that when a being takes birth, there are fortunate times followed by times of grief, and then after undergoing a time of misery, God benevolently gives a time of some happiness.
4. If all times were fortunate, then everyone would be kings. Some times are fortunate, and some times are unfortunate. This is the natural order of life.
5. If one utilizes proper discrimination in worldly life and in spiritual life, many wondrous things naturally happen. This is a gift of God.
6. It is never seen nor heard on earth that one understands without listening, or that one becomes wise without learning.
7. Everything can be understood by listening. By knowing more and more, one's state of mind becomes clear and peaceful, and Essence and non-essence is properly understood in the mind.
8. Listening (shravana) means to hear correctly, and reflection (manana) means to retain what has been heard and to consider it again and again in the mind. This is the natural way of understanding in the three worlds.
9. While listening, many disturbances arise. There are so many such things, how can they all be mentioned? By remaining attentive, what is being told can be understood.
10. When people come to sit and listen, they become more attentive as the discourse progresses. However, when someone new arrives late, he is not as attentive.
11. Some people come to listen who have been to many different places and have heard different things from various people. Because they are confused, they are restless and cannot sit quietly.
12. There are very few people who act appropriately according to the situation. There are many disturbances that happen while listening. Please listen to some of them now.
13. Some people who come to listen to the discourse begin to feel physically uncomfortable and start making noise, or start yawning and falling asleep.
14. Some come and make the mind ready for listening, but their mind does not hear what is being said. Instead they only sit and think about various things that have been heard previously.
15. Some come and make the body ready for listening, but their mind is full of thoughts and they get caught up in concepts and imagination. How many such concepts and imaginings can be enumerated?
16. Only when what has been heard is properly considered and understood, can it be said that listening to the explanations has been worthwhile.
17. If the mind were visible and it was possible to hold it, then it would be easy to control. Control of the mind comes through discrimination. In this way, one retains the inner meaning of what is heard.

18. If someone comes to listen to the discourse after having just eaten a large meal, he soon becomes restless due to being thirsty for water.
19. If he asks for water and then drinks it profusely, he begins to feel nauseous and gets up and leaves.
20. There are some who let out foul smelling burps, some get the hiccups, some let out farts and feel very awkward, and some get up frequently to urinate.
21. Some become uncomfortable feeling the need to have a bowel movement, and forget about the discourse and make a run for the toilet. These types of things always occur.
22. Sometimes, if the speaker gives an extraordinary example, the mind of the listener gets stuck there. Some get carried away thinking about something that has been heard or read previously, and do not grasp the meaning of what is being said.
23. If someone comes and sits for the explanation, but by chance an insect stings or bites him, he gets distracted by the pain and cannot stay focused on the explanation.
24. For some, there may arise a pain in the stomach, or some pain in the back, or some discomfort in the knee joints, or an infection between the toes, or a boil on the rear-end, and they cannot sit for listening.
25. If someone happens to get bit by fleas, he becomes restless and leaves, or if there is some commotion outside, someone runs out to see what is happening.
26. Some people come to listen, but they get distracted by sexual attraction and cannot stop looking at the opposite sex. Sometimes thieves come and steal the footwear of the listeners.
27. Some come and make arguments, saying that one thing is true and that another thing is false, thus causing confusion and mixed feelings. Sometimes someone comes and says hurtful and abusive things. By doing so, he misses the explanations.
28. Sometimes people come and then after some time begin to start talking amongst themselves. Sometimes a speaker gives talks just for the sake of making money.
29. Sometimes when there are many knowledgeable people present they speak nonstop, one after the other, not caring about whether or not the needs of the listeners are being met.
30. Some people are always in the habit of saying, "I'm right, and you are wrong." In doing so, they abandon propriety and good ethics and behave improperly.
31. For the sake of proving their greatness, they babble on without any self control. Because there is no sense of propriety in their behavior, they only prove that they do not know how to act appropriately.
32. Some people are rigid with pride while others flare up in anger. Who can say whether such listeners are intelligent or dull-minded?
33. Therefore, those who are knowledgeable cleverly present themselves initially as being ignorant. They humbly act slightly foolish and unassuming, as if they do not know anything.
34. One who has understood that God is greater than oneself knows how to please and take care of the people in the world because God resides within all.
35. If there is quarreling and commotion going on at the place of a gathering, the knowledgeable person takes the blame. If one does not know how to please the minds of others, he has not learned anything. How can such a person be called someone who is in union with God (a yogi)?

36. Enmity increases with enmity and one only suffers grief because of this. Therefore, the wise understand the secret of remaining humble.
37. Such people of wisdom take care to not allow themselves to become petty-minded. The wise and great people always know the importance of being peaceful and forgiving.
38. When a virtuous person sits next to a person without any virtue, the lack of virtue is immediately apparent. A discerning person always behaves with consideration.
39. The greatness of a person is known to the one who recognizes ways of providing solutions and alternatives, and who makes discrete efforts to achieve goals.
40. How can someone be considered wise if he gets dragged into arguments with an evil-minded person, or comes down to the level of lowly people by giving up proper discernment?
41. What does a foolish person understand about propriety or offering various alternatives and solutions to a problem? A foolish person makes a mess of a good meeting.
42. In that case, a wise person intervenes and corrects the situation. With patience and forbearance he teaches people to be tolerant. He knows how to do things himself as well as how to get things done through others.
43. There are many people on the earth, and among them there are a few who are truly virtuous. It is due to those few, that satisfaction comes to living beings.
44. He understands the many aspects of the minds of others, and knows how to respect others according to the situation and circumstances. He knows many ways of pacifying those who are agitated and angry.
45. Such a knowledgeable person is powerful and exercises discretion. The nature of his actions are not easily known by ordinary people.
46. He knows how to move people to action, and how to motivate various groups of people. Such a person achieves a powerful position through the power of discrimination.
47. Practice discrimination in solitude and hold firmly to continuous meditation on God. There should not be any distinction made of calling some people as "one's own" and some as "others" (or "us" and "them").
48. Proper discrimination and efforts made are successful when one is in solitude. In solitude one's power of reason can become so sharp that one can understand the entire universe.
49. Meditate in solitude on God and the important things that were forgotten will be found, and you will realize that you are the all-pervading Inner-Self.
50. The one who enjoys being in solitude understands everything before others do. For achieving greatness, there is no substitute for solitude.

Thus in Shri Dasbodh, a dialogue between the Guru and disciple, Sub-Chapter 10 of Chapter 18, named "The Negative Signs of Listeners" is concluded.

Chapter 19. The Teaching

Chapter: 19, Sub-Chapter: 1

The Art of Writing

|| ShriRam ||

1. One should practice one's writing and be able to write the letters of the alphabet so that they look beautiful, and wise people feel pleased when seeing them.
2. The letters should have nice curves, and the lines should be straight with correct spacing between the letters and words. The writing should be done in black ink, and the rows should look nice, like a string of pearls.
3. Every letter should be neat with proper spacing and distance between letters and horizontal rows. The vowels and letters should be formed properly and made easy to recognize.
4. From the first word of the text to the last word, the writing should be uniform. It should look as if everything was written by one pen all at the same time.
5. The blackness and boldness of the letters, and the style and shape of the letters, should be consistent.
6. The lines should be straight and not touch each other. The letters and markings should not mix with or touch the letters of other words, or spill over into the rows.
7. The student should use a clean writing surface and the distance between all of the rows should be equal.
8. If a reader were to search for errors anywhere in the text, he should not be able to find any careless mistakes made by the writer.
9. If the writer is young, he must write carefully so people are attracted to his writing.
10. The writer should not write so small that older readers will have difficulty reading. Therefore, it is best that the writing is of a medium size.
11. There should be a nice space on the sides of the paper. The writing should look gracefully placed in the center. This way, even if the paper begins to become worn out, the writing will not be damaged.
12. The text should be written with great care so that the readers will hold it in high regard and want to meet the writer.
13. Use the body to put in good efforts so that you leave behind a good name for yourself, and so that many people will be eager to read what you have written.
14. Your writing should be on good quality paper, and the body of the text should be bound together carefully and neatly. There should be a good variety of writing materials available.
15. The pages should be cut properly, and nice colors should be chosen so that they look good together.
16. Choose a good selection of writing pens from different sources that are firm, thin and straight. Select a variety of colors and qualities of writing tools.
17. Keep various instruments nearby so they are ready and available when needed.
18. Make sure that you have the paper and ink readily available for when they are needed.
19. At the end of the text write a formal phrase of completion. Make use of appropriate drawings and pictures in the text.

20. Keep a variety of wrappings and coverings ready for when you put the books away. Keep them in safe places so they are well protected.

Thus in Shri Dasbodh, a dialogue between the Guru and disciple, Sub-Chapter 1 of Chapter 19, named "The Art of Writing" ends.

Chapter: 19, Sub-Chapter: 2

Discourse on Giving Explanations

|| ShriRam ||

1. In the previous sub-chapter, emphasis was put on the art of writing. Now, listen to the explanation about how to give different interpretations that are appropriate to various conversations so that the listeners can understand correctly
2. Understand that there are many different words, differences in their meanings, many types of expressions, various forms of composition, and different connotations of various words.
3. There are many doubts, many replies and counter-replies, many varied experiences, and many different ways of seeing things that people find amazing.
4. There are many preliminary propositions and final conclusions that need to be verified through experience. Do not speak in a manner which is not methodical or is disorganized, and do not make speculations based on imagination.
5. Whether it is in regard to worldly activity or renunciation, if something is not verifiable it should be considered as merely delusional talk. Just like rubbish that is thrown in a ditch cannot be lit, the flame of knowledge cannot be kindled by conjecture and guesswork.
6. The main sign of wisdom is that one answers a question only after understanding the mind of the questioner, and the motivation behind the question being asked.
7. If any activity is undertaken without using proper discernment, one's accumulated knowledge is worthless. How can anyone gain satisfaction by only arguing with others in a gathering?
8. Where there is a lot of talking going on, simply listen and keep silent. Come to understand the minds of others by noticing little indications.
9. Don't sit around with the foolish people, don't quarrel with people who are arrogant, and don't disturb other people's contentment simply for the sake of your own selfish motives.
10. Don't give up the appearance of being ignorant in some matters, and don't act arrogantly, all puffed up with knowledge. Open up the hearts and minds of many people with soft words.
11. It is important to understand situations correctly. If you continue to argue with people too long, you can spoil the whole occasion even though what you say may be true.
12. Don't be lazy when investigating something, and don't sit around with corrupt and degraded people. If you do happen to sit with them, don't point out their faults and false statements.

13. Find out the mental state of the one who is in sorrow. In such a situation, read something to him. By easing people's minds like this, they will be attracted to you.
14. Don't take a prominent seat at a meeting, and don't simply go to a meeting because meals are being served. Going to meetings only to fill your belly is not dignified behavior.
15. Exhibit your best qualities so that when you speak, people will value what you say. Seek out good people and become friends with them.
16. Speak in accordance with your study and practice. Try to please all of the people, and maintain good relations with everyone.
17. When going to a new place, try to find out the conditions there before arriving. Speak to all living beings in a loving and affectionate manner.
18. Speak in order to pacify everyone's heart without making distinctions that some are superior and some are inferior. Try not to go to strange places unnecessarily after sunset.
19. If one wants to be friendly with everyone in the world, the secret is in the way you speak to people. If you search, you will eventually find some good people.
20. Go to places where explanations about God are taking place. Sit at a distance in a humble manner, and take in the essence of what is being said.
21. There you will come across good people, and you will come to know who is open-minded. In this way, you can slowly and gradually know the people in the crowd.
22. Among all the practices, listening is the most important. More important than listening is reflection. Through reflection many people become content.
23. Very shrewdly and wisely come to understand what is within the minds of others. Without understanding the minds of others, what is the point in tiring yourself out for no reason?

Thus in Shri Dasbodh, a dialogue between the Guru and disciple, Sub-Chapter 2 of Chapter 19, named "Discourse on Giving Explanations" is concluded.

Chapter: 19, Sub-Chapter: 3

Signs of an Unfortunate Person

|| ShriRam ||

1. Making your mind attentive, listen to the signs of an unfortunate person. By abandoning these qualities, the signs of a fortunate person are obtained.
2. By committing wrongful deeds one becomes impoverished, and poverty gives rise to an accumulation of more wrongful deeds. This cycle continues on and on.
3. Therefore, listen to the signs of an unfortunate person and abandon them so that the signs of good fortune can be gained.
4. The unfortunate person likes to be lazy, and does not like to make any effort. His desires always move him to do improper things.
5. Such a person is always sleepy and confused. He constantly speaks unnecessarily about many irrelevant things, and is not liked in anyone's mind.

6. He does not understand the importance of reading or writing, and does not know how to conduct business transactions. He cannot keep track of accounts or do any record keeping, and he does not have a good memory.
7. He loses things, drops things, falls down and breaks things, he is forgetful, he makes many mistakes, and he has many bad habits. Such a person never likes to keep the company of good and virtuous people.
8. He makes friends with mischievous people and trouble-makers, and he associates with people who are hypocrites, thieves, and wrong-doers.
9. Such a person quarrels with everyone. Being a thief himself, he deceives and steals from others, and being a bully, he causes trouble for everyone he meets.
10. Such a person has no forethought, he does not have any appreciation for justice and propriety, and he always has a keen desire to take the belongings of others.
11. He pampers his body by being lazy, but as a result of his laziness he does not even have any means for getting good food, or to buy decent clothing or bedding.
12. In his laziness he sits around picking and scratching at his body, or he just merely lies around sleeping.
13. Such a person does not develop any meaningful friendships with other people because he is always speaking harsh words to others. He is uncontrollable by anyone because of his foolishness.
14. He feels ashamed and shy to meet virtuous people, yet he freely runs around with lowly people. His mind feels delighted when he is criticized by others about his actions.
15. How can such a person be helpful to others? He is a destructive person who does many wrongful deeds, and he brings a great deal of calamity into the lives of others. He behaves eccentrically and brings disorder to everything that he does.
16. He is undisciplined in his speech and never carefully considers what he is talking about before he speaks. Thus, nobody cares about anything that he says.
17. He doesn't trust anyone, and nobody trusts him or feels close to him. Such a person has no knowledge or prosperity. The only thing that he has is useless stubbornness and pride.
18. If someone pleases the minds of many people, fortune comes naturally. However, an unfortunate person will never listen to this type of thoughtful advice.
19. He does not understand anything, and does not listen when someone is trying to teach him. What is the use of using various means to try to teach such a person the solutions to his problems?
20. His imagination runs wild, but he never actually achieves anything because his mind is continuously engaged in imagination and doubt.
21. When the mind of such a person has abandoned the path virtue, how can his wrongful-mindedness be cleansed? Because he has no determination, his life is spoiled by doubts.
22. He does not have any complete understanding about anything, but that does not keep him from speaking out in gatherings. Because of this, people can easily see his ignorance and masquerade.
23. When people can see the substance of a person's knowledge, that person becomes respected and appreciated by many people in the world.
24. One cannot earn a good name without doing any hard work. Honor and respect do not come for free. When a person only displays negative qualities, he is scorned and disrespected everywhere.

25. Such an unfortunate person does not keep the company of good people, and does nothing to become wise. Understand that such a person does not understand what is in his own best interest and is basically his own worst enemy,
26. If you do good things for people, you naturally are repaid with good things in return. However, this simple principle is not understood by the unfortunate ones.
27. Recognize that where none of the best qualities are found, this is the sign of an unfortunate person. Such a person is not respected by many people. This is clearly a sign of misfortune.
28. The principle of cause and effect shows us that nothing is achieved without doing some work. The person who does not do anything gets carried away by grief and sorrow.
29. A person who is not liked by anyone is like someone who has no footwear. Being without any shelter, an unfortunate person is exposed everywhere he goes.
30. Therefore, recognize and abandon your bad qualities and adopt good qualities. In this way, one gets everything that is needed in life.

Thus in Shri Dasbodh, a dialogue between the Guru and disciple, Sub-Chapter 3 of Chapter 19, named "Signs of an Unfortunate Person" is concluded.

Chapter: 19, Sub-Chapter: 4

The Signs of a Fortunate Person

|| ShriRam ||

1. In the last chapter, the signs of an unfortunate person have been described. Using proper discernment, those qualities should be dropped completely. Now, listen to the attributes of a fortunate person that provide contentment in life.
2. Some people have good qualities from the time of birth that enable them to help others in many ways. Such a person is appreciated in the minds of all.
3. Such a person knows how to write beautifully, can read quickly while comprehending the inner meaning, and is quite naturally able explain what he has understood.
4. Such a person never harms anyone's mind, nor does he give up the company of good people. He is easily able to deduce the signs of good fortune and exhibit them as an example to others.
5. He is respected by all people and admired wherever he goes. He does not exhibit any foolishness, and does not get entangled in confusion or imagination.
6. He has many of the best qualities and is a virtuous person. Such a person is a friend of the world. His greatness is clearly evident and has been earned by his own good efforts. His greatness does not depend upon the efforts of others.
7. He understands very well how to please the minds of others. He has learned many things by heart, and is not negligent with regard to propriety in his behavior.
8. He knows how to ask about things in a polite manner, and can convey exact meaning in his replies. He understands what the best actions are, and his actions are in accordance with his speech.

9. He is genuinely liked by many people, and is rarely criticized by anyone. He is a truly great person of brilliant virtue.
10. Such a person spends his life helping others, each according to their needs. What can be lacking in life for such a person?
11. Many people are eager to see him, and he is always available to help in times of need. Such a person of good fortune cannot bear to see anyone suffering because they do not have what they need.
12. He is well versed in the various streams of knowledge, art, and music, and he has a great love for Self-Knowledge.
13. He is humble to everyone in his speech, and is able to easily understand the minds of others. His nature is such that he makes efforts to see to it that nobody is lacking for anything.
14. He upholds the values of justice, propriety, and praising God. He is disciplined in his conduct and makes worthwhile use of his time. How can such a person suffer from calamity and poverty?
15. Such a person is adorned with the best qualities and is a shining example among people everywhere. His appearance is glorious like a rising sun.
16. When such a knowledgeable person is present, how can any chaos arise? Those who do not possess the best qualities are truly the unfortunate ones.
17. In family life, he knows how to maintain good relations, and in spiritual life he knows how to give satisfying explanations. He recognizes and takes delight in the best qualities that are present in all people.
18. He is not contradictory in his speech or behavior, and does not say one thing to one person and something different to another. People marvel at his attitude of equality towards all.
19. A fortunate person does not behave in a way that is hurtful to others. Wherever he goes, he exhibits discretion and proper discernment.
20. Such a person understands the significance of right actions, worship, Self-Knowledge, and detachment. His intellect is steeped in Self-knowledge, so how can he ever be lead astray?
21. When the best qualities are clearly evident in him, who can can find fault in him? He is the same as the fullness of the Self which resides within all.
22. Everyone, young and old, is always eager to do anything according to their own selfish motives, but he is not like that. He takes great pleasure in selflessly doing things for others out of the kindness of his heart.
23. He feels sorrow when he sees the pain and sorrow of others, and feels pleased when he sees that others are happy. His sincere wish is that everyone should be happy.
24. He is like a father who is concerned about the welfare and various needs of his children. This is the nature of such a great person.
25. Such a person cannot bear to see the sufferings of others, and eagerly does whatever he can to help them without any expectation or desire to be rewarded. Even when he is berated by others, he does not berate anyone. This is the nature of such a great person.
26. He knows that the body is unreal, so he does not matter to him if the body or its actions are criticized or insulted. Such a knowledgeable person never feels subjugated by bodily misidentification.

27. Bodily identification is a sign of misfortune. The knowledgeable person is bodiless even though he has a body. A fortunate person always shows at least some of the best qualities when among the people.
28. People feel attracted to the best qualities, and feel repulsed towards negative bad qualities. One who has a keen intellect understands this and can easily win over the hearts and minds of the people. How can the common people understand this?
29. When people have experienced the kindness and forgiving nature of such a person, they stand behind him and are supportive in many ways.
30. Many people think that they are great, but greatness is something that must be recognized and agreed upon by all. The truly great person is generous, supportive and serene.
31. The best qualities that have been described are the signs of a truly powerful person. The lack of virtue and negative qualities can naturally be seen to be the signs of an unfortunate person.

Thus in Shri Dasbodh, a dialogue between the Guru and disciple, Sub-Chapter 4 of Chapter 19, named "Signs of a Fortunate Person" is concluded.

Chapter: 19, Sub-Chapter: 5

The Importance of the Body

|| ShriRam ||

1. There are many images of God. Some are made of clay, stone, gold, silver, brass, or copper, and some are painted images.
2. There are images of God that are made from various types of wood, coral, precious stones, pearls, stones from rivers, etc.
3. Some people worship images of God on copper coins, gold coins, and stones with markings on them that are brought from various places of pilgrimage.
4. There are so many different varieties of worship, how many should be told? People are attracted to the type of worship according to what they like.
5. However, one should see the root cause of all worship, which is the Inner-Self, and remember Him. Remember the Self and know that all of the many deities that are seen in the world are but a fraction of Him.
6. At the root, there is the one God that has become many, and it is He who is the seer of all. When this point is comprehended and one begins to see with discrimination, this is the beginning of understanding.
7. Without the body, devotion is not possible, and without the body, one cannot realize God. Thus, the body is the origin of devotion to God.
8. If the care for the body is totally neglected, where is the place for devotion to God? Therefore, the capacity to worship God lies in the connection of the body with the Self.
9. How can one praise or worship God without the body? Without the body, how can one rejoice in God or celebrate his glory?

10. Without the body, how would it be possible to utilize various articles of worship such as perfumes, sandalwood, flowers, fruits, incense, lamps, and various other things?
11. How could there be any appreciation of sacred water, the application of sandalwood paste, the offering of flowers, or the repetition of mantras, without the body?
12. What would be possible without the body? Devotion and worship of God are possible only because of the body.
13. God and the various deities have some basic power that is associated with them. Respect and have reverence for the different gods according to their power.
14. Even if many different gods are praised, ultimately that praise is received by the one Original Existence. Therefore, the various gods should all be respected.
15. The vine of Illusion has proliferated extensively bearing the fruit of many bodies. It is through these fruits in the form of bodies that is possible to realize the Original Existence.
16. Therefore one should not neglect the body. Recognize that it is only with the body that one can realize God and become content in life.
17. Many human beings give up their family life and wander around searching for God. However, wherever they go, they only end up becoming entangled in imagination and doubt.
18. Seeing the many different customs of people at various places, they make various offerings to God and see images of God that are located at places of pilgrimage.
19. Or, they listen to many stories about incarnations of God and hold on to beliefs that come from those stories. But all of those incarnations appeared in ancient times and then disappeared.
20. When people hear about Brahma, Vishnu, and Shiva they say that they are especially great gods. However, it is the one Lord of the Universe (Jagadisha) that is without attributes which must be recognized.
21. There is no one place where the one God resides, so where is it that He should be worshipped? When one begins to think about this concept one begins to get carried away by speculation and imagination.
22. Thus, the question arises, "Without having a glimpse of God that is without attributes, how can one realize Him?" Blessed are the sages who understand this.
23. There are many gods in the world, and it is not possible to disregard their power. Because of this, the one main God is not easily known.
24. If one gives up the sense of individual doership, then the one God can be seen. Only then can something can be understood about his secret and mysterious existence.
25. The one God cannot be seen or perceived, and does not get destroyed even at the time of the final destruction of the universe. If one does not have any virtue, how can there be any faith in his existence?
26. The mind conceives and imagines many things, and it is always preoccupied with many desires and habits. They are like continuous waves that arise and subside in the mind.
27. Therefore, understand that only "That" which is without any imagination is alone the eternal Reality. There is no end to it, therefore it is called limitless.

28. See this with the eyes of Knowledge and become That after you have seen. With constant contemplation and verification, one becomes one with That, free of any attachment.
29. The amazing acts and the play of God cannot be understood by ignorant beings. Its only by keeping the company of saints that one gains the experience of the Self, and comes to realize it for oneself.
30. This is the means for realizing the subtle state of the Self. Understanding this allows one to avoid downfall in life. By the grace of the Sadguru, one becomes liberated from worldly bondage in no time.

Thus in Shri Dasbodh, a dialogue between the Guru and disciple, Sub-Chapter 5 of Chapter 19, named "The Importance of the Body" is concluded.

Chapter: 19, Sub-Chapter: 6

Explanation of Intelligence

|| ShriRam ||

1. The actions of the one who is living a life of spirituality and who utilizes the power of discrimination are respected by the world. With thoughtfulness and careful consideration, he avoids making many mistakes.
2. Such a person does not harbor the doubts that are felt by most people. With forethought, he carefully analyzes situations thoroughly and acts accordingly.
3. When a person is not free of selfish desires and motives, the things that he says are not acceptable to others. It is very difficult to keep the people of the world pleased.
4. Some people try to force their teachings on others, and some enlist the help of others to propagate their teachings. It is only natural that such people gradually experience a downfall because of their greed.
5. If someone tries to give such people teachings about discrimination, he is met with great opposition. The result of his good intentions is that those people become his enemies and the whole affair is a disaster.
6. Sometimes a person tries to give advice to his brother but is only ridiculed. Therefore, it is not wise to try to teach or exhibit qualities of spiritual leadership among family or mere acquaintances.
7. Initially there may appear to be some agreement, but soon the relationship starts to fall apart. The discerning person is careful to avoid this kind of situation when there is a gathering of people lacking discernment.
8. It is also not wise for a husband to become a disciple of his wife. The lack of careful consideration and discernment with regard to this type of situation will tend to lead to a disregard for propriety.
9. Such teachers do not speak of discrimination. Instead they conceal many things, and do not reveal the truth to people. Such teachers do not offer the principle determinations or any firm conclusions to seekers.
10. Such people get carried away by various whimsical ideas and do not exercise any discernment. Such people give no forethought to anything, and are definitely not sages.

11. A good teacher does not ask for anything from anyone. He enhances the spreading of devotion to God by instilling the power of discrimination in people.
12. To win over and please the hearts and minds of others, and to reveal the power of discrimination to many people is very difficult. All of the people in the world live according to their own desires and their own customs.
13. If a person of low caliber becomes a fake guru and takes on many lowly people as disciples, the whole group becomes spoiled due to ignorance and lack of virtue.
14. However, when a group of real knowers of Brahman comes together, many worthy devotees gather around them. Therefore, seek out the company of the saintly people on the earth.
15. Accept what is noble and grand, and give up those things that are insubstantial and useless in life. Through desirelessness become great on the earth.
16. Writing, reading, giving clear explanations, singing and dancing in joy, and learning many things by heart are worthwhile activities in life.
17. Initiation into Knowledge (Jnana), friendliness, sharp intellect, and maintaining good relations with others are good qualities. A person with such qualities knows how to be engaged in many activities while remaining detached.
18. Such a person is always interested in hearing explanations about God, and delights in inspiring people to chant the name of God. His explanations are clear and he is brilliant like the sun.
19. He knows how to please evil-minded people and pacify the virtuous. He knows how to reach the minds of everyone according to their disposition.
20. People change in his company and the best qualities arise in them by coming into contact with him. By being in his company, many people are inspired to study spiritual texts.
21. Wherever he goes he brings a freshness with him and he is appreciated by the people that gather around him. However, he never allows himself to become entangled in greed.
22. His devotion, knowledge, wisdom, and praising of God is intense. He is established in union with God, and engages in great undertakings everywhere he goes.
23. For the one who remains desirelessness, his greatness extends in all directions. People everywhere are pacified by his devotion.
24. Without some kind of effort, no greatness can be achieved. Nothing is achieved by unnecessarily wandering around aimlessly.
25. There is no guarantee of when the life of the body will end. Who knows what kinds of situations in which one may find oneself?
26. Therefore be alert. Do as much work as you can to fill the world with praise for God's greatness and glory.
27. Whatever can easily be accomplished should be done immediately, and understand clearly through proper discernment what cannot be accomplished.
28. There is nothing that cannot be understood through proper discernment. By utilizing the power of discrimination in solitude one is able to come up with good conclusions.
29. When one is thoughtful and carefully considers situations, one is able to find solutions to many problems. What can be lacking for such a person? How can living beings acquire intelligence without taking the time to reflect in solitude?

30. Utilize the power of discrimination in solitude, and recognize the Inner-Self that is Lord Rama. In this way, you will not become confused from the beginning to the end in any situation.

Thus in Shri Dasbodh, a dialogue between the Guru and disciple, Sub-Chapter 6 of Chapter 19, named "Explanation of Intelligence" is concluded.

Chapter: 19, Sub-Chapter: 7

Discourse on Making Effort

|| ShriRam ||

1. In spiritual discourse and when giving explanations about God, the speaker should speak with great enthusiasm and be able to give clear examples so that there is nothing lacking in his explanations.
2. If the speaker makes mistakes in his explanations, those who are knowledgeable will recognize what he has done, but the ignorant people will merely continue to look on without gaining any understanding.
3. If the speaker hesitates when giving an answer to a question, the listeners will recognize this, and the speaker will begin to lose his credibility.
4. The speaker should be able to satisfy the listeners with short and direct answers. Even if some irritation arises in his mind, he must control himself. His speech should be such that everyone remains interested in what he has to say.
5. The speaker who cannot tolerate any disturbances from the listeners and becomes angry will lose the listener's interest in the discourse.
6. The speaker should examine from time to time who among the listeners are attentive and pleased with the discourse, and whose mind is distracted.
7. When a disciple begins doubting and his mind runs in the wrong direction, if the guru tries to argue with him, this will create doubts in the minds of everyone who sees the discourse going in the wrong direction.
8. If a spiritual leader is bound by expectations, he does not display signs of wisdom and endlessly engages in senseless arguments.
9. Such spiritual leaders are useless and get into trouble everywhere they go. How can anyone gain any satisfaction in the company of such a person?
10. A good speaker should be able to please the minds of the people everywhere. In this way, his fame will spread and he will be respected by people of all types of dispositions.
11. He should remain out of the world, and observe the congregation from a higher level of consciousness, not asking or demanding anything from anyone.
12. He should understand full well that the Lord of the Universe resides everywhere. Those who utilize the power of discrimination take care to remember this at all times.
13. If a speaker takes it for granted that everyone that he sees are entirely useless people, how can it be true that he is the only good person?

14. A spiritual leader should not go off to some barren land and separate himself from the people. He should not behave eccentrically, and he should maintain a humble demeanor in order to please people.
15. One who cannot live and behave well among people is of no use as a spiritual leader. Such a person should spend his time listening to discourses about spirituality and doing spiritual practice to gain knowledge.
16. For example, if one does not know how to swim oneself, why should he make others drown? Acting in such a manner, the interest and attraction towards spirituality becomes lost and listeners become doubtful.
17. A speaker should only present himself to others if he has studied and can impart proper knowledge. Otherwise, he should remain quiet. One should not present oneself as being knowledgeable if he is not.
18. How can someone who walks very slowly catch up with someone who walks quickly? One who wants to ride a fast horse should be capable and competent to do so.
19. The teaching of spiritual matters requires a great deal of effort which needs to be done by those with keen and sharp intellect. How can such work be done by the simple-minded who easily get carried away by their emotions and drowned by false beliefs?
20. Of what use is a speaker who gathers people together but cannot hold their attention or clear away their doubts? It is like one who sows a field but does not cultivate and harvest the crop, or a jeweler who collects gems but does not bring them to the market.
21. Spiritual meaning becomes evident when there is an increasing interest and attraction to spiritual life aroused within the listeners. Otherwise, people only get fed up with arguing and lose interest.
22. If what the speaker says is not acceptable to the people, then the listeners come to be regarded as not being acceptable by the speaker. If there is doubt in everyone's minds, how can anyone gain any satisfaction?
23. If the initiation into Knowledge is given by those who have no virtue, and if the people receiving the initiation are not sincere, how can there be any proper use of the power of discrimination? Where the lack of discrimination prevails, one should not remain in such a place of false teachings.
24. If one cannot take on the responsibility of making sure that things are done correctly, what is the point of organizing some undertaking? Even if one works hard for many days, all of the effort merely turns out to be wasted in the end.
25. To ensure that everything runs smoothly takes a lot of work, and if things do not turn out well, it creates a lot of dissent and anger among people from one moment to the next. There are so many obstacles to success, how many of them can be enumerated?
26. The foolish people get carried away in their foolishness, and the knowledgeable quarrel out of pride in their knowledge. In both ways, a ridiculous situation develops among the people.
27. What can be said about such people who cannot manage and control the entire affair, yet cannot remain quiet?
28. Such a person who is not capable of managing responsibilities should give up attachment to titles and honors, and instead put some effort into making his life worthwhile by traveling to some new places.

29. If one cannot travel to new places, nor can he tolerate dealing with other people, he will experience a great deal of suffering and doubt in life.
30. All of this depends upon one's own disposition. Each person must give careful consideration as to what is right for oneself. Consider what is most beneficial for yourself and act accordingly.

Thus in Shri Dasbodh, a dialogue between the Guru and disciple, Sub-Chapter 7 of Chapter 19, named "Discourse on Making Effort" is concluded.

Chapter: 19, Sub-Chapter: 8

The Description of Endeavors

|| ShriRam ||

1. There are many varieties of people in the world. By traveling, one can come to know of them and appreciate them, as well as discover that there are many varieties of discerning wisdom that can be found.
2. There are many people who are householders who live in a detached state. Their contentment does not become shaken by the joys and sorrows of life.
3. Their nature is such that they say only what is required to be said, and behave in a natural and appropriate manner. Their manner of speaking is such that they are respected by all.
4. Some people have a natural knowledge of rhythm and music that emanates from them very easily, and some people have a natural understanding of justice and propriety.
5. There are very few extraordinary people found among many who are loved by living beings and who always emanate a radiance of their presence.
6. Sometimes, by rare chance, such a person of great virtue is found. The significance of the greatness of such a person is felt immediately.
7. When such a person is found, it is marvelous to see his grand qualities. His actions and speech are always appropriate and consistent with his experiential understanding.
8. The worst among all vices is to consider one's vices to be virtues. When one makes such a great mistake as this, misfortune cannot be avoided.
9. Some people can accomplish great tasks easily without encountering any obstacles or difficulties, while some cannot achieve any success even when making great efforts.
10. What comes effortlessly and naturally for some cannot be obtained by others even after long and hard study. Such is the greatness of the activity of God which cannot be known.
11. There are many politicians who make mistakes in their political strategies that create many problems for them. Because of their mistakes, they are publicly disgraced, and are ridiculed everywhere they go.
12. Thus, if one does not make big political mistakes, there will be an abundance of solutions to various problems. If mistakes are made while trying to implement solutions, the attempted solutions will cause more harm than good.

13. If one is not able to understand what has gone wrong, it is not possible to make the situation clear in the minds of those involved, and the people on both sides will not let go of their positions due to pride.
14. As a result, the entire event and the relationships between the involved parties get spoiled, and people's minds become aggravated. Because of the lack of skill, nobody understands what went wrong.
15. If an endeavor is undertaken without proper planning and management, the whole affair will begin to deteriorate due a lack of forethought and an inability to exercise any control over the situation.
16. Some people are not endowed with any ability to get things accomplished. They are powerless because they have fallen into a web of wrong beliefs.
17. Such a person does not understand situations correctly and is therefore incapable of making anyone else understand. His mind is constantly running out of control, entangled in doubt and imagination.
18. Who knows what hidden imaginings are running through his mind, and who can bring them under control? It is up to each person to bring one's own mind under control with a strong intellect.
19. One who cannot manage large undertakings should not expand his activities. Such a person should keep his mind attentive to his current duties and be content in that.
20. If one carries out one's endeavors in haste, he becomes distressed and also creates troubles for others. Carrying out one's work in this way only creates trouble and turmoil all around.
21. If someone creates many problems for other people, and only becomes troubled himself, what is the point of engaging in such useless endeavors?
22. Understand that the nature of undertaking endeavors is like this. Sometimes everything works out well, and at other times endeavors do not meet with success. Knowing this, do your best according to the situation while being aware that your endeavors may or may not be successful.
23. People generally do not have any faith and are not inspired. It is up to you to awaken it in them at the same time taking care to make sure that nobody suffers any humiliation as a result.
24. Everything that happens, whether good or bad, is received by the Inner-Self, while That which is without attributes is not affected by anything. Understand that all of the various type of dangers and pitfalls happen only in the activity of Illusion.
25. The place of peaceful repose is pure and untainted stillness. It is there, in that changelessness, that all changes come to rest.
26. There, all sorrows and disappointments fall away, and the mind settles into peaceful repose. Such is the nature of Parabrahman which must be realized as being one's own True Form through the utilization of the power of discrimination.
27. Your realization should be such that you have no attachment to any titles or endeavors, any past relations or events, and there is no feeling of disturbance with regard to whether anyone comes or goes.
28. One who becomes wearied or disgusted with an endeavor should take some time away to sit and rest in peace. Why should one continue to be engaged in activity which is not getting accomplished?
29. It is natural that there should be times of activity and also times of peaceful relaxation. In this way, one is sure to get the proper rest that is required.

30. Any work or endeavor that is undertaken will not last forever. It is important to remember that there is nothing greater than being content in one's life. The human body is not acquired so easily, so one should use it wisely.

Thus in Shri Dasbodh, a dialogue between the Guru and disciple, Sub-Chapter 8 of Chapter 19, named "The Description of Endeavors" is concluded.

Chapter: 19, Sub-Chapter: 9

Discourse on Politics

|| ShriRam ||

1. One who is knowledgeable and detached from the world, yet who likes to be with friends and attend gatherings of the people, should first be able to easily remain in solitude.
2. In solitude, one comes up with new ideas and is able to consider various plans and strategies. It also gives one the opportunity to come to understand the various situations and progress of the people.
3. If one does not spend time in reflection, then nothing can be realized. It is like a businessman who does not keep an eye on his accounts and ends up bankrupt.
4. Some people acquire the rights and titles to their property, while some foolishly lose land that is in their possession. This is similar to the various situations among people who think and reflect, and those who do not.
5. When one takes time to reflect on situations in the mind, one can understand the possible outcomes before they happen. In this way, one can easily avoid being deceived.
6. If one continuously remains in one place in close intimacy with other people, it often happens that there is too much familiarity and people start to feel resentment or contempt towards each other. Therefore, one who is spiritual leader should not spend too much time in one place.
7. If one takes too much rest or begins to neglect work that needs to be done, the entire project begins to fall apart and the inner motivation to gather other people around him is lost.
8. Various types of spiritual practices and other activities should be organized and performed regularly. This will leave little time for people to gossip or get involved in other kinds of mischief.
9. For example, a person who is in the habit of stealing should be put in charge of managing a store. When he makes a mistake due to the force of habit, he should be admonished and corrected so he gradually learns step by step how to leave behind his foolish behavior.
10. These types of things have been going on for a long time. Do not harass anyone or cause them to suffer, instead use political skill to get people everywhere to change their ways.
11. Arrange it so a mean-spirited person is used to comfort another mean-spirited person, and that a disruptive person who causes disputes is confronted by another

disruptive person. Meanwhile, remain aloof from the situation yourself so no blame or criticism falls on you.

12. Remove one thorn with another thorn, but do not allow anyone to know. Allow people to remain with the impression that you are not involved in the situation.
13. If some activity is done without anyone's knowledge, it easily gets accomplished immediately. However, if it becomes revealed and known to everyone, then it doesn't get accomplished even by some miracle.
14. People should become interested in a spiritual leader just by hearing about him. Upon seeing him they will develop a growing affinity towards him, and they will be eager to volunteer to do service for him.
15. If one sets out to do some work, it will get done. However, if one does not set out to do anything, nothing will be accomplished. For this reason, there should be no laxity about carrying out any work.
16. If a person depends on somebody else to do his work, he does not become successful, while the one who does the work himself is wise, and goes on to become successful.
17. If everyone comes to know everything about the project, then the work tends not to get done. Therefore, care should be taken to make sure that this does not happen.
18. Control of the project should be kept in one's own hands, and efforts should be made to see to it that the work gets completed through others, and that troublemakers are handled tactfully with political skill.
19. There are some people who are overly talkative bullies who instigate arguments and create problems. Such people should be challenged so that good relationships are not ruined and hindrances don't get created because of their mischievous ways.
20. Such bullies should be exposed and their activities should be crushed by taking away their power. However, after their power is taken away, they should be supported and allowed to work without being completely ruined.
21. If, because of fear of the mischief makers and bullies, the leader does not protect the social relationships and maintain the political strategies, then everything will be revealed, both the good and the bad aspects of the situation.
22. If the group is large, then there should be strict codes of conduct. If a leader establishes a temple or ashram, he should be humble, and not harbor any pride.
23. The troublemakers in the group should be identified, but do not expose them as such. Rather, treat them like good and virtuous people, and they should be given some importance in the group.
24. If the troublemakers are openly exposed among the people, they will always be a source of problems. Therefore, their capacity to create problems should be shut down permanently.
25. When seeing the army of an enemy approaching, the warriors of the kingdom should be brave and eager to fight them. Similarly, a king should be equally eager to uphold and support the spirituality of the people.
26. A great leader should be such that upon seeing him, evil-minded men are struck with the fear that he will make them experience the severe blows of admonishment. With such power as this, any plans of rebellion effortlessly get destroyed.
27. These are activities that must be carried out carefully and wisely. Political activity is something that needs to be done routinely. It is important not to give the wrong impression because of negligence.

28. It is not possible for a leader to be seen at all places at all times, but his name and greatness should be known everywhere. The whole world is uplifted by the eloquence of his speech.
29. Let a complainer confront another complainer, let an obstinate person go up against another obstinate person, and let a clever person confront another clever person.
30. Put a strong person in front of another strong person, let an arrogant person be met by another arrogant person, and let a troublemaker be met with another troublemaker.
31. When two people of similar qualities are put together, there is a certain entertainment in the political game. However, when all of this happens, the politician who makes it happen should remain out of sight, not to be seen anywhere.

Thus in Shri Dasbodh, a dialogue between the Guru and disciple, Sub-Chapter 9 of Chapter 19, named "Discourse on Politics" is concluded.

Chapter: 19, Sub-Chapter: 10

The Signs of Discrimination

|| ShriRam ||

1. In the company of a great sage or spiritual leader (mahanta), there is ongoing discourse on various subjects, ongoing reflection on many opinions, and ongoing consideration of various political philosophies in the minds of those present.
2. There, the best qualities in the world are discussed and explained, and not a single moment is wasted in empty talk.
3. In such places there is discussion about various doubts, the resolution to the questions about what is true and what is false, and many discussions about statements that are made in various scriptures.
4. The path of devotion is properly explained, the meaning of worship becomes clearly understood, and the path of Knowledge is made clear.
5. The spiritual leader takes great delight in desirelessness and has an attitude of disinterestedness in the world. Although he is involved in many activities, he is not attached to them.
6. He can quote passages from many books that he knows by heart. His answers are methodical and relevant to the questions, and his precise speech pacifies the hearts and minds of the listeners.
7. He is loved by many people and his critics can not sidetrack him. There is always a crowd around him, but his inner state cannot be fathomed by anyone.
8. It is natural for him to travel to many places to propagate the path of worship. Therefore he becomes well known to all of the people in the world.
9. He is well known, yet he cannot be found at any one location. Nobody knows what he does, but he is visited by people from many different countries that come and go.

10. He understands the dispositions and minds of many people, and instills thoughtfulness and discrimination within them. With great skill and tact in his explanations, he clears away the doubts from people's minds.
11. Nobody knows how many people follow him. It cannot be estimated how large his group is, or how many people he has put on the path of listening and reflecting.
12. By using relevant examples from prose and poetry he gives many explanations that pleases the minds of the people gathered around him.
13. With such a regular routine of attentive discrimination is always going on around him, how can anyone who comes to him fall into a lack of discrimination?
14. Whatever is known by him is gradually and patiently taught to the people. In this way, all of the people who come to him are made wiser.
15. He teaches others repeatedly in many ways, clearing away the difficulties and doubts of the desireless person.
16. Whatever is possible to be done by himself, he does, and what he cannot do, he gets done through other people. All the while, he never neglects his practice of praising God.
17. By his example, he does what needs to be done. Through his thoughtfulness and investigation, he gets others to think and investigate. By holding to the path of devotion, he inspires others to follow the path of devotion.
18. If he becomes tired of the same old group of people, he moves on and finds a new place. He does not become lazy with respect to doing whatever he can for others.
19. If the spiritual studies and devotional practices are given up by the spiritual leader, then he will surely lose his status. In such a situation, he should find new people to teach the path of devotion to without delay.
20. He should not get caught up in worldly activities, while at the same time he should not become tired of starting new endeavors. Laziness is of no use in any situation.
21. Sometimes, even when many efforts are made, an endeavor gets spoiled and is a failure, and an ignorant person just helplessly looks on. How can a lazy and dull-minded fool know what needs to be done?
22. To be a leader requires effort and being able to deal with many situations. How can one who is weak in body and mind do such work? Therefore, a person who is strong must be taught in various ways.
23. The leader remains at a place as long as the activities can be managed. When the activity becomes unmanageable, he happily moves on to some other place.
24. One who is free of attachment to worldly activities becomes stronger in desirelessness. He leisurely goes wherever the conditions are favorable.
25. If one seeks greatness, he must be able to set aside comforts. If one only wants comforts, he will not become great. Nothing can be achieved without doing something or without putting in some effort.
26. However much needs to be done, the appropriate amount of work needs to take place. However, the weak and incapable simply make excuses.
27. If the enthusiasm is given up in the beginning, or one loses confidence while the work is going on, how can one achieve any success in worldly life?
28. Worldly life is basically a rotten and destructible thing. However, by utilizing the power of discrimination, it becomes a decent and worthwhile thing, and it gradually loses its power to affect the mind.
29. Such is the nature of worldly life. The mind can understand this through proper observation. One should never give up the perseverance to understand correctly.

30. If perseverance is given up, one suffers over everything. Only the wise person understands the many various opinions and ways of wisdom.

Thus in Shri Dasbodh, a dialogue between the Guru and disciple, Sub-Chapter 10 of Chapter 19, named "The Signs of Discrimination" ends.

Chapter 20. The Chapter of Completion

Chapter: 20, Sub-Chapter: 1

The Complete and the Incomplete

|| ShriRam ||

1. "The numbers of living beings is vast. The mind is vast. The five elements of earth, water, fire, wind, and space, the three gunas (rajas, tamas, sattva), the Inner-Self, and the Primal Illusion are all vast and spread out all over.
2. The attributeless (nirguna) Brahman is also vast and all-pervading. Thus the question arises, "Is there only one vastness that is entirely undifferentiated, or is there some differentiation in their qualities and expanse?"
3. The Self is unseen, and this gives rise to the doubt, "Is the Self (Atman) with attributes (saguna), or is the Self pure, without attributes (nirguna)?
4. The listener gets this doubt and the doubt persists, and he begins speculating about "What is the Self?," and "How is the Self?"
5. Please listen now to the answer to the first doubt. Be attentive and don't make everything confusing in your mind. Let the power of discrimination allow you to look and see for yourself in your own experience
6. Living beings function according to the capacity of the physical body and the capacity of one's power to do activities and make decisions, and we can see that nothing is more swift than the mind.
7. However, the swiftness of the mind is limited. It is not limitless in its expanse. If we look, we see that the expanse of the earth is also limited.
8. Similarly, we can naturally see that water and light are not complete in their expanse. Understand that even the swiftness of the wind is limited in its expanse.
9. Space and Parabrahman are both complete in their expanse, invisibility, and density. There is no imagination in this.
10. The three attributes (rajas, tamas, sattva), the stirring movement of three attributes, and the entire Illusion itself, all come to an end. Their expanse is incomplete, and limited. It is not possible to say that they are complete in their expanse.
11. The Self (Atman) and Reality (Brahman) are the two names that are always used to represent two sides of the individual self (Jiva) and the Self in the form of pure untainted Consciousness (Shiva). In order to aid in the understanding of the meaning of this, something must said in order to convey some meaning.
12. The Self and the mind together are very fast, and their expanse is very vast, but their expanse is not limitless. This can be seen by observing with a clear and tranquil mind.
13. If the attention is to the space above, the mind and Self are absent in the space below, and if the attention is to the space below, they are not in present in the space above. They do not pervade everywhere at all times.
14. If looking ahead, they are not looking behind, and when looking back, they are not not looking ahead. If looking to the left, they are not looking right. Thus, the Self and the mind do not pervade all directions.

15. For example, if flags are placed on all sides of you, how can you touch all of them at the same time? After understanding this, experience for yourself that the mind and the Self are not complete in their expanse.
16. Sometimes it is said that the sun rises and its reflection appears in the water. However, this simile is not entirely appropriate for what is called "Attributeless Absolute Reality" (Nirguna Parabrahman).
17. The simile of "the space in the pot" (at the level of the Self) and "the space in the room" (at the level of Universal Consciousness) is also used, but there is no accurate comparison that can be used to assign any similarity of Parabrahman to the expanse of anything.
18. The space element is but a small fraction of Brahman, and similarly, the mind is but a small part of the Self. The experience and realization of this can be gained from this indication.
19. How can space and the mind be similar? Those who use subtle thought about this are the great ones who understand completely.
20. If the attention of the mind is looking ahead, what is behind is non-existent. What comparison can used to compare the expanse of the mind to the complete expanse of Space?
21. Parabrahman, the Supreme Reality, is unmoving. A mountain can also be said to be unmoving, but can one say that they are the same?
22. How can one say that knowledge, ignorance, and wrong-knowledge are the same? Reflect on this and see in your own experience.
23. Knowledge means "to know," and ignorance means "not knowing." Wrong-knowledge means "seeing something and taking it to be something else."
24. When the "knowing" and the "not knowing" are kept aside, what remains is only the five gross elements. When this play of the five elements is thought to be real, this is what is called the "wrong-knowledge" of living beings.
25. The Inner-Self is the witness, the observer. That which is the individual self (Jivatma), becomes the Pure Self (Shivatma), and moreover, it is the Pure Self that takes birth as the individual self.
26. The individual self is subject to birth and death, and it cannot escape the cycle of birth and death. Therefore, God has stated, "I will come in every age taking birth."
27. The individual self is a limited being. Through investigation and the power of discrimination, the "Universal Self," or God, is seen to be filling the entire universe. This Universal Self cannot escape the appearance of the worldly existence.
28. Knowledge (Jnana) and Ignorance (Ajnana) are equal in that they both exist in the form of attitudes, or states (vritti). Pure Knowledge (Vijnana) is the withdrawal from states, or the absence of states (nivritti). This Supreme Knowledge can be recognized without delay.
29. The universe has been created out of Knowledge. Knowledge has expanded to a great extent, and has taken the form of many changes. This is the nature of Jnana.
30. The eighth body, or the Great Causal Body, at the level of universal awareness, is the Primal Illusion. This is this highest level of Jnana. "Supreme Knowledge" or Vijnana, is bodiless (and inconceivable).

Thus in Shri Dasbodh, a dialogue between the Guru and disciple, Sub-Chapter 1 of Chapter 20, named "The Complete and the Incomplete" is concluded.

Chapter: 20, Sub-Chapter: 2

The Three-Fold Creation

|| ShriRam ||

1. When the Primal Illusion, which is of the nature of motion, does not exist, only the unmoving Brahman without attributes remains, like space, spread out everywhere.
2. The visible creation appears and disappears, but Brahman remains as it is, permeating everywhere like space.
3. Wherever you look, it is there. It is endless, and has no limit to its expanse. It is alone by itself. There is no other thing that exists.
4. If you sit above and beyond the universe you see only empty space. Nothing of the vast expanse of movement can be found there. There is only emptiness.
5. When the visible is removed through the power of discrimination, only Parabrahman pervades everywhere. It is not possible for anyone to imagine it at anytime as it is beyond the scope of the mind.
6. When looking above or below and everywhere in all directions, it is only the attributeless Brahman which is seen. Wherever the mind runs, it cannot see its limitlessness.
7. The visible moves, and Brahman is unmoving. The visible is known, and Brahman is unknown. The visible is understood, and Brahman cannot be comprehended with concepts in imagination.
8. Imagination means "that which does not exist." Brahman pervades everywhere. This is best understood by keeping in mind the essential meaning of the Great Statements ("Only Brahman Exists").
9. There is nothing as great as Parabrahman, there is no practice greater than listening, and there is no true contentment without understanding.
10. With the path of meditation, the "Ant's Way" (Piplika Marg), one gains realization slowly like an ant that makes progress little by little. However, one can fly like a bird with the "Bird's Way" (Vihangam Marg), using the wings of discrimination, and can reach the fruit immediately. The aspirant should understand the meaning of this in the mind.
11. There is nothing else that is real except Parabrahman. Praise and blame do not exist in Parabrahman.
12. Parabrahman is one homogeneous whole. There is nothing that can be used as a comparison to it. Only the great ones who are full of virtue understand it.
13. To be identified with the moving results in sorrow and suffering. There is no other peace than repose in the unmoving. Only those with "Great Experience" (MahaAnubhava) see and understand this.
14. Only one who earnestly inquires about everything from beginning to end gains the firm determination and inner experience of Parabrahman.
15. The entire creation is born out of conceptual imagination, and appears to be manifest in three ways. With sharp intellect one must reflect upon this with the mind.
16. The three attributes (three gunas) are born out the Primal Illusion (Moolamaya) and are limited in their expanse. It is evident that the five elements are also limited in their expanse.

17. The four types of species that have their origin on the earth with all of their various types of behavior that have propagated in creation, are found only in Illusion. The activities of creation end in Illusion, and there is nothing found beyond it.
18. The threefold signs found in creation can be understood by analyzing the explanation given about them. The listeners are asked to please listen with a clear inner-mind.
19. The Primal Illusion is of the nature of awareness. The root of this awareness is a subtle stirring of imagination, similar to the state of the subtle speech (Para Speech), which is prior to words in the form of an inspiration.
20. The root of the eightfold creation (the three gunas and five elements) is the Primal Illusion alone. Everything exists in it in a subtle seed form.
21. The Primal Illusion stimulates gross inert matter with its Life-Energy, thus it is called Chaitanya. This can be understood through subtle indications.
22. Through inquiry, one can realize that Purusha and Prakriti, the half-male and half-female principle, and the eightfold creation exist entirely in the Primal Illusion.
23. Intermingled together, the three gunas in their subtle hidden form are indicated as the being the "Great Element" (Mahat Tattva). This Primal Illusion is the hidden "Pure Consciousness" (Shuda Sattva) itself.
24. From where the three gunas become manifest is called the disturbance in the Primal Illusion (Gunakshobhini). Blessed are those sages who understand the nature of these three qualities.
25. The three gunas in hidden unmanifest form are very subtle in an intermixed state of balanced equilibrium. This subtle indication is difficult to understand, and is not understood by many people.
26. The three gunas arise from the Primal Illusion which is of the nature of motion that is limited in its expanse. By seeing this within, one gains experiential understanding.
27. From this motion arises the activity of the five elements which proliferates to a vast expanse. From these five elements the Earth is formed.
28. The first step of creation is the Primal Illusion. From this, the three gunas arise and give rise to the creation of the five elements and all of the objects in the universe. This is the second step of creation. Now, please listen to the third step of creation.
29. The Earth is the seed of many things. All living beings arise from the four streams of birth; from eggs, from blood (placenta), from moisture (the combination of heat and moisture), and that sprout from the ground (seeds). All beings, along with the four types of speech have spontaneously been created from the Earth.
30. All of the many species of living beings, and the four types of speech appear and disappear, but the universe remains. Like this, it can be seen that a great many beings have come and gone from this world.

Thus in Shri Dasbodh, a dialogue between the Guru and disciple, Sub-Chapter 2 of Chapter 20, named "The Threefold Creation', is concluded.

Chapter: 20, Sub-Chapter: 3

Subtle Terms

|| ShriRam ||

1. From the beginning to the end, the expanse of the universe has been explained in many ways. These explanations should be reflected upon again and again until there is a withdrawal from all mental states and they are dissolved in the Primal Illusion.
2. All of the four types of speech, and all of the 8.4 millions species of living beings arising from the four streams of birth have been born from the Earth.
3. All beings that are formed from the Earth get destroyed and return to the Earth. Many beings come and go, but the Earth remains as it is.
4. This is the third part of creation that is the Earth, which is like the tips of the branches of the Primal Illusion. The vast expanse of the five elements is the second aspect of creation. The first aspect of creation is very subtle and has many names.
5. Whatever is gross must be given up and left off to fall away. Then one must look with subtle vision into the nature and qualities of the three gunas.
6. The three gunas are in the forms of Knowledge (sattva), of Ignorance (tamas), and a mixture of both (rajas). One must look repeatedly into the thought of this. From here, subtle vision must be applied with skill in order to understand further.
7. Pure Ignorance is the quality of tamas (tamoguna). Pure Knowledge is the quality of sattva (sattvaguna), and the quality of rajas (rajoguna) is the mixture of Knowledge and Ignorance.
8. When one begins to understand correctly that the form of the three gunas is like this, one can go to the origin of the three gunas. This is the homogeneous intermingled mixture that is called the stirring of the three gunas (Gunakshobhini; the stimulation or arousal of the three manifest attributes).
9. Understand that here, the three qualities of rajas, tamas and sattva exist in a homogeneous form known as the "Principle Element" (Mahat Tattva; also called the Cosmic Intelligence).
10. This is called Purusha/Prakriti, or Shiva/Shakti that is the half-male and half-female principle. However, its true nature is a state of a homogeneous intermixture of attributes in Oneness.
11. There, the gunas are intermingled in balance in subtle form, This is called the equilibrium of the gunas (Gunasamya). This is the Life-Energy, or Chaitanya, which exists in a very subtle form and is difficult to comprehend.
12. The Primal Illusion contains many things. It is the Great Causal Body of the universe. It must be seen correctly with subtle vision.
13. The four streams of living beings, the five elements, and the fourteen subtle indications of the Primal Illusion are what are seen here. One must look with subtle vision and see this for oneself.
14. By looking superficially, this cannot be understood. If one only casually thinks about this for a short time, it cannot understood. The common people look superficially like this, and many doubts arise in their minds.

15. The fourteen names of the Primal Illusion[60] together with the five elements make nineteen, and when the four types of living beings are added, it becomes twenty-three. Among these twenty-three, the fourteen Brahmans must be seen again and again as being the origin.
16. One who analyzes this understands and becomes doubtless. Any talk that is without understanding is meaningless and only causes confusion.
17. The seed of all of creation spontaneously arises in the Primal Illusion. When all of this is understood, spiritual life is fulfilled.
18. The one who has understood will never be confused, and because of his firm conviction he will never hold on to any imagination. Such a person can never be confused or fall into speculation about "Supreme Truth" (Paramartha).
19. When one uses words to speak about That which is beyond words, it is called the word meaning. The pure untainted Reality that is being indicated, is not an object that can be perceived. It can only be understood through the power of discrimination.
20. The primary premise (purvapaksha) presented in the *Vedas* is that everything is Illusion. The "final conclusion" (siddhanta) is the dissolution of Illusion. What can be said about That which exists when Illusion is not present?
21. The discrimination regarding the appearance and disappearance of objects is the primary premise of the *Vedas*. The final conclusion, or siddhanta, means that there is only the oneness of "Pure Reality" which admits to nothing "other."
22. By looking downwards, the distinctions in duality increase, while looking upwards, duality falls away. The great yogi who gives up everything remains attributeless.
23. When one understands that Illusion is false, why does one get caught up in Illusion? The attraction to Illusion is what makes one feel that one has slipped down from the state of one's True Form (Swaroopa).
24. What a wonder it is that one would give up the firm determination about Absolute Reality because of being attracted to Illusion.
25. There are many people in the world, and among them, there are some good and virtuous people. However, only a true sage can recognize another sage.
26. Therefore attachment to worldly life must be given up, and one should search for a sage. By going from place to place, one should find a true sage.
27. One must seek out many saintly people and find one who is experienced, and a great leader (Mahanta). If a teacher who is without any experience is found, there will not be any true benefit for one's best self-interest.
28. Whether in worldly life or in spiritual life, if there is no experience everything is useless. One whose Knowledge is based in experience is the most "Powerful" (Samartha) among all.
29. One who looks day and night, and sees "Supreme Meaning" is the one who is Samartha. One's own best interest is secured when one stands beyond the world.
30. Therefore, one must look and see, and find out what is true. When the entire truth is known, all doubt is effortlessly destroyed.

Thus in Shri Dasbodh, a dialogue between the Guru and disciple, Sub-Chapter 3 of Chapter 20, named "Subtle Terms" is concluded.

---

[60]The fourteen names given to the Primal Illusion are: 1) Life-Energy or Chaitanya, 2) The equilibrium of the gunas, or Gunasamya, 3) The half-male/half-female principle, 4) Prakriti/Purusha, 5) Shiva/Shakti, 6) The Gunas in their pure form as God, or Shadguneshwara, 7) The Principle Element, or Mahat Tattva, 8) The stirring of the gunas, or Gunakshobhini, 9) Sattva, 10) Rajas, 11) Tamas, 12) Mind, 13) Illusion, or Maya, and 14) Jiva.

Chapter: 20, Sub-Chapter: 4

Explanation of the Self

|| ShriRam ||

1. The listeners are requested not to unnecessarily feel sad or depressed. Bring the attention of your mind to the explanation and gain the realization of what is being said.
2. If realization and direct experience is on one side, and one runs to the other side, how can there be any discrimination between the Essence and non-essence?
3. When looking casually and superficially the whole creation appears as chaos to the eyes. However, there is always a state of powerful authority that is quite extraordinary.
4. All of the bodies that live in this world are the many houses of God. These bodies are the doorways through which many pleasures are enjoyed by God.
5. Who will understand his greatness? It is God himself who has distributed his benevolence through the loving feelings of mothers. It is God, the "Lord of the World," who is the protector of the world.
6. It is the power of God that is distributed everywhere in the world. The entire universe functions by only a fraction of his power.
7. It is his power that is the Primordial Awareness that has been distributed among all bodies. All skills and wisdom reside in this Awareness.
8. It is God that is Pure Being that is present in all bodies, and is present in the world. He functions through all bodies with great ease.
9. If the construction of the universe is examined, it is seen that everything cannot be done with only one body. It is the one God alone who does everything by residing in all bodies and making then function.
10. God does not consider any bodies to be superior or inferior, or good or bad. All that he is concerned with is that everything continues to function naturally.
11. Some bodies experience hindrance due to ignorance, and some are occupied with knowledge and self-study. Only God himself knows how all of this happens.
12. If we see the Self of the world with the inner attention of the mind, this is real meditation. This meditation and Self-Knowledge are one and the same.
13. When a living being is born into this worldly life he begins to gain a little bit of wisdom and begins analyzing the world.
14. The glory of Lord Rama is the fullness of the Knowledge of the Inner-Self. He is the Lord who permeates the universe and is present everywhere. Through great fortune, this comes to be understood.
15. If one seeks to worship God, that desire for worship is adopted. In this way, the desire to worship God as being separate gets prolonged, and the greatness of God is not comprehended.
16. Recognize God in his endless forms. He is the observer who sees, and he is the witness who is the knower.
17. Keep the company of good people and be in the habit of listening to the narrations and explanations about God. This brings peace and some repose to the mind.

18. In addition to that, knowledge based in experience burns up all speculation and guesswork. How can one gain contentment without experience?
19. The original volition, or desire, is the volition of God (Vishnu). All of the activity of the Primal Illusion seen as the form of the world is itself the Inner-Self of the world.
20. The worship of God is in the form of Knowledge (Jnana). The fourth body is this formless body of Knowledge. Therefore, all desire should be given up and left behind.
21. When desires are given up, afterwards, there is only the Absolute Reality, Parabrahman, which is vast and empty like space. It can be said to be dense and spread out everywhere, or delicate and soft, but what can really be said about it?
22. Worship and spiritual practice means Knowledge (Jnana). With Knowledge one realizes the pure untainted Reality. This is the contentment of the yogis.
23. When one constantly inquires into one's True Form, this is the worship of the Self by the Self. At the time of death, some go away (merged in Self-Knowledge), and some remain, holding on to the attachment to the body.
24. Such turbulence of duality has been taking place continuously from time immemorial. Now also, the process of creation and sustenance continues on in the same way.
25. The wild animals dominate in the forest, the aquatic animals have control in the water, and kings dictate on earth. In the same way, God rules the universe.
26. Thus, there is power in all of the activity in the universe among those who exercise it. However, here it must be firmly established that everything is done only by the power and support of God.
27. It is true that it is only God who is the doer of everything, and he has distributed himself in the many forms that appear on earth. Therefore, one should not become affected by the madness of the pride of ego.
28. It is God who is the giver, and it is he who is the enjoyer. Like this, is the principle that is the functioning of everything. This should be seen now through investigation and thoughtfulness.
29. The Supreme God, Parameshwar, is the doer of all. The thought about oneself as being an individual is illusory. Whatever the level of one's understanding is, one will act accordingly in the world.
30. There is nothing that is as swift as God, and nothing is unmoving like Brahman. Proceeding step by step, one can see to the root.

Thus in Shri Dasbodh, a dialogue between the Guru and disciple, Sub-Chapter 4 of Chapter 20, named "Explanation of the Self" is concluded.

Chapter: 20, Sub-Chapter: 5

The Four Substances

|| ShriRam ||

1. From here to the end of the exposition, there are four principle elements to keep in the mind. First is Parabrahman, the second is the fourteen aspects of the Primal Illusion, the third is the five elements, and the fourth is the four streams of living species.
2. Parabrahman, the Absolute Reality, is entirely of a nature different from everything. The Absolute is distinct from everything else. It is free of any kind of imaginings.
3. The nature of Parabrahman is beyond any conceptualization. It is pure, unmoving, changeless, and continuous.
4. Nothing can be compared with Parabrahman. It is the one principle substance. The second substance is the Primal Illusion (Moolamaya) which consists of many concepts and imaginings.
5. The Primal Illusion occurs in a very subtle form. It is in the form of one homogeneous subtle mixture. The original inspiration of "I Am" that took place in Parabrahman is what is called the Primal Illusion.
6. The Primal Illusion is the original desire of God, which is the Inner-Self of all that is Lord Rama (AtmaRama). There are many names and indications that are given to describe its nature.
7. In the unmoving Reality, movement came to life. Therefore, it is called Life-Energy, or Chaitanya. From that Life-Energy came the three gunas in a subtle state of equilibrium, and thus, the three attributes became established in a state of equal balance. This state of equilibrium of the gunas is called "Gunasamya."
8. The Primal Illusion is God who is sometimes called the half-male and half-female principle, God with six qualities, and Prakriti-Purusha. It is also called Shiva-Shakti.
9. It is initially in the form of "Pure Sattva" that is indicated by the crescent mark on the OM symbol (ॐ) which represents the initial stirring of the three gunas (Gunakshobhini). Afterwards, the activity of the three gunas being distinct from each other became apparent.
10. Mind, Illusion, and the Inner-Self are also names given to it. All of this is called the fourteen names of the Primal Illusion. It is of the nature of Self-Knowledge which exists everywhere.
11. Like this, is the second substance, which is given fourteen names. The third substance is the five elements.
12. Here, with the five elements, the principle of Awareness is less predominant. At the beginning (in the Primal Illusion) and at the end (in the four streams of living species) the principle of Awareness is evident. The fourth substance, which has been explained previously, is the four streams of living species.
13. The four types of living species which are endless in number have proliferated everywhere on the earth, each with its own type of awareness. At this point in the exposition, all of the four substances have been named.
14. When only a small quantity of seeds are sown, a large crop arises from them. Similarly, the same thing has happened with the Self. From the one Self, the four streams of living beings and the four types of speech have arisen.

15. Like this, the Power has expanded. It was subtle and singular in the beginning, but then proliferated in many forms. In the form of a human being it enjoys creation in many ways.
16. An animal kills another living being and then moves on. Its understanding of life is limited to the functions related to survival. With the human body, the Self is able to enjoy a great many things.
17. There are many special words and sounds, many different special sensations of touch, many special forms, many special tastes, and many special fragrances. The special qualities of these various objects of the senses can only be understood with the human body.
18. There are many precious gems, various types of clothing, different types of vehicles, and various streams of knowledge, art, and science, that are only appreciated with the human body.
19. The Power of the Self fills all places and controls all things, but it is only through the human body that the many streams of knowledge, the arts, and various ideas and concepts are comprehended.
20. Through the human body, it is possible to see the visible world, to protect one's status and honor, and to utilize the power of discrimination.
21. With the human body, it is possible to think about the worldly life and the spiritual life, as well as exercise various types of discernment and lack of discernment.
22. Only with a human body is it possible to understand the structure of the universe, the nature of the Primal Illusion, and various abstract ideas and concepts.
23. Only human beings can enjoy the eight types of pleasures, the nine types of emotions, the many types of recreation, and the essential hidden meaning which lies behind the apparent meaning of words.
24. The human being has control over other living beings, and the human being is protected by God. This can only be understood fully because of the human body.
25. The human body is extremely difficult to obtain, and with it comes many rare benefits. What is difficult is made easy with the human body.
26. All of the other bodies of living beings only lead a life of mundane existence and toil, but the human body is a great treasure. However, to understand its value one must utilize the power of discrimination.
27. One who is lazy and neglects the capacity for discrimination becomes ruined in all respects. One cannot recognize God without utilizing the power of discrimination.
28. The human being is himself Lord Narayana. This realization comes by listening and with continuous meditation of the inner-mind.
29. One who knows how to swim does not require any support. Such a person can independently investigate and find out anything and everything.
30. After having investigated everything, one remains free of doubt. Thereafter, his own state is known only to himself.

Thus in Shri Dasbodh, a dialogue between the Guru and disciple, Sub-Chapter 5 of Chapter 20, named "The Four Substances" is concluded.

Chapter: 20, Sub-Chapter: 6

The Attributes of the Self

|| ShriRam ||

1. If we look at the Earth, we see that there is water found at many places, and there are many places where the land is dry.
2. Similarly, the visible creation is expansive, and in it, some beings are adorned with a greater awareness, and many appearances have remained inanimate without any awareness.
3. The ancient scriptures of spiritual science (*Shastras*) have described the four streams of living beings, the four speeches, and the 8.4 million species of creatures.
4. In the *Shastras* it is also mentioned that there are four hundred thousand types of human beings, two million types of wild animals, and one million one hundred thousand types of worms and insects.
5. Furthermore, the *Shastras* state that there are one million types of birds, nine hundred thousand types of aquatic animals, and three million types of stationary beings.
6. All together, this makes up eight million four hundred thousand species of living beings. All of these living beings have some degree of awareness within them. The actual numbers of such bodies that have taken form are cannot be counted.
7. Innumerable beings appear and disappear, and this Universal Light (Primal Illusion) is the basic support for all of them. There is no other support for them other than this Universal Light.
8. Looking more subtly, we find the five elements. Some are manifest in a gross state and are visible, and some are simply known to be present.
9. The Inner-Self is recognized to be of the nature of motion. Now, please listen attentively to the explanation of the resting place of consciousness.
10. The living being, the jiva, is the knower of happiness and sorrow. Similarly, the "Pure Awareness," or Sada-Shiva is also the knower of happiness and sorrow. In both jiva and Shiva, the inner-mind (antahkarana) with its five aspects (inner-mind, mind, intellect, thinking, and ego), is present as a wondrous aspect of the Self.
11. In the gross body, the qualities of the sky (desire, anger, fear, greed, enticement, and sorrow) are manifested. Understand that these, along with the three gunas are also attributes of the Self.
12. The many ways of thinking and discrimination, many firm determinations, the nine types of devotion, the four types of liberation, the state of detachment, and the effortless Natural State are also all qualities of the Self.
13. Being the Seer, the witness, the density of Knowledge, Power, Life-Energy, the most ancient, and the attributes of listening, reflecting, and explaining are all qualities of the Self.
14. The seen, the seer, and the act of seeing; the object of meditation, the mediator, and meditation, as well as the known, the knower, and knowledge, are all qualities of the Self.
15. The hidden meanings of the *Vedas*, the *Shastras*, the *Puranas*, and spiritual life, as well as omniscience and power are all qualities of the Self.

16. The one who feels bound, the seeker, the aspirant, and the accomplished one, as well as the investigation and the seeing of purity, Knowledge, and understanding, are all attributes of the Self.
17. The waking state, the dream state, the state of deep sleep, and the Turya state, as well as Prakriti-Purusha, the Primal Illusion, the body, and the eight bodies of the universe, are all attributes of the Self.
18. The Supreme Self (Paramatman), the Supreme Goddess (Parameshwari), the Universal Self, the "Lord of the Universe," as well as Shiva and Parvati are all attributes of the Self.
19. Whatever is subtle, as well as all that has name and form, is only the Self. There is no limit to the innumerable names that are used to indicate the Self.
20. Primordial Power, the Absolute with its power, the "Power of the Primal Illusion," the all-powerful, the genesis of the many substances in creation and their sustenance, are all attributes of the Self.
21. The primary premise of the *Vedas*, the final conclusion (siddhanta), many types of singing, the playing of musical instruments, and the various streams of knowledge are all marvelous attributes of the Self.
22. Knowledge, ignorance, and wrong-knowledge, as well as negative dispositions and positive dispositions, knowingness, pure Knowledge, and detachment from the world are all attributes of the Self.
23. Understanding of the body, the universe, the elements, as well as making decisions and clear thinking, are all attributes of the Self.
24. The many various types of meditation, as well as the contemplation on various states, situations, different types of knowledge, self-surrender, and the oneness of God are all attributes of the Self.
25. The three hundred and thirty million gods, the eighty-eight thousand sages, as well as countless animals and birds are all attributes of the Self.
26. The various forms of spirits, angels, and goddesses are all attributes of the Self.
27. The moon, the sun, the galaxies of stars, constellations, planetary systems, as well as the divine serpent and tortoise, and huge cloud formations are all attributes of the Self.
28. Gods, demons, human beings, many varieties of living beings, as well as the states of being and not being, are all attributes of the Self.
29. The Self has many attributes, but Brahman is changeless and without attributes. The main quality of the Self is to know, whether it is partial knowledge or complete Knowledge.
30. Through contemplation and the worship of the Inner-Self, one realizes the unseen Reality. There, there is no doubt, or any place for imagination.

Thus in Shri Dasbodh, a dialogue between the Guru and disciple, Sub-Chapter 6 of Chapter 20, named "The Qualities of the Self" is concluded.

Chapter: 20, Sub-Chapter: 7

Explanation of Self

|| ShriRam ||

1. The indescribable contentment that is gained must somehow be spoken of in words. Even if it is spoken about, it can never be lost.
2. It is not required to actually give up anything, nor it is necessary to make or create something new. With investigation, one finds out for oneself and understands what is true.
3. There are many temples of God. The temple of Lord Shiva at Kashi is considered to be the principle temple. After that, the temple of Lord Rama in the south at Malikarjuna is considered to be second in importance, and after that the temple of Bhimashankar is considered to be third. These are all qualities of the Self.
4. There are twelve main Shiva Lingams (symbols for Pure Consciousness), and aside from these, there are many other Shiva Lingams that are well known. Many people have understood and experienced the significance of their sacredness. These are all qualities of the Self.
5. There are an endless number of powers on the earth, and many ways in which Self-realization and various miracles happen. There are also many powerful images of God. These are all attributes of the Self.
6. There are many powerful and accomplished people, there are many mantras and chants, and there are of many powerful medicinal herbs and gemstones. These are all attributes of the Self.
7. There are many powerful places of pilgrimage, powerful streams and rivers, and many other places of power on the Earth. All of these are attributes of the Self.
8. Whatever are considered to be the best qualities, good qualities, or negative qualities are all only attributes of the Self.
9. The Pure Self is the best in quality, however, because of the intermingling of the three gunas, there appears to be good and bad qualities in it. Understand that all of this is the activity of the Self.
10. Holding on to various things because of pride, the manifestation of many similar creations, and the giving and receiving of various curses are all attributes of the Self.
11. By examining one's own body, one should find out the elements that make up the body. When one discovers the primary elements that make up the body, one gains understanding of the entire body.
12. The gross body is made up of the five elements and the quality of motion that is the nature of the Self. However, there is nothing which is not pervaded by the unmoving Brahman.
13. Analyze the unmoving and the moving with the aid of the gross body. Without having actual experience, one's speech does not carry any weight.
14. When the Self leaves the gross body, one understands the distinction between the gross and the subtle. It is easily seen that the gross body falls inert very quickly.
15. When the inert gross body falls down, that which is moving leaves it. By observing this, the nature of that which is gross and inert, and of that which is moving can be realized.

16. The unmoving Reality is present everywhere. It is not required to be seen in order to be realized as there is no modification of the gunas present in the unmoving stillness.
17. The structure of the body is the same as the structure of the universe. This can clearly be seen through inquiry. When the inert and moving Illusion disappears, what remains is the all-pervading Parabrahman.
18. The mixture of the five elements combine to make a firm structure for the Self. When the Self is integrated into this structure the activity of the body becomes alive. It is in this same way that the activity of creation functions.
19. All activity is the functioning of Illusion and the Self, however, people attribute this activity to Brahman. The one who analyses everything and gains experiential understanding is the truly wise person.
20. Brahman is continuous and all-pervading. Other things which appear to be vast are limited in their expanse, and are not continuous. Through investigation and observation, there is nothing that is difficult to understand.
21. It is not possible to divide or break the continuity of space. Even if everything is dissolved and the entire universe is destroyed, how can space be destroyed?
22. Those who get caught up in the destructible easily get destroyed. Those who are knowledgeable should solve this mystery.
23. It appears as a mystery if not understood, but once it is understood, then everything becomes obvious. Therefore, one must reflect upon this in solitude and see for oneself.
24. Moreover, in addition to just remaining in solitude, when one meets with a saint with actual experience, one must engage in many discourses with him with an attentive mind.
25. That which cannot be seen is not easily understood. As understanding increases, doubts disappear. Seeing with the power of discrimination, there is no entanglement of Illusion found anywhere.
26. Clouds appear in the sky and then disappear on their own. It is in the same way that the visible creation is formed in the Self, and disappears by itself.
27. The one who utilizes the power of discrimination is able to discern and analyze everything from the root to the end. He alone arrives at the firm resolution of That which does not move.
28. Other determinations are superficially based upon speculation and imagination. One does not lose anything by speaking from speculation, but those who have wisdom based in experience do not give any credence to such talk.
29. Any talk that is based on speculation is useless. Of what use can it be to anyone? Common thinking and logic cannot succeed when applied to the realization of Reality.
30. Commonplace worldly ways of thinking are not correct inquiry. Many people say that everything is One and indistinguishable. Do not make this mistake, as this is incorrect thinking.
31. Whatever is artificial and created by imagination should be given up, and that which is pure should be accepted. With knowledge and understanding select the Essence and leave the non-essence.

Thus in Shri Dasbodh, a dialogue between the Guru and disciple, Sub-Chapter 7 of Chapter 20, named "Explanation of Self" is concluded.

Chapter: 20, Sub-Chapter: 8

The Field of the Body

|| ShriRam ||

1. The tree of worldly life sown by Brahma has proliferated, and with its continuous growth, it has expanded extensively. Its growth came to rest and many living beings enjoy the fruits of this creation.
2. The tree of creation produced many juicy fruits and sweet things, and many bodies were created in order to enjoy the sweetness and to experience the many sense pleasures.
3. Many very nice objects were created, but without bodies there was no enjoyment of them. Therefore, as a solution to this, many bodies were created.
4. The various sense organs were created, each with their different qualities. They are all attached to one body, yet they are separated from each other.
5. When sound falls on the sense organ of hearing, it is able to differentiate sounds and words. This is the type of arrangement that has been created among the sense organs.
6. The sense organ of touch can feel hot and cold. With the sense organ of the eyes, all forms can be seen. It is like this that the capacity and the quality of the functioning of the various sense organs is differentiated.
7. With the sense organ of the tongue many tastes are experienced, and through the sense organ of the nose many smells are experienced. Like this, are the differences in quality and function of the sense organs.
8. In the five aspects of wind, the five aspects of the inner-mind get intermixed and move around without doubts, and circulate freely, and the inner-mind naturally observes the functioning of the sense organs and the organs of action.
9. Through the sense organs, living beings eagerly enjoy the many various sense objects. Such is the arrangement that God has created in the world.
10. Many nice objects have been created, but how can they be enjoyed without a body? For this reason, many types of bodies were created.
11. The body is made of bones and flesh, and it has many various qualities present in it. There is no other instrument or machine that is as refined as the body.
12. Like this, many bodies were created and were made to grow and develop according to their capacity to enjoy the various sense objects relating to the sense organs. Many small and large bodies have been created in this manner.
13. Many bodies made of bones and flesh were created by God with consideration to the capacity of each to discern the qualities of the sense objects.
14. The body is like a statue made of flesh and bones which has knowledge of many arts and skills. However, there are differences among all of the bodies found everywhere.
15. The differences in the bodies are based on cause and effect. There are many aspects to this which cannot be understood without a sharp intellect.
16. God has created everything, and it is because of the will of God that there are many differences found in his creation. However, if we look beyond appearances, there is no differentiation to be found.

17. Differentiation was necessary for creating the universe. Upon the destruction of the universe, there is no differentiation. The talk of differentiation and the absence of differentiation is only due to Illusion.
18. The Inner-Self is the Illusion, but its greatness cannot be understood. Even the creator, Lord Brahma, gets doubts about it.
19. When thinking about the intricacies of the Self there is much confusion that arises in the mind. Even when using very sharp common logic, the mind becomes exhausted trying to analyze it.
20. With regard to the Self, it is required to think and inquire into everything. However, with regard to the invisible Reality, thinking is of no use. In order to realize this, it is useful to spend time contemplating in solitude.
21. The Lord of the Universe gets everything done according to the capacity and power of the body. Those bodies which are filled with great power are called incarnations of God.
22. Various incarnations, such as those of the divine serpent Shesha, the great tortoise, and the great boar, have huge bodies that support the universe. Due to these incarnations, the structure of the universe continues to function.
23. See what a great and wondrous creation God has made. He made the sun that moves across the sky, and the cloud formations that hold huge amounts of water.
24. He has created clouds as huge as mountains that obscure the sun, and the wind that exists everywhere with its own swiftness.
25. Wind runs with such speed and force that it feels is as if it is the agent of death. It disperses the clouds allowing the sun to fully reappear.
26. God has created the lightening which strikes so hard that living beings suddenly feel frightened. It feels as if the sky is crashing down everywhere with a huge rumbling.
27. God has created one very marvelous thing in the world. This is that each element has some influence on each of the other elements. Thus all of the elements are equally balanced and because of this all of creation functions smoothly.
28. There are an endless number of differences in the Self. How can all of its differences be known? By careful analysis again and again, the mind gets ripped apart.
29. Ramdas says, that my worship is like this. The worshipper should bring to mind the greatness and immensity of it, which is not fully known to even Lord Brahma himself.
30. The invocation of the presence of God and the immersion into him is the sign of the worship of God. The knowledgeable and virtuous people know and understand this. What more can be said to them?

Thus in Shri Dasbodh, a dialogue between the Guru and disciple, Sub-Chapter 8 of Chapter 20, named "The Field of the Body" is concluded.

Chapter: 20, Sub-Chapter: 9

Explanation of the Subtle

|| ShriRam ||

1. It is not acceptable to the inner-mind that one should worship an idol made of clay and try to immerse oneself in it.
2. The worship of God in the form of an image that can be thrown away is not deemed to be proper by living beings. This must be carefully considered and seen with the inner-mind.
3. It is not possible that God can be made, destroyed, or thrown away. Therefore, one must investigate into the nature of God and see for oneself.
4. God resides in many bodies and then after some time gives them up. One must recognize this God for oneself through the power of discrimination.
5. There are many spiritual practices and many explanations that are given so that aspirants may find God. Everything must be understood with one's inner-mind.
6. The Knowledge of Brahman cannot be given to others without experiential understanding. It is not an object that can be given and taken away.
7. All people feel in their minds that they must meet God personally. However, the answer that lies in the utilization of the power of discrimination is something altogether different.
8. The mere thinking about an idea of God cannot be sustained. An idea about God is not God. However, people do not agree with this, and do not want to let go of their ideas about God. What to do?
9. When great people die, the common people make statues in their likeness and look to those statues with faith as if the person was still alive. This is the way of worship for most people.
10. If a person cannot succeed in a large business, he turns to a small business in order to make money. How can anyone acquire great wealth like that of a king with this kind of approach?
11. This is an example of simple and blind faith which is of the nature of ignorance. How can one realize the "God of gods" through ignorance?
12. Knowledge (Jnana) is not acceptable to the ignorant person, and for a knowledgeable person, speculation and imagination is not acceptable. Therefore, Knowledge must be gained through the indications of one who is accomplished.
13. Give up Illusion and go to the root. It is only in this way that one gains contentment, otherwise one gets carried away in the wrong direction.
14. There are many ways to cross beyond Illusion and realize God. The path of listening to spiritual knowledge must be followed in order to gain actual experience.
15. By not following this way, worldly people go astray and miss recognizing God. Therefore, the aspirant must recognize the correct and incorrect types of spiritual practice.
16. Do not follow the path of falsehood, avoid the company of people who say false things, and do not accumulate false beliefs of any kind.
17. Whatever is false, will always be false. The false cannot survive in the light of the True. The tendency of the mind to flow downwards towards the objects of the world must be reversed and one's attention must be turned towards Parabrahman.

18. Continue to listen to spiritual discourses and everything can be understood. Listening clears away many types of confusion and entanglement.
19. Just as a tangled thread is disentangled by untying its knots, in the same way, the mind should be unraveled step by step by turning it towards its root.
20. Everything in creation is all mixed together. All of creation is formed from the unified mixture of the elements and gunas, and the same is true for the body.
21. Whatever one wants to see should be looked at and discovered at the level of the body. The meaning of the fourteen names of the Primal Illusion must be understood from the level of the body.
22. That which is changeless and without any attributes pervades all places. One must discover that this untainted Reality permeates the body in the same way.
23. The Primal Illusion is in the form of desire. This is the true nature of the inner-mind. It is ignited in the form of Life-Energy which is also present in the body.
24. The state where the gunas are in equilibrium is called "the equilibrium of the gunas," or Gunasamya. This is a subtle principle which is not easy to comprehend. Those sages who understand the subtle are worthy to be praised by everyone.
25. The body appears to have two sides, the left and the right. Similarly, the half-male and half-female principle should be recognized in the body.
26. Understand what Purusha-Prakriti is, and recognize the homogeneous mixture that is called God with six qualities.
27. This is called the "Principle Element" wherein lies the hidden three gunas. The half crescent mark of the OM symbol (ॐ) represents this Pure Sattva quality, which is the origin of the stirring of the three gunas.
28. The body functions because of the three gunas, this can be directly perceived. Understand that the mixture of all the qualities that has just now been explained is what is called the field of the body.
29. Mind, Illusion, and the living being (jiva) are also naturally in the field of the body. The meaning of the fourteen names of Brahman must be seen from the level of the body.
30. When the body falls dead, everything disappears, but Parabrahman, the Absolute Reality remains. Knowing that Parabrahman is eternal, hold steadfastly to it.

Thus in Shri Dasbodh, a dialogue between the Guru and disciple, Sub-Chapter 9 of Chapter 20, named "Explanation of the Subtle" is concluded.

Chapter: 20, Sub-Chapter: 10

Explanation of Pure Brahman

|| ShriRam ||

1. If one tries to hold it, it cannot be held. If one tries to give it up, it cannot be given up. Parabrahman is always present everywhere.
2. It exists everywhere in all directions. Even if trying to turn away from it, it is always in front of us. It is not possible to turn away from it in any direction.

3. When a person who is sitting down stands up and walks away, the space that is there always remain the same. Even if we look in all directions, space is always there in front of us.
4. In whatever direction beings turn, space is all around them in every direction. Even with great effort, it is not possible to move out of space.
5. Living beings see in all directions, and space is present there, facing them. It stands on the heads of all, like the midday sun.
6. However, the sun is only in one place, so this simile is not entirely fitting for Parabrahman. This example was just given in order to make some analogy.
7. Many pilgrimage places are visited and pilgrims go to a lot of trouble to see them. Nothing like that is required to realize Parabrahman. It is always in the same place that one is sitting.
8. Whether a living being remains sitting in one place or goes running about with great speed, Parabrahman is always there with that being.
9. Just as a bird flies around in the sky, and there is only sky all around it, in the same way, Parabrahman pervades everywhere.
10. Parabrahman is empty, yet it is also densely permeating everywhere. It is the end of everything that ends, and is always present in everyone at all times.
11. The entire visible creation is permeated by Brahman, both outwardly and inwardly. What can be used as a comparison to its purity?
12. It permeates the abode of Vishnu, of Shiva, of heaven, in the kingdom of Indra, in the fourteen worlds, and in the netherworld which is the domain of the divine serpent Shesha.
13. From Kashi to Rameshvar (these are holy places, but also metaphors for the Pure Consciousness and the Self), it permeates everywhere without limitation. Even by going beyond all appearances, there is no end to it that can be found.
14. Parabrahman is One, and alone. It permeates everything at the same time. It touches everyone, and resides in all places.
15. Parabrahman does not get wet in the rain, nor does it get soiled by mud, nor does it get carried away by floodwater.
16. It is always present in front, behind, and to left and the right. It permeates all beings, high and low.
17. The container that is space is full but it is never over-filled. It is spread out everywhere beyond imagination.
18. Space is one substance which is indifferent to everything, and it is not touched by the visible appearances that appear within it. However, understand that Parabrahman is different from space in that it has no appearance or perceptible objects in it.
19. Understand that for the saints and sages with the highest experience, for the gods and demons, and for human beings, Parabrahman is the place of rest and peace for all.
20. Where can one go, or what can one see, that can be called the end of Parabrahman? It is impossible to define it as anything.
21. It is neither gross nor subtle. It is not like any other substance. Without seeing with the eyes of Knowledge, there can be no contentment.
22. When the body and the universe are dissolved, Parabrahman remains without any appearance. From here to eternity it is like empty space.

23. It is true that Parabrahman is all-pervading, but this statement is only true as long as there is a visible creation. Without the visible creation, how can it be said to be pervading anything?
24. There is no word that can describe Parabrahman, and the imagination cannot conceive of it. That invisible Reality which is beyond imagination must be recognized with the power of discrimination.
25. Pure Essence is in the listening, and can be experienced through meditation. Upon gaining Supreme Knowledge, one effortlessly becomes "no-mind" (unmana).
26. The fruit of spiritual practice has been obtained, and the worldly life has been fulfilled when the attributeless unmoving Reality is firmly realized within.
27. The nature of Illusion and all of the elements has been explained and analyzed completely. When the goal has been reached, there is no further need for spiritual practice.
28. Whatever was seen in the dream has disappeared upon awakening, and one naturally becomes speechless, unable to describe That which cannot be told.
29. Like this, understand through the power of discrimination. The indications about it should be used to gain actual experience. In that experiential understanding, the cycle of birth and death is reduced to nothing.
30. Being pleased with his devotees, Lord Rama has benevolently given his blessing, and these words have flowed out by his power, in the form of this text named *Dasbodh*.
31. By listening to and studying the twenty chapters of this *Dasbodh*, one who reflects on what is contained here, gains "Divine Understanding" (Paramartha).
32. By studying the twenty chapters and two hundred sub-chapters of *Dasbodh* with perseverance and patience, one begins to understand the exceptional Knowledge that is beyond the intellect.
33. There is a custom to praise this book, but what is the purpose of only praising the text? One must verify the evidence that is presented here and gain the experience of what is explained in this book.
34. The body is made up of the five elements, and the doer of everything is the Self. How then can it be said that this poetic composition was created by a human being?
35. God is the doer of everything, so how can it claimed that this poetic skill came from a human being? Do not even entertain such a statement as being true.
36. When all of the eight bodies are discarded, and when the elements are dissolved one into another, everything disappears. What then remains that can then be called as one's own?
37. Now, the activities of investigation and reflection have been explained. Don't unnecessarily become deluded by Illusion. God has now narrated everything step by step in a methodical sequence.

Thus in Shri Dasbodh, a dialogue between the Guru and disciple, Sub-Chapter 10 of Chapter 20, named "Explanation of Pure Brahman" is concluded.

The End of Dasbodh

www.ingramcontent.com/pod-product-compliance
Lightning Source LLC
Chambersburg PA
CBHW031053080526
44587CB00011B/667